12,000 WORDS

12,000 WORDS

A Supplement to Webster's Third New International Dictionary

A Merriam-Webster®
MERRIAM-WEBSTER INC., *Publishers*
Springfield, Massachusetts, U.S.A.

Contents

Library of Congress Cataloging in Publication Data

12,000 words.

1. Words, New — English — Dictionaries. 2. English language — Dictionaries. I. Webster's third new international dictionary of the English language, unabridged. II. Title: Twelve thousand words.
PE1630.A17 1986 423 86-12598

ISBN 0-87779-207-0

MADE IN THE UNITED STATES OF AMERICA

123RRD888786

Preface

A dictionary begins to go out-of-date as soon as it is published. When Webster's Third New International Dictionary appeared in 1961, it provided as complete a coverage of contemporary American English as was then available. But the editing of the Third had begun more than a decade earlier; the language did not stand still during the editing, nor has it since. To try to keep abreast of the living language, Merriam-Webster editors added an eight-page Addenda Section to Webster's Third in 1966, increased it to sixteen pages in 1971, to thirty-two in 1976, to forty-eight in 1981, and to fifty-six in 1986.

The Addenda Section serves two purposes: to record as many as space will permit of the new words and meanings that have become established since Webster's Third was edited and to enter those older words that for various reasons had been passed over in the earlier editing. 12,000 Words is simply the most recent Addenda Section of Webster's Third New International Dictionary without any difference from what appears in Webster's Third except larger type. Like the Addenda Section, moreover, 12,000 Words cannot be self-contained; the reader will find it necessary to consult another dictionary for terms—especially technical terms—which are unfamiliar. Every word used in 12,000 Words can be found in Webster's Third or in 12,000 Words; most can be found in a good desk dictionary like Webster's Ninth New Collegiate Dictionary.

In order to get such satisfaction and pleasure as a dictionary affords, one must learn how to use it—that is, how to interpret the information contained in each entry. This knowledge involves mainly an ability to recognize different typefaces, a number of abbreviations that occur over and over, and a few traditional dictionary devices. Every reader is therefore urged to read the Explanatory Notes that follow this preface carefully. They contain, in brief form, the essential information given in the corresponding section of Webster's Third. After these the reader will find an informative section on the recent growth of English vocabulary, the fields which yield new words, the processes of word-formation, and the means by which Merriam-Webster editors record and define new words and meanings, then a list of pronunciation symbols and a list of abbreviations.

In addition to the contributions of the present members of the staff, listed below, those of former staff member Kara L. Noble deserve acknowledgment.

Editorial Staff

Explanatory Notes

NOTE: In all but a few minor respects (as the use of the asterisk and the word *herein*) the policies and styles embodied in this dictionary are exactly the same as those of its parent, Webster's Third New International Dictionary. Consequently, these notes repeat much of what is said in the Explanatory Notes of Webster's Third. They have been kept as brief as possible, but it is believed that they will answer all the questions a user is likely to have in the normal course of trying to find and make use of the information in this book. If occasionally more detail is needed, however, it should be sought in the Explanatory Notes, Guide to Pronunciation, and other parts of the front matter of Webster's Third.

Entries

A boldface letter or a combination of such letters set flush with the left-hand margin of each column of type is a main entry. The main entry may consist of letters set solid (as **anchorperson**), of letters joined by a hyphen (as **pro-life**), or of letters separated by one or more spaces (as **quick fix**).

The main entries follow one another in alphabetical order letter by letter. Those containing an Arabic numeral are alphabetized as if the numeral were spelled out. Entry words beginning with abbreviated forms of *Mac-* (as **mcluhanesque**) are alphabetized as if spelled *mac-*. Entries often beginning with *St.* in common usage have the abbreviation spelled out *saint* (as **saint emilion**).

A main entry marked with an asterisk (as **bad***) is not a new word, but a new sense of a word already entered in Webster's Third New International Dictionary. A main entry marked with two asterisks (as **callback****) is also a sense of a word entered in Webster's Third, but the entry in this dictionary differs in form (as the style of compounding or the presence or absence of an accent mark) from the entry in the Third.

When one new main entry has exactly the same written form as another, the two are distinguished by superscript numerals preceding each word (as **¹photochromic** *adj* and **²photochromic** *n*). Main entries marked with asterisks are not given such superscript numerals. The order of homographs is usually historical: the one first used in English, insofar as the dates can be established, is entered first.

The centered periods within entry words indicate points at which a hyphen may be put at the end of a line of print or writing. They are not shown at the second and succeeding homographs of a word or for asterisked entries. There are acceptable alternative end-of-line divisions just as there are acceptable variant spellings and pronunciations, but for reasons of space no more than one division is shown for any entry in this dictionary. Centered periods are not given here for asterisked entries or for parts of solid, hyphened, or open compounds that are entered in the body of Webster's Third. Division points for such forms can be found there.

A double hyphen ⸗ at the end of a line in this dictionary stands for a hyphen that belongs at that point in a hyphened word and that is retained when the word is written as a unit on one line.

When a main entry is followed by the word *or* and another form (as **flextime** *or* **flexitime**), the two forms are equal variants. Both are standard, and either one may be used according to personal inclination. When another form is joined to the main entry by the word *also* (as **thrustor** *also* **thruster***), the form after *also* is a secondary variant and occurs less frequently than the first. Secondary variants belong to standard usage and may be used according to personal inclination. If there are two secondary variants, the second is joined to the first by *or* (as **maven** *also* **mavin** *or* **mayvin**).

Variants whose spelling puts them alphabetically more than a column away from the main entry are entered at their own alphabetical places (as **lite** *var of* LIGHT *herein*).

A main entry may be followed by one or more words (as **cablecast** *n* and **cablecaster** *n* at **cablecast** *vt*) derived from it by the addition of a suffix or by a change of grammatical function. These are run-on entries. Each is introduced by a lightface dash and each has a functional label. They are not defined, however, since their meanings can readily be derived from the meaning of the root word.

A few main entries may be followed by one or more phrases (as **get one's act together** and **get on the stick** at **get***) containing the entry word or an inflected form of it. These are also run-on entries. Each is introduced by a lightface dash but there is no functional label. They are, however, defined since their meanings are more than the sum of the meanings of their elements.

Boldface words that appear within parentheses (as **Yayoi ware** at **yayoi**) are run-in entries. They are related to the entry word in an obvious way and their meaning should be clear from the context in which they occur.

Pronunciation

The matter between a pair of reversed virgules \ \ following the entry word indicates the pronunciation. The symbols used are explained in the chart printed on pages 22a and 23a.

Pronunciations are shown for most entries in this book, though two important groups are exceptions. Entries with asterisks have their pronunciations shown in Webster's Third, and so none are shown for them in this book. Similarly, open compounds consisting entirely of words entered in the body of Webster's Third have no pronunciations here. However, a pronunciation is shown for any element of an open compound that is not entered in the body of Webster's Third, e.g., **alfvén wave** \¦al(f)¦vān-, -ven-\.

All the pronunciation variants shown for entries or parts of entries may be considered acceptable in educated English speech. Variation in pronunciation falls into two main categories, predictable and unpredictable. Predictable variants are those for which one speaker's pronunciation differs from another's because their dialects or speech patterns are different. This type of variation may be predicted from the speaker's pronunciation of other words. One type of predictable variation often recorded in this book is the so-called "loss" of \r\ before a consonant or pause in the speech of many Americans from New England, New York City, and much of the South and in that of most southern British speakers. Unpredictable variation, on the other hand, may occur in any dialect, and there is no certain way of telling from a speaker's treatment of other words which variant he might use for a particular utterance of a word with unpredictable variants. For instance, some speakers put more stress on the first syllable of **academese** than on the second; others stress the second syllable more than the first. The order of pronunciation variants in this book does not mean that the first is to be preferred over the second or even that it is necessarily more frequent; of two equally common variants one must be printed before the other. Variants preceded by *also* are appreciably less frequent than unlabeled variants, and those preceded by *sometimes* are infrequent; however, no variant with either of these labels should be considered unacceptable simply on the basis of relative infrequency.

Entries labeled *abbr* are not normally given a pronunciation respelling in this work; the pronunciation may be assumed to be that of its individual constituent letters: **VLSI** *abbr*, **CPR** *abbr*. However, abbreviations are given a pronunciation respelling if evidence of a pronunciation other than that of the constituent letters appears in the Merriam-Webster pronunciation files: **GIGO** \ˈgī,gō, ˈgē-\ *abbr*, **TEFL** \ˈtefəl\ *abbr*. For these it can be assumed that some people may pronounce the constituent letters, even though such a pronunciation is not shown. Some abbreviations are not initialisms but are shortened forms of words or parts of words. Many of these are automatically expanded in speech; for instance, **kbar** is probably most often pronounced like **kilobar**, though it may possibly also be pronounced in a way analogous to the pronunciation of the noun **krad** \ˈkāˌrad\. In entries of this class no pronunciation is shown unless evidence appears in our pronunciation files.

Words of foreign origin whose pronunciations have not been anglicized are shown with a transcription approximating the pronunciation of the original language. Some French pronunciations in this book indicate greater duration by doubling the appropriate vowel symbol, as at **dacquoise** \dȧkwȧȧz\ and **fièvre boutonneuse** \fyeevrᵊ bütȯnœ̄œ̄z\. Similarly, consonantal lengthening or gemination in Italian pronunciations is indicated by doubling the appropriate consonant symbol, as at **agnolotti** \ˌänyəˈlȯttē\.

The following devices are used in the pronunciation transcriptions in addition to the character symbols:

\, ;\ A comma separates pronunciation variants, e.g., **sandinista** \ˌsandəˈnēstə, ˌsän-\. A semicolon separates groups of variants, as at **medullin** \məˈdələ̇n, me-; ˈmedᵊl-, ˈmejəl-\ where the variants transcribed in full would be \məˈdələ̇n, meˈdələ̇n, ˈmedᵊlə̇n, ˈmejələ̇n\.

\(), (\ Parentheses indicate that the enclosed symbols are present in some utterances and not in others; for example, \ˈp(y)ülə\ indicates two pronunciation variants for **pula**, \ˈpyülə\ and \ˈpülə\. In entries such as **lekvar** \ˈlekˌvär, -ˌvȧ(r\ where the pronunciation of so-called "*r*-droppers" is distinguished from that of "*r*-keepers," \(r\ with no closing parenthesis indicates that the *r*-dropper may pronounce the \r\ when a vowel initial word or suffix follows without pause.

\-\ A hyphen is used at the beginning or end of a pronunciation respelling to show that not all of the boldface entry is transcribed. The missing part may be supplied from another entry, from a preceding variant within the same pair of reversed virgules, or from the pronunciation of a common word which is not entered separately in this dictionary but may be found in the body of Webster's Third.

\ˈ ˌ ¦\ Three levels of stress are indicated in this dictionary: primary stress \ˈ\ as in **kir** \ˈki(ə)r\, secondary stress \ˌ\ as in the first syllable of **langoustine** \ˌlaŋgəˈstēn\, and no stress at all, as in the second syllable of **signage** \ˈsīnij\. The stress marks stacked together \¦\ mean "either \ˈ\ or \ˌ\." Items with a stress pattern like that of **aflatoxin** \¦afləˈtäksə̇n\ should be interpreted as indicating that when one of the stressed syllables has primary stress the other has secondary, or that both may have secondary stress, as is common in running speech for adjectives and even nouns in attributive position where the primary stress may fall on the word being modified. Thus the transcription for **aflatoxin** represents \ˌafləˈtäksə̇n, ˈafləˌtäksə̇n, ˌaflaˌtäksə̇n\. The occurrence of \(ˈ)\ on the first syllable and of \¦\ on a later syllable indicates that in some contexts the first syllable has little or no stress and the later syllable has primary stress but that in other contexts the first syllable has primary stress and the later syllable has secondary stress, e.g., **hydronautics** \(ˈ)hīdrə¦nȯd·iks\. Stress is especially variable in compounds, depending on context, emphasis, and personal preference. Fully French pronunciations are shown without any stress marks, as in the usual practice of transcribers of French. Heaviest stress generally falls on the last syllable of French words pronounced in isolation, though no such precise rule can be given for French pronunciation in running speech. The placement of stress marks in this book is not intended to indicate syllable division; see the section on \·\ below.

_\ The low-set minus sign cancels a stress at the same point in a pronunciation shown elsewhere, as in a preceding variant or in a pronunciation for a preceding entry, e.g., **dopamine** \ˈdōpəˌmēn, -_mə̇n\ and **planetology** \ˌplanəˈtäləjē\ . . . —**planetological**\-_tᵊlˈäjə̇kəl\.

\·\ Syllable division is not regularly indicated in the pronunciation transcriptions. However, we have found it desirable to indicate what we will here call syllable division in some cases where confusion might arise otherwise. This is shown by the use of a centered period \·\. It occurs, for instance, between the third and fourth syllables of the plural of **corpus allatum, corpora allata** \ˌkȯrpərə·əˈlād·ə, . . . \, to indicate that the two adjacent vowels are in separate syllables. In the entry **fortran** \ˈfȯr·ˌtran\ the centered period indicates that the variety of \t\ used in this word is that heard at the beginning of a word or syllable as in *tan* or *train,* and not that heard at the end of a word or syllable as in *foot* or *fort.* That is to say, the centered period shows that the *tr* in **fortran** is pronounced as in *four transoms,* not as in *Fort Ransom.* The centered period following the character in the symbol \d·\ is not meant to represent syllable division. The use of this symbol is explained in some detail in the Pronunciation Guide to Webster's Third. \d·\ should be thought of as a single character representing a sound heard in the speech of most Americans in both *madder* and *matter.*

\|\ The lightface vertical bar is used occasionally to assist understanding of variant pronunciations. It is placed just before or just after a variation to serve as a point of reference. In the entry **zuppa inglese** \¦tsüpə·iŋˈglā|(ˌ)zā, ¦zü, -inˈg-, |(ˌ)sā, |sē, |zē\ the vertical bar appears before each of the four variant final syllables of the compound. This device makes it possible to show economically a number of variant pronunciations for *zuppa inglese.*

\=\ A slanted double hyphen is used frequently in this book to represent all the sounds of a syllable. The syllable or syllables to be supplied may be those of a preceding entry but more often are those of an entry in the body of Webster's Third. An example of the first kind is **saluretic** \ˌsalyəˈred·ik\ *n* . . . —**saluretic** \¦==¦==\ *adj.* An example of the second kind is **one–up** \¦=ˈ=\. Solid or hyphened compounds whose parts are entered in Webster's Third are typically represented in this dictionary by a combination of slanted double hyphens and stress marks.

\"\ A ditto mark in a pronunciation stands for the sounds of the nearest preceding pronounced entry. The pronunciation of **²macho** \"\ is thus the same as that of **¹macho** \ˈmä(ˌ)chō\.

\+\ When a word is composed of a combining form or prefix and a whole English word, the pronunciation often consists of a transcription of the first part followed by a plus sign. The plus sign means that the sounds for the second element will be found at the entry for that word in Webster's Third. If other compounds with the same first element follow, their pronunciation may be shown by a ditto mark followed by a plus sign, e.g., **bioenvironmental** \¦bīō+\, **bioethics** \"+\, **biofeedback** \"+\. The plus sign also appears in the formula "+V," which means "when a vowel sound follows without a pause," e.g., **watergate** \ˈwȯ|d·ə(r)ˌgāt, ˈwä|, |tə(-, *usu* -ād·+V\.

\R, –R\ The first of these symbols indicates the pronunciation of speakers who consistently pronounce postvocalic \r\; the second indicates the pronunciation of speakers who consistently have no \r\ sound where educated usage sanctions its absence, e.g., **martin luther king day** \R ˌmartᵊnˌlüthərˈkiŋ-, –R ˌmȧtᵊnˌlüthəˈk-\.

\. . .\ The three-dot ellipsis is sometimes used after a plus sign to stand for the second part of a three-part compound of which the first two parts form a solid unit. In this use it is a space-saving device, and the part represented by the ellipsis will be found at its own place in Webster's Third. Thus, in the pronunciation shown at **para influenza virus** \¦parə+ . . .-\, the dots stand for \ˌinˌflüˈenzə\, found at **influenza** in Webster's Third.

\÷\ The symbol \÷\ preceding a variant indicates that although the variant occurs in educated speech many people consider it unacceptable, e.g., the variant \ ÷ -kyələ͵rīz\ at the entry for **denuclearize**.

Functional Labels

An italic label indicating a part of speech or some other functional classification follows the pronunciation or, if no pronunciation is given, the main entry. The eight traditional parts of speech are abbreviated thus: *adj* (adjective), *adv* (adverb), *conj* (conjunction), *interj* (interjection), *n* (noun), *prep* (preposition), *pron* (pronoun), *vb* (verb).

Other italicized labels used to indicate functional classifications that are not traditional parts of speech include these: *vi* (verb intransitive), *vt* (verb transitive), *abbr* (abbreviation), *comb form* (combining form), *prefix, service mark, suffix, symbol, trademark.* Functional labels are sometimes combined.

In entries for verbs that have both transitive and intransitive uses, a boldface swung dash ~ appears before the second functional label to stand for the boldface entry word (as **²shuck**. . . *vi* . . . ~ *vt* . . .).

Inflected Forms

NOUNS

The plurals of nouns are shown in full in this dictionary when the noun has an irregular plural or a zero plural (i.e., one whose form is unchanged from the singular) or a foreign plural, when the noun is a compound that pluralizes any element but the last, when the noun has variant plurals, and when it is believed that the dictionary user might have reasonable doubts about the spelling of the plural.

dong . . . *n, pl* **dong**
granum . . . *n, pl* **grana**
prelate nullius . . . *n, pl* **prelates nullius**
halala . . . *n, pl* **halala** *or* **halalas**
bialy . . . *n, pl* **bialys**
goofy-foot . . . *n, pl* **goofy-foots**

A noun that has only a regular English plural has its plural indicated by the suffixal cross-reference -S or -ES following the label *n.* Asterisked entries and compounds whose final element is regular and is entered in Webster's Third have no plural shown in this dictionary.

Nouns that are plural in form and that regularly occur in plural construction are labeled *n pl* (as **granny glasses** *n pl*). Nouns that are plural in form but that do not always take a plural verb are appropriately labeled:

cliometrics . . . *n pl but sing in constr*
cardiodynamics . . . *n pl but sing or pl in constr*

VERBS

The principal parts of verbs are shown in full in this dictionary when suffixation brings about a doubling of a final consonant, when the inflection is irregular, when there are variant inflected forms, when it is desirable to show the pronunciation of one of the inflected forms, and when it is believed that the dictionary user might have reasonable doubts about the spelling of an inflected form.

> [2]**rap** . . . *vt* **rapped**; **rapped**; **rapping**; **raps**
> **epoxy** . . . *vt* **epoxied** *or* **epoxyed**; **epoxied** *or* **epoxyed**; **epoxying**; **epoxies**
> **beaver** . . . *vi* **beavered**; **beavered**; **beavering** \-v(ə)riŋ\; **beavers**
> **yo-yo** . . . *vi* **yo-yoed**; **yo-yoed**; **yo-yoing**; **yo-yos**

Verbs that have only regular inflected forms (including those whose past-tense formation involves dropping a final *-e* or changing a final *-y* to *-i-*) have their inflected forms indicated by the suffixal cross-reference -ED/-ING/-S or -ED/-ING/-ES following the functional label. Asterisked entries and compounds whose final element is regular and is entered in Webster's Third have no inflected forms shown in this dictionary.

If one or more inflected forms cannot be recorded for lack of evidence, the ones recorded are identified with italic labels (as [2]**MIRV**. . .*vb, past or past part* **MIRVed**; *pres part* **MIRVing**).

ADJECTIVES & ADVERBS

The comparative and superlative forms of adjectives and adverbs are shown in full in this dictionary when suffixation brings about a doubling of a final consonant, when the inflection is irregular, when there are variant inflected forms, and when it is believed that a dictionary user might have reasonable doubts about the spelling of an inflected form.

> **bad*** *adj* **badder**; **baddest**
> **dicey** . . . *adj* **dicier**; **diciest**
> **dyke** *or* **dike** . . . *n* . . .— **dykey** *or* **dikey** . . . *adj* **dykier** *or* **dikier**; **dykiest** *or* **dikiest**
> **kooky** *also* **kookie** . . . *adj* **kookier**; **kookiest**

Adjectives and adverbs that have only regular inflected forms have their inflected forms indicated by the suffixal cross-reference -ER/-EST following the functional label. Asterisked entries and compounds whose final element is regular and is entered in Webster's Third do not have their comparative and superlative forms shown in this dictionary.

The inclusion of inflected forms in *-er* and *-est* at adjective and adverb entries does not mean that *more* and *most* cannot be used with these adjectives and adverbs; their comparative and superlative degrees may be expressed in either way.

Inflected forms whose spelling puts them alphabetically more than a column away from the main entry are also entered at their own alphabetical places (as **makuta** *pl of* LIKUTA *herein*).

Capitalization

Most of the entries in this dictionary are set entirely lowercase. Exceptions are trademarks and service marks, some abbreviations and symbols, and some words (as nouns and verbs) derived from such abbreviations.

> **Dumpster** . . . *trademark*
> **CAD** *abbr*

Lr *symbol*
MIA . . . *n*
[2]OD . . . *vi*

For lowercase entries the extent to which usage calls for an initial uppercase letter is indicated by one of four italic labels.

cap = almost always capitalized initially
usu cap = more often capitalized than not; capitalized approximately two to one
often cap = as likely to be capitalized as not; acceptable one way or the other
sometimes cap = more often not capitalized than capitalized; not usually capitalized

Absence of a label and of an initial capital indicates that the word is almost never capitalized except under irrelevant circumstances (as beginning a sentence).

yinglish . . . *n* . . . *cap*
mahlerian . . . *adj, usu cap*
verdicchio . . . *n* . . . *often cap*
tabbouleh . . . *n* . . . *sometimes cap*
freebase . . . *vb*

When an entry has more than one letter in question, the label specifies the capitalization indicated by usage.

steak diane . . . *n, usu cap D*
creutzfeld–jacob disease . . . *n, usu cap C & J*
zip code . . . *n, often cap Z & I & P*
totten trust . . . *n, usu cap 1st T*

For a word that is capitalized in some senses and lowercase in others, variation from the form of the main entry is shown by the use of an italicized label at the appropriate sense (as **kwanza** . . . *n* . . . **3** *usu cap*).

Etymology

The matter in square brackets preceding the definition is the etymology. Meanings given in roman type within these brackets are not definitions of the entry, but are meanings of the italicized words within the brackets.

The etymology gives the language from which a word borrowed into English has come. It also gives the form or a transliteration of the word in that language, if the form in that language differs from that in English.

Many abbreviations are used in etymologies. Their meanings will be found in "Abbreviations in This Work" on page 24a.

Whenever a language name appears in an etymology without an expressed form or without an expressed meaning, the form or meaning of the etymon in that language is the same as that of the word immediately preceding. If a language name which begins an etymology has no expressed form or meaning, the form of the word in that language is the same as the form of the entry word, or the meaning is the same as that of the first definition of the entry. When an italicized word appears in an etymology with no language label, that word belongs to the same language as the word immediately preceding.

ekistics . . . *n pl but sing in constr* [NGk *oikistikē,* fr. fem. of *oikistikos* relating to settlement, fr. Gk, fr. *oikizein* to settle, colonize, fr. *oikos* house . . .]

In the example above, the unglossed New Greek noun *oikistikē* has the same meaning as that defined for the entry word **ekistics**; the unlabeled adjective *oikistikos* is, like *oikistikē,* a New Greek word; the unspecified Greek word from which New Greek *oikistikos* descended was also spelled *oikistikos*; and the unlabeled words *oikizein* and *oikos* are both Greek.

When no language label at all appears ahead of a word, it is assumed to be English. English words that are entered in the body of Webster's Third are not specially marked when they appear in an etymology, but those that are entries in this book are followed by "(herein)." Superscript numbers preceding forms in an etymology identify them in each case as a numbered homographic entry in Webster's Third or, if followed by "(herein)," in this book. Such numbers are normally used with unlabeled (Modern English) forms; but sometimes, for convenience, they are used with forms that are labeled (as with ISV or NL), provided these are identical in spelling with the corresponding Modern English form.

reverse transcriptase . . . *n* [*transcript*ion (herein) + *-ase*]
brushback . . . *n* . . . [^{6}*brush* + *back*]
high–riser . . . *n* . . . [^{1}*high-rise* (herein) + ^{2}*-er*]
graviton . . . *n* . . . [ISV *gravity* + ^{2}*on*]

Small superscript numerals following words or syllables in an etymology refer to the tone of the word or syllable which they follow. They are, therefore, used only with forms cited from tone languages, e.g., **chiao** . . . *n* . . . [Chin (Pek) *chiao*^{3}].

An etymology is often not given for a word formed in English especially by compounding of free forms. Such an absence indicates that the etymology is expected to be self-evident. When the source of a word is not known, the formula "origin unknown" is used.

At some entries an etymology gives cognates from other Indo-European languages. Such cognates are introduced by the phrase "akin to." A special application of this phrase occurs when it is preceded by the name of a group of languages rather than the name of a particular language and a form from that language. Then it indicates that a word was borrowed from some language belonging to the indicated group but that it is not possible to say with confidence that the word in question is a borrowing of a particular attested word in a particular language of the group. The words following "akin to" are, in this situation, attested cognates of the word in question. Considerations of space preclude a full display of cognates at every possible entry; usually the reader is directed by a "more at" cross-reference to an entry in the body of Webster's Third where such a full display of cognates is given.

spiedino . . . *n* . . . [It, lit., skewer, fr. *spiedo* spit, spear, fr. OF *espiet* lance, fr. (assumed) Frankish *speut* lance; akin to G *spies* spit, Sp *espeto* skewer . . .]
kalimba . . . *n* . . . [of African origin; akin to Bemba *akalimba* zanza, Kimbundu *marimba* xylophone]
circadian . . . *adj* [L *circa* about + *dies* day + E *-an* —more at CIRCA, DEITY]

Usage

Two types of status labels are used in this dictionary—regional and stylistic—to signal that a word or a sense of a word is not part of the standard vocabulary of English.

A word or sense limited in use to one of the other countries of the English-speaking world has an appropriate regional label:

shortlist . . . *vt* . . . *Brit*

The stylistic label *slang* is used with words or senses that are especially appropriate in contexts of extreme informality:

ralph . . . *vb* . . . *slang*

There is no satisfactory objective test for slang, especially with reference to a word out of context. No word, in fact, is invariably slang, and many standard words can be given slang applications.

When the application of a word or sense is very limited, the definition may be preceded by an italic guide phrase that points out the limitation:

scramble* *vi, of a football quarterback*

Definitions are sometimes followed by usage notes that give supplementary information about such matters as idiom, syntax, and semantic relationship. A usage note is introduced by a lightface dash:

factor* . . . *vt* . . .— used with *in* or *into*
mao . . . adj . . .— usu. used of a jacket
sweep* *n* . . .— usu. used in pl.

Definitions are frequently followed by illustrative quotations and verbal illustrations that show a typical use of the word in context. These illustrations are enclosed in angle brackets, and the word being illustrated is either represented by a lightface swung dash (to which an italicized suffix may be added) or is spelled out in italics.

bit-mapped . . . *adj* : being or produced on a computer display in which each pixel of the display is controlled by a bit in the computer's memory ⟨*bit-mapped* graphics⟩
giveback . . . *n* . . . : a previous gain (as an increase in wages or benefits) given back to management by workers (as in a labor contract) ⟨union workers . . . agreed to ∼*s* to avoid layoffs—Lawrence Ingrassia⟩

Definitions

A boldface colon is used in this dictionary to introduce a definition; it is also used to separate two or more definitions of a single sense. If there is no boldface colon, there is no definition. At some entries a usage note may take the place of a definition:

gangle . . . *vi* . . . : to walk or move with or as if with a loose-jointed gait : move like a gangling person
no way . . . *adv* — used interjectionally to express emphatic negation

Boldface Arabic numerals separate the senses of a word that has more than one sense, boldface letters separate subsenses, and lightface numbers in parentheses indicate further division of subsenses.

A particular semantic relationship between meanings is sometimes suggested by the use of one of the italic sense dividers *esp, specif, also,* or *broadly.*

The sense divider *esp* (for *especially*) is used to introduce the most common meaning included in the more general preceding definition. The sense divider *specif* (for *specifically*) is used to introduce a common but highly restricted meaning subsumed in the more general preceding sense.

The sense divider *also* is used to introduce a meaning that is closely related to the preceding sense but that may be considered less important. The sense divider *broadly* is used to introduce an extended or wider meaning of the preceding definition.

lander* *n* : one that lands; *esp* : a space vehicle that is designed to land on a celestial body (as the moon or a planet)
vital signs *n pl* : signs of life; *specif* : the pulse rate, respiratory rate, body temperature, and sometimes blood pressure of a person
dreamscape . . . *n* . . . : a dreamlike usu. surrealistic scene . . .; *also* : a painting of a dreamscape
hang–up* *n* : a source of mental or emotional difficulty; *broadly* : PROBLEM

The order of senses is basically historical: the sense our evidence shows to have been first used in English is usually entered first.

When an italicized label follows a boldface numeral, the label applies only to that specific numbered sense. It does not apply to any other boldface numbered senses. Thus, only the first sense of **clean*** *adj* is slang; the second and third senses are standard.

Cross-References

Five different kinds of cross-references are used in this dictionary: directional, synonymous, cognate, inflectional, and suffixal. Suffixal cross-references are discussed in the section on Inflected Forms above. In each instance a cross-reference is readily recognized by the lightface small capitals in which it is printed. In most cases the occurrence of small capitals refers the reader to an entry in Webster's Third. A cross=reference followed by the word *herein* in italics, however, refers the reader to an entry in this dictionary.

A cross-reference following a lightface dash and beginning with either *compare* or *see* is a directional cross-reference. It directs the dictionary user to look elsewhere for further information.

plateglass . . . *adj* . . .—compare OXBRIDGE *herein*, REDBRICK *herein*
ekuele . . . *n* . . . **1** . . .—see MONEY table *in the Dict*

A cross-reference following a boldface colon is a synonymous cross-reference:

triple jump *n* : HOP, STEP, AND JUMP
apocynthion . . . *n* . . . : APOLUNE *herein*

A synonymous cross-reference indicates that a definition at the entry cross-referred to can be substituted as a definition for the entry or the sense in which the cross-reference appears. A lightface numeral following a synonymous cross-reference refers to a sense number at the entry cross-referred to. A superscript numeral preceding a synonymous cross-reference refers to a numbered homographic entry.

genetic map *n* : MAP 1 *herein*
flak* *n* . . . **3** : ^{3}FLACK

A synonymous cross-reference sometimes accounts for a usage note introduced by "called also" at the entry cross-referred to.

spin wave *n* : . . . —called also *magnon*
magnon . . . *n* . . . : SPIN WAVE *herein*

A cross-reference following an italic label that identifies an entry as an inflected form is an inflectional cross-reference, e.g., **maloti** *pl of* LOTI *herein.*

Abbreviations & Symbols

Abbreviations and symbols are included as main entries in the vocabulary. What follows is an expansion rather than a definition. No boldface colon is used. If the expansion is followed by the word "herein" in italics, the expansion is also an entry in the vocabulary of this book.

ICU *abbr* intensive care unit
p* *symbol* **1** momentum of a particle . . .
EER *abbr* energy efficiency ratio *herein*

Abbreviations have been normalized to one form. In practice, however, there is considerable variation in the use of periods and in capitalization (as *bpi, b.p.i., BPI, B.P.I.*), and stylings other than those given in this dictionary are often acceptable.

The Recent Growth of English Vocabulary

The vocabulary of English, like that of every other living language, is constantly growing. This growth is certainly not new. Always, as people have met with new objects and new experiences and have developed new ideas, they have needed new words to describe them. New words and new meanings for old words are the reason for this book. In the sections that follow, we will indicate some of the areas that produce new words, the ways in which new words are formed, and how new words get into the dictionary.

Where Do They All Come From?

Science and technology are probably the most prolific providers of new words today. Most spectacularly, perhaps, they have combined to make possible the flights of *space shuttles,* to take men to the moon and bring them back, and to send robot craft even farther into space and to planets. The exploration of the moon has given us words for novel experiences: *moonshot, moonwalk, earthrise.*

It is not only the more direct exploration of *deep space* which adds to our extraterrestrial vocabulary. Earthbound astronomers continue to make new discoveries and formulate new theories. We hear about *quasars, pulsars, neutron stars, black dwarfs,* and the mysterious *black hole.* The *big bang theory* and the *steady state theory* offer us alternative explanations of the origin of the universe. We learn that the earth moves in a mysterious way, *Chandler's wobble,* not yet explained. And on a more terrestrial scale, we find *plate tectonics* gaining increasing acceptance on the basis of geological observations.

Other fields of scientific study are also adding to the English vocabulary. For all the years men have lived on the earth, they have not exhausted the study of the earth's natural history. It is true that discoveries of undescribed and uncataloged animals and plants are not as frequent as they were in earlier ages, when whole continents were being opened up for scientific exploration. Nor have we yet discovered living things in our exploration of outer space. But we shall probably never feel confident that we know all the forms of life. Few new discoveries are as striking or as controversial as that, as yet unconfirmed, of a large nonhuman primate in the Pacific Northwest. Whether or not he exists, the animal's names, *Sasquatch* and *bigfoot,* are now a part of our language. Other animals, although not new to science, are new to America. For example, two immigrants from abroad, the *walking catfish* and the *imported fire ant,* are making their presence felt in the southeastern United States, and their names have become established in American English.

The discovery of the mechanism of protein synthesis has made genetics a fertile provider of new terms, giving us the *Watson-Crick model* of DNA, the *genetic code, messenger RNA,* and a new meaning for *template* among many others. And as physicists pry deeper and deeper into the atomic nucleus they have discovered more subatomic particles: *kaon, lambda,* and the several varieties of *quarks,* for example. They have discovered *antiparticles,* studied *isospin,* and used *spark chambers.* Medicine too is a major contributor of new terms such as *AIDS, busulfan, Legionnaires' disease, open-heart* surgery, the *sudden infant death syndrome, toxic shock syndrome,* and the famous *pill.* Mathematics has become more noticeable especially since the revising of the subject as taught in school. *Open sentence, onto, truth set,* and *category* are among the mathematical terms that will be found herein.

High-tech sophistication seems to make things faster or smaller, as such terms as *computerize* and *microminiaturization* attest. Programmers communicate with computers in *Logo, C,* or *Pascal,* and computers talk to each other in *ASCII* or *EBCDIC.* Other computer-related terms include *bubble memory, number crunching, printwheel,* and *spreadsheet.* Technical improvement in *microforms* has made possible the business of *micropublishing.* Tiny *microchips* make the pocket calculator and the *microcomputer* possible. And in even more familiar applications technology has supplied the *flashcube,* the *microwave oven,* the *videocassette,* the *compact disc,* and the *solar collector.*

Some technological advances are less benevolent than these, however. Our capacity for military destructiveness is constantly increasing, and with it our military vocabulary. We have *ABMs, SAMs* and *MIRVs.* We have *cruise missiles, smart bombs,* and *AWACS.* We have *overkill.* We can talk almost casually about the possibility of nuclear war, and we have a new unit of measurement to use in such discussions, the *megadeath.* Our long military involvement in Vietnam also increased our vocabulary. We sought to justify our actions by the *domino theory.* We disparaged the *Cong* by calling them *dinks.* The *Green Berets* became a household word, and the common foot soldier became a *grunt.* The division of American opinion on our undeclared war gave us *doves* and *hawks.* And the words we brought out of the war were not only military: the appearance in American English of such words as *ao dai* and *hootch* was a by-product of our military involvement in Southeast Asia.

But science and technology are not the only sources of new words. The two decades since the publication of Webster's Third has seen considerable political and social ferment, and this ferment has left its mark on the language. Besides *hippies, teenyboppers,* and *flower people* we have *preppies, pro-lifers,* and *whistle-blowers, Hare Krishnas, Moonies,* and *yuppies.* We have been exposed to *skyjacking* and *ayatollah,* to *white flight* and *gentrification,* to *redlining* and *supply-side* economics, to *culture shock,* and *future shock.*

So many people have become involved with the drug subculture that the jargon of drugs has won a prominent place in the consciousness of contemporary America. We talk of *uppers* and *downers, acid, free base, jays, dexies,* and *smack,* of people who have *OD'd,* and of people *busted* by *narcs* for trying to smuggle in a couple of *keys.*

Minorities have also made themselves heard. The civil rights movement that began with *freedom rides* has made us all more aware of black culture. Black culture itself have given us many new words. A new academic subject, *black studies,* has been added to the curriculum of many schools. And *Afro, dashiki,* the *Black Panthers,* the *Black Muslims,* and *soul* are familiar to most of us. Other minorities have also become more politically active and more visible: we are now familiar with both *Chicanos* and *Native Americans.* From the women's movement we get such terms as *Ms., sexism,* and *chairperson.* Rounding out the group are politically active *golden-agers* who call themselves *Gray Panthers* and fight *ageism.*

The changing attitude of Americans toward sexual matters and materials has also contributed to the language. Movies are now rated *G, PG, PG-13, R,* or *X,* and people may be *AC/DC.* The homosexual subculture has become more open, bringing into general use such terms as *homophile, gay, butch, drag queen,* and *camp.*

Education is another source of new vocabulary, giving us *underachiever, open classroom, TA, grade point average, CAI,* and *pass-fail* grading. Increasing interest in the consumer has given us *consumerism, callback, unit pricing,* and *generic.*

Entertainment has always been a source of new words. We have *sitcoms, docudramas, videos,* and *shoot-'em-ups* on television and *call-in* programs on radio; at the neighborhood movie theater we might watch a *spaghetti western.* We might see *break dancing* or listen to *salsa, punk rock, rap, reggae,* or *zydeco.* Sports continues its steady production of vocabulary with new sports such as *roller hockey* and new ways of playing old ones, such as baseball's *designated hitter.* Television coverage of football fills weekends with *blitzes, play-action passes, square outs,* and *squib kicks.* Those who care *zilch* about football may go to the track and play the *perfecta, superfecta,* or *trifecta.* The *martial arts* of the Far East have given us *aikido* and *kung fu* along with *dan, dojo,* and *black belt.*

Cooking too has added to the English vocabulary. From *aioli* to *zuppa inglese* English has borrowed a host of terms from foreign cuisines, including *caldo verde, frijoles refritos, souvlakia, tabbouleh,* and *wok.* The vocabulary of food has also been increased by such domestic contributors as the *corn chip, lane cake, green goddess dressing,* and *sloppy joe.*

How Are They Formed?

English gets its new vocabulary from many fields, some very new. But these new words are, for the most part, created or derived in a number of time-honored ways. Not all new words, in fact, are really new. Old words are frequently given new meanings to fit new situations. *Angel,* for example, is the name of a spiritual being believed by many to be able to exert an influence on humans without their being aware of his presence. Now the word *angel* is used also for a radar echo whose cause is not visually discernible. Because the dove is a traditional symbol of peace and the hawk is a predatory bird, *dove* has come to be used for a conciliatory person, *hawk* for one who is militant. We have long been familiar with the *Mafia* as a secret criminal society; now the use of the word has been extended so that any clique may be called a *mafia.*

Some new words are new not in form but in function. By functional shift an old noun, for example, may come to be used as a new verb. The noun *clone* was first used for "an aggregate of the asexually produced progeny of an individual." *Clone* has now been made into a verb, meaning "to propagate a clone from." The noun *update,* meaning "an updating," comes by functional shift from the verb *update.* Similarly, the adjective *soul* comes from the noun, the noun *commute* from the verb, the verb *format* from the noun.

Of course the words most obviously new are those whose forms have not been used before, whether in earlier senses or in other functions. One common method of forming new words is compounding, combining two (or more) old words to form a new one. Typical compounds are such words as *fake book, pantsuit, uptight, goof-off, acidhead, bag lady, debit card, floating decimal, water bed, courseware, splashdown.* Some of these occur in more than one styling—closed (*acidhead*), hyphened (*acid⸗head*), or open (*acid head*)—but only the most common styling will appear in the dictionary. Some new words are compounds of parts of older words. *Gridlock,* for example, adds the *-lock* from *deadlock* to *grid. Underwhelm* is formed from *under* and the *-whelm* of *overwhelm.*

Sometimes words which are combined seem to overlap. Two words which have letters or sounds in common may be blended. Typical blends are such new words as *cremains,* from *cremated* and *remains, gasohol,* from *gasoline* and *alcohol,* and *Franglais,* blended in French of *français* (French) and *anglais* (English).

Many word elements occur only in combinations, never alone. There are affixes (prefixes and suffixes) and combining forms. Many old affixes and combining forms are very prolific. The prefix *anti-*, for example, has given us *antihero, antiparticle, antipollution, antisatellite, antismog,* and a host of other new words. From *non-* we derive such words as *nonbook, nondiscrimination, nonnegative,* and *nonperson.* The suffix *-ese,* which denotes a jargon, has formed *academese, computerese, educationese, sociologese.* The combining form *-logy* has been especially prolific in recent years, yielding terms for such studies as *erotology, Pekingology,* and *planetology.* Nor is the English language content with its already large hoard of affixes and combining forms; it creates or borrows new ones like the suffix *-manship,* taken from *sportsmanship* and used to form such words as *grantsmanship*; like the suffix *-nik,* borrowed from Yiddish and used in *peacenik, computernik,* and their relatives; like the combining form *-in,* which we find not only in the original *sit-in,* but very widespread, as in *love-in, teach-in,* and *smoke-in,* and like the very frequently used new combining form *mini-,* in *minibike, minibus, minicomputer, miniseries,* and *ministate.*

Many new words are simply shortened forms, or clippings, of older words. By shortening we derive *deli* from *delicatessen, mayo* from *mayonnaise, mod* from *modern, sci-fi* from *science fiction.* Some words are formed as acronyms from the initial letters of the parts of a compound term. In this way we have created *COBOL* from *common business oriented language, PG* from *parental guidance, WASP* from *white Anglo-Saxon Protestant,* and *AIDS* from *acquired immune deficiency syndrome.*

A process somewhat similar to clipping is known as back-formation. A back-formation is formed from an already existing word by subtracting a real or supposed affix. *Gangling,* for example, looks as if it ought to be the present participle of a verb, so we create a new verb *gangle,* removing the supposed derivative suffix *-ing. Laser,* although it is an acronymic formation from *light amplification by stimulated emission of radiation,* looks like an agent noun formed from a verb. So we remove the apparent agent suffix and form the verb *lase.* In like manner, we have created the back-formations *free-associate* from *free association* and *one-up* from *one-upmanship.*

Many new English words are not products of English word formation at all. They are borrowed from other languages. For much of its history English has been a great borrower, building its vocabulary by culling languages all over the world for new and useful terms. From the French, English has taken such words as *après-ski, extraordinaire, bidonville,* and *yé-yé* (the last borrowed earlier by French from English *yeah-yeah*). We have borrowed Italian *autostrada* and *ciao,* Portuguese *cachaça,* German *gemütlich* and *gemütlichkeit,* Swedish *ombudsman,* Mexican Spanish *machismo,* Hindi *tabla,* Sanskrit *tala,* Chinese *wok,* Japanese *ikebana,* Tahitian *mai tai,* Persian *ayatollah.*

We have borrowed such words as *flokati* from modern Greek and gone back to classical Greek for *lexis.* One language from which Enlish has borrowed extensively is in a unique position. Yiddish is a language foreign to English, but it is spoken by many English-speaking American Jews, who often lard their English with Yiddish words. And many Yiddish words have passed into the speech of non-Yiddish-speaking Americans. Especially prominent among these borrowings are pejorative terms like *klutz, kvetch, nebbish,* and *schlock.* But also from Yiddish come *chutzpah* (perhaps pejorative), *bialy, maven, mensch,* and *nosh.*

Sometimes English compounds are borrowed from other languages, but their components are translated into English. These are called loan translations. *Black humor* is a loan translation from French *humour noir.* French *objet trouvé* has entered English both as a straight borrowing and as a loan translation (*found object*). Occasionally we translate only part of a compound we are borrowing. *Auteur theory,* for example, is a part translation of French *politique des auteurs.*

Some new words come from the names of people or places. The *Alfvén wave,* for instance, was named for Swedish astrophysicist Hannes Alfvén, *Chandler's wobble* for American astronomer Seth Carlo Chandler. The *Heimlich maneuver* was named for Henry J. Heimlich, an American surgeon. *A-go-go* comes from a café and discotheque in Paris, the Whisky à Gogo.

Trademarks are another source of new words. Although a trademark is owned by a particular company and used for a specific class of products, some trademarks become so familiar that they are used by many people for similar products. Of course a company that owns a trademark will try to protect its property and maintain the association of the trademarked name with its product alone. But occasionally a trademark does become generic. *Granola,* formerly a trademark, is now a generic name for a cereal mixture whose basic component is rolled oats. Sometimes a trademark for one product is borrowed and used as a general word for something else. *STP* is a trademark for a motor fuel additive, but it is commonly applied to a psychedelic drug. Other trademarks, although they do not become generic, do produce derivatives by functional shift. The trademark *Mace,* for example, has given us the verb *mace.* Some trademarks which have not become generic occur so often in speech and writing that they deserve a place in a dictionary, even though they cannot really be considered a part of the general vocabulary of English. Those entries known to be trademarks or service marks are so labeled and are treated in accordance with a formula approved by the United States Trademark Association. No entry in this dictionary, however, should be regarded as affecting the validity of any trademark or service mark.

Many new words are onomatopoeic, imitative of sound. *Chugalug* imitates the sound of swallowing liquid, *bleep* a high-pitched sound of electronic equipment, *zap* the sound of a gun. Some words are simply coined ex nihilo, but these are relatively rare. One such is *grok,* which was coined by the American author Robert A. Heinlein in his 1961 science fiction novel *Stranger in a Strange Land.*

How Do They Get Into Merriam-Webster Dictionaries?

It is one thing for a word to get into the language and quite another for it to get into a dictionary. The definitions in this book, as in all Merriam-Webster dictionaries, are based upon our voluminous files of citations. The editorial staff regularly reads a variety of periodicals, as well as fiction and nonfiction books in many fields. Every editor spends a part of each working day reading and marking. When a word that is not in our dictionaries or that is used in a new or striking way is noted, the editor underlines the word and brackets enough of its context to make the word's meaning clear. (Sometimes, it is true, a word's meaning will not be clear no matter how much context surrounds it. When this happens, the only thing an editor can do is mark it anyway, simply for its occurrence, and hope that the word will turn up elsewhere, more intelligibly used.) The passages marked in this manner are put on 3 × 5 slips of paper, called citation slips, and filed alphabetically. Citations are also stored in machine-readable form. When a new dictionary is being written, a definer will take all the citations for a particular word, sort them according to grammatical function (such as noun or verb) and possible separable segments of meaning, read them carefully to determine the meaning of the word as it is used, and write a definition. The definitions, then, are based not on an editor's idea of what words ought to mean but rather on the meanings actually given to words by the speakers and writers of English who use them.

Not every word that is represented in the citation files will be entered in a dictionary. A single citation or two is not normally considered evidence of a word's establishment as part of the general vocabulary. We look for the use of a word in a variety of sources, and for its occurrence over several years. Some words enjoy a brief vogue, when they are on practically every tongue, then disappear. In the mid 1960s the division of British youth into *Mods* and *Rockers* seemed destined to add these terms to the general vocabulary. But after a couple of years the division faded away and with it the words. Such words as *Mod* and *Rocker* are items of interest for a historical dictionary, but are unlikely to enter a general dictionary.

Some of our 12,000 Words are older than the 1960s. They appear here because, for one reason or another, they were not entered in Webster's Third New International Dictionary. Some words, although they had been in the spoken language for years, did not appear in print until recently or appeared so rarely as to be caught only once or twice, or not at all, by our reading and marking program. *Mayo* has probably been heard at lunch counters for forty years or more, but it was only in the early 1960s that we began to see it in print. Another word, *frog* "a spiked or perforated holder used to keep flowers in a position in a vase," is quite old. Even now it has been cited only very rarely by our readers and markers. But after the appearance of Webster's Third, a number of correspondents questioned its absence from that book, so it was entered among the addenda.

In some fields, our reading and marking program was fairly weak in the past. In mathematics, for example, such words as *counterexample* and *Fibonacci number,* although they are not new, have only recently caught the attention of the markers and definers. Some older words did not appear in Webster's Third because they were rejected by outside consultants. One such is *sprechstimme,* which was rejected by the music consultant with the note "The time will come . . . when this word will or must, be entered." His note is dated 1957 and the citational evidence, now more than three times what it was in 1957, shows that *sprechstimme* deserves entry.

Some words have an air of antiquity not because they themselves are old but because the objects with which they are associated are old. The controversial *Homo habilis,* for example, although he is a fossil about two million years old, was not discovered until 1964. And though typists have been taught for years with the aid of such sentences as "The quick brown fox jumps over the lazy dog," we knew of no word for such sentences until 1964, when we first met *pangram* in print.

Pronunciation Symbols

ə in unstressed syllables as in banan**a**, c**o**llide, **a**but, mak**e**r; in stressed syllables as in h**u**mdr**u**m, ab**u**t, and by *r*-keepers in b**i**rd

ə̄ alternative pronunciation used by *r*-droppers in stressed positions where *r*-keepers have \ər\ as in b**ir**d

ə̇ two-value symbol meaning \ə\ or \i\ in unstressed syllables only

ᵊ immediately preceding \l\, \n\, \m\ as in batt**le**, cott**on**, and one pronunciation of op**en** \ˈōpᵊm\; immediately following\l\, \m\, \r\as often in French tab**le**, pris**me**, tit**re**

əi alternative pronunciation used by *r*-droppers in stressed positions where *r*-keepers have \ər\ as in b**ir**d

a m**a**t, m**a**p, m**a**d, m**a**n, p**a**ss, st**a**mp

ā d**ay**, f**a**de, **a**orta, dr**a**pe, c**a**pe, d**a**te

ä b**o**ther, c**o**t, and with most Americans f**a**ther, c**a**rt

ȧ f**a**ther as pronounced by speakers who do not rhyme it with *bother*; **au**nt as pronounced by speakers who do not rhyme it with *pant* or *font*; f**ar**ther, c**ar**t as pronounced by *r*-droppers; French p**a**tte

au̇ n**ow**, l**ou**d, **ou**t, some pronunciations of t**al**cum (see \u̇\)

b **b**a**b**y, ri**b**

ch **ch**in, nature ˈnā**ch**ə(r)\ (actually, this sound is \t\ + \sh\)

d el**d**er, un**d**one, gla**d**

d· as in the usual American pronunciation of du**t**y, la**tt**er; \t\ is always to be understood as an alternative

e b**e**d, p**e**t

ē in stressed syllables as in b**ea**t, nosebl**ee**d, **e**venly, sl**ee**py; in unstressed syllables as in one pronunciation of evenl**y**, sleep**y**, envious, ign**e**ous (alternative \i\)

f **f**i**f**ty, cu**ff**

g **g**o, bi**g**

h **h**at, a**h**ead

hw **wh**ale as pronounced by those who do not have the same pronunciation for both *whale* and *wail*

i b**i**d, t**i**p, one pronunciation of act**i**ve, evenl**y** (alternative unstressed \ē\)

ī s**i**te, s**i**de, b**uy** (actually, this sound is \ä\ + \i\ or \ȧ\ + \i\)

j **j**ob, **g**em, **j**u**dge** (actually, this sound is \d\ + \zh\)

k **k**in, **c**oo**k**, a**che**

k̲ as in one pronunciation of lo**ch** (alternative \k\); German i**ch**, bu**ch**

l **l**i**l**y, poo**l**, co**l**d

m **m**ur**m**ur, di**m**, ny**m**ph

n **n**o, ow**n**

ⁿ indicates that a preceding vowel or diphthong is pronounced with open nasal passages as in French *un bon vin blanc* \œⁿbōⁿvaⁿbläⁿ\

ŋ si**ng** \ˈsiŋ\, si**ng**er \ˈsiŋə(r)\, fi**ng**er \ˈfiŋgə(r)\, i**n**k \ˈiŋk\

ō b**o**ne, kn**ow**, b**eau**

ȯ s**aw**, **a**ll, gn**aw**

œ French b**œu**f, German H**ö**lle

œ̄ French f**eu**, German H**öh**le

ȯi c**oi**n, destr**oy**, s**awi**ng

p pe**pp**er, li**p**

r **r**a**r**ity, **r**ead; ca**r** and ca**r**d as pronounced by *r*-keepers

s sour**ce**, le**ss**

sh with nothing between, as in **sh**y, mi**ss**ion, ma**ch**ine, spe**ci**al (actually this is a single sound, not two)

t **t**ie, a**tt**ack; one pronunciation of la**tt**er (alternative \d·\)

th with nothing between, as in **th**in, e**th**er (actually this is a single sound, not two)

th̲ **th**en, ei**th**er, **th**is (actually this is a single sound, not two)

ü r**u**le, y**ou**th, union \ˈyünyən\, few \ˈfyü\

u̇ p**u**ll, w**oo**d, t**oo**k, curable \ˈkyu̇rəbəl\

ue German f**ü**llen, h**ü**bsch

ue̅ French r**ue**, German f**üh**len

v **v**i**v**id, gi**ve**

w **we**, a**w**ay; in some words having final \(ˌ)ō\ or \(ˌ)yü\ variant \əw\ occurs before vowels as in foll**ow**ing \ˈfäləwiŋ\

y **y**ard, **y**oung, cue \ˈkyü\, union \ˈyünyən\

\ marks the beginning and end of a transcription

, ; a comma separates pronunciation variants; a semicolon separates groups of variants (see page 7a)

(), (indicate that what is symbolized between or after is present in some utterances but not in others (see page 7a)

\- used at the beginning or end of a partially transcribed pronunciation (see page 8a)

ˈ ˌ ˈˌ \ˈ\ precedes a syllable with strongest stress; \ˌ\ precedes a syllable with next= strongest stress; combined marks \ˈˌ\ precede a syllable whose stress may be either of these (see page 8a)

_ indicates that the following syllable is unstressed: *riemann integral* \irēˌmän-, -_mən-\

· used to indicate syllable division where confusion might otherwise arise (see also \d·\ above and page 8a)

+V means "when a vowel sound follows without pause, as in a suffix or another word"

| facilitates the placement of a variant pronunciation: *flightily* \ˈflīd·|ᵊlē, -īt|, |ᵊli, |əl-\

z **z**one, rai**se**

zh with nothing between, as in vi**si**on, azure \ˈazhə(r)\ (actually this is a single sound, not two)

= represents a syllable whose pronunciation is given elsewhere: *airbus* \ˈ=ˌ=\

" indicates that a preceding pronunciation is to be repeated: *¹poise* \ˈpȯiz\ *vb,* *²poise* \"\ *n*

\+ indicates a part of a pronunciation to be sought elsewhere in the vocabulary: *alloantibody* \ˌalo+\ (pronunciation of *-antibody* is to be sought at ANTIBODY)

R labels certain pronunciations used by speakers who do not drop *r*

–R labels certain pronunciations used by speakers who drop *r*

. . . indicates omitted material to be supplied from another entry: *antiballistic missile* \"+. . .-\ (pronunciation of *-ballistic* is to be sought at BALLISTIC)

÷ indicates that many regard as unacceptable the one pronunciation immediately following, as in *escalate* \ˈeskəˌlāt, ÷-kyə-\

Special Symbols

[ ] boldface square brackets contain etymology

: boldface symbolic colon signals a definition or sense

~ boldface or lightface swung dash stands for the preceding boldface entry word

⟨⟩ lightface angle brackets contain a verbal illustration

= lightface double hyphen at end-of-line is a hyphen that should be retained

\+ plus sign in etymology joins words or word elements

† daggers precedes a death date

Abbreviations in This Work

ab	about
abbr	abbreviation
adj	adjective
adv	adverb
advt	advertisement
Alta	Alberta
alter	alteration
Am, Amer	American
AmerSp	American Spanish
Ar	Arabic
Assoc	Association
Austral	Australian
AV	Authorized Version
b	born
B.C.	before Christ
Belg	Belgian
Biog	Biography
Biol	Biological
Brit	British
Bull	Bulletin
C	centigrade
cal	caliber
Canad	Canadian
CanF	Canadian French
Cant	Cantonese
cap	capital, capitalized
Cat, Catal	Catalan
cent	century
Chem	Chemical
Chin	Chinese
Co	Company
comb	combining
conj	conjunction
constr	construction
contr	contraction
Corp	Corporation
Czech	Czechoslovak, Czechoslovakia Czechoslovakian
D	Dutch
Dan	Danish
D.C.	District of Columbia
deriv	derivative
dial	dialect
Dict	Dictionary
dim	diminutive
Du	Dutch
E, Eng	English
Esk	Eskimo
esp	especially
et al	and others
Eve	Evening
Explan	Explanatory
F	French
fem	feminine
fl	flourished
Fla	Florida
Flem	Flemish
fr	from
Fr	French
freq	frequentative
G, Ger	German
Gk	Greek
Gmc	Germanic
GT & E	General Telephone & Electronics
Heb	Hebrew
Hung	Hungarian
Icel	Icelandic
Ill	Illinois
imit	imitative
interj	interjection
Introd	Introduction
Ir	Irish
irreg	irregular
ISV	International Scientific Vocabulary
It, Ital	Italian
Jap	Japanese
Jour	Journal
Jr.	Junior
L	Latin
La	Louisiana
LHeb	Late Hebrew
lit	literally
Lit	Literary
LL	Late Latin
Mag	Magazine
Mass	Massachusetts
MD	Middle Dutch
MexSp	Mexican Spanish
MF	Middle French
MHG	Middle High German
ML	Medieval Latin
MLG	Middle Low German
modif	modification
n	noun
N.C.	North Carolina
NE	northeast
neut	neuter
Nev	Nevada
NGk	New Greek
NHeb	New Hebrew
NL	New Latin
No	North
Norw	Norwegian
NY	New York
obs	obsolete
OE	Old English
OF	Old French
OHG	Old High German
OIt	Old Italian
ON	Old Norse
orig	originally
Pa	Pennsylvania
part	participle
Pek	Pekingese
Per	Persian
perh	perhaps
Pg	Portuguese
pl	plural
Pol	Polish
prep	preposition
Pro	Professors
prob	probably
pron	pronoun
Prov	Provençal
redupl	reduplication
Rev	Review
Russ	Russian
Sat	Saturday
Sc	Scots
Scand	Scandinavian
Scot	Scottish
sing	singular
Skt	Sanskrit
Slav	Slavic
So	South
So Afr	South Africa
Sp	Spanish
specif	specifically
Supp	Supplement
Sw, Swed	Swedish
Tenn	Tennessee
trans	translation
Turk	Turkish
Univ	University
U.S.	United States
U.S.S.R.	Union of Soviet Socialist Republics
usu	usually
v	verb, versus
var	variant
vb	verb
vi	verb intransitive
VL	Vulgar Latin
vt	verb transitive
Vt	Vermont
W	Welsh

A Supplement to Webster's Third New International Dictionary

A

a* *abbr* atto- *herein*

A and R *abbr* artists and repertory

a band *n, usu cap A* [fr. *a*nisotropic *band*] **:** one of the cross striations of striated muscle that contains myosin filaments and appears dark under the light microscope and light in polarized light

ABD \ˌā(ˌ)bēˈdē\ *n* -s [*a*ll *b*ut *d*issertation] **:** a doctoral candidate who has completed the required course work and examinations but not the dissertation

abe·lian \əˈbēlyən, -lēən\ *adj, often cap* [Niels *Abel* †1829 Norw. mathematician + E *-ian*] **:** COMMUTATIVE 2 ⟨~ ring⟩ ⟨the real numbers under addition comprise an ~ group⟩

abio·gen·ic \ˌāˌbīōˈjenik\ *adj* **:** not produced by the action of living organisms — **abio·gen·i·cal·ly** \-nək(ə)lē\ *adv*

ab·la·tor \aˈblād·ə(r)\ *n* -s [LL, one that removes, fr. *ablatus* (suppletive past part. of *auferre* to remove) + *-or* — more at ABLATE] **:** a material that provides thermal protection (as to the outside of a spacecraft on reentry) by ablating

ABM \ˌā(ˌ)bēˈem\ *n* -s **:** ANTIBALLISTIC MISSILE *herein*

aboard* *adv or adj* **1 :** in or into a group, association, or organization ⟨her second promotion since coming ~⟩ **2** *baseball* **:** on base

abort* *n* **:** the premature termination of an action, procedure, or mission relating to a rocket or spacecraft ⟨a launch ~⟩

ABS \ˈāˈbēˈes\ *n* **:** a tough rigid plastic used esp. for automobile parts and building materials

ab·scis·ic acid \(ˌ)abˌsizik-\ *n* [*abscisic* fr. *abscis*ion + *-ic*] **:** a growth-inhibiting plant hormone widespread in nature and made synthetically that typically promotes leaf abscission and dormancy and has an inhibitory effect on cell elongation — called also *abscisin II, dormin*

ab·scis·in *also* **ab·scis·sin** \abˈsisᵊn\ *n* -s [*abscis*ion, *abscis*sion + *-in*] **:** any of a group of plant hormones (as abscisic acid) orig. found in young cotton bolls that tend to promote leaf abscission and inhibit various growth processes

ab·seil \ˈäpˌzīl, -īəl\ *vi* -ED/-ING/-S [*abseil,* n.] *chiefly Brit* **:** [2]RAPPEL — **ab·seil·er** \-ə(r)\ *n* -s

absolute convergence *n* **:** convergence of a mathematical series when the absolute values of the terms are taken

absurd* *adj* **1 :** having no rational or orderly relationship to man's life **:** MEANINGLESS; *also* **:** lacking order or values ⟨adults have condemned them to live in what must seem like an ~ universe —Joseph Featherstone⟩ **2 :** dealing with the absurd or with absurdism

absurd *n* -s [*absurd,* adj. (herein)] **:** the state or condition in which man exists in an irrational and meaningless universe and in which man's life has no meaning outside his own existence

ab·surd·ism \əbˈsərdˌizəm, ab-, -ˈz-\ *n* -s [*absurd* (herein) + *-ism*] **:** a philosophy based on the belief that man exists in an irrational and meaningless universe and that his search for order brings him into conflict with his universe

[1]**ab·surd·ist** \-dəst\ *n* -s [*absurd* (herein) + *-ist*] **:** a proponent or adherent of absurdism; *esp* **:** a writer who deals with absurdist themes

[2]**absurdist** \"\ *adj* **:** of, relating to, or dealing with absurdism

-ac \ˌak, *in a few words* ik *or* ək\ *n suffix* -s [NL *-acus* of or relating to, fr. Gk *-akos*] **:** one affected with ⟨nostalgiac⟩

AC* *abbr* **1** air conditioning **2** area code *herein*

aca·de·mese \əˌkadəˈmēz, ˌakəd-, -ēs\ *n* -s [*academ*ic + [2]*-ese*] **:** a style of writing held to be characteristic of those in academic life

academic* *n* **academics** *pl* **:** academic subjects

aca·pul·co gold \ˌäkəˈpül(ˌ)kō, ˌak-, -ül-\ *n, usu cap A & often cap G* [*Acapulco,* Mexico] **:** marijuana grown in Mexico that is held to be very potent

acathisia *var of* AKATHISIA *herein*

acceptable* *adj* **:** capable of being endured **:** TOLERABLE ⟨maximum ~ damage from nuclear attack⟩ ⟨~ level of risk⟩

access *vt* -ED/-ING/-ES [*access,* n.] **:** to get at **:** gain access to ⟨index registers can be ~*ed* by the programmer —*Datamation*⟩

access time *n* **1 :** the lag between the time stored information (as in a computer) is requested and the time it is delivered **2 :** television airtime during prime viewing hours that is reserved for exclusive use by local broadcasters

¹ac·com·mo·da·tion·ist \ə,kämə'dāsh(ə)nəst\ *n* -s [*accommodation* + ¹-*ist*] **:** a black who adapts to the ideals or attitudes of whites ⟨making Uncle Toms, compromisers, and ~*s* . . . thoroughly ashamed —Ossie Davis⟩

²accommodationist *adj* **:** favoring or practicing accommodation or compromise

AC/DC \¦ā(,)sē¦dē(,)sē\ *adj* [so called fr. the likening of a bisexual person to an electrical appliance which can operate on either alternating or direct current] **:** BISEXUAL 1b

ace* *vt* **:** to earn the grade of A on (an examination)

ac·e·tab·u·lo·plas·ty \¦asə¦tabyə(,)lō,plastē, -i\ *n* -ES [*acetabulum* + -*plasty*] **:** a plastic operation on the acetabulum intended to restore its normal state (as by repairing or enlarging its cavity)

ac·et·amin·o·phen \ə,sēd·ə'minəfən, ,asəd·-\ *n* -s [*acet-* + *amin-* + *phen*ol] **:** a crystalline compound $C_8H_9NO_2$ that is a hydroxy derivative of acetanilide and is used in chemical synthesis and in medicine instead of aspirin to relieve pain and fever

ac·e·to·hex·amide \¦asəd·ō¦heksəməd, ə¦sē-, -,heks¦aməd, -,mīd\ *n* -s [N-(p-*acetyl*phenylsulfonyl)-N′-cyclo*hexyl*urea + *amide,* chemical family to which ureas belong] **:** a sulfonylurea drug $C_{15}H_{20}N_2O_4S$ used in the oral treatment of some of the milder forms of diabetes in adults to lower the level of glucose in the blood

ace·tyl–coA \ə¦sēd·ᵊl¦kō'ā; ¦asəd·ᵊl-, -ə,tēl-\ *abbr or n* -s [*acetyl* coenzyme *A*] acetyl coenzyme A

acetylcysteine \≐¦≐≐¦≐(≐) ≐, ¦≐≐(,)≐-\ *n* [*acetyl* + *cysteine*] **:** a mucolytic agent $C_5H_9NO_3S$ used esp. to reduce the viscosity of abnormally viscid respiratory tract secretions

acid* *n* **:** LSD

acidhead \'≐≐,≐\ *n* [*acid* (herein) + *head*] **:** a person who frequently uses LSD

acid precipitation *n* **:** precipitation (as rain or snow) whose increased acidity is caused by environmental factors (as sulfur dioxide and nitrogen oxides from the combustion of fossil fuels)

acid rain *n* **:** acid precipitation esp. in the form of rain

acid rock *n* [*acid* (herein) + *rock*] **:** rock music with lyrics and sound relating to or suggestive of drug-induced experiences

acid·uria \,asə'd(y)u̇rēə, ,aas-, -ür-\ *n* -s [*acid* + -*uria*] **:** the condition of having acid in the urine esp. in abnormal amounts — see AMINOACIDURIA *herein*

acoustic* *adj* **1** *also* **acoustical*** **:** of, relating to, or being a musical instrument whose sound is not electronically modified **2a :** being a musical group or performer that uses acoustic instruments **b :** being or involving a musical performance on acoustic instruments

acoustic *n* -s **:** an acoustic musical instrument (as a guitar)

acoustic microscope *n* **:** a microscope in which ultrasound is used to scan a sample and then is converted to an electrical signal from which an image is reconstructed on a video screen — **acoustic microscopy** *n*

acous·to·electric \ə¦küstō +\ *adj* [¹*acoustic* + -*o-* + *electric*] **:** ELECTROACOUSTIC

acous·to–optic \ə¦küstō+\ *also* **acous·to–optical** \"+\ *adj* [¹*acoustic* + -*o-* + *optic, optical*] **:** of or relating to the use of ultrasound to modulate or change the direction of light in solids

acquire* *vt* **:** to locate and hold (a desired object) in a detector ⟨~ a target by radar⟩

acquired immune deficiency syndrome *n* **:** AIDS *herein*

acquired immunodeficiency syndrome *n* **:** AIDS *herein*

ac·ro·lect \'akrə,lekt, -rō-\ *n* -s [*acr-* + -*lect* (as in *dialect*)] **:** the most prestigious language variety of a community — compare BASILECT *herein* — **ac·ro·lect·al** \,≐≐'lektᵊl\ *adj*

acro·mio·clavicular \ə¦krōmē(,)ō, a¦- +\ *adj* [*acromio-* + *clavicular*] **:** relating to or being the joint connecting the acromion and the clavicle ⟨~ arthritis⟩

acrylic* *n* **1 :** a paint in which the vehicle is an acrylic resin **2 :** a painting done in an acrylic resin

actinomycin D *n* **:** DACTINOMYCIN *herein*

ac·ti·no·spec·ta·cin \ak,tinō'spektəsən, ,≐(,)≐-, ,≐tən-\ *n* -s [*actino*mycete + NL *specta*bilis (specific epithet of *Streptomyces spectabilis,* species of actinomycete) + E -*mycin* substance obtained from a fungus, fr. *streptomycin*] **:** SPECTINOMYCIN *herein*

action* *n* **:** the most vigorous, productive, or exciting activity in a particular field, area, or group ⟨go where the ~ is⟩

action painting *n* **:** nonrepresentational painting marked esp. by thickly textured surfaces and by the use of improvised techniques (as dribbling, splattering, or smearing) to create apparently accidental pictorial effects — **action painter** *n*

action potential *n* **:** a momentary change in electrical potential (as between the inside of a nerve cell and the extracellular medium) that occurs when a cell or tissue has been activated by a stimulus

activation analysis *n* **:** a method of analyzing a material for chemical elements by bombarding it with nuclear particles or gamma rays to produce radioactive atoms whose radiations indicate the identity and quantity of the parent elements

active* *adj* **1 :** requiring the expenditure of energy ⟨~ calcium ion uptake⟩ **2 :** of or relating to the collection, storage, and redistribution of the sun's heat esp. with the aid of pumps and blowers ⟨an ~ solar energy system⟩

active transport *n* **:** a movement of a chemical substance by the expenditure of energy through a gradient (as across a cell membrane) in concentration or electrical potential and opposite to the direction of normal diffusion

acu·pressure \'akyu̇ +,\ *n* [*acu-* (as in *acupuncture*) + *pressure*] **:** SHIATSU *herein* — **acu·pres·sur·ist** \,≐≐¦preshərəst\ *n* -s

ACV *abbr* **1** actual cash value **2** air-cushion vehicle

acy·clo·vir \,ā'sīklō,vir\ *n* [²*a-* + *cyclo-* + *vir*us; fr. its containing less cyclic structure than its naturally occurring analogue guanosine] **:** a cyclic nucleoside $C_8H_{11}N_5O_3$ used esp. to treat the symptoms of the genital form of herpes simplex

ADA \'ādə\ *trademark* — used for a structured computer programming language

add* *n* **:** an instance of addition ⟨the computer does an ~ in 7 microseconds⟩

additive identity *n* **:** an identity element (as 0 in the group of whole numbers under the operation of addition) that in a given mathematical system leaves unchanged any element to which it is added

additive inverse *n* **:** a number of opposite sign with respect to a given number so that addition of the two numbers gives zero ⟨the *additive inverse* of 4 is –4⟩

¹add–on \ˈ=,=\ *adj* **1 :** being or able to be added on ⟨~ accessories for an electric train⟩ **2 :** of or relating to add-ons **3 :** that can be added to ⟨an ~ certificate of deposit⟩

²add–on \ˈ=,=\ *n* -s **:** something added on: as **a :** a sum or amount added on **b :** something (as an accessory or an added feature) that enhances the thing it is added to

ad·dress·able \əˈdresəbəl\ *adj* [¹*address* + *-able*] **1 :** able to be addressed **:** directly accessible **2 :** of or relating to a subscription television system that uses decoders addressable by the system operator

ad·e·no·acanthoma \ˈadᵊn(,)ō+\ *n, pl* **adenoacanthomas** *or* **adenoacanthomata** [*aden-* + *acanthoma*] **:** an adenocarcinoma with epithelial cells differentiated and proliferated into squamous cells

ad·e·no·ma·toid \,adᵊnˈōmə,tȯid\ *adj* [*adenomat-* (as in *adenomatosis*), fr. *adenoma* + ¹*-oid*] **:** relating to or resembling an adenoma ⟨~ tumors of the fallopian tube⟩

adenosine mo·no·phos·phate \-,mänəˈfäs,fāt, -,mōnə-\ *n* [*mon-* + *phosphate*] **:** AMP *herein*

ad·e·no·sis \,adᵊnˈōsəs\ *n, pl* **adeno·ses** \-ˈō,sēz\ [NL, fr. Gk *aden-* + *-osis*] **:** a disease of glandular tissue; *esp* **:** one involving abnormal proliferation or occurrence of glandular tissue

ade·no·syl·methionine \əˈdenəsəl, ,adᵊnˈōs-, -,sil+\ *n* [*adenosine* + *-yl* + *methionine*] **:** the active sulfonium form of methionine which gives up a methyl group in various metabolic reactions; *S*-adenosylmethionine

ad·e·no·virus \ˈadᵊnō+\ *n* [*adenoid* + *-o-* + *virus*] **:** any of a group of DNA-containing icosahedral animal viruses orig. identified in human adenoid tissue, causing respiratory diseases (as catarrh), and including some capable of inducing malignant tumors in experimental animals — **ad·e·no·viral** \" +\ *adj*

ad·e·nyl·ate cy·clase \əˈdenᵊlətˈsī,klās, ˈadᵊn(ˈ)il-, -l,āt-, -āz\ *n* [*adenylate* fr. *adenyl* + ¹*-ate; cyclase* fr. *cyclic* AMP (herein) + *-ase*] **:** an enzyme that catalyzes the formation of cyclic AMP from ATP

adenyl cy·clase \-ˈsī,klās, -āz\ *n* **:** ADENYLATE CYCLASE *herein*

ad·ho·cra·cy \(ˈ)adˈhäkrəsē, -ōk-, -si\ *n* -ES [*ad hoc* + *-cracy*] **:** a temporary organization or committee set up to accomplish a specific task; *also* **:** a system of government composed of such organizations

adipocyte* *n* **:** a fat-containing cell of adipose tissue

adip·sia \āˈdipsēə, əˈ-\ *n* -s [NL, fr. Gk *a-* + *dipsa* thirst + ¹*-ia*] **:** loss of thirst; *also* **:** abnormal and esp. prolonged abstinence from the intake of fluids

¹admass \ˈ=,=\ *n* [*advertising* + *mass*] *chiefly Brit* **:** a system of commercial marketing that attempts to influence great masses of consumers by mass-media advertising; *also* **:** a society thus influenced

²admass \"\ *adj, chiefly Brit* **:** of, characterized by, or influenced by admass

ado·bo \əˈdōbō, *Sp* äˈthōbō\ *n* -s [Sp] **:** a dish of Spanish origin consisting of meat (as chicken or pork) marinated in a spicy sauce, browned, and then simmered in the marinade

ad·re·no·cor·ti·co·steroid \əˈdrēnō,kȯrd·əkōˈsti(ə)-,rȯid, -ren-, -te(-\ *n* [*adrenocortical* + *-o-* + *steroid*] **:** a steroid (as cortisone or hydrocortisone) obtained from, resembling, or having physiological effects like those of the adrenal cortex

ad·re·no·cor·ti·co·tro·pin \-ˈtrōpən, -äp-\ *or* **ad·re·no·cor·ti·co·tro·phin** \-ˈtrōfən, -äf-\ [*adrenocorticotropic* or *adrenocorticotrophic* + *-in*] **:** ADRENOCORTICOTROPIC HORMONE

ad·re·no·medullary \əˈdrēnō, -ren-+\ *adj* [*adren-* + *medullary*] **:** relating to or derived from the medulla of the adrenal glands ⟨~ extracts⟩

adri·a·my·cin \,ādrēəˈmīsᵊn\ *n* -s [*Adria* Laboratories + *-mycin*] **:** an antibiotic with antitumor activity that is obtained from a bacterium of the genus *Streptomyces* (*S. peucetius*) and is administered as the hydrochloride $C_{27}H_{29}NO_{11}{\cdot}HCl$ — called also *doxorubicin*

adult* *adj* **:** dealing in or with explicitly sexual material **:** PORNOGRAPHIC ⟨~ bookstore⟩ ⟨~ movie⟩

advanced level *n, usu cap A* **:** A LEVEL *herein*

advance man* *n* **:** an aide (as of a political candidate) who makes a security check or handles publicity in advance of personal appearances by his employer

ad·vect \(ˈ)adˈvekt\ *vt* -ED/-ING/-S [back-formation fr. *advection*] **:** to transport esp. horizontally by the movement of tides, currents, or air masses ⟨~ heat⟩ ⟨~ plankton⟩

ad·ver·bi·al \(ˈ)adˈvərbēəl, adˈv-, -əb-\ *n* -s **:** a word or phrase that functions as an adverb

ad·ver·sar·i·al *R* ,advə(r)ˈserēəl, —*R* -vəˈs-\ *adj* [*adversary* + ¹*-al*] **:** of, relating to, or characteristic of an adversary

advocacy journalism *n* **:** journalism that advocates a cause or expresses a viewpoint

aeon* *n* **:** a unit of geologic time equal to one billion years

ae·quo·rin \ēˈkwȯrən, -ōr-\ *n* -s [*Aequorea* + *-in*] **:** a bioluminescent protein of jellyfish (genus *Aequorea*) that emits light in response to the addition of calcium or strontium and is used to demonstrate the presence and distribution of calcium in cells

aer·o·bics \ˈa(ə)ˈrōbiks, ˈe(ə)-, ˈāə-\ *n pl but sing or pl in constr* [fr. *aerobic*, after such pairs as *calisthenic: calisthenics*] **:** a system of physical conditioning designed to improve respiratory and circulatory function by exercises (as running, walking, or swimming) that increase oxygen consumption

aer·on·o·my \a(ə)ˈränəmē, e(ə)ˈ-, ,āəˈ-\ *n* -ES [*aer-* + *-nomy*] **:** a science that deals with the physics and chemistry of the upper atmosphere of planets — **aer·on·o·mer** \-mə(r)\ *n -s* — **aer·o·nom·ic** \,a(ə)rəˈnämik, ,e(ə)r-, ,āər-\ *also* **aer·o·nom·i·cal** \-məkəl\ *adj* — **aer·on·o·mist** \a(ə)ˈränəməst, e(ə)ˈ-, ,āəˈ-\ *n* -s

aero·plankton \ˈa(ə)rə, ˈe(ə)rə, ˈāərə, -rō +\ *n* [*aer-* + *plankton*] **:** small airborne organisms (as flying insects)

¹aero·space \ˈa(ə)rə, ˈe(ə)r-, ˈāər-, -rō +,\ *n* [*aer-* + *space*] **1 :** space comprising the earth's atmosphere and the space beyond **2 :** a branch of physical science that deals with aerospace **3 :** the industry involved in the manufacture of aerospace vehicles

²aerospace \"\ *adj* **:** of or relating to aerospace, to vehicles used in aerospace or the manufacture of such vehicles, or to travel in aerospace ⟨~ research⟩ ⟨~ medicine⟩

aero·train \-rə‚trān\ *n* [*aer-* + *train*] **:** a propeller-driven vehicle that rides on a cushion of air astride a single rail
AFDC *abbr* aid to families with dependent children
affective fallacy *n* **:** the error in literary criticism of judging a work on the basis of its effect on the reader
affirmative action *n* **:** an active effort to improve employment or educational opportunities for members of minority groups and women
af·ford·able \ə'fō(ə)rdəbəl, -ȯ(ə)rd-, -ōəd-, -ȯəd-\ *adj* [*afford* + *-able*] **:** that can be afforded ⟨~ housing⟩ ⟨~ prices⟩ — **af·ford·abil·i·ty** \=‚=='bilədē, -ətē, -i\ *n* -ES
af·ghan·i·stan·ism \af'ganə‚sta‚nizəm, -taa‚n-, -ˌstə‚-\ *n* -s *usu cap* [*Afghanistan* + *-ism;* fr. the remoteness of Afghanistan from America] **:** the practice (as by a journalist) of concentrating on problems in distant parts of the world while ignoring controversial local issues
af·la·tox·in \ˌaflə¦täksən\ *n* [NL *Aspergillus flavus,* species of mold + E *toxin*] **:** any of several carcinogenic mycotoxins that are produced esp. in agricultural crops (as peanuts) by molds (as *Aspergillus flavus*)
a–frame* *n, cap A* [fr. the resemblance of the shape of the facade to a capital A] **:** a building (as a house) that typically has a triangular front and rear wall and a roof reaching to or nearly to the level of the ground floor
af·ri·cana \ˌafrə'känə, -'kanə, -'kaa(ə)nə\ *n pl, usu cap* [*Africa* + *-ana*] **:** materials (as books, documents, or artifacts) relating to African history and culture
[1]**af·ro** \'a(ˌ)frō\ *adj, usu cap* [*Afro-*] **:** having the hair shaped into a round bushy mass ⟨an *Afro* hairstyle⟩
[2]**afro** \"\ *n* -s *usu cap* **:** an Afro hairstyle — **afroed** \'a(ˌ)frōd\ *adj, usu cap*
afterburner* *n* **:** a device for burning or catalytically destroying unburned or partially burned carbon compounds in exhaust (as from an automobile)
after–tax \¦==¦=\ *adj* [[2]*after* + *tax*] **:** remaining after payment of taxes and esp. of income tax
agar·ose \'ägə‚rōs, -ōz\ *n* -s [*agar* + [2]*-ose*] **:** a polysaccharide obtained from agar that is used esp. as a supporting medium in electrophoresis and chromatography
age·ism *also* **agism** \'ā(ˌ)jizəm\ *n* -s [[1]*age* + *-ism* (as in *racism*)] **:** prejudice or discrimination against a particular age-group and esp. against the elderly — **age·ist** *also* **agist** \-əst\ *adj*
agent orange *n, usu cap A&O* **:** an herbicide widely used as a defoliant in the Vietnam War that is composed of 2,4-D and 2,4,5-T and contains dioxin as a contaminant
ag·gior·na·men·to \əˌjȯrnə'men(ˌ)tō\ *n* -s [It, fr. *aggiornare* to bring up to date, fr. *a-* to (fr. L *ad-*) + *giorno* day, fr. LL *diurnum* — more at JOURNEY] **:** a bringing up to date ⟨the enthusiasts of ~ and the defenders of older, stricter ways —*Time*⟩
ag·grieve·ment \ə'grēvmənt *also* a'-\ *n* -s [*aggrieve* + [1]*-ment*] **:** the quality or state of being aggrieved
ag·gro *also* **ag·ro** \'ag(ˌ)rō\ *n* -s [by shortening & alter. of *aggravation*] **1** *Brit* **:** EXASPERATION, IRRITATION ⟨in any case it is not worth the ~ it causes —*The Sun* (*London*)⟩ **2** *Brit* **:** a rivalry or grievance esp. public in nature marked by mistrust, rancor, and often violence ⟨the railwaymen could cause trouble again in May . . . even if their ~ about inter-union differentials is resolved — *Economist* ⟩ ⟨a lot of Town-versus-Gown ~: bricks flew . . . the atmosphere was edgy —Ann Leslie & Geoffrey Dickinson⟩ **3** *Brit* **:** violence against persons and property that is usu. deliberate but not specific in its aims ⟨shots fired and tyres let down as the ~ flares —Gilbert Johnson⟩
agin·ner \ə'ginə(r)\ *n* -s [[2]*agin* + *-er*] *slang* **:** one who opposes change
ag·no·lot·ti \ˌänyə'lȯt(t)ē\ *n, pl* **agnolotti** [It *agnellotto,* fr. *agnello* lamb, fr. LL *agnellus,* dim. of L *agnus* lamb] **:** a crescent-shaped dumpling usu. filled with meat
[1]**a–go–go** \ä'gō(ˌ)gō, ə'g-\ *n* -s [*Whisky à Gogo,* café and discotheque in Paris, France, fr. F *whisky* whiskey + *à gogo* galore, fr. MF] **:** a nightclub for dancing to live or recorded pop music **:** DISCOTHEQUE
[2]**a–go–go** \"\ *adj* **1 :** of, relating to, or being an a-go-go or the music or dances performed there ⟨*a-go-go* dancers⟩ **2 :** being in the latest style ⟨psychiatry *a-go-go* —Charles Schulz⟩
agonist* *n* **:** a chemical substance capable of combining with a receptor on a cell and initiating a reaction or activity — compare ANTAGONIST 2b *in the Dict*
agonistic* **:** of, relating to, or being aggressive or defensive social interaction (as fighting, fleeing, or submitting) between individuals usu. of the same species ⟨~ behavior⟩
ago·ra \ägə'rä\ *n, pl* **ago·rot** \-'rōt\ [NHeb *ăgōrāh,* fr. Heb, a small coin] **1 :** a monetary unit of Israel representing $^{1}/_{100}$ of a shekel — see MONEY table *in the Dict* **2 :** a coin representing one agora
agrav·ic \(ˈ)ā¦gravik\ *adj* [[2]*a-* + *gravity* + *-ic*] **:** of or relating to a theoretical condition of no gravitation
ag·ri·power \'agrə+\ *n* [*agri*culture + *power*] **:** the economic and political power of an agriculturally productive nation
ag·ro·chemical \¦a(ˌ)grō'===\ *also* **ag·ri·chemical** \¦agrə+\ *n* [*agrochemical* fr. *agro-* + *chemical; agrichemical* fr. *agri-* + *chemical*] **:** an agricultural chemical (as an herbicide or an insecticide) — **agrochemical** *adj*
ag·ro–industrial \¦a(ˌ)grō=¦===\ *adj* [*agro-* + *industrial*] **1 :** of or relating to production for both industrial and agricultural purposes ⟨a nuclear-powered *agro-industrial* complex for producing electric power and desalted seawater⟩ **2 :** of or relating to an industry (as the production of farm tools or fertilizer) directly related to agriculture — **agro–industry** \¦=(ˌ)=¦=(ˌ)==\ *n*
ag·ro·nome \'agrə‚nōm\ *n* -s [Russ or F; Russ *agronom,* fr. F *agronome,* after such pairs as F *astronomie* astronomy : *astronome* astronomer] **:** AGRONOMIST
AI* *abbr* artificial intelligence *herein*
AIDS \'ādz\ *n* **:** a condition of acquired immunological deficiency that is associated with infection of the cells of the immune system with a retrovirus, that occurs esp. in male homosexuals and intravenous drug abusers, and that is usu. recognized by the presence of a life-threatening infection (as pneumonia or candidiasis) or of Kaposi's sarcoma in individuals under 60 years of age who have not been subjected to immunosuppressive drugs or an immunosuppressive disease — called also *acquired immune deficiency syndrome, acquired immunodeficiency syndrome*
ai·ki·do \¦īkē¦dō, ī'kē(ˌ)dō\ *n* -s [Jap *aikidō,* fr. *ai-* together, mutual + *ki* spirit + *dō* district] **:** a Japanese art of self-defense employing locks and holds and utilizing the principle of nonresistance to cause an opponent's own momentum to work against him
ai·o·li \(ˈ)ī¦ōlē, (ˈ)ā¦-, -li, *F* àyȯlē\ *n* -s [Prov, fr. *ai* garlic (fr. L *allium*) + *oli* oil, fr. L *oleum* — more at ALLIUM, OIL] **:** a sauce made of crushed garlic, egg yolks, olive oil,

and lemon juice and sometimes potato : garlic mayonnaise

air bag *n* : a bag designed to inflate automatically in front of riders in an automotive vehicle in case of accident to protect them from pitching forward into solid parts (as the windshield or dashboard) — called also *air cushion*

air ball *n* : a shot in basketball that misses the rim and the backboard

airbus \ˈ=,=\ *n* : a short-range or medium-range subsonic jet passenger airplane

air cavalry *or* **air cav** \-ˈkav\ *n* **1** : an army unit that is transported in air vehicles and carries out the traditional cavalry missions of reconnaissance and security **2** : an army unit that is esp. equipped and adapted for transportation in air vehicles but is organized for sustained ground combat

air–cushion vehicle *n* : a vehicle that is supported above the surface of land or water by a cushion of air produced by downwardly directed fans

air date *n* : the scheduled date of a broadcast

air·er \ˈe(ə)rə(r), ˈa(-\ *n* -s *Brit* : a frame on which clothes are aired or dried

airfall \ˈ=,=\ *n* : the deposition of material (as ash) ejected from a volcano

airfare \ˈ=,=\ *n* : fare for travel by airplane

airhead \ˈ=,=\ *n* : a mindless or stupid person

airmobile \ˈ=ˈ==, ,=ˈ=,=\ *adj* [*air* + *mobile,* adj] : of, relating to, or being a military unit whose members are transported to combat areas usu. by helicopter

air piracy *n* : the hijacking of an airplane — **air pirate** *n*

airplay \ˈ=,=\ *n* : the playing of a phonograph record on the air by a radio station

airshed \ˈ=,=\ *n* -s [*air* + *-shed* (as in *watershed*)] : the air supply of a given region; *also* : the geographical area covered by such an air supply

air taxi *n* : a small commercial airplane used to transport passengers on short flights between localities not served by scheduled airlines

air·tel \ˌa(ə)rˈtel, ˌe(-\ *n* -s [*air* + ho*tel*] : a hotel situated at or close to an airport

airtime \ˈ=,=\ *n* : the time or any part thereof that a radio or television station is on the air

aka *abbr* also known as

aka·thi·sia *also* **aca·thi·sia** \ˌäkaˈthizh(ē)ə, ˌa-, -ēzh-\ *n* -s [[2]*a-* + Gk *kathisis* a sitting down + [1]*-ia*] : a condition characterized by uncontrollable motor restlessness

àla grecque \ˌäləˈgrek, ˌal-\ *adj, often cap G* [F, lit., in the Greek manner] : served in a sauce of olive oil, lemon juice, and seasonings

albatross* *n* [fr. the albatross killed by the ancient mariner and subsequently hung about his neck in the poem *The Rime of the Ancient Mariner* (1798) by S. T. Coleridge †1834 Eng. poet] **1** : something that causes persistent deep concern or anxiety ⟨an ~ of guilt that he has volunteered to carry —Jack Holland⟩ **2** : something that makes accomplishment particularly difficult : ENCUMBRANCE ⟨this regulatory ~ inhibits any marketing scheme that might lure commuters —Charles Luna⟩

al den·te \(ˌ)älˈden·(ˌ)tā, -ál-, -al-\ *adj* [It, lit., to the tooth] *of food* : cooked just enough to retain a somewhat firm texture ⟨fresh pasta cooked *al dente —Vogue*⟩ ⟨hosannahs for precisely *al dente* carrots —Gael Greene⟩

al·do·ste·ron·ism \alˈdästə,rō,nizəm, ˌaldōstəˈr-\ *n* -s [*aldosterone* + *-ism*] : a condition that is characterized by excessive production and excretion of aldosterone and typically by loss of body potassium, muscular weakness, and elevated blood pressure

ale·a·tor·ic \ˌālēəˌtórik\ *adj* [L *aleator* dice player, gambler (fr. *alea* dice game) + E *-ic*] : characterized by chance or random elements ⟨~ music⟩

aleatory* *adj* : ALEATORIC *herein*

a level *n, usu cap A* : the later of two standardized British examinations in a secondary school subject used as a qualification for university entrance; *also* : the level of education required to pass such an examination — called also *advanced level;* compare O LEVEL *herein*

alf·vén wave \ˌal(f)ˌvān-, -ven-\ *n, usu cap A* [after Hannes *Alfvén* b1908 Swed. astrophysicist] : a transverse electromagnetic wave that propagates along the lines of force in a magnetized plasma

ALG *abbr* antilymphocyte globulin; antilymphocytic globulin

algebra* *n* : LINEAR ALGEBRA 2 *herein*

al·gol \ˈal,gäl, -gȯl\ *n* -s *usu cap A or all cap* [*algo*rithmic *l*anguage] : an algebraic and logical language for programming a computer

algorithm* *n* : a procedure for solving a mathematical problem (as finding the greatest common divisor) in a finite number of steps that frequently involves repetition of an operation; *broadly* : a step-by-step procedure for solving a problem or accomplishing an end — **algorithmic*** *adj* — **al·go·rith·mi·cal·ly** \-mək(ə)lē, -mēk-, -li\ *adv*

al·gor mor·tis \ˌalgȯ(ə)rˌmórtəs\ *n* [NL, fr. L, lit., coldness of death] : the gradual cooling of the body following death

al·ice–in–won·der·land \ˌ===ˈ==,=\ *adj, usu cap A & W* [fr. *Alice's Adventures in Wonderland* (1865) by Lewis Carroll †1898 Eng. storywriter] : suitable to a world of fantasy or illusion

alien* *n* : EXTRATERRESTRIAL *herein*

ali·es·ter·ase \ˌalēˌestə,rās, -āz\ *n* [*ali*phatic + *esterase*] : an esterase that promotes the hydrolysis of ester links esp. in aliphatic esters of low molecular weight

a–line \ˈ=,=\ *adj, cap A* [fr. the resemblance of such a garment's outline to that of a capital A] : having a flared bottom and a close-fitting top — used of a garment ⟨an *A-line* skirt⟩

alin·gual \(ˈ)āˌliŋgwəl *sometimes* -gyəw-\ *adj* [[2]*a-* + *-lingual* (as in *bilingual*)] : not fluent in any language

ali·yah* *or* **ali·ya** \ˌäléˈ(y)ä, äˈlē(ˌ)(-, əˈlē(y)ə\ *n* -s : immigration of Jews into Israel

al·le·lo·path·ic \ə,lēləˈpathik, -ˌlel-\ *adj* [*allelopathy* + *-ic*] : of or relating to allelopathy

all–night·er \(ˌ)=ˈnīd·ə(r)\ *n* -s : something (as a party or a study session) that lasts throughout the night

al·lo·antibody \ˌalō+\ *n* [*all-* + *antibody*] : ISOANTIBODY

al·lo·antigen \"+\ *n* [*all-* + *antigen*] : ISOANTIGEN — **al·lo·antigenic** \"+\ *adj*

al·lo·ge·ne·ic \ˌaləjəˌnēik, -lō-\ *also* **al·lo·gen·ic*** \-ˌjenik\ *adj* [*allogeneic* fr. *all-* + *-geneic* (as in *syngeneic* — herein); *allogenic* fr. *all-* + *-genic*] : involving or derived from individuals of the same species that are sufficiently unlike genetically to interact antigenically ⟨~ skin grafts⟩ — compare SYNGENEIC *herein,* XENOGENEIC *herein*

al·lo·graft \ˈalō,=, ˈalə,=\ *n* [*all-* + *graft;* fr. its being a graft from another individual] : a homograft between allogeneic individuals — **allograft** *vt*

al·lo·immune \ˈalō+\ *adj* [*all-* + *immune*] **:** of, relating to, or characterized by isoimmunization ⟨~ reactivity⟩

al·lo·pu·ri·nol \ˌalōˈpyu̇rəˌnȯl, -ˌnōl\ *n* -s [*all-* + *purine* + *-ol*] **:** a drug $C_5H_4N_4O$ used to promote excretion of uric acid esp. in the treatment of gout

al·lo·ste·ric \ˈaləˈsterik, -ti(ə)r-\ *adj* [*all-* + *steric*] **:** of, relating to, or being alteration of the activity of a protein (as an enzyme) by combination with another substance at a point other than the chemically active site — **al·lo·ste·ri·cal·ly** \-rək(ə)lē\ *adv* — **al·los·te·ry** \aˈlästərē, ˈaləˈ-sterē\ *n* -ES

al·lo·transplant \ˈal(ˌ)ō+\ *vt* [*allo-* + *transplant*] **:** to transplant between genetically different individuals — **allotransplant** *n* — **al·lo·transplantation** \"+\ *n*

allotype* *n* **:** an alloantigen that is part of a plasma protein (as an immunoglobulin) — compare IDIOTYPE *herein*, ISOTYPE *herein* — **al·lo·typic** \ˌalə+\ *adj* — **al·lo·typically** \"+\ *adv* — **al·lo·typy** \ˈ==ˌtīpē\ *n*

al·lo·zyme \ˈ==ˌzīm\ *n* -s [*all-* + *-o-* + *-zyme*] **:** any of the variants of an enzyme that are determined by alleles at a single genetic locus — **al·lo·zy·mic** \ˌ==ˈzīmik\ *adj*

all–terrain vehicle \ˈ==ˈ=-\ *n* **:** a small amphibious motor vehicle that has a boatlike bottom, rides on four or more soft rubber tires or on endless rubber belts, and is designed to travel over all types of terrain

àl'orange \àlòränzh\ *adj* [F] **:** prepared or served with oranges

alpha* *n* **:** ALPHA WAVE

alpha* *adj* **:** socially dominant esp. in a group of animals

al·pha \ˈalfə, ˈau̇fə\ *adj* [by shortening] **:** ALPHABETIC ⟨an ~ sort⟩

alpha–adrenergic \ˈ==ˌ==ˈ==\ *adj* **:** of, relating to, or being an alpha-receptor ⟨*alpha-adrenergic* blocking action⟩

alphabet soup* *n* **:** a hodgepodge esp. of initials (as of the names of organizations)

alpha decay *n* **:** the radioactive decay of an atomic nucleus by emission of an alpha particle

alpha–fe·to·protein \ˌ==ˌfēd·ō+\ *n* [[2]*alpha* + *feto-* + *protein*] **:** a fetal antigen that appears in adults with some forms of cancer (as of the liver) and in the amniotic fluid of pregnant women carrying fetuses with some birth defects esp. of the neural tube

alpha–helix *n* **:** the coiled structural arrangement of many proteins consisting of a single chain of amino acids that is stabilized by hydrogen bonds — compare DOUBLE HELIX *herein* — **alpha–helical** \ˌ==ˈ===\ *adj*

alpha–ketoglutaric acid \ˈ==ˈ===ˈ==-\ *n* [[2]*alpha* + *ketoglutaric acid*] **:** the alpha keto isomer of ketoglutaric acid formed in various metabolic processes (as the Krebs cycle)

al·pha·met·ic \ˈalfəˈmed·ik\ *n* -s [*alpha*betic + arith*metic*] **:** a mathematical puzzle consisting of a numerical computation with letters substituted for numbers which are to be restored through mathematical reasoning

alpha–1–antitrypsin \ˈ==ˈwənˈ=(ˌ)=+\ *n* [[2]*alpha* + [1]*anti-* + *trypsin*] **:** a trypsin-inhibiting serum protein whose deficiency has been implicated as a factor in emphysema

alpha–receptor \ˈ===ˌ==\ *n* **:** any of a group of receptors on cell membranes that are held to be associated with vasoconstriction, relaxation of intestinal muscle, and contraction of the nictitating membrane, iris dilator muscle, splenic smooth muscle, and muscular layer of the wall of the uterus — compare BETA-RECEPTOR *herein*

alpine* *adj, usu cap* **:** of, relating to, or being competitive ski events consisting of slalom and downhill racing — compare NORDIC *herein*

alternating series *n* **:** a mathematical series in which consecutive terms are alternatively positive and negative

alternative* *adj* **:** existing or functioning outside the established cultural, social, or economic system ⟨~ newspaper⟩ ⟨whose kids went to the same ~ nursery school —Cyra McFadden⟩

alternative school *n* **:** an elementary or secondary school with a nontraditional curriculum

altruism* *n* **:** behavior by an animal that is not beneficial to or may be harmful to itself but that benefits the survival of its species

al·ve·o·lo·plas·ty \alˈvēə(ˌ)lōˌplastē\ *or* **al·veo·plas·ty** \ˈalvē- (ˌ)ō- \ *n* -ES [*alveoloplasty* fr. *alveol-* + *-plasty*; *alveoplasty* fr. L *alve*us cavity + *-o-* + E *-plasty*] **:** surgical shaping of the dental alveoli and alveolar processes esp. after extraction of several teeth or in preparation for dentures

am·a·ni·tin \ˌaməˈnētᵊn\ *n* -s [ISV *amanit-* + *-in*; orig. formed in G] **:** a highly poisonous cyclic peptide produced by the death cup that selectively inhibits RNA polymerase in mammalian cells

aman·ta·dine \əˈmantəˌdēn\ *n* -s [*amantad-* (fr. anagram of *adamantane*) + *amine*] **:** a drug used esp. as the hydrochloride $C_{10}H_{17}N{\cdot}HCl$ to prevent infection (as by an influenza virus) by interfering with virus penetration into host cells and in the treatment of Parkinson's disease

am·a·ret·to \ˌaməˈred·ō, -etō\ *n* [It, dim. of *amaro* bitter, fr. L *amarus* bitter] **1 amaret·ti** \-dē, -tē\ *pl* **:** macaroons made with bitter almonds **2** -s *often cap* **:** an almond-flavored liqueur

am·bi·plasma \ˈambə, ˈaam-, -bē +\ *n* [*ambi-* + *plasma*] **:** a hypothetical plasma that is held to consist of matter and antimatter

am·bi·polar \"+\ *adj* [*ambi-* + *polar*] **:** relating to or consisting of both electrons and positive ions moving in opposite directions ⟨~ diffusion⟩

am·er·asian \ˈamər+\ *n, cap* [*Amer-* + *Asian*] **:** a person of mixed American and Asian descent

american dream *n, usu cap A & often cap D* **:** an American social ideal that stresses egalitarianism and esp. material prosperity

amer·i·can·o·pho·bia \əˌmerəkənəˈfōbēə, -ˌkan-\ *n, usu cap* [*American* + *-o-* + *-phobia* (as in *claustrophobia*)] **:** hatred of the U.S. or American culture — **amer·i·cano·phobe** \=ˈ===əˌfōb, =ˌ==ˈkanəˌfōb\ *n* -s *usu cap*

american shorthair *n, usu cap A&S* **:** SHORTHAIR

american sign language *n, usu cap A&S&L* **:** a sign language for the deaf in which meaning is conveyed by a system of articulated hand gestures and their placement relative to the upper body

american staffordshire terrier *n, usu cap A&S* **:** a strong stocky terrier of a breed orig. developed for dogfighting

amer·i·ka \əˈmerəkə\ *n* -s *usu cap* [G *Amerika*; fr. the likening of the U.S. to Nazi Germany] **:** the fascist or racist aspect of American society — **amer·i·kan** \-kən\ *adj, usu cap*

ameslan \ˈaməˌslan\ *n* -s *usu cap* **:** AMERICAN SIGN LANGUAGE *herein*

am·e·thop·ter·in \ˌaməˈthäpt(ə)rən\ *n* -s [*amin-* + *meth-* + *pteroyl* + *-in*] **:** METHOTREXATE *herein*

ami·cus \əˈmēkəs\ *n, pl* **ami·ci** \-ē(ˌ)kē\ **:** AMICUS CURIAE

ami·no·ac·id·uria \=ˈ==ˌasəˈdyu̇rēə, -u̇r-\ *n* -s [NL, fr. *amino acid* + *-uria*] **:** a condition in which one or more amino acids are excreted in excessive amounts

ami·no·transferase \⸗¦⸗⸗+\ *n* [*amin-* + *transferase*] **:** TRANSAMINASE

ami·no·triazole \⸗¦⸗⸗+\ *n* [*amin-* + *triazole*] **:** AMITROLE *herein*

am·i·trip·ty·line \ˌamə·ˈtriptəˌlēn\ *n* -s [*amin-* + *tript-* (alter. of *trypt-* — as in *tryptophan*) + *-yl* + ²*-ine*] **:** a tricyclic antidepressant drug $C_{20}H_{23}N$ administered as the hydrochloride salt

am·i·trole \ˈamə·ˌtrōl\ *n* -s [*amin-* + *triazole*] **:** a systemic herbicide $C_2H_4N_4$ used in areas other than food croplands

am·nio·cen·te·sis \ˌamnēōsen·ˈtēsəs\ *n, pl* **amnio·cente·ses** \-ˈtēˌsēz\ [NL, fr. *amnio-* + *centesis*] **:** the surgical insertion of a hollow needle through the abdominal wall and into the uterus of a pregnant female to obtain amniotic fluid esp. to examine the fetal chromosomes for an abnormality and for the determination of sex

am·ni·og·ra·phy \ˌamnēˈägrəfē\ *n* -ES [*amnio-* + radio*graphy*] **:** radiographic visualization of the outlines of the uterine cavity, placenta, and fetus after injection of a radiopaque substance into the amniotic sac

am·ni·os·co·py \ˌ⸗⸗ˈäskəpē\ *n* -ES [*amnio-* + *-scopy*] **:** visual examination of the amniotic cavity and its contents by means of an endoscope — **am·nio·scope** \ˈamnēəˌskōp\ *n*

amp \ˈamp, ˈaa(ə)-\ *n* -s [by shortening] **:** AMPLIFIER

AMP \ˌāˌemˈpē\ *n* -s [*a*denosine *m*ono*p*hosphate] **:** a mononucleotide of adenine $C_{10}H_{12}N_5O_3H_2PO_4$ that was orig. isolated from mammalian muscle and is reversibly convertible to ADP and ATP in metabolic reactions — called also *adenosine monophosphate;* see CYCLIC AMP *herein*

am·phi·path·ic \ˌamfəˈpathik\ *adj* [*amphi-* + *-pathic*] **:** AMPHIPHILIC *herein*

am·phi·phil·ic \-ˈfilik\ *adj* [*amphi-* + *-philic*] **:** of or relating to compounds (as glycolipids and sphingolipids in biological membranes and surfactants) consisting of molecules having a polar water-soluble terminal group attached to a water-insoluble hydrocarbon chain

am·pho·ter·i·cin \ˌamfəˈterəsən\ *n* -s [*amphoteric* + *-in*] **:** either of two antibiotic drugs obtained from a soil actinomycete of the genus *Streptomyces* (*S. nodosus*); *esp* **:** AMPHOTERICIN B *herein*

amphotericin B *n* **:** the amphotericin that is useful against deep-seated and systemic fungal infections

am·pi·cil·lin \ˌampəˈsilən\ *n* -s [*amin-* + *penicillin*] **:** a penicillin that is effective against gram-negative and gram-positive bacteria and is used to treat various infections of the urinary, respiratory, and intestinal tracts

amyg·da·lot·o·my \əˌmigdəˈlätəmē\ *n* -ES [*amygdal-* + *-o-* + *-tomy*] **:** destruction of part of the amygdala of the brain (as for the control of epilepsy) esp. by surgical incision

am·y·lo·bar·bi·tone \ˌaməlō+\ *n* [*amyl-* + *barbitone*] *Brit* **:** AMOBARBITAL

amyotrophic lateral sclerosis *n* **:** a rare fatal progressive degenerative disease that affects pyramidal motor neurons, usu. begins in middle age, and is characterized esp. by increasing and spreading muscular weakness — called also *Lou Gehrig's disease*

anabolic steroid *n* **:** any of a group of usu. synthetic hormones that increase constructive metabolism and are sometimes taken by athletes in training to increase temporarily the size of their muscles

an·a·dama bread \ˌanəˈdamə-, -dȧm-\ *n* [origin unknown] **:** a leavened bread made with flour, cornmeal, and molasses

anagenesis* *n* **:** linear evolutionary change in which one group replaces another without branching into distinct forms **:** phyletic evolution — compare CLADOGENESIS *herein* — **anagenetic*** *adj* — **ana·ge·net·i·cal·ly** \ˌanəjəˈned·ək(ə)lē\ *adv*

an·a·log *also* **an·a·logue** \ˈanᵊlˌȯg, -äg\ *adj* **1 :** of, relating to, or being an analogue **2 a :** of or relating to the representation of data by continuously variable physical quantities **b :** being a watch having both hour and minute hands **c :** of or relating to an analog computer

analogue* *also* **analog*** *n* **1 :** a chemical compound that is similar in structure to another but differs in composition in the matter of one element **2 :** a synthetic food product made of vegetable matter (as soybeans) and used as a meat substitute

analytic* *adj* **1** *of a function of a real variable* **:** capable of being expanded in a Taylor's series in powers of $x - h$ in some neighborhood of the point h **2** *of a function of a complex variable* **:** differentiable at every point in some neighborhood of a given point or points

anamnestic* *adj* **:** of or relating to a second rapid increased production of antibodies in response to an immunogenic substance after serum antibodies from a first response can no longer be detected in the blood

ana·plas·tic \ˌanəˈplastik\ *adj* [NL, fr. Gk *ana-* again + *-plastic*] **:** characterized by or composed of cells which have reverted to a relatively undifferentiated state ⟨~ carcinomas⟩

an·a·tom·i·co- \ˌanə·ˌtämə̇(ˌ)kō\ *or* **anat·o·mo-** \əˌnad·ə(ˌ)mō\ *comb form* [*anatomic*] **:** anatomical and **:** anatomical ⟨*anatomico*pathological⟩ ⟨*anatomo*clinical⟩

an·autogenous \ˌan+\ *adj* [*an-* + *autogenous* (herein)] **:** requiring a meal esp. of blood to produce eggs ⟨~ mosquitoes⟩

anchor* *n* **:** an anchorman or anchorwoman

anchor* *vt* **:** to act or serve as anchorman for ⟨~ the evening news⟩

an·chor·man \ˈ⸗⸗ˌman, -ˌmən\ *n, pl* **anchormen** **1 :** a broadcaster (as on a newscast) who introduces reports by other broadcasters and usu. reads the news **2 :** MODERATOR 3d

anchorpeople \ˈ⸗⸗ˌ⸗⸗\ *n pl* **:** ANCHORPERSONS *herein*

anchorperson \ˈ⸗⸗ˌ⸗⸗\ *n* **:** an anchorman or anchorwoman

anchorwoman \ˈ⸗⸗ˌ⸗⸗\ *n, pl* **anchorwomen** **:** a woman who anchors a broadcast

AND \ˈand\ *n* -s **:** a logical operator equivalent to the sentential connective *and* ⟨~ gate in a computer⟩

an·dra·go·gy \ˈandrəˌgäjē, -ˌgōjē, -ˌgägē\ *n* -ES [*andr-* + *-agogy* (as in *pedagogy*)] **:** the art or science of teaching adults

an·dro·gen·ize \anˈdräjəˌnīz\ *vt* -ED/-ING/-S [*androgen* + *-ize*] **:** to treat or influence with male sex hormone esp. in excessive amounts ⟨neonatally *androgenized* female rats⟩

androgynous* *adj* **1 a :** neither specifically feminine or masculine ⟨the ~ pronoun *them*⟩ ⟨the themes cross the sexual divide to the darkest place of our ~ soul — Anne Roiphe⟩ **b :** suitable to or for either sex ⟨an ~ school of clothing design —Angelo d'Arcangelo⟩ ⟨the best fiction is ~: designed by a writer . . . for a reader of either sex —Doris Grumbach⟩ **2 :** having traditional male and female roles obscured or reversed ⟨the possibility of a new ~ way of life —Gerda Lerner⟩

an·dro·stene·di·one \ˌandrəˈstēnˈdīˌōn, -ˈstēndē,-\ *n* -s [*androsterone* + *-ene* + *-dione*] **:** a steroid sex hormone that is secreted by the testis, ovary, and adrenal cortex and acts more strongly in the production of male characteristics than testosterone

angel* *n* **:** a radar echo caused by something not visually discernible

angel dust *n* **:** PHENCYCLIDINE *herein*

an·gi·op·a·thy \ˌanjēˈäpəthē, anˈjäp-\ *n* -ES [*angi-* + *-pathy*] **:** a disease of the blood or lymph vessels

an·gio·sarcoma \ˌanj(ē)ō, -jēə+\ *n* [*angi-* + *sarcoma*] **:** a rare malignant tumor affecting esp. the liver

an·gio·ten·sin \ˌ≈(≈)≈ˈten(t)sən\ *n* -s [blend of *angiotonin* and *hypertensin*] **1 :** either of two forms of a kinin of which one has physiological activity; *esp* **:** ANGIOTENSIN II **2 :** a synthetic amide derivative of angiotensin II used to treat some forms of hypotension

an·gio·ten·sin·ase \-səˌnās, -āz\ *n* -s [*angiotensin* + *-ase*] **:** any of several enzymes in the blood that hydrolyze angiotensin

angiotensin II \-ˈtü\ *n* **:** a protein with vasoconstrictive activity that is composed of a chain of eight amino-acid residues and is the physiologically active form of angiotensin

[1]**an·glo·phone** \ˈaŋgləˌfōn\ *or* **an·glo·phon·ic** \ˌ≈≈ˈfänik\ *adj, usu cap* [*Anglophone* fr. F, fr. *anglo-* Anglo- + *-phone* (as in *francophone*); *Anglophonic* fr. *Anglophone* + *-ic*] **:** having or belonging to an English-speaking population esp. in a country where two or more languages are spoken

[2]**anglophone** \"\ *n* -s *usu cap* **:** an English-speaking person esp. in a country where two or more languages are spoken

angry young man *n* [*Angry Young Man,* autobiography (1951) of Leslie A. Paul *b*1905 Eng. journalist] **1 :** one of a group of mid-20th century British writers whose works express the bitterness of the lower classes toward the established sociopolitical system and toward the mediocrity and hypocrisy of the middle and upper classes **2 :** an outspoken critic of or protester against a social or economic condition or injustice

angular perspective *n* **:** TWO-POINT PERSPECTIVE

ankylosing spondylitis *n* **:** RHEUMATOID SPONDYLITIS

anneal* *vb* ~ *vt* **:** to heat and then cool (nucleic acid) in order to separate strands and induce combination at lower temperatures esp. with complementary strands of a different species ~ *vi* **:** to be capable of combining with complementary nucleic acid by a process of heating and cooling ⟨some bacterial nucleic acid ~*s* well with eukaryotic DNA⟩

annihilate* *vb* ~ *vi* **:** to undergo annihilation ⟨an elementary particle and its antiparticle ~ when they meet⟩

annual percentage rate *n* **:** a measure of the annual percentage cost of consumer credit (as in installment buying or a charge account) that is required by law to appear on statements of credit accounts and is variously computed but always takes into consideration the amount financed, the amount of the finance charges, and the schedule of repayment

anod·al \ˈaˌnōdᵊl, ˌaˈ-\ *adj* [*anode* + *-al*] **:** of, relating to, or attracted to an anode **:** ANODIC 3a ⟨~ potentials⟩ — used esp. in the life sciences — **anod·al·ly** \-ē\ *adv*

anointing of the sick : EXTREME UNCTION

[1]**an·o·rex·ic** \ˌanəˈreksik, -nōˈ-\ *adj* [*anorexia* + *-ic*] **:** ANORECTIC; *also* **:** affected with anorexia nervosa

[2]**anorexic** *n* -s **:** a person affected with anorexia nervosa

an·ovu·lant \aˈnävyələnt, -ōv-\ *n* -s [*an-* + *ovulation* + *-ant*] **:** an anovulatory drug — **anovulant** *adj*

an·ovulation \(ˈ)an+\ *n* [*an-* + *ovulation*] **:** failure or absence of ovulation

anovulatory* *adj* **:** suppressing ovulation ⟨~ drugs⟩

answer* *n* **:** one that imitates, matches, or corresponds to another ⟨picture books — the book business's ~ to the movies —Edward Hoagland⟩

answering service *n* **:** a commercial service that answers telephone calls for its clients

antenna* *n* **:** a special sensitivity, alertness, or receptiveness — usu. used in pl. ⟨helped in her career by sensitive political *antennae*⟩

an·tero·lateral \ˈantə(ˌ)rō, -ˌrə+\ *adj* [*antero-* + *lateral*] **:** situated or occurring in front and to the side ⟨~ wall of the left ventricle of the heart⟩ — **anterolaterally** *adv*

an·tero·posterior \"+\ *adj* [*antero-* + *posterior*] **:** concerned with or extending along a direction or axis from front to back or from anterior to posterior — **anteroposteriorly** *adv*

an·thro·po·nym \anˈthräpəˌnim, ˈan(t)thrəpə-\ *n* [*anthrop-* + *-onym*] **:** a person's name; *esp* **:** SURNAME 2a — **an·thro·po·nym·ic** \≈ˌ≈≈ˈnimik, ˌ≈≈≈-\ *adj*

an·thro·po·sere \anˈthräpə, ˈan(t)thrəpə+ˌ\ *n* [*anthrop-* + [5]*sere*] **:** NOOSPHERE *herein*

an·thro·po·sphere \"+ˌ\ *n* [*anthrop-* + *sphere*] **:** NOOSPHERE *herein*

an·ti·abortion \ˈanˌtī, ˈantē, ˈantə̇+\ *adj* [[1]*anti-* + *abortion*] **:** opposed to abortion — **antiabortionist** \"+\ *n*

an·ti·allergic \"+\ *also* **an·ti·allergenic** \"+\ *adj* [[1]*anti-* + *allergic* or *allergenic*] **:** tending to relieve or control allergic symptoms — **antiallergic** *also* **antiallergenic** *n* -s

anti–american \"+\ *adj, usu cap 2d A* **:** opposed or hostile to the people or the government policies of the U.S. — **anti–americanism** \"+\ *n, usu cap 2d A*

an·ti·androgen \"+\ *n* [[1]*anti-* + *androgen*] **:** a substance that tends to inhibit the production, activity, or effects of a male sex hormone — **an·ti·androgenic** \"+\ *adj*

an·ti·anginal \"+\ *adj* [[1]*anti-* + *anginal*] **:** used or tending to prevent or relieve angina pectoris ⟨~ drugs⟩

an·ti·anxiety \"+\ *adj* [[1]*anti-* + *anxiety*] **:** tending to prevent or relieve anxiety ⟨~ drugs⟩

an·ti·arrhythmic \"+\ *adj* [[1]*anti-* + *arrhythmia* + *-ic*] **:** counteracting or preventing cardiac arrhythmia ⟨an ~ agent⟩ — **antiarrhythmic** *n* -s

an·ti–art \ˈanˌtī, ˈantē, ˈantə̇ +ˌ\ *n* [[1]*anti-* + *art*] **:** art based on premises antithetical to traditional or popular art forms; *specif* **:** DADA

an·ti·arthritic \ˈ≈(ˌ)≈+\ *adj* [[1]*anti-* + *arthritic*] **:** tending to relieve or prevent arthritic symptoms — **antiarthritic** *n*

an·ti·atom \ˈ≈(ˌ)≈+ˌ\ *n* [[1]*anti-* + *atom*] **:** an atom comprised of antiparticles

an·ti·authoritarian \ˈanˌtī, ˈantē, ˈantə̇+\ *adj* [[1]*anti-* + *authoritarian*] **:** opposed or hostile to authoritarians or authoritarianism — **an·ti·authoritarianism** \"+\ *n*

an·ti·auxin \"+\ *n* [[1]*anti-* + *auxin*] **:** a plant substance that opposes or suppresses the natural effect of an auxin

an·ti·ballistic missile \"+ . . .-\ *n* [[1]*anti-* + *ballistic missile*] **:** a missile for intercepting and destroying a ballistic missile

an·ti·baryon \"+\ *n* [[1]*anti-* + *baryon* (herein)] **:** an antiparticle of a baryon (as an antiproton or antineutron)

an·ti·black \"+\ *adj* [[1]*anti-* + *black*] **:** opposed or hostile to people belonging to the Negro race — **an·ti·black·ism** \-ˌizəm\ *n* -s

an·ti·busing \"+\ *adj* [[1]*anti-* + *busing* (herein)] **:** opposed to the busing of schoolchildren ⟨~ parents⟩ ⟨~ campaign⟩

an·ti·cancer \"+\ *adj* [[1]*anti-* + *cancer*] **:** used or effective against cancer ⟨~ drugs⟩ ⟨~ treatments⟩

an·ti·carcinogenic \"+\ *adj* [[1]*anti-* + *carcinogenic*] **:** tending to inhibit or prevent the activity of a carcinogen or the development of carcinoma ⟨an ~ substance counteracting the carcinogenic potential of estrogens in birth control pills⟩

an·ti·caries \"+\ *adj* [[1]*anti-* + *caries*] **:** tending to inhibit the formation of caries ⟨~ effects⟩ ⟨an ~ toothpaste additive⟩

an·ti·coagulation \"+\ *n* [[1]*anti-* + *coagulation*] **:** the process of hindering the clotting of blood esp. by treatment with an anticoagulant — **an·ti·coagulate** \"+\ *vt* — **an·ti·coagulatory** \"+\ *adj*

an·ti·codon \"+\ *n* [[1]*anti-* + *codon* (herein)] **:** a triplet of nucleotide bases in transfer RNA that identifies the amino acid carried and binds to a complementary codon in messenger RNA during protein synthesis at a ribosome

an·ti·convulsant \"+\ *also* **an·ti·convulsive** \"+\ *adj* [[1]*anti-* + *convulsant* or *convulsive*] **:** used or tending to control or prevent convulsions (as in epilepsy) — **anticonvulsant** *also* **anticonvulsive** *n* -s

an·ti·crop \"+\ *adj* [[1]*anti-* + *crop*] **:** destructive to or directed against crops ⟨~ chemical weapons⟩

[1]**an·ti·depressant** \ˌanˌtī, ˌantē, ˌantə +\ *also* **an·ti·depressive** \"+\ *adj* [[1]*anti-* + *depressant* or *depressive*] **:** used or tending to relieve psychic depression

[2]**antidepressant** *n* **:** an antidepressant drug — called also *energizer, psychic energizer*

an·ti·deuteron \"+\ *n* [[1]*anti-* + *deuteron*] **:** the antimatter counterpart of a deuteron

an·ti·diabetic \"+\ *adj* [[1]*anti-* + *diabetic*] **:** tending to relieve diabetes ⟨~ drugs⟩ — **antidiabetic** *n*

an·ti·diuresis \"+\ *n* [[1]*anti-* + *diuresis*] **:** reduction in or suppression of the excretion of urine

antidiuretic hormone *n* **:** VASOPRESSIN

an·ti·dumping \"+\ *adj* [[1]*anti-* + *dumping*] **:** designed to discourage the importation and sale of foreign goods at prices substantially lower than domestic prices ⟨~ tariffs⟩

an·ti·electron \"+\ *n* [[1]*anti-* + *electron*] **:** POSITRON

an·ti·emetic \"+\ *adj* [[1]*anti-* + *emetic*] **:** used or tending to prevent or check vomiting ⟨~ drugs⟩ — **antiemetic** *n*

an·ti·epileptic \"+\ *adj* [[1]*anti-* + *epileptic*] **:** tending to suppress or prevent epilepsy ⟨~ treatment⟩

an·ti·establishment \"+\ *adj* [[1]*anti-* + *establishment* (herein)] **:** opposed or hostile to the social, economic, and political principles of a ruling class (as of a nation)

an·ti·establishmentarian \"+\ *adj* [*antiestablishment* (herein) + *-arian*] **:** ANTIESTABLISHMENT *herein* — **antiestablishmentarian** *n* -s

an·ti·estrogen \"+\ *n* [[1]*anti-* + *estrogen*] **:** a substance that inhibits the physiological action of an estrogen — **an·ti·estrogenic** \"+\ *adj*

an·ti·feminist \"+\ *adj* [[1]*anti-* + *feminist*] **:** opposed to feminism — **an·ti·feminism** \"+\ *n* — **antifeminist** *n*

an·ti·fertility \"+\ *adj* [[1]*anti-* + *fertility*] **:** having the capacity or tending to reduce or destroy fertility **:** CONTRACEPTIVE ⟨~ agents⟩ ⟨~ action⟩

an·ti·flu·o·ri·da·tion·ist \ˌ=(ˌ)=ˌflu̇rəˈdāsh(ə)nəst, -ōr-, -ȯr-\ *n* -s [[1]*anti-* + *fluoridation* + *-ist*] **:** a person who is vigorously opposed to the fluoridation of public water supplies

an·ti·foul·ant \ˌ=(ˌ)=ˈfau̇lənt\ *n* -s [[1]*anti-* + [4]*foul* + [1]*-ant*] **:** a substance (as paint for use on the bottom of a boat) designed to prevent, reduce, or eliminate fouling

an·ti·fungal \ˌanˌtī, ˌantē, ˌantə +\ *adj* [[1]*anti-* + *fungal*] **:** used or effective against fungi **:** FUNGICIDAL ⟨~ drugs⟩ ⟨~ chemotherapy⟩ — **antifungal** *n*

an·ti·globulin \"+\ *n* [[1]*anti-* + *globulin*] **:** an antibody that combines with and precipitates globulin

[1]**an·ti·gravity** \"+\ *adj* [[1]*anti-* + *gravity*] **:** reducing, canceling, or protecting against the effect of gravity

[2]**antigravity** \"+\ *n* **:** a hypothetical effect resulting from cancellation or reduction of a gravitational field

an·ti·helium \"+\ *n* [[1]*anti-* + *helium*] **:** the antimatter counterpart of helium

an·ti·hemophilic factor *also* **antihemophilic globulin** \"+ . . .-\ *n* [[1]*anti-* + *hemophilic*] **:** a glycoprotein of blood plasma that is essential for blood clotting and is absent or inactive in hemophilia — called also *factor VIII*

an·ti·hero \"+\ *n* [[1]*anti-* + *hero*] **:** a protagonist who is notably lacking in heroic qualities — **an·ti·heroic** \"+\ *adj*

an·ti·heroine \"+\ *n* [[1]*anti-* + *heroine*] **:** a female antihero

an·ti·human \"+\ *adj* [[1]*anti-* + *human*] **:** acting or being against man; *also* **:** reacting strongly with human antigens

an·ti·hydrogen \"+\ *n* [[1]*anti-* + *hydrogen*] **:** the antimatter counterpart of hydrogen

an·ti·hypertensive \"+\ *adj* [[1]*anti-* + *hypertension* + *-ive*] **:** used or effective against high blood pressure — **antihypertensive** *n*

an·ti–immunoglobulin \"+\ *adj* [[1]*anti-* + *immunoglobulin*] **:** acting against specific antibodies ⟨*anti-immunoglobulin* sera⟩ — **an·ti–immunoglobulin** *n*

an·ti–infective \"+\ *adj* [[1]*anti-* + *infective*] **:** used against or tending to counteract or prevent infection ⟨*anti-infective* agents⟩ — **anti–infective** *n* -s

an·ti–inflammatory \ˌanˌtī, ˌantē, ˌantə +\ *adj* [[1]*anti-* + *inflammatory*] **:** counteracting inflammation — **anti–inflammatory** *n* -ES

an·ti–intellectual \"+\ *adj* [[1]*anti-* + *intellectual*] **:** opposing or hostile to intellectuals or to an intellectual view or approach ⟨an *anti-intellectual* know-nothingism: forget politics, forget art, forget history —Samuel Hynes⟩ — **anti–intellectual** *n*

an·ti·lepton \"+\ *n* [[1]*anti-* + [3]*lepton*] **:** an antiparticle (as a positron or an antineutrino) of a lepton

an·ti·leukemic \"+\ *also* **an·ti·leukemia** \"+\ *adj* [[1]*anti-* + *leukemic* or *leukemia*] **:** counteracting the effects of leukemia

an·ti·life \"+\ *adj* [[1]*anti-* + *life*] **:** antipathetic to normal, full, or healthy life; *also* **:** favoring birth control

an·ti·litter \"+\ *adj* [[1]*anti-* + *litter*] **:** serving to prevent or discourage the littering of public areas ⟨~ laws⟩

an·ti·lymphocyte globulin \"+ . . .-\ *n* [[1]*anti-* + *lymphocyte*] **:** serum globulin containing antibodies against lymphocytes that is used similarly to antilymphocyte serum

an·ti·lymphocyte serum \"+ . . .-\ *n* **:** a serum containing antibodies against lymphocytes that is used for suppressing graft rejection caused by lymphocyte-controlled immune responses in organ or tissue transplant recipients

an·ti·lymphocytic globulin \"+ . . .-\ *n* [[1]*anti-* + *lymphocytic*] **:** ANTILYMPHOCYTE GLOBULIN *herein*

an·ti·lymphocytic serum \"+ . . .-\ *n* [[1]*anti-* + *lymphocytic*] **:** ANTILYMPHOCYTE SERUM *herein*

an·ti·missile \"+\ *adj* [[1]*anti-* + *missile*] **:** designed as a defense against missiles ⟨an ~ system⟩

antimissile missile *n* **:** a missile for intercepting another missile in flight; *esp* **:** ANTIBALLISTIC MISSILE *herein*

an·ti·mitotic \ˌan‚tī, ˌantē, ˌantə +\ *adj* [[1]*anti-* + *mitotic*] **:** inhibiting or disrupting mitosis ⟨~ drugs⟩ ⟨~ activity⟩ — **antimitotic** *n* -s

an·ti·mutagenic \"+\ *adj* [[1]*anti-* + *mutagenic*] **:** reducing the rate of mutation ⟨~ substances⟩

an·ti·mycotic \"+\ *adj or n* [[1]*anti-* + *mycotic*] **:** ANTIFUNGAL *herein*

an·ti·neoplastic \"+\ *adj* [[1]*anti-* + *neoplastic*] **:** inhibiting or preventing the growth and spread of neoplasms or malignant cells — **antineoplastic** *n* -s

an·ti·noise \"+\ *adj* [[1]*anti-* + *noise*] **:** designed or acting to reduce noise level ⟨an ~ ordinance⟩

an·ti·novel \"+\ *n* [[1]*anti-* + *novel*] **:** a work of fiction that lacks most or all of the traditional features (as coherent structure or character development) of the novel — **an·ti·novelist** \"+\ *n*

an·ti·nuclear \"+\ *adj* **1** [[1]*anti-* +*nucleus* +*-ar*] **:** tending to react with cell nuclei or their components (as DNA) ⟨~ antibodies⟩ **2** [[1]*anti-* +*nuclear*] **:** opposing the use or production of nuclear power plants or nuclear weapons

an·ti·nuke \ˌ≈(ˌ)≈ˌn(y)ük\ *adj* [by shortening & alter] **:** ANTINUCLEAR 2 *herein*

an·ti·obscenity \"+\ *adj* [[1]*anti-* + *obscenity*] **:** designed to prevent or restrict the dissemination of obscene materials

an·ti·ozon·ant \ˌ≈(ˌ)≈ˌō‚zōnənt\ *n* -s [[1]*anti-* + *ozone* + [2]*-ant*] **:** a substance that opposes ozonization or protects against it

an·ti·parasitic \"+\ *adj* [[1]*anti-* + *parasite* + *-ic*] **:** acting against parasites ⟨~ drugs⟩

an·ti·parkinsonian \"+\ *also* **an·ti·parkinson** \ˌ≈(ˌ)≈ˈpärkənsən\ *adj* [[1]*anti-* + *parkinsonian* or *parkinson*'s disease] **:** tending to relieve parkinsonism ⟨~ drugs⟩

an·ti·particle \ˈan‚tī, ˈantē, ˈantə +ˌ\ *n* [[1]*anti-* + *particle*] **:** an elementary particle that is identical to another elementary particle in mass but opposite to it in electric and magnetic properties (as sign of charge) and that when brought together with its counterpart produces mutual annihilation; *specif* **:** an elementary particle not found in ordinary matter

an·ti·political \ˌan‚tī, ˌantē, ˌantə+\ *adj* [[1]*anti-* + *political*] **:** opposing or reacting against traditional political policies and principles

an·ti·politician \"+\ *n* [[1]*anti-* + *politician*] **:** a politician who appears to be antipolitical

an·ti–politics \"+\ *n pl but sing or pl in constr* [[1]*anti-* + *politics*] **:** reaction against or rejection of the practices or attitudes associated with traditional politics

an·ti·pollution \"+\ *adj* [[1]*anti-* + *pollution*] **:** intended to prevent, reduce, or eliminate pollution — **an·ti·pol·lu·tion·ist** \-əst\ *n* -s

an·ti·poverty \"+\ *adj* [[1]*anti-* + *poverty*] **:** of or relating to action designed to relieve poverty ⟨~ programs⟩

an·ti·psychotic \"+\ *adj* [[1]*anti-* + *psychotic*] **:** tending to alleviate psychosis or psychotic states ⟨an ~ drug⟩ — **antipsychotic** *n*

an·ti·quark \"+\ *n* [[1]*anti-* + *quark* (herein)] **:** the antiparticle of the quark

antique* *vb* ~ *vi* **:** to shop around for antiques

an·ti·racism \"+\ *n* [[1]*anti-* + *racism*] **:** adherence to the view that racism is a social evil — **an·ti·racist** \"+\ *n or adj*

an·ti·radical \"+\ *adj* [[1]*anti-* + *radical*] **:** opposed to radicals or radicalism

an·ti·satellite \"+\ *adj* **:** of, relating to, or being a system designed for the destruction or incapacitation of satellites

an·ti·science \"+\ *n* [[1]*anti-* + *science*] **:** a system or attitude or cult that rejects scientific methods or the value of science to man; *also* **:** one that denies the value of basic scientific research — **an·ti·scientific** \"+\ *adj*

an·ti·sex \"+\ *or* **an·ti·sexual** \"+\ *adj* [[1]*anti-* + *sex* or *sexual*] **:** antagonistic toward sex; *esp* **:** tending to reduce or eliminate the sex drive or sexual activity

an·ti·skid \"+\ *adj* [[1]*anti-* + *skid*] **:** designed to prevent skidding

an·ti·smog \"+\ *adj* [[1]*anti-* + *smog*] **:** designed to reduce pollutants that contribute to the formation of smog

an·ti·static \ˌan‚tī, ˌantē, ˌantə +\ *also* **an·ti·stat** \ˌan‚tīˌstat, ˌantē-, ˌantə-\ *adj* [*antistatic* fr. [1]*anti-* + *static,* n.; *antistat* short for *antistatic*] **:** reducing, removing, or preventing the buildup of static electricity — **antistatic** *n*

an·ti·streptococcal *or* **an·ti·streptococcic** \ˌan‚tī, ˌantē, ˌantə+\ *adj* [[1]*anti-* + *streptococcal* or *streptococcic*] **:** tending to destroy or inhibit the growth and reproduction of streptococci ⟨~ antibodies⟩

antisymmetric* *adj* **:** relating to or being a relation (as "is a subset of") that implies equality of any two quantities for which it holds in both directions ⟨the relation *R* is ~ if *aRb* and *bRa* implies *a* = *b*⟩

an·ti·thrombotic \"+\ *adj* [[1]*anti-* + *thrombotic*] **:** used against or tending to prevent thrombosis ⟨~ agents⟩ ⟨~ therapy⟩

an·ti·tuberculous \"+\ *or* **an·ti·tuberculosis** \"+\ *or* **an·ti·tubercular** \"+\ *adj* [[1]*anti-* + *tuberculous* or *tuberculosis* or *tubercular*] **:** used or effective against tuberculosis ⟨~ drugs⟩

an·ti·tumor \"+\ *also* **an·ti·tumoral** \"+\ *adj* [[1]*anti-* + *tumor* or *tumoral*] **:** ANTICANCER *herein* ⟨~ agents⟩ ⟨~ activity⟩

antitussive* *n* -s **:** an antitussive agent

an·ti·ulcer \"+\ *adj* [[1]*anti-* + *ulcer*] **:** tending to prevent or heal ulcers ⟨~ drug research⟩

an·ti–utopia \"+\ *n* [[1]*anti-* + *utopia*] **:** DYSTOPIA *herein* — **an·ti–utopian** \"+\ *adj or n*

an·ti·war \"+\ *adj* [[1]*anti-* + *war*] **:** opposed to war ⟨~ demonstrations⟩

an·ti·white \"+\ *adj* [[1]*anti-* + *white*] **:** opposed or hostile to people belonging to a light-skinned race — **an·ti·whit·ism** \ˌ≈(ˌ)≈ˌ(h)wīd‚izəm\ *n* -s

an·ti·world \'an,tī, 'antē, 'antə+,\ *n* [[1]*anti-* + *world*] **:** the hypothetical antimatter counterpart of a world

anx·io·lyt·ic \,aŋzēō'lid·ik, ,aŋ(k)sē-, -itik, -ēk\ *n* -s [*anxiety* + *-o-* + *-lytic* (perh. influenced by *analytic, catalytic*)] **:** a drug that relieves anxiety — **anxiolytic** *adj*

ao dai \'äō'dī, 'a-\ *n, pl* **ao dais** [Vietnamese *áo dài,* fr. *áo* jacket, tunic (of Chinese origin — akin to Chin (Pek) *ao*[3] jacket) + *dai* long] **:** the traditional dress of Vietnamese women that consists of a long tunic with slits on either side and wide trousers

A–OK \'ā(,)ō'kā\ *adj* [[1]*a* + *OK*] **:** very definitely OK

aor·to·il·i·ac \,ā,ȯrd·ō'ilē,ak, -rtō-\ *adj* [*aort-* + *iliac*] **:** of, relating to, or joining the abdominal aorta and the iliac arteries

ape \'āp\ *adj* [[1]*ape*] **:** being beyond restraint **:** CRAZY, WILD — usu. used in the phrase *go ape* ⟨went ~ over another girl —*Boston Sunday Globe Mag.*⟩

aperture card *n* **:** a punched card for data processing in which one or more frames of a microfilmed document are mounted

aperture synthesis *n* **:** a technique in radio astronomy in which two or more radio telescopes are varied in position and spacing to simulate a large telescope having a collecting area with a diameter approximately equal to the largest spacing between the smaller telescopes

APEX \'ā,peks\ *n* -ES [*a*dvance *p*urchase *ex*cursion] **:** a class of reduced air fares requiring payment a specified number of days in advance and a round trip of specified duration

Ap·gar score \'ap,gär, -,gȧ(r\ *n* [after Virginia *Apgar* †1974 Am. anesthesiologist] **:** an index used to evaluate the condition of a newborn infant based on a rating of 0, 1, or 2 for each of the five characteristics of color, heart rate, response to stimulation of the sole of the foot, muscle tone, and respiration with 10 being a perfect score

apha·si·ol·o·gy \ə'fāz(h)ē'äləjē, -ji\ *n* -ES [*aphasia* + *-ology*] **:** the study of aphasia including its linguistic, psychological, and neurological aspects — **apha·si·ol·o·gist** \-jəst\ *n* -s

aph·ox·ide \(')a'fäk,sīd *also* -ksəd\ *n* [prob. fr. aziridinyl + *ph*osphine, a chemical compound + *oxide*] **:** TEPA *herein*

apo·apsis \'apō +\ *n, pl* **apo·apsides** \"+\ [NL, fr. *apo-* + *apsis*] **:** the apsis that is farthest from the center of attraction **:** the high point in an orbit — compare PERIAPSIS *herein*

apo·cyn·thi·on \'apə'sin(t)thēən\ *n* -s [NL, fr. *apo-* + *Cynthia,* goddess of the moon (fr. Gk *Kynthia*) + *-on* (as in *aphelion*)] **:** APOLUNE *herein*

apo·lipoprotein \'apə, 'apō +\ *n* [*apo-* + *lipoprotein*] **:** a protein that combines with a lipid to form a lipoprotein

apo·lune \'apə,lün\ *n* -s [*apo-* + *-lune* (fr. L *luna* moon — more at LUNAR] **:** the point in the path of a body orbiting the moon that is farthest from the center of the moon

apo·protein \'apə, 'apō +\ *n* [*apo-* + *protein*] **:** a protein that combines with a prosthetic group to form a conjugated protein

ap·pa·la·chian \,apə'lāchən, -ach-, -āsh-, -chēən\ *n* -s *cap* **:** a white native or resident of the Appalachian mountain area

apple–pie* *adj* [fr. the tradition that apple pie is a quintessentially American dish] **:** of, relating to, or characterized by traditionally American values ⟨concerned with the recovery of a lot of *apple-pie* virtues after an era of turmoil and flux —E. B. Fiske⟩

approach–approach conflict \=¦==′=-\ *n* **:** psychological conflict that results when a choice must be made between two desirable alternatives — compare APPROACH-AVOIDANCE CONFLICT *herein,* AVOIDANCE-AVOIDANCE CONFLICT *herein*

approach–avoidance conflict \=¦==′==-\ *n* **:** psychological conflict that results when a goal is both desirable and undesirable — compare APPROACH-APPROACH CONFLICT *herein,* AVOIDANCE-AVOIDANCE CONFLICT *herein*

appropriate technology *n* **:** technology that is suitable to the social and economic conditions of the geographic area in which it is to be applied, is environmentally sound, and promotes self-sufficiency on the part of those using it

[1]**après–ski** \'ä,prā'skē, 'a-\ *n* [F, fr. *après* after + *ski* ski, skiing — more at APRÈS] **:** social activity (as at a ski lodge) after a day's skiing

[2]**après–ski** \"\ *adj* **:** of, relating to, or suitable for après-ski

aqua·cul·tur·ist *also* **aqui·cul·tur·ist** \'akwə'kəlch(ə)rəst, 'äk-\ *n* **:** a person who specializes in aquaculture

aqua·naut \'akwə,nȯt, 'äk-, -nät\ *n* -s [*aqua-* + *-naut* (as in *astronaut*)] **:** a scuba diver who lives beneath the surface of water for an extended period and carries on activities both inside and outside his underwater shelter

aquaplane* *vi* **:** HYDROPLANE *herein*

aquarian* *n, usu cap* **:** AQUARIUS *herein*

aquar·i·an \ə'kwa(a)rēən, -wer-, -wār-\ *adj, usu cap* [*aquarian,* n. (herein)] **:** relating to or characteristic of an Aquarius ⟨that little bit of *Aquarian* perversity — *Annabel*⟩

aquarius* *n, usu cap* **:** one born under the astrological sign Aquarius

arabesque* *n* **:** a contrived intricate pattern of verbal expression ⟨~*s* of alliteration —C.E.Montague⟩

ara·chid·o·nate \,arə'kidᵊn,āt\ *n* -s [*arachidonic* + [1]*-ate*] **:** a salt or ester of arachidonic acid

ar·a·mid \'arəməd\ *n* -s [*ar*omatic poly*amide*] **:** any of a group of lightweight but very strong heat-resistant synthetic aromatic polyamide materials that are fashioned into fibers and used esp. in textiles; *also* **:** a fiber manufactured from an aramid

ar·bo·vi·rol·o·gy \,ärbə,vī'räləjē\ *n* [*arbovirus* + *-ology*] **:** a branch of virology that deals with the arboviruses — **ar·bo·vi·rol·o·gist** \-jəst\ *n* -s

ar·bo·vi·rus \'ärbə'vīrəs\ *n* [*ar*thropod-*bo*rne *virus*] **:** any of various viruses transmitted by arthropods and including the causative agents of encephalitis, yellow fever, and dengue

arcade* *n* **:** an amusement center having coin-operated games

ar·chaeo·astronomy \'==(,)= *or* =¦== *at* ARCHAE- +\ *n* [*archae-* + *astronomy*] **:** the study of the astronomy of ancient cultures — **ar·chaeo·astronomer** \"+\ *n*

architecture* *n* **:** the manner in which the components of a computer or computer system are organized and integrated

ar·cho·saur \'ärkə,sȯ(ə)r\ *n* -s [NL *Archosauria*] **:** a member of the reptilian subclass Archosauria

ar·col·ogy \är'käləjē\ *n* -ES [*ar*chitectural e*cology*] **:** a city intended to be contained in a single structure

arc second *n* **:** [4]SECOND 1

arcuate nucleus *n* **:** any of several cellular masses in the thalamus, hypothalamus, or medulla oblongata

area code *n* [so called fr. its designation of major subdivisions of the territory of the United States] **:** a 3-digit code used in dialing long-distance telephone calls

area rug *n* **:** a rug covering only part of a floor

arena stage *n* **:** a theater stage surrounded or nearly surrounded by the audience; *specif* **:** the stage of an arena theater

ar·eo·cen·tric \ˌa(a)rēōˈsen·trik, -ēə-\ *adj* [*areo-* + *-centric*] **:** having or relating to the planet Mars as a center

ar 15 \ˈāˈär(ˈ)fifˈtēn\ *or* **ar 15 rifle** *n* -s *usu cap A & R* [fr. *Ar*malite, the manufacturer] **:** a .223 caliber gas-operated semiautomatic rifle that is essentially a civilian version of the M16

arguable* *adj* **:** that can be plausibly or convincingly argued — **arguably*** *adv*

Ar·gy·rol \ˈärjəˌrȯl, -ˌrōl\ *trademark* — used for a silver-protein compound whose aqueous solution is used as a local antiseptic esp. for mucous membranes

arhythmic \ˈā+\ *also* **arhythmical** \"+\ *adj* [²*a-* + *rhythmic* or *rhythmical*] **:** marked by the absence of rhythm ⟨struck by the ~ quality of their reading — Charles Drake⟩

ar·i·an \ˈa(a)rēən, ˈer-, ˈär-\ *n* -s *usu cap* [fr. *Aries* + E *-an*] **:** ARIES *herein*

aries* *n, usu cap* **:** one born under the astrological sign Aries

arm and a leg *n* **:** an exorbitant price ⟨have fun without shelling out an *arm and a leg* —Genevieve Stuttaford⟩

arm–twist·ing \ˈ=ˌ==\ *n* **:** the use of direct personal pressure in order to achieve a desired end ⟨for all the *arm-twisting,* the . . . vote on the measure was unexpectedly tight —*Newsweek*⟩

arm wrestling *n* **:** INDIAN WRESTLING 2b

ar·nold·ian \ärˈnōldēən\ *adj, usu cap* [Matthew *Arnold* †1888 Eng. poet & critic + E *-ian*] **:** of or relating to Matthew Arnold or his works

around the world *n* **:** the action of orally stimulating many parts of the body for sexual gratification

array* *n* **1 :** an arrangement of computer memory elements in a single plane **2 :** a group of elements forming a complete unit ⟨an ~ of solar cells⟩

array processor *n* **:** a computer peripheral designed to perform fast numerical calculations on large amounts of data

ar·res·tant \əˈrestənt\ *n* -s [¹*arrest* + *-ant*] **:** a substance or stimulus that causes an insect to stop locomotion and begin to feed

art de·co \ˌär(t)dāˈkō; (ˈ)är(t)ˈdā(ˌ)kō, -de-; -ȧ(t)-\ *n, often cap A&D* [F *Art Déco,* fr. *Exposition Internationale des Arts Décoratifs et Industriels Modernes,* an exposition of modern decorative and industrial arts held in Paris, France, in 1925] **:** a popular architectural and decorative style of the 1920s and 1930s characterized esp. by bold outlines and colors, by streamlined and geometric forms, and by the use of man-made materials

ar·thro·gry·po·sis \ˌärˌthrōgrəˈpōsəs, ˌȧˌth-\ *n* [NL, fr. *arthr-* + *gryposis*] **:** permanent flexure of a joint

ar·throl·o·gy \ärˈthrälәjē\ *n* -ES [*arthr-* + *-logy*] **:** a science concerned with the study of joints

ar·thros·co·py \-ˈthräskəpē\ *n* -ES [ISV *arthr-* + *-scope* + *-y*] **:** visual examination of the interior of a joint (as the knee) with a special surgical instrument — **ar·thro·scope** \ˈärthrəˌskōp\ *n* — **ar·thro·scop·ic** \ˌ==ˈskäpik\ *adj*

ar·throt·o·my \ärˈthrätəmē\ *n* -ES [ISV *arthr-* + *-tomy*] **:** incision into a joint

ar·tic \ȧˈtik\ *n* -s [short for *articulated lorry*] *Brit* **:** SEMITRAILER 2

artificial intelligence *n* **:** the capability of a machine to imitate intelligent human behavior (as reasoning, learning, or the understanding of speech)

art·mo·bile \ˈärtmōˌbēl, ˈȧt-\ *n* -s [*art* + *-mobile*] **:** a trailer that houses an art collection designed for exhibition on road tours

art mo·derne \ˌär(t)mȯˈde(ə)rn\ *n, often cap A & M* [F, lit., *modern art*] **:** ART DECO *herein*

aru·gu·la \əˈrüg(y)ələ\ *n* [prob. from It dial. *arugula,* fr. L *ērūca* colewort; akin to Sp *ruqueta,* Cat *oruga,* F *roquette*] **:** GARDEN ROCKET 1

ary·te·noi·dec·to·my \ˌarəˌtēˌnȯiˈdektəmē, əˌritᵊnˌȯi-\ *n* -ES [²*arytenoid* + *-ectomy*] **:** excision of an arytenoid cartilage

ASAP *abbr* as soon as possible

ascending colon *n* **:** the part of the large intestine that extends from the cecum to the bend on the right side below the liver — compare DESCENDING COLON *herein,* TRANSVERSE COLON *in the Dict*

ASCII \ˈas(ˌ)kē\ *n* [*A*merican *S*tandard *C*ode for *I*nformation *I*nterchange] **:** a code for representing alphanumeric information

as far as *prep* **:** with reference to **:** as for — not often in formal use; used in speech and speechlike prose ⟨*as far as* being mentioned in the Ten Commandments, I think it is —Billy Graham⟩

ash* *n* [OE *æsc,* lit., ash tree, name of the corresponding runic letter] **:** the ligature æ used in Old English to represent a low front vowel

ASL *abbr* American Sign Language *herein*

as·par·tame \ˈaspə(r)ˌtām, əˈspärˌtām\ *n* -s **:** a noncarbohydrate crystalline compound $C_{14}H_{18}N_2O_5$ that is formed from the amino acids phenylalanine and aspartic acid and is used as a low-calorie sweetener

as·par·to·kinase \əˌspärd·ō +\ *n* [*aspart*ic acid + *-o-* + *-ki- nase*] **:** an enzyme that catalyzes the phosphorylation of aspartic acid by ATP

asphalt jungle *n* **:** a big city or a specified part of a big city ⟨the *asphalt jungle* around Times Square — E.R.Bentley⟩

¹-ass \ˌas, ˌaa(ə)s, ˌais *also* ˌȧs\ *adj or adv comb form* [⁴*ass*] — used as a derogatory intensive ⟨fancy-*ass*⟩; often considered vulgar

²-ass \ˌ=\ *n comb form* -ES [⁴*ass*] **:** a contemptible person ⟨smart-*ass*⟩ — often considered vulgar

as·sem·blage* \əˈsemblij; ˌaˌsä(ⁿ)mˈbläzh\ *n* **1 :** an artistic composition made from scraps, junk, and odds and ends (as of paper, cloth, wood, stone, or metal) **2 :** the art of making assemblages — **as·sem·blag·ist** \-jə̇st, -zhə̇-\ *n* -s

assembler* *n* **1 :** a computer program that automatically converts instructions written in assembly language into the equivalent machine language **2 :** ASSEMBLY LANGUAGE

assembly* *n* **:** the translation of assembly language to machine language by an assembler

assembly language *n* **:** a symbolic language for programming a computer that is a close approximation of machine language

assertiveness training *n* **:** a method of training individuals to act in a bold self-confident manner

asshole \ˈ=ˌ=\ *n* [⁴*ass* + *hole*] **1 :** ANUS — usu. considered vulgar **2 :** a stupid or incompetent person **:** BLOCK-

HEAD — usu. considered vulgar **3 :** the least attractive or desirable part or area — usu. considered vulgar

assist* *n* **:** a mechanical device that provides assistance

ass–kissing \'⸗ˌ⸗⸗\ *n* **:** obsequious flattery or attentiveness — usu. considered vulgar

associative neuron *n* **:** a neuron that conveys nerve impulses from one neuron to another

as·ti spu·man·te \ˌästē(ˌ)spü'män(ˌ)tā, ˌas-, -sti-, -spə'-, -tē\ *n, usu cap A & often cap S* [It, lit., sparkling Asti] **:** a sweet sparkling white wine made in and around the village of Asti in Piedmont

astral projection *n* **:** out-of-body travel

as·tro·biology \ˌas(ˌ)trō +\ *n [astr- + biology]* **:** EXOBIOLOGY *herein* — **as·tro·biological** \"+\ *adj* — **as·tro·biologist** \"+\ *n*

as·tro·bleme \'astrəˌblēm\ *n* -s [*astr-* + Gk *blēma* throw, missile, wound from a missile, fr. *ballein* to throw — more at DEVIL] **:** a scar on the earth's crust made by the impact of a meteorite

as·tro·chemistry \ˌastrō +\ *n [astr- + chemistry]* **:** the chemistry of celestial bodies and interstellar space — **as·tro·chemist** \"+\ *n*

as·tro·dynamics \ˌas(ˌ)trō +\ *n pl but sing or pl in constr* [*astr-* + *dynamics*] **:** dynamics that deals with objects in outer space — **as·tro·dynamic** \"+\ *adj* — **as·tro·dy·nam·i·cist** \ˌas(ˌ)trōdī'naməsə̇st *sometimes* -də̇-\ *n* -s

as·tro·geology \ˌas(ˌ)trō +\ *n* [*astr-* + *geology*] **:** a branch of geology that deals with celestial bodies — **as·tro·geologic** \ˌastrō +\ *adj* — **as·tro·geologist** \ˌas(ˌ)trō +\ *n*

As·tro·turf \'astrəˌtərf\ *trademark* — used for an artificial grass that resembles carpeting

atemporal \(ˈ)ā+ˌ\ *adj* [²*a-* + *temporal*] **:** independent of or unaffected by time **:** TIMELESS

atheoretical \ˌā+\ *adj* [²*a-* + *theoretical*] **:** not based on or concerned with theory

ath·ero·genesis \ˌathərō +\ *n* [*athero-* + *genesis*] **:** the production of atheroma

ath·ero·gen·ic \ˌathərōˌjenik\ *adj* [*athero-* + *-genic*] **:** relating to or tending to produce degenerative changes in arterial walls — **ath·ero·ge·nic·i·ty** \-ˌjəˌnisəd·ē, -ətē\ *n* -ES

athymic \(ˈ)ā+ˌ\ *adj* [²*a-* + *thymic*] **:** lacking a thymus ⟨congenitally ~ babies⟩

at·lan·ti·cism \ət'lantəˌsizəm\ *n* -s *usu cap* [*Atlantic* + *-ism*] **:** a policy of military, political, and economic cooperation between European and North American powers — **at·lan·ti·cist** \-ntəsə̇st\ *n* -s *usu cap*

at·mo·sphe·ri·um \ˌatmə'sfirēəm\ *n* -s [*atmosphere* + *-ium* (as in *planetarium*)] **1 :** an optical device for projecting images of meteorological phenomena (as clouds) on the inside of a dome **2 :** a room housing an atmospherium

atoxic \(ˈ)ā+ˌ\ *adj* [²*a-* + *toxic*] **:** not toxic ⟨~ antibiotics⟩

ATPase \ˌāˌtē'pēˌās, -ˌāz\ *n* -s [*ATP* + *-ase*] **:** ADENOSINE TRIPHOSPHATASE

at·ra·zine \'a·trəˌzēn\ *n* -s [ISV *atr-* (perh. fr. L *atr-, ater* black, dark) + tri*azine*] **:** a photosynthesis-inhibiting persistent herbicide $C_8H_{14}ClN_5$ used esp. to kill annual weeds and quack grass

at·ro·pin·iza·tion \ˌa·trəpənə̇'zāshən, -ˌpēn-, -ˌī'z-\ *n* -s [*atropine* + *-ization*] **:** the physiological condition of being under the influence of atropine

attackman \'⸗ˌ(ˌ)⸗\ *n, pl* **attackmen :** a player (as in lacrosse) assigned to an offensive zone or position

at·to- \ˌad·(ˌ)ō, ˌatə\ *comb form* [ISV, fr. Dan or Norw *atten* eighteen (fr. ON *āttjān*) + *-o-* — more at EIGHTEEN] **:** one quintillionth (10^{-18}) part of ⟨*atto*gram⟩

at·trit \ə'trit, a·'-\ *or* **at·trite** \-'trīt\ *vt* -ED/-ING/-S [back-formation fr. *attrition*] **:** to weaken or reduce by attrition

attrition* *n* **:** a usu. gradual loss of personnel from causes normal or peculiar to a given situation (as death, retirement, and resignation in a labor force or failure and dropout among students) often without filling the vacancies

au bleu \(ˌ)ō'blœ, -'blə, -'blü\ *adj (or adv)* [F, lit., to the blue; fr. the fact that the skin of fish cooked in this manner turns blue] **:** cooked by boiling in acidulated water immediately after being killed and cleaned but without being washed or scaled — used esp. of trout

au·di·al \'ódēəl\ *adj* [*audio-* + *-al* (as in *visual*)] **:** of, relating to, or affecting the sense of hearing **:** AURAL

audible *n* -s [*audible,* adj.] **:** a substitute offensive play or defensive formation called at the line of scrimmage in football

au·dio·cassette \ˌódē(ˌ)ō+\ *n* [*audio-* + *cassette*] **:** an audio recording mounted in a cassette

au·dio–lingual \ˌódē(ˌ)ō +\ *adj* [*audio-* + *lingual*] **:** involving the use of listening and speaking drills in language learning

au·dio·tape \'ódēōˌtāp\ *n* [*audio-* + *tape*] **:** a tape recording of sound

au·dio·visuals \ˌódēō +\ *n pl* [*audiovisual*] **:** instructional materials (as filmstrips accompanied by recordings) that make use of both hearing and sight

au gra·tin \ō'grätᵊn, ó'-, -rat-\ *n, pl* **au gratins :** a container in which au gratin dishes may be cooked and served

auntie* *n* **:** a usu. middle-aged male homosexual who seeks the companionship of younger men

aunt sally* *n, usu cap A & S, Brit* **:** an object of criticism or contention; *esp* **:** a person, condition, or argument set up to invite criticism or be easily refuted

au pair *or* **au pair girl** *n* **:** a foreign girl who does domestic work for a family in return for room and board and the opportunity to learn the family's language

aus·form \'ósˌfó(ə)rm, -ó(ə)m\ *vt* -ED/-ING/-S [*aus*tenitic + de*form;* fr. the deformation's taking place while the steel is still in the austenitic form] **:** to subject (steel) to deformation and then to quenching and tempering in order to increase the strength, ductility, and resistance to fatigue failure

aus·tral \ó'sträl\ *n* -s [Sp] **:** the basic monetary unit of Argentina — see MONEY table *in the Dict*

Australia antigen *also* **Australian antigen** *n* **:** HEPATITIS B SURFACE ANTIGEN *herein*

aus·tra·li·ana \óˌstrālē'änə, äˌ-, əˌ-, -'anə\ *n pl, usu cap* [*Australia* + E *-ana*] **:** collected material (as books) relating to Australia

au·teur \ō'tər, -tœr\ *n* -s **:** a film director whose practice accords with the auteur theory

au·teur·ism \-ˌizəm\ *n* -s [*auteur* (herein) + *-ism*] **:** AUTEUR THEORY *herein* — **au·teur·ist** \-ə̇st\ *n or adj*

auteur theory *n* [part trans. of F *politique des auteurs,* fr. *auteur* author, fr. OF *autor;* fr. the view that the director is the true author of a film — more at AUTHOR] **:** a view of film making in which the director is considered the primary creative force in a motion picture

au·to·ci·dal \ˌȯd-ə̇ˈsīdᵊl\ *adj* [[1]*auto-* + *-cide* + [1]*-al*] **:** controlling or eradicating populations of noxious insects (as the screwworm) by reducing their capacity to produce viable or fertile offspring (as by the introduction of sterile males) ⟨~ procedures⟩ ⟨~ effects⟩

au·to·cide \ˈ==ˌsīd\ *n* -s [[2]*auto-* + *-cide*] **:** suicide by crashing one's automobile

au·to·clav·able \ˌ==ˌklāvəbəl\ *adj* [[2]*autoclave* + *-able*] **:** able to withstand the action of an autoclave

au·to·correlation \ˌ==+\ *n* [*aut-* + *correlation*] **:** the correlation between the two members of pairs of values of a function of a mathematical or statistical variable taken at usually constant time intervals that indicates the degree of periodicity of the function

au·to·cross \ˈ==+ˌ\ *n* -ES [[2]*auto* + *cross*-country, n.] **:** an automobile gymkhana

au·to·focus \ˈ==+ˌ\ *n* [*aut-* + *focus*] **:** a system by which a camera automatically focuses on an object in its field of view

autogenous* *also* **autogenic*** *adj* **:** not requiring a meal of blood to produce eggs ⟨~ mosquitoes⟩ — **autogeny*** *n*

au·to·ges·tion \ˌ==ˌjes(h)chən\ *n* -s [F *autogestion*, fr. Gk *autos* self + F *gestion* administration, fr. L *gestio* managing, performing, fr. *gerere* to perform, accomplish] **:** control and management of an enterprise (as a factory) by representatives of the workers

au·to·immune \ˌȯd-ō, ˌȯtō+\ *adj* [back-formation fr. *autoimmunization*] **:** of, relating to, or caused by antibodies or lymphocytes that attack molecules, cells, or tissues of the organism producing them ⟨~ diseases⟩ — **au·to·immunity** \"+\ *n* — **au·to·immunization** \"+\ *n* — **au·to·immunize** \"+\ *vt*

au·to·ionization \ˌ==+\ *n* [*aut-* + *ionization*] **:** a process by which an excited atom becomes ionized and goes to a lower energy state by emitting one of two or more excited electrons that together possess energy exceeding the atom's ionization energy; *esp* **:** such a process yielding an electron having an energy equivalent to that of a photon of optical wavelength — compare AUGER EFFECT *in the Dict* — **au·to·ionize** \"+\ *vb*

au·to·ma·nia \ˌȯd-ə̇ˈmānyə, ˌȯt|, -nēə\ *n* [[2]*auto* + *mania*] **:** undue dependence on or concern with having an automobile esp. for recreation

au·to·manipulation \" +\ *n* [*aut-* + *manipulation*] **:** physical stimulation of the genital organs by oneself — **au·to·manipulative** \"+\ *adj*

automatic* *n* **:** AUDIBLE *herein*

au·toph·a·gy \ȯˈtäfəjē\ *n* -ES [*aut-* + *-phagy*] **:** digestion of cellular constituents by enzymes of the same cell — **au·toph·a·gic** \-jik\ *adj*

au·to·regulation \ˌȯd-(ˌ)ō, ˌȯ(ˌ)tō, -ə+\ *n* [*aut-* + *regulation*] **:** the maintenance of relative constancy of a physiological process under varying conditions by an organ or tissue; *esp* **:** the maintenance of a constant supply of blood to an organ in spite of varying arterial pressure ⟨the influence of vasoactive agents on ~ of renal flow —P.C. Johnson *et al*⟩ — **au·to·regulative** \"+\ *adj* — **au·to·regulatory** \"+\ *adj*

au·to·route \ˈȯd-əˌrüt, -d-ō-, ˈäd-; *F* ȯtȯrüt, ō-\ *n* [F, fr. *auto* automobile (fr. *automobile*) + *route* road, fr. OF — more at ROUTE] **:** a high-speed multilane motor road in France

au·to·stra·da \ˌau̇d-ōˈsträdə, ˌȯd-\ *n, pl* **autostradas** *or* **autostra·de** \-äd(ˌ)ā\ [It, fr. *auto*mobile automobile (fr. F) + *strada* street, fr. LL *strata* paved road — more at STREET] **:** a high-speed multilane motor road first developed in Italy

autoworker \ˈ==ˌ==\ *n* [[2]*auto* + *worker*] **:** a person employed in the automobile manufacturing industry

auxo·troph \ˈȯksəˌtrōf, -äf\ *n* -s [*auxo-* + *-troph*, prob. fr. Gk *trophos* one that feeds] **:** an auxotrophic strain or individual

auxo·tro·phic \ˌȯksəˈtrōfik, -äf-\ *adj* [*auxo-* + *-trophic*] **:** requiring a specific growth substance beyond the minimum required for normal metabolism and reproduction of the parental or wild-type strain ⟨~ mutants of bacteria⟩ — **aux·ot·ro·phy** \ȯkˈsätrəfē\ *n* -ES

avale·ment \ävál(ə)mäⁿ\ *n* -s [F, lit., swallowing, fr. *avaler* to lower, swallow, fr. MF — more at AVALE] **:** the technique of allowing the knees to flex and thus absorb bumps when skiing and turning at high speed so that the skis will remain in constant contact with the snow

aversion* *n* **:** a tendency to extinguish a behavior or to avoid a thing or situation and esp. a usu. pleasurable one because it is or has been associated with a noxious stimulus ⟨conditioning of food ~s by drug injection⟩

aversion therapy *n* **:** therapy intended to change habits or antisocial behavior by inducing a dislike for them through association with a noxious stimulus

aversive* *adj* **:** tending to avoid or causing avoidance of a noxious or punishing stimulus ⟨behavior modification by ~ stimulation⟩ ⟨~ conditioning⟩ — **aver·sive·ly** \-lē\ *adv* — **aver·sive·ness** *n*

av·go·lem·o·no \ˌävgōˈleməˌ(ˌ)nō\ *n* -s [NGk *augolemono*, fr. *augon* egg + *lemonion* lemon] **:** a soup or sauce made of chicken stock, egg yolks, and lemon juice

aviator glasses *n pl* **:** eyeglasses having a lightweight metal frame and usu. tinted lenses

avoidance* *n* **:** an anticipatory response undertaken to avoid a noxious stimulus ⟨conditioned ~ in mice⟩

avoidance–avoidance conflict \=ˌ===ˈ==-\ *n* **:** psychological conflict that results when a choice must be made between two undesirable alternatives — compare APPROACH-APPROACH CONFLICT *herein*, APPROACH-AVOIDANCE CONFLICT *herein*

avoid·ant \əˈvȯidᵊnt\ *adj* [*avoid* + [2]*-ant*] **:** characterized by turning away or by withdrawal or defensive behavior ⟨the ~ detached schizophrenic patient — Norman Cameron⟩

AWACS \ˈāˌwaks\ *n, pl* **AWACS** [*a*irborne *w*arning *a*nd *c*ontrol *s*ystem] **:** a long-range military surveillance system for use in an airplane

ax* *or* **axe*** *n* **:** any of several musical instruments (as a guitar or a saxophone)

aya·tol·lah \ˌīəˈtōlə, -tälə, -tələ, ˈ==ˌ==; ˌīəˌtəˈlä\ *n* -s [Per, lit., sign of God, fr. Ar *āyat* sign, miracle + *allāh* God] **:** a religious leader among Shiite Muslims — used as a title of respect esp. for one who is not an imam

aza·thi·o·prine \ˌazəˈthīəˌprēn, -ˌprən\ *n* -s [*aza-* + *thio-* + *purine*] **:** a purine antimetabolite $C_9H_7N_7O_2S$ that is used esp. as an immunosuppressant

azin·phos·meth·yl \ˌāzᵊn(ˌ)fäsˈmethəl, ˌaz-\ *n* [*azine* + *phos*phorus + *methyl*] **:** an organophosphorus pesticide $C_{10}H_{12}N_3O_3PS_2$ used against insects and mites

azy·gog·ra·phy \ˌā(ˌ)zīˈgägrəfē, əˌzīˈgäg-\ *n* -ES [ISV *azygo-* + *-graphy*] **:** roentgenographic visualization of the azygous system of veins after injection of a radiopaque medium

B

bab·ka \ˈbäbkə, ˈbab-\ *n* -s [Pol *babka* old woman, grandmother] **:** a glazed sweet bread made with dried fruit (as raisins)

baby boom *n* **:** a marked rise in birthrate (as in the U.S. immediately following the end of World War II) — **baby boom·er** *n*

baby–sit* *vi* **:** to stay with and care for any offspring ⟨the male *baby-sits,* uncovering the eggs if the mound gets too hot — *Nat'l Geographic World* ⟩ ~ *vt* **:** to stay with and look after the welfare of ⟨*baby-sit* the children⟩

bach·e·lor·ette \ˌbach(ə)ləˈret\ *n* -s [*bachelor* + *-ette*] **:** a young unmarried woman

back* *vt* **:** to provide a musical accompaniment for — often used with *up* ⟨a song is categorized as "country" if it is ~*ed* up with a steel guitar —Robert Windeler⟩

backbeat \ˈ=ˌ=\ *n* [*back*ground + *beat*] **:** a steady pronounced rhythm that is the characteristic driving force esp. of rock music

back burner *n* [fr. the custom of allowing food to simmer on the back burner] **:** the condition of being out of active consideration or development ⟨directed the board to put on a *back burner* follow-up studies —Dan Berger⟩ ⟨*back burner* projects⟩

back forty *n* [[3]*back* + [3]*forty*] **:** a remote and uncultivated or undeveloped piece of land of indefinite size (as on a farm)

back·ground·er \ˈbakˌgraündə(r)\ *n* [*background* + [2]*-er*] **:** an informal off-the-record news conference in which a government official provides reporters with background information on a particular government policy or action

back judge *n* **:** a football official whose duties include keeping the official time and identifying eligible pass receivers

backlash* *n* **:** a strong adverse reaction (as to a recent political or social development) ⟨a national white ~ in which the aspirations of blacks are meeting increased resistance —Wayne King⟩

backmarker \ˈ=ˌ==\ *n* [[1]*back* + *marker*] **:** ALSO-RAN

back of beyond *chiefly Brit* **:** an extremely remote place; *esp* **:** the outback of Australia

back·pack·er \ˈ=ˌ=ə(r)\ *n* -s [[2]*backpack* + [2]*-er*] **:** one who backpacks

back–street \ˈ=(ˌ)=\ *adj* [*back street*] **:** SURREPTITIOUS ⟨*back-street* abortions⟩

backup* *n* **:** one that serves as a substitute or alternative ⟨the second spacecraft would be a ~ in case of failure⟩

backup \ˈ=ˌ=\ *adj* **1 :** serving as a backup ⟨a ~ guidance system⟩ **2 :** serving as an accompaniment ⟨he records as a soloist with ~ musicians —Ellen Sander⟩

backwrap \ˈ=ˌ=\ *n* [[1]*back* + *wrap*] **:** a wraparound garment (as a skirt) designed so that the ends of the garment are at the back

bac·te·rio·cin \bakˈtirēəsən\ *n* -s [ISV *bacteri-* + *-cin* (as in *colicin*)] **:** an antibacterial agent (as colicin) produced by bacteria

bac·te·rio·rhodopsin \=ˈ===+\ *n* [ISV *bacterio-* + *rhodopsin*] **:** a purple-pigmented protein that is found in the outer membrane of a bacterium (*Holobacterium halobium*) and converts light energy into chemical energy in the synthesis of ATP

bad* *adj* **badder; baddest** *slang* **:** GOOD, GREAT ⟨one of the *baddest* songwriters to be found anywhere —*Black Collegian*⟩

badass \ˈ=ˌ=\ *adj* [[2]*bad* + [1]*-ass* (herein)] *slang* **:** ready and willing to cause or get into trouble **:** MEAN ⟨down on the ground in a great big ring lived a ~ lion who knew he was king—*The Signifying Monkey*⟩ ⟨pretending to be a ~ gunslinger—L. L. King⟩ — sometimes used as a term of approval — **badass** *n, slang*

bad–mouth \ˈ=ˌmaůth, -t͟h\ *vt* [[2]*bad* + *mouth*] **:** to criticize severely **:** make disparaging remarks about

bad news *n pl but sing in constr* **:** a troublesome situation or person

bafflegab \ˈ==ˌ=\ *n* [[2]*baffle* + [3]*gab*] **:** GOBBLEDYGOOK

bag* *n* **1 :** frame or state of mind ⟨when a person acts stupidly, he is "in his stupid ~" —Junius Griffin⟩ **2 :** something suited to one's taste **:** something one likes or does well **:** SPECIALTY ⟨hasn't been my ~ so far, but I'm a very dedicated actor —Dick Van Dyke⟩ **3 a :** an individual's typical way of life ⟨can't expect people who are in another ~ to accept my ~ —Jerry Rubin⟩ **b :** a characteristic manner of expression ⟨more than any other singer in the soul ~ —Albert Goldman⟩ **4 :** something that frustrates or impedes **:** HANG-UP **5 :** a small packet of a narcotic drug (as heroin or marijuana)

bag lady *n* **:** a homeless woman who roams the streets of a large city carrying her possessions in a shopping bag

baguette* *n* **:** a long thin loaf of French bread; *also* **:** a long thin roll

bagwash \ˈ=ˌ=\ *n* [[1]*bag* + *wash*] *Brit* **:** LAUNDRY 1b; *esp* **:** WET WASH

ba·ha·sa in·do·ne·sia \bəˌhäsəˌindəˈnēzhə, -ēshə, -ēzēə, -ēsēə\ *n, cap B&I* [Indonesian *bahasa indonésia,* fr. *bahasa* language (fr. Skt *bhāṣā,* fr. *bhāṣate* he speaks; akin to Gk *phanai* to say) + *indonésia* Indonesian, fr. *Indonesia,* republic in Malay archipelago — more at BAN] **:** INDONESIAN 3b

bailout* *n* **:** a rescue (as of a corporation) from financial distress ⟨massive Government ~*s* of big business — *Time*⟩

bail out *vi* [[6]*bail* + *out*] **1 :** to back away from a pitch in baseball **2 :** to jump off a surfboard or skis in order to avoid an accident **3 :** to get out **:** LEAVE, DEPART ⟨some guests *bailed out* early —Laura Stevenson⟩

bait and switch *n* **:** a sales tactic in which a customer is attracted by the advertisement of a low-priced item but is then encouraged to buy a higher-priced one

ba·jan \ˈbājən\ *n* -s *cap* [fr. *Barbadian,* by shortening & alter.] **:** a native or inhabitant of Barbados

ba·ker–nunn camera \ˌbākə(r)ˈnən-\ *n, usu cap B&N* [after James G. *Baker* b1914 & Joseph *Nunn,* Am. optical designers] **:** a large camera for tracking earth satellites

bake sale *n* **:** a fund-raising event at which homemade foods (as cakes and cookies) are offered for sale

balancing act *n* **:** an attempt to cope with several often conflicting factors or situations at the same time ⟨social life . . . becomes a *balancing act* between the realms of politics, economics and religion —Mark Lilla⟩

balinese* *n, usu cap* **:** a domestic cat of a breed that originated as a spontaneous mutation of the Siamese and is identical to it in type and in coat color and eye color but has a long silky coat and plumelike tail

ball* *n* **balls** *pl, slang* **:** NERVE 3b, c ⟨don't have enough ~*s* to try out their new material in front of a real audience —*East Village Other*⟩

ball* *vb* [[1]*ball* (testis)] *vt* **:** to have sexual intercourse with — often considered vulgar ~ *vi* **:** to have sexual intercourse — often considered vulgar

ball control *n* **:** an offensive strategy (as in football or basketball) in which a team tries to maintain possession of the ball for extended periods of time

ball game* *n* **1 :** a set of circumstances **:** SITUATION ⟨letter answering is a whole new *ball game* —Goodman Ace⟩ **2 :** CONTEST, COMPETITION ⟨the big powers will have to play the decisive role. . . . It's a U.S.-Soviet *ball game* —G.S. Wills⟩

ball of wax : a vaguely specified set of objects or circumstances ⟨will you go to the file safe, please, get the whole *ball of wax,* and lay it out here —*New Yorker*⟩ ⟨knows who's having troubles, who's sleeping with who, the whole *ball of wax* —Grover Lewis⟩

ballpark** *n* **:** a range (as of prices, views, or capabilities) within which comparison, compromise, or competition is possible ⟨the views of the two sides are being brought closer. . . . We are in the same general ~ —H.A. Kissinger⟩ ⟨price of $3500 puts it in the same ~ —*Datamation*⟩ — **in the ballpark :** approximately correct

ballpark \ˈ=,=\ *adj* **:** approximately correct ⟨a 20 percent increase would be a good ~ figure —H. L. MacOdrum⟩

ballsy \ˈbȯlzē, -zi\ *adj* -ER/-EST [*balls* (pl. of [1]*ball*) + *-y*] **:** aggressively tough **:** GUTSY ⟨a ~ little guy, and . . . the most perfect writer of my generation —Norman Mailer⟩

bal·lute \bəˈlüt, ˈba,lüt\ *n* -s [*ball*oon + parach*ute*] **:** a small inflatable parachute for stabilization and deceleration of a jumper or object usu. before a conventional parachute opens

bal mu·sette \bålmüezet\ *n* [F, bagpipe dance] **:** a French dance hall with an accordion band

baltimore chop *n, usu cap B* [so called fr. its perfection by the Baltimore baseball team of the 1890s] **:** a batted ball in baseball that usu. bounces too high for an infielder to make a putout at first base

ba·nach algebra \ˈbä,näk-, -,nək-\ *n, usu cap B* [Stefan *Banach* †1945 Pol. mathematician] **:** a linear algebra over the field of real or complex numbers that is also a Banach space for which the norm of the product of *x* and *y* is less than or equal to the product of the norm of *x* and the norm of *y* for all *x* and *y* belonging to it

ban·ach space *n, usu cap B* **:** a normed vector space for which the field of multipliers comprises the real or complex numbers and in which every Cauchy sequence converges to a point in the space

ba·nal·ize \bəˈnäl,īz, -ˈnȧl-; bəˈnal-, ba-, bā-; ˈbānᵊl-\ *vt* -ED/-ING/-S [[1]*banal* + *-ize*] **:** to make banal ⟨*banalized* the art . . . by mass-producing a few popular designs —Bernard Leach⟩

ba·nan·as \bəˈnanəz\ *adj* [fr. pl. of *banana*] **:** CRAZY ⟨spelling the English language drives everyone ~ —G. H. Poteet⟩

banana seat *n* **:** an elongated bicycle saddle that often has an upward-curved back — called also *banana saddle*

bananas fos·ter \-ˈfȯstə(r), -ˈfäs-\ *n pl but sing in constr, often cap B & usu cap F* [prob. fr. the name *Foster*] **:** a dessert of bananas flamed (as with rum) and served with ice cream

band–aid \ˈ=,=\ *adj* [fr. *Band-Aid,* a trademark] **:** serving as a temporary or expedient remedy or solution

B and B *abbr or n* bed-and-breakfast *herein*

B and D *abbr or n, sometimes not cap* [bondage *and d*iscipline] **:** sadomasochistic practices

B and E *abbr* breaking and entering

band·gap \ˈ=,=\ *n* [[1]*band* + *gap*] **:** the difference in energy between the valence band and the conduction band of an atom (as an insulator or semiconductor) that consists of the range of energy values forbidden to electrons of the atom

bang·er \ˈbaŋə(r), -aiŋ-\ *n* -s [[1]*bang* + [2]*-er*] **1** [prob. fr. the noise sausages often make while frying] *Brit* **:** SAUSAGE **2** *Brit* **:** FIRECRACKER **3** *Brit* **:** a noisy dilapidated automobile

ban·jax \ˈban,jaks\ *vt* -ED/-ING/-ES [origin unknown] *chiefly Irish* **:** DAMAGE, RUIN; *also* **:** SMASH

bankable* *adj* **:** sure to bring in a profit ⟨only one ~ female star whose name can guarantee financing of a movie —Judy Klemesrud⟩

bankcard \ˈ=,=\ *n* [[4]*bank* + [3]*card*] **:** a credit card issued by a bank

bankers'hours *n pl* **:** short working hours

banquet lamp *n* **:** a tall elaborate kerosene table lamp

ban·tu·stan \ˈban·(,)tü,stan, ˈbantə,s-, ˈbän·(,)tü,stän, ,=(,)=ˈ=\ *n* -s *usu cap* [*Bantu* + *-stan* land (as in *Hindustan*)] **:** any of several all-black enclaves in the Republic of So. Africa that have a limited degree of self-government

barcelona chair *n, usu cap B* [fr. *Barcelona,* Spain, site of the 1929 International Exposition for which the chair was designed] **:** an armless chair with leather-covered cushions on a stainless steel frame

bar code *n* **:** a code made up of a group of printed and variously patterned bars and spaces and sometimes numerals that is designed to be scanned and read into computer memory as identification for the object it labels — see UNIVERSAL PRODUCT CODE *herein*

bar·do·li·no \,bärdᵊlˈē(,)nō, -dəˈlē-\ *n* -s *usu cap* [It, fr. *Bardolino,* village on Lake Garda, Italy] **:** a light red Italian wine

barefoot doctor *n* **:** an auxiliary medical worker trained to provide health care in rural areas of the People's Republic of China

barf \ˈbärf, ˈbȧf\ *vi* -ED/-ING/-S [origin unknown] **:** VOMIT — **barf** *n* -s

bargaining chip *n* **:** something that can be used to gain concessions in a negotiation

bar·gel·lo \bärˈjelō\ *n* -s [fr. the *Bargello,* museum in Florence, Italy; fr. the use of this stitch in the upholstery of 17th cent. chairs at the Bargello] **:** a needlepoint stitch that produces a zigzag pattern

bar girl *n* **1 :** BARMAID **2 :** a prostitute who frequents bars **3 :** B-GIRL

bar·iat·rics \,barēˈa·triks\ *n pl but sing in constr* [*bar-* + *-iatrics*] **:** a branch of medicine that deals with the treatment of obesity — **bar·iat·ric** \-ik\ *adj* — **bar·ia·tri·cian** \-ēə·ˈtrishən\ *n* -s

bar mitzvah *vt* **bar mitzvahed; bar mitzvahed; bar mitzvahing; bar mitzvahs** *often cap B&M* **:** to administer the ceremony of bar mitzvah to

barn burner *n* **:** one that arouses much interest or excitement ⟨the game promises to be a real ~⟩

barn sale *n* **:** GARAGE SALE *herein*

ba·ro·lo \bä'rō(,)lō, bə-\ *n* -s *usu cap* [fr. *Barolo*, village in the Piedmont region, Italy] **:** a dry red Italian wine

baro·re·cep·tor \¦barōrə̇¦septə(r), -ōrē¦-\ *also* **bar·o·cep·tor** \'barō,s-\ *n* -s [*bar-* + *receptor*] **:** a neural receptor (as of the arterial walls of the carotid sinus) sensitive to changes in pressure

barr body \'bär-, 'bá(r-\ *n, usu cap 1st B* [after Murray Llewellyn *Barr b*1908 Canad. anatomist] **:** material from the inactivated X chromosome that is present in each somatic cell of most mammals and is used as a test of genetic femaleness (as in a fetus or an athlete) — called also *sex chromatin*

bar·tók·ian \,bär'täkyən, -tòk-, -kēən\ *adj, usu cap* [Béla *Bartók* †1945 Hung. composer + E *-ian*] **:** of, relating to, or suggestive of Béla Bartók or his musical compositions

barware \'=,=\ *n* [[1]*bar* + [4]*ware*] **:** glassware or utensils used in serving alcoholic beverages

bary·on \'barē,än\ *n* -s [ISV *bary-* + [2]*-on*] **:** any of a group of elementary particles (as a nucleon or a lambda particle) that undergo strong interactions and are held to be a combination of three quarks — **bary·on·ic** \¦barē¦änik\ *adj*

baryon number *n* **:** a number equal to the number of baryons minus that of antibaryons in a system of elementary particles

base* *n* **1 :** a number that is multiplied by a rate or of which a percentage or fraction is calculated ⟨to find the interest on $90 at 10% multiply the ~ 90 by .10⟩ **2 :** the economic factors on which in Marxist theory all legal, social, and political relations are formed **3 :** a price level at which a security previously actively declining in price resists further price decline **4 :** a point to be considered ⟨is covering . . . detailed material and is trying to touch every ~ —R.L. Tobin⟩

base angle* *n* **:** either of the angles of a triangle that have one side in common with the base

[1]**base·band** \'=,=\ *n* [[3]*base* + [1]*band*] **:** the band of frequencies that carries information in electronic communications and usu. modulates a carrier signal

[2]**baseband** *adj* **:** of or relating to a communications system in which information is transmitted using a single unmodulated band of frequencies — compare BROADBAND *herein*

base exchange *n* **:** a post exchange on a naval or an air force base

baseline** \'=,=\ *n* **:** a set of critical observations or data used for comparison or a control

base pair *n* **:** one of the pairs of chemical bases composed of a purine on one strand of DNA joined by hydrogen bonds to a pyrimidine on the other that hold together the two complementary strands much like the rungs of a ladder and include adenine linked to thymine, adenine linked to uracil, and guanine linked to cytosine

BA·SIC \'bāsik, -zik\ *n* -s [*B*eginner's *A*ll-purpose *S*ymbolic *I*nstruction *C*ode] **:** a simplified language for programming and interacting with a computer

basi·lect \'bazə̇,lekt, 'bāzə̇-, -sə̇-\ *n* -s [*basi-* + *-lect* (as in *dialect*)] **:** the least prestigious language variety of a community — compare ACROLECT *herein* — **basi·lec·tal** \,=='lekᵊl\ *adj*

basis* *n* **:** a set of linearly independent vectors in a vector space such that any vector in the vector space can be expressed as a linear combination of them with appropriately chosen coefficients

basket* *n* **1** *slang* **:** male genitalia **2 :** a ring around the lower end of a ski pole that keeps the pole from sinking too deep in snow

basket case* *n* **:** one that is totally worn out, incapacitated, or inoperable ⟨dad's a *basket case* by the time he gets out to Yellowstone from the East —Harold Graham⟩ ⟨reveal the Northeast to be an economic *basket case* —Michael Kramer⟩ ⟨many models end up emotional *basket cases* —Gwen Kinkead⟩

bass–ack·ward \¦bas¦akwə(r)d, -aa(ə)s-, -ais- *sometimes in NE* -ás-\ *or* **bass–ackwards** \-dz\ *adv (or adj)* [anagram for *ass-backward*] **:** in a backward or inept way

batch* *n* **:** a group of jobs to be run on a computer at one time with the same program ⟨~ processing⟩

ba·tracho·toxin \bə·,trakə, ,ba·trəkō +\ *n* [ISV *batrach-* + *toxin*] **:** a very powerful steroid venom $C_{31}H_{42}N_2O_6$ extracted from the skin of a So. American frog (*Phyllobates aurotaenia*)

battered child syndrome *n* **:** the complex of grave physical injuries (as fractures, hematomas, and contusions) that results from gross abuse (as by a parent) of a young child

baud* *n, pl* **baud** *also* **bauds :** a variable unit of data transmission speed (as one bit per second)

baud·e·lair·ean *also* **baud·e·lair·ian** \bōd'lerēən, ,bōdᵊl'er-, -a(a)r-\ *adj, cap* [Charles Pierre *Baudelaire* †1867 Fr. poet + *-an*] **:** of, relating to, or characteristic of Baudelaire or his writings

bayes·ian \'bāzēən, -āzhən\ *adj, usu cap* [Thomas *Bayes* †1761 Eng. mathematician + E *-ian*] **:** being or relating to a theory (as of decision or of statistical inference) in which probabilities are associated with individual events or statements and not merely with sequences of events (as in frequency theories)

bayes'theorem \'bāz-\ *n, usu cap B* [Thomas *Bayes*] **:** a theorem about conditional probabilities: the probability that an event A occurs given that another event B has already occurred is equal to the probability that the event B occurs given that A has already occurred multiplied by the probability of occurrence of event A and divided by the probability of occurrence of event B

ba·zoom \bə'züm\ *n* -s [prob. alter. of *bosom*] **:** a woman's breast

BBA \,bē(,)bē'ā\ *abbr or n* -s **:** a bachelor of business administration

BCD \,bē(,)sē'dē\ *n* -s [*b*inary *c*oded *d*ecimal] **:** a code for representing alphanumeric information (as on magnetic tape); *also* **:** a code for representing decimal digits in a computer

b cell *n, usu cap B* [bone-marrow-derived *cell*] **:** any of the lymphocytes that have immunoglobulin molecules on the surface and comprise the antibody-secreting plasma cells when mature — called also *b lymphocyte;* compare T CELL *herein*

beach bag *n* **:** a capacious bag for articles used at the beach

beach bunny *n* **:** a girl who joins a surfing group but does not engage in surfing

beachwear \'=,=\ *n* **:** clothing for wear at the beach

beamwidth \'=,=\ *n* **:** the angular diameter of the region adjoining an antenna through which the reception of the signal is best

bean* *n* **1 beans** *pl* **:** EXUBERANCE — used in the phrase *full of beans* **2 beans** *pl* **:** NONSENSE — used in the phrase *full of beans*

beanbag* *n* **:** any of various pellet-filled bags used for furniture (as a chair) or for household articles (as the base of an ashtray)

bearded collie *n* **:** any of a breed of large working dogs that originated in Scotland and have a long rough coat and drooping ears

beat off* *vb* ~ *vi* **:** MASTURBATE — usu. considered vulgar

beautiful people *n pl, often cap B&P* **:** people who are identified with high society ⟨to this festival came the stars, the magnates, the *beautiful people,* and the crowds —Roland Gelatt⟩

beauty contest* *n* **:** a presidential primary election in which the popular vote does not determine the number of convention delegates a candidate receives

beaver* *n* [[1]*beaver*] **:** the pudenda of a woman — often considered vulgar

bea·ver \'bēvə(r)\ *vi* **beavered; beavered; beavering** \-v(ə)riŋ\; **beavers** [fr. the proverbial energy of the animal] *chiefly Brit* **:** to work diligently — usu. used with *away* ⟨my subconscious, ~*ing* away independently, suddenly came up with that dazzlingly brilliant punch line —*Yorkshire Post*⟩

beck·ett·ian \be'ketēən\ *adj, usu cap* [Samuel *Beckett* *b*1906 Ir. author + E *-ian*] **:** of, relating to, or suggestive of the works or characters of Samuel Beckett

bed-and-breakfast *n* **:** an establishment (as an inn or guesthouse) offering lodging and breakfast

bed·da·ble \'bedəbəl\ *adj* [[2]*bed* + *-able*] **:** suitable for taking to bed ⟨tolerated brains in women who were too old to be ~ —Peter Quennell⟩

[1]**bed·dy-bye** \ˌbedēˌbī\ *n* [baby talk, fr. *bed*] **:** [3]BYE-BYE

[2]**beddy-bye** \"\ *adv* **:** [4]BYE-BYE

bed-sit \'=ˌ=\ *n* [by shortening] *Brit* **:** BED-SITTING-ROOM

[1]**bed·so·nia** \bed'sōnēə\ [NL, fr. Samuel P. *Bedson* †1969 Brit. bacteriologist + *-ia*] *syn of* CHLAMYDIA

[2]**bedsonia** \"\ *n, pl* **bedsoni·ae** \-nēˌī\ **:** any of a group of microorganisms that are related to the rickettsias, include the causative agents of psittacosis, lymphogranuloma venereum, and trachoma, and are now classified in the genus *Chlamydia* of the family Chlamydiaceae

bedworthy \'=ˌ==\ *adj* [[1]*bed* + *worthy*] *chiefly Brit* **:** BEDDABLE *herein*

beef·alo \'bēfəˌlō\ *n, pl* **beefalos** *or* **beefaloes** [[1]*beef* + buff*alo*] **:** a hybrid between beef cattle and the buffalo (*Bison bison*) of No. America that was developed in No. America and is typically 3/8 buffalo and 5/8 domestic bovine

beef wellington *n, usu cap W* [prob. fr. the name *Wellington*] **:** a fillet of beef covered with pâté de foie gras and enclosed in pastry

beehive* *n* **:** a woman's hairdo in a conical shape

beeper* *n* **:** a portable electronic device used to page the person carrying it that beeps when it receives a special radio signal

beeswax* *n* **:** BUSINESS — used chiefly by children in the phrases *mind your own beeswax, none of your beeswax*

beggar's chicken *n* **:** a traditional Chinese dish of marinated and stuffed chicken wrapped in lotus leaves and roasted in a shell of clay

behavioral scientist *n* **:** a specialist in behavioral science

behavior therapy *n* **:** psychotherapy that emphasizes the application of the principles of learning to substitute desirable responses and behavior patterns for undesirable ones — called also *behavior modification* — **behavior therapist** *n*

belgian malinois *n, usu cap B & M* **:** MALINOIS

belgian tervuren \-(ˌ)tər'vyu̇rən, -ter-\ *n, usu cap B & T* [fr. *Tervuren,* commune in Brabant, Belgium] **:** any of a breed of working dogs closely related to the Belgian sheepdog but having abundant long straight fawn-colored hair with black tips

belle epoque *or* **belle époque** \ˌbelā'pȯk\ *n* [F *belle époque* beautiful age] **:** a period that represents the height of artistic or cultural development (as for a society); *specif* **:** the period in France around the turn of the century

bells \'belz\ *n pl* [by shortening] **:** BELL-BOTTOMS

bells and whistles *n pl* **:** items that are useful or decorative but not essential **:** FRILLS

bell-shaped \'=ˌ=\ *adj* **:** relating to, being, or approximating a normal curve or a normal distribution

bellyboard \'==ˌ=\ *n* [[1]*belly* + *board*] **:** a small buoyant board usu. less than three feet long that is used in surf riding

belly dancer *n* **:** one who performs a belly dance — **belly dance** *vi*

belly-up \ˌ=='=\ *adj* **:** done for; *esp* **:** BANKRUPT ⟨twelve thousand businesses have gone *belly-up* this year —L.A. Iacocca⟩

belted-bias tire \ˌ=='==-\ *n* **:** BIAS-BELTED TIRE *herein*

belt up *vi, Brit* **:** to shut up

be·me·gride \'beməˌgrīd, -ēm-\ *n* -s [*be*ta + *e*thyl + *me*thyl + glutal*r*ic acid + im*ide*] **:** an analeptic drug $C_8H_{13}NO_2$ used esp. to counteract the effect of barbiturates

bench mark* *n, usu* **benchmark** \'=ˌ=\ **:** a standardized problem by which computer systems or programs are compared

benchmark \'=ˌ=\ *vt* **:** to test (as a computer system) by a benchmark problem

bench press* *n* **:** a lift in weight lifting in which from a supine position on a bench a lifter presses the weight from chest level straight up to full extension of the arms; *also* **:** a competitive event involving this lift — **bench-press** \'=ˌ=\ *vt*

bench seat *n* **:** a seat in an automotive vehicle that extends the full width of the passenger section

Benedict's solution *n* [after Stanley Rossiter *Benedict* †1936 Am. chemist] **:** a blue solution containing sodium carbonate, sodium citrate, and cupric sulfate which yields a red, yellow, or orange precipitate upon warming with a reducing sugar (as glucose or maltose)

benign neglect *n* **:** an attitude or policy of ignoring an often undesirable situation that one is perceived to be responsible for dealing with

be·nin \bə'nin, -'nēn; 'benən\ *adj, usu cap* **:** of or relating to Benin **:** of the kind or style prevalent in Benin

ben·ning·ton \'beniŋtən\ *or* **bennington ware** *also* **bennington pottery** *n* -s *usu cap B* **:** ceramic ware including earthenware, stoneware, and Parian ware produced at Bennington, Vt.; *esp* **:** earthenware with brown or mottled glaze

ben·o·myl \'benəˌmil, -nōˌ-\ *n* -s [*benz-* + *-o-* + *-myl* (by shortening & alter. fr. *methyl*)] **:** a derivative $C_{14}H_{18}N_4O_3$ of carbamate and benzimidazole used esp. as a systemic fungicide on agricultural crops and ornamental plants

bent* *adj, slang* **1 :** different from what is normal or usual: as **a** *chiefly Brit* **:** DISHONEST, CORRUPT ⟨a basically straight guy making it in an unrepentantly ~ world —

Times Lit. Supp.〉 **b :** ECCENTRIC, CRAZY 〈she was so ~ that she's probably a woman who ought to be locked up somewhere —Robert Redford〉 **c :** HOMOSEXUAL **2 :** extremely upset or angry — often used in the phrase *bent out of shape*

ben·zo·di·az·e·pine \ˌbenzōˌdīˌazəˌpēn, -ˌpən\ *n* -s [*benz-* + *diaze-* pam (herein) + [1]*-ine*] **:** any of a group of aromatic lipophilic amines (as diazepam and chlordiazepoxide) used as tranquilizers

ben·zo·mor·phan \ˌbenzō'mȯrˌfan\ *n* -s [*benz-* + *-morph* + [3]*-an*] **:** any of a group of synthetic compounds whose best-known members are analgesics (as phenazocine or pentazocine)

ben·zyne \'benˌzīn\ *n* -s [*benzene* + *-yne*] **:** an unsaturated cyclic hydrocarbon C_6H_4 derived from and structurally similar to benzene but having one of the double bonds of benzene replaced by a triple bond

be·rim·bau \bā'rēⁿ(m)ˌbau̇\ *n* [Pg *berimbau* Jew's harp] **:** a musical instrument of the Indians of Brazil that consists of a gourd resonator and a single string which is struck with a stick

bermuda bag *n, usu cap 1st B* **:** a round or oval handbag with a wooden handle and removable cloth covers

bermuda petrel *n, usu cap B* **:** CAHOW

ber·noul·li trial \bər'nülē-, ber-\ *n, usu cap B* [after Jacques *Bernoulli* †1705 Swiss mathematician] **:** one of the repetitions of a statistical experiment having two mutually exclusive outcomes with constant probability of occurrence

be·som \'bēzəm, 'biz-, 'bis-\ *n* [origin unknown] **:** a welting or edging around a pocket opening

best boy *n* **:** the chief assistant to the gaffer in motion-picture or television productions

best–efforts \ˌ≈ˌ≈\ *adj, of security underwriting* **:** not involving a firm commitment on the part of an underwriter to take up any unsold shares or bonds of an issue being underwritten

beta* *n* **:** a measure of the risk potential of a stock or investment portfolio expressed as a ratio of the stock's or portfolio's volatility to the volatility of the market as a whole

beta–adrenergic \ˌ≈ˌ≈ˌ≈\ *adj* [[2]*beta* + *adrenergic*] **:** of, relating to, or being a beta-receptor 〈*beta-adrenergic* blocking action〉

beta–adrenergic receptor *n* **:** BETA-RECEPTOR *herein*

beta–blocker \'≈'≈\ *n* [[2]*beta* + *blocker*] **:** an agent (as propranolol) that combines with and blocks the activity of a beta-receptor

beta decay *n* **1 :** a radioactive transformation of an atomic nucleus in which the atomic number is increased or decreased by 1 by the simultaneous emission of a beta particle and a neutrino or antineutrino without change in the mass number **2 :** the decay of an unstable elementary particle in which an electron or positron is emitted

beta–en·dor·phin \ˌ≈enˌdȯrfən\ *n* [[2]*beta* + *end-* + m*orphine*] **:** an endorphin of the pituitary gland with much greater analgesic potency than morphine that occurs free and as the terminal sequence of 31 amino acids in the polypeptide chain of beta-lipotropin

beta–lipotropin \ˌ≈ˌ≈ˌ≈\ *n* [[2]*beta* + *lipotropin* (herein)] **:** a lipotropin of the anterior pituitary that contains beta-endorphin as the terminal sequence of 31 amino acids in its polypeptide chain

be·ta·meth·a·sone \ˌ≈ˌmethəˌzōn, -ˌsōn\ *n* -s [[2]*beta* + *meth*ylprednisol*one* (herein)] **:** a potent glucocorticoid $C_{22}H_{29}FO_5$ that is isomeric with dexamethasone and has anti-inflammatory activity

beta–oxidation \ˌ≈ˌ≈ˌ≈\ *n* [[2]*beta* + *oxidation*] **:** stepwise catabolism of fatty acids in which two-carbon fragments are successively removed from the carboxyl end of the chain

beta particle* *n* **:** an electron or positron ejected from the nucleus of an atom during beta decay; *also* **:** a high-speed electron or positron

beta–receptor \ˌ≈ˌ≈\ *n* [[2]*beta* + *receptor*] **:** any of a group of receptors on cell membranes that are held to be associated esp. with positive effects on the beat and muscular contractility of the heart, with vasodilation, and with inhibition of smooth muscle in the bronchi, intestine, and muscular layer of the wall of the uterus — compare ALPHA-RECEPTOR *herein*

be·tha·ne·chol \bə'thānəˌkȯl, -ōl\ *n* -s [*beth-* (blend of [2]*beta* and *methyl*) + *-ane* + *-ol*] **:** a parasympathomimetic agent administered in the form of its chloride $C_7H_{17}ClN_2O_2$ and used esp. to treat gastric and urinary retention

beurre blanc \'bər'bläⁿ\ *n* [F, white butter] **:** a sauce made from a base of wine, vinegar, or lemon juice cooked down and flavored with herbs and often stock and blended with softened butter

BFA *abbr* bachelor of fine arts

BHA \ˌbēˌāch'ā\ *n* [*b*utylated *h*ydroxy*a*nisole] **:** a phenolic antioxidant $C_{11}H_{16}O_2$ used to preserve fats and oils in food, cosmetics, and pharmaceuticals

BHT \ˌbēˌāch'tē\ *n* [*b*utylated *h*ydroxy*t*oluene] **:** a crystalline phenol $C_{15}H_{24}O$ used esp. to preserve fats and oils in food, cosmetics, and pharmaceuticals

bi \'bī\ *adj* **:** BISEXUAL 1b — **bi** *n -s*

bi·a·fran \bē'afrən, bī-, -äf-, -áf-\ *n* -s *cap* [*Biafra,* name assumed by seceding region of Nigeria (1967–1970) + E *-an*] **:** a native or inhabitant of the onetime secessionist Republic of Biafra — **biafran** *adj, usu cap*

bi·aly \bē'alē\ *n, pl* **bialys** [Yiddish, short for *bialystoker,* fr. *bialystoker* of Bialystok, fr. *Bialystok,* city in northeast Poland] **:** a flat roll that has a depressed center and is usu. covered with onion flakes

bias–belted tire \ˌ≈ˌ≈-\ *n* **:** a pneumatic tire with a belt of cord, steel, or fiber glass around the tire underneath the tread and on top of the ply cords laid at an acute angle to the center line of the tread

biased* *adj* **1 :** tending to yield or select one outcome more frequently or less frequently than others in a statistical experiment 〈a ~ coin〉 〈a ~ sample〉 **2 :** having an expected value different from the quantity or parameter estimated 〈a ~ estimate〉 **3 :** not having minimum probability of rejecting the null hypothesis when it is true 〈a ~ statistical test〉

bias–ply tire \ˌ≈ˌ≈-\ *n* **:** a pneumatic tire having crossed layers of ply cord set diagonally to the center line of the tread

bi·ath·lon \bī'athlən, -ˌlän\ *n* -s [ISV [1]*bi-* + *-athlon* (as in *pentathlon*)] **:** a composite athletic contest consisting of cross-country skiing and rifle sharpshooting

bibb lettuce \'bib-\ *n, usu cap B* [after Major John *Bibb,* 19th cent. Am. grower] **:** lettuce of a variety that has a small head and dark green color

bib·lio·ther·a·py \ˌbiblēə'therəpē\ *n* [*biblio-* + *therapy*] **:** the use of reading materials for help in solving personal problems or for psychiatric therapy

bi·carpellate \(ˈ)bī'kärpəˌlāt, -ˌlət\ *adj* [[1]*bi-* + *carpellate*] **:** having two carpels

bi·chon fri·se \bē¦shōⁿfrē'zā\ *n, pl* **bichon frises** *or* **bichons fries** \-ōⁿfrē'zā(z)\ [modif. of F *bichon à poil frisé* curly-furred lap dog] **:** any of a small sturdy breed of dogs of Mediterranean origin having a thick wavy white coat

bi·coastal \¦bī+\ *adj* [¹*bi-* + *coastal*] **:** of or relating to or living or working on both the East and West coasts of the U.S. ⟨pioneers in ~ living, continuing to write for the theater in New York, our home, and going out West periodically to do a movie —Betty Comden & Adolph Green⟩

bi·cu·cul·line \(ˈ)bī¦k(y)ükyə,lēn, -‚lə̇n\ *n* -s [¹*bi-* + *cucull-* (fr. *Dicentra cucullaria,* species of fungus in which the substance occurs) + *-ine*] **:** a convulsant alkaloid $C_{20}H_{17}NO_6$ obtained esp. from plants of the family Fumariaceae and having the capacity to antagonize the action of gamma-aminobutyric acid in the central nervous system

bi·cultural \¦bī +\ *adj* [¹*bi-* + *cultural*] **:** of, relating to, or including two distinct cultures ⟨~ education⟩ — **bi·cul·tur·al·ism** \¦bī¦kəlch(ə)rə(‚)lizəm\ *n* -s

bi·dialectal \" +\ *adj* [¹*bi-* + *dialectal*] **:** fluent in the use of two dialects of the same language — **bidialectal** *n* -s

bi·dialectalism \" +\ *or* **bi·di·a·lect·ism** \(¦)bī¦dīə‚lekt(‚)izəm\ *n* -s **:** facility in using two dialects of the same language

bi·di·a·lec·tal·ist \¦bī‚dīə¦lektələ̇st\ *n* [*bidialectal* (herein) + *-ist*] **:** a person who favors the promotion and development of bidialectalism by schools esp. for speakers whose primary dialects are not standard

bi·don·ville \‚bē‚dōⁿ'vē(ə)l\ *n* -s [F, fr. *bidon* tin can (fr. MF, canteen, fr. OF) + *ville* city, fr. OF, village — more at VILLAGE] **:** a settlement of jerry-built dwellings on the outskirts of a city (as in France or Africa)

bi·functional \¦bī+\ *adj* [¹*bi-* + *functional*] **:** having two functions ⟨~ reagents⟩ ⟨~ neurons⟩

big bang *n* **:** the cosmic explosion that marked the beginning of the universe according to the big bang theory

big bang theory *n* **:** a theory in astronomy: the universe originated billions of years ago in an explosion from a single point of nearly infinite energy density — compare STEADY STATE THEORY *herein*

big beat *n, often cap both Bs* **:** ROCK 'N' ROLL

big C \¦=¦=\ *n, usu cap B* **:** CANCER 2

big daddy *n, often cap B & D* **:** one preeminent esp. by reason of power, size, or seniority **:** one representing paternalistic authority

big deal *n* **:** something of special importance

bigfoot \'=‚=\ *n, often cap* [fr. the size of the footprints ascribed to it] **:** SASQUATCH *herein*

big one* *n* **:** a thousand dollars ⟨pulling down 30 *big ones* as an "up-and-coming" vice-president —Howard Anderson⟩

bi·jec·tion \bī'jekshən\ *n* -s [¹*bi-* + *-jection* (as in *injection*)] **:** a mathematical function that is a one-to-one and onto mapping — compare INJECTION *herein,* SURJECTION *herein* — **bi·jec·tive** \-ktiv, -ēv\ *adj*

bike* *n* **1 :** MOTORCYCLE **2 :** MOTORBICYCLE 2 **3 :** a light 2-wheeled cart used at horse shows and in harness races **:** SULKY

biker* *n* **:** MOTORCYCLIST; *esp* **:** one who belongs to an organized gang

bikeway \'=‚=\ *n* **:** a thoroughfare for bicycles

bik·ie \'bīkē\ *n* -s [*bike* + *-ie*] **:** BIKER *herein*

bikini* *n* **1 :** a man's brief swimsuit **2 :** a man's or woman's low-cut briefs

bi·ki·nied \bə'kēnēd\ *adj* **:** wearing a bikini

bi·layer \¦bī +\ *n* [¹*bi-* + *layer*] **:** a film or membrane with two molecular layers ⟨a ~ of phospholipid molecules⟩ — **bilayer** *adj*

[1]**bi–level** \'=¦==\ *adj* [¹*bi-* + *level*] **1 :** having two levels of freight or passenger space **2 :** having two floors with a ground-level entry situated between the floors

[2]**bi–level** \" +\ *n* **:** a bi-level house

bilingual education *n* **:** education in an English-language school system in which minority students with little fluency in English are taught in their native tongue

bill·able \'biləbəl\ *adj* [⁵*bill* + *-able*] **:** that can be billed ⟨a lawyer's ~ hours⟩ ⟨time ~ to a specific project⟩

bil·li–bi *also* **bil·ly–bi** \¦bilē¦bē, -li¦-\ *n* -s [F, alter. of *Billy B.,* William B. Leeds, Jr. †1972 Am. industrialist; fr. his partiality for it] **:** a soup made of mussel stock, white wine, and cream and served hot or cold

bi·lo·qui·al·ism \(ˈ)bī¦lōkwēə‚lizəm\ *n* -s [¹*bi-* + *-loquial* (as in *colloquial*) + *-ism*] **:** BIDIALECTALISM *herein* — **bi·lo·qui·al·ist** \-kwēələ̇st\ *n or adj*

binary* *adj* **1 :** involving a choice or condition of two alternatives only (as on-off or yes-no) **2 :** involving binary notation **3 :** utilizing two harmless ingredients that upon combining form a lethal substance (as a gas) ⟨~ weapon⟩

binary notation *n* **:** expression of a number with a base of 2 using only the digits 0 and 1 with each digital place representing a power of 2 instead of a power of 10 as in decimal notation

bio–* *comb form* **:** being such biologically ⟨*bio*mother⟩ ⟨*bio*parent⟩

bio– *comb form* [*bio*] **:** biographical ⟨*bio*drama⟩ **:** biographical and ⟨*bio*critical⟩

bio·accumulation \¦bīō+\ *n* [²*bi-* + *accumulation*] **:** the accumulation of a substance (as a pesticide) in a living organism

bio·active \"+\ *adj* [²*bi-* + *active*] **:** having an effect on a living organism ⟨~ pharmaceuticals and pesticides⟩ — **bio·activity** \"+\ *n*

bio·astronautics \" +\ *n pl but sing or pl in constr* [²*bi-* + *astronautics*] **:** the medical and biological aspect of astronautics — **bio·astronautical** \" +\ *adj*

bio·au·tog·ra·phy \‚bīō ȯ'tägrəfē\ *n* -ES [²*bi-* + *autograph* + *-y*] **:** the identification or comparison of organic compounds separated by chromatography by means of their effect on living organisms and esp. microorganisms — **bio·au·to·graph** \-'ȯd·ə‚graf\ *n* — **bio·au·to·graph·ic** \¦bīō‚ȯd·ə¦grafik\ *adj*

bio·availability \¦bīō+\ *n* [²*bi-* + *availability*] **:** the degree and rate at which a substance (as a drug) is absorbed into a living system or is made available at the site of physiological activity

bio·cid·al \¦bīə¦sīdᵊl\ *adj* [²*bi-* + *-cidal*] **:** destructive to life

bio·clean \¦bīō +\ *adj* [²*bi-* + *clean*] **:** free or almost free of harmful or potentially harmful organisms (as bacteria) ⟨a ~ room⟩

bio·compatibility \"+\ *n* [²*bi-* + *compatibility*] **:** the condition of being compatible with living tissue or a living system by not being toxic or injurious and not causing immunological rejection — **bio·compatible** \"+\ *adj*

bio·conversion \"+\ *n* [²*bi-* + *conversion*] **:** conversion of organic materials (as wastes) into an energy source (as methane) by processes (as fermentation) involving living organisms

bio·critical \"+\ *adj* [*bio-* (herein) + *critical*] **:** of, relating to, or being a study of the life and work of someone (as a writer or moviemaker)

bio·degradable \¦bīō +\ *adj* [^{2}*bi-* + *degradable* (herein)] **:** capable of being broken down esp. into innocuous products by the action of living things (as microorganisms) — **bio·de·grad·abil·i·ty** \¦==,=¦biləd·ē\ *n* — **bio·degradation** \¦bīō +\ *n* — **bio·degrade** \"+\ *vb*

bio·electronics \¦bīō +\ *n pl but sing in constr* [^{2}*bi-* + *electronics*] **1 :** a branch of the life sciences that deals with electronic control of physiological function esp. as applied in medicine to compensate for defects of the nervous system **2 :** a branch of science that deals with the role of electron transfer in biological processes — **bio·electronic** \"+\ *adj*

bioenergetics* *n pl but sing in constr* **:** a system of therapy that combines breathing and body exercises, psychological therapy, and the free expression of impulses and emotions and that is held to increase well-being by releasing blocked physical and psychic energy — **bioenergetic*** *adj*

bioengineering* *n* **:** the application to biological or medical science of engineering principles (as the theory of control systems in models of the nervous system) or engineering equipment (as in the construction of artificial organs) — called also *biomedical engineering* — **bio·engineer** \¦bīō +\ *n*

bio·environmental \¦bīō +\ *adj* [^{2}*bi-* + *environmental*] **:** of, relating to, affecting, or utilizing living things, their environment, and the interactions between them ⟨~ effects of pollution⟩ ⟨~ pest control⟩

bio·ethics \"+\ *n pl but usu sing in constr* [^{2}*bi-* + *ethics*] **:** a discipline dealing with the ethical implications of biological research and applications esp. in medicine — **bio·ethic** \"+\ *n* — **bio·ethical** \"+\ *adj* — **bio·ethicist** \"+\ *n* -s

bio·feedback \" +\ *n* [^{2}*bi-* + *feedback*] **:** the technique of making unconscious or involuntary bodily processes (as heartbeat or brainwaves) perceptible to the senses (as by use of an oscilloscope) in order to manipulate them by conscious mental control

bio·gas \"+\ *n* [^{2}*bi-* + *gas*] **:** a mixture of methane and carbon dioxide produced by the bacterial decomposition of animal and vegetable wastes and used as a fuel

bio·geo·ce·nose *or* **bio·geo·coe·nose** \ˌbīō¦jēōsə¦nōz, -nōs\ *n* -s [Russ *biogeotsenoz,* fr. NL *bi-* ^{2}bi- + *ge-* + *-coenosis* (as in *biocoenosis*)] **:** BIOGEOCOENOSIS *herein*

bio·geo·coe·no·sis *or* **bio·geo·ce·no·sis** \-¦jēōsə¦nōsəs\ *n, pl* **biogeocoeno·ses** *or* **biogeoceno·ses** \-ōˌsēz\ [NL, fr. ^{2}*bi-* + *ge-* + *-coenosis* (as in *biocoenosis*)] **:** ECOSYSTEM — **bio·geo·coe·not·ic** \-näd·ik\ *adj*

bio·hazard \¦bīō +\ *n* [^{2}*bi-* + *hazard*] **:** a biological agent or condition (as an infectious organism or insecure laboratory procedures) that constitutes a hazard to man or his environment; *also* **:** a hazard posed by such an agent or condition — **bio·hazardous** \"+\ *adj*

bio·inorganic \"+\ *adj* [^{2}*bi-* + *inorganic*] **:** of, relating to, or concerned with the application of inorganic chemistry and its techniques to the study of biological processes and substances in which inorganic substances are important constituents or play important roles

bio·instrumentation \"+\ *n* [^{2}*bi-* + *instrumentation*] **:** the development and use of instruments for recording and transmitting physiological data (as from astronauts in flight); *also* **:** the instruments themselves

biological clock *n* **:** an inherent timing mechanism that is inferred to exist in some living systems (as a cell) in order to explain various cyclical behaviors and physiological processes

biomass* *n* **:** plant materials and animal waste used as a source of fuel

bio·material \¦bīō +\ *n* [^{2}*bi-* + *material*] **:** material used for or suitable for use in prostheses that come in direct contact with living tissues

bio·medical \" +\ *adj* [^{2}*bi-* + *medical*] **1 :** of or relating to biomedicine ⟨~ studies⟩ **2 :** of, relating to, or involving biological, medical, and physical science — **bio·medically** \"+\ *adv*

biomedical engineering *n* **:** BIOENGINEERING *herein*

bio·medicine \¦bīō+\ *n* [^{2}*bi-* + *medicine*] **:** a branch of medical science concerned esp. with the capacity of human beings to survive and function in abnormally stressing environments and with the protective modification of such environments

bio·membrane \"+\ *n* [^{2}*bi-* + *membrane*] **:** a membrane either on the surface or in the interior of a cell that is composed of protein and lipid esp. in sheets only a few molecules thick and that limits the diffusion and transport of materials

bio·molecular \"+\ *adj* [^{2}*bi-* + *molecular*] **:** of or relating to organic molecules and esp. macromolecules in living organisms

bi·on·ic \(ˈ)bī¦änik\ *adj* [^{2}*bi-* + *-onic* (as in *electronic*)] **1 :** of or relating to bionics **2 a** (1) **:** having natural biological capability or performance enhanced by or as if by electronic or electromechanical devices ⟨our future may lie not with the ~ man but with natural man —Susan Schiefelbein⟩ (2) **:** comprising or made up of artificial body parts that enhance or substitute for a natural biological capability ⟨a ~ heart⟩ **b :** better than ordinary **:** SUPER ⟨the developer of this ~ tuber . . . admits that it's not the perfect potato —*Saturday Rev.*⟩

bi·on·ics \bīˈäniks\ *n pl but sing in constr* [^{2}*bi-* + *-onics* (as in *electronics*)] **:** a branch of science concerned with the application of data about the functioning of biological systems to the solution of engineering problems

bio·organic \¦bīō +\ *adj* [^{2}*bi-* + *organic*] **:** of, relating to, or concerned with the organic chemistry of biologically significant substances

bio·pharmaceutics \"+\ *n pl but sing in constr* [^{2}*bi-* + *pharmaceutics*] **:** the study of the relationships between the physical and chemical properties, the dosage, and the form of administration of a drug and its activity in the living animal — **bio·pharmaceutical** \"+\ *adj*

bio·pic \ˈbīōˌpik\ *n* -s [*bio-* (herein) + *pic*ture] **:** a movie about the life of a usu. famous person

bio·polymer \¦bīō +\ *n* [^{2}*bi-* + *polymer*] **:** a polymeric substance (as a protein or a polysaccharide) formed in a biological system

bio·research \" +\ *n* [^{2}*bi-* + *research*] **:** research in biological science

bio·rhythm \"+\ *n* [^{2}*bi-* + *rhythm*] **:** an innately determined rhythmic biological process or function (as sleep behavior); *also* **:** an innate rhythmic determiner of such a process or function — **bio·rhythmic** \"+\ *adj* — **bio·rhythmicity** \"+\ *n*

bio·satellite \" +\ *n* [^{2}*bi-* + *satellite*] **:** an artificial satellite for carrying a living human being, animal, or plant

bio·science \ˌbīō +\ *n* [²*bi-* + *science*] **:** BIOLOGY 1a; *also* **:** LIFE SCIENCE *herein* — **bio·scientific** \"+\ *adj* — **bio·scientist** \"+\ *n*

bio·sensor \" +\ *n* [²*bi-* + *sensor*] **:** a device sensitive to a physical stimulus (as heat or a particular motion) and transmitting information about a life process (as of an astronaut)

bio·speleology \" +\ *n* [²*bi-* + *speleology*] **:** the biological study of cave-dwelling organisms — **bio·speleologist** \" +\ *n*

bio·synthesize \"+\ *vt* [²*bi-* + *synthesize*] **:** to produce by biosynthesis

bio·technical \"+\ *adj* [²*bi-* + *technical*] **:** BIOTECHNOLOGICAL

bio·telemetry \" +\ *n* [²*bi-* + *telemetry*] **:** the remote detection and measurement of a biological function, activity, or condition of a man or animal — **bio·telemetric** \" +\ *adj*

bio·transformation \" +\ *n* [²*bi-* + *transformation*] **:** the transformation of chemical compounds within a living system

bipolar* *adj* **:** characterized by the alternation of manic and depressive states ⟨a ~ affective disorder⟩

bi·quinary \(ˈ)bī +\ *adj* [¹*bi-* + *quinary*] **:** of, based on, being, or relating to a mixed-base system of numbers in which each decimal digit *n* is represented as a pair of digits *xy* where $n = 5x + y$ and *x* is written in base 2 as 0 or 1 and *y* is written in base 5 as 0, 1, 2, 3, or 4 ⟨decimal 9 is represented by ~ 14⟩

birch·er \ˈbərchər\ *n* -s *usu cap* [the John *Birch* Society, conservative political organization + E *-er*] **:** a member or adherent of the John Birch Society — **birch·ite** \-ˌchīt, *usu* -īd· +V\ *n or adj, usu cap*

bird* *n* **1 :** something (as an aircraft, rocket, or satellite) resembling a bird esp. in flying or being aloft **2 :** an obscene gesture of contempt made by pointing the middle finger upward while keeping the other fingers down — usu. used with *the;* called also *finger*

birman* *n, usu cap* **:** a long-haired domestic cat of a breed originating in Burma and resembling the Siamese in eye color and coat pattern but much stockier in build and with paws symmetrically marked with white

birr \ˈbi(ə)r\ *n, pl* **birr** *also* **birrs** [native name in Ethiopia] **1 :** the basic monetary unit of Ethiopia — see MONEY table *in the Dict* **2 :** a note representing one birr

birth defect *n* **:** a physical or biochemical defect (as cleft palate or phenylketonuria) that is present at birth and may be inherited or environmentally induced

biryani *also* **biriani** \bi(ə)rˈyänē, ˌbirēˈänē, -i\ *n* -s [prob. fr. Per *biryān* roasted] **:** an Indian dish of meat, fish, or vegetables cooked with rice flavored esp. with saffron or turmeric

bis·cot·to \bəˈskäd·ō, -ä(ˌ)tō\ *n, pl* **biscot·ti** \-äd·ē, -ä(ˌ)tē, -i\ [It — more at BISCUIT] **:** a crisp cookie or biscuit of Italian origin flavored usu. with anise and filberts or almonds

bi·stable \(ˈ)bī +\ *adj* [¹*bi-* + *stable,* adj.] **:** having two stable states ⟨a ~ electrical element⟩ — **bi·stability** \ˌbī +\ *n*

bi·static \" +\ *adj* [¹*bi-* + *static*] **:** involving the use of a transmitter and receiver at separate locations ⟨~ radar⟩

bi-swing \"+\ *adj* [¹*bi-* + *swing;* perh. because of the freedom allowed by this garment] *of a coat or jacket* **:** made with a pleat or gusset at the back of the arms to permit more freedom of movement

bit* *n* [³*bit*] **1 :** a characteristic situation, appearance, behavior, or action ⟨book burning, unless it's an embassy library, is strictly a Fascist ~ —Gene Williams⟩ ⟨I never have dates or call up a girl and meet her and take her out, that whole ~ —Arthur Garfunkle⟩ **2 :** an action or mode of behavior likened to a theater role or sketch ⟨starts in with one of her crazy lunatic ~*s* —Judith Rossner⟩ **3 :** subject under consideration **:** MATTER ⟨as for the ~ about marriage being a woman's be-all and end-all —Letty C. Pogrebin⟩ — often used as a general indirect reference to something specified or implied ⟨the blouson top . . . matches exactly. The blouson ~ is piped in suede —Lois Long⟩

bit* *n* [⁷*bit*] **:** the physical representation (as in a computer tape or memory) of a bit by an electrical pulse, a magnetized spot, or a hole whose presence or absence indicates data

bite* *vb* — **bite the bullet :** to face up to an unpleasant situation by taking action ⟨we are now seeing responsible industries beginning to *bite the bullet* and clean up waste sites —Harold Gershowitz⟩

bite plate *n* **:** a dental appliance that is usu. made of plastic and wire, is worn in the palate or sometimes on the lower jaw, and is used in orthodontics and prosthodontics to assist in therapy and diagnosis

bit-mapped \ˈ=ˌ=\ *adj* **:** being or produced on a computer display in which each pixel of the display is controlled by a bit in the computer's memory ⟨*bit-mapped* graphics⟩

bi·unique \(ˈ)bī +\ *adj* [¹*bi-* + *unique*] **:** being a correspondence between two sets that is one-to-one in both directions ⟨the ~ correspondence between the points on a straight line and the real numbers⟩ ⟨a phonemic transcription should be ~⟩ — **biuniqueness** \" +\ *n*

bi·zen ware \bēˈzen-\ *n, usu cap B* [part trans. of Jap *bizen-yaki,* fr. *Bizen,* former province in Japan, where it was made + Jap *yaki* pottery] **:** a Japanese ceramic ware produced since the 14th century that is typically a dark bronzy stoneware often with smears of natural ash glaze

black* *adj* **1 :** of or relating to covert intelligence operations **2 :** employed in covert intelligence operations

black* *vt, chiefly Brit* **:** to declare (as a business or industry) subject to boycott by trade-union members

¹**black belt** *n* **1 :** an area characterized by rich black soil **2** *often cap both Bs* **:** an area densely populated by blacks

²**black belt** \ˈ=ˌ=\ *n* [so called fr. the color of the belt of the uniform worn by the holder of the rating] **1 :** a rating of expert in various arts of self-defense (as judo and karate) **2 :** one who holds a black belt

blackboard jungle *n* **:** an urban school whose students are generally belligerent and disorderly

black box *n* **:** a usu. complicated electronic device that functions and is packaged as a unit and whose internal mechanism is usu. hidden from or mysterious to the user; *broadly* **:** anything that has mysterious or unknown internal functions or mechanisms ⟨the secrecy of Soviet society makes it a *black box* to Western observers —James Fallows⟩ ⟨the cancer cell is no longer an impenetrable *black box* —R.A. Weinberg⟩

black comedy *n* [trans. of F *comédie noire*] **:** comedy that employs black humor

black dwarf *n, pl* **black dwarfs :** a very small star that gives off no detectable light either because it has cooled from a white dwarf or because it was never massive enough for fusion to begin

black english *n, usu cap B & cap E* **:** a variety of English spoken by many American blacks

black forest cake *n, usu cap B&F* [*Black Forest,* region in Germany] **:** a rich usu. chocolate layer cake with cherries

black hole *n* **1 :** a hypothetical invisible region in space with a small diameter and intense gravitational field that is held to be caused by the collapse of a massive star **2 :** one that resembles a black hole: as **a :** one into which something disappears ⟨do not foresee the international debt situation dragging the banking system into a financial *black hole* —*Business Week*⟩ **b :** something unseen or undetected ⟨the *black hole* of error revealed —Mavis Gallant⟩ **c :** an empty space **:** VOID ⟨paused, as if he had suddenly come upon a *black hole* in the space of his ambition —Anatole Broyard⟩

black humor *n* [trans. of F *humour noir*] **:** humor marked by the use of usu. morbid, ironic, grotesquely comic episodes — **black–humored** \ˌ-ˈ-ˌ--\ *adj* — **black humorist** *n*

blacklight trap \ˈ-ˌ-ˌ-\ *n* **:** an insect trap using a form of black light for attraction

black lung *n* **:** a disease of the lungs caused by habitual inhalation of coal dust (as by miners) — called also *black lung disease*

black money *n* **:** income (as from gambling) that is not reported to the government for tax purposes

black muslim *n, usu cap B & M* **:** a member of a chiefly black group that professes Islamic religious belief

black nationalist *n, often cap B&N* **:** one of a group of militant blacks who advocate separatism from the whites and the formation of self-governing black communities — **black nationalism** *n, often cap B&N*

blackness* *n* **1 :** the aggregate of qualities characteristic of the Negro race **2 :** NEGRITUDE *herein*

black panther *n, usu cap B&P* **:** a member of an organization of militant American blacks

black power *n, often cap B & P* **:** the power of American blacks esp. as applied to the achieving of their political and economic rights

black studies *n pl* **:** studies (as in history and literature) relating to the culture of American blacks

blacktown \ˈ-ˌ-\ *n* [[2]*black* + *town*] **:** the predominantly black section of a city

blahs \ˈbläz, -àz\ *n pl* **:** a feeling of boredom, discomfort, or general dissatisfaction — usu. used with *the*

blanc de blancs *or* **blanc de blanc** \ˌbläⁿdəˈbläⁿ\ *n, pl* **blanc de blancs** [F, lit., white of whites] **:** a still or sparkling white wine made from white grapes only

blast* *n* **1 :** an enjoyably exciting experience, occasion, or event ⟨have a ~⟩; *esp* **:** PARTY ⟨beer ~⟩ **2 :** HOME RUN

blast \ˈblast\ *n* -s [*-blast*] **:** an immature or imperfectly developed cell — **blast·ic** \ˈblastik\ *also* **blast** *adj*

blast cell *n* **:** a precursor of a blood cell in the earliest stage of development in which it is recognizably committed to development along a particular cell lineage

blastogenesis* *n* **:** the transformation of lymphocytes into larger cells capable of undergoing mitosis

blas·to·my·cin \ˌblastōˈmīsᵊn\ *n* -s [*blast-* + *-mycin*] **:** a preparation of growth products of the causative agent (*Blastomyces dermatitidis*) of No. American blastomycosis that is used esp. to test for this disease

blax·ploi·ta·tion \ˌblakˌsplȯiˈtāshən\ *n* -s [blend of *blax* (alter. of *blacks*) and *exploitation*] **:** the exploitation of blacks by producers of black-oriented films

[1]**bleep** \ˈblēp\ *n* -s [imit.] **1 :** a short high-pitched sound (as from electronic equipment) **2** — used in place of an obscene or vulgar expletive

[2]**bleep** \"\ *vt* -ED/-ING/-S **:** BLIP *herein*

[3]**bleep** \"\ *interj* — used in place of an expletive

bleeper \-ə(r)\ *n* -s [[1]*bleep* + *-er*] *chiefly Brit* **:** a device that emits bleep signals

blended family *n* **:** a family in which one parent is a stepparent

bleo·my·cin \ˌblēəˈmīsᵊn\ *n* -s [*bleo-* (of unknown origin) + *-mycin*] **:** a mixture of polypeptide antibiotics derived from a streptomyces (*Streptomyces verticillus*) and used in the form of its sulfate as an antineoplastic agent

bleph·a·ro·plas·ty \ˈblefərōˌplastē\ *n* -ES [*blephar-* + *-plasty*] **:** a plastic operation on an eyelid esp. to remove fatty or excess tissue

blind side* *n* **:** the side away from which one is looking

blindside *vt* **1 :** to hit from the blind side **2 :** to strike suddenly and unexpectedly **:** surprise unpleasantly ⟨was *blindsided* by the news of his colleague's disloyalty⟩

blind trust *n* **:** an arrangement by which a person in a sensitive position protects himself from possible conflict of interest charges by placing his financial affairs in the hands of a fiduciary and giving up all right to know about or intervene in their handling

blip* *n* **:** a temporary sharp move up or down (as on a graph)

blip* *vt* **:** to remove (recorded matter) from a magnetic tape so that there is an interruption in the reproduced sound or picture ⟨swearwords *blipped* by a censor⟩

bliss out *vt* **:** to send into a state of bliss **:** make ecstatic

blister pack *n* **:** a package holding and displaying merchandise in a clear plastic case sealed to a sheet of cardboard

blitz* *n* **:** a rush on a passer in football by the linebackers or safetymen

blitz* *vb* ~ *vt* **1 :** to rush (a passer) in football from a position as a linebacker or defensive back **2 :** to have (as a linebacker) blitz ~ *vi, of a linebacker or defensive back* **:** to make a rush on the passer in football — **blitz·er** *n* -s

block* *vt* **:** to work out (as the principal positions and movements) for the performers (as of a play); *also* **:** to work out the players' positions and movements for (as a scene or a play)

block·bust·ing \ˈ-ˌbəstiŋ\ *n* -s [[1]*block* (space in a city) + *-busting,* gerund of [2]*bust*] **:** profiteering by first inducing white property owners to sell hastily and often at a loss by appeals to fears of depressed values because of threatened minority encroachment and then reselling at inflated prices — **block·bust·er** \-ə(r)\ *n*

block club *n* **:** an organized group of residents in an urban neighborhood

block grant* *n* **:** an unrestricted federal grant

blocking* *n* **:** the planning and working out of the principal positions and movements of stage performers (as for a play) ⟨camera shots, musical cues, ~, makeup, costumes and the rest were run through —Robert Jacobson⟩

blood* *n* **:** a black American — used esp. among blacks

blood–brain barrier \ˌ-ˈ-ˌ-\ *n* **:** a barrier postulated to exist between brain capillaries and brain tissue to explain the relative inability of many substances to leave the blood and cross the capillary walls into the brain tissues

bloody–minded \ˌ--ˈ--\ *adj* **1 :** willing to accept violence or bloodshed **2** *chiefly Brit* **:** stubbornly contrary or obstructive **:** CANTANKEROUS

bloom* *n* **:** an abundant or excessive growth of plankton

bloop* *vt* **:** to hit (a fly ball) usu. just beyond the infield in baseball ⟨~*ed* a single to center field⟩

bloop \'blüp\ *adj* [*bloop*, v.t. (herein)] *of a baseball* **:** hit in the air just beyond the infield

blouse* *vb* ~ *vt* **:** to cause to blouse ⟨trousers are *bloused* over the boots⟩ ⟨big, loose shapes (which the fainthearted may ~ over a belt) —Anne-Marie Shiro⟩

blou·son \'blau̇ˌzän, -ˌsän, -ˌsᵊn; 'blüˌzän\ *n* -s [F, dim. of *blouse* blouse] **:** a garment (as a dress or blouse) having a close waistband with a blousing of material over it

blow* *vt* **1 :** FELLATE *herein* — usu. considered vulgar **2 :** SMOKE ⟨a few had started ~*ing* grass in their early teens —Daniel Greene⟩ — **blow one's cool :** to lose one's composure — **blow one's cover :** to reveal one's real identity **:** give one's cover away — **blow one's mind 1 :** to overwhelm with wonder or bafflement **2 :** to undergo or cause to undergo a psychedelic experience

blow* *n* [perh. fr. ⁵*blow*] *slang* **:** COCAINE

blow away* *vt* **1 :** to kill by gunfire **:** shoot dead **2 :** to overwhelm emotionally **:** STUN

blow–dry \(ˈ)=ˌ=\ *vt* [back-formation fr. *blow-dryer*] **:** to dry and usu. style (hair) with a hand-held hair dryer — **blow–dry** \'=ˌ=\ *n*

blower* *n, Brit* **:** TELEPHONE

blowjob \'=ˌ=\ *n* **:** the act of stimulating the penis orally usu. to orgasm — usu. considered vulgar

BLS \ˌbē(ˌ)el'es\ *abbr or n* -s **1 :** a bachelor of liberal studies **2 :** a bachelor of library science

BLT \ˌbē(ˌ)el'tē\ *n* -s **:** a bacon, lettuce, and tomato sandwich

blue box *n* **:** an electronic device attached to a telephone that emits signals enabling the user to make illegal free long-distance calls

blue flu *n* [fr. the color of a police uniform] **:** SICK-OUT *herein; specif* **:** a sick-out staged by policemen

bluegrass* *n* [fr. the *Blue Grass Boys*, performing group, fr. *Bluegrass State*, nickname of Kentucky] **:** country music played on unamplified stringed instruments (as banjo, fiddle, guitar, and mandolin) and characterized by free improvisation and close usu. high-pitched harmony

blue heaven *n, slang* **:** amobarbital or its sodium derivative in a blue tablet or capsule

blue point *adj, of a domestic cat* **:** having a bluish cream body coat with dark gray points

blue shift *n* **:** the displacement of the spectrum of an approaching celestial body toward shorter wavelengths as a consequence of the Doppler effect — compare RED SHIFT *in the Dict* — **blue·shift·ed** \'=ˌ==\ *adj*

bluesman \'=(ˌ)=\ *n, pl* **bluesmen :** a musician who plays or sings the blues

blues–rock \ˌ=ˈ=\ *n* **:** music combining blues and rock 'n' roll

blue stellar object *n* **:** any of various blue celestial bodies that do not emit appreciable radio waves

bluesy \'blüzē, -i\ *adj* -ER/-EST [²*blues* + -*y*] **:** resembling, characteristic of, or suited to the blues

blusher* *n* **:** a cosmetic applied to the face to give a usu. pink color or to accent the cheekbones

b lymphocyte *n, usu cap B* [bone-marrow-derived *lymphocyte*] **:** B CELL *herein*

BM* *abbr or n* **:** a bachelor of music

BME \ˌbē(ˌ)em'ē\ *abbr or n* -s **1 :** a bachelor of mechanical engineering **2 :** a bachelor of mining engineering **3 :** a bachelor of music education

board* *n* **1 :** BLACKBOARD **2a boards** *pl* **:** the low wooden wall enclosing a hockey rink **b** (1) **:** BACKBOARD — usu. used in pl. (2) **:** a rebound in basketball **c :** SURFBOARD **3 :** a sheet of insulating material carrying circuit elements and terminals so that it can be inserted in an electronic apparatus — **on board* :** in or into a working relationship

boat* *n* **:** a conformation of a six-membered cyclic molecule (as of cyclohexane) in which two opposite atoms are both on the same side of the plane of the molecule — compare CHAIR *herein*

boa·tel \(ˈ)bōˈtel\ *n* -s [blend of *boat* and *hotel*] **:** a waterside hotel equipped with docks to accommodate persons traveling by boat

boat people *n pl* **:** refugees fleeing by boat

bob·bing \'bäbiŋ\ *n* -s [⁹*bob*] **:** BOBSLEDDING

bocage* *n* **:** a supporting and ornamental background (as of shrubbery and flowers) for a ceramic figure

bod* *n* [by shortening] **:** BODY

body bag *n* **:** a zippered bag (as of rubber) in which a human corpse is placed (as for transportation)

body builder *n* **:** one who engages in body building

body building *n* **:** the developing of the body through physical exercises and diet; *specif* **:** the developing of the physique for competitive exhibition

body checker *n* **:** one that body checks

body count *n* **:** a count of or as if of the bodies of killed enemy soldiers

body language *n* **:** the bodily gestures and mannerisms by which a person communicates with others

body mechanics *n pl but sing or pl in constr* **:** systematic exercises designed esp. to develop coordination, endurance, and poise

body shirt *n* **1 :** a woman's close-fitting top made with a sewn-in or snapped crotch **2 :** a close-fitting shirt or blouse

body stocking *n* **:** a sheer close-fitting one-piece garment for the torso that often has sleeves and legs

bodysuit \'==ˌ=\ *n* **:** a close-fitting one-piece garment for the torso

bodysurf \'==ˌ=\ *vi* [¹*body* + *surf*] **:** to ride on a wave without a surfboard by planing on the chest and stomach — **bodysurfer** \'==ˌ==\ *n*

bof·fo \'bäf(ˌ)ō\ *adj* [*boffo*, n., short for *boffola*] **:** extraordinarily successful **:** SENSATIONAL

bog \'bäg\ *n* -s [obs. *boghouse* privy, of unknown origin] *Brit* **:** TOILET, LOO

bohr effect \'bō(ə)r-, 'bȯ(ə)r-\ *n, usu cap B* [Christian *Bohr* †1911 Dan. physiologist] **:** the decrease in oxygen affinity of hemoglobins and some invertebrate respiratory pigments (as hemocyanin) in response to increased carbon dioxide concentration and consequent increased acidity of the blood

boiloff \'=ˌ=\ *n* -s **:** the vaporization of a liquid (as liquid oxygen)

bok choy \'bäk'chȯi, -'jȯi\ *n* [modif. of *pakchoi*] **:** a Chinese cabbage (*Brassica chinensis*) that forms an open head with long white stalks and green leaves

bok·mål \'bu̇kˌmȯl, 'bōk-\ *n* -s *usu cap* [Norw, fr. *bok* book (fr. ON *bōk*) + *mål* language, fr. ON *māl* — more at BOOK, MAIL] **:** RIKSMÅL

bol·li·to mis·to \bȯˈlēd·ō'mē(ˌ)stō, -ētō'-\ *n, pl* **bol·li·ti mis·ti** \-ēd·ē'mēstē, -ētē'-\ [It, fr. *bollito*, past part. of *bollire* boil + *misto* mixed] **:** a dish of mixed meats (as lamb, veal, beef, and sausage) boiled with vegetables

bo·lo tie \'bō(,)lō-\ *or* **bola tie** *n* [prob. fr. *bola*] **:** a cord fastened around the neck with an ornamental clasp and worn as a necktie

bomb* *n* **1** *sometimes cap* **:** ATOM BOMB; *also* **:** nuclear weapons in general — usu. used with *the* ⟨when the ~ has taken the place of God . . . as the ultimate disposer of the earth —H. C. Schonberg⟩ **2 :** an unsuccessful performance or production **:** FLOP ⟨a terrible ~ of a movie —Paul Newman⟩; *broadly* **:** FAILURE **3** *chiefly Brit* **:** an old car **4** *Brit* **:** a lot of money **:** FORTUNE ⟨demonstrating how to avoid the flu and save a ~ on the central heating —Richard Gordon⟩ **5** *Brit* **:** a great success **:** HIT — often used in the phrases *go a bomb* or *go like a bomb* **6 :** a long pass in football

bomb* *vb* ~ *vi* **1 :** FAIL; *esp* **:** to fail to win audience approval **2** *slang* **:** to move rapidly ⟨realized that there was more to [ski] racing than ~*ing* down her native hill —Adam Shaw⟩

bom·bay \bäm'bā\ *n* -s *usu cap* [fr. *Bombay,* India] **:** a domestic cat of a breed originating as a cross between the American Shorthair and the Burmese that is characterized by a shiny black short-haired coat and gold or copper eyes

bombed \'bämd\ *adj* **:** intoxicated by alcohol or drugs **:** HIGH, DRUNK

bomber jacket *n* **:** FLIGHT JACKET *herein*

bomb·let \'bämlət\ *n* -s [[1]*bomb* + *-let*] **:** a small bomb

bona fides* \'bōnə¦fī,dēz, -,fīdz\ *n* **:** evidence of one's good faith or genuineness — usu. pl. in constr. ⟨when the war ended . . . [his] *bona fides* were unambiguously established —E.J. Epstein⟩

bonce* *n, Brit* **:** HEAD, PATE

bondage* *n* **:** sadomasochistic sexual practices involving the physical restraint of one partner

bonded* *adj* **:** composed of two or more layers of the same or different fabrics held together by an adhesive ⟨~ jersey⟩

bonding* *n* **:** the formation of a close personal relationship (as between a mother and child) esp. through frequent or constant association

bonehead \'=,=\ *adj* **:** being a college course intended for students lacking fundamental skills **:** REMEDIAL ⟨teaches ~ English⟩

bong \'bȯŋ, 'bäŋ\ *n* -s [origin unknown] **:** a simple water pipe for smoking marijuana that consists of a bottle or vertical tube partially filled with a liquid (as water or liqueur) and a smaller offset tube ending in a bowl

bonk \'bäŋk, 'bȯŋk\ *vt* [imit.] **:** HIT ⟨baseball players getting ~*ed* on the head by routine fly balls —Gary Cartwright⟩

bon·kers \'bäŋkə(r)z, 'bȯŋ-\ *adj* [origin unknown] **:** CRAZY, MAD ⟨if I don't work, I go ~ —Zoe Caldwell⟩

boo \'bü\ *n* -s [origin unknown] **:** MARIJUANA

boob* *n, Brit* **:** MISTAKE, BLOOPER

boob \'büb\ *n* -s [short for [2]*booby*] **:** BREAST — sometimes considered vulgar

boob tube *n* [[1]*boob* + television *tube;* fr. the belief that a taste for television viewing indicates stupidity] **:** TELEVISION; *esp* **:** a television set

boo·gie *also* **boo·gy** \'bu̇gē, 'bügē\ *vi* **boogied; boogieing** or **boogying; boogies** [short for *boogie-woogie*] **:** to dance to rock music

book* *vt, Brit, of a referee* **:** to note the name or number of (as a soccer player) because of a flagrant foul

boom* *n* **:** a temporary floating barrier used to contain an oil spill

boonies \'bünēz, -iz\ *n pl* [alter. of *boondocks*] *slang* **:** BACKCOUNTRY, BOONDOCKS

boot \'büt\ *vb* **boot·ed; boot·ing** [short for *bootstrap* (herein)] *vt* **1 :** to enter (a program) into a computer by a bootstrap **2 :** to ready for use by booting a program ⟨~ a floppy disk⟩ ~ *vi* **:** to become ready for use ⟨a disk guaranteed to ~ properly⟩

bootstrap* *n* **:** a computer routine consisting of a few initial instructions by means of which the rest of the instructions are brought into the computer

bootstrap* *adj* **1 :** being or relating to a process that is self-generated or self-sustaining **2 :** being or relating to a device that is self-acting **3 :** of or relating to a hypothesis of particle physics which assumes that all strongly interacting particles are composite systems made up of other strongly interacting particles

bootstrap \'=,=\ *vt* **1 :** BOOT *vt herein* **2 :** to work or develop by individual initiative and effort with little or no assistance ⟨the junior-grade professional woman may face stiff opposition when she tries to ~ her way up — Lisa C. Wohl⟩

bop* *n* **:** JIVE 1

bop *vi* **bopped; bopped; bopping; bops** [prob. fr. *bop,* n. (herein)] **1 :** to go quickly or unceremoniously **:** POP **2 :** to dance or shuffle along to or as if to bop music

borderline* *adj* **:** characterized by psychological instability in several areas (as interpersonal relations, behavior, mood, and identity) often with impaired social and vocational functioning but with brief or no psychotic episodes ⟨a ~ personality disorder⟩

bor·de·tel·la \,bȯrdā'telə\ *n, cap* [after Jules *Bordet* †1961 Belg. bacteriologist] **:** a genus of bacteria comprising minute and very short gram-negative strictly aerobic coccuslike bacilli and including the causative agent (*B. pertussis*) of whooping cough

born–again \,==,=\ *adj* [fr. the statement "Except a man be *born again,* he cannot see the Kingdom of God" — John 3:3 (AV)] **1 :** of, relating to, or being a Christian who has made a renewed or confirmed commitment of faith esp. after an intense religious experience **2 :** having returned to a former conviction or activity ⟨a *born-again* conservative⟩ ⟨a *born-again* jogger⟩ **3 :** restored to an earlier condition ⟨proud of their *born-again* Victorian house⟩

borough* *n* **:** a civil division of the state of Alaska corresponding to a county in other states

bor·sa·li·no \,bȯrsə'lē(,)nō\ *or* **borsalino hat** *n* -s *usu cap B* [It, fr. *Borsalino,* the manufacturer] **:** a wide-brimmed soft felt hat for men

borscht belt *or* **borsch belt** *n* [fr. the popularity of borscht on menus of the resorts] **:** BORSCH CIRCUIT

bos·sa no·va \,bäsə'nōvə, ,bȯs-\ *n* [Pg, lit., new trend, fr. *bossa* hump, bump, trend (fr. F *bosse* hump, fr. OF *boce*) + *nova,* fem. of *novo* new, fr. L *novus* — more at BOSS, NEW] **1 :** a Brazilian dance characterized by the sprightly step pattern of the samba and a subtle bounce **2 :** music resembling the samba with jazz interpolations

boston arm *n, usu cap B* [so called fr. its development by four institutions in Boston, Mass.] **:** an artificial arm that is activated by an amputee's nerve impulses which are electrically amplified and transmitted to a motor operating the arm

bo·ta \'bōd·ə, -ōtə\ *n* -s [Sp, fr. LL *buttis* cask, flask] **:** a leather pouch for carrying wine

bo·tan·i·ca \bə'tanikə, bō-, -nēkə\ *n* -s [Sp *botánica* botanical] **:** a shop that specializes in articles (as herbs, charms, and statues) relating esp. to voodoo or the occult

bot·ti·cel·lian \,bäd·ə'cheléən, -ätə-, -lyən\ *adj, usu cap* [fr. Alessandro *Botticelli* †1510 Ital. painter + *-an*] **:** of, relating to, or having the characteristics of the painter Botticelli or his work

bottle–feed \'==,=\ *vt* **:** to feed (as an infant) with a bottle

bottleneck* *or* **bottleneck guitar** *n* **:** a style of guitar playing in which an object (as a metal bar or the neck of a bottle) is pressed against the strings for a glissando effect

bottling* *n* **:** a bottled beverage; *esp* **:** WINE

bottom* *n* **:** the base or baritone instruments of a band

bottom* *adj* **:** having a quantum characteristic that accounts for the existence and lifetime of upsilon particles and that has a value of zero for most known particles ⟨~ quark⟩

bot·tomed \'bäd·əmd, -ätə-\ *adj* **:** having a bottom esp. of a specified kind — usu. used in combination ⟨a broad= *bottomed* boat⟩

bottomless* *adj* **1 :** NUDE **2 :** featuring nude entertainers ⟨a ~ bar⟩

bottom line *n* **1 a :** the line at the bottom of a financial report that shows the net profit or loss **b :** financial considerations (as cost or profit or loss) **c :** the final result **:** OUTCOME, UPSHOT **d :** final statement **:** SUMMARY, CONCLUSION **2 a :** the essential or salient point **:** CRUX **b :** the primary or most important consideration

bottom–line \,==,=\ *adj* **1 :** concerned only with cost or profits ⟨*bottom-line* publishing, with little real concern for editorial values —*Newsweek*⟩ **2 :** PRAGMATIC, REALISTIC ⟨a realist, dealing in facts, in *bottom-line* emotions —Allene Talmey⟩

bottom out *vi* **1** *of a security market* **:** to decline to a point where demand begins to exceed supply and a rise in prices is imminent **2 :** to reach a point where a decline is halted or reversed

bottom woman *n, slang* **:** a pimp's favorite or most dependable prostitute

bou·bou \'bü,bü\ *n* -s [native name in Mali] **:** a long flowing garment worn in parts of Africa

bouillabaisse* *n* **:** POTPOURRI ⟨a ~ of essays⟩

boul·der·ing \'bōld(ə)riŋ\ *n* -s [[1]*boulder* + *-ing*] **:** practice in the techniques of rock climbing

boulevard* *adj* **:** produced primarily to entertain ⟨~ farce⟩

bounce* *vt* **:** to write (a check) on an account having insufficient funds

bouncer* *n* **:** a batted baseball that bounces

bouque·tière \,bük(ə)'tye(ə)r, -tē'e(-\ *adj* [F, woman who sells flowers, fem. of *bouquetier* flower seller, fr. *bouquet* bouquet + *-ier* -eer] **:** garnished with vegetables ⟨rack of lamb ~⟩

bour·gui·gnonne \,bürgēn'yòn\ *also* **bour·gui·gnon** \-'yōⁿ\ *adj, often cap* [F, fr. *Bourgogne* Burgundy, region in France] **:** prepared or served in the manner of Burgundy (as with a sauce made with red Burgundy wine) ⟨beef ~⟩

bour·ride \bü'rēd, bə-\ *n* -s [Prov *bourrido, boulido* something boiled; akin to *bouillon*] **:** a fish stew similar to bouillabaisse that is usu. thickened with egg yolks and strongly flavored with garlic

bou·zou·ki *also* **bou·sou·ki** \bü'zükē, bə'-\ *n, pl* **bouzoukia** \-kēə\ *also* **bouzoukis** [NGk *mpouzouki*] **:** a long-necked stringed musical instrument of Greek origin

bow shock \'baü-\ *n* [fr. a similarity to the wave pattern produced at the bow of a ship] **:** the shock wave formed by the collision of the supersonic charged particles of the solar wind with the magnetosphere of a planet

box* *n* **1 :** the female genitalia — usu. considered vulgar **2 :** TELEVISION; *esp* **:** a television set

BP *abbr or n* -s beautiful people *herein*

bpi *abbr* bits per inch; bytes per inch

bps *abbr* bits per second

brace* *n* **brac·es** *pl* **:** orthodontic wire used to exert pressure to straighten misaligned teeth

brachio·ce·phal·ic artery \¦brakē(,)ōsə¦falik-\ *n* [*brachi-* + *-cephalic*] **:** INNOMINATE ARTERY

brachiocephalic trunk \"...-\ *n* [*brachi-* + *-cephalic*] **:** INNOMINATE ARTERY

brachiocephalic vein \"...-\ *n* [*brachi-* + *-cephalic*] **:** INNOMINATE VEIN

bra·ci·o·la \,bräch(ē)'ōlə\ *or* **bra·ci·o·le** \-lā\ *n* -s [*braciola* fr. It, fr. *brace* live coal (fr. OIt *bragia*) + *-ola* -ole, fr. L; *braciole* fr. It, pl. of *braciola* — more at BRAZE] **:** a thin slice of meat (as steak) that is usu. wrapped around a filling of meat, chopped vegetables, and seasonings and often cooked in wine

bra·dy·ki·nin \¦brādə¦kīnən\ *n* [*brady-* + *kinin* (herein)] **:** a kinin that is formed locally in injured tissue, acts in vasodilation of small arterioles, is held to play a part in inflammatory processes, and is composed of a chain of nine amino acids

brain* *n* **:** an automatic device (as a computer) that performs one or more of the functions of the human brain for control, guidance, or computation ⟨the ~ of a missile⟩

brain death *n* **:** final cessation of activity in the central nervous system esp. as indicated by a flat electroencephalogram for a predetermined length of time — **brain–dead** \'=¦=\ *adj*

brain drain *n* **:** the departure of educated or professional people from one country, economic sector, or field for another usu. for better pay or living conditions

brain–drain \'=¦=\ *vt* **:** to entice to move to another country or job for a higher salary or better working conditions

brain hormone *n* **:** a hormone that is secreted by neurosecretory cells of the insect brain and that stimulates the prothoracic glands to secrete ecdysone

bra·less \'bräləs, -rål-, *sometimes* -ròl-\ *adj, of a woman* **:** wearing no bra — **bralessness** *n* -ES

branch* *n* **:** a part of a computer program executed as a result of a program decision

branch* *vi* **:** to follow one of two or more branches (as in a computer program)

bran·dade \brän'dád\ *n* -s [F, fr. Prov *brandado,* past part. of *brandar* shake, agitate, fr. Gmc *brand* sword — more at BRANDISH] **:** a seasoned puree of fish and esp. of salt cod

Bran·gus \'braŋgəs, -aiŋ-\ *trademark* — used for registered polled solid black beef cattle that are 3/8 Brahman and 5/8 Angus, for the offspring of crosses between such animals which conform to breed specifications, and for registered purebred Brahman and Angus used to produce such stock

brassware \'=,=\ *n* [[1]*brass* + *ware*] **:** articles made of brass

breadboard \'=,=\ *vt* **:** to make an experimental arrangement of (an electronic circuit) on a flat surface

break* *n* **1 :** a usu. solo instrumental passage in jazz, folk, country, or popular music **2 :** BREAKDOWN 2a

break–bulk \'⸗,⸗\ *adj* **:** of or relating to materials shipped in conventional individual packages and not containerized

break dancing *n* [perh. fr. *break* 1 (herein)] **:** dancing in which individual dancers perform a series of often acrobatic moves

break out* *vi* **:** to make a break from a restraining condition or situation ⟨*broke out* of a slump⟩ ~ *vt* **:** to separate from a mass of data ⟨*break out* newsstand sales⟩

breakout* *n* **:** a breakdown of statistical data

breathable* *adj* **:** allowing air to pass through ⟨a ~ synthetic fabric⟩

breathe* *vi, of wine* **:** to develop flavor and bouquet by exposure to air

brecht·ian \'brektēən, -k̲-\ *adj, usu cap* [Bertolt *Brecht* †1956 Ger. dramatist + E *-ian*] **:** of, relating to, or suggestive of Bertolt Brecht or his writings

bride's basket \'⸗,⸗⸗\ *n* [so called fr. such bowls' frequently being given as wedding presents in the late 19th century] **:** an ornate usu. colored glass bowl fitted with a handle and mounted on a silver-plated base

bridesmaid* *n* **:** one that finishes just behind the winner

bringdown \'⸗,⸗\ *n* [*bring* + *down*] **:** COMEDOWN, LETDOWN

brit \'brit\ *n* -s *cap* [by shortening] **:** BRITON 2

british shorthair *n, usu cap B&S* **:** any of a breed of domestic cats resembling the American Shorthair but stockier in build with a closer-lying coat

broad·band \'⸗,⸗\ *adj* **1 :** operating at, responsive to, or including a wide band of frequencies **2 :** of, relating to, or being a communications network in which a frequency range is divided into multiple independent channels for simultaneous transmission of signals (as voice, data, or video) usu. by cable — compare BASEBAND *herein*

broken* *adj* **:** disunited by divorce, separation, or the desertion of one parent ⟨~ homes⟩ ⟨a ~ family⟩

broker* *n* **:** POWER BROKER *herein*

broker* *vt* **:** to arrange, settle, or control as a broker ⟨~ a convention⟩ ⟨accustomed to diversity and disagreement, to ~*ing* policy between the various factions —*Wall Street Jour.*⟩

bro·kered \'brōkə(r)d\ *adj* [*broker,* n. (herein)] **:** arranged or controlled by power brokers ⟨a ~ political convention⟩

bro·mo·crip·tine \,brōmō'krip,tēn\ *n* -s [alter. of 2-*bromo-α-ergocryptine,* fr. *brom-* + [2]*ergo-* + [1]*crypt* (gland) + [2]*-ine*] **:** a polypeptide alkaloid $C_{32}H_{40}BrN_5O_5$ that is a derivative of ergot and mimics the activity of dopamine in selectively inhibiting the secretion of prolactin by the pituitary gland

bro·mo·de·oxy·uridine \¦brōmō(,)dē¦äksē+\ *n* [*brom-* + *deoxy-* + *uridine*] **:** a mutagenic analogue $C_9H_{11}O_5NBr$ of thymidine that induces chromosomal breakage esp. in heterochromatic regions and has been used to selectively destroy actively dividing cells — abbr. *BUdR*

bro·mo·ura·cil \,brōmō'yu̇rə,sil, -mə'-, -,səl\ *n* [*brom-* + *uracil*] **:** a mutagenic uracil derivative $C_4H_3N_2O_2Br$ that is an analogue of thymine and pairs readily with adenine and sometimes with guanine during bacterial or phage DNA synthesis

bron·cho·constriction \¦bräŋ(,)kō, -än(- +\ *n* [*bronch-* + *constriction*] **:** constriction of the bronchial air passages

bron·cho·constrictor \"+\ *adj* [*bronch-* + *constrictor*] **:** causing or involving bronchoconstriction ⟨~ effects⟩ ⟨~ responses⟩

bron·cho·pulmonary \"+\ *adj* [*bronch-* + *pulmonary*] **:** of, relating to, or affecting the bronchi and the lungs ⟨arterial branches that supply the ~ segments of the lungs⟩

bronzer* *n* **:** a cosmetic esp. for men that makes the skin look tanned

brown bag·ging \'brau̇n'bagiŋ\ *n* [*brown bag* + *-ing;* fr. the brown paper bag used] **1 :** the practice of carrying a bottle of liquor into a restaurant or club where setups are available but where the sale of liquor by the drink is illegal **2 :** the practice of carrying one's lunch (as to work) usu. in a brown paper bag — **brown–bag** \'⸗,⸗\ *vb or adj* — **brown bag·ger** \-gə(r)\ *n*

brown fat *n* **:** a mammalian heat-producing tissue occurring esp. in hibernators

brownie point *n, often cap B* **:** a credit regarded as earned esp. by currying favor with a superior

brown lung disease *or* **brown lung** *n* **:** BYSSINOSIS

brown recluse spider *also* **brown recluse** *n* [*recluse* prob. fr. NL *reclusa,* specific epithet, fr. LL, fem. of *reclusus* shut up; fr. its living chiefly in dark corners — more at RECLUSE] **:** a venomous spider (*Loxosceles reclusa*) introduced into the southern U.S. that has a violin⸗shaped mark on the cephalothorax and produces a dangerous neurotoxin

brownware \'⸗,⸗\ *n* [[1]*brown* + *ware*] **1 :** a brown⸗glazed earthenware formerly widely used for utility pottery **2 :** typically primitive pottery that fires to a brown or reddish color

browser* *n* **:** an open case for holding phonograph records that is designed for ease in browsing

brush back *vt* **:** to throw a brushback to ⟨hard to set up a hitter if you can't *brush* him *back* —Red Schoendienst⟩

brushback \'⸗,⸗\ *n* [[6]*brush* + *back*] **:** a pitch thrown near the batter's head in baseball in an attempt to make him move back from home plate

bru·tal·ism \'brüd·ᵊl,izəm, -üt̲ᵊl-\ *n* -s [*brutal* + *-ism*] **:** a style in art and esp. architecture using exaggeration and distortion to create its effect (as of massiveness or power) — **bru·tal·ist** \-ᵊləst\ *adj or n*

BS* *abbr, often not cap* bullshit

BSEE \,bē,es,ē'ē\ *abbr or n* -s **1 :** a bachelor of science in electrical engineering **2 :** a bachelor of science in elementary education

b side *n, usu cap B* **:** FLIP SIDE *herein; also* **:** a song on the flip side of a record

bubble* *n* **1 :** something (as a plastic structure) that is more or less semicylindrical or dome-shaped **2 :** MAGNETIC BUBBLE *herein*

bubble car *n* **:** an automobile having a transparent bubble top

bubblegum** *n* **:** bubble-gum rock music

bubble–gum \'⸗⸗,⸗\ *adj* [fr. the fact that bubble gum is chewed chiefly by children] **:** appealing to, characteristic of, or being preteens or adolescents ⟨a TV star's ~ looks⟩ ⟨~ songs⟩ ⟨the ~ set⟩

buc·co·lingual \¦bəkō+\ *adj* [*bucco-* + *lingual*] **1 :** relating to or affecting the cheek and the tongue **2 :** of or relating to the buccal and lingual aspects of a tooth ⟨the ~ width of a molar⟩ — **buc·co·lingually** \"+\ *adv*

buck* *n* **:** a sum of money esp. to be gained ⟨greed and the desire to make a quick ~ —*London Times*⟩ ⟨pursuing the tourist ~ —Albin West⟩ ⟨it entreats in the name of art; it hopes to make a ~, too —John Corry⟩ ⟨agents who look only for the biggest ~ —Sol Stein⟩; *also* **:** MONEY ⟨tactics . . . the Pentagon has used in its pursuit of the public ~ —Robert Claiborne⟩ — usu. used in pl. ⟨for the big ~*s* you've got to give people meaningful material —Russell Baker⟩ ⟨the public image of art as ~*s* —Barbara Rose⟩

bu·do \ˈbüd(ˌ)ō\ *n* -s [Jap *budō* martial arts] **:** the Japanese martial arts (as karate, aikido, and kendo)

BUdR *abbr* bromodeoxyuridine

buffer* *vt* **1 :** to supply with a buffer ⟨~*ed* computer terminals⟩ **2 :** to collect (as data) in a buffer

bug off \ˌbəgˈȯf, *also* -äf\ *vi* [short for *bugger*] **:** to go away **:** LEAVE — usu. used as a command

bug out* *vi* **1 :** to depart esp. in a hurry **2 :** to evade a responsibility ⟨an excuse to *bug out* of exams⟩

building society *n, Brit* **:** SAVINGS AND LOAN ASSOCIATION

bul·bo·spon·gi·o·sus muscle \ˌbəl(ˌ)bōˌspənjēˈōsəs-, -ˌspän-\ *n* [NL, fr. *bulb-* + L *spongiosus* spongy] **:** BULBOCAVERNOSUS

[1]**bu·lim·ic** \b(y)üˈlimik\ *adj* [*bulimia* + *-ic*] **:** of, relating to, or affected with bulimia ⟨~ patients⟩

[2]**bulimic** *n* -s **:** a person affected with bulimia

bull dyke *n* **:** an aggressively masculine lesbian

bull·shot \ˈbu̇lˌshät\ *n* [shortening and alter. of *bouillon* + [1]*shot*] **:** a drink made of vodka and bouillon

bum·mer \ˈbəmə(r)\ *n* -s [[8]*bum* + [2]*-er*] **1 :** something bad or unpleasant; *esp* **:** an unpleasant experience (as a bad drug trip) **2 a :** something of low quality **:** STINKER **b :** something that is a disappointment

bumper sticker *n* **:** a strip of adhesive paper or plastic bearing a printed message (as a candidate's name or a slogan) and designed to be stuck on a vehicle's bumper

bun* *n* **:** BUTTOCKS — usu. used in pl.

BUN \ˌbēˌyüˈen\ *n* -s [*b*lood *u*rea *n*itrogen] **:** the concentration of nitrogen in the form of urea in the blood

bun·ga·ro·toxin \ˌbəŋgərōˈtäksən\ *n* [*Bungarus* (genus name of the krait) + *-o-* + *toxin*] **:** a potent polypeptide neurotoxin that is obtained from krait venom and yields three electrophoretic fractions of which the one designated α is used esp. to label acetylcholine receptors at neuromuscular junctions because it binds irreversibly to them and blocks their activity — often used with one of the Greek prefixes α-, β-, or γ- to indicate the electrophoretic fractions

bunny* *n* [fr. *Bunny,* a service mark used for a waitress whose minimal attire includes a tail and ears resembling those of a rabbit] **:** a pretty girl esp. considered as an object of sexual desire

bun·ra·ku \bu̇nˈrä(ˌ)kü, ˈbu̇n(ˌ)r-\ *n* -s *usu cap* [Jap] **:** Japanese puppet theater featuring large costumed wooden puppets, onstage puppeteers, and a chanter who speaks all the lines

buq·sha \ˈbu̇kshə *also* ˈbək-\ *n, pl* **buqsha** *or* **buqshas** [Ar] **1 :** a monetary unit of the Yemen Arab Republic equal to 1/40 rial — see MONEY table *in the Dict* **2 :** a note or coin representing one buqsha

bu·reau·cra·tese \ˌbyu̇rəˌkradˌēz, ˈbyü-, -rō-, -aˈtēz; byüˌ- räkrəˌtēz, byu̇-; *also* -ˈēs\ *n* [*bureaucrat* + [2]*-ese*] **:** a style of language held to be characteristic of bureaucrats and marked by the prevalence of abstractions, jargon, euphemisms, and circumlocutions

bur·kitt's lymphoma \ˌbərkəts-, ˌbək-\ *also* **burkitt lymphoma** \-kət-\ *n, usu cap B* [after Denis Parsons Burkitt *b*1911 Brit. surgeon] **:** a malignant lymphoma that affects primarily the upper and lower jaws, orbit, retroperitoneal tissues situated near the pancreas, kidneys, ovaries, testes, thyroid, adrenal glands, heart, and pleura, that occurs esp. in children of central Africa, and that is associated with Epstein-Barr virus

burkitt's tumor *also* **burkitt tumor** \ˌ==-\ *n, usu cap B* **:** BURKITT'S LYMPHOMA *herein*

burn* *n* **1 :** the firing of a spacecraft rocket engine in flight **2** *slang* **:** an instance of dishonest dealing **:** SWINDLE, GYP

burn bag *n* **:** a bag for holding classified papers that are to be destroyed by burning

burnout* *n* **1 a :** the process or an instance of burning out **b :** the cessation of operation of a jet engine as the result of exhaustion of or shutting off of fuel **2 :** the point in the trajectory of a rocket engine at which burnout occurs **3 :** exhaustion of physical or emotional strength **4 :** a person showing the results of drug abuse

burrito* *n* **:** a flour tortilla rolled or folded around a filling (as of meat, beans, or cheese) and usu. baked

bur·sec·to·my \ˌbərˈsektəmē, ˌbə(r)ˈ-\ *n* -ES [[1]*bursa* + *-ectomy*] **:** excision of a bursa (as the bursa of Fabricius of a chicken) — **bur·sec·to·mize** \(ˌ)=ˈ==ˌmīz\ *vt* -ED/-ING/-S

burst* *vt* **:** to separate (as a perforated continuous paper form) into sheets

burster* *n* **:** the celestial source of an outburst of radiation (as X rays)

bus* *n* **1 :** a spacecraft or missile that carries one or more detachable devices (as probes or warheads) **2 :** a set of parallel conductors in a computer or computer system that forms a main data transmission path

bush \ˈbu̇sh\ *adj* [[1]*bush*] **:** MEDIOCRE, UNPROFESSIONAL ⟨the travesty was not that the speedway went the show= business route, but that the execution was so ~ —J.S. Radosta⟩

bush hat *n* [[1]*bush* (backcountry)] **:** a broad-brimmed hat worn orig. as part of an Australian military uniform

bush·hog \ˈ=ˌhȯg, -äg\ *vi* [[1]*bush* + *hog,* fr. ON *hoggva* to hew or cut down; akin to E *hew,* Scot *hag* to chop wood] *chiefly South & Midland* **:** to clear land of trees and brush

businessman's risk *n* **:** an investment (as a stock) with a moderately high risk factor that is bought with an eye to growth potential and capital gains or sometimes tax advantages rather than for income

bus·ing *or* **bus·sing** \ˈbəsiŋ\ *n* -s [fr. gerund of [2]*bus*] **:** the act of transporting by bus; *specif* **:** the transporting of children to a school outside their residential area as a means of establishing racial balance in the school

bust* *vt* **1** *slang* **:** ARREST **2** *slang* **:** RAID — **bust one's ass** *slang* **:** to make an all-out effort to do something

bust* *n* **1** *slang* **:** a police raid **2** *slang* **:** the act or an instance of arresting or of being arrested

bustout \ˈ=ˌ=\ *n* -s [[2]*bust* + *out*] *slang* **:** a confidence scheme in which an established business is taken over, a large stock of merchandise is purchased on credit and quickly sold, and the business is then abandoned or bankruptcy is declared

bust–up* *n, chiefly Brit* **:** an outbreak of dissension or hostility **:** ALTERCATION; *also* **:** a rough argument or fight **:** SCUFFLE

bu·sul·fan \byüˈsəlfən\ *n* -s [*butane* + *sulfonyl*] **:** an antineoplastic agent $C_6H_{14}O_6S_2$ used in the treatment of chronic myelogenous leukemia

busway* *n* **:** an expressway or a lane of one that is reserved for the exclusive use of commuter buses

Bu·ta·zol·i·din \ˌbyüd·əˈzäləˌdēn, -ˌdən\ *trademark* — used for a preparation of phenylbutazone

butch* *n* [*butch,* adj. (herein)] **:** one who is butch

¹butch \ˈbu̇ch\ *adj* [prob. fr. *Butch,* a nickname for boys, esp. tough boys] **1** *of a homosexual* **:** playing the male role in a homosexual relationship **2 :** very masculine in appearance or manner

²butch \"\ *n* -ES [by shortening] **:** BUTCHER 5

butcher block *n* **:** a heavy board made by bonding together thick strips of hardwood

butcher–block \ˈ≈≈ˌ≈\ *adj* **:** having a top made of or resembling butcher block

but·ter·fly·er \ˈbəd·ərˌflī(ə)r, ˈbəd·əˌflīə, -ətə-\ *n* -s [¹*butterfly* + ²*-er*] **:** a swimmer who specializes in the butterfly

button* *n* **:** a mescal button chewed for its hallucinogenic effect

button–down* *also* **but·toned–down** \ˈbətᵊnˌdau̇n\ *adj* [fr. the fact that button-down shirts are felt to be conservative] **:** lacking originality and imagination and adhering to conventional standards esp. in dress and behavior

buttondown \ˈ≈≈ˌ≈\ *n* -s **:** a shirt with a button-down collar

button man *n* [earlier *button boy* page, errand boy; fr. the buttons on a page's uniform] **:** a low-ranking member of an underworld organization who is given disagreeable and often dangerous assignments

bu·tut \ˈbüˌtüt\ *n, pl* **butut** *or* **bututs** [native name in Gambia] **1 :** a monetary unit of Gambia equal to $^1/_{100}$ dalasi — see MONEY table *in the Dict* **2 :** a coin representing one butut

butylated hy·droxy·anisole \-hīˌdräksē+\ *n* [ISV *hydroxy-* + *anisole*] **:** BHA *herein*

butylated hy·droxy·toluene \"+\ *n* [ISV *hydroxy-* + *toluene*] **:** BHT *herein*

bu·ty·ro·phe·none \ˌbyüd·ə(ˌ)rōfəˈnōn, -ˈfēˌnōn\ *n* [*butyr-* + *phen-* + *-one*] **:** any of a class of neuroleptic drugs (as haloperidol) used esp. in the treatment of schizophrenia

buyback \ˈ≈ˌ≈\ *n* -s [*buy back*] **:** the repurchase by a corporation of shares of its own common stock on the open market (as in an effort to avert a take-over by another corporation)

buy–in \ˈbīˌin\ *n* -s [*buy in,* v.] **:** the act or process of buying in to cover a short on a stock or commodity exchange

buyout \ˈ≈ˌ≈\ *n* -s [*buy out*] **:** an act or instance of buying out ⟨a ~ of residual rights⟩ ⟨a leveraged ~ of a corporation⟩

buzz off *vi* **:** to leave forthwith **:** go away — usu. used as a command

buzz session *n* **:** a small informal group discussion

buzz word *n* **1 :** an important-sounding and often technical word or phrase associated with a special group or activity and used chiefly to impress others **2 :** a word enjoying a popular vogue

BX \(ˈ)bēˈeks\ *abbr or n, pl* **BXs** \-eksəz\ base exchange *herein*

BY *abbr, usu not cap* billion years

BYOB *abbr* bring your own booze; bring your own bottle

byte \ˈbīt\ *n* -s [alter. of ²*bite* (morsel)] **:** a group of adjacent binary digits often shorter than a word that a computer processes as a unit ⟨an 8-bit ~⟩

byzantine* *adj, usu cap* **1 :** of, relating to, or characterized by a devious and usu. surreptitious manner of operation ⟨the government, with its own *Byzantine* sources of intelligence —Wesley Pruden⟩ **2 :** intricately involved **:** LABYRINTHINE ⟨searching in the *Byzantine* complexity of the record —B.L. Collier⟩

BZ \(ˈ)bēˈzē\ *n* [*BZ,* army code name] **:** a gaseous benzilic acid ester $C_{21}H_{23}NO_3$ that when breathed produces incapacitating physical and mental effects

C

c* *n* **1** *usu cap, slang* **:** COCAINE **2** *cap* **:** a structured programming language designed to produce compact and efficient object code after compilation and to allow access to hardware functions of a computer

c* *symbol, cap* charge conjugation *herein*

cabana set *n* **:** a two-piece beachwear ensemble for men consisting of loosely fitting shorts and a short-sleeved jacket

cable* *n* **:** CABLE TELEVISION *herein*

ca·ble·cast \ˈ==,=\ *vt* **cablecast** *also* **cablecasted; cablecast** *also* **cablecasted; cablecasting; cablecasts** [*cable* (*television*) (herein) + tele*cast*] **:** to telecast by cable television — **cablecast** *n* — **ca·ble·cast·er** \-ə(r)\ *n*

cable television *or* **cable TV** *n* **:** a system of television reception in which signals from distant stations are picked up by a master antenna and sent by cable to the individual receivers of paying subscribers

cablevision \ˈ==,==\ *n* **:** CABLE TELEVISION *herein*

ca·cha·ça *or* **ca·cha·ca** \kəˈshäsə\ *n* -s [Pg] **:** a clear Brazilian rum

cache* *or* **cache memory** *n* **:** a computer memory with a very low access time used for storage of frequently used instructions or data

cack–hand·ed \ˈkak¦handəd\ *adj* [prob. fr. ON *keikr* bent backwards; akin to Dan *keite* left-handed] **1** *Brit* **:** LEFT-HANDED **2** *Brit* **:** CLUMSY, AWKWARD

CAD *abbr* computer-aided design

cad·il·lac \ˈkadᵊl,ak\ *n, usu cap* [fr. *Cadillac,* a trademark] **:** something that is the most outstanding or prestigious of its kind

caer·phil·ly \ke(ə)rˈfilē, kär-, kī(ə)r-, kə(r)-\ *n* -ES *usu cap* [fr. *Caerphilly,* urban district in Wales] **:** a mild white friable cheese of Welsh origin

cae·sar salad \¦sēzə(r)-\ *n, usu cap C* [fr. *Caesar's,* restaurant in Tijuana, Mexico, where it originated] **:** a tossed salad made typically with romaine, garlic, anchovies, and croutons and served with a dressing of olive oil, coddled egg, lemon juice, and grated cheese

ca·fé filtre \¦ka,fāˈfiltə(r), *F* kàfāfiltrᵊ\ *n* [F] **:** coffee made by passing hot water through ground coffee and a filter

caff \ˈkaf\ *n* -s [by shortening and alter.] *Brit* **:** CAFÉ

cage* *n* **:** a sheer one-piece dress that has no waistline, is often gathered at the neck, and is worn over a close-fitting underdress or slip

CAGS *abbr* certificate of advanced graduate study

CAI *abbr* computer-aided instruction; computer-assisted instruction

cal·a·mari \kaləˈmärē, kä-; ˈkala,merē, -ri\ *n* -s [It, pl. of *calamaro,* fr. ML *calamarium* pen-case, fr. L *calamus* reed pen; so called fr. the inky substance that the squid secretes and the shape of its shell — more at CALAMUS] **:** squid used as food

cal·ci·phy·lax·is \,kalsəfəˈlaksəs\ *n, pl* **calciphylax·es** \-ak-,sēz\ [NL, fr. *calc-* + *-phylaxis* (as in *prophylaxis*)] **:** an adaptive response that follows systemic sensitization by a calcifying factor (as a D-vitamin) and a challenge (as with a metallic salt) and involves local inflammation and sclerosis with calcium deposition — **cal·ci·phy·lac·tic** \¦===¦laktik\ *adj* — **cal·ci·phy·lac·ti·cal·ly** \-tək(ə)lē, -li\ *adv*

cal·ci·to·nin \,kalsəˈtōnən\ *n* -s [*calc-* + [1]*tonic* + *-in*] **:** a polypeptide hormone esp. from the thyroid gland that tends to lower the level of calcium in the blood plasma — called also *thyrocalcitonin*

calculus* *n* **:** a system or arrangement of intricate or interrelated parts ⟨the ~ of forces in world affairs — Martin Mayer⟩

cal·do ver·de \,kaldōˈve(ə)rdā, ,kälduˈverdē\ *n* [Pg, green broth] **:** a soup that is a puree of potatoes and greens served with smoked sausages

calibrate* *vt* **:** ADJUST, TUNE ⟨each airport's systems are *calibrated* at least every five months —J.N. Wilford⟩

cal·i·for·ni·ana \kalə,fȯrnēˈänə, -,fȯ(ə)n-, -ˈanə, -ˈaa(ə)nə\ *n pl, usu cap* [*California* + *-ana*] **:** materials concerning or characteristic of California, its history, or its culture

caliper* *n* **:** a device consisting of two plates lined with a frictional material that press against the sides of a rotating wheel or disk in some brake systems

call* *vt* **1 :** to indicate and keep track of balls and strikes in (a baseball game) **2 :** to manage (as an offensive game) by giving the signals or orders ⟨that catcher ~*s* a good game⟩ **3 :** to temporarily transfer control of computer processing to (as a subroutine) — **call forth :** to bring into being or action **:** ELICIT ⟨these events *call forth* great emotions⟩ — **call on* :** to solicit a response (as an answer or comment) from ⟨the teacher always *called on* her first⟩

call* *n* **:** a temporary transfer of control of computer processing to a particular set of instructions (as a subroutine)

[1]**cal·la·loo** *also* **cal·a·loo** *or* **calalu*** *or* **cal·la·lou** \¦kalə¦lü\ *n* -s [*calalu*] **:** a soup or stew made with greens (as calalu or spinach), okra, and crabmeat

[2]**callaloo** *var of* CALALU

callback** *n* **:** a recall by a manufacturer of a recently sold product (as an automobile) for correction of a defect

call boy** *n* **:** a male homosexual prostitute

cal·li·graph \ˈkalə,graf\ *vt* -ED/-ING/-s [back-formation fr. *calligraphy*] **:** to produce or reproduce in a calligraphic style

call in* *vb* — **call in sick :** to report by telephone that one will be absent because of illness

call–in \ˈ=(,)=\ *adj* [*call in*] *of a radio program* **:** allowing listeners to engage in on-the-air telephone conversations with the host

call up* *vt* **:** to retrieve from the memory of a computer esp. for display and user interaction

cal·zo·ne \kalˈzȯ(,)nā, -ˈzō(-\ *n, pl* **calzone** *or* **calzones** *or* **cal·zo·ni** \-(,)nē\ [It, sing. back-formation fr. *calzoni* trousers; fr. its shape] **:** a turnover filled with cheese and ham

CAM *abbr* computer-aided manufacturing

cam·e·lot \ˈkamə,lät\ *n* -s *usu cap* [fr. the musical *Camelot* by Alan J. Lerner *b*1918 Am. playwright and Frederick Loewe *b*1901 Am. (Austrian-born) composer which portrayed an ideal world in the Arthurian setting] **:** a time, place, or atmosphere of idyllic happiness

cameo* *n* **:** a brief dramatic role performed by a well-known actor or actress and often limited to a single scene

camerawork \'=(=)=ˌ=\ *n* [*camera* + [1]*work*] **:** the photography produced by a motion-picture or television camera

[1]**camp** \'kamp, -aa(ə)-, -ai-\ *n* -s [origin unknown] **1 :** exaggerated effeminate mannerisms (as of speech or gesture) exhibited esp. by homosexuals; *also* **:** a homosexual displaying such mannerisms **2 :** something that is so outrageously artificial, affected, inappropriate, or out-of-date as to be considered amusing **3 :** something self-consciously exaggerated or theatrical — **camp·i·ly** \-pəlē, -li\ *adv* — **camp·i·ness** *n* -ES — **campy** *adj* -ER/-EST

[2]**camp** \"\ *adj* **1 :** of, relating to, or displaying camp **2 :** of, relating to, or being a camp

[3]**camp** \"\ *vi* -ED/-ING/-S **:** to engage in camp **:** exhibit the qualities of camp ⟨he . . . was ~*ing,* hands on hips, with a quick eye to notice every man who passed by —R. M. McAlmon⟩

camper* *n* **:** a portable dwelling (as a collapsible structure folded into a small trailer or a specially equipped automotive vehicle) for use during casual travel and camping

camphor glass *n* **:** glass with a cloudy white appearance resembling gum camphor in lump form

camp·to·the·cin \ˌkamptə'thēsən\ *n* [*Camptotheca* + *-in*] **:** an alkaloid $C_{20}H_{16}N_2O_4$ from the wood of a Chinese tree (*Camptotheca acuminata*) of the family Nyssaceae that has shown some antileukemic and antitumor activity in animal studies

cam·pylo·bac·ter \ˌkampəlō'baktər, kam'pilə,-\ *n* [ISV *campylo-* + *-bacter*] **1** *cap* **:** a genus of slender spirally curved rod bacteria that are gram-negative, microaerophilic, and motile with a characteristic motion resembling a corkscrew, that do not form spores, and that include forms formerly included in the genus *Spirillum* or *Vibrio* of which some are pathogenic for domestic animals or man **2** -s **:** a bacterium of the genus *Campylobacter*

can* *n, slang* **:** an ounce of marijuana

canalization* *n* **:** the developmental buffering and homeostatic processes by which a particular kind of organism forms a relatively constant phenotype although individuals may have a variety of genotypes and environmental conditions may vary

canard* *n* **:** a small airfoil in front of the wing of an aircraft that increases the aircraft's stability

cancer* *n, usu cap* **:** one born under the astrological sign Cancer

can·cer·ian \kan'sərēən, -'si(ə)r-\ *n* -s *usu cap* [*cancer* + E *-ian*] **:** CANCER *herein*

C and W *abbr* country and western *herein*

candy ass *n* **:** SISSY 2b — usu. considered vulgar — **candy–assed** *adj*

candy floss *n* **1** *chiefly Brit* **:** COTTON CANDY **2** *usu* **candyfloss** *chiefly Brit* **:** something attractive but insubstantial

candy strip·er \-ˌstrīpə(r)\ *n* [*candy stripe* + *-er;* fr. the red and white stripes of her uniform] **:** a teenage volunteer nurse's aide

can·na·bi·noid \'kanəbəˌnȯid, kə'nabə-\ *n* [*cannabis* + *-n-* (as in *cannabinol* or L *cannabinus* hempen) + [1]*-oid*] **:** any of various chemical constituents (as THC or cannabinol) of cannabis or marijuana

cannibalize* *vt* **1 :** to use or draw on material of (as earlier work or another person) ⟨chose to ~ existing technology rather than build a new model from the ground up —Thomas O'Donnell & Jill Andresky⟩ **2 :** to make use of (a part taken from one thing) in building something else

can·no·li \kə'nōlē, ka-\ *n pl but sing or pl in constr* [It, pl. of *cannolo* small cylinder, tube, dim. of *canna* tube, fr. L *canna* reed, fr. Gk *kanna* pole, reed — more at CANE] **:** a tube of pastry fried in deep fat and filled with a sweetened mixture of ricotta cheese, cream, and flavoring

cannon net *n* **:** a net that is left on the ground until birds or mammals are in position and then is spread over them by the simultaneous firing of several projectiles

can of worms : PANDORA'S BOX

canonical form *n* **:** the simplest form of a matrix; *specif* **:** the form of a square matrix that has zero elements everywhere except along the principal diagonal

canton china *n, usu cap 1st C* **:** porcelain Canton ware esp. when blue and white

canton enamel *n, usu cap C* [fr. *Canton,* China] **:** Chinese enamelware of Limoges type

cap* *n* [[1]*cap*] **1** *Brit* **:** DUTCH CAP *herein* **2 :** the symbol ∩ indicating the intersection of two sets — compare CUP *herein* **3 :** a cluster of molecules or chemical groups bound to one end or a region of a cell, virus, or molecule ⟨the cell surface receptors were redistributed into ~*s*⟩

cap* *vt* **:** to form a chemical cap on ⟨the *capped* end of a messenger RNA⟩ ~ *vi* **:** to form or produce a chemical cap ⟨erythrocytes and fibroblasts usually do not ~⟩

capacitate* *vt* **:** to cause (sperm) to undergo capacitation

capacitation* *n* **:** the change undergone by sperm in the female reproductive tract that enables them to penetrate and fertilize an egg

capital gains distribution *n* **:** the part of the payout of an investment company to its shareholders that consists of realized profits from the sale of securities and technically is not income

capital–intensive \ˌ=(=)=(')=ˌ==\ *adj* **:** having a high capital cost per unit of output; *esp* **:** requiring greater expenditure in the form of capital than of labor

capital structure *n* **:** the makeup of the capitalization of a business in terms of the amounts and kinds of equity and debt securities **:** the equity and debt securities of a business together with its surplus and reserves

cap·i·tate \'kapəˌtāt\ *n* -s **:** CAPITATUM

ca·po \'kä(ˌ)pō, 'ka-, 'kȧ-\ *n* -s [It, head, chief, fr. L *caput* — more at HEAD] **:** the head of a branch of a crime syndicate

ca·po·na·ta \ˌkäpə'näd·ə, -ätə\ *n* -s [It (Sicilian dial.)] **:** a relish of chopped eggplant and assorted vegetables

cap·puc·ci·no \ˌkapə'chēnō, ˌkäpü-\ *n* -s [It, lit., Capuchin; fr. the likeness of its color to that of a Capuchin's habit] **:** espresso coffee topped with frothed hot milk or cream and often flavored with cinnamon

cap·reo·my·cin \ˌkaprēə'mīsᵊn\ *n* -s [NL, fr. L *capreo*lus + ISV *-mycin*] **:** an antibiotic obtained from a bacterium of the genus *Streptomyces* (*S. capreolus*) that is used to treat tuberculosis

capricorn* *n, usu cap* **:** one born under the astrological sign Capricorn

cap·ri·cor·ni·an \ˌkaprə'kȯrnēən, -rē'k-, -ȯ(ə)n-\ *n* -s *usu cap* [*capricorn* + E *-ian*] **:** CAPRICORN *herein*

capri pants *n pl, often cap C* [fr. *Capri,* island in the Bay of Naples, Italy] **:** close-fitting pants that have tapered legs with a slit on the outside of the leg bottom, extend almost to the ankle, and are used for informal wear esp. by women

cap·sid \ˈkapsəd\ *n* -s [L *capsa* case + E *-id* — more at CASE] **:** the outer protein shell of a virus particle — **cap·sid·al** \-dᵊl\ *adj*

cap·so·mer \ˈkapsəmər\ *or* **cap·so·mere** \-ˌmi(ə)r\ *n* -s [*caps*id (herein) + *-o-* + *-mer, -mere*] **:** one of the subunits making up a viral capsid

cap·su·li·tis \ˌkaps(y)əˈlīd·əs, -ītəs\ *n* -ES [[1]*capsule* + *-itis*] **:** inflammation of a capsule (as that of the crystalline lens)

cap·su·lot·o·my \ˌkaps(y)əˈläd·əmē, -ätə-, -mi\ *n* -ES [[1]*capsule* + *-o-* + *-tomy*] **:** incision of a capsule esp. of the crystalline lens (as in a cataract operation)

cap·tan \ˈkapˌtan\ *n* -s [perh. fr. *mercaptan*] **:** a fungicide $C_9H_8Cl_3NO_2S$ that is used on agricultural crops and as a bacteriostat in soaps

car·a·van·eer \ˌkarə(ˌ)vaˈni(ə)r, -ˌvəˈ-, -niə(r\ *n* -s [*caravan* + *-eer*] **:** CARAVANNER *herein*

car·a·van·ner \ˈkarəˌvanə(r), -vaan- *also* ˈker- *esp Brit* ˌ==ˈ==\ *n* -s [*caravan* + *-er*] **1** *or* **car·a·van·er :** one that travels in a caravan **2** *Brit* **:** one that goes camping with a trailer

car·ba·maz·e·pine \ˌkärbəˈmazəˌpēn\ *n* -s [*carb-* + *am*ide + *-azepine* (chemical designation)] **:** a tricyclic anticonvulsant and analgesic $C_{15}H_{12}N_2O$ used in the treatment of trigeminal neuralgia and epilepsy

car·ba·ryl \ˈkärbəˌril, -ˌrəl\ *n* -s [*carb*amate + *aryl*] **:** a nonpersistent carbamate insecticide $C_{12}H_{11}O_2N$ effective against numerous crop, forage, and forest pests

car bed *n* **:** a portable bed for an infant that is designed for use in an automobile

carbene* *n* **:** any of a class of usu. highly reactive chemical compounds containing an uncharged divalent carbon atom that are formed esp. as intermediates in chemical reactions

car·ben·i·cil·lin \ˌkär(ˌ)benəˈsilən\ *n* -s [*car*boxy*benz*yl-pen*icillin*] **:** a broad-spectrum semisynthetic penicillin that is effective against gram-negative bacteria (as pseudomonas) and that acts esp. by inhibiting cell-wall synthesis

car·bo·line \ˈkärbəˌlēn\ *n* -s [*carb-* + ind*ole* + pyrid*ine*] **:** any of various isomers that have the formula $C_{11}H_8N_2$ and are structurally related to indole and pyridine

car bomb *n* **:** an explosive device concealed in an automobile for use as a weapon of terrorism

car·bo·na·ra \ˌkärbəˈnärə\ *n* -s [It, fr. *alla carbonara* from the charcoal grill] **:** a pasta dish made with a white cheese sauce that incorporates bits of bacon and ham ⟨spaghetti ~⟩

carbon dating *n* **:** the determination of the age of old material (as of an archaeological find) by means of the content of carbon 14 — called also *carbon 14 dating, radiocarbon dating* — **carbon–date** \ˈ==ˌ=\ *vt*

car·bon·nade \ˌkärbəˈnäd\ *n* -s [F, grilled (meat), fr. It *carbonata,* fr. *carbone* carbon] **:** a stew usu. of beef cooked in beer

carbon spot* *n* **:** a small black spot on a coin

carbon star *n* **:** a reddish star of low surface temperature containing a high proportion of carbon and other heavier elements

car·bo·rane \ˈkärbəˌrān\ *n* -s [blend of *carbon* and *borane*] **:** any of a class of thermally stable compounds $B_nC_2H_{n+2}$ that are used in the synthesis of polymers and lubricants

car·byne \ˈkärˌbīn\ *n* -s [*carb-* + *-yne*] **:** any of several crystalline forms of carbon in which it is linked in chains containing alternating single and triple bonds

car·ci·no·embryonic antigen \ˌkärsᵊn(ˌ)ō+ . . .-\ *n* [*carcino-* + *embryonic*] **:** a glycoprotein present in fetal gut tissues during the first two trimesters of pregnancy and in peripheral blood of patients with some forms of cancer (as of the digestive system or breast) — abbr. *CEA*

car coat *n* **:** a three-quarter-length overcoat

card* *n* **1 :** CREDIT CARD **2 :** a flat stiff piece of material (as plastic) bearing electronic circuit components for insertion into a larger electronic device (as a computer)

card–car·ry·ing \ˌ=ˌ===\ *adj* [so called fr. the assumption that such a member carries a membership card] **1 :** being a full-fledged member esp. of a Communist party **2 :** being a member of a group ⟨to me and other *card-carrying* hypochondriacs —Grace H. Glueck⟩

card·enol·ide \kärˈdēnᵊlˌīd\ *n* -s [*card*iac + but*enolide* ring, a constituent of cardenolide] **:** any of numerous organic compounds with a characteristic ring structure many of which are found in plants (as some milkweeds), have an effect on the vertebrate heart like that of digitalis, and cause vomiting

car·di·nal·i·ty \ˌkärdᵊnˈaləd·ē\ *n* -ES [[2]*cardinal* + *-ity*] **:** the number of elements in a given mathematical set

cardinal number* *n* **:** the property that a mathematical set has in common with all sets that can be put into one-to-one correspondence with it

cardinal's hat *n* **:** GALERO *herein*

car·dio·accelerator *also* **car·dio·acceleratory** \ˌkärdē(ˌ)ō +\ *adj* [*cardi-* + *accelerator* or *acceleratory*] **:** speeding up the action of the heart — **car·dio·acceler·ation** \"+\ *n*

car·dio·active \"+\ *adj* [*cardi-* + *active*] **:** having an influence on the heart ⟨~ drugs⟩ — **car·dio·activity** \"+\ *n*

car·dio·circulatory \"+\ *adj* [*cardi-* + *circulatory*] **:** of or relating to the heart and circulatory system ⟨temporary ~ assist⟩

car·dio·dynamics \"+\ *n pl but sing or pl in constr* [*cardi-* + *dynamics*] **:** the dynamics of the heart's action in pumping blood — **car·dio·dynamic** \"+\ *adj*

car·dio·gen·ic \ˌ==(ˌ)=ˈjenik *also* -jēn-\ *adj* [*cardi-* + *-genic*] **:** originating in the heart **:** caused by a cardiac condition ⟨~ shock⟩

car·dio·meg·a·ly \ˌkärdēōˈmegəlē\ *n* -ES [*cardi-* + *-megaly*] **:** enlargement of the heart

car·dio·myopathy \ˌkärdē(ˌ)ō+\ *n* [*cardi-* + *myopathy*] **:** a typically chronic disorder of heart muscle that may involve hypertrophy and obstructive damage to the heart

car·dio·pulmonary \"+\ *adj* [*cardi-* + *pulmonary*] **:** of or relating to the heart and lungs ⟨the ~ system⟩ ⟨a ~ bypass that diverts blood from the entrance to the right atrium through an oxygenator directly to the aorta⟩

cardiopulmonary resuscitation *n* **:** a procedure designed to restore normal breathing after cardiac arrest that includes the clearance of air passages to the lungs, heart massage by the exertion of pressure on the chest, and the use of drugs — abbr. *CPR*

car·dio·sclerosis \ˌkärdē(ˌ)ō+\ *n, pl* **cardioscleroses** [*cardi-* + *sclerosis*] **:** induration of the heart caused by formation of fibrous tissue in the cardiac muscle

car·dio·toxic \"+\ *adj* [*cardi-* + *toxic*] **:** having a toxic effect on the heart — **car·dio·toxicity** \"+\ *n*

car·dio·ver·sion \ˌ==(ˌ)=ˈvərzhən *also* shən\ *n* -s [*cardi-* + *-version* (fr. L *version-, versio* action of turning)] **:** application of an electric shock in order to restore normal heartbeat

cargo pocket *n* **:** a large pocket usu. with a flap and a pleat

car·io·static \ˌka(a)rēō+\ *adj* [*cario-* + *static*] **:** tending to inhibit the formation of dental caries ⟨the ~ action of fluorides⟩

ca·ri·so·pro·dol \kəˌrīsə'prōˌdȯl, -īzə-, -dōl\ *n* -s [*car-* (prob. fr. *carbamate*) + *isopropyl* + *diol*] **:** a drug $C_{12}H_{24}N_2O_4$ related to meprobamate that is used to relax muscle and relieve pain

carnival glass *n, often cap C* [so called fr. its frequent use for prizes at carnival booths] **:** pressed glass with an iridescent finish mass-produced in a variety of colors (as frosty white or deep purple) in the U. S. in the early 20th century

carp \'kärp, 'kȧp\ *n* -s [[1]*carp*] **:** COMPLAINT

car·pac·cio \kär'päch(ē)ō\ *n* -s [It *filetto Carpaccio* fillet Carpaccio, after Vittore *Carpaccio* †1525 Venetian painter known for his use of reds and whites] **:** slices of raw beef served with a sauce

carpal tunnel *n* **:** a passage between the flexor retinaculum of the hand and the carpal bones that is sometimes a site of compression of the median nerve

carpal tunnel syndrome *n* **:** a condition caused by compression of the median nerve in the carpal tunnel and characterized esp. by discomfort and disturbances of sensation in the hand

carpetbag steak *n* **:** a thick piece of steak in which a pocket is cut and stuffed with oysters

carpool \'=ˌ=\ *vb* [[1]*car* + [4]*pool*] *vt* **:** to take turns driving ⟨~*ed* their way from New Mexico —*Reader's Digest*⟩ ⟨~ children to school⟩ ~ *vi* **:** to participate in a car pool — **car pool·er** \'=ˌpülə(r)\ *n*

carrier* *n* **:** an entity (as a hole or an electron) capable of carrying an electric charge

carrier bag *n, Brit* **:** SHOPPING BAG *herein*

carrot-and-stick \ˌ===ˌ=\ *adj* **:** characterized by the alternating use of reward and punishment

carry* *vb* — **carry the can** *chiefly Brit* **:** to bear alone and in full an often hazardous responsibility

carry* *n* **:** a quantity that is transferred in addition from one number place to the adjacent one of higher place value

carry-cot \'==ˌ=\ *n, Brit* **:** a portable bed for an infant

carryon \'==ˌ=\ *n* -s [[1]*carry* + [2]*on*] **:** a piece of luggage suitable for being carried aboard an airplane by a passenger — **carry-on** \ˌ==ˌ=\ *adj*

carryout \ˌ==ˌ=\ *adj* **:** TAKE-OUT *herein* — **carryout** \'==ˌ=\ *n* -s

cartesian plane *n, usu cap C* **:** a plane whose points are labeled with Cartesian coordinates

cartesian product *n, usu cap C* **:** a set that is constructed from two given sets and comprises all pairs of elements such that one element of the pair is from the first set and the other element is from the second set

car·toon·ish \kär'tünish\ *adj* **:** resembling a cartoon

car·top·per \'kärˌtäpər; 'kȧˌ-, -pə(r\ *n* -s [*cartop* + [2]*-er*] **:** a small boat that may be transported on top of a car

cartridge* *n* **1 :** a removable case containing a magnetic tape or one or more disks and used as a computer storage medium **2 :** a case for holding integrated circuits containing a computer program ⟨a video-game ~⟩

case* *n* **1 :** one of a set of relational semantic categories in the deep structure of a sentence that help determine the meaning of the sentence **2 :** oneself considered as an object of harassment ⟨get off my ~⟩ ⟨they'd been on his ~ ever since his school grades had started to drop —*New Yorker*⟩

casebook* *n* **:** a compilation of primary and secondary documents relating to a central topic together with scholarly comment, exercises, and study aids that is often designed to serve as a source book for short papers (as in a course in composition) or as a point of departure for a research paper

case grammar *n* **:** a grammar that describes the deep structure of sentences in terms of the relation of a verb to a set of semantic cases

ca·sette \kə'set, ka-\ *n* -s [by alter.] **1 :** CASSETTE 3 **2 :** CASSETTE *herein*

cash bar *n* **:** a bar (as at a wedding reception) at which drinks are sold — compare OPEN BAR *herein*

cash desk *n, Brit* **:** a counter at which a cashier works

cash flow *n* **1 :** a measure of an organization's liquidity that usu. consists of net income after taxes plus noncash charges (as depreciation) against income **2 :** a flow of cash ⟨maintaining an international *cash flow* —C. H. Stern⟩ ⟨the faster the speed of *cash flow,* the better the fiscal health of the publishing company —*Book Production Industry*⟩; *esp* **:** one that provides solvency ⟨colleges obtained bank loans in July to maintain a *cash flow* until tuition money came in —L. B. Mayhew⟩

ca·si·no \kə'sē(ˌ)nō\ *adj* [*casino,* n.] **:** baked or broiled on the half shell usu. with a topping of green pepper and bacon ⟨clams ~⟩ ⟨oysters ~⟩

cas·sa·ta \kə'säd·ə, ka-, -ätə\ *n* -s [It dial. (Sicilian) *cassata,* perh. fr. L *caseus* cheese] **:** a cake filled with ricotta cheese, candied fruit, and chocolate

cas·se·grain \'kasəˌgrān, *F* kȧsgraⁿ\ *also* **casse·grainian** *adj, usu cap C* **:** of, relating to, or being the system of optics used in a Cassegrainian telescope ⟨~ focus⟩

cassette* *n* **:** a usu. flat case or container that holds a substance, device, or material which is difficult, troublesome, or awkward to handle and that can be easily changed; *esp* **:** a usu. plastic cartridge containing magnetic tape with the tape on one reel passing to the other without having to be threaded

Cas·si·ni division \kəˌsēnē-\ *n* [after Gian Domenico *Cassini* †1712 Ital. astronomer] **:** the dark region between the two brightest rings of Saturn

cas·tro·ism \'kas(ˌ)trōˌizəm *sometimes* -äs-\ *n* -s *usu cap* [Fidel *Castro b*1927 Cuban political leader + E *-ism*] **:** the political, economic, and social principles and policies of Fidel Castro — **cas·tro·ist** \-ōˌist, -ō̤əst\ *n or adj, usu cap* — **cas·tro·ite** \-ōˌīt\ *n or adj, usu cap*

CAT *abbr* **1** clear-air turbulence *herein* **2** computed axial tomography *herein;* computerized axial tomography *herein*

catalytic converter *n* **:** a device in the exhaust system of an automobile that contains a catalyst for converting gases into harmless or less harmful products (as water and carbon dioxide)

catchment area* *n* **:** the geographical area served by an institution ⟨describe the *catchment areas* and social backgrounds of the various schools she examined —*Times Lit. Supp.*⟩

catch-22 \ˌ=ˌ==ˌ=\ *n, pl* **catch-22's** *or* **catch-22s** *often cap C* [fr. *Catch-22,* the paradoxical rule found in the novel *Catch-22* (1961) by Joseph Heller *b*1923 Am. author, fr. [2]*catch* + *22*] **1 :** a problematic situation for which the only solution is denied by a circumstance inherent in the problem or by a rule ⟨the show-business *catch-22* — no work unless you have an agent, no agent unless you've worked —Mary Murphy⟩; *also* **:** the circumstance or rule that denies a solution ⟨this *Catch-22* principle of the tax code: . . . any transaction which has no substantive object other than to reduce one's taxes — does not qualify to reduce one's taxes —Andrew Tobias⟩ **2 a :** an illogical, unreasonable, or senseless situation ⟨continuing the *Catch-22* logic, he explained that the agents busted in with guns drawn "to reduce the potential for violence" —Michael Drosnin⟩ **b :** a measure or policy whose effect is the opposite of what was intended ⟨a medical *catch-22:* some experts now believe that the examination . . . may actually cause more cases of breast cancer than it helps to cure —*Newsweek*⟩ **c :** a situation presenting two equally undesirable alternatives **:** DILEMMA ⟨"*catch-22*" If I don't jog, it's bad. If I jog in polluted city air, it's bad —Jim Berry⟩ **3 :** CATCH 7 ⟨the puritanical *Catch-22* that runs through our society — pleasure, it warns, must be paid for —Janet S. King⟩

catch–up *adj* **:** intended to catch up to a theoretical norm or a competitor's accomplishments

catechism* *n* **:** something resembling a catechism esp. in being a rote response or formulaic statement

cat·e·chol·amine \ˌkad·əˈkōləˈmēn, -äl-\ *n* [*catechol* + *amine*] **:** any of various substances (as epinephrine, norepinephrine, and dopamine) that contain a benzene ring with two adjacent hydroxyl groups and a side chain of ethylamine and that function as hormones or neurotransmitters or both

cat·e·chol·amin·er·gic \ˌ==ˈ==(ˌ)mēˈnərjik, -ˌməˈ-\ *adj* [ISV *catecholamine* + *-ergic* (herein)] **:** involving, liberating, or mediated by catecholamine ⟨~ neurons in the brain⟩ ⟨~ transmission in the nervous system⟩

category* *n* **:** a mathematical class of objects (as groups or topological spaces) together with a set of structure-preserving mappings (as homomorphisms or continuous functions) between the members of the class such that the operation of applying one mapping after another to produce a single combined mapping is associative and the set of mappings includes an identity element — **categorical*** *adj*

cat·e·na·tive \ˈkad·əˌnād·iv, ˈkatᵊnˌād·iv, -atə-, -ātiv\ *or* **catenative verb** *also* **catenative auxiliary** *n* -s [[1]*catenate* + [2]*-ive*] **:** a verb often followed by a function word (as *to* or *on*) that occupies a position other than final in a succession of two or more verbs together forming the main part of the predicate of a sentence (as *ought* in "I ought to go home now" and *try* and *keep* in "they tried to keep on working")

cathedral* *adj, of women's formal apparel* **:** having a length that reaches the floor and trails behind ⟨~ veil⟩

ca·tho·dal \ˈkathˌōdᵊl, kathˈ-\ *adj* [*cathode* + [1]*-al*] **:** of, relating to, or attracted to a cathode **:** CATHODIC 1a ⟨~ potentials⟩ ⟨~ hemoglobins⟩ — used esp. in the life sciences — **ca·tho·dal·ly** \=ˈ=ᵊlē\ *adv*

CAT scan \ˈkat-, ˌsēˌāˈtē-\ *n* [*c*omputed *a*xial *t*omography] **:** a sectional view of the body made by computed tomography

CAT scanner *n* **:** a medical instrument consisting of integrated X-ray and computing equipment and used for computed tomography

cattle call *n* **:** a mass audition

CATV *abbr* community antenna television *herein*

cau·chy sequence \ˈkōshē-, kōˈshē-\ *n, usu cap C* [Augustin-Louis *Cauchy* †1857 Fr. mathematician] **:** a sequence of elements in a metric space such that for any positive number no matter how small there exists a term in the sequence for which the distance between any two consecutive or nonconsecutive terms beyond this term is less than an arbitrarily small positive number ⟨the sequence 1, $^1/_2$, $^1/_3$, $^1/_4$, . . . , $^1/_n$, . . . is a *Cauchy sequence*⟩

cau·ri \ˈkau̇rē\ *n, pl* **cauris** [native name in Guinea] **:** a monetary unit of Guinea equal to $^1/_{100}$ syli — see MONEY table *in the Dict*

CB \ˌsēˈbē\ *n* -s **:** CITIZENS BAND *herein*

cber \(ˌ)sēˈbēə(r)\ *n* -s *usu cap C & B* [*CB* (herein) + [2]-er] **:** one that operates a CB radio

CBW *abbr* chemical and biological warfare

CCD \ˈsēˈsēˈdē\ *n* -s **:** CHARGE-COUPLED DEVICE *herein*

CCTV *abbr* closed-circuit television

CD *abbr* compact disc *herein*

cDNA \ˈsēˈdēˈenˈā\ *n* [complementary] **:** single-stranded DNA complementary to a given messenger RNA which serves as a template for production of the messenger RNA in the presence of a reverse transcriptase

CDP *abbr* certificate in data processing

CEA *abbr* carcinoembryonic antigen *herein*

ce·co·pexy \ˈsēkəˌpeksē, -kō-\ *n* -ES [*cec-* + *-pexy*] **:** a surgical operation to fix the cecum to the abdominal wall

ce·di \ˈsādē\ *n* -s [Akan *sedie* cowrie] **1 :** the basic monetary unit of Ghana — see MONEY table *in the Dict* **2 :** a note representing one cedi

cell* *n* **1 :** a basic subdivision of a computer memory that is addressable and can hold one basic operating unit (as a word) **2 :** FUEL CELL *herein*

cell cycle *n* **:** the complete series of events from one cell division to the next — see G1 PHASE *herein,* G2 PHASE *herein,* M PHASE *herein,* S PHASE *herein*

cell–mediated immunity *n* **:** immunity that is conferred on the body by the activities of T cells and esp. cytotoxic T cells

cellular* *adj* **:** of, relating to, or being a radiotelephone system in which a geographical area (as a city) is divided into small sections (**cells**) each served by a transmitter of limited range so that any available radio channel can be used in different parts of the area simultaneously

cel·lu·lite \ˈselyəˌlīt, -ˌlēt\ *n* -s [F, fr. *cellule* cell + *-ite* [1]-ite] **:** lumpy fat found in the thighs, hips, and buttocks of some women

center* *n* **:** the center of the circle inscribed in a regular polygon

centerfold \ˈ==ˌ=\ *n* [[1]*center* + *fold*] **1 :** a foldout that is the center spread of a magazine **2 :** a picture (as of a nude model) on a centerfold

center–of–mass system* *n* **:** a frame of reference in which the center of mass is at rest

centerpiece* *n* **:** one (as an event, concept, or policy) that is of central importance or interest within a larger whole ⟨some women make a husband or lover the ~ of their lives —Carol Tavris⟩

centime* *n* **:** a monetary unit of Equatorial Guinea equivalent to $^1/_{100}$ ekuele — see MONEY table *in the Dict*

central angle *n* **:** an angle formed by two radii of a circle

central dogma *n* **:** a theory in genetics and molecular biology subject to several exceptions that genetic information is coded in self-replicating DNA and undergoes unidirectional transfer to messenger RNAs in transcription which act as templates for protein synthesis in translation

central limit theorem *n* **:** any of several fundamental theorems of probability and statistics giving the conditions under which the distribution of a sum of independent random variables can be found approximately by using the normal distribution; *esp* **:** a special case of the central limit theorem which is much applied in sampling: the distribution of the mean of a sample from a population with finite variance approaches the normal distribution as the number in the sample becomes large

central processing unit *n* **:** PROCESSOR 1b *herein*

central tendon *n* **:** a 3-lobed aponeurosis located near the central portion of the diaphragm caudal to the pericardium and composed of intersecting planes of collagenous fibers

cen·tri·lobular \ˌsen·trə+\ *adj* [*centri-* + *lobular*] **:** relating to or affecting the center of a lobule ⟨~ necrosis in the liver⟩; *also* **:** affecting the central parts of the secondary pulmonary lobules of the lung ⟨~ emphysema⟩

cen·trism \ˈsen·ˌtrizəm\ *n* -s [*centr-* + *-ism*] **:** a political philosophy of avoiding extremes of right or left

CEO \ˌsēˌēˈō\ *n* -s *sometimes not cap* **:** the chief executive officer of a business concern or corporation

ceph·a·lex·in \ˌsefəˈleksən\ *n* -s [NL, fr. *cephalo*sporin (herein) + *-ex-* (arbitrary infix) + *-in*] **:** a semisynthetic cephalosporin $C_{16}H_{17}N_3O_4S$ with a spectrum of antibiotic activity similar to the penicillins

ceph·a·lopelvic disproportion \ˌsefə(ˌ)lō+ . . .-\ *n* [*cephalo-* + *pelvic*] **:** a condition in which a maternal pelvis is small in relation to the size of the fetal head

ceph·a·lor·i·dine \ˌsefəˈlòrəˌdēn, -ˈlär-\ *n* -s [prob. fr. *cephalo-* spo*rin* (herein) + *-idine*] **:** a broad-spectrum antibiotic $C_{19}H_{17}$- $N_3O_4S_2$ derived from cephalosporin

ceph·a·lo·spo·rin \ˌsefələˈspōrən, -ˈspòr-\ *n* -s [*Cephalosporium* + *-in*] **:** any of several antibiotics produced by an imperfect fungus of the genus *Cephalosporium*

ceph·a·lo·thin \ˈsefələ(ˌ)thin\ *n* -s [*cephalo*sporin (herein) + *thi-* + *-in*] **:** a semisynthetic broad-spectrum antibiotic $C_{16}H_{15}N_2$- NaO_6S_2 that is an analogue of a cephalosporin and is effective against penicillin-resistant staphylococci

cer·amide \ˈse(ə)rəˌmīd, ˈsi(ə)r-, -ˌməd; səˈramˌīd, -məd\ *n* [*cere*broside + *amide*] **:** any of a group of amides formed by linking a fatty acid to sphingosine and found widely but in small amounts in plant and animal tissue

cereal leaf beetle *n* **:** a small reddish brown black-headed Old World chrysomelid beetle (*Oulema melanopus*) that feeds on cereal grasses and is a serious threat to U. S. grain crops

ce·re·bral–pal·sied \=ˈ==ˈpòlzēd, ˈ===-\ *adj* [*cerebral palsy* + [1]*-ed*] **:** affected with cerebral palsy

ce·ren·kov *also* **che·ren·kov** \chərˈ(y)eŋkəf\ *adj, usu cap C* **1 :** of, relating to, or being Cerenkov radiation or the process that produces such radiation **2 :** being a device that makes use of Cerenkov radiation ⟨*Cerenkov* counter⟩

ce·ru·lo·plas·min \səˌrülōˌplazmən, ˌser(y)əl-\ *n* -s [ISV *cerulo-* (fr. L *caeruleus* dark blue) + *plasma* + *-in;* prob. orig. formed in Sw] **:** an alpha globulin active in the biological storage and transport of copper

cer·vico·thoracic \ˌsərvə(ˌ)kō+\ *adj* [*cervico-* + *thoracic*] **:** of or relating to the neck and thorax ⟨~ sympathectomy⟩

cer·vico·vaginal \"+\ *adj* [*cervico-* + *vaginal*] **:** of or relating to the uterine cervix and the vagina ⟨~ flora⟩ ⟨~ carcinoma⟩

cesium clock *n* **:** an atomic clock regulated by the natural vibration frequency of cesium atoms

cesium 137 *n* **:** a radioactive isotope of cesium that has the mass number 137 and a half-life of about 12 months and that is present in fallout

ce·tol·o·gist \sēˈtäləjəst\ *n* -s **:** a zoologist who is a specialist in cetology

ce·tri·mide \ˈsē·trəˌmīd, ˈse·t-\ *n* [fr. *ce*tyl + *tri-* + *m*ethyl + *-ide*] **:** a mixture of bromides of ammonium used esp. as a detergent and antiseptic

CFA *abbr* certified financial analyst

chain printer *n* **:** a line printer in which the printing element is type carried on a continuous chain

chain rule *n* **:** a mathematical rule concerning the differentiation of a function of a function (as $f[u(x)]$) by which under suitable conditions of continuity and differentiability one function is differentiated with respect to the second considered as an independent variable and then the second function is differentiated with respect to the independent variable ⟨if $v = u^2$ and $u = 3x^2 + 2$ the derivative of v by the *chain rule* is $2u(6x)$ or $12x(3x^2 + 2)$⟩

chainwheel \ˈ=ˌ=\ *n* **:** SPROCKET WHEEL

chair* *n* **:** a conformation of a six-membered cyclic molecule (as of cyclohexane) in which two opposite atoms are also on opposite sides of the plane of the molecule — compare BOAT *herein*

chairperson \ˈ=ˌ==\ *n* [[1]*chair* + *person*] **1 :** the presiding officer of a meeting or an organization or a committee **2 :** the administrative officer of a department of instruction (as in a college)

chairside \ˈ=ˌ=\ *adj* [[1]*chair* + *side* (as in *bedside*)] **:** relating to, performed in the vicinity of, or assisting in the work done on a patient in a dentist's chair ⟨a dental ~ assistant⟩ ⟨a good ~ manner⟩

chakra* *n* **:** any of several points of physical or spiritual energy in the human body according to yoga philosophy

chamberlain* *n* **:** an often honorary papal attendant; *specif* **:** a priest having a rank of honor below domestic prelate

cham·pers \ˈshampə(r)z\ *n pl but sing in constr* [by alter.] *Brit* **:** CHAMPAGNE

chan·dler wobble \ˈchan(d)lər-\ *also* **chan·dler's wobble** \-lərz-\ *n, usu cap C* [after Seth Carlo *Chandler* †1913 Am. astronomer] **:** an elliptical oscillation of the earth's axis of rotation with a period of 14 months whose cause has not been determined

Chan·dra·se·khar limit \ˌchəndrəˈshā(ˌ)kär-\ *n* [after Subrahmanyan *Chandrasekhar b*1910 Am. (Indian-born) physicist] **:** the mass above which a star near the end of its life cycle will collapse to form a neutron star or black hole rather than a white dwarf **:** a stellar mass equal to about 1.4 solar masses

changing room *n, Brit* **:** CHANGEROOM; *esp* **:** LOCKER ROOM

channel* *n* **1 :** a path along which information passes or an area (as of magnetic tape) on which it is stored **2 :** a transition passage in jazz **:** BRIDGE

chao·tro·pic \ˌkāəˌtrōpik, -ˌträp-\ *adj* [*chaos* + *-tropic*] **:** disrupting the structure of water, macromolecules, or a living system so as to promote activities inhibited by such structure

character* *n* **:** a symbol (as a letter or number) that represents information; *also* **:** a representation (as in binary form) of such a character that may be accepted by a computer

characteristic* *n* **:** the smallest positive integer *n* which for an operation in a ring, integral domain, or field yields 0 when any element is used *n* times with the operation and which is arbitrarily denoted by 0 or ∞ if no such integer exists

characteristic equation *n* **:** an equation in which the characteristic polynomial of a matrix is set equal to 0

characteristic polynomial *n* **:** the determinant of a square matrix in which an arbitrary variable (as *x*) is subtracted from each of the elements along the principal diagonal

characteristic root *n* **:** EIGENVALUE *herein*

characteristic value *n* **:** EIGENVALUE *herein*

characteristic vector *n* **:** EIGENVECTOR

char·ac·to·nym \ˈkarəktəˌnim *also* ˈker-\ *n* -s [*character* + *-onym*] **:** a name esp. for a fictional character (as Mistress Quickly or Caspar Milquetoast) that suggests a distinctive trait of the character

char·broil \ˈchärˌbrȯil, ˈcháˌ-\ *vt* [*char*coal + *broil*] **:** to broil on a rack over hot charcoal — **char·broil·er** \ˈ=ˌbrȯilə(r)\ *n*

charge card *n* **:** CREDIT CARD 1

charge conjugation *n* **:** an operation in mathematical physics in which each particle in a system is replaced by its antiparticle

charge–coupled device *n* **:** a semiconductor device that is used esp. as an optical sensor and that stores charge and transfers it sequentially to an amplifier and detector — called also *CCD*

charismatic* *adj* **:** of or relating to the religious movement that emphasizes the extraordinary power (as of healing) given a Christian by the Holy Spirit

char·is·mat·ic \ˌkarəzˈmad·ik\ *n* -s [*charismatic,* adj. (herein)] **:** a member of a charismatic religious group or movement

charm* *n* **:** a quantum characteristic of subatomic particles that accounts for the unexpectedly long lifetime of the J/psi particle, explains various difficulties in the theory of weak interactions, and is conserved in electromagnetic and strong interactions

charmed* *adj* **:** having the quantum characteristic of charm ⟨a ~ antiquark⟩

char·mo·ni·um \chärˈmōnēəm\ *n, pl* **charmonium** [*charm* (herein) + *-onium* (as in *positronium*)] **:** any of a group of fundamental particles that are held to consist of a charmed quark-antiquark pair

chart* *n* **:** a listing by rank (as of sales) — often used in pl. ⟨number one on the ~*s*⟩

chartbuster \ˈ=ˌ==\ *n* [¹*chart* + *buster*] **:** BEST SELLER; *esp* **:** a best-selling phonograph record

charter* *n* **:** a travel arrangement in which transportation (as a bus or plane) is hired by and for a specific group of people

chartreux* \(ˈ)shärˈtrüs, -äˈt-, -üz *sometimes* -ärˈtrərs *or* -äˈtrəs\ *n, pl* **chartreux** *usu cap* **:** any of a breed of short-haired domestic cats of French origin having a bluish gray coat and gold or orange eyes

chat show *n, Brit* **:** TALK SHOW *herein*

chauvinism* *n* **:** an attitude of superiority toward members of the opposite sex; *also* **:** behavior expressive of such an attitude

cheapo *adj* [alter. of ³*cheap*] **:** CHEAP

cheap shot *n* **1 :** an act of deliberate roughness against a defenseless opponent esp. in a contact sport **2 :** an unfair statement that takes advantage of a known weakness of the target

checkbook journalism *n* **:** the practice of paying someone for a news story and esp. for granting an interview

check off* *vt* **:** to change a play at the line of scrimmage in football by calling an audible

checkoff* *n* **:** designation by a taxpayer of a dollar of income tax to be used for public financing of political campaigns

checkout** *n* **1 :** the process of examining and testing something as to readiness for intended use ⟨the ~ of a spacecraft⟩ **2 :** the process of familiarizing oneself with the operation of a mechanical thing (as an airplane)

che·diak–hi·ga·shi syndrome \shādˈyäkhēˈgäshē-\ *n, usu cap C & H* [after Moises *Chediak fl*1952 Fr. physician and Ototaka *Higashi fl*1954 Jap. physician] **:** a genetic disorder inherited as an autosomal recessive and characterized by partial albinism, abnormal granules in the white blood cells, and marked susceptibility to bacterial infections

chef's knife *n* **:** a large kitchen knife with a curved triangular blade

chef's salad \ˌshefˈsaləd\ *n* **:** a meal-size salad that includes lettuce, tomatoes, celery, hard-boiled eggs, and julienne strips of meat and cheese

che·la·tor \ˈkēˌlād·ə(r)\ *n* -s **:** a binding agent that suppresses chemical activity by forming chelates

chemi·osmotic \ˌkemē+\ *adj* [*chem-* + *osmotic*] **:** relating to or being a hypothesis that seeks to explain the mechanism of ATP formation in oxidative phosphorylation by mitochondria and chloroplasts without recourse to the formation of high-energy intermediates by postulating the formation of an energy gradient of hydrogen ions across the organelle membranes that results in the reversible movement of hydrogen ions to the outside and is generated by electron transport or the activity of electron carriers

che·mo·nuclear \ˌkēmō, ˌkemō+\ *adj* [*chem-* + *nuclear*] **:** being or relating to a chemical reaction induced by nuclear radiation or fission fragments

che·mo·nucleolysis \"+\ *n* [*chem-* + *nucleolysis*] **:** treatment of a slipped disk by the injection of chymopapain to dissolve the displaced nucleus pulposus

che·mo·sensory \"+\ *adj* [*chem-* + *sensory*] **:** of, relating to, or functioning in the sensory reception of chemical stimuli ⟨~ hairs⟩ ⟨insect ~ behavior⟩

che·mo·sphere \ˈkēmə, ˌkemə+ˌ\ *n* [*chem-* + *sphere*] **:** a stratum of the upper atmosphere in which photochemical reactions are prevalent and which begins about 20 miles above the earth's surface

che·mo·sterilant \ˌkēmō, ˌkemo+\ *n* [*chem-* + *sterilant*] **:** a substance that produces irreversible sterility (as of an insect) without marked alteration of mating habits or life expectancy — **che·mo·sterilization** \"+\ *n* — **che·mo·sterilize** \"+\ *vb*

che·mo·surgery \"+\ *n* [*chem-* + *surgery*] **:** removal by chemical means of diseased or unwanted tissue — **che·mo·surgical** \"+\ *adj*

che·mo·taxonomy \"+\ *n* [*chem-* + *taxonomy*] **:** the classification of plants and animals based on similarities and differences in biochemical composition — **che·mo·taxonomic** \"+\ *adj* — **che·mo·taxonomist** \"+\ *n*

cheong·sam \ˈcheuŋˈsäm, ˈchȯŋ-\ *n* -s [Chin (Cant) *cheung shaam,* lit., long gown] **:** a dress with a slit skirt and a mandarin collar worn esp. by Oriental women

chet·rum \ˈchē·trəm, ˈche-\ *n* -s [native name in Bhutan] **1 :** a monetary unit of Bhutan equal to 1/100 ngultrum — see MONEY table *in the Dict* **2 :** a coin representing one chetrum

chiao \ˈjaů\ *n, pl* **chiao** [Chin (Pek) *chiao³*] **1 :** a monetary unit of China equal to $^1/_{10}$ yuan **2 :** a coin or note representing one chiao

chi·ca·na \chiˈkänə, shi-, -kȧn-\ *n* -s *cap* [modif. of MexSp *mexicana,* fem. of *mexicano*] **:** a female Chicano — **chicana** *adj, usu cap*

chicane* *n* **:** a series of tight turns in opposite directions in an otherwise straight stretch of a road-racing course

chi·ca·nis·mo \chiˌkäˌniz(ˌ)mō, shi-, -kȧ-, -is(-\ *n* -s *often cap* [*Chicano* + *-ismo* (fr. Sp, -ism)] **:** strong ethnic pride exhibited by Chicanos

chi·ca·no \chiˈkän(ˌ)ō, shi-, -kȧn-\ *n* -s *cap* [modif. of MexSp *mexicano* Mexican] **:** an American of Mexican descent — **chicano** *adj, usu cap*

chicken–and–egg \ˌchik(ə)nən(d)ˌeg, -ˌäg\ *adj* [so called fr. the proverbial question "which came first, the chicken or the egg?"] **:** of, relating to, or being a cause-and-effect dilemma

chicken kiev *n, usu cap K* [fr. *Kiev,* U.S.S.R.] **:** a boneless chicken breast that is stuffed with seasoned butter and deep fried

chick·en·shit \ˈ=,=\ *adj* **1 :** PETTY, INSIGNIFICANT — often considered vulgar ⟨jailed . . . on the ~ charge of loitering —Tim Cahill⟩ **2 :** lacking courage, manliness, or effectiveness — often considered vulgar ⟨too ~ to raise his voice —D.A. Latimer⟩; often used as a generalized term of contempt ⟨a useless mob of ignorant, ~ ego-junkies whose only accomplishment was to embarrass the whole tradition of public protest —H.S. Thompson⟩

chi·com \ˈchīˌkäm\ *n* -s *usu cap* [[1]*chinese* + *communist*] **:** a communist Chinese

chief of staff **1 a :** the ranking officer of a staff in the armed forces serving as principal adviser to a commander **b :** the senior official of a staff serving a civilian executive (as the president of the United States) **2 :** the commanding officer of the army or air force serving on the Joint Chiefs of Staff

chien ware \chēˈen,-\ *also* **chien yao** \-nˌyaů\ *n, usu cap C* [Chin (Pek) *ch'ien yao²,* fr. *Ch'ien-an,* locality in China where it was first made + Chin (Pek) *yao²* pottery] **:** a dark Chinese stoneware dating from the Sung period that usu. has a black brown-mottled glaze and is used esp. for tea wares

childproof \ˈ=,=\ *adj* **:** designed to prevent tampering by children ⟨a ~ door lock⟩

chili·burger \ˈ==,==\ *n* -s [*chili* + *-burger*] **:** a hamburger topped with chili

chili dog *n* **:** a hot dog topped with chili

chill factor *n* **:** WINDCHILL *herein*

chil·tern hundreds \ˌchiltə(r)n-\ *n pl, usu cap C&H* [fr. *Chiltern Hundreds,* three hundreds in the Chiltern hills of England appointment to the stewardship of which is a disqualification for membership in Parliament] **:** a nominal appointment granted by the British crown that serves as a legal fiction to enable a member of Parliament to relinquish his seat

chi·me·rism \ kīˈmi(ə)rˌizəm, kə̇-; ˈkīməˌriz- \ *n* -s [*chimera* + *-ism*] **:** the state of being a genetic chimera

chinaman* *n* **:** an off-break in cricket bowled by a left-handed bowler to a right-handed batsman

china syndrome *n, usu cap C* [so called fr. the notion that the molten reactor contents could theoretically sink through the earth to reach China] **:** the accidental melting of the core of a nuclear reactor so that it passes through the bottom of its container and down into the earth

chinese fire drill *n, usu cap C* **1 :** a state of great confusion or disorder **2 :** a prank in which a number of people jump out of an automobile stopped at a red traffic light, run around to the opposite side, and jump back in often in a different seat before the light changes to green

chinese parsley *n, usu cap C* **:** CILANTRO *herein*

chinese restaurant syndrome *n, usu cap C* **:** a group of symptoms that may include numbness of the neck, arms, and back with headache, dizziness, and palpitations and that is held to affect susceptible persons ingesting monosodium glutamate often used to season Chinese food

chip* *n* **1 :** INTEGRATED CIRCUIT *herein* **2 a :** a soft high pass or shot over a defender's head in soccer **b :** a return shot in tennis made by hitting down on the ball to give it backspin **3 :** a small wafer of semiconductor material that forms the base for an integrated circuit

chip* *vt* **1 :** to hit (a return in tennis) with backspin **2 :** to kick (a soccer ball) in a soft high arc ~ *vi* **:** to make a chip (as in soccer or tennis)

chi·ral \ˈkī(ə)rəl\ *adj* [*chir-* + [1]*-al*] **:** of or relating to a molecule that is nonsuperimposable on its mirror image — **chi·ral·i·ty** \kīˈralə̇d·ē, kə̇ˈ-\ *n*

chi–square distribution *n* **:** a probability density function that gives the distribution of the sum of the squares of a number of independent random variables each having a normal distribution with zero mean and unit variance, that has the property that the sum of two random variables with such a distribution also has one, and that is widely used in testing statistical hypotheses esp. about the theoretical and observed values of a quantity and about population variances and standard deviations

chit·lin circuit \ˈchitlə̇n-\ *n* [so called fr. the assumption that chitterlings are eaten chiefly by blacks] **:** a group of theaters and nightclubs that cater to black audiences and feature black entertainers

chlor–alkali \ˌklōr, -ȯr+\ *n* [*chlor-* + *alkali*] **:** any of a group of chemicals (as chlorine and sodium hydroxide) that are manufactured by the electrolytic decomposition of sodium chloride — usu. used in pl.

chlor·am·bu·cil \klōrˈambyəˌsil, klȯr-\ *n* -s [*chloro*ethyl + *am-* in- + *bu*tyric + *-il*] **:** an anticancer drug $C_{14}H_{19}Cl_2NO_2$ that is a derivative of nitrogen mustard and is used esp. to treat leukemias and Hodgkin's disease

chlor·di·az·epox·ide \ˌklōrdīˌazə̇ˈpäkˌsīd, ˌklȯr-\ *n* [*chlor-* + *diaz-* + *epoxide*] **:** a benzodiazepine $C_{16}H_{14}ClN_3O$ structurally and pharmacologically related to diazepam that is used in the form of its hydrochloride esp. as a tranquilizer and to treat the withdrawal symptoms of alcoholism — see LIBRIUM *herein*

chlor·hex·i·dine \klōrˈhexə̇ˌdīn, klȯr-, -ˌdēn\ *n* -s [ISV *chlor-* + *hex-* + *-idine*] **:** a biguanide derivative $C_{22}H_{30}Cl_2N_{10}$ used as a local antiseptic esp. in the form of its hydrochloride or acetate

chlor·mer·o·drin \klōrˈmerədrə̇n, klȯr-\ *n* -s [*chlor-* + *mercury* + *-o-* + *-hydrin*] **:** a mercurial diuretic $C_5H_{11}ClHgN_2O_2$ used in the treatment of some forms of edema, ascites, and nephritis

chlo·ro·fluorocarbon \ˌklōrə, -lȯrə+\ *n* [ISV *chlor-* + *fluorocarbon*] **:** CHLOROFLUOROMETHANE *herein*

chlo·ro·flu·o·ro·methane \ˌklōrəˌflů(ə)(ˌ)rō, ˌklȯr-, -ˌflōr(ˌ)ō, ˌflȯ(ˌ)rō+\ *n* [ISV *chlor-* + *fluor-* + *methane*] **:** any of several gaseous compounds that are derivatives of methane, contain chlorine and fluorine, and are used esp. as aerosol propellants and refrigerants

chlo·ro·phy·tum \ˌklōrəˈfīd·əm, ˌklȯr-\ *n* [NL *chlor-* + *-phytum*] **1** *cap* **:** a genus of perennial tropical herbs of the family Liliaceae **2** -s **:** a plant of the genus *Chlorophytum; esp* **:** SPIDER PLANT *herein*

chlo·ro·thiazide \ˌklōrə, -lȯrə+\ *n* [*chlor-* + *thiazide*] **:** a thiazide diuretic $C_7H_6ClN_3O_4S_2$ used esp. to treat edema and to increase the effectiveness of antihypertensive drugs

chlo·ro·tri·anis·ene \ˌklōrōˌtrīˈanəˌsēn, ˌklȯr-\ *n* -s [*chlor-* + *tri-* + ²*anis-* + *-ene*] **:** a synthetic compound $C_{23}H_{21}ClO_3$ that is converted to a potent estrogenic substance in the living system and is used esp. orally to treat menopausal symptoms

chlor·prop·amide \-ˈpräpəˌmīd, -prōp-, -ˌməd\ *n* [*chlor-* + *propane* + *amide*] **:** a sulfonylurea compound $C_{10}H_{13}ClN_2O_3S$ used to reduce blood sugar in the treatment of mild diabetes

chlor·thal·i·done \klōrˈthaləˌdōn, klȯr-\ *n* -s [*chlor-* + *thalidone,* fr. ph*thal*imide + ket*one*] **:** a sulfonamide $C_{14}H_{11}ClN_2O_4S$ that is a long-acting diuretic used esp. in the treatment of edema associated with congestive heart failure, renal disease, cirrhosis of the liver, pregnancy, and obesity

choke* *vi* **:** to lose one's composure and fail to perform effectively in a critical situation

cho·le·cyst·agogue \ˌkōləˈsistəˌgäg, ˈkäl-, -ȯg\ *n* -s [*cholecyst* + *-agogue*] **:** an agent (as cholecystokinin) that causes the gallbladder to discharge bile

cho·le·cyst·ec·to·mized \ˌkōlə(ˌ)sisˈtektəˌmīzd, ˌkäl-\ *adj* [*cholecystectomy* + *-ize* + ²*-ed*] **:** having had the gallbladder removed

¹**cho·le·cys·to·kinetic** \ˌkōləˌsistō, ˈkäl-+\ *adj* [*cholecyst* + *-o-* + *kinetic*] **:** tending to cause the gallbladder to contract and discharge bile

²**cholecystokinetic** \"\ *n* -s **:** CHOLECYSTAGOGUE *herein*

cho·le·sta·sis \ˌkōləˈstāsəs, ˌkäl-\ *n, pl* **cholesta·ses** \-āˌsēz\ [NL, fr. *chol-* + *-stasis*] **:** a checking or failure of bile flow — **cho·le·stat·ic** \ˌkōləˈstad·ik, ˈkäl-\ *adj*

cho·le·styr·amine \ˌkōləˈstīrəˌmēn, kōˈlestirəˌmēn\ *n* [perh. *chol-* + *styr-* (alter. of *sterol*) + *amine*] **:** a basic resin that forms insoluble complexes with bile acids and has been used to lower cholesterol levels in hypercholesterolemic patients

cho·li·no·lyt·ic \ˌkōlənōˈlid·ik, ˈkäl-\ *adj* [ISV acetyl*choline* + *-o-* + *-lytic*] **:** interfering with the action of acetylcholine or cholinergic agents — **cholinolytic** *n* -s

cho·li·no·mimetic \"+\ *adj* [ISV acetyl*choline* + *-o-* + *mimetic*] **:** resembling acetylcholine or simulating its physiologic action — **cholinomimetic** *n* -s

cho·li·no·receptor \"+\ *n* [acetyl*choline* + *-o-* + *receptor*] **:** a receptor for acetylcholine in a postsynaptic membrane

chom·skyan *or* **chom·skian** \ˈchäm(p)skēən, -ȯm-, -kyən\ *adj, usu cap* [Avram Noam *Chomsky* b1928 Am. linguist + E *-an*] **:** of, relating to, based on, or being the linguistic theories of Noam Chomsky

chopper* *n* **1 :** a high-bouncing batted baseball **2 :** a customized motorcycle

chop·per \ˈchäpə(r)\ *vb* -ED/-ING/-S [¹*chopper*] **:** HELICOPTER

chop shop *n* **:** a place where stolen automobiles are stripped of salable parts

chor·do·ma \kōrˈdōmə, kȯr-\ *n, pl* **chordomas** *or* **chordoma·ta** \-məd·ə, -ətə\ [noto*chord* + *-oma*] **:** a malignant tumor that is derived from remnants of the embryonic notochord and occurs along the spine attacking esp. the bones at the base of the skull or near the coccyx

chord organ *n* **:** an electronic or reed organ with buttons for producing simple chords

choreograph* *vt* **:** to arrange or direct the movement, progress, or details of ⟨clashes with police, ~*ed* to feed the mass media's hunger for sensation —Irving Howe⟩

choreography* *n* **:** something resembling choreography ⟨a snail-paced ~ of delicate high diplomacy —Wolfgang Saxon⟩

chorion fron·do·sum \-fränˈdōsəm\ *n* [NL, fr. *chorion* + L *frondosum* leafy, fr. *frond-, frons* foliage + *-osum* -ose] **:** the part of the chorion that has persistent villi and that with the attached portions of the endometrium forms the placenta

cho·roi·de·re·mia \ˌkōrˌȯidəˈrēmēə, ˈkȯr-\ *n* -s [¹*choroid* + Gk *erēmia* desolation] **:** progressive degeneration of the choroid that is controlled by a sex-linked gene

christmas tree* *n, usu cap C* **:** a legislative bill under consideration esp. near the end of a session that contains a variety of amendments unrelated to the main purpose of the bill

chromatograph* *n* **:** an instrument for producing chromatograms

chrome* *n* **:** something plated with an alloy of chromium

chro·mo·dynamics \ˌkrōmō+\ *n pl but sing in constr* [*chrom-* + *dynamics*] **:** QUANTUM CHROMODYNAMICS *herein*

chro·no·biology \ˌkränə, ˈkrō-, -nō+\ *n* [*chron-* + *biology*] **:** the study of biological rhythms — **chro·no·bi·ologic** \"+\ *or* **chro·no·biological** \"+\ *adj* — **chro·no·biologist** \"+\ *n*

chryso·phyte \ˈkrisəˌfīt\ *n* -s [*chrys-* + *-phyte*] **:** GOLDEN-BROWN ALGA *herein*

chuffed \ˈchəft\ *adj* [³*chuff* + ¹*-ed*] *Brit* **:** PROUD, SATISFIED

chug·a·lug \ˈchəgəˌləg\ *vb* **chugalugged; chugalugged; chugalugging; chugalugs** [imit.] *vt* **:** to drink a container of (as beer) without pause; *also* **:** to drink quickly or copiously **:** GUZZLE ⟨chain-smoking cigarettes and *chugalugging* tea —Melvin Maddox⟩ ~ *vi* **:** to drink a container (as of beer) without pause

church key *n* **:** an implement with a triangular pointed head at one end for piercing the tops of cans (as of beer) and usu. a rounded head at the other end for removing bottle caps

churn* *vt* **:** to subject (a client's security account) to excessive numbers of purchases and sales primarily to generate additional commissions

churn out *vt* **:** to produce mechanically or copiously **:** grind out ⟨the usual pap which has been *churned out* about this superstar —W.S. Murphy⟩ ⟨computers *churn out* gaudy parlay cards at peak efficiency —Pete Axthelm⟩

chutz·pah *also* **chutz·pa** *or* **hutz·pah** *or* **hutz·pa** \ˈkutspə, ˈhu-, -(ˌ)spä\ *n* -s [Yiddish, fr. LHeb *ḥuṣpāh*] **:** supreme self-confidence **:** NERVE, GALL

chvos·tek's sign \(kə)ˌvȯsˌtek(s)-\ *or* **chvostek sign** \-ˌtek-\ *n, usu cap C* [after Franz *Chvostek* †1884 Austrian surgeon] **:** a twitch of the facial muscles following gentle tapping over the facial nerve in front of the ear that indicates hyperirritability of the facial nerve

chy·lo·mi·cro·ne·mia \ˌkīlōˌmīkrə'nēmēə\ *n* -s [*chylomicron* + *-emia*] **:** an excessive number of chylomicrons in the blood ⟨postprandial ~⟩

chy·lo·thorax \ˈkīlə+\ *n* [*chyl-* + *thorax*] **:** an effusion of chyle or chylous fluid into the thoracic cavity

chy·mo·papain \ˈkīmō+\ *n* [*chyme* + *-o-* + *papain*] **:** a proteolytic enzyme from the latex of the papaya that is used in meat tenderizer and has been used medically in chemonucleolysis

chy·mo·tryp·tic \ˈkīmōˈtriptik\ *adj* [*chymotrypsin* + *-tic* (as in *tryptic*)] **:** of, relating to, produced by, or performed with chymotrypsin ⟨~ peptide mapping⟩

ciao \'chaů\ *interj* [It, fr. It dial., alter. of *schiavo* (I am your) slave, fr. ML *sclavus* slave — more at SLAVE] — used conventionally as an utterance at meeting or parting

ci·gua·tox·in \ˈsēgwəˈtäksən, ˈsig-\ *n* [*ciguatera* + *toxin*] **:** a potent lipid neurotoxin associated with ciguatera that has been found widely in normally edible fish

ci·lan·tro \sə'lantrō, -län-\ *n* -s [Sp, coriander, fr. LL *coliandrum*, alter. of L *coriandrum* — more at CORIANDER] **:** leaves of coriander used as a flavoring or garnish — called also *Chinese parsley*

ci·met·i·dine \sī'med·əˌdēn, -etə-\ *n* -s [*ci-* (alter. of *cyan-*) + *methyl* + *-idine*] **:** a histamine analogue $C_{10}H_{16}N_6S$ that has been used esp. in the short-term treatment of duodenal ulcers

cine·angiocardiography \ˈsinē +\ *n* [*cine-* + *angiocardiography*] **:** motion-picture photography of a fluoroscopic screen recording passage of a contrasting medium through the chambers of the heart and large blood vessels — **cine·angiocardiographic** \"+\ *adj*

cine·angiography \"+\ *n* [*cine-* + *angiography*] **:** motion-picture photography of a fluorescent screen recording passage of a contrasting medium through the blood vessels — **cine·an·gio·graph·ic** \ˈ==ˌanjēəˈgrafik, -ēk\ *adj*

cinema ve·ri·té \ˈsinəməˌverəˈtā, -nāˌmäˌ-\ *n* [F *cinéma-vérité* truth cinema] **:** the art or technique of filming a motion picture (as a documentary) so as to convey candid realism

cine·phile \'sinəˌfīl\ *n* -s [*cine-* + *-phile*] **:** a devotee of motion pictures **:** CINEAST

cin·gu·late gyrus \'siŋgyələt-, -ˌlāt-\ *n* **:** a medial gyrus of each cerebral hemisphere that partly surrounds the corpus callosum

cin·gu·lec·to·my \ˌ=='lektəmē\ *n* -ES [*cingulum* + *-ectomy*] **:** CINGULOTOMY *herein*

cin·gu·lot·o·my \-'läd·əmē, -ätə-\ *n* -ES [*cingulum* + *-o-* + *-tomy*] **:** surgical removal of all or part (as the cingulum) of the cingulate gyrus

CIP *abbr* cataloging in publication

cir·ca·di·an \(ˌ)sər'kādēən, ˈsərkəˈdēən\ *adj* [L *circa* about + *dies* day + E *-an* — more at CIRCA, DEITY] **:** being, having, characterized by, or occurring in approximately 24-hour periods or cycles (as of biological activity or function) ⟨~ oscillations⟩ ⟨~ periodicity⟩ ⟨~ rhythms in activity⟩ ⟨~ leaf movements⟩ — **circadianly** *adv*

circ·an·nu·al \(')sərˈkanyə(wə)l\ *adj* [L *circa* about + E *annual*] **:** having, characterized by, or occurring in approximately yearly periods or cycles (as of biological activity or function) ⟨~ rhythmicity⟩

circle* *n* **:** a residential street that curves and typically loops back on itself — used chiefly in the names of streets

circuit breaker* *n* **:** a provision (as in an insurance contract or tax law) that limits financial obligations beyond a specified amount for covered individuals

circular dichroism *n* **1 :** the property (as of an optically active medium) of unequal absorption of right and left circularly plane-polarized light so that the emergent light is elliptically polarized **2 :** a spectroscopic technique that makes use of circular dichroism

circular file *n* **:** WASTEBASKET

circular polarization *n* **:** polarization in which the mutually perpendicular components of a transverse wave radiation have equal amplitudes but differ in phase by 90 degrees — **circularly polarized** *adj*

cir·cum·planetary \ˈsərkəm +\ *adj* [*circum-* + *planet* + *-ary*] **:** surrounding and relatively close to a planet ⟨~ space⟩

cir·cum·solar \"+\ *adj* [*circum-* + *solar*] **:** revolving about or surrounding the sun

cir·cum·stellar \"+\ *adj* [*circum-* + *stellar*] **:** surrounding or occurring in the vicinity of a star

cir·cum·terrestrial \"+\ *adj* [*circum-* + *terrestrial*] **:** revolving about or surrounding the earth

cir·cus·iana \ˌsərkəsē'äna, -'anə\ *n pl* [*circus* + *-ana*] **:** materials or objects relating to circuses or circus life

cis·lunar \(')sis +\ *adj* [*cis-* + *lunar*] **:** of or relating to the space between the earth and the moon or the moon's orbit

cisterna* *n* **:** one of the interconnected flattened vesicles or tubules comprising the endoplasmic reticulum — **cisternal*** *adj*

cis·tron \'siˌsträn\ *n* -s [*cis-trans* + *-on* (herein)] **:** a segment of DNA which specifies a single functional unit (as a protein or enzyme) and within which two heterozygous and closely linked recessive mutations are expressed in the phenotype when on different homologous chromosomes but not when on the same chromosome — compare OPERON *herein* — **cis·tron·ic** \si'stränik\ *adj*

citizen's arrest *n* **:** an arrest made by a citizen who derives his authority from the fact that he is a citizen

citizens band *n, sometimes cap C & B* **:** a range of radio-wave frequencies that in the U.S. is allocated officially for private radio communications

citrus red mite *n* **:** a comparatively large mite (*Panonychus citri*) that is a destructive pest on the foliage of citrus — called also *citrus red spider*

city·bil·ly \'sid·ēˌbilē, -d·iˌ-, -li\ *n* -ES [*city* + *hillbilly*] **:** a musician or singer brought up in a city who performs country music

clad *n* -s **:** CLADDING

clade \'klād\ *n* -s [Gk *klados* sprout; influenced by *grade*] **:** a group of biological taxa (as species) including organisms descended from a common ancestor

cla·dis·tic \klə'distik, kla'-\ *adj* [*clad-* (fr. Gk *klados* branch) + *-istic*] **:** based on phylogenetic relationships ⟨a ~ system of classification⟩ — compare PHENETIC *herein* — **cla·dis·ti·cal·ly** \-tək(ə)lē\ *adv*

cla·dis·tics \-iks\ *n pl but sing in constr* **:** biological systematics based on phylogenetic relationships — **cla·dist** \'kladəst\ *n* -s

clado·genesis \ˈkladō +\ *n* [NL, fr. Gk *klados* branch + *genesis* — more at GLADIATOR] **:** evolutionary change characterized by treelike branching of lines of descent — compare ANAGENESIS *herein* — **clado·genetic** \"+\ *adj* — **clado·genetically** \"+\ *adv*

clado·gram \'kladəˌgram\ *n* -s [*clad-* + *-gram*] **:** a branching diagrammatic tree used in biological classification to illustrate phylogenetic relationships — compare PHENOGRAM

clam* *n* **1 :** DOLLAR ⟨it cost me seventy-five ~*s,* and I wore it only twice —Ethel Merman⟩ **2 :** a sour note ⟨hit a ~ during the first few bars —Nat Hentoff⟩

clam·digger \ˈ⸗,⸗⸗\ *n* [[5]*clam* + *digger;* fr. the fact that one can wear such a garment while wading without getting it wet] **:** a pant that reaches to mid-calf — usu. used in pl.

clang·er \ˈklaŋə(r)\ *n* -s [[2]*clang* + *-er*] *Brit* **:** a conspicuous blunder — often used in the phrase *drop a clanger*

clapped–out \ˌklapˈdau̇t, -aptˈau̇t\ *adj* [fr. past part. of [1]*clap* + *out*] *Brit* **:** WORN-OUT; *also* **:** TIRED

class* *n* **1 :** a group of adjacent and discrete or continuous values of a random variable **2 :** a mathematical set; *esp* **:** a collection of all the sets having a particular property ⟨the ~ of groups includes all possible mathematical groups⟩ — see CATEGORY *herein*

class action *n* **:** a legal action undertaken by one or more plaintiffs on behalf of themselves and all other persons having an identical interest in the alleged wrong

classical conditioning *n* **:** conditioning in which the conditioned stimulus (as the sound of a bell) is paired with and precedes the unconditioned stimulus (as the sight of food) until the conditioned stimulus alone is sufficient to elicit the response (as salivation in a dog)

clathrate *n* -s [*clathrate,* adj.] **:** a clathrate compound

clath·ra·tion \klaˈthrāshən\ *n* -s [*clathrate* + *-ion*] **:** the process of clathrate formation

claus·tro·phil·ia \ˌklȯstrəˈfilēə\ *n* -s [NL, fr. *claustro-* (fr. L *claustrum* bar, bolt) + *-philia*] **:** an abnormal desire for confinement in an enclosed space

clean* *adj* **1** *slang* **:** smartly dressed **2 :** free from drug addiction **3 :** having no contraband (as drugs) in one's possession

clean* *vb* — **clean one's clock :** to beat or whip one in a fight or competition ⟨she played one of her best matches. . . . She really *cleaned my clock* —Chris Evert Lloyd⟩

clean room \ˈ⸗,⸗\ *n* **:** a room for the manufacture or assembly of objects (as precision parts) that is maintained at a high level of cleanliness by special means

clean up* *vt* — **clean up one's act :** to behave in a more acceptable manner (as by discarding questionable practices)

clear–air turbulence \ˌ⸗ˈ⸗-\ *n* **:** sudden severe turbulence occurring in cloudless regions that causes violent jarring or buffeting of aircraft passing through

clearway \ˈ⸗,⸗\ *n, Brit* **:** FREEWAY

cleaver* *n* **:** a rock ridge protruding from a glacier or snowfield

cleft sentence *n* **:** a sentence that emphasizes one part of a simple sentence (as "Kathy likes cognac") typically by transforming it into two clauses with the noun phrase to be emphasized in the first clause if it begins with *it* (as in "It is cognac that Kathy likes" or "It is Kathy who likes cognac") or following a form of *be* if the first clause begins with *what* (as in "What Kathy likes is cognac")

clem·en·tine \ˈklemən,tēn, -tīn\ *n* [F *clémentine*] **:** a small nearly seedless citrus fruit that is prob. a hybrid between a tangerine and an orange and has a stiff skin and slightly acid pink-tinged flesh

client state *n* **:** a country that is economically, politically, or militarily dependent on another country

clin·da·my·cin \ˌklindəˈmīsᵊn\ *n* -s [chlor- + *lindamycin,* alter. (influenced by *deoxy-*) of *lincomycin* (herein)] **:** a semisynthetic antibacterial antibiotic $C_{18}H_{33}ClN_2O_5S$ chemically related to lincomycin and used esp. against gram-positive organisms

clio* *n* -s *usu cap* **:** any of several statuettes awarded annually by a professional organization for notable achievement in radio and television commercials

clio·met·rics \ˌklīəˈme·triks\ *n pl but sing in constr* [*Clio,* muse of history + *-metric* + [1]*-s*] **:** the application of methods developed in other fields (as economics, statistics, and data processing) to the study of history — **clio·met·ric** \-ik\ *adj* — **clio·met·ri·cian** \-me·ˈtrishən, -mə-\ *n* -s

clip art *n* **:** ready-made illustrations sold in books from which they may be cut and pasted as artwork

clock* *n* **1 :** a synchronizing device (as in a computer) that produces pulses at regular intervals **2 :** BIOLOGICAL CLOCK *herein* — **kill the clock** *or* **run out the clock :** to use up as much as possible of the playing time remaining in a game (as football) while retaining possession of the ball or puck esp. to protect a lead

clock radio *n* **:** a combination clock and radio device in which the clock can be set to turn on the radio at a designated time

clo·fi·brate \klōˈfīb,rāt, -ˈfib-\ *n* -s [perh. fr. *chlor-* + *fibr-* + propion*ate*] **:** a synthetic drug $C_{12}H_{15}ClO_3$ used esp. to lower abnormally high concentrations of fats and cholesterol in the blood

clo·mi·phene \ˈklōmə,fēn\ *n* -s [*chlor-* + *amine* + *-phene* (fr. *phenyl*)] **:** a synthetic drug $C_{26}H_{28}ClNO$ used in the form of its citrate to induce ovulation

clone* *n* **1 :** an individual grown from a single somatic cell of its parent and genetically identical to it **2 :** one that is or appears to be a copy of an original

clone *vb* -ED/-ING/-S *vt* **1 :** to propagate a clone from ⟨frogs have been successfully *cloned* by transplanting nuclei from body cells to enucleated eggs⟩ **2 :** to make a copy of ~ *vi* **:** to produce a clone

clo·ni·dine \ˈklänə,dēn, ˈklōn-, -,dīn\ *n* -s [*chlor-* + *-nidine,* alter. fr. *imidazoline*] **:** an antihypertensive drug $C_9H_9Cl_2N_3$ used to treat essential hypertension and to prevent migraine headache

closed* *adj* **1 :** traced by a moving point that returns to an arbitrary starting point ⟨~ curve⟩; *also* **:** so formed that every plane section is a closed curve ⟨~ surface⟩ **2 a :** containing all the limit points of every subset ⟨a ~ set⟩ **b** *of an interval* **:** containing its endpoints **3 :** characterized by mathematical elements that when subjected to an operation produce only elements of the same set ⟨the set of whole numbers is ~ under addition and multiplication⟩ **4** *of the universe* **:** having enough mass to stop expanding and eventually collapse

closed–captioned \ˈ⸗ˈ⸗⸗\ *adj, of a television program* **:** broadcast so that captions appear only on the screen of a receiver equipped with a decoder

closed loop *n* **:** an automatic control system for an operation or process in which feedback in a closed path or group of paths acts to maintain the output at the desired level

closet* *n* **:** a state or condition of secrecy, privacy, or obscurity ⟨he comes out of the ~ and unabashedly urges socialism — *New Times*⟩

closet* *adj* **:** being so in private **:** SECRET ⟨a ~ racist⟩ ⟨a ~ reader . . . during her years in the limelight as a dancer —John Updike⟩

closet queen *n* **:** one who is a latent or a covert homosexual

closing* *n* **:** a meeting between parties to a real-estate deal usu. together with their attorneys and interested parties (as a mortgagor) for the purpose of formally transferring title

closing costs *n pl* **:** expenses (as for appraisal, title search, and title insurance) connected with the purchase of real estate that usu. constitute a charge against the purchaser additional to the cost of the property purchased

closure* *n* **1 :** the property that a number system or a set has when it is mathematically closed under an operation **2 :** a set that contains all its limit points

clothesline \ˈ=,=\ *vt* **:** to knock down (as a football player) by catching by the neck with an outstretched arm — **clothesline** *n*

clotting factor *n* **:** any of several plasma components (as fibrinogen, prothrombin, and thromboplastin) that are involved in the clotting of blood

cloud nine *n* [perh. so called fr. the ninth and highest heaven of Dante's Paradise, whose inhabitants are most blissful because nearest to God] **:** a state of feeling extreme elation — usu. used with *on* ⟨was on *cloud nine* after his victory⟩

clout* *n* **:** PULL, INFLUENCE ⟨had a lot of ~ with the governor⟩

clo·vis \ˈklōvəs\ *adj, usu cap* [*Clovis,* New Mexico] **:** of or relating to a widely distributed prehistoric culture of No. America characterized by leaf-shaped flint projectile points having fluted sides

clox·a·cil·lin \ˌkläksəˈsilən\ *n* -s [*chl*orophenol + is*ox*-*a*zole + peni*cillin*] **:** a semisynthetic oral penicillin $C_{19}H_{17}ClN_3NaO_5S$ effective esp. against staphylococci because of resistance to their penicillinases

cloze \ˈklōz\ *adj* [by shortening & alter. fr. *closure*] **:** of, relating to, or being a test of reading comprehension that involves having the person being tested supply words which have been systematically deleted from a text

club* *n* **:** a group identified by some common characteristic ⟨the nations in the nuclear ~⟩

clunker* *n* **:** an effort or performance that is notably unsuccessful

clunky \ˈkləŋkē\ *adj* -ER/-EST [*clunk* + *-y*] **:** clumsy in style, form, or execution ⟨a ~ thriller⟩ ⟨~ earrings⟩

cluster* *n* **1 :** a group of buildings and esp. houses built close together on a sizable tract in order to preserve open spaces larger than the individual yard for common recreation **2 :** a group of two or more atoms chiefly of the same usu. metallic element that are bonded together in usu. polyhedral form

cluster college *n* **:** a small residential college constituting a semiautonomous division of a university and usu. specializing in one branch of knowledge (as history and the social sciences)

cluster headache *n* **:** a headache that is characterized by severe unilateral pain in the eye or temple and tends to recur in a series of attacks

clut·ton's joints \ˈklətᵊnz-\ *n pl, usu cap C* [after Henry Hugh *Clutton* †1909 Eng. surgeon] **:** symmetrical hydrarthrosis esp. of the knees or elbows that occurs in congenital syphilis

CMA *abbr* certified medical assistant

CMOS \ˌsēˌemˌōˈes, ˈsēˌmōs\ *n, often attrib* [*c*omplementary *m*etal-*o*xide *s*emiconductor] **:** a technology for making integrated circuits using metal-oxide semiconductor devices in which flip-flops are made up of pairs of two different types of transistor connected in such a way that power is used only when the state is changed

CN* *abbr* chloroacetophenone

co·adapted \ˌkō +\ *adj* [*co-* + *adapted,* past part. of [1]*adapt*] **:** mutually adapted esp. by natural selection ⟨~ gene complexes⟩

co·ag·u·lop·a·thy \(ˌ)kōˌagyəˈläpəthē\ *n* -ES [*coagul*ation + *-o-* + *-pathy*] **:** a disease affecting blood coagulation

coalesce* *vi* **:** to arise from the combination of distinct elements ⟨an organized and a popular resistance immediately *coalesced* —C.C. Menges⟩

co–anchor \(ˈ)kō+\ *n* [*co-* + *anchor* (herein)] **:** a newscaster who shares the duties of anchoring a news broadcast — **co–anchor** \"+\ *vt*

co·an·da effect \kōˈandə-, -än-\ *n, usu cap C* [after Henri *Coanda* †1972 Romanian engineer] **:** the tendency of a jet of fluid emerging from an orifice to follow an adjacent flat or curved surface and to entrain fluid from the surroundings so that a region of lower pressure develops

cobblers \ˈkäblə(r)z\ *n pl* [fr. *cobblers' awls,* rhyming slang for *balls*] *Brit* **:** NONSENSE, BUNK

co·bol \ˈkōˌbȯl\ *n* -s *usu cap C or all cap* [*co*mmon *b*usiness *o*riented *l*anguage] **:** a computer programming language designed for business applications

co·chromatograph \ˌkō +\ *vb* [*co-* + *chromatograph*] *vi* **:** to undergo separation out of a mixed sample by cochromatography ~ *vt* **:** to subject to cochromatography

co·chromatography \"+\ *n* [*co-* + *chromatography*] **:** chromatography of two or more samples together; *esp* **:** identification of an unknown substance by chromatographic comparison with a known substance

cock·a·ma·mie *also* **cock·a·ma·my** \ˈkäkəˌmāmē\ *adj* [prob. alter. of earlier *cockamanie* decal, alter. of *decalcomania*] **:** RIDICULOUS, INCREDIBLE ⟨of all the ~ excuses I ever heard —Leo Rosten⟩

cock·a·poo \ˈkäkəˌpü\ *n* -s [*cocka-,* shortening and alter. of *cocker* spaniel + *poo*dle] **:** a dog that is a cross between a cocker spaniel and a poodle

cocksucker \ˈ=ˌ==\ *n* **:** one who fellates — usu. considered obscene; often used as a generalized term of abuse — **cocksucking** \ˈ=ˈ==\ *adj*

cockteaser \ˈ=ˌ==\ *n* **:** a female who excites a male sexually and then refuses intercourse — usu. considered obscene

co·cultivation \ˌkō+\ *n* [*co-* + *cultivation*] **:** cultivation of two types of cell or tissue in the same medium — **cocultivate** \"+\ *vt*

code* *n* **:** GENETIC CODE *herein*

code* *vi* **:** to specify the genetic code ⟨the DNA sequence of the gene that ~*s* for that protein —Gina B. Kolata⟩

code–switching \ˈ=ˌ==\ *n* **:** the switching from the linguistic system of one language or dialect to that of another

code word* *n* **:** EUPHEMISM ⟨interpreting "compatability" as a *code word* for stifling dissent, the faculty denounced the memorandum —Robert Griffith⟩

co·di·col·o·gy \ˌkōdiˈkäləjē, ˌkäd-\ *n* -ES [L *codic-, codex* book + *-o-* + E *-logy*] **:** the study of manuscripts as cultural artifacts for historical purposes — **co·di·co·log·i·cal** \-ˌkəˈläjikəl\ *adj*

codominant* *adj* **:** being fully expressed in the heterozygous condition

co·don \ˈkōˌdän\ *n* -s [[2]*code* + [2]*-on*] **:** a specific sequence of three consecutive nucleotides that is part of the genetic code and that specifies a particular amino acid in a protein or starts or stops protein synthesis — called also *triplet*

cods·wal·lop \'kädz,wäləp, -wȯl-\ *n* [origin unknown] *chiefly Brit* : NONSENSE, DRIVEL

co·enzymatic \¦kō+\ *adj* [*coenzyme* + *-atic* (as in *enzymatic*)] : of or relating to a coenzyme ⟨~ activity⟩ — **co·enzymatically** \"+\ *adv*

coenzyme Q *n* [*Q* prob. fr. *quinone*] : UBIQUINONE *herein*

coes·ite \'kō,zīt\ *n* -s [Loring *Coes*, Jr., *b*1915 Am. chemist + E *-ite*] : a dense crystalline silica formed from quartz under great heat and pressure and found in meteorite craters

co·evolution \,kō,evə'lüshən, *esp Brit* -,ēv-\ *n* [*co-* + *evolution*] : evolution involving successive changes in two or more ecologically interdependent species (as of a plant and its pollinators) that affect their interactions — **co·evolutionary** \"+\ *adj* — **co·evolve** \"+\ *vi*

coffee lightener *or* **coffee whitener** *n* : a nondairy product used as a substitute for cream in coffee

coffee–table \'=¦=\ *adj* : of, relating to, or being an expensive lavishly illustrated oversize book

co·generation \¦kō+\ *n* [*co-* + *generation*] : the production of electricity using waste heat (as in steam) from an industrial process or the use of steam from electric power generation as a source of heat

cognitive dissonance *n* : psychological conflict resulting from incongruous beliefs and attitudes (as a fondness for smoking and a belief that it is harmful) held simultaneously

coherence* *n* : the property of being coherent

co·he·sion·less \kō'hēzhənləs\ *adj* : composed of particles or granules that tend not to cohere ⟨~ soils⟩

coincident* *or* **coincident indicator** *n* : an economic indicator (as level of personal income or of retail sales) that more often than not correlates directly with the state of the economy

COLA *abbr* cost-of-living adjustment

cold* *adj* : low in energy ⟨~ neutrons⟩

cold call *n* : a telephone call soliciting business made directly to a potential customer without prior contact or without a lead

cold duck *n* [trans. of G *kalte ente*, a drink made of a mixture of fine wines] : a beverage that consists of a blend of sparkling burgundy and champagne

cold weld** *vi* : to adhere on contact without application of pressure or heat — used of metals in the vacuum of outer space

col·i·ci·no·ge·nic \¦käləsənə¦jenik, -,sēn-\ *adj* [*colicin* + *-o-* + *-genic*] **1** : producing or having the capacity to produce colicins ⟨~ bacteria⟩ **2** : conferring the capacity to produce colicins ⟨~ genetic material⟩ — **col·i·ci·no·ge·nic·i·ty** \-nəjə'nis(ə)d·ē\ *n* -ES

col·i·ci·nog·e·ny \,===='näjənē\ *n* -ES [*colicin* + *-o-* + *-geny*] : the capacity to produce colicins

colinear* *adj* : having corresponding parts arranged in the same linear order ⟨good evidence is accumulating that the gene and its polypeptide product are ~ —J.D. Watson⟩ — **co·lin·ear·i·ty** \(,)kō,linē'arəd·ē\ *n* -ES

co·lis·tin \kə'listən, kō-\ *n* -s [NL *colistinus*, specific epithet of the bacterium producing it] : a polymyxin antibiotic produced by a bacterium of the genus *Bacillus* (*B. polymyxa* var. *colistinus*) and used against some gram-negative pathogens esp. of the genera *Pseudomonas, Escherichia*, and *Aerobacter*

collage* *n* : a work (as a film) having disparate scenes in rapid succession without transitions

col·lage \kə'läzh\ *vt* -ED/-ING/-s [*collage*, n.] : to assemble or create a collage from; *also* : to make a collage on

col·la·gen·o·lyt·ic \,käləjənə'lid·ik, -,jen-\ *adj* [*collagen* + *-o-* + *-lytic*] : relating to or having the capacity to break down collagen ⟨~ activity⟩ ⟨~ enzymes⟩

col·lap·sar \kə'lap,sär\ *n* -s [[1]*collapse* + *-ar* (as in *quasar* — herein)] : BLACK HOLE 1 *herein*

collateral ligament *n* : any of various ligaments on one or the other side of a hinge joint (as the knee, elbow, or the joints between the phalanges of the toes and fingers); *esp* : either of two ligaments of the knee that help stabilize it by preventing lateral dislocation

col·lect·ible *or* **col·lect·able** \kə'lektəbəl\ *n* -s [*collectible* or *collectable*, adj.] : an object that is collected by fanciers; *esp* : one other than such traditionally collectible items as art, stamps, coins, and antiques

collegiality* *n* : the participation of bishops in the government of the Roman Catholic Church in collaboration with the pope

col·li·sion·less \kə'lizhənləs\ *adj* : of, relating to, or being a plasma in which particles interact through charge rather than collision ⟨a ~ shock wave⟩

co·lon·ic \(')kō¦länik, kə'l-\ *n* -s [*colonic*, adj.] : irrigation of the colon : ENEMA

co·lon·o·scope \kō'länə,skōp, kə'-\ *n* [[1]*colon* + *-o-* + *-scope*] : a flexible tube containing a fiberscope for visual inspection of the colon and apparatus for taking tissue samples

co·lo·nos·co·py \,kōlə'näskəpē\ *n* -ES [[1]*colon* + *-o-* + *-scopy*] : endoscopic examination of the colon — **co·lon·o·scop·ic** \kō¦länə¦skäpik, kə-\ *adj*

color* *n* : a hypothetical property of quarks that differentiates each type into three forms that are identical in mass, spin, electric charge, and all other measurable quantities but that have distinct roles in the strong interactions that bind quarks together

color–blind* *adj* : not recognizing differences of race; *esp* : free from racial prejudice

color center *n* : a defect in the lattice structure of a usu. transparent crystal that causes light of only one color to be transmitted by the part of the crystal in which the defect is located

color–code \¦=¦=\ *vt* : to color (as wires or pipes) according to a key designed to facilitate identification

co·lo·rec·tal \¦kōlə¦rektᵊl\ *adj* [[1]*colon* + *rectal*] : relating to or affecting the colon and the rectum ⟨~ cancer⟩ ⟨~ surgery⟩

color–field \¦=¦=\ *adj* : of, relating to, or being abstract painting in which color is emphasized and form and surface are correspondingly de-emphasized ⟨*color-field* abstractionists⟩

colorpoint shorthair \'==¦=-\ *n* : any of a breed of domestic cats of Siamese type and coat pattern but occurring in different colors

col·por·rha·phy \käl'pȯrəfē, -ȯr-\ *n* -ES [Gk *kolpos* vagina + *rhaphē* suture] : surgical repair of the vaginal wall

column chromatography *n* : chromatography in which the substances to be separated are absorbed in layers as they pass in solution through a column packed with the absorbing medium (as silica gel or alumina) — compare PAPER CHROMATOGRAPHY *in the Dict*, THIN-LAYER CHROMATOGRAPHY *herein*

COM *abbr* computer-output microfilm; computer-output microfilmer

comb filter *n* **:** a filter that passes only distinctly separated narrow ranges of wavelengths

combinatorial* *adj* **:** of or relating to the arrangement of, operation on, and selection of discrete mathematical elements belonging to finite sets (as the set of possible states making up a digital computer) or making up geometric configurations

combinatorial topology *n* **:** a study that deals with geometric forms based on their decomposition into combinations of the simplest geometric figures

com·bi·na·to·rics \ˌkämbənəˈtōriks, -ȯr- *also* kəmˌbīn-\ *n pl but sing in constr* [*combinatorial* mathemat*ics*] **:** combinatorial mathematics

comb–out* *n* **:** the combing of hair into a desired hairdo

come* *vb* — **come off*** **:** to return to a regular activity after (a particular condition, experience, or performance) ⟨an injury-prone wide receiver *coming off* his only good season in five —D.P. Anderson⟩ —**come to :** to be a question of ⟨when it *comes to* pitching horseshoes, I'm the champ⟩

come* *n* **1 :** ORGASM — usu. considered vulgar **2 :** SEMEN — usu. considered vulgar

come·back·er \ˈkəmˌbakə(r)\ *n* -s [*come back* + *-er*] **:** a grounder in baseball hit directly to the pitcher

come down* *vi* **:** to recover from the effects of drugs or alcohol

come on* *vi* **1 :** to project an indicated personal image ⟨*comes on* gruff and laconic . . . on the telephone — Robert Craft⟩ **2 :** to show sexual interest in someone; *also* **:** to make sexual advances — usu. used with *to* or *with* ⟨didn't get the feeling that [she] was interested in him or that he was *coming on* strong to her —Ellen J. Willis⟩ ⟨in his own inept way was trying to *come on* to her —*East Village Other*⟩ **3** \ˈ=ˈ=\ — used to express astonishment, incredulity, or recognition of an obvious put-on

come out* *vi* **:** to openly declare one's homosexuality

come up* *vi* **:** to turn out to be ⟨the coin *came up* heads⟩ — **come up roses :** to turn out far better than expected

comix \ˈkämiks\ *n pl* [by alter.] **:** comic books or comic strips

command* *n* **1 :** an electrical or electronic signal that actuates a device (as a control mechanism in a spacecraft or one step in a computer) **2 :** the activation of a device in or the control of a vehicle (as a spacecraft) by means of a command

command module *n* **:** a space vehicle module designed to carry the crew, the chief communication equipment, and the equipment for reentry

commentator* *n* **:** a layman who leads a congregation in prayer at Mass or explains the rituals performed by the priest

common market *n* **:** an economic association (as of nations) formed to remove trade barriers among members

common si·tus picketing \-ˈsīd·əs-\ *n* [fr. L *situs* site] **:** picketing of an entire construction site by a trade union having a grievance with only a single subcontractor working at the site — compare SECONDARY BOYCOTT *in the Dict*

common trust fund *n* **:** a fund which is managed by a bank or trust company and in which the assets of many small trusts are handled as a single portfolio with individual beneficiaries receiving returns proportionate to their share of the principal

communication theory *also* **communications theory** *n* **:** a theory that deals with the technology of the transmission of information (as in the printed word or a computer) between men or men and machines or machines and machines

community antenna television *n* **:** CABLE TELEVISION *herein*

com·mu·ta·tiv·i·ty \kəˌmyüd·əˈtivəd·ē, ˌkämyəd·əˈti-\ *n* -ES [*commutative* + *-ity*] **:** the property of being commutative ⟨the ~ of a mathematical operation⟩

commutator* *n* **:** an element of a mathematical group that when used to multiply the product of two given elements either on the right side or on the left side but not necessarily on both sides yields the product of the two given elements in reverse order ⟨$c = a^{-1}b^{-1}ab$ is a right ~ of *ba* because $bac = ab$⟩

commute* *vi* **:** to yield the same result regardless of order — used of two mathematical elements undergoing an operation or of two operations on elements

com·mute \kəˈmyüt\ *n* -s [*commute*, v.] **1 :** an act or instance of commuting ⟨his usual morning ~ to work —*Newsweek*⟩ **2 :** the distance covered in commuting ⟨about an hour's ~ from the university —*College Composition & Communication*⟩

¹comp \ˈkämp, ˈkəmp\ *vi* [short for *accompany*] **:** to play an irregular rhythmic chord accompaniment for jazz

²comp \ˈkämp\ *n* -s [by shortening] **:** a complimentary ticket; *broadly* **:** something provided free of charge ⟨flying them here free on charters and supplying them with other ~*s* — a room, meals and liquor — Hal Lancaster⟩

compact* *adj* **:** being a topological space (as a metric space) with the property that for any collection of open sets which contains it there is a subset of the collection with a finite number of elements which also contains it — **com·pact·ness*** *n*

compact disc *n* **:** a small plastic optical disc usu. containing recorded music — abbr. *CD*

com·pact·ible \kəmˈpaktəbəl\ *adj* [²*compact* + *-ible*] **:** capable of being compacted ⟨~ soils⟩ — **com·pac·ti·bil·i·ty** \-ˌpaktəˈbiləd·ē, -ətē\ *n* -ES

comparative advertising *n* **:** advertising in which a competitor's product is named and compared with the advertiser's product

comparison shop *vi* **:** to compare prices of competing brands or competing dealers or stores in order to find the best value

compensatory education *n* **:** educational programs intended to make up for cultural experiences or educational stimulation lacked by disadvantaged children

competence* *n* **1 :** readiness of bacteria to undergo genetic transformation **2 :** the knowledge which enables a person to speak and understand a language — compare PERFORMANCE

competent* *adj* **:** having the capacity to respond (as by producing an antibody) to an antigenic determinant ⟨immunologically ~ cells⟩

competitive* *adj* **:** being or causing inhibition of an enzyme in which an analogue of the substrate inhibits the activity of the enzyme by binding to its active site and which increases in effectiveness with increased concentration of the analogue ⟨~ enzymatic inhibition⟩ ⟨~ inhibitor⟩

competitive exclusion *or* **competitive exclusion principle** *n* **:** a generalization in ecology: two species cannot coexist in the same ecological niche for very long without one becoming extinct or being driven out because of competition for limited resources

compile* *vt* **:** to run (as a program) through a compiler

compiler* *n* **:** a computer program that translates an entire set of instructions written in a higher-level language (as Fortran) into machine language so that the instructions can be executed

complement* *n* **:** the set of all elements that do not belong to a given set and are contained in a particular mathematical set containing the given set

complementarity* *n* **:** the correspondence between complementary strands or nucleotides of DNA or sometimes RNA that permits their precise pairing

complementary* *adj* **:** characterized by molecular complementarity; *esp* **:** characterized by the capacity for precise pairing of purine and pyrimidine bases between strands of DNA and sometimes RNA such that the structure of one strand determines the other

complementary DNA *n* **:** CDNA *herein*

complementation* *n* **1 :** the determination of the complement of a given mathematical set **2 :** production of normal phenotype in an individual heterozygous for two closely related mutations with one on each homologous chromosome and at a slightly different position

complete* *adj* **1** *of insect metamorphosis* **:** having a pupal stage intercalated between the motile immature stages and the adult — compare INCOMPLETE *herein* **2** *of a metric space* **:** having the property that every Cauchy sequence of elements converges to a limit in the space

complex* *adj* **:** of, concerned with, being, or containing complex numbers ⟨a ~ root⟩ ⟨~ analysis⟩

complex conjugate *n* **1 :** CONJUGATE COMPLEX NUMBER **2 :** a matrix whose elements and the corresponding elements of a given matrix form pairs of conjugate complex numbers

com·plex·o·met·ric \kəm,pleksə'me·trik, (,)käm-\ *adj* [¹*complex* + *-o-* + *-metric*] **:** of, relating to, or being a titration in which a complexing agent (as EDTA) is used as the titrant — **com·plex·om·e·try** \,käm,plek'sämətrē, kəm-\ *n* -ES

com·plic·it \(,)kəm'plisə̇t\ *adj* [back-formation fr. *complicity*] **:** having complicity ⟨who, having abjured killing in revulsion against the war, finds himself guiltily ~ in it in the revolution —C. E. Schorske⟩

com·plic·i·tous \(,)kəm'plisə̇d·əs, -ətəs\ *adj* [*complicit* + *-ous*] **:** COMPLICIT *herein*

component* *n* **:** a coordinate of a vector; *also* **:** either member of an ordered pair of numbers

com·po·nent·ry \kəm'pōnən·trē, käm-\ *n* -ES **:** the parts that make up a system or device

composite* *adj, of a statistical hypothesis* **:** specifying a range of values for one or more statistical parameters — compare SIMPLE *herein*

composite function *also* **composite*** *n* **:** a function whose values are found from two given functions by applying one function to an independent variable and then applying the second function to the result and whose domain consists of those values of the independent variable for which the result yielded by the first function lies in the domain of the second

composition* *n* **:** the operation of forming a composite function; *also* **:** COMPOSITE FUNCTION *herein*

computation* *n* **:** the use or operation of a computer

computational linguistics *n pl but usu sing in constr* **:** linguistic research carried out by means of a computer

compute* *vt* **:** to determine or calculate by means of a computer ~ *vi* **:** to use a computer

computed tomography *or* **computerized tomography** *also* **computed axial tomography** *or* **computerized axial tomography** *n* **:** radiography in which a three-dimensional image of a body structure is constructed by computer from a series of plane cross-sectional images made along an axis

com·put·er·ese \kəm¦pyüd·ə¦rēz, -ütə-, -ēs\ *n* -s [*computer* + *-ese*] **1 :** a language designed to be used with or by a computer **2 :** jargon used by computer experts

computerise *Brit var of* COMPUTERIZE *herein*

com·put·er·ist \kəm'pyüd·ərə̇st, -ütə-\ *n* -s **:** a person who uses or operates a computer

com·put·er·ize \kəm'pyüd·ə,rīz, -ütə-\ *vb* -ED/-ING/-s [*computer* + *-ize*] *vt* **1 :** to carry out, control, or produce by means of a computer ⟨*computerized* typesetting⟩ ⟨*computerized* music⟩ **2 :** to equip with computers **3 a :** to store in a computer ⟨will soon ~ all available information on the buyers and sellers of property — Ward Morehouse III⟩ **b :** to put into a form that a computer can use ~ *vi* **:** to use computers — **com·put·er·iz·able** \-¦pyüd·ə¦rīzəbəl\ *adj* — **com·put·er·iza·tion** \-,pyüd·ərə̇'zāshən, -,rī'z-\ *n* -s

com·put·er·ized \=ˈ==,rīzd\ *adj* **:** run or produced as if by computer — used as a generalized term of disapproval ⟨arguments against ~ America with its ~ language — T.L. Gross⟩

computerlike \=¦==,=\ *adj* **:** resembling or characteristic of a computer

com·put·er·nik \=ˈ==,nik\ *n* -s [*computer* + *-nik* (herein)] **:** a person who works with or has a deep interest in computers

Com·sat \'käm,sat\ *service mark* — used for communications services involving an artificial satellite

com·symp \'käm,simp\ *n* -s *often cap* [¹*com*munist + *symp*athizer] **:** a person who sympathizes with communist causes — usu. used disparagingly

conative* *adj* **:** of or relating to the function of a message to influence the one receiving it — **conatively** *adv*

concave* *n* **:** a concave line or surface

conceptual* *adj* **:** of, relating to, or being conceptual art

conceptual art *n* **:** an art form in which the artist's intent is to convey a concept rather than to create an art object — **conceptual artist** *n*

con·clu·so·ry \kən'klüs(ə)rē, -üz(-\ *adj* **:** relating to, based on, or consisting of a conclusion (sense 8) ⟨we agree plaintiff's petition is ~ and does not adequately state the factual basis for its assertion —*Lavergne v. Western Company of North America*⟩

con·cord \kən'kȯ(ə)rd, kän-\ *vt* -ED/-ING/-s [back-formation fr. *concordance*] **:** to prepare a concordance of

concrete* *adj* **:** of or relating to concrete poetry ⟨~ poet⟩

concrete* *n* **1 :** CONCRETE POETRY *herein* **2 :** a concrete poet

concrete jungle *n* **:** ASPHALT JUNGLE *herein*

concrete poetry *n* **:** poetry in which the poet's intent is conveyed by the graphic patterns of letters, words, or symbols rather than by the conventional arrangement of words

concretism* *n* -s **:** the theory or practice of concrete poetry — **con·cret·ist** \-ēd·ə̇st, -ētə̇-\ *n* -s

conditional* *adj* **1 :** involving or yielding values that are conditional probabilities ⟨a ~ distribution⟩ **2 :** eliciting a conditional response ⟨a ~ stimulus⟩ **3 :** permitting survival only under special growth or environmental conditions ⟨~ lethal mutations⟩

conditional probability *n* **:** the probability that a given event will occur if it is certain that another event has taken place or will take place

conditioned* *adj* **:** CONDITIONAL 2 *herein*

con·do \ˈkän(ˌ)dō\ *n* -s [by shortening] **:** CONDOMINIUM

conduction band *n* **:** the range of permissible energy values that allow an electron of an atom to dissociate from the atom and become a free charge carrier — compare VALENCE BAND *herein*

conference call *n* **:** a telephone call by which a caller can speak to several people at the same time

confessional* *adj* **:** of, relating to, or being intimately autobiographical writing or fiction ⟨~ books⟩ ⟨~ journalism⟩

configuration* *n* **:** something (as a figure, contour, pattern, or apparatus) that results from a particular arrangement of parts or components; *esp* **:** a set of interconnected equipment forming a computer system

configure* *vt* **:** to set up for operation or use esp. in a particular way

conflagration* *n* **:** something like a large disastrous fire; *esp* **:** WAR

con·for·ma·tion·al \ˌkän(ˌ)fȯ(r)ˈmāshnəl, -ˌfə(r)-, -shənᵊl\ *adj* [*conformation* + [1]*-al*] **:** of, relating to, or being molecular conformation ⟨~ changes in proteins⟩ — **con·for·ma·tion·al·ly** \-lē, -li\ *adv*

cong \ˈkäŋ, ˈkȯŋ\ *n, pl* **cong** *usu cap* [by shortening] **:** VIETCONG

conglomerate* *n* **:** a widely diversified company; *esp* **:** a corporation that acquires other companies whose activities are unrelated to the corporation's primary activity

con·glom·er·a·tor \kənˈglämə̦rād·ə(r)\ *n* -s [*conglomerate* (herein) + [1]*-or*] **:** one who forms or heads a conglomerate

congruence* *n* **:** a statement that two numbers, mathematical expressions (as polynomials), or geometric figures are congruent

congruent* *adj* **:** related in such a way that the difference is divisible by a given modulus ⟨12 is ~ to 2 (modulo 5) since 12 − 2 = 2·5⟩

conjugate* *adj* **:** relating to or being conjugate complex numbers ⟨complex roots occurring in ~ pairs⟩

conjugate* *n* **1 :** CONJUGATE COMPLEX NUMBER **2 :** an element of a mathematical group that is equal to a given element of the group multiplied on the right by another element and on the left by the inverse of the latter element

conjugation* *n* **:** the one-way transfer of DNA between bacteria in cellular contact

conk \ˈkäŋk, ˈkȯŋk\ *vt* -ED/-ING/-s [prob. by shortening and alter. fr. *congolene,* a preparation for straightening hair, prob. fr. *congolene,* a hydrocarbon produced from Congo copal, fr. *Congolese* + *-ene*] **:** to treat (as kinky hair) so as to straighten — **conk** *n* -s

connected* *adj, of a set* **:** having the property that any two of its points can be joined by a line completely contained in the set; *also* **:** incapable of being separated into two or more closed disjoint subsets — **con·nect·ed·ness*** *n*

consciousness–raising \ˈ==ˌ==\ *n* **:** an increasing of concerned awareness esp. of some social or political issue

conservation of angular momentum : a principle in physics: the total angular momentum of a system free of external torque remains constant irrespective of transformations and interactions within the system

conservation of baryons : a principle in physics: the number of baryons in an isolated system of elementary particles remains constant irrespective of transformations or decays

conservation of charge : a principle in physics: the total electric charge of an isolated system remains constant irrespective of whatever internal changes may take place

conservation of leptons : a principle in physics: the number of leptons in an isolated system of elementary particles remains constant irrespective of transformations or decays

conserve* *vt* **:** to maintain (a quantity) constant during a process of chemical, physical, or evolutionary change ⟨~ angular momentum⟩ ⟨a DNA sequence that has been *conserved*⟩

consistent* *adj* **:** tending to be arbitrarily close to the true value of the parameter estimated as the sample becomes large ⟨a ~ statistical estimator⟩ — **consistency*** *n*

console* *n* **1 :** a small storage cabinet between bucket seats in an automobile **2 :** the part of a computer used for communication between the operator and the computer

consolidation* *n* **:** a period of backing and filling in a security or commodity market usu. following a strong run-up of prices and typically preceding a further active advance

con·sta·tive \kənˈstād·iv, ˈkänstəd·iv\ *adj* [*constate* + *-ive*] **:** making an assertion and thus capable of being judged as to truth ⟨~ utterance⟩ — **constative** *n* -s

constituent structure *n* **:** a formal representation of the grammatical structure of a sentence in terms of its individual constituents; *also* **:** the structure which such a representation describes

constitutive* *adj* **1 a :** of, relating to, or being an enzyme or protein produced in relatively constant amounts in all cells of an organism without regard to cell environmental conditions (as the concentration of a substrate) **b :** controlling production of or coding genetic information for a constitutive enzyme or protein ⟨~ genes⟩ ⟨~ mutations⟩ **2 :** being chromatin of a chromosomal region that is condensed into heterochromatin in all cells of an organism rather than just some — **constitutively*** *adv*

con·sul·tan·cy \kənˈsəltənsē\ *n* -ES [*consultant* + *-cy*] **1 :** CONSULTATION **2 :** an agency that provides consulting services **3 :** the position of a consultant

consumer* *n* **:** an organism requiring complex organic compounds for food which it obtains by preying on other organisms or by eating particles of organic matter — compare PRODUCER *herein*

con·sum·er·ism \kənˈsümə̦rizəm\ *n* -s [*consumer* + *-ism*] **1 :** the promotion of the consumer's interests **2 :** the theory that an increasing consumption of goods is economically desirable; *also* **:** a preoccupation with and an inclination toward the buying of consumer goods — **con·sum·er·ist** \-ˌrəst\ *n* -s

consummatory* *adj* **:** of, relating to, or being a response or act (as eating or copulating) that terminates a period of usu. goal-directed behavior

contact inhibition *n* **:** cessation of cellular undulating movements upon contact with other cells with accompanying cessation of cell growth and division

con·tain·er·iza·tion \kən̦tānərəˈzāshən, -̦rīˈz-\ *n* -s [*containerize* (herein) + *-ation*] **:** a method of shipping whereby a considerable amount of material (as merchandise) is packed in large containers for more efficient handling

con·tain·er·ize \kən'tānə,rīz\ *vt* -ED/-ING/-S [*container* + *-ize*] **1** : to ship by containerization ⟨*containerized* freight⟩ **2** : to pack in containers

containerport \=ˈ==,=\ *n* [*container* + *port*] : a shipping port specially equipped to handle containerized cargo

containership \=ˈ==,=\ *n* [*container* + [1]*ship*] : a ship esp. designed or equipped for carrying containerized cargo

con·tex·tu·al·ize \kən'teksch(wə),līz, kän-\ *vt* -ED/-ING/-S [*contextual* + *-ize*] : to place (as a word or activity) in a context — **con·tex·tu·al·iza·tion** \=,==(=)lə'zāshən, -,lī'-\ *n*

continental* *n* : a person born on the mainland of the United States and living in Puerto Rico or the Virgin Islands

continental seating *n, often cap C* : theater seating with no center aisle and with room enough between rows to allow easy passage

continuing education *n* : formal courses of study for part-time students : ADULT EDUCATION

continuous creation theory *n* : STEADY STATE THEORY *herein*

continuous–tone *adj* : of or relating to artwork (as a photograph) that consists of varying shades of gray — see HALFTONE *in the Dict*

continuum* *n* : a compact set which cannot be separated into two sets neither of which contains a limit point of the other ⟨any closed interval of the real numbers is a ~⟩

con·toid \'kän·,toid\ *n* -s [*consonant* + *-oid*] : a speech sound of a phonetic rather than phonemic classification that includes most sounds traditionally treated as consonants and that excludes those (as English \y\, \w\, \r\, and \h\) which like vowels are characterized by the escape of air from the mouth over the center of the tongue without oral friction — compare VOCOID *in the Dict*

contract* *n* : an arrangement whereby an assassin is paid to murder a particular person ⟨the mob put out a ~ on the man's life — Patricia Burstein⟩

con·tra·cyclical \¦kän·trə+\ *adj* [*contra-* + *cyclical*] : being or acting in opposition to an economic cycle ⟨~ fiscal policies⟩

con·trar·i·an \kən·'trerēən, (,)kän-\ *n* [*contrary* + [1]*-an*] : a person who buys shares of stock when most other investors are selling and sells when they are buying

con·tra·test \¦==,=\ *adj* [*contra-* + *test*] : of, relating to, or serving as an experimental control

con·tre·fi·let \kōⁿ·trəfēlā; ¦kōn·trəfə¦lā, ¦kän-, -'fi(,)lā\ *n* [F] : CLUB STEAK

control chart *n* : QUALITY CONTROL CHART

controlled* *adj* : regulated by law with regard to possession and use ⟨marijuana and cocaine are ~ substances⟩ ⟨~ drugs⟩

conus med·ul·lar·is \-,medyù'lerəs, -,mejə'-\ *n* [NL, lit., cone situated in the pith] : a tapering lower part of the spinal cord at the level of the first lumbar segment

convection oven *n* : an oven having a fan that circulates hot air uniformly and continuously around food

convenience *adj* : designed for quick and easy preparation or use ⟨~ food⟩

convenience store *n* : a small often franchised market that is open long hours

conventional* *adj* : not making use of nuclear weapons ⟨~ warfare⟩

convergent lady beetle *also* **convergent** *n* -s [so called fr. the two converging white lines on its prothorax] : a periodically migratory beneficial lady beetle (*Hippodamia convergens*) that feeds on various crop pests (as aphids)

conversation* *n* : an exchange similar to conversation; *esp* : real-time interaction with a computer esp. through a keyboard

conversation pit *n* : a usu. sunken area (as in a living room) with intimate seating that facilitates conversation

converse* *vi* : to carry on an exchange similar to a conversation; *esp* : to interact with a computer

converter* *n* : a device that accepts data in one form and changes it to another ⟨analog-digital ~⟩

convex* *adj* **1** : being a continuous function or part of a continuous function with the property that a line joining any two points on its graph lies on or above the graph **2 a** *of a set of points* : containing all points in a line joining any two constituent points **b** *of a geometric figure* : comprising a convex set when combined with its interior ⟨a ~ polygon⟩

convolution* *n* : a function $h(y)$ that for two given functions f and g is given by

$$h(y) = \int_a^b f(y-x)\, g(x)\, dx$$

where in various applications (as in finding the probability density function of the sum of two independent and continuous random variables) the lower limit of integration is taken as $-\infty$ or O and the upper limit is taken as $+\infty$ or the variable y — called also *convolution integral*

cook* *vi* [[2]*cook*] **1** : to play music extremely well and entertainingly; *specif* : SWING 4b **2** : to go or do well : proceed successfully ⟨the party is ~*ing*⟩

cookbook* *n* : a book of detailed instructions

cooker* *n* : a small and often makeshift container (as a bottlecap) in which a drug (as heroin) is heated and dissolved in water

cooking top *n* : a built-in cabinet-top cooking apparatus consisting usu. of four heating units for gas or electricity

cook–off \'=,=\ *n* -s [[1]*cook* + *off*] : an organized cooking competition

cooktop \'=,=\ *n* [[2]*cook* + *top*] **1** : the flat top of a range **2** : COOKING TOP *herein*

cool* *adj* : employing understatement and a minimum of detail to convey information and usu. requiring the listener, viewer, or reader to complete the message ⟨another indication of the very ~ . . . character of this medium — H.M. McLuhan⟩

cool* *vb* — **cool it** : to keep or regain control of one's emotions

cooldown \'=,=\ *n* [fr. *cool down*, vb.] : a reduction in temperature esp. to cryogenic temperatures

coombs'test \¦kümz-\ *n, usu cap C* [after R. R. A. *Coombs* *b*1921 Brit. immunologist] : an agglutination test used to detect proteins and esp. antibodies on the surface of red blood cells

coon·ass \'kün,as\ *n, sometimes cap* [[1]*coon* (Negro) + [2]*-ass* (herein); perh. fr.the Cajuns' energetic work habits when newly hired on Louisiana oil fields] *chiefly in Louisiana* : ACADIAN 2a — often used disparagingly

cooper pair \'küpər-\ *n, usu cap C* [after Leon H. *Cooper* *b*1930 Am. physicist] : a pair of electrons in a superconductor that are attractively bound and have equal and opposite momentum and spin

co–opt* *vt* : to take in and make part of a group, movement, or culture : ABSORB ⟨the students are *co-opted* by a system they serve even in their struggle against it —A.C. Danto〉; *also* **:** to take over **:** APPROPRIATE 〈many people now view television as a kind of virus, *co-opting* the healthy brain cells of our young —Robert Pattison〉

co–optation* *n* **:** the act or action or an instance of co-opting

coordinate* *adj* **:** of, relating to, or being a system of indexing by two or more terms so that documents may be retrieved through the intersection of index terms

coordinate* *n* **coordinates** *pl* **:** articles (as of clothing or furniture) designed to be used together and to attain their effect through pleasing contrast (as of color, material, or texture)

cop out* *vi* **:** to back out (as of an unwanted responsibility) **:** EVADE — often used with *on* or *of* 〈young Americans who *cop out* on society —*Christian Science Monitor*〉 〈*copping out* of jury duty through a variety of machinations —H.F. Waters〉

cop–out \ˈ=,=\ *n* -s **1 :** an excuse for copping out **:** PRETEXT **2 :** the means for copping out **3 :** one who cops out **4 :** the act or an instance of copping out

copperware \ˈ==,=\ *n* [²*copper* + *ware*] **:** articles made of copper

cop·ro·antibody \ˌkäprō+\ *n* [*copr-* + *antibody*] **:** an antibody whose presence in the intestinal tract can be demonstrated by examination of an extract of the feces

co·processor \ˌkō+\ *n* [*co-* + *processor*] **:** an extra processor in a computer that is designed to perform specialized tasks (as input/output functions or mathematical calculations)

copy* *n* **— a copy** *also* **per copy :** APIECE 〈tickets selling for $15 *a copy*〉

coq au vin \ˌkōkōˈvaⁿ, ˌkäk-, ˌkōk-, -kȯˈv-, *F* kȯkōvaⁿ\ *n* [F, cock with wine] **:** chicken cooked in usu. red wine

coquille saint jacques \-saⁿˈzhäk\ *n, pl* **coquilles saint jacques** *usu cap S&J* [fr. *Saint Jacques* St. James the apostle, whose identifying token is a scallop shell] **:** a dish of scallops usu. served with a wine sauce

cor·al·ene \ˈkȯrəˌlēn, ˈkär-\ *n* -s [irreg. fr. ¹*coral*] **1 :** a raised decoration of glass beading on glassware **2 :** glassware with coralene decoration

cord blood *n* **:** blood from the umbilical cord of a fetus or newborn

cord·less \ˈkȯ(ə)rdləs, -ȯ(ə)d-\ *adj* [¹*cord* + *-less*] **:** having no cord; *esp* **:** powered by a battery 〈~ tools〉

cordon bleu* *adj, often cap C&B* **1 a :** of, relating to, or being a cook of great skill **b :** of, relating to, or being the food prepared by such a cook **2 :** stuffed with ham and Swiss cheese 〈veal *cordon bleu*〉

cor·dy·cep·in \ˌkȯ(r)dəˈsepən\ *n* -s [*cordyceps* + *-in*] **:** an adenosine analogue $C_{10}H_{13}N_5O_3$ with antibiotic activity used esp. to study gene regulation because of its ability to inhibit transcription

core* *n* **1 :** a tiny doughnut-shaped piece of magnetic material (as ferrite) used in computer memories — called also *magnetic core* **2** *or* **core memory** *or* **core storage :** a computer memory consisting of an array of cores strung on fine wires; *broadly* **:** the internal memory of a computer

co·repressor \ˌkō +\ *n* [*co-* + *repressor* (herein)] **:** a substance that activates a particular genetic repressor by combining with it

corn chip *n* **:** a piece of a crisp dry snack food prepared from a seasoned cornmeal batter

cor·neo·scleral \ˌkȯ(r)nē(ˌ)ō+\ *adj* [*cornea* + *-o-* + *scleral*] **:** of, relating to, or affecting both the cornea and the sclera 〈posterior to the ~ junction〉

corner* *adj* **:** of, relating to, or being a defensive football player who covers one of the flanks 〈~ linebacker〉 〈~ positions〉

cornerback \ˈ==,=\ *n* [*corner* (herein) + ¹*back*] **:** a defensive back in football whose duties include defending the flank and covering a wide receiver

cor·ner·man \ˈ==,man\ *n, pl* **cornermen** [*corner* + *man*] **:** one that is in a corner: as **a :** CORNERBACK *herein* **b :** a basketball forward **c :** a boxer's second

corn–fed* *adj* **:** CORNY

cornhole \ˈ=,=\ *vt* [¹*corn* + *hole;* perh. fr. the practice of using corncobs in place of modern toilet paper] **:** to perform anal intercourse with **:** BUGGER — usu. considered vulgar

cor·ni·chon \kȯrnēshōⁿ\ *n* -s [F, gherkin] **:** a sour gherkin usu. flavored with tarragon

cornish rex *n, usu cap C* **:** any of a breed of rex cats with a short plushy coat that curls esp. on the back and tail and a face that is straight in profile

cornrow \ˈ=,=\ *vt* [¹*corn* + *row;* fr. the fancied resemblance of the braids to rows of corn] **:** to style (hair) by dividing into sections that are braided usu. flat to the scalp in rows — **cornrow** *n*

co·ro·na·virus \kəˌrōnə+\ *n* [*corona* + *virus,* fr. their shape as seen under an electron microscope] **:** any of a group of viruses that resemble myxoviruses, have widely spaced club-shaped projections, and include some causing respiratory symptoms in man

co·rotate \(ˈ)kō +\ *vi* [*co-* + *rotate*] **:** to rotate in conjunction with or at the same rate as another rotating body — **co·rotation** \ˌkō +\ *n*

cor·pus al·la·tum \ˌkȯrpəsəˈlād·əm, -äd-\ *n, pl* **corpo·ra al·la·ta** \ˌkȯrpərə·əˈlād·ə, -äd-\ [NL, lit., applied body] **:** one of a pair of separate or fused bodies in many insects that are sometimes closely associated with the corpora cardiaca and secrete hormones (as juvenile hormone)

corpus car·di·a·cum \-pəskärˈdīəkəm\ *n, pl* **cor·po·ra car·di·a·ca** \-pərəkärˈdīəkə\ [NL, lit., cardiac body] **:** one of a pair of separate or fused bodies of nervous tissue in many insects that lie posterior to the brain and dorsal to the esophagus and function in the storage and secretion of brain hormone

corpus spon·gi·o·sum \-ˌspənjēˈōsəm, -ˌspän-\ *n* [NL, lit., spongy body] **:** the median longitudinal column of erectile tissue of the penis that contains the urethra and is ventral to the two corpora cavernosa

correction fluid *n* **:** a liquid used to paint over typing errors

corresponding angles *n pl* **:** any pair of angles each of which is on the same side of one of two lines cut by a transversal and on the same side of the transversal

corticotropin–releasing factor *n* **:** a substance secreted by the median eminence of the hypothalamus that regulates the release of ACTH by the anterior lobe of the pituitary gland

co–script \ˈkō+ˌ\ *vt* [*co-* + *script*] **:** to collaborate in the preparation of a script for

co·set \ˈkōˌset\ *n* [*co-* + *set*] **:** any of the subsets of a mathematical group of which each consists of all the products obtained by multiplying one of the elements of the group on the right side by each of the elements of the subgroup or of the products obtained by such multiplication on the left and which partition the group into subsets of which any two are either identical or disjoint

cosmetic* *adj* **:** lacking in depth or thoroughness **:** SUPERFICIAL

cos·met·i·cize \käz'med·ə,sīz\ *vt* -ED/-ING/-S [²*cosmetic* + *-ize*] **:** to make (something unpleasant or ugly) superficially attractive

cos·mo·drome \'käzmə,drōm\ *n* -s [Russ *Kosmodrom,* fr. *Kosmo*navt cosmonaut + *-drom* ¹-drome] **:** a Soviet aerospace center; *esp* **:** a Soviet spacecraft launching installation

cos·mo·gen·ic \¦käzmə¦jenik\ *adj* [*cos*mic (*ray*) + *-o-* + *-genic*] **:** produced by the action of cosmic rays ⟨~ carbon 14⟩

cos·mo·nau·tics \,käzmə'nȯd·iks, -näd-\ *n pl but usu sing in constr* [*cosmonaut* + *-ics*] **:** ASTRONAUTICS — **cos·mo·nau·tic** \-d·ik\ *or* **cos·mo·nau·ti·cal** \-d·ə̇kəl\ *adj*

cossack hat *n* **:** an oblong visorless folding cap usu. made of fur or imitation fur

cost–benefit \¦=¦===\ *adj* **:** of, relating to, being, or resembling economic analysis that assigns a numerical value to the cost-effectiveness of an operation, procedure, or program

cost–effective \¦==¦==\ *adj* **:** economical in terms of tangible benefits produced by money spent — **cost–effectiveness** *n*

cost–push \'=¦=\ *n* **:** an increase or upward trend in production costs (as wages) that tends to result in increased consumer prices irrespective of the level of demand — compare DEMAND-PULL *herein* — **cost–push** *adj*

cot death *n, chiefly Brit* **:** SUDDEN INFANT DEATH SYNDROME *herein*

co·te·chi·no \,kōd·ā'kē(,)nō\ *n* -s [It] **:** a smoked and dried pork sausage

co·terminal \(ˈ)kō +\ *adj* [*co-* + *terminal*] **:** having different angular measure but with the vertex and sides identical — used of angles generated by the rotation of lines about the same point in a given line whose values differ by an integral multiple of 2π radians or of 360° ⟨~ angles measuring 30° and 390°⟩

co·transduction \¦kō+\ *n* [*co-* + *transduction*] **:** transduction involving two or more genetic loci carried by a single bacteriophage

cotton candy* *n* **:** something attractive but insubstantial

cou·chette \kü'shet\ *n* -s [F, berth, bunk, dim. of *couche* bed, fr. MF — more at COUCH] **1 :** a compartment on a European passenger train so arranged that berths can be provided at night **2 :** one of the berths in a couchette

cou·li·biac \,külēb'yäk, -ák\ *n* -s [F, fr. Russ *kulebyaka*] **:** fish rolled in pastry dough and baked ⟨~ of salmon⟩

cou·lom·bic \(ˈ)kü¦läm(b)ik, kə¦l-, -lōm-\ *adj* [ISV *coulomb* + *-ic*] **:** of or relating to electrostatic coulomb forces

cou·ma·phos \'kümə,fäs, -fōs\ *n* -ES [*couma*rin + *phos*phorus] **:** an organophosphorus systemic insecticide and anthelmintic $C_{14}H_{16}ClO_5PS$ used esp. on cattle and poultry

count·abil·i·ty \,kaůn(t)ə'biləd·ē\ *n* **:** the quality or state of being countable

count·ably \'kaůn(t)əblē\ *adv* **:** in a way that is countable ⟨a ~ infinite subset⟩

counter* *n* **:** a football play in which the ballcarrier goes in a direction opposite to the flow of play

counteradvertising \'==¦==,==\ *n* [*counter-* 1 + *advertising*] **:** COUNTERCOMMERCIALS *herein*

countercommercial \'===¦==\ *n* [*counter-* + *commercial*] **:** a commercial that rebuts the claims of another commercial

coun·ter·con·di·tion·ing \¦kaůn(t)ə(r)kən¦dish(ə)niŋ\ *n* [*counter-* + *conditioning,* gerund of *condition*] **:** conditioning in order to replace an undesirable response (as fear) to a stimulus (as an engagement in public speaking) by a favorable one

coun·ter·culture \'==,==\ *n* [*counter-* + *culture*] **:** a culture with values and mores that run counter to those of established society — **coun·ter·cultural** \¦== +\ *adj* — **coun·ter·culturist** \"+\ *n*

coun·ter·electrophoresis \¦==+\ *n* [*counter-* + *electrophoresis*] **:** an electrophoretic method of testing blood esp. for antigens associated with hepatitis

coun·ter·example \"+\ *n* [*counter-* + *example*] **:** an example that disproves a theorem or proposition; *broadly* **:** an example that is inconsistent with or contrary to what is typical or usual

coun·ter·force \'==¦=\ *adj* [*counter-* + *force*] **:** of, relating to, or being an attack directed against enemy military targets rather than civilian targets ⟨~ weapons⟩ ⟨a ~ strategy⟩

coun·ter·insurgency \"+\ *n* [*counter-* + *insurgency*] **:** organized activity designed to combat insurgency — **coun·ter·insurgent** \"+\ *n*

coun·ter·intuitive \"+\ *adj* [*counter-* + *intuitive*] **:** contrary to intuition ⟨complex systems are ~. They behave in ways opposite to what most people expect —J.W. Forrester⟩

coun·ter·phobic \"+\ *adj* [*counter-* + *phobic*] **:** relating to or characterized by a preference for or the seeking out of a situation that is feared ⟨~ reaction patterns⟩

coun·ter·productive \"+\ *adj* [*counter-* + *productive*] **:** tending to hinder the attainment of a desired goal ⟨violence as a means to achieve an end is ~ —W.E. Brock *b*1930⟩

coun·ter·program \"+\ *vb* [*counter-* + *program*] *vi* **:** to engage in counterprogramming ~ *vt* **:** to run against (another television program)

coun·ter·programming \'==+\ *n* [*counter-* + *programming*] **:** the scheduling of programs by television networks so as to attract audiences away from simultaneously telecast programs of competitors

coun·ter·pulsation \¦==+\ *n* [*counter-* + *pulsation*] **:** a technique for reducing the work load on the heart by the automatic lowering of systemic blood pressure just before or during expulsion of blood from the ventricle and by the automatic raising of blood pressure during diastole — see INTRA-AORTIC BALLOON COUNTERPULSATION *herein*

coun·ter·shock \"+\ *n* [*counter-* + *shock*] **:** therapeutic electric shock applied to the heart for the purpose of altering a disturbed rhythm (as in chronic atrial fibrillation)

counting number *n* **:** NATURAL NUMBER

country* *n* **:** COUNTRY MUSIC

country* *adj* **1 :** of or relating to country music ⟨~ singer⟩ **2 :** featuring country music ⟨~ radio stations⟩ **3 :** of, relating to, or having the characteristics of early American rustic or informal furniture

country and western *adj, sometimes cap C&W* **:** having or using lyrics, style, or string instrumentation identified with country music of western U.S. origin

country rock *n* **:** ROCKABILLY *herein*

cou·pon·ing \'k(y)ü,pänin\ *n* -s [*coupon* + ³-*ing*] **:** the distribution or redemption of coupons

cour·gette \kü(ə)r'zhet, küə'zhet\ *n* -s [F dial., dim. of *courge* gourd — more at COURGE] *chiefly Brit* **:** ZUCCHINI

course·ware \'=,=\ *n* [¹*course* + ⁴*ware*] **:** educational software

courtesy light *n* **:** an interior automobile light that goes on automatically when a door is opened

couth \'küth\ *n* -s [²*couth*] **:** POLISH, REFINEMENT ⟨I expected kindness and gentility and I found it, but there is such a thing as too much ~ —S.J. Perelman⟩

cover–up* *n* **1 :** a usu. concerted effort to keep an illegal or unethical act or situation from being made public **2 :** a loose outer garment

cover version *or* **cover*** *n* **:** a recording made by one performer or aimed at one market of a tune orig. recorded by a different performer or aimed at a different market

cow·boy·ing \'kaù,bòi(·i)ŋ\ *n* -s [¹*cowboy* + ³-*ing*] **:** the work or occupation of a cowboy

cowshed \'=,=\ *n* **:** a shed for the housing of cows

CP \'sē'pē\ *n* -s [charge conjugation, parity] **:** the combination of the theoretical operations of charge conjugation and inversion of parity for all particles involved in a nuclear or electromagnetic interaction that is used as a test of the symmetry of the interaction under the laws of quantum mechanics

CPI *abbr* consumer price index

CPR *abbr* cardiopulmonary resuscitation

CPS* *abbr* **1** certified professional secretary **2** *usu not cap* characters per second

CPU \,sē(,) pē'yü\ *abbr or n* -s *often not cap* central processing unit *herein*

crackback \'=,=\ *n* [¹*crack* + *back*] **:** a blind-side block on a defensive player in football by a pass receiver who starts downfield and then cuts back toward the middle of the line

crack up *vi* **:** to laugh out loud ~ *vt* **:** to cause to laugh out loud

crambe* *n* **:** an annual Mediterranean herb of the genus *Crambe* (*C. abyssinica*) cultivated as an oilseed crop

cranberry glass *n* **:** clear ruby glass usu. with a blue-violet tint

cra·nio·pha·ryn·gi·oma \,krānē(,)ō,farənjē'ōmə, -,fə,rin-\ *n, pl* **craniopharyngiomas** *or* **craniopharyngioma·ta** \-məd·ə, -ətə\ [*crani-* + *pharyng-* + *-i-* + *-oma*] **:** a tumor of the brain near the pituitary gland that develops esp. in children or young adults and is often associated with increased intracranial pressure

crapshoot \'=,=\ *n* [⁵*crap* + ²*shoot*] **:** a risky business venture

crash* *vi* **1** *slang* **:** to experience the aftereffects (as dysphoria or depression) of drug intoxication **2** *slang* **:** SLEEP ⟨sometimes we can't pay the rent and we ~ around town, sleep in yards or at friends' houses —*East Village Other*⟩ — **crash*** *n*

crash pad* *n* **:** a place where free temporary lodging is available

crashworthy \'=,==\ *adj* [²*crash* + *-worthy* (as in *seaworthy*)] **:** resistant to the effects of a collision ⟨~ cars⟩ — **crashworthiness** *n*

cra·ter·iza·tion \,krād·ərə'zāshən, -ātə-, -r,ī'z-\ *n* -s [*crater* + *-ize* + *-ation*] **:** surgical excision of a crater-shaped piece of bone

crawl* *n* **:** lettering that moves vertically or horizontally across a television or movie screen to give information (as credits or news bulletins)

crawlerway \'==,=\ *n* [*crawler* + *way;* fr. its slow-moving traffic] **:** a road built esp. for moving heavy rockets and spacecraft

crawlway \'=,=\ *n* [¹*crawl* + *way*] **:** a low passageway (as in a cave) that can be traversed only by crawling

cray·fish·ing \'=,==\ *n* -s [*crayfish* + ³-*ing*] **:** the occupation or pastime of catching crayfish

crazy* *adj* — **like crazy :** to an extreme degree ⟨everyone dancing *like crazy*⟩

cra·zy \'krāzē, -zi\ *n* -ES [*crazy,* adj.] **:** one who is or acts crazy; *esp* **:** such a one associated with a radical or extremist political cause

C–re·ac·tive protein \'=(,)=,==-\ *n* [*C-polysaccharide* (a polysaccharide found in the cell wall of pneumococci and precipitated by this protein), fr. *carbohydrate*] **:** a protein present in blood serum in various abnormal states (as inflammation or neoplasia)

creamer* *n* **:** a nondairy product used as a substitute for cream (as in coffee)

creatine kinase *n* **:** an enzyme of vertebrate skeletal and myocardial muscle that catalyzes the transfer of a high-energy phosphate group from phosphocreatine to ADP with the formation of ATP and creatine

creatine phos·pho·kinase \-¦fäsfō+\ *n* [*phospho-* + *kinase*] **:** CREATINE KINASE *herein*

cre·den·tial \krə'denchəl, krē-\ *vt* **cre·den·tialed** *also* **cre·den·tialled; cre·den·tial·ing** *also* **cre·den·tial·ling** \-ch(ə)liŋ;\ **cre·den·tials** [*credential,* n.] **:** to furnish with credentials

cre·den·tial·ism \krə'denchə,lizəm, krē'-\ *n* -s [²*credential* + *-ism*] **:** undue emphasis on credentials (as college degrees) as prerequisites to employment

credibility gap *n* **1 a :** lack of trust ⟨a special *credibility gap* is likely to open between the generations — Kenneth Keniston⟩ **b :** lack of believability ⟨a *credibility gap* created by contradictory official statements — Samuel Ellenport⟩ **2 :** DISCREPANCY ⟨the *credibility gap* between the professed ideals . . . and their actual practices —Jeanne L. Noble⟩

creditworthy \'==,==\ *adj* [¹*credit* + *worthy*] **:** being financially sound enough to justify the extension of credit **:** having an acceptable credit rating — **creditworthiness** *n*

creeping* *adj* **:** developing or advancing slowly over a period of time ⟨~ urbanization⟩ ⟨~ senility⟩

cre·mains \krə'mānz, krē'-\ *n pl* [blend of *cremated* and *remains*] **:** the ashes of a cremated human body

crème brûlée \¦krembrüē'lā, ¦kräm-, ¦krem-, -brü-\ *n* [F, lit., scorched cream] **:** a rich custard topped with caramelized sugar

crème fraîche *or* **crème fraiche** \-'fresh\ *n* [F, lit., fresh cream] **:** heavy cream thickened and slightly soured with buttermilk and often served on fruit

creosote* *n* **:** a dark brown or black flammable tar deposited from esp. wood smoke on the walls of a chimney

creutz·feldt–ja·kob disease *also* **creutz·feld–ja·cob disease** \,kròits,felt¦yä(,)kōb-, -(,)kòp-\ *n, usu cap C&J* [Hans G. *Creutzfeldt* †1964 Ger. psychiatrist and Alfons M. *Jakob* †1931 Ger. psychiatrist] **:** a rare progressive fatal encephalopathy caused by a slow virus and marked by premature dementia in middle age and gradual loss of muscular coordination

crew sock *n* [so called fr. its use by rowing crews] **:** a short bulky usu. ribbed sock

crib death *n* **:** SUDDEN INFANT DEATH SYNDROME *herein*

[1]**cri·co·thyroid** \ˌkrīkə+\ *adj* [*crico-* + *thyroid*] **:** relating to or connecting the cricoid cartilage and the thyroid cartilage ⟨a ~ muscle⟩

[2]**cricothyroid** \"\ *n* **:** a cricothyroid muscle

cri du chat syndrome \ˌkrēdüˈshä-, -dəˈ-\ *n* [*cri du chat* fr. F, cry of the cat] **:** an inherited condition that is characterized by a mewing cry, mental retardation, physical anomalies, and the absence of part of a chromosome

crisis center *n* **:** a facility run usu. by nonprofessionals who counsel those who telephone for help in a personal crisis

crista* *n* **:** any of the inwardly projecting folds of the inner membrane of a mitochondrion

critical mass *n* [*critical* (capable of sustaining a chain reaction) + [2]*mass*] **:** a size, number, or amount large enough to produce a desired or expected result ⟨wants to achieve the *critical mass* of a major company —*Business Week*⟩ ⟨women may have to reach a point of *critical mass* in any institution to raise that different voice —Betty Friedan⟩

critical region *n* **:** the set of outcomes of a statistical test for which the null hypothesis is to be rejected

CRNA *abbr* certified registered nurse anesthetist

crock* *n* [fr. the phrase *crock of shit*] **:** BUNKUM, BALONEY, BULL — usu. used with *a* ⟨those awards are a ~, a PR stunt —Irma Lipkin⟩

Crockpot \ˈ=ˌ=\ *trademark* — used for an electric cooking pot

cro·quem·bouche \krȯkäⁿbüsh\ *n* -s [F] **:** a cone-shaped stack of cream puffs coated with caramelized sugar

cross·court \ˌkrȯs+\ *adv or adj* [[4]*cross* + *court*] **:** to or toward the opposite side of a court (as in tennis or basketball)

cross–disciplinary \ˌ=ˈ===ˌ==\ *adj* [[5]*cross*] **:** of, relating to, or involving two or more disciplines **:** INTERDISCIPLINARY

cross–dress \ˌ=ˈ=\ *vi* [[5]*cross*] **:** to dress in the clothes of the opposite sex

cross multiply *vi* [back-formation fr. *cross multiplication*] **:** to find the two products obtained by multiplying the numerator of each of two fractions by the denominator of the other

cross–na·tion·al \ˌkrȯs+\ *adj* [[5]*cross*] **:** of or relating to two or more nations

crossover* *n* **1 :** a voter registered as a member of one political party who votes in the primary of the other party **2 :** a broadening of popular musical appeal that is often the result of a change of musical style; *also* **:** a musician who has achieved such a crossover

crossover* *adj* **1 :** CRITICAL 2 ⟨~ point⟩ ⟨~ date⟩ **2 :** permitting voting by crossovers ⟨~ primary⟩ **3 :** involving or using interchange of the control group and the experimental group during the course of an experiment ⟨a double-blind ~ study⟩

cross product* *n* **:** either of the two products obtained by multiplying together the two means or the two extremes of a proportion

cross–reactivity \ˌ=(ˌ)=ˈ=ˈ===\ *n* [[3]*cross*] **:** the capability of undergoing cross-reaction — **cross–react** \"+\ *vi* — **cross–reactive** *adj*

cross–train \ˌ=ˈ=\ *vt* [[5]*cross* + *train*] **:** to train (a person) to do more than one specific job

crow·die \ˈkrau̇dē\ *n* -s [Sc, alter. of ME *crud* curds — more at CURD] **:** a Scottish cottage cheese that is partially cooked

crown of thorns *or* **crown–of–thorns starfish :** a starfish (*Acanthaster planci*) of the Pacific region that is covered with long spines and is destructive to the coral of coral reefs

crucible* *n* **:** a place or situation in which concentrated forces interact to cause or influence change or development ⟨conditioned by having grown up within the ~ of Chinatown —Tom Wolfe⟩

cru·di·tés \krüēdētā\ *n pl* [F, pl. of *crudité* raw food, fr. MF, indigestibility, crudity — more at CRUDITY] **:** pieces of raw vegetables (as celery, carrots, or cauliflower) served as an hors d'oeuvre often with a dip

cruise* *vi* **:** to search (as in public places) for a sexual partner ~ *vt* **:** to search in (a public place) for a sexual partner

cruise control *n* **:** an electronic device in an automobile that controls the throttle so as to maintain a constant speed

cruise missile *n* **:** a guided missile that has a terrain-following radar system and that flies at moderate speed and low altitude

crumb structure *n* [trans. of G *krümelstruktur*] **:** a soil condition suitable for farming in which the soil particles are aggregated into crumbs

crunch* *vt* **:** PROCESS; *esp* **:** to perform mathematical computations on ⟨~ numbers⟩

crunch* *n* **:** a tight or critical situation: as **a :** a critical point in the buildup of pressure between opposing elements **b :** a severe economic squeeze (as on credit) **c :** SHORTAGE ⟨energy ~⟩

cryo·biology \ˌkrīō +\ *n* [*cry-* + *biology*] **:** the study of the effects of extremely low temperature on biological systems (as cells or organisms) — **cryo·biological** \"+\ *adj* — **cryo·biologically** \"+\ *adv* — **cryo·biologist** \"+\ *n*

cryo·electronics \"+\ *n pl but sing in constr* [*cry-* + *electronics*] **:** a branch of electronics that employs cryogenic methods to bring about a desired effect (as superconductivity) — **cryo·electronic** \"+\ *adj*

cryo·extraction \"+\ *n* [*cry-* + *extraction*] **:** extraction of a cataract through use of a cryoprobe whose refrigerated tip adheres to and freezes tissue of the lens permitting its removal

cryo·extractor \"+\ *n* [*cry-* + *extractor*] **:** a cryoprobe used for removal of cataracts

cryogenic* *adj* **1 :** being or relating to a very low temperature ⟨a ~ temperature of −50° C⟩ **2 a :** requiring or involving the use of a cryogenic temperature ⟨~ surgery⟩ **b :** requiring cryogenic storage **c :** suitable for the storage of a cryogenic substance ⟨a ~ container⟩ — **cry·o·gen·i·cal·ly** \-nək(ə)lē\ *adv*

cryo·glob·u·li·ne·mia \ˌkrīōˌgläbyələˈnēmēə\ *n* -s [*cryoglobulin* + *-emia*] **:** the condition of having abnormal quantities of cryoglobulins in the blood

cry·on·ics \krīˈäniks\ *n pl but usu sing in constr* [*cryo*biology (herein) + *-onics* (as in *electronics*)] **:** the practice of freezing a dead diseased human being in hopes of bringing him back to life at some future time when a cure for his disease has been developed — **cry·on·ic** \(ˈ)krīˈänik\ *adj*

cryo·precipitate \ˌkrīō +\ *n* [*cry-* + *precipitate*] **:** a precipitate that is formed by cooling a solution — **cryo·precipitation** \"+\ *n*

cryo·preservation \"+\ *n* [*cry-* + *preservation*] **:** preservation (as of cells) by subjection to extremely low temperatures — **cryo·preserve** \"+\ *vt*

cryo·probe \'krīə +,\ *n* [*cry-* + *probe*] **:** a blunt chilled instrument used to freeze tissues in cryosurgery

cryo·protective \ˌkrīō +\ *adj* [*cry-* + *protective*] **:** serving to protect against freezing ⟨an extracellular ~ agent⟩ — **cryo·protectant** \"+\ *n or adj*

cryo·pump \'krīō,=\ *n* [*cry-* + *pump*] **:** a vacuum pump whose operation involves the freezing and adsorption of gases on cold surfaces at very low temperatures — **cryo·pump** *vi*

cryo·sorption \ˌkrīō +\ *n* [*cry-* + *sorption*] **:** the adsorption of gases onto the cold surfaces of a cryopump

cryo·surgery \"+\ *n* [*cry-* + *surgery*] **:** surgery in which the tissue to be dissected is frozen (as by the use of liquid nitrogen) — **cryo·surgeon** \"+\ *n* — **cryo·surgical** \"+\ *adj*

cryp·to·biosis \ˌkrip(ˌ)tō +\ *n, pl* **cryptobioses** [NL, fr. *crypt-* + *-biosis*] **:** the reversible cessation of metabolism under extreme environmental conditions (as low temperature)

crystal* *n* **:** powdered methamphetamine

CT *abbr* computed tomography *herein*; computerized tomography *herein*

c–type \'sē,tīp\ *adj, usu cap C* **:** TYPE C *herein*

cuat·ro \'kwä·trō\ *n* -s [Sp *cuatro* four] **:** a Puerto Rican stringed instrument similar to a small guitar

cu·chi·fri·to \ˌküchi'frēd·ō, -chē'-\ *n* -s [AmerSp, fr. *cuche, cuchi* hog, pig (fr. Sp *cochino*) + Sp *frito* fried, past part. of *freir* to fry, fr. L *frigere* — more at FRY] **:** a deep-fried cube of pork

cued speech *n* **:** a form of communication for the deaf in which lipreading is enhanced by hand signals that distinguish between similar lip movements

cui·se·naire rod *also* **cuisenaire colored rod** \ˌkwēzᵊn¦a(ə)r-, -¦e(-\ *n, usu cap 1st C* [fr. *Cuisenaire*, a trademark] **:** any of a set of colored rods that are usu. of 1 centimeter cross section and of 10 lengths from 1 to 10 centimeters and that are used for teaching number concepts and the basic operations of arithmetic

cuisine min·ceur \-maⁿsœœr\ *n* [F, slimness cooking] **:** a low-calorie form of French cooking

cui–ui \'kwē,wē\ *n* -s [prob. fr. Paiute] **:** an endangered sucker (*Chasmistes cujus*) of the family Catostomidae that is found only in Lake Pyramid, Nevada

cul·dot·o·my \(ˌ)kəl'däd·əmē, kůl-, -ätə-, -mi\ *n* -ES [*cul-do-* + *-tomy*] **:** surgical incision of the pouch of Douglas

cu·li·coi·des \ˌkyülə'kȯiˌdēz\ *n, cap* [NL, fr. L *culicis*, gen. of *culex* gnat + L *-oides* -oid] **:** a genus of bloodsucking midges of the family Ceratopogonidae of which some are intermediate hosts of filarial parasites

cul·tur·a·ti \ˌkəlchə'rä|d·(ˌ)ē, -'rä|, |(ˌ)tē, *also* -'rāˌtī\ *n pl* [fr. *culture* + *-ati* (as in *literati*)] **:** people intensely interested in cultural affairs

culture shock *n* **:** a sense of confusion and uncertainty sometimes with feelings of anxiety that may affect people exposed to an alien culture without adequate preparation

culture–vulture \'==¦==\ *n* **:** a person who avidly attends cultural events

cumberland sauce *n, usu cap C* [after *Cumberland* county, England] **:** a cold sauce flavored with orange, lemon, currant jelly, port wine, and spices that is often served with game

cumulative* *adj* **:** summing or integrating over all data or values of a random variable less than or less than or equal to a specified value ⟨~ normal distribution⟩ ⟨~ frequency distribution⟩

cumulative distribution function *n* **:** DISTRIBUTION FUNCTION

cup* *n* **:** the symbol ∪ indicating the union of two sets — compare CAP *herein*

cup·pa \'kəpə\ *n* -s [fr. *cuppa tea*, pronunciation spelling of *cup of tea*] *chiefly Brit* **:** a cup of tea

cupule* *n* **:** an outer integument partially enclosing the seed of some seed ferns

cu·rate's egg \ˌkyůrəts¦=\ *n* [so called fr. the story of a curate who was given a stale egg by his bishop and declared that parts of it were excellent] *Brit* **:** something with both good and bad parts or qualities

curb weight *n* **:** the weight of an automobile with standard equipment and fuel, oil, and coolant

curl* *n* **:** a hollow arch of water formed when the crest of a breaking wave spills forward — called also *tube, tunnel*

cur·sil·lo \kůr'sē(l)yō\ *n* -s *often cap* [Sp, short course, dim. of *curso* course] **:** a movement in Roman Catholicism designed to deepen the spiritual life and bring about Christian involvement in daily activities through participation in a 3-day gathering usu. followed by weekly or monthly meetings; *also* **:** the 3-day gathering

cursor* *n* **1 :** a visual cue (as a flashing rectangle) on a video display that indicates position esp. for entry of data or manipulation of information **2 :** a usu. transparent movable object with cross hairs used to mark position on a tablet for entry of graphic data into a computer

curve* *vt* **:** to throw a curve to (a batter) in baseball

custard glass *n* **:** opaque glass of creamy buff color

custom–make \'==¦=\ *vt* [back-formation from *custom=made*] **:** to make to order

cut* *vb* — **cut it :** to manage or perform something successfully

cut* *n* **:** a single song or musical piece on a phonograph record

cutability \ˌ=='===\ *n* -ES [¹*cut* + *-ability*] **:** the proportion of lean salable meat yielded by a carcass

cutback* *n* **:** a surfing maneuver in which a surfboard is turned back toward the crest of the wave

cute·sy *also* **cute·sie** \'kyütsē\ *adj* **cutesier; cutesiest** [²*cute* + *-sy* (as in *folksy*)] **:** self-consciously cute ⟨tries . . . to be bright and often ends up merely ~ — Newgate Callendar⟩ — **cute·sy·ness** *n* -ES

cut·offs \'kəd·ˌȯfs, -ət| *also* |ˌäfs\ *n pl* [short for *cut-off blue jeans*] **:** trousers (as of blue denim) cut off at the knee or higher — **cut–off** \ˌ=¦=\ *adj*

cutting edge *n* **1 :** the forefront of an art, science, or movement **:** VANGUARD, FRONTIER ⟨the *cutting edge* of American industrial prowess —P.J. Schuyten⟩ **2 :** a sharp effect or quality

cy·a·no·acrylate \ˌsīənō +\ *n* [*cyan-* + *acrylate*] **:** any of several liquid acrylate monomers that readily undergo anionic polymerization and are used as adhesives in industry and on living tissue in medicine to close wounds as an adjunct to surgery

cy·ber·culture \'sībə(r) +,\ *n* [*cybernetics* + *culture*] **:** a society that is served by cybernated industry — **cy·ber·cultural** \ˌsībə(r)+\ *adj*

cy·ber·nat·ed \'sībə(r),nād·əd, -ātəd\ *adj* [fr. *cybernation* (herein); after such pairs as E *automation: automated*] **:** characterized by or involving cybernation ⟨a ~ factory⟩ ⟨a ~ society⟩

cy·ber·na·tion \ˌsībə(r)ˈnāshən\ *n* -s [*cyber*netics + *-ation*] **:** the automatic control of a process or operation (as in manufacturing) by means of computers

cy·borg \ˈsīˌbȯrg\ *n* -s [*cyb*ernetic + *org*anism] **:** a human being who is linked (as for temporary adaptation to a hostile space environment) to one or more mechanical devices upon which some of his vital physiological functions depend

cy·ca·sin \ˈsīkəsən\ *n* -s [*cycas* + *-in*] **:** a glucoside $C_8H_{16}N_2O_7$ that occurs in cycads and results in toxic and carcinogenic effects when introduced into mammals

cy·clan·de·late \ˌsīˈkland^{ə}lˌāt, -ˌət\ *n* -s [fr. *cyclo*hexyl + m*andelate*] **:** an antispasmodic drug $C_{17}H_{24}O_3$ used esp. as a vasodilator in the treatment of diseased arteries

cy·clase \ˈsīˌklās, -āz\ *n* -s [*cycl-* + *-ase*] **:** an enzyme (as adenylate cyclase) that catalyzes cyclization of a compound

cy·claz·o·cine \sīˈklazəˌsēn, -sən\ *n* -s [*cycl-* + *azocine,* a compound C_7H_7N, fr. *benzacocine,* derivative of azobenzene, prob. irreg. fr. *azobenzene*] **:** an analgesic $C_{18}H_{25}NO$ that inhibits the effect of morphine and related addictive drugs and is used in the treatment of drug addiction

cycle* *n* **:** a permutation of a set of ordered elements in which each element takes the place of the next and the last becomes first

cy·cle·ry \ˈsīkəl(ˌ)rē, -klə(-\ *n* -ES [[1]*cycle* + *-ery*] **:** a place where bicycles are sold and serviced

cyclic* *adj* **:** being a mathematical group that has an element such that every element of the group can be expressed as one of its powers

cyclic adenosine monophosphate *n* **:** CYCLIC AMP *herein*

cyclic AMP *n* **:** a cyclic mononucleotide of adenosine that has been implicated as a second messenger in addition to hormones in the control of cellular processes (as lipid metabolism, membrane transport, and cell proliferation); adenosine 3′,5′-monophosphate

cyclic GMP \-ˌjē(ˌ)emˈpē\ *n* **:** a cyclic mononucleotide of guanosine that has been implicated with cyclic AMP as a second messenger in addition to hormones in the control of cellular processes; guanosine 3′,5′-monophosphate — called also *guanosine monophosphate*

cyclic guanosine mono·phosphate \-ˌmänəˈfäsˌfāt, -ˌmōn-\ *n* [*mono-* + *phosphate*] **:** CYCLIC GMP *herein*

cy·clo \ˈsē(ˌ)klō, ˈsik(ˌ)lō\ *n* -s [prob. fr. F, short for (assumed) *cyclotaxi,* fr. moto*cycl*ette motorcycle + *-o-* + *taxi*] **:** a 3-wheeled motor-driven taxi

cy·clo·diene \ˈsī(ˌ)klō+, *also* ˈsik(ˌ)lō+\ *n* -s [*cycl-* + *-diene*] **:** an organic insecticide (as aldrin, dieldrin, chlordane, or endosulfan) with a chlorinated methylene group forming a bridge across a 6-membered carbon ring

cy·clo·oxygenase \"+\ *n* [*cycl-* + *oxygenase*] **:** an enzyme that catalyzes the conversion of arachidonic acid into prostaglandins of which some are associated with arthritic inflammation and that is held to be inactivated by aspirin giving temporary partial relief of arthritic symptoms

cy·clo·phos·pha·mide \ˌsīkləˈfäsfəˌmīd, ˌsik-, -ˌməd\ *n* -s [prob. fr. *cycl-* + *phosph-* + *amide*] **:** an immunosuppressive and antineoplastic drug $C_7H_{15}Cl_2N_2O_2P$ used esp. against lymphomas and some leukemias

cy·clo·spo·rine *or* **cy·clo·spo·rin A** \ˌsīklōˈspȯrən-(ā)\ *n* -s [ISV *cycl-* + *spor-* + *-in* or *-ine*] **:** an immunosuppressive drug $C_{62}H_{111}N_{11}O_{12}$ that is a polypeptide obtained from various imperfect fungi (as *Tolypocladium inflatum Gams* syn. *Trichoderma polysporum*) and is used esp. to prevent rejection of transplanted organs

cyclotomic* *adj* **:** relating to, being, or containing a polynomial of the form $x^{p-1} + x^{p-2} + \ldots + x + 1$ where p is a prime number

cyclotron resonance *n* **:** the absorption of electromagnetic energy by a charged particle orbiting in a magnetic field when the electromagnetic and orbital frequencies are equal

cymric* *n, usu cap* **:** any of a breed of domestic cats that prob. originated as a spontaneous mutation of the Manx and that differs from it only in having a long coat

cy·pro·hep·ta·dine \ˌsīprōˈheptəˌdēn\ *n* -s [*cycl-* + *pro*pyl + *hepta-* + piper*idine*] **:** a drug $C_{21}H_{21}N$ that acts antagonistically to histamine and serotonin and is used esp. in the treatment of asthma

cy·pro·ter·one \sīˈprōd·əˌrōn *also* -ˈpräd·-\ *n* -s [prob. fr. *cy*clic + *progesterone*] **:** a synthetic steroid used in the form of its acetate to inhibit androgenic secretions (as testosterone)

cys·ta·mine \ˈsistəˌmēn, -ˌmən\ *n* [*cyst*ine + *amine*] **:** a cystine derivative $C_4H_{12}N_2S_2$ used in the prevention of radiation sickness (as of cancer patients)

cys·ta·thi·o·nine \ˌsistəˈthīəˌnēn, -ˌnən\ *n* -s [irreg. fr. *cyst*eine + me*thionine*] **:** a sulfur-containing amino acid $C_7H_{14}N_2O_4S$ formed as an intermediate in the conversion of methionine to cysteine in animals

cys·te·amine \sisˈtēəmən\ *n* [*cyste*ine + *amine*] **:** a cysteine derivative C_2H_7NS that has been used in the prevention of radiation sickness (as in cancer patients)

cys·ti·no·sis \ˌsistəˈnōsəs\ *n, pl* **cystino·ses** \-ōˌsēz\ [NL *cystine* + *-osis*] **:** a recessive autosomally inherited disease characterized esp. by cystinuria and deposits of cystine throughout the body — **cys·ti·not·ic** \-ˈnäd·ik\ *adj*

cys·to·ure·throg·ra·phy \ˌsistəˌyu̇rəˈthrägrəfē\ *n* -ES [*cyst-* + *urethrograph* + *-y*] **:** roentgenography for the purpose of preparing a cystourethrogram — **cys·to·ure·thro·graph·ic** \-ˌyəˌrēthrəˈgrafik\ *adj*

cy·to·cha·la·sin \ˌsīd·ōkəˈlāsən\ *n* -s [*cyt-* + Gk *chalasis* slackening + *-in*] **:** any of a group of metabolites isolated from fungi (esp. *Helminthosporium dematioideum*) that inhibit various cell processes

cy·to·chimera \ˈsīd·ō +\ *n* [NL, fr. *cyt-* + *chimera*] **:** an individual (as a plant, an organ, or a tissue) having cells of varied genetic constitution and esp. of various ploidy levels

cy·to·differentiation \"+\ *n* [*cyt-* + *differentiation*] **:** the development of specialized cells (as muscle, blood, or nerve cells) from undifferentiated precursors

cy·to·kinin \"+\ *n* [*cyt-* + *kinin* (herein)] **:** any of various plant growth substances that are usu. derivatives of adenine

cy·to·me·gal·ic \ˈsīd·ōməˈgalik\ *adj* [NL *cytomegalia* condition of having enlarged cells (fr. *cyt-* + *megal-* + *-ia*) + E *-ic*] **:** characterized by or causing the formation of enlarged cells

cytomegalic inclusion disease *n* **:** a severe disease esp. of newborns that is caused by a cytomegalovirus and usu. affects the salivary glands, brain, kidneys, liver, and lungs

cy·to·meg·a·lo·vi·rus \ˌsīd·əˈmegəlōˈvīrəs\ *n* [NL, fr. *cytomegalia* + *-o-* + *virus*] **:** any of several herpesviruses that cause cellular enlargement and formation of eosinophilic inclusion bodies esp. in the nucleus and include one causing cytomegalic inclusion disease

cy·to·membrane \ˌsīd·ə +\ *n* [*cyt-* + *membrane*] **:** one of the cellular membranes including those of the plasmalemma, endoplasmic reticulum, nuclear envelope, and Golgi apparatus; *specif* **:** UNIT MEMBRANE *herein*

cy·tom·e·try \sīˈtämə·trē\ *n* -ES [*cyt-* + *-metry*] **:** a technical specialty concerned with the counting of cells and esp. blood cells — **cy·to·met·ric** \ˌsīd·əˈme·trik\ *adj*

cy·to·morphology \ˌsīd·ō +\ *n* [*cyt-* + *morphology*] **:** the morphology of cells — **cy·to·morphological** \"+\ *adj*

cy·to·pathogenic \"+\ *adj* [*cyt-* + *pathogenic*] **:** pathologic for or destructive to cells — **cy·to·pathogenicity** \"+\ *n*

cy·to·photometer \"+\ *n* [*cyt-* + *photometer*] **:** a photometer for use in cytophotometry

cy·to·photometry \"+\ *n* [*cyt-* + *photometry*] **:** photometry applied to the study of the cell or its constituents — **cy·to·photometric** \"+\ *adj* — **cy·to·photometrically** \"+\ *adv*

cy·to·physiology \"+\ *n* [*cyt-* + *physiology*] **:** the physiology of cells — **cy·to·physiological** \"+\ *adj* — **cy·to·physiologically** \"+\ *adv*

cytosine arabinoside *n* **:** a synthetic cytotoxic antineoplastic agent $C_9H_{13}N_3O_5$ that is an isomer of the naturally occurring nucleoside of cytosine and arabinose and is used esp. in the treatment of acute myelogenous leukemia in adults

cy·to·skeletal \"+\ *adj* [*cyt-* + *skeletal*] **:** of, relating to, or being the cytoskeleton of a cell

cy·to·sol \ˈsīd·ə +ˌ\ *n* [*cyt-* + [6]*sol*] **:** the fluid portion of the cytoplasm exclusive of organelles and membranes that is usu. obtained as the supernatant fraction from high-speed centrifugation of a tissue homogenate — **cy·to·sol·ic** \ˌsīd·əˌsälik, -sōl-, -sȯl-\ *adj*

cy·to·spectrophotometry \ˌsīd·ō+\ *n* [*cyt-* + *spectrophotometry*] **:** the application of spectrophotometry to the study of cells and esp. to the quantitative estimation of their constituents (as DNA)

cy·to·stat·ic \ˌsīd·əˌstad·ik\ *adj* [*cyt-* + Gk *statikos* causing to stand — more at STATIC] **:** tending to retard cellular activity and multiplication ⟨~ treatment of tumor cells⟩ — **cytostatic** *n* — **cy·to·stat·i·cal·ly** \-ad·ək(ə)lē\ *adv*

cy·to·tech \ˈ⸗ˌtek\ *n* -s [by shortening] **:** CYTOTECHNOLOGIST *herein*

cy·to·technologist \ˌsīd·ō +\ *also* **cy·to·technician** \"+\ *n* [*cyt-* + *technologist* or *technician*] **:** a medical technician trained in cytotechnology

cy·to·technology \"+\ *n* [*cyt-* + *technology*] **:** a specialty in medical technology concerned with the identification of cells and cellular abnormalities (as in cancer)

cy·to·vi·rin \ˌsīd·əˈvī(ə)rən\ *n* -s [*cyt-* + *virus* + *-in*] **:** a compound that is produced by a bacterium of the genus *Streptomyces* (*S. olivochromogenes*) and that is active against some plant viruses (as tobacco mosaic virus)

D

da* *abbr* deka-

DA \ˈdēˈā\ *n* -s [*d*uck's *a*ss; fr. its resemblance to the tail of a duck] **:** DUCKTAIL

DA \ˌdēˈā\ *abbr or n* -s **:** a doctor of arts

dab* *n, slang Brit* **:** FINGERPRINT

dac·quoise \dȧkwȧȧz\ *n* -s [F *Dacquoise* of or relating to Dax, a town in southern France] **:** a dessert made of layers of baked nut meringue with a filling usu. of buttercream

dac·ryo·cys·to·rhi·nos·to·my \ˌdakrē(ˌ)ōˌsis(ˌ)tōrīˈnästəmē\ *n* -ES [*dacryocyst* + *rhin-* + ²*-stomy*] **:** surgical creation of a passage for drainage between the lacrimal sac and the nasal cavity

dac·ti·no·mycin \ˈdaktənōˈmīsᵊn\ *n* -s [alter. of *actinomycin D*] **:** a toxic antineoplastic drug $C_{62}H_{86}N_{12}O_{16}$ of the actinomycin group — called also *actinomycin D*

dag·wood \ˈdagˌwu̇d\ *n* -s *often cap* [after *Dagwood* Bumstead, character who made such sandwiches in the comic strip *Blondie* by M.B. Young †1973] **:** a many-layered sandwich

daisy chain* *n* **:** a group sexual activity in which each person attends to the one in front while being attended to by the one behind

daisy wheel *n* [fr. its resemblance to the flower] **:** a printing element of an electric typewriter or printer that consists of a disk with spokes bearing type

dal·a·pon \ˈdaləˌpän\ *n* -s [prob. fr. *di-* + *al*pha + *pro*pionic acid] **:** an herbicide $C_3H_4Cl_2O_2$ that kills monocotyledonous plants selectively and is used esp. on unwanted grasses

da·la·si \däˈläsē\ *n, pl* **dalasi** *or* **dalasis** [native name in Gambia] **1 :** the basic monetary unit of Gambia — see MONEY table *in the Dict* **2 :** a coin or note representing one dalasi

Dal·mane \ˈdalˌmān, ˈdäl-\ *trademark* — used for a preparation of flurazepam hydrochloride

dal·ton \ˈdȯltᵊn\ *n* -s [after John *Dalton* †1844 Eng. chemist and physicist] **:** ATOMIC MASS UNIT — used chiefly in biochemistry

damsel bug *n* **:** any of a family (Nabidae) of small brown or black predaceous bugs that feed on pest insects

dan \ˈdän, ˈdan\ *n* -s [Jap, step, grade] **:** the expert level in Oriental arts of self-defense (as judo and karate) and games (as shogi)

D & C *abbr* dilatation and curettage

dap·sone \ˈdapˌsōn, -ˌzōn\ *n* -s [*di*aminodi*p*henyl *s*ulf*one*] **:** DIAMINODIPHENYL SULFONE

dar·ier's disease \därˈyāz, dȧ(r)-\ *n, usu cap 1st D* [J. F. *Darier* †1938 Fr. dermatologist] **:** a genetically determined skin condition characterized by patches of keratotic papules — called also *keratosis follicularis*

dar·win's finches \ˈdärwənz-\ *n pl, usu cap D* [after Charles *Darwin* †1882 Eng. naturalist] **:** finches of a subfamily (Geospizinae) characterized by great variation in bill shape and confined mostly to the Galapagos islands

das *abbr* dekastere *herein*

da·shi \ˈdäsh(ˌ)ē, däˈshē\ *n* -s [Jap, lit., broth] **:** a fish broth made from dried bonito

da·shi·ki \däˈshēkē, dəˈ-\ *also* **dai·shi·ki** \dīˈ-\ *n* -s [alter. of Yoruba *danshiki*] **:** a usu. brightly colored loose-fitting tunic of African origin worn esp. by black men

data bank *n* **1 :** DATA BASE *herein* **2 :** an institution whose chief concern is building and maintaining a data bank

data base *n* **:** a collection of data organized esp. for rapid search and retrieval (as by a computer)

data processing *n* **:** the conversion of raw data to machine-readable form and its subsequent processing (as storing, updating, combining, rearranging, or printing out) by a computer — **data processor** *n*

dating bar *n* **:** SINGLES BAR *herein*

dau·no·my·cin \ˌdȯnəˈmīsᵊn, ˌdau̇-\ *n* -s [(assumed) It *daunomicina,* fr. *Dauni*a, ancient region of Apulia, Italy + It *-o-* + *-micina* (as in *streptomicina* streptomycin)] **:** an antibiotic $C_{27}H_{29}NO_{10}$ that is a nitrogenous glycoside and is used experimentally as an antineoplastic agent

dau·no·ru·bi·cin \ˌ==ˈrübəsən\ *n* -s **:** DAUNOMYCIN *herein*

day care *n* **1 :** supervision of and care for children that is provided during the day by a person or organization other than the children's parents **2 :** a program, facility, or organization that provides day care

day–care \ˈ=ˌ=-\ *adj* **:** of, relating to, or providing day care ⟨*day-care* centers⟩

Day–Glo \ˈdāˌglō\ *trademark* — used for fluorescent materials

day·glow \ˈdāˌglō\ *n* -s [*day* + air*glow*] **:** airglow seen during the day

day one *also* **day I** \ˈ=ˈ=\ *n, often cap D&O* **:** the first day of something **:** the beginning of an activity or enterprise ⟨the trip was great from *day one*⟩

day release *n, Brit* **:** a program whereby employees are permitted to spend part of the workday attending courses to develop needed job skills

day sailer *n* **:** a small sailboat without sleeping accommodations

day·side* *n* **:** the side of a planet in sunlight

day trader *n* **:** a speculator who seeks profit from the intraday fluctuation in the price of a security or commodity and therefore completes double trades of buying and selling or selling and covering in the course of single sessions of the market — **day–trade** \ˈ=ˌ=\ *n or vb*

day–tripper *n* **:** one (as a tourist) who takes a trip that does not last overnight — **day–trip** *n or vb*

DBA *abbr* doctor of business administration

DBMS \ˈdēˈbēˈemˈes\ *abbr or n* -s [*d*ata *b*ase *m*anagement *s*ystem] **:** software designed to facilitate the creation, update, and retrieval of information in a data base

DC *abbr* doctor of chiropractic

DDE \ˈdē(ˌ)dēˈē\ *n* -s [*d*ichloro*d*iphenyldichloro*e*thylene] **:** a persistent organochlorine $C_{15}H_8Cl_4$ that is produced by the metabolic breakdown of DDT

DDVP \ˈdē(ˌ)dēˈvēˈpē\ *n* -s [*d*imethyl + *d*ichlor- + *v*inyl + *p*hosphate] **:** DICHLORVOS *herein*

de–accession \ˈdē+\ *also* **de–ac·cess** \ˈdeakˈses\ *vb* [*de-accession* fr. *de-* + *accession*; *de-access* by shortening] *vt* **:** to remove and sell (a work of art) from a museum's collection esp. to raise funds to purchase other works of art ~ *vi* **:** to de-accession a work of art or part of a collection — **de·accession** *n*

de·acylate \(,)≈+\ *vt* [*de-* + *acylate*] **:** to remove an acyl group from (a compound) — **de·acylation** \ˌ≈+\ *n*

dead drop *n* [so called fr. the absence of personal contact between the agents] **:** a prearranged hiding place for the deposit and pickup of information obtained through espionage

dead lift* *n* **:** a lift in weight lifting in which the weight is lifted from the floor to hip level; *also* **:** a competitive event involving this lift

dead–on \(ˈ)≈ˈ≈\ *adj* [[4]*dead* + *on*] **:** precisely correct **:** extremely accurate ⟨*dead-on* timing⟩ ⟨*dead-on* in his contention that effective worker-education programs need firm intellectual . . . underpinnings —Benjamin DeMott⟩

dear john *n, usu cap D&J* **:** a letter (as to a soldier) in which a wife asks for a divorce or a girl friend breaks off an engagement or a friendship

deb·by \ˈdebē, -i\ *adj* [*deb* + *-y*] *chiefly Brit* **:** being, relating to, or resembling a debutante

debit card *n* **:** a card like a credit card by which money may be withdrawn or the cost of purchases paid directly from the holder's bank account without the payment of interest

de·boost \(ˈ)dē, dә +\ *n* [*de-* + *boost*] **:** the process of slowing down a spacecraft ⟨before ~ into low orbit —C.J. Sitomer⟩

debrief* *vt* **:** to instruct not to reveal classified information after release from a sensitive position

debug* *vt* **1 :** to remove a concealed microphone or wiretapping device from ⟨~ a room⟩ **2 :** to make (concealed microphones) ineffective by electronic means

de·bug·ger \(ˈ)dēˈbәgәr\ *n* -s **:** one that debugs

deca·met·ric \ˌdekәˌme·trik\ *adj* [*decameter* + *-ic;* fr. the wavelength range being between 1 and 10 decameters] **:** of, relating to, or being a radio wave of high frequency

deca·peptide \ˌ≈≈+\ *n* [*deca-* + *peptide*] **:** a polypeptide (as angiotensin I) that consists of a chain of 10 amino acids

dec·ath·lete \dәˈkath,lēt\ *n* -s [blend of *decathlon* and *athlete*] **:** an athlete who competes in the decathlon

dec·ca \ˈdekә\ *n, usu cap* [*Decca* Co., British firm which developed it] **:** a system of long-range navigation utilizing the phase differences of continuous-wave signals from synchronized ground transmitters

deciding *adj* [fr. pres. part. of *decide*] **:** having the effect of settling a contest or controversy ⟨the ~ run⟩ ⟨the ~ vote⟩

de·cid·u·o·ma \dә,sijәˈwōmә, dē-\ *n, pl* **deciduomas** *or* **deciduo·ma·ta** \-mәd·ә, -әtә\ [NL, fr. *decidua* + *-oma*] **1 :** a mass of tissue formed in the uterus following pregnancy that contains remnants of chorionic or decidual tissue **2 :** decidual tissue induced in the uterus (as by trauma) in the absence of pregnancy

decision theory *n* **:** a branch of statistical theory that attempts to quantify the process of making choices between alternatives

deck* *n* **1 :** TAPE DECK 1b *herein* **2 :** a layer of clouds

declining–balance method \≈ˌ≈≈ˌ≈≈-\ *n* **:** a method of calculating periodic depreciation that involves the determining at regular (as annual) intervals throughout the expected life of an asset of equal percentage amounts of a cost balance which is progressively decreased by subtraction of each prior increment of depreciation from the original cost of the asset — compare STRAIGHT-LINE METHOD *in the Dict*

de·clot \(ˈ)dē, dә+\ *vt* [*de-* + *clot*] **:** to remove blood clots from

deco *n* -s *often cap* **:** ART DECO *herein*

decoder* *n* **:** an electronic device for unscrambling a television transmission

decollate* *vt* **:** to separate the copies of (as a computer printout produced in multiple copies) — **de·collator** \ˌdē+\ *n*

de·colonize \(ˈ)dē, dә +\ *vb* [*de-* + *colonize*] *vt* **:** to free from colonial status ~ *vi* **:** to grant independence to colonies — **de·colonization** \"+\ *n*

de·commitment \ˌdē+\ *n* [*de-* + *commitment*] **:** a dropping or turning away from a prior commitment

decomposer* *n* **:** any of various organisms (as many bacteria and fungi) that return constituents of organic substances to ecological cycles by feeding on and breaking down dead protoplasm

de·conglomerate \ˌdē+\ *vi* [*de-* + [2]*conglomerate*] **:** to divide a corporate conglomerate into independent companies — **de·conglomeration** \"+\ *n*

de·construct \ˌdē+\ *vt* [*de-* + *construct*] **:** to discuss (as a work of literature) using the methods of deconstruction

de·construction \"+\ *n* [*de-* + *construction*] **:** a method of literary criticism that interprets texts on the basis of the philosophical, political, or social implications of the way that language is used in the text rather than on the basis of the intentional use to which the language is being put — **de·con·struc·tion·ism** \ˌ≈≈ˈ≈shә,nizәm\ *n* — **de·con·struc·tion·ist** \-sh(ә)nәst\ *n or adj* — **de·constructive** \"+\ *adj*

de·convolution \ˌdē+\ *n* [*de-* + *convolution*] **:** simplification of a complex signal (as instrumental data) usu. by removal of instrument noise

de·couple \(ˈ)dē, dә+\ *vt* [*de-* + *couple*] **1 :** to reduce or eliminate the coupling of (as circuits or mechanical parts) **2 :** to decrease the seismic effect of (a nuclear explosion) by explosion in an underground cavity — **de·coupler** \"+\ *n*

de·creolization \ˌdē+\ *n* -s [*de-* + *creolization*] **:** the process of evolving from a creole into a standard language or a variety of a standard language

de·crim·i·nal·ize \(ˈ)dēˈkrimәnᵊl,īz, dәˈ-, -m(ә)nәl-\ *vt* -ED/-ING/-S [*de-* + *criminal* + *-ize*] **:** to remove or reduce the criminal classification or status of; *esp* **:** to repeal a strict ban on while keeping under some form of regulation ⟨wanted to ~ the possession of marijuana⟩ — **de·crim·i·nal·iza·tion** \-ˌkrimәnᵊlәˈzāshәn, -mnәl-, -līˈ- \ *n* -s

de·cumulation \ˌdē+\ *n* [*de-* + *cumulation*] **:** disposal of something accumulated

DEd *abbr* doctor of education

deep* *adj* **:** LARGE ⟨~ discounts⟩ ⟨~ cuts in the budget⟩

deep* *adv* **:** at the farther limits of the normal position of play ⟨the shortstop was playing ~⟩

deep space* *also* **deep sky** *n* **:** space well beyond the limits of the earth's atmosphere including space outside the solar system

deep structure *n* **:** a formal representation of the underlying semantic content of a sentence; *also* **:** the structure which such a representation specifies

de–escalate \(ˈ)dē +\ *vb* [*de-* + *escalate*] *vi* **:** to decrease in extent, volume, number, amount, or scope **:** DIMINISH ~ *vt* **:** to decrease the extent, volume, number, amount, or scope of ⟨my sister . . . tried to *de-escalate* our feud —H.A.Smith⟩ — **de–escalation** \(ˌ)dē +\ *n*

de-es·ca·la·tor \(ˈ)dēˌeskəˌlād·ə(r), -ātə-, ÷-kyə-\ *n* -s [*de-escalate* + *-or*] **:** an advocate of de-escalation

de-es·ca·la·to·ry \-ˌləˌtōrē\ *adj* [*de-escalate* + *-ory*] **:** of or relating to de-escalation ⟨took the first *de-escalatory* step⟩

deet \ˈdēt\ *n* -s [fr. *d. t.* (abbr. of *diethyl toluamide*)] **:** a colorless oily liquid insect repellent $C_{12}H_{17}NO$ — called also *diethyl toluamide*

defang* *vt* **:** to make harmless or less powerful **:** WEAKEN

defensive* *adj* **:** of, relating to, or being industries (as foods, utilities, and insurance) which provide essential needs to the ultimate consumer and in which business activity is relatively insensitive to changes in general business activity

deferred income* *n* **:** current income forgone to produce a later higher income (as at retirement)

de·fibrillation \(ˈ)dē, də+\ *n* **:** restoration of the rhythm of a fibrillating heart — **de·fibrillate** \(ˌ)dē, də+\ *vt* — **de·fi·bril·la·tor** \dēˈfibrəˌlād·ə(r)\ *n* -s

[1]**de·focus** \(ˈ)dē, də +\ *vb* [*de-* + *focus*] *vt* **:** to cause (as a beam of radiation or a lens) to be out of focus ⟨~*ed* his eye⟩ ⟨a ~*ed* image⟩ ~ *vi* **:** to lose accuracy of focus **:** become defocused

[2]**defocus** \"\ *n* **:** a result of defocusing; *esp* **:** an image (as on motion-picture film) deliberately blurred for dramatic effect

de·fog \(ˈ)dē, də +\ *vt* [*de-* + *fog*] **:** to remove fog or condensed moisture from **:** keep free of fog — **de·fog·ger** *n* -s

defuse* *vt* **:** to make less dangerous, potent, or tense **:** CALM

degeneracy* *n* **:** the coding of an amino acid by more than one codon of the genetic code

degenerate* *adj* **1 :** being mathematically simpler (as by having a factor or constant equal to zero) than the typical case ⟨the graph of a second degree equation yielding two intersecting lines is a ~ hyperbola⟩ **2 a :** having two or more states or subdivisions esp. of the same energy or frequency ⟨~ orbital⟩ ⟨~ oscillation⟩ **b** *of a semiconductor* **:** having a sufficient concentration of impurities to conduct electricity as a semimetal **3 :** having more than one codon representing an amino acid; *also* **:** being such a codon **4 :** consisting of degenerate matter ⟨a ~ star⟩

de·grad·able \dəˈgrādəbəl, dē-\ *adj* [*degrade* + *-able*] **:** capable of being chemically degraded ⟨~ detergents⟩

de·granulation \(ˌ)dē, də +\ *n* [*de-* + *granulation*] **:** the process of losing granules ⟨~ of leukocytes⟩

de·hire \"+\ *vt* [*de-* + *hire*] **:** to dismiss esp. from an executive position

de·hy·drase \dēˈhīˌdrās, -āz\ *n* -s [*dehydr-* + *-ase*] **1 :** DEHYDROGENASE **2 :** DEHYDRATASE *herein*

de·hy·dra·tase \-ˌdrəˌtās, -āz\ *n* -s [*dehydrate* + *-ase*] **:** an enzyme that catalyzes the removal of oxygen and hydrogen from metabolites in the proportion in which they form water

de·hy·dro·chlo·ri·nase \(ˌ)dēˌhīdrəˈklōrəˌnās, -lȯr-, -āz\ *n* -s [*dehydrochlorinate* (herein) + *-ase*] **:** an enzyme that dehydrochlorinates a chlorinated hydrocarbon (as DDT) and is found esp. in some DDT resistant insects

de·hy·dro·chlo·ri·na·tion \-ˌklōrəˈnāshən, -lȯr-\ *n* [*de-* + *hydr-* + *chlorine* + *-ation*] **:** the process of removing hydrogen and chlorine or hydrogen chloride from a compound — **de·hy·dro·chlo·ri·nate** \-ˈklōrəˌnāt, -lȯr-\ *vt*

de·hy·dro·epi·androsterone \(ˌ)dēˌhīdrōˌepē+\ *n* [*dehydr-* + *epi-* + *androsterone*] **:** an androgenic ketosteroid $C_{19}H_{28}O_2$ found in human urine and the adrenal cortex that is thought to be an intermediate in the biosynthesis of testosterone

de·hy·dro·iso·androsterone \-ˌī(ˌ)sō+\ *n* [*dehydr-* + *iso-* + *androsterone*] **:** DEHYDROEPIANDROSTERONE *herein*

de·individualize \(ˈ)dē+\ *vt* [*de-* + *individualize*] **:** to remove or destroy the individuality of **:** deprive of individuality — **de·individualization** \"+\ *n*

de·industrialization \ˌdē+\ *n* [*de-* + *industrialization*] **:** the reduction or destruction of a nation's industrial capacity; *also* **:** the loss of industrial plants and jobs — **de·industrialize** \"+\ *vb*

de·institutionalization \"+\ *n* [*de-* + *institutionalization*] **1 :** the release of institutionalized individuals (as mental patients) from institutional care to care in the community **2 :** the reform or modification of an institution to remove or disguise its institutional character — **de·institutionalize** \"+\ *vt*

deix·is \ˈdīksės\ *n* -ES [Gk, lit., demonstrative force] **:** the pointing or specifying function of some words (as definite articles and demonstrative pronouns)

déjàvu* *n* **1 :** a feeling that one has seen or heard something before ⟨a nightmarish *déjà vu* hit us as we sat in on the . . . conference —*Wall Street Jour.*⟩ **2 :** something overly or unpleasantly familiar ⟨the appointment seems like a case of *déjà vu* —E.B. Fiske⟩

déjàvu *adj* **:** so familiar as to be uninteresting **:** COMMONPLACE ⟨much of what was blasted as revolutionary in 1931 has long since become *déjà vu* —J.J. Lamberts⟩

deka·gram *n* [by alter.] **:** DECAGRAM

deka·li·ter *n* [by alter.] **:** DECALITER

deka·me·ter *n* **:** [2]DECAMETER

deka·met·ric *adj* [by alter.] **:** DECAMETRIC *herein*

deka·stere *n* [by alter.] **:** DECASTERE

delay* *n* **:** a play in football in which a ballcarrier or potential receiver delays momentarily as if to block before receiving a handoff or running a prescribed pattern

de·legitimate \ˌdē+\ *vt* [*de-* + [2]*legitimate*] **:** to diminish or destroy the prestige or authority of — **de·legitimation** \"+\ *n*

deli *also* **del·ly** \ˈdelē, -li\ *n, pl* **del·is** *also* **del·lies** [by shortening] **:** DELICATESSEN

delicacy* *n* **:** the degree of differentiation between subcategories of linguistic categories ⟨by increase in ~, the primary class is broken down into secondary classes —M.A.K. Halliday⟩

delimiter* *n* **:** a character that marks the beginning or end of a unit of data (as on a magnetic tape)

deliver* *vt* **1 :** to cause (oneself) to produce something as if by giving birth ⟨~*ed* himself of half an autobiography —H.C. Schonberg⟩ **2 :** to come through with **:** PRODUCE ⟨the new car ~*s* high gas mileage⟩ ~ *vi* **:** to produce the promised, desired, or expected results **:** come through ⟨failed to ~ on their promises⟩

de·localized \ˌdē+\ *adj* [*de-* + *localized*] **:** relating to, containing, or being a charge or charge carrier that can reside at any of several locations within a molecule ⟨~ electron⟩

delta wave *also* **delta*** *or* **delta rhythm** *n* **:** a high amplitude electrical rhythm of the brain with a frequency of less than 6 cycles per second that occurs esp. in deep sleep, in infancy, and in many diseased conditions of the brain

deltoid tuberosity *n* **:** a rough triangular bump on the outer side of the middle of the humerus that is the site of insertion of the deltoid muscle

de·magnify \(ˈ)dē, də̇ +\ *vt* [*de-* + *magnify*] **:** to reduce the size of (as a photographic image or an electron beam) — **de·magnification** \(ˌ)dē, də̇ +\ *n*

demand–pull \ˌ=ˈ=\ *n* [^{1}*demand* + ^{2}*pull*] **:** an increase or upward trend in spendable money that tends to result in increased competition for available goods and services and a corresponding increase in consumer prices — compare COST-PUSH *herein* — **demand–pull** *adj*

de·marketing \(ˌ)dē, də̇+\ *n* [*de-* + *marketing*] **:** the use of advertising to decrease demand for a product that is in short supply

de·masculinize \"+\ *vt* [*de-* + *masculinize*] **:** to remove the masculine character or qualities of ⟨~ the behavior of young men⟩ — **de·masculinization** \"+\ *n*

dem·e·ton \ˈdeməˌtän\ *n* -s [prob. fr. *d*iethyl + *me*rcapt- + *th*io*n*ate] **:** a mixture of organophosphorus insecticides used as a systemic on plants

demi–pen·sion \ˌdemē(ˈ)pä^{n}ˌsyō^{n}, -ˌpä^{n}sēˌō^{n}\ *n* [F, fr. *demi-* half + *pension* board] **:** MODIFIED AMERICAN PLAN *herein*

de·mist·er \dēˈmistə(r), də̇-\ *n* -s [*de-* + *mist* + *-er*] *Brit* **:** DEFROSTER

demo* *n* **1 :** DEMONSTRATION **2 :** DEMONSTRATOR

demographic* *adj* **:** of or relating to demographics; *esp* **:** relating to or intended for a segment of the population identified by demographics ⟨a ~ edition of a magazine⟩ ⟨~ advertising⟩

de·mo·graph·ics \ˌdēməˈgrafiks, ˌdem-\ *n pl* [*demographic* + ^{1}*-s*] **:** statistical characteristics (as age, sex, income, educational level) of a segment of a human population used esp. to identify markets; *also* **:** a market or a segment of the population so identified

demolition derby *n* **:** a contest in which drivers ram old cars into one another until only one car remains running

de·mothball \(ˈ)dē+\ *vt* [*de-* + *mothball*] **:** to remove the preservative covering in order to reactivate (as ships)

de·mystify \"+\ *vt* [*de-* + *mystify*] **:** to eliminate the mystifying features of ⟨his novels . . . ~ death, confronting us with the omnipresent reality of it —Harriet Blodgett⟩ — **de·mystification** \"+\ *n*

demythologize* *vt* **:** to divest of mythical elements or associations

den·dro·dendritic \ˌdendrō+\ *adj* [*dendr-* + *dendritic*] **:** relating to or being a nerve synapse between a dendrite of one cell and a dendrite of another

de·ni·abil·i·ty \də̇ˌnīəˈbiləd·ē, dē-\ *n* -ES **:** the ability of an official to deny something esp. on the basis of being officially uninformed

density function *n* **:** PROBABILITY DENSITY FUNCTION

den·som·e·ter \denˈsäməd·ə(r)\ *n* [ISV *dens-* (fr. L *densus* dense) + *-o-* + *-meter*] **1 :** an instrument for measuring the porosity of paper by forcing air through it **2 :** DENSIMETER

den·tur·ist \ˈdenchərə̇st\ *n* -s [*denture* + *-ist*] **:** a dental technician who makes, fits, and repairs dentures directly for the public

de·nu·cle·ar·ize \(ˈ)dēˈn(y)üklēəˌrīz, ÷-kyələˌrīz\ *vt* -ED/-ING/-s *see -ize in Explan Notes* [*de-* + *nuclear* + *-ize*] **:** to remove nuclear arms from **:** prohibit the use of nuclear arms in — **de·nu·cle·ar·iza·tion** \(ˌ)dēˌn(y)üklēərə̇ˈzāshən, ÷-kyələr-, -ˌrīˈz-\ *n*

denver boot *n, usu cap D* **:** a metal clamp that locks onto one of the wheels of an automobile and must be unlocked before a motorist can drive off (as after payment of a fine)

de·orbit \(ˈ)dē +\ *vb* [*de-* + *orbit*] *vi* **:** to go out of orbit ~ *vt* **:** to cause to deorbit ⟨~ a spacecraft⟩ — **deorbit** *n*

de·oxy·cytidine \(ˌ)dēˌäksē+\ *n* [*deoxy-* + *cytidine*] **:** a nucleoside consisting of cytosine combined with deoxyribose that occurs esp. as a component of DNA

de·oxy·ri·bo·nucleotide \(ˌ)dēˌäksēˌrī(ˌ)bō +\ *n* [*deoxyribose* + *nucleotide*] **:** a nucleotide that contains deoxyribose and is a constituent of DNA

dependence* *also* **dependance*** *n* **1 :** a drug addiction **2 :** HABITUATION 2b

dependent* *adj* **1 :** affected with a drug dependence **2 a :** not mathematically or statistically independent ⟨a ~ set of vectors⟩ ⟨~ events⟩ **b :** EQUIVALENT 1 *herein* ⟨~ equations⟩

de·pic·ture \də̇ˈpikchə(r), dē-, -ksh-\ *vt* [blend of *depict* and ^{2}*picture*] **1 :** DEPICT **2 :** IMAGINE — **de·pic·ture·ment** \-mənt\ *n* -s

de·politicize \ˌdē +\ *vt* [*de-* + *politicize*] **:** to remove the political character from **:** take out of the realm of politics — **de·po·lit·i·ci·za·tion** \ˌdēpəˌlid·əsə̇ˈzāshən, -ˌsīˈ-\ *n* -s

de·pollute \"+\ *vt* [*de-* + *pollute*] **:** to remove the pollution from — **de·pollution** \"+\ *n*

depression glass *n, usu cap D* **:** glassware mass-produced in a variety of colors and patterns during the late 1920s and 1930s

de·pressurize \(ˈ)dē +\ *vt* [*de-* + *pressurize*] **:** to release pressure from — **de·pressurization** \"+\ *n*

de·program \"+\ *vt* [*de-* + *program*] **:** to dissuade or try to dissuade from convictions usu. of a religious nature often with the use of force ⟨parents lure their children away from the communes so that he can ~ them —Kenneth Woodward⟩ — **de·programmer** \"+\ *n* — **de·programming** \"+\ *n*

de·pro·tein·ate \(ˈ)dēˌprōˌtēˌnāt *also* -ˌprōd·ēə̇ˌn- *or* -ōtēə̇ˌn-\ *vt* -ED/-ING/-s [*de-* + *protein* + ^{4}*ate*] **:** DEPROTEINIZE — **de·pro·tein·ation** \(ˈ)dēˌprōˌtēˈnāshən *also* -ˌprōd·ēə̇ˈn- *or* -ōtēə̇ˈn-\ *n* -s

de·quer·vain's disease \dəkerˌva^{n}z-\ *n, usu cap Q* [after Fritz *de Quervain* †1940 Swiss surgeon] **:** inflammation of tendons and their sheaths at the styloid process of the radius that often causes pain in the thumb side of the wrist

de·rail·leur \də̇ˈrālə(r), dē-\ *n* -s [F *dérailleur,* fr. *dérailler* to throw off the track (fr. *dé-* de- + *rail* rail, fr. E) + *-eur* -or] **:** a mechanism for shifting gears on a bicycle that operates by moving the chain from one set of exposed gears to another ⟨10-speed ~⟩

de·regulate \(ˈ)dē, də̇ +\ *vt* [*de-* + *regulate*] **:** DECONTROL ⟨proposals to ~ natural-gas prices —*Wall Street Jour.*⟩ — **de·regulation** \(ˌ)dē, də̇ +\ *n* — **de·regulator** \"+\ *n* — **de·regulatory** \"+\ *adj*

de·repress \ˌdē +\ *vt* [*de-* + *repress*] **:** to activate (a gene or protein synthesis) by releasing from a blocked state — **de·repression** \"+\ *n*

derm·abrasion \ˌdərm+\ *n* [*derm-* + *abrasion*] **:** surgical removal of skin blemishes or imperfections (as scars or tattoos) by abrasion (as with sandpaper or wire brushes)

der·mom·e·ter \ (ˌ)dərˈmäməd·ər, -ətər\ *n* -s [*derm-* + *-meter*] **:** an instrument used to measure the electrical resistance of the skin

der·mo·necrotic \ˌdər(ˌ)mō+\ *adj* [*derm-* + *necrotic*] : relating to or causing necrosis of the skin ⟨a ~ toxin⟩ ⟨~ effects⟩

de·romanticize \ˌdē+\ *vt* [*de-* + *romanticize*] : to remove the romance from : make mundane

DES \ˌdē(ˌ)ē'es\ *n* -ES : DIETHYLSTILBESTROL

de·sa·li·nate \(ˈ)dēˈsalə̦nāt, -sā-\ *vt* -ED/-ING/-S [*de-* + *salin-* + *-ate*] : to remove salt from ⟨~ seawater⟩ — **de·sa·li·na·tor** \-nād·ə(r)\ *n* -S

de·salinize \(ˈ)dē, dȯ +\ *vt* [*de-* + *salinize*] : DESALINATE *herein*

descending colon *n* : the part of the large intestine on the left side that extends from the bend below the spleen to the sigmoid flexure — compare ASCENDING COLON *herein*, TRANSVERSE COLON *in the Dict*

de·school \(ˈ)dē +\ *vt* [*de-* + *school*] : to eliminate traditional schools from ⟨the movement to ~ society —John Holt⟩

descriptor* *n* **1** : a word or phrase (as an index term) used to identify an item (as a subject or document) esp. in an information retrieval system; *also* : an alphanumeric symbol so used **2** : something (as a word or phrase or a characteristic feature) that serves to describe or identify

de·select \ˌdē +\ *vt* [*de-* + *select*] : DISMISS, REJECT

de·sert·i·fi·ca·tion \də̇ˌzərd·əfə̇'kāshən\ *n* -S [¹*desert* + *-ification* (as in *saponification*)] : the process of becoming arid land or desert (as from land mismanagement or climate change)

designated hitter *n* : a baseball player designated at the start of the game to bat in place of the pitcher without causing the pitcher to be removed from the game

de·si·pra·mine \də̇'ziprəˌmēn\ *n* -S [*des*methyl (fr. *des-* + *methyl*) + imi*pramine* (herein)] : a tricyclic antidepressant $C_{18}H_{22}N_2$ administered as the hydrochloride esp. in the treatment of endogenous depressions (as a manic-depressive psychosis)

desktop \'=ˌ=\ *adj* : of a size that can be conveniently used on a desk or table ⟨~ computer⟩

des·mo·some \'dezməˌsōm\ *n* -S [*desm-* + *-some*] : a specialized local thickening of the cell membrane of an epithelial cell that serves to anchor contiguous cells together

des·mos·ter·ol \dez'mästəˌrȯl, -ˌrōl\ *n* [*desm-* + *sterol*] : DEHYDROCHOLESTEROL

de·spin \(ˈ)dē +\ *vt* [*de-* + *spin*] : to stop the rotation of or reduce the speed of rotation of (as a satellite)

de–sta·lin·iza·tion \(ˌ)dēˌstälənə̇ˈzāshən, -tal-, -ˌnīˈz-\ *n* -S *usu cap S* [*destalinize* + *-ation*] : the discrediting of Stalin and his policies

de·struct \'dēˌstrəkt, də̇'s-, dē's-\ *n* -S [short for *destruction*] : the deliberate destruction of a rocket after launching esp. during a test; *also* : such destruction of a device or material (as to prevent its falling into enemy hands)

de·synchronization \(ˈ)dē+\ *n* [*de-* + *synchronization*] : the process or result of getting out of synchronization — **de·synchronize** \"+\ *vt*

deterrence* *n* : the maintaining of vast military power and weaponry in order to discourage war

detonate* *vt* : to set off in a burst of activity : SPARK ⟨programs that *detonated* controversies⟩

de·tox \'dēˈtäks\ *adj* [by shortening] : of or used for detoxification ⟨an alcohol ~ clinic⟩ ⟨a ~ program⟩

detoxify* *vt* : to free (as a drug user or an alcoholic) from an intoxicating or an addictive substance in the body or from dependence on or addiction to such a substance ⟨the clinic started ~*ing* him by gradually lowering his dosage —J.M. Markham⟩ **2** : NEUTRALIZE 2 ⟨~*ing* tensions that arise between people of divergent tastes and goals — M. B. Duberman⟩ ~ *vi* : to become free of addiction to a drug or alcohol — **detoxification*** *n*

de·tumescent \ˌdē +\ *adj* [L *detumescere* to cease swelling + E *-ent*] : characterized by detumescence

deu·ter·ate \'d(y)üd·əˌrāt\ *vt* -ED/-ING/-S [*deuter*ium + *-ate*] : to introduce deuterium into (a compound)

de·vel·op·ing *adj* : UNDERDEVELOPED 3 ⟨~ nations⟩

de·volatilize \(ˈ)dē, də̇ +\ *vt* [*de-* + *volatilize*] : to remove volatile material from (as coal) — **de·volatilization** \"+\ *n*

devon rex *n, usu cap D* : any of a breed of rex cats with a very short curly coat and a strongly marked stop

dex \'deks\ *n* -ES [short for *Dexedrine* (herein)] : the sulfate of dextroamphetamine

dexa·meth·a·sone \ˌdeksə'methəˌsōn, -ˌzōn\ *n* -S [perh. fr. *Dexa*myl, a trademark + *meth*yl + *-sone* (as in *cortisone*)] : a synthetic glucocorticoid $C_{22}H_{29}FO_5$ used esp. as an anti-inflammatory and antiallergic agent

dex·amphetamine \ˌdeks +\ *n* [alter. of *dextroamphetamine*] *chiefly Brit* : DEXTROAMPHETAMINE

Dex·e·drine \'deksə̇ˌdrēn, -drən\ *trademark* — used for a preparation of the sulfate of dextroamphetamine

dex·ies \'deksēz\ *n pl* [*dex* (herein) + *-ie* + *-s*] : tablets or capsules of the sulfate of dextroamphetamine

dex·tran·ase \-strəˌnās, -ˌnāz\ *n* -S [*dextran* + *-ase*] : a hydrolase that prevents tooth decay by breaking down dextran and eliminating dental plaque

dex·tro·propoxyphene \ˌdekstrə +\ *n* [*dextr-* + *propoxyphene*] : PROPOXYPHENE *herein*

DH *abbr* designated hitter *herein*

diagnosis related group *n* : DRG *herein*

di·ag·o·nal·ize \dī'agənᵊlˌīz, -gnəl-\ *vt* -ED/-ING/-S [¹*diagonal* + *-ize*] : to convert (a matrix) to a diagonal matrix — **di·ag·o·nal·iz·able** \-ˈīzəbəl\ *adj* — **di·ag·o·nal·iza·tion** \-ˌag(ə)nᵊl-ə̇'zāshən, -gnəl-\ *n* -S

diagonal matrix *n* : a matrix that has all the nonzero elements located along the diagonal from upper left to lower right

di·az·e·pam \dī'azəˌpam\ *n* -S [*diaz-* + *e*poxide + *-am*] : a synthetic tranquilizer $C_{16}H_{13}ClN_2O$ used esp. to relieve anxiety and tension and as a muscle relaxant — see VALIUM *herein*

Di·az·i·non \dī'azə̇ˌnän\ *trademark* — used for an organophosphate insecticide $C_{12}H_{21}N_2O_3PS$ that is a cholinesterase inhibitor dangerous to human beings if ingested

di·azo·benzenesulfonic acid \(ˈ)dīˈazō, -ˈāzō + . . .-\ *n* [*diaz-* + *benzene* + *sulfonic*] : a white or reddish crystalline acid derivative $C_6H_4N_2O_3S$ of sulfanilic acid that is used as the reagent in the diazo reaction

di·az·ox·ide \ˌdīˌaz'äkˌsīd\ *n* [*diaz-* + *oxide*] : an antihypertensive drug $C_8H_7ClN_2O_2S$ that has a structure similar to chlorothiazide but no diuretic activity

dice* *n* : a close contest between two racing-car drivers for position during a race

dice* *vi* : to engage in a dice

di·cen·tric \(ˈ)dīˈsen·trik\ *n* -S : a dicentric chromosome

dic·ey \'dīsē\ *adj* **dic·i·er; dic·i·est** [²*dice* + *-y*] : RISKY, UNPREDICTABLE ⟨consumer loans, which are becoming *dicier* with rising unemployment —*Business Week*⟩

di·chlor·vos \(ˈ)dīˈklō(ə)rˌväs, -lȯ(-, -vəs\ *n* -ES [*dichlor-* + *v*inyl + pho*s*phate] : a nonpersistent organophosphorus pesticide $C_4H_7Cl_2O_4P$ that is used esp. against insects and is of low toxicity to man — called also *DDVP*

dich·otic \(ˈ)dī¦kōd·ik, -käd·-\ *adj* [*dich-* + *-otic*] **:** affecting or relating to the two ears differently in regard to a conscious aspect (as pitch or loudness) or a physical aspect (as frequency or energy) of sound — **dich·oti·cal·ly** \-d·ək(ə)lē\ *adv*

dictionary* *n* **:** a list (as of data items or words) stored in a computer for reference (as for information retrieval or word processing)

diddle* *vi* **:** FIDDLE, TOY — usu. used with *with* ⟨*diddling* around with the tape machine —Michael Stephens⟩

did·dly–squat \ˈdid(ᵊ)lē+\ *n* [perh. alter. of *doodley-squat* (herein)] *slang* **:** the least amount **:** NOTHING ⟨if everyone ignores it, it won't be worth *diddly-squat* —Andrew Tobias⟩

die·sel·ing \ˈdēz(ə)liŋ, ˈdēs(-\ *n* -s [[1]*diesel* + *-ing*] **:** the continued operation of an internal-combustion engine after the ignition is turned off

diethyl tolu·amide \-¦täl(ˌ)yü +\ *n* [*diethyl* + *tol-* + *amide*] **:** DEET *herein*

difference* *vt* **:** to compute the difference between

di·functional \(ˈ)dī+\ *adj* [*di-* + *functional*] **:** of, relating to, or being a compound with two sites in the molecule that are highly reactive — **di·functionality** \(ˌ)dī+\ *n*

di·ges·tif \ˌdēzhesˈtēf\ *n* -s [F, lit., digestive] **:** an alcoholic drink (as brandy or a liqueur) usu. taken after a meal

digital* *adj* **1 :** providing a readout in numerical digits ⟨a ~ voltmeter⟩ ⟨a ~ clock radio⟩ **2 :** relating to or being a phonograph record made from a digital recording with the result that wow and flutter are eliminated and background noise is greatly reduced

dig·i·tal·ize \ˈdijəd·ᵊlˌīz\ *vt* -ED/-ING/-S [[1]*digital* + *-ize*] **:** DIGITIZE

digital recording *n* **:** the process of recording sound usu. on magnetic tape by the digital representation of sound waves as the sum of minute increments in amplitude

di·glos·sia \(ˈ)dī¦gläsēə, -lȯs-\ *n* -s [NL, fr. F *diglossie* (fr. *di-* di- + *-glossie,* fr. Gk *glōssa* language, tongue) + L *-ia* -y] **:** the use of two languages or dialects for different functions or at different social levels — **di·glos·sic** \-sik\ *adj*

di·hy·droxy·acetone \ˌdīhīˌdräksē+\ *n* [*dihydroxy-* + *acetone*] **:** a glyceraldehyde isomer $C_3H_6O_3$ that is used esp. to stain the skin to resemble a tan

di·hy·droxy·cholecalciferol \"+\ *n* [*dihydroxy-* + *cholecalciferol*] **:** a physiologically active vitamin D derivative $C_{27}H_{44}O_3$ that is synthesized in the kidney

di·hy·droxy·phenylalanine \"+\ *n* [*dihydroxy-* + *phenylalanine*] **1 :** DOPA **2 :** L-DOPA *herein*

dike *var of* DYKE *herein*

di·lu·tive \(ˈ)dī¦l(y)üd·iv, dəˈl-\ *adj* [[1]*dilute* + [1]*-ive*] **:** reducing or involving reduction of per share income of a corporate stock ⟨the ~ effect of stock options and convertible securities⟩

dime* *n* **1** *slang* **a :** 10 dollars **b** *or* **dime bag :** a packet containing 10 dollars worth of an illicit drug (as marijuana) **2** *slang* **:** a sentence of 10 years in prison

dimension* *n* **:** the number of elements in a basis of a vector space

di·meth·o·ate \dīˈmethəˌwāt\ *n* -s [*dimethyl* + *-thioic* + [1]*-ate*] **:** an organophosphorus insecticide $C_5H_{12}NO_3PS_2$ used on livestock and various crops

dimethylhydrazine \¦÷¦÷÷¦÷÷,÷\ *n* [*dimethyl* + *hydrazine*] **:** either of two flammable corrosive isomeric liquids $C_2H_8N_2$ which are methylated derivatives of hydrazine and of which one is used in rocket fuels

dimethylnitrosamine \¦÷¦÷÷(ˌ)nī·ˈtrōsəˌmēn\ *n* [*dimethyl* + *nitrosamine*] **:** a carcinogenic nitrosamine $(CH_3)_2N_2O$ that occurs esp. in tobacco smoke

dimethylsulfoxide \¦÷¦÷÷,÷¦÷(ˌ)÷\ *n* [*dimethyl* + *sulfoxide*] **:** a compound $(CH_3)_2SO$ obtained as a by-product in wood-pulp manufacture and used as a solvent and in experimental medicine — called also *DMSO*

dimethyl terephthalate *n* **:** a chemical $C_{10}H_{10}O_2$ used for making polyester film and fiber

dimethyltryptamine \¦÷¦÷÷¦÷÷(ˌ)÷\ *n* [*dimethyl* + *tryptamine*] **:** an easily synthesized hallucinogenic drug $C_{12}H_{16}N_2$ that is chemically similar to but shorter acting than psilocybin — called also *DMT*

dim sum \ˈdimˈsəm\ *n pl* [Chin (Cant) *tím sam,* lit., small center] **:** traditional Chinese refreshments consisting of steamed or fried dumplings with a savory filling

dinch \ˈdinch\ *vt* -ED/-ING/-ES [origin unknown] **:** to extinguish by crushing ⟨~ a cigarette⟩

diner–out \¦÷÷ˈ÷\ *n, pl* **diners–out** [*dine out* + *-er*] **:** one that dines out ⟨a constant *diner-out* —Thomas Wolfe⟩

ding* *n* -s **:** minor surface damage (as a dent)

ding–a–ling* *n* **:** NITWIT, KOOK

dingbat* *n* **:** DING-A-LING *herein*

dink \ˈdiŋk\ *n* -s [origin unknown] *slang* **:** VIETNAMESE — used disparagingly

dinner theater *n* **:** a restaurant in which a play is presented after the meal is over

dinosaur* *n* **:** one that resembles a dinosaur esp. in having been made out-of-date or outmoded by changing conditions

di·ox·in \dīˈäksən\ *n* -s [*di-* + [1]*ox-* + *-in*] **:** any of several heterocyclic hydrocarbons that occur esp. as persistent toxic impurities in herbicides; *esp* **:** a teratogenic impurity $C_{12}H_4O_2Cl_4$ in 2, 4, 5-T — see AGENT ORANGE *herein,* TCDD *herein*

di·phe·nox·y·late \ˌdīˌfēnˈäksəˌlāt, -ˌfen-\ *n* -s [fr. *diphenyl*propyl + carb*oxyl*ic acid + *-ate*] **:** an antidiarrheal agent chemically related to meperidine and administered as the hydrochloride $C_{30}H_{32}N_2O_2{\cdot}HCl$

di·phosphoglycerate \(ˈ)dī+\ *n* [*di-* + *phosphoglycerate*] **:** an isomeric ester of diphosphoglyceric acid that occurs in human erythrocytes and facilitates release of oxygen by decreasing the oxygen affinity of hemoglobin

di·phos·pho·glyceric acid \(ˈ)dī¦fäsfō+ . . .-\ *n* [*di-* + *phosph-* + *glyceric acid*] **:** a diphosphate $C_3H_8O_9P_2$ of glyceric acid that is an important intermediate in photosynthesis and in glycolysis and fermentation

dipshit \ˈ÷¦÷\ *n* [[2]*dip* + *shit*] **:** a stupid or incompetent person **:** NITWIT — usu. considered vulgar

di·py·rid·am·ole \ˌdīpīˈridəˌmōl, -ˈpirədə,-\ *n* -s [*di-* + *pyrid*ine + *am*ine + *-ol*] **:** a drug $C_{24}H_{40}N_8O_4$ used as a coronary vasodilator

di·quat \ˈdīˌkwät\ *n* -s [*di-* + *quat*ernary] **:** a powerful nonpersistent herbicide $C_{12}H_{12}Br_2N_2$ that has been used to control water weeds (as the water hyacinth)

directly proportional *adj* **:** related by direct variation — compare INVERSELY PROPORTIONAL *herein*

director's chair *n* [so called fr. its use by movie directors] **:** a lightweight usu. folding armchair with a back and seat usu. of cotton duck

direct product *n* **:** CARTESIAN PRODUCT *herein; esp* **:** a group that is the Cartesian product of two other groups

direct sum *n* **:** CARTSIAN PRODUCT *herein*

direct variation *n* **1 :** mathematical relationship between two variables that can be expressed by an equation in which one variable is equal to a nonzero constant times the other **2 :** an equation or function expressing direct variation — compare INVERSE VARIATION 2 *herein*

dirhem* *n, usu* **dirham*** **1 a :** the basic monetary unit of Morocco and the United Arab Emirates — see MONEY table *in the Dict* **b :** a monetary unit of Iraq equal to $^1/_{20}$ dinar **c :** a monetary unit of Libya equal to $^1/_{1000}$ dinar — see MONEY table *in the Dict* **2 :** a coin or note representing one dirham

dirt bike *n* **:** a usu. lightweight motorcycle designed for operation on unpaved surfaces

dirty old man *n* **:** a lecherous mature man

dirty pool *n* [[3]*pool*] **:** underhanded or unsportsmanlike conduct

disaggregate* *vb* ~ *vi* **:** to break up or apart ⟨the molecules of a gel ~ to form a sol⟩ — **dis·aggregative** \(ˈ)dis+\ *adj*

dis·am·big·u·ate \ˌdis(ˌ)amˈbigyəˌwāt\ *vt* -ED/-ING/-S [[1]*dis-* + *ambiguous* + [4]*-ate*] **:** to establish a single semantic or grammatical interpretation for — **dis·am·big·u·ation** \-ˌbigyə-ˈwāshən \ *n* -s

dis·arm·er \ˈdisˈärmər\ *n* **:** a person who favors disarmament ⟨a nuclear ~⟩

disastrous* *adj* **:** extremely bad **:** TERRIBLE ⟨she was a ~ mother —Garry Wills⟩

dis·benefit \ˈdis+\ *n* [[1]*dis-* + *benefit*] **:** something disadvantageous or objectionable **:** DRAWBACK ⟨noise nuisance was the main ~ —Philip Howard⟩

dis·bound \(ˈ)dis+\ *adj* [[1]*dis-* + [4]*bound*] **:** no longer having a binding ⟨a ~ pamphlet⟩

disc brake *n* **:** a brake that operates by the friction of a caliper pressing against the sides of a rotating disc

disclosing *adj* **:** being or using an agent (as a tablet or liquid) that contains a usu. red dye that stains dental plaque

[1]dis·co \ˈdis(ˌ)kō\ *n* -s [short for *discotheque*] **1 :** a nightclub for dancing to live and recorded music often featuring flamboyant decor, special lighting effects, and live disc jockeys **2 :** popular dance music characterized by strong steady rhythms, repetitive lyrics, and usu. a predominance of electronically produced sounds

[2]disco *vi* -ED/-ING/-S **:** to dance to disco music

[1]dis·co·theque \ˈdiskəˌtek, ˈdēs-, -kōˌ-, ˌ==ˈ=\ *n* -s [F *discothèque* collection of phonograph records, discotheque, fr. *disque* disk (fr. L *discus*) + *-o-* + *thèque* (as in *bibliothèque* library, fr. L *bibliotheca*) — more at DISH, BIBLIOTHECA] **:** a usu. small intimate nightclub for dancing to recorded music; *also* **:** DISCO 1 *herein*

[2]discotheque *vi* -ED/-ING/-S **:** to dance at a discotheque

discretionary account *n* **:** a security or commodity market account in which an agent (as a broker) is given power of attorney allowing him to make independent decisions and buy and sell for the account of his principal

discretionary income *n* **:** the part of personal income left after payment of basic expenses (as taxes and the cost of food and shelter)

dis·cret·iza·tion \(ˌ)disˌkrēd·əˈzāshən, -ētə-\ *n* -s [*discrete* + *-ization*] **:** the action of making mathematically discrete

discriminant function *n* **:** a function of a set of variables (as measurements of taxonomic specimens) that is evaluated for samples of events or objects and used as an aid in discriminating between or classifying them

dis·habituation \ˈdis+\ *n* [[1]*dis-* + *habituation*] **:** restoration to full strength of a response that has become weakened by habituation — **dis·habituate** \"+\ *vb*

dishware \ˈ=ˌ=\ *n* [[1]*dish* + *ware*] **:** tableware (as of china) used in serving food

dishy \ˈdishē, -i\ *adj* -ER/-EST [*dish* + *-y*] **:** ATTRACTIVE

dis·information \ˈdis+\ *n* [trans. of Russ *dezinformatsiya* misinformation] **:** false information deliberately and often covertly spread (as by the planting of rumors) in order to influence public opinion or obscure the truth

dis·in·sec·tion \ˌdisənˈsekshən, -ˌinˈs-\ *n* -s [[1]*dis-* + *insect* + *-ion*] **:** DISINSECTIZATION

dis·in·ter·me·di·a·tion \(ˌ)disˌintə(r)ˌmēdēˈāshən\ *n* [[1]*dis-* + *intermediate* + *-ion;* fr. the investor's bypassing of the intermediate institution] **:** diversion of savings from institutions with governmentally imposed interest ceilings (as savings banks) to direct investment in higher-yielding instruments

dis·intoxicate \ˈdis+\ *vt* [*dis-* + *intoxicate*] **:** DETOXIFY 1 *herein*

disjoint* *adj* **:** having no elements in common ⟨~ mathematical sets⟩

disk* *or* **disc*** *n* **1 :** a round flat plate (as of metal) coated with a magnetic substance on which data for a computer can be stored — called also *magnetic disk* **2 :** a circular grid in a photocomposer **3** *usu disc* **a :** OPTICAL DISC *herein* **b :** COMPACT DISC *herein* **c :** VIDEODISC *herein*

disk·ette \ˌdisˈket\ *n* -s [[1]*disk* + *-ette*] **:** FLOPPY DISK *herein*

disk pack *n* **:** a storage device for a computer that consists of a stack of magnetic disks mounted on a central hub and their removable protective cover and that can be handled and stored as a unit

dis·ney·esque \ˈdiznēˈesk\ *adj, usu cap* [after Walt *Disney* †1966, Am. cartoonist] **:** resembling or suggestive of the films, television productions, or amusement parks made by Walt Disney or his organization

dis·par·lure \ˈdispärˌlu̇(ə)r\ *n* [NL *dispar* (specific epithet of the gypsy moth *Porthetria dispar*) + E *lure*] **:** a pheromone $C_{19}H_{38}O$ produced by female gypsy moths that has been made synthetically and used to attract males to traps

displacement* *n* **:** the substitution of another form of behavior for what is usual or expected esp. when the usual response is nonadaptive

display* *n* **:** an electronic device (as a cathode-ray tube or a liquid-crystal readout) that presents information in visual form; *also* **:** the visual information

disposable *n* -s [*disposable,* adj.] **:** something (as a paper blanket) that is disposable

dissonance* *n* **:** inconsistency between the beliefs one holds or between one's actions and one's beliefs **:** DISCORD

dis·tal* *adj* **:** of, relating to, or being the surface of a tooth that is most distant from the middle of the front of the jaw and is usu. next to the tooth behind it — compare MESIAL *herein,* PROXIMAL *herein* — **dis·tal·ly*** *adv*

dis·to·buccal \ˈdistō+\ *adj* [*dist-* + *buccal*] **:** relating to or located on the distal and buccal surfaces of a molar or premolar ⟨the ~ cusp of the first molar⟩ — **dis·to·buc·cally** \"+\ *adv*

dis·to·lingual \"+\ *adj* [*dist-* + *lingual*] **:** relating to or situated on the distal and lingual surfaces of a tooth ⟨the ~ cusp of a tooth⟩

distracter* *or* **distractor*** *n* **:** an incorrect answer given as a choice in a multiple-choice test

distribute* *vt* **:** to use in or as an operation so as to be mathematically distributive ⟨addition is not *distributed* over multiplication⟩ ~ *vi* **:** to be mathematically distributive ⟨multiplication ~*s* over addition⟩

distributed *adj* [fr. past part. of *distribute*] **1 :** characterized by a statistical distribution of a particular kind ⟨independently ~ random variables⟩ **2 :** of, relating to, or being a computer network in which at least some of the processing is done by the individual workstations and information is shared by and often stored at the workstations

distribution* *n* **1 :** FREQUENCY DISTRIBUTION **2 :** PROBABILITY FUNCTION **3 :** PROBABILITY DENSITY FUNCTION 2

distribution function *n* **:** a function that gives the probability that a random variable is less than or equal to the independent variable of the function

distributive education *n, often cap D & E* **:** a vocational program set up between schools and employers in which the student receives both classroom instruction and on-the-job training

di·sul·fo·ton \(ˌ)dī'səlfəˌtän\ *n* -s [*di*ethyl + *sulfo-* + *-ton* (prob. fr. *thio*nate)] **:** an organophosphorus systemic insecticide $C_8H_{19}O_2PS_3$ used esp. on cultivated plants

dit·sy *also* **dit·zy** \'ditsē\ *adj* -ER/-EST [origin unknown] **1 :** eccentrically silly, giddy, or inane **:** DIZZY ⟨the ~ but nice blond who may deserve the guy but seldom gets him —Rebecca Bricker⟩ **2 :** overly decorative **:** FUSSY ⟨a ~ pattern⟩

di·uron \'dīyəˌrän\ *n* -s [*di-* + *ur*ea + [1]*-on*] **:** a persistent herbicide $C_9H_{10}Cl_2N_2O$ used esp. to control annual weeds

diverge* *vi* **:** to be mathematically divergent

divergence* *n* **:** the state of being mathematically divergent

divide* *vt* **1 :** to be used as a divisor with respect to (a dividend) ⟨4 ~*s* 16 evenly⟩ **2 :** to use as a divisor — used with *into* ⟨~ 14 into 42⟩

divide* *n* **:** an instance of division performed by a computer; *also* **:** the means for performing division

division sign *n* **1 :** the symbol ÷ used to indicate division **2 :** a diagonal / used to indicate a fraction

di·vor·cé \də̇ˌvȯr'sā*also* -'sē, ≈'≈ˌ≈\ *n* -s [F] **:** a divorced man

DMA *abbr or n* -s **:** a doctor of musical arts

DMSO \ˌdē(ˌ)emˌes'ō\ *n* -s [*di*methyl*s*ulf*o*xide] **:** DIMETHYLSULFOXIDE *herein*

DMT \ˌdēˌem'tē\ *n* -s [*d*i*m*ethyl*t*ryptamine] **:** DIMETHYLTRYPTAMINE *herein*

DMZ *abbr* demilitarized zone

DNA polymerase *n* **:** any of several polymerases that promote replication or repair of DNA usu. using single-stranded DNA as a template

DN·ase \(ˈ)dēˌenˌās, -ˌāz\ *also* **DNA·ase** \(ˌ)dēˌen'āˌās, -ˌāz\ *n* -s [*DNase,* blend of *DNA* and *-ase; DNAase* fr. *DNA* + *-ase*] **:** DEOXYRIBONUCLEASE

DNF *abbr* did not finish

do* *vt* **:** to consume or take regularly **:** USE ⟨doesn't ~ cocaine⟩ — **do a number on 1 :** to defeat or confound thoroughly esp. by indirect or deceptive means **2 :** MOCK, RIDICULE

dobra* *n* **:** the basic monetary unit of Sao Tome and Principe — see MONEY table *in the Dict*

Do·bro \'dō(ˌ)brō\ *trademark* — used for an acoustic guitar having a metal resonator

dock* *vt* **:** to join mechanically (as two spacecraft) while in space ~ *vi* **:** to become docked

doctor* *vt* **:** CASTRATE, SPAY ⟨have your pet cat ~*ed*⟩

docu·drama \'däkyu̇, -yə+\ *n* [[2]*docu*mentary + *drama*] **:** a television or motion-picture drama dealing freely with historical events and esp. those of a recent and controversial nature

documentation* *n* **:** the usu. printed instructions, comments, and other information on the use of a particular piece or system of computer software or hardware

dodgy* *adj* **1** *Brit* **:** not sound, stable, or reliable ⟨there were thirteen planes, all brand new. And I had to pick the one with the ~ engine —Susan Saggers⟩ **2** *Brit* **:** requiring skill or care in handling or coping with **:** AWKWARD, TRICKY ⟨it was a little ~ getting her home and into the parsonage without anyone noticing —R.F. Delderfield⟩; *also* **:** CHANCY, RISKY ⟨bringing out a restaurant guide is a ~ business, since it has been prepared so far in advance —Alison Mitchell⟩

dog and pony show *n* **:** an often elaborate public relations or sales presentation

doggie bag *or* **doggy bag** *n* [[2]*doggy* + *bag;* fr. the original assumption that such leftovers were destined for the diner's dog] **:** a bag used for carrying home leftover food and esp. meat from a meal eaten at a restaurant

do–good·ing \'düˌgu̇diŋ\ *n* -s **:** the activities of a do-gooder — **do–gooding** *adj*

dogs·body \'dȯgzˌbädē *sometimes* 'däg-\ *n* [Brit. naval slang, midshipman, fr. slang *dog's body* pease pudding] *chiefly Brit* **:** one who performs menial tasks **:** DRUDGE

do–it–your·self \ˌdüə̇chə(r)ˌself, -ə̇tyə-\ *adj* **:** of, relating to, or designed for use in construction, repair, or artistic work done by an amateur or hobbyist ⟨a *do-it-yourself* car model kit⟩

do–it–your·self·er \-fə(r)\ *n* -s [*do-it-yourself* (herein) + [2]*-er*] **:** one who engages in do-it-yourself projects

do·jo \'dō(ˌ)jō\ *n* -s [Jap *dōjō,* fr. *dō* way, art + *-jō* ground] **:** a school for training in oriental martial arts

Dol·by \'dȯlbē, 'dōl-\ *trademark* — used for an electronic device that eliminates noise from recorded sound or sound broadcast on FM radio

dol·ce vi·ta \ˌdōlchē'vē(ˌ)tä, -(ˌ)chā-\ *n* [It, lit., sweet life] **:** a life of indolence and self-indulgence

dolly bird *n, Brit* **:** a pretty young woman

DOM \ˌdē(ˌ)ō'em\ *n* -s [prob. fr. *d*imethoxy- + *m*ethyl] **:** STP *herein*

dome car *n* **:** a railroad car with a raised glassed-in seating section

domestic prelate *n* **:** a priest having permanent honorary membership in the papal household and ranking above a papal chamberlain

dom·i·na·trix \ˌdämə̇'nā·triks\ *n, pl* **dominatri·ces** \-'nā·trəˌsēz, -nə'trīˌsēz\ [L, fem. of *dominator* — more at DOMINATOR] **:** a woman who physically and psychologically dominates and abuses her partner in sadomasochistic sex

domino effect *n* [so called fr. the fact that if a number of dominoes are stood on end one behind the other with a slight intervening space, a slight push on the first one will result in the toppling of all the others] **:** a cumulative effect produced when one event initiates a succession of similar events — compare RIPPLE EFFECT *herein*

domino theory *n* [*domino* (*effect*) (herein)] **1 :** the theory that if one nation becomes Communist-controlled the neighboring nations will also become Communist-controlled **2 :** the theory that if one act or event is allowed to take place a succession of similar acts or events will follow

done·ness \ˈdənnəs\ *n* -ES [²*done* + *-ness*] **:** the condition of being cooked to the desired degree ⟨test the meat for ~⟩

dong \ˈdȯŋ\ *n, pl* **dong** [Annamese] **1 :** the basic monetary unit of Vietnam — see MONEY table *in the Dict* **2 :** a coin or note representing one dong

dood·ley–squat \ˈdüd(ᵊ)lē+\ *n* [prob. fr. *doodle* + *-y* + *squat* (excretion, nothing —herein), prob. influenced by *doo-doo* (excrement)] *slang* **:** DIDDLY-SQUAT *herein*

do·pa·mine \ˈdōpəˌmēn, -ˌmən\ *n* [*dopa* + *amine*] **:** a monoamine $C_8H_{11}NO_2$ that is a decarboxylated form of dopa and occurs esp. as a neurotransmitter in the brain and as an intermediate in the biosynthesis of epinephrine

do·pa·min·er·gic \ˌdōpəˌmēˈnərjək, -məˈn-\ *adj* [*dopamine* + *-ergy* + *-ic*] **:** relating to, participating in, or activated by the neurotransmitter activity of dopamine or related substances ⟨a ~ pathway in the nervous system⟩ ⟨~ activity⟩

dop·ant \ˈdōpənt\ *n* -s [²*dope* + ¹*-ant*] **:** an impurity added usu. in minute amounts to a pure substance to alter its properties

dope* *vt* **:** to treat with a dopant ⟨*doped* semiconductor⟩

doper* *n* **:** an habitual or frequent drug user

dopp·ler \ˈdäplə(r)\ *adj, usu cap* **:** of, relating to, or utilizing a shift in frequency in accordance with the Doppler effect; *also* **:** of or relating to Doppler radar

doppler radar *n, usu cap D* **:** a radar system utilizing the Doppler effect for measuring velocity

do–rag \ˈdüˌrag\ *n* [*do* (as in *hairdo*) + *rag*] **:** a kerchief worn over the hair

dork \ˈdȯrk, ˈdȯ(ə)k\ *n* -s [perh. alter. of ¹*dick*] **1 :** PENIS — usu. considered vulgar **2** *slang* **:** a stupid or foolish person **:** JERK

dor·min \ˈdȯrmən\ *n* -s [*dormancy* + *-in*] **:** ABSCISIC ACID *herein*

DOS *abbr* disk operating system

dosage compensation *n* **:** the genetic mechanism by which the same effect on the phenotype is produced by a pair of identical sex-linked genes in the sex (as the human female) having the two sex chromosomes of the same type as by a single gene in the sex (as the human male) having the two sex chromosomes of different types or having only one sex chromosome (as in the males of some insects)

dot matrix *n* **:** a pattern of dots in a grid from which alphanumeric characters can be formed (as in printing)

double bind *n* **:** a psychological dilemma in which a usu. dependent person (as a child) receives conflicting interpersonal communications from a single source or faces disparagement no matter what his or her response to a situation; *broadly* **:** DILEMMA 2

double–blind \ˌ==ˈ=\ *adj* **:** of, relating to, or being an experimental procedure in which neither the subjects nor the experimenters know the makeup of the test and control groups during the actual course of the experiments — compare SINGLE-BLIND *herein*

double–cover \ˌ==ˈ==\ *vt* **:** DOUBLE-TEAM

double–digit \ˌ==ˈ==\ *adj* [¹*double* + *digit*] **:** of 10 percent or more ⟨*double-digit* inflation⟩ ⟨*double-digit* price increases⟩

double dip *vi* [*double-dip* cone with two scoops of ice cream] **:** to obtain money from two sources at the same time or by two separate accounting methods; *esp* **:** to draw a pension from one government department while working for another — **double–dipper** \ˌ==ˈ==\ *n*

double gloucester *n, usu cap D&G* **:** a firm mild orange-colored English cheese similar to cheddar

double helix *n* **:** a helix or spiral consisting of two strands in the surface of a cylinder that coil around its axis; *esp* **:** the structural arrangement of DNA in space that consists of paired polynucleotide strands stabilized by cross-links between purine and pyrimidine bases — compare ALPHA-HELIX *herein*, WATSON-CRICK MODEL *herein* — **double–helical** \ˌ==ˈ===\ *adj*

double knit *n* **:** a knitted fabric (as of wool or polyester) made with a double set of needles to produce a double thickness of fabric with each thickness joined by interlocking stitches; *also* **:** an article of clothing made of such fabric

double–precision \ˌ===ˈ==\ *adj* **:** using two computer words rather than one to represent a number

double reverse *n* **:** an offensive play in football consisting of a reverse with an additional handoff so that the ultimate ballcarrier is running in the direction in which the play started

doublespeak \ˈ==ˌ=\ *n* **:** DOUBLE-TALK 2

doublet* *n* **1 a :** a pair of atomic, molecular, or nuclear quantum states that are usu. close together in energy and arise from two possible orientations of spin **b :** a pair of spectral frequencies of light arising from transitions to or from such quantum states **2 :** a pair of otherwise similar elementary particles (as a proton and a neutron) with different charge **3 :** any of nine pairs of microtubules found in cilia and flagella

doug·las bag \ˈdəgləs-\ *n, usu cap D* [C. G. *Douglas* †1963 Eng. physiologist] **:** an inflatable bag used to collect expired air for the determination of oxygen consumption and basal metabolic rate

dove* *n* **:** one who takes a conciliatory attitude (as in a dispute) and advocates negotiations and compromise; *esp* **:** an opponent of war — compare HAWK *herein* — **dov·ish** \ˈdəvish\ *adj* — **dov·ish·ness** *n* -ES

down* *adj* **:** being a constituent of nucleons and having the quantum characteristics of an electric charge of $-\frac{1}{3}$ and a baryon number of $\frac{1}{3}$ ⟨~ quark⟩ — compare UP *herein*

down–and–out* *n* **:** a pass pattern in football in which the receiver runs straight downfield and then cuts to the outside

downer* *n* **1 :** a depressant drug; *esp* **:** BARBITURATE — compare UPPER *herein* **2 :** someone or something depressing

downhole \ˈ=ˌ=\ *adj* [³*down* + *hole*] **:** of, relating to, or used in a hole in the earth and esp. in a borehole

down–home \ˌ=ˈ=\ *adj* [³*down* + *home*] **:** of, relating to, or having qualities (as informality, simplicity, and earthiness) associated with the common people esp. of the southern U.S.

downlink \ˈ=ˌ=\ *adj* [⁴*down* + *link*] **:** of or relating to transmissions from a spacecraft or satellite to earth — compare UPLINK *herein*

download \ˈ=ˌ=\ *vt* [²*down* + *load*] **:** to transfer (information) from a usu. large remote computer to the memory of another device (as a smaller computer)

downplay \ˈ=ˌ=\ *vt* **:** to play down **:** DE-EMPHASIZE

downrange \ˌ=ˈ=\ *adv (or adj)* [³*down* + ¹*range*] **:** away from a launching site and along the course of a test range

downsize \'⸗,⸗\ *vt* [²*down* + *size*] **:** to reduce in size; *esp* **:** to design or produce in smaller size — **down·siz·ing** *n*

down's syndrome \'daün(z)-\ *n, usu cap D* [after J. L. H. *Down* †1896 Eng. physician] **:** MONGOLISM

downstream* *adv (or adj)* **:** of, relating to, in, or toward the later stages of a usu. industrial process ⟨~ products⟩ ⟨improve profits ~⟩

downtick \'⸗,⸗\ *n* [⁴*down* + ²*tick*] **:** a stock market transaction at a price below the last previous transaction in the same security — compare UPTICK *herein*

downtime \'⸗,⸗\ *n* [⁴*down* + *time*] **:** time during which production is stopped (as in a factory or on a machine) esp. during setup for an operation or when making repairs ⟨few moving parts and, thus, low maintenance costs and ~ —J. C. Friedlander⟩

dox·e·pin \'däksə,pin, -,pən\ *n* -s [fr. *d*imethyl + *ox-* + *-ep-* (arbitrary infix) + *-in*] **:** a tricyclic antidepressant administered as the hydrochloride salt $C_9H_{21}NO{\cdot}HCl$

dox·o·ru·bi·cin \,däksō'rübəsən\ *n* -s [fr. *doxo-*, alter. of *deoxy-* + *-rubi-* (perh. alter. of ISV *rube-* reddish) + *-cin* (as in *-mycin*)] **:** ADRIAMYCIN *herein*

dox·y·cy·cline \,däksə'sī,klēn, -,klən\ *n* -s [*d*eoxy- + *oxy-* + tetra*cycline*] **:** a broad-spectrum tetracycline antibiotic $C_{22}H_{24}N_2O_8$ that is administered orally and is used esp. to treat bronchial infections and gonorrhea

dozen* *n* **dozens** *pl* **:** a game that consists of exchanging often obscene insults usu. about the members of the opponent's family — often used in the phrase *play the dozens*

d phase *n, usu cap D* **:** M PHASE *herein*

draft* *vi* **:** to drive close behind another car while racing at high speed in order to take advantage of the reduced air pressure created by the leading car

drag* *n* **1 :** ⁶BORE b ⟨their work . . . is a ~ a good deal of the time —Nora Johnson⟩ **2 :** COSTUME, OUTFIT, GETUP ⟨dresses hundreds in full clown ~ — Bill Cardoso⟩ **3 :** DRAG QUEEN *herein* **4 :** man's clothing worn by a woman ⟨a lesbian can also wear ~; that is . . . clothing designed for men —Julia P. Stanley⟩

drag queen *n* **:** a male homosexual who dresses as a woman

drag racing *n* [¹*drag*] **:** the sport of holding acceleration contests for vehicles over a straight course

drawdown* *n* **1 :** a lowering of the water level (as in a reservoir) **2 :** DEPLETION, REDUCTION

dreadlocks \'⸗,⸗\ *n pl* [perh. fr. ³*dread* + *locks*] **:** long braids of hair worn esp. by Rastafarians

dream·scape \'drēm,skāp\ *n* -s [¹*dream* + *-scape*] **:** a dreamlike usu. surrealistic scene ⟨seemed greener than he had remembered any jungle to be: a ~ out of neverland —Frank Yerby⟩; *also* **:** a painting of a dreamscape

DRG \,dē,är'jē\ *n* -s [*d*iagnosis *r*elated *g*roup] **:** any of 470 payment categories that are used to classify patients and esp. Medicare patients for the purpose of reimbursing hospitals for each case in a given category with a fixed fee regardless of the actual costs incurred and that are based esp. on the principal diagnosis, surgical procedure used, age of patient, and expected length of stay in the hospital — called also *diagnosis related group*

drillship \'⸗,⸗\ *n* **:** a ship equipped for drilling (as for oil) in the ocean floor

drink·er respirator \'driŋkə(r)-\ *n, usu cap D* [after Philip *Drinker* †1972 Am. public health engineer] **:** IRON LUNG

drive* *n* **:** a device including an electric motor and heads for reading or writing on a magnetic medium (as magnetic tape or disks)

driveline \'⸗,⸗\ *n* **:** the parts including the universal joint and the drive shaft that connect the transmission with the driving axles of an automotive vehicle

driver* *n* **:** a piece of computer software that controls input and output operations

drive time *n* **:** the time during rush hour when radio audiences are swelled by commuters listening to car radios

drivetrain \'⸗,⸗\ *n* [²*drive* + *train*] **:** DRIVELINE *herein*

drive–up \'⸗,⸗\ *adj* [*drive up*, v.] **:** designed to allow patrons or customers to be served while remaining in their automobiles ⟨two *drive-up* windows at the bank⟩

drone* *n* **:** one who does menial, routine, or boring work **:** DRUDGE

drop* *vt* **:** to take (a drug) through the mouth **:** SWALLOW

drop–dead \'⸗,⸗\ *adj* **:** sensationally striking, attractive, or impressive ⟨a *drop-dead* evening gown⟩

drop–in \'drä,pin\ *n* -s [fr. the verb phrase *drop in*] **1 :** one who drops in **:** a casual visitor **2 :** an informal social gathering at which guests are invited to drop in

drop–in center *n* **:** an establishment designed to provide recreational, educational, and counseling services to a particular group

drop out* *vi* **:** to withdraw from conventional society because of disenchantment with its values and mores

dropout* *n* **1 :** one who drops out of conventional society **2 :** a spot on a magnetic tape or disk from which information has disappeared

drop pass *n* **:** a pass in ice hockey in which the dribbler skates past the puck leaving it for a teammate following close behind

drown·proof·ing \'draün,prüfiŋ\ *n* -s [*drown* + ²*proof* + *-ing*] **:** a technique for staying afloat in water for an extended period with minimum effort by using one's natural buoyancy

drug·gie *also* **drug·gy** \'drəgē\ *n, pl* **drug·gies** [¹*drug* + *-ie*] **:** one who habitually uses drugs

drug·gy \'drəgē\ *adj* -ER/-EST [¹*drug* + *-y*] **:** relating to, associated with, or affected by drugs or drug use

drug·ola \,drəg'ōlə\ *n* -s [¹*drug* + *-ola* (as in *payola*)] **:** payola in the form of illicit drugs

drumbeat* *n* **:** DRUMBEATING

drum printer *n* **:** a line printer in which the printing element is a revolving drum

drunk tank *n* **:** a large detention cell for arrested drunks

dry–eyed \'⸗,⸗\ *adj* **1 :** not moved to tears or to sympathy **2 :** marked by the absence of sentimentalism or romanticism ⟨an exercise in *dry-eyed* nostalgia —Edith Oliver⟩

dry out *vt* **:** to subject to withdrawal from the use of alcohol or drugs **:** DETOXIFY 1 *herein* ~ *vi* **:** to undergo an extended period of withdrawal from alcohol or drug use esp. at a special clinic **:** DETOXIFY *herein*

dry sink *n* **:** a wooden cabinet with a tray top for holding a wash basin

dual–purpose fund *n* **:** a closed-end investment company with two classes of shares one of which is entitled to all dividend income and the other to all gains from capital appreciation

duck's ass *n* **:** DA *herein* — often considered vulgar

dude* *n* **:** FELLOW, GUY

du·en·de \dü'en(,)dā\ *n* -s [Sp dial., charm, fr. Sp, ghost, goblin, fr. *duen de casa,* prob. fr. *dueño de casa* owner of a house] **:** the power to attract through personal magnetism and charm

duke \ˈdük\ *vb* -ED/-ING/-S [*duke* (fist), fr. *Duke of York,* rhyming slang for *fork* hand, fist] **:** FIGHT — **duke it out** **:** to have a fight and esp. a fistfight

dulls·ville \ˈdəlz,vil, -ˌvəl\ *n* [[1]*dull* + -*s,* alter. of -*'s,* + -*ville* (herein)] **:** something or some place that is dull or boring

dumb* *adj* **:** not having the capability to process data ⟨a ~ terminal⟩ — compare INTELLIGENT 1 *herein*

dum–dum \ˈdəmˌdəm\ *n* -S [redupl. of *dum,* alter. of [1]*dumb*] **:** a stupid person **:** DUMMY

dummy variable *n* **:** an arbitrary mathematical symbol or variable that can be replaced by another without affecting the value of the expression in which it occurs

dump* *vt* **1 :** to copy (data in a computer's internal storage) to an external storage or output device **2 :** to lose (a game or match) on purpose **:** THROW — **dump on** **:** to treat disrespectfully: as **a :** to take unfair advantage of ⟨feeling overworked and *dumped on* —Joan Sackett⟩ **b :** to abuse verbally **:** DISPARAGE, BELITTLE ⟨if they want to *dump on* people's work, let them become reviewers —Stephen Sondheim⟩

dump* *n* **:** an instance of dumping data stored in a computer

Dump·ster \ˈdəmpstər\ *trademark* — used for a large trash receptacle

dumpy* *adj* **:** being in a dirty or shabby condition **:** GRUNGY *herein* ⟨~ hotel rooms⟩

dune buggy *n* **:** a motor vehicle with oversize tires for use on sand

dunk* *vt* **:** to make a dunk shot with

dun·ny \ˈdənē, -ni\ *n* -ES [alter. of earlier *dunikin,* of unknown origin] *Austral* **:** TOILET; *esp* **:** one outdoors **:** PRIVY

duplicate* *vi* **:** to become duplicate **:** REPLICATE ⟨DNA in chromosomes ~*s*⟩

duplication* *n* **:** a part of a chromosome in which the genetic material is repeated; *also* **:** the process of forming a duplication

durable press *n* **:** PERMANENT PRESS *herein* — **durable–press** \ˈ≈≈ˈ≈\ *adj*

dutch cap* *n, usu cap D* **:** a molded contraceptive cap that fits over the uterine cervix

duvet* *n* **:** COMFORTER 3b

DWI \ˌdēˌdəbə(l)yəˈwī, -byəˈ-\ *abbr or n* -S **1 :** driving while intoxicated **2 :** one who is charged with driving while intoxicated

dye laser *n* **:** a laser in which light is emitted by a fluorescent organic dye and which can be tuned to radiate at any of a wide range of frequencies

dyke *or* **dike** \ˈdīk\ *n* -S [origin unknown] **:** LESBIAN; *esp* **:** one assuming an aggressively masculine role — **dyk·ey** *or* **dik·ey** \-kē, -ki\ *adj* **dyk·i·er** *or* **dik·i·er; dyk·i·est** *or* **dik·i·est**

dys·au·to·no·mia \(ˌ)disˌȯd·əˈnōmēə, -ˌäd·-\ *n* -S [*dys-* + [2]*autonomic* + [1]-*ia*] **:** a familial disorder of the nervous system characterized esp. by multiple sensory deficiency (as of taste and pain) and by excessive sweating and salivation — **dys·autonomic** \(ˌ)dis +\ *adj*

dys·ba·rism \ˈdisbəˌrizəm\ *n* -S [*dys-* + *bar-* + *-ism*] **:** the complex of symptoms (as bends, headache, or mental disturbance) that accompanies exposure to excessively low or rapidly changing environmental air pressure

dys·cal·cu·lia \ˌdiskalˈkyülēə\ *n* -S [NL, fr. *dys-* + L *calcul*are to compute + E [1]-*ia*] **:** impairment of mathematical ability due to an organic condition of the brain

dys·genesis \(ˈ)dis +\ *n* [*dys-* + *genesis*] **:** defective development esp. of the gonads (as in Klinefelter's syndrome or Turner's syndrome)

dys·graph·ia \disˈgrafēə\ *n* -S [NL, fr. *dys-* + *-graphia*] **:** impairment of the ability to write caused by brain damage

dys·pro·tein·emia \ˌdisˌprōˌtēˈnēmēə *also* -ōd·ēəˈn- *or* -ōtēəˈn-\ *n* -S [NL, fr. *dys-* + *protein* + *-emia*] **:** any abnormality of the protein content of the blood — **dys·pro·tein·emic** \-ˈnēmik\ *adj*

dysrhythmia* *n* **:** JET LAG *herein*

dys·to·pia \diˈstōpēə\ *n* -S [*dys-* + *-topia* (as in *utopia*)] **1 :** an imaginary place which is depressingly wretched and whose people lead a fearful existence **2 :** a work describing a dystopia — **dys·to·pi·an** \-ēən\ *adj*

E

eames chair \'ēmz-, 'āmz-\ *n, usu cap E* [after Charles *Eames* †1978 Am. designer] **:** any of several chairs designed by Charles Eames to fit the contours of the body and to be made from modern materials (as molded plywood or fiber glass)

earthrise \'=,=\ *n* [*earth* + *rise*] **:** the rising of the earth above the horizon of the moon as seen from the moon

earth tone *n* **:** any of various rich dark colors containing some brown

eat* *vt* **1 :** to perform fellatio or cunnilingus on — usu. considered vulgar **2 :** to bear the expense of **:** take a loss on ⟨if a drive-in taco stand opens next door, you ~ the loss in asset value of your house —Susan Lee⟩

EBCDIC \'epsə,dik, 'ebs-\ *n* [extended *b*inary *c*oded *d*ecimal *i*nterchange *c*ode] **:** a code for representing alphanumeric information (as on magnetic tape)

eb·ul·lism \'eb(y)ə,lizəm\ *n* -s [L *ebullire* to come bubbling out + E *-ism* — more at EBULLIENT] **:** the formation of bubbles in body fluids under sharply reduced environmental pressure

ec·cle·si·al \ə'klēzēəl, e'k-, -zhəl\ *adj* [*ecclesi-* + [1]*-al*] **:** ECCLESIASTICAL 1a ⟨these differences of ~ belief . . . are not an absolute prohibition of intercommunion — W.W. Bassett⟩

ec·dy·sone \'ekdə,sōn\ *n* -s [*ecdy*sis + horm*one*] **:** any of several arthropod hormones that in insects are produced by the prothoracic gland and that trigger molting and metamorphosis

echo·cardiogram \'e(,)kō +\ *n* [[1]*echo* + *cardiogram*] **:** a visual record made by echocardiography

echo·cardiography \"+\ *n* [[1]*echo* + *cardiography*] **:** a noninvasive and painless diagnostic procedure for making a record of cardiac structure and functioning by means of high frequency sound waves reflected back from the heart — **echo·cardiographic** \"+\ *adj*

echo·encephalography \"+\ *n* [ISV, fr. L *echo* + ISV *encephalography*] **:** the use of ultrasound in the examination and measurement of internal structures (as the ventricles) of the skull and in the diagnosis of abnormalities — **echo·encephalographic** \"+\ *adj*

echog·ra·phy \e'kägrəfē\ *n* -ES [[1]*echo* + *-graphy*] **:** ULTRASOUND 1 *herein* — **echo·graph·ic** \,ekə'grafik, ,e(,)kō-, -ēk\ *adj* — **echo·graph·i·cal·ly** \-ik(ə)lē, -li\ *adv*

echolocate \¦ekō +\ *vb* [[1]*echo* + *locate*] *vt* **:** to find by echolocation ⟨a bat ~*s* food⟩ ~ *vi* **:** to utilize or have the capacity for echolocation

echo·virus \"+\ *n* [*e*nteric *c*ytopathogenic *h*uman *o*rphan + *virus*] **:** any of a group of picornaviruses that are found in the gastrointestinal tract, that cause cytopathic changes in cells in tissue culture, and that are sometimes associated with respiratory ailments and meningitis

eco·catastrophe \¦ē(,)kō, ¦e(,)kō +\ *n* [[2]*ec-* + *catastrophe*] **:** a major destructive upset in the balance of nature esp. when caused by the intervention of man

eco·cide \'ēkə,sīd, 'ek-, -(,)kō,-\ *n* -s [[2]*ec-* + *-cide*] **:** the destruction and esp. the deliberate destruction (as in war) of large areas of the natural environment — **eco·cid·al** \¦==¦sīdᵊl\ *adj*

eco·geographic *or* **eco·geographical** \¦ekō, ¦ēkō +\ *adj* [[2]*ec-* + *geographic* or *geographical*] **:** of or relating to both ecological and geographical aspects of the environment — **eco·geographically** \" +\ *adv*

economy *adj* **:** designed to save the buyer money ⟨~ cars⟩

eco·physiology \¦ēkō, ¦ekō +\ *n* [[2]*ec-* + *physiology*] **:** the science of the interrelationships between the physiology of organisms and their environment — **eco·physiological** \" +\ *adj* — **eco·physiologist** \" +\ *n*

eco·sphere \'ēkō, 'ekō +,\ *n* [[2]*ec-* + *sphere*] **:** the parts of the universe habitable by living organisms; *esp* **:** BIOSPHERE 1 — **eco·spheric** \¦ēkō, ¦ekō +\ *adj*

ec·to·crine \'ektəkrən; -,krin, -rīn, -rēn\ *n* -s [*ect-* + *-crine* (as in *endocrine*)] **:** a metabolite produced by an organism of one kind and utilized by one of another kind

ec·to·hormone \¦ektə +\ *n* [*ect-* + *hormone*] **:** PHEROMONE *herein* — **ec·to·hormonal** \" +\ *adj*

ecu·me·nop·o·lis \,ekyəmə'näpələs, e,kyüm-\ *n* -ES [NGk *oikoumenopolis*, fr. Gk *oikoumenē* world + *-polis* — more at ECUMENE] **:** a single city encompassing the whole world that is held to be a possibility of the future

EDB *abbr* ethylene dibromide

ed·it \'edət\ *n* -s [*edit*, v.] **:** an instance or the result of editing

editor* *n* **:** a computer program that permits the user to create or modify data (as text or graphics) esp. on a display screen

EDP *abbr* electronic data processing

edro·pho·nium \,edrə'fōnēəm\ *n* -s [*e*thyl + hy*dr*oxy + *ph*enyl + amm*onium*] **:** an anticholinesterase $C_{10}H_{16}ClNO$ used esp. to stimulate skeletal muscle and in the diagnosis of myasthenia gravis — called also *edrophonium chloride*

educational park *n* **:** a large centralized educational complex of elementary and secondary schools

educational psychologist *n* **:** a specialist in educational psychology

educational television *n* **1 :** PUBLIC TELEVISION *herein* **2 :** television that provides instructional material esp. for students sometimes by closed circuit

ed·u·ca·tion·ese \,ejə,kāshə'nēz, -ēs\ *n* -s [*education* + [2]*-ese*] **:** the jargonistic language used esp. by educational theorists

EEO *abbr* equal employment opportunity

EER *abbr* energy efficiency ratio *herein*

effectively* *adv* **:** in effect **:** VIRTUALLY ⟨the civil war ~ partitioned Lebanon —J.M. Markham⟩

EFTS *abbr* electronic funds transfer systems

egg* *n* — **with egg on one's face :** in a state of embarrassment or humiliation

egg cream *n* **:** a drink consisting of milk, a flavoring syrup, and soda water

ego–dystonic \¦==dis'tänik\ *adj* [*ego* + *dyston*ia + *-ic*] **:** incompatible with or unacceptable to the ego ⟨*ego-dystonic* acts or thoughts —J. L. Singer⟩ — compare EGO-SYNTONIC *in the Dict*

ego trip *n* **:** something that enhances and satisfies one's ego

ego–trip \'≈,≈\ *vi* **:** to behave in a self-seeking manner ⟨never overplayed, never *ego-tripped,* never grabbed the spotlight — Bob Palmer⟩ — **ego–tripper** \'≈,≈\ *n* -s

egyptian mau \-'maů\ *n, usu cap E&M* [*mau* of imit. origin] **:** any of a breed of short-haired domestic cats developed in the U.S. and characterized by a spotted coat and light green or amber eyes

EHV *abbr* extra high voltage

eigenvalue* *n* **:** a scalar associated with a given linear transformation of a vector space and having the property that there is some nonzero vector which when multiplied by the scalar is equal to the vector obtained by letting the transformation operate on the vector ⟨If $T(v) = \lambda v$, where T is a linear transformation, v is a nonzero vector, and λ is a scalar, then λ is an ~ of T, and v is an eigenvector of T corresponding to λ⟩; *specif* **:** a root of the characteristic equation of a matrix

ei·gen·vector \'īgən+,\ *n* [ISV *eigen-* (fr. G *eigen*) + *vector*] **:** a nonzero vector that is mapped by a given linear transformation of a vector space onto a vector that is the product of a scalar multiplied by the original vector — called also *characteristic vector*

eightfold way *n* [fr. the *Eightfold Way* Eightfold Path; fr. the fact that the most common grouping contains eight interacting particles] **:** a unified theoretical scheme for classifying the relationship among strongly interacting elementary particles on the basis of isospin and hypercharge

eighty–six \¦≈¦≈\ *or* **86** \"\ *vt* -ED/-ING/-ES [rhyming slang for ⁴*nix*] *slang* **:** to refuse to serve (a customer); *also* **:** EJECT

ekis·tics \ə̇'kistiks, ē'k-\ *n pl but sing in constr* [NGk *oikistikē,* fr. fem. of *oikistikos* relating to settlement, fr. Gk, fr. *oikizein* to settle, colonize, fr. *oikos* house — more at VICINITY] **:** a science dealing with human settlements and drawing on the research and experience of professionals in various fields (as architecture, engineering, city planning, and sociology) — **ekis·tic** \-tik\ *adj* — **ekis·ti·cian** \ə̇,ki'stishən, (,)ē,k-\ *n* -s

ek·man dredge \'ekmən-\ *n, usu cap E* [prob. after V.W. *Ekman* †1954 Swed. oceanographer] **:** a dredge that has opposable jaws operated by a messenger traveling down a cable to release a spring catch and that is used in ecology for sampling the bottom of a body of water

ekt·exine \(')ekt+\ *n* [Gk *ekto-* outside + E *exine* — more at ECT-] **:** a structurally variable outer layer of the exine

ekue·le \ā'kwā(,)lā\ *also* **ek·pwe·le** \ek'pwā(,)lā\ *n, pl* **ekuele** *also* **ekpweles** [native name in Equatorial Guinea] **1 :** the basic monetary unit of Equatorial Guinea — see MONEY table *in the Dict* **2 :** a coin or note representing one ekuele

El·a·vil \'elə,vil\ *trademark* — used for amitriptyline

el chea·po \el'chē(,)pō\ *adj* [pseudo-Spanish alter. of ³*cheap*] *slang* **:** CHEAP 3

el·der·ly \'eldə(r)lē\ *n, pl* **elderly** *or* **elderlies :** an elderly person

elect·able \ə̇'lektəbəl, ē'l-\ *adj* [³*elect* + *-able*] **:** capable of being elected — **elect·abil·i·ty** \ə̇,lektə'biləd·ē, ē,l-, -ətē\ *n* -ES

elective* *adj* **:** beneficial to the patient but not essential for his survival ⟨an ~ appendectomy⟩

electric* *adj* **:** being or involving a musical performance on electric instruments ⟨loud fast ~ blues⟩

electric broom *n* **:** a lightweight upright vacuum cleaner

elec·tro·an·ten·no·gram \ə̇¦lektrō,an'tenə,gram\ *n* [*electr-* + *antenna* + *-o-* + *-gram*] **:** a record of electrical activity in an antenna esp. of an insect

elec·tro·cor·ti·cog·ra·phy \≈¦≈,kōrtə̇¦kägrəfē, -kȯr-\ *n* -ES [*electr-* + *cortico-* + *-graphy*] **:** the process of recording electrical activity in the brain by placing electrodes in direct contact with the cerebral cortex — **elec·tro·cor·ti·co·graph·ic** \-tə̇kə¦grafik\ *adj* — **elec·tro·cor·ti·co·graph·i·cal·ly** \-k(ə)lē\ *adv*

electrode* *n* **:** a semiconductor-device element that emits or collects electrons or holes or that controls their movements

elec·tro·dermal \ə̇¦lektrō, ē¦l- +\ *adj* [*electr-* + *dermal*] **:** of or relating to electrical activity in or electrical properties of the skin

elec·tro·diagnostic \"+\ *adj* [*electr-* + *diagnostic*] **:** involving or obtained by the recording of responses to electrical stimulation or of spontaneous electrical activity (as in electromyography) for purposes of diagnosing a pathological condition ⟨~ studies⟩ — **elec·tro·diag·nostically** \"+\ *adv*

elec·tro·en·ceph·a·log·ra·pher \ə̇¦lektrōə̇n,sefə'lägrəfər\ *n* -s **:** one who makes electroencephalograms

elec·tro·fishing \"+\ *n* [*electr-* + *fishing*] **:** the taking of fish by a system based on their tendency to respond positively to a source of direct electric current

elec·tro·gas·dynamics \"+\ *n pl but sing in constr* [*electr-* + *gas* + *dynamic* + *-s*] **:** a method of generating electrical energy that is based on the conversion of the kinetic energy of the flow of a high pressure charged combustion gas — **elec·tro·gas·dynamic** \"+\ *adj*

elec·tro·genesis \"+\ *n* [*electr-* + *genesis*] **:** the production of electrical activity esp. in living tissue

elec·tro·genic \"+\ *adj* [*electr-* + *-genic*] **:** of or relating to the production of electrical activity in living tissue ⟨an ~ pump causing movement of sodium ions across a membrane⟩

elec·tro·hydraulic \ə̇¦lektrō, ē¦l- +\ *adj* [*electr-* + *hydraulic*] **1 :** of, relating to, or involving a combination of electric and hydraulic mechanisms ⟨an ~ elevator⟩ **2 :** involving or produced by the action of very brief but powerful pulse discharges of electricity under a liquid resulting in the generation of shock waves and highly reactive chemical species ⟨an ~ effect⟩ — **elec·tro·hy·draulically** \"+\ *adv*

elec·tro·less \ə̇'lektrōlə̇s, -,les\ *adj* [*electro*lytic + *-less*] **:** being or involving chemical deposition of metal instead of electrodeposition

electromagnetic interaction *n* **:** a fundamental interaction experienced by most elementary particles that is responsible for the emission and absorption of photons and for electric and magnetic forces

electromagnetic pulse *n* **:** high-intensity electromagnetic radiation generated by a nuclear blast high above the earth's surface that is held to disrupt electronic and electrical systems

electronic* *adj* **1 :** of, relating to, or being music that consists of sounds electronically generated or modified **2 :** of, relating to, or being a medium (as television) transmitted electronically ⟨~ journalism⟩

electronic funds transfer *n* **:** the transfer of money from one location or account to another by computerized means

electronic mail *n* **1 :** messages sent and received electronically (as through a telecommunications network) **2 :** mail that is transmitted electronically to a receiving station where it is printed or reproduced as graphic matter and delivered to the addressee (as by messenger or through the postal system)

electron paramagnetic resonance *n* **:** ELECTRON SPIN RESONANCE *herein*

electron spin resonance *n* **:** the resonance of unpaired electrons in a magnetic field

electron transport *n* **:** the sequential transfer of electrons esp. by cytochromes in cellular respiration from an oxidizable substrate to molecular oxygen by a series of oxidation-reduction reactions

elec·tro·nys·tag·mog·ra·phy \ə̦lektrō,nis,tag'mägrəfē, ē̦l-\ *n* -ES [*electr-* + *nystagmus* + *-o-* + *-graphy*] **:** the use of electrooculography to study nystagmus — **elec·tro·nys·tag·mo·graph·ic** \=¦==,=,=mə¦grafik\ *adj*

elec·tro·oc·u·lo·gram \=¦==¦äkyələ,gram\ *n* [*electr-* + *ocul-* + *-gram*] **:** a record of the standing voltage between the front and back of the eye that is correlated with eyeball movement (as in REM sleep) and obtained by electrodes suitably placed on the skin near the eye

elec·tro·ocu·log·ra·phy \=¦==,äkyə'lägrəfē\ *n* -ES [*electr-* + *ocul-* + *-graphy*] **:** the preparation and study of electrooculograms — **elec·tro·ocu·lo·graph·ic** \=,==,=yələ'-grafik\ *adj*

elec·tro·pho·rese \ə,lektrəfə'rēs, ē,l-, -'träfə,-, -ēz\ *vt* -ED/-ING/-S [back-formation fr. *electrophoresis*] **:** to subject to electrophoresis

elec·tro·pho·reto·gram \ə,lektrəfə'red·ə,gram, ē,l-\ *or* **elec·tro·phero·gram** \=,=='ferə,gram\ *n* [*electrophoretogram* fr. *electrophoretic* + *-o-* + *-gram; electropherogram* fr. *electr-* + ISV *phero-* (fr. Gk *pherein* to carry) + *-gram*] **:** a record that consists of the separated components of a mixture (as of proteins) produced by electrophoresis in a supporting medium (as filter paper)

elec·tro·ret·i·no·graph \ə¦lektrō¦ret(ᵊ)nə,graf, ē¦l-\ *n* [*electr-* + ²*retin-* + *-graph*] **:** an instrument for recording electrical activity in the retina — **elec·tro·ret·i·no·graph·ic** \-,ret(ᵊ)nə¦grafik\ *adj* — **elec·tro·ret·i·nog·ra·phy** \-(ᵊ)n'ägrəfē\ *n* -ES

elec·tro·sensitive \"+\ *adj* [*electr-* + *sensitive*] **:** being or using sensitive paper on which an image is produced by the passage of electric current through it

elec·tro·sleep \"+\ *n* [*electr-* + *sleep*] **:** profound relaxation or a state of unconsciousness induced by the passage of a very low voltage electric current through the brain

electrostatic precipitator *n* **:** an electrostatic device in chimney flues that removes particles from escaping gases

electrostatic printing *n* **:** a process (as xerography) for printing or copying in which electrostatic forces are used to form the image (as with powder or ink) directly on a surface

electrotonic* *adj* **:** of, relating to, or being the spread of electrical activity through living tissue or cells in the absence of repeated action potentials ⟨an ~ junction between cells⟩ — **electrotonically*** *adv*

el·e·doi·sin \,elə'dȯisᵊn\ *n* -S [irreg. fr. NL *Eledone,* genus name + *-in*] **:** a small protein $C_{54}H_{85}N_{13}O_{15}S$ from the salivary glands of several octopuses (genus *Eledone*) that is a powerful vasodilator and hypotensive agent

elementary particle* *n* **:** OXYSOME *herein*

eleven–plus *or* **11–plus** \=,=='=\ *n, Brit* **:** an examination taken between the ages of 11 and 12 that determines the type of secondary education to which a student is assigned

el·hi \¦el,hī\ *adj* [*el*ementary school + *hi*gh school] **:** of, relating to, or designed for use in grades 1 through 12

emalangeni *pl of* LILANGENI *herein*

em·battled \əm, em +\ *adj* [ME *embatailled,* fr. past part. of *embatailen* to battle] **1 a :** ready to fight **:** prepared to give battle ⟨here once the ~ farmers stood —R. W. Emerson⟩ **b :** engaged in battle, conflict, or controversy ⟨lends psychological support to an ~ president — R. J. Whalen⟩ **2 a :** being a site of battle, conflict, or controversy ⟨defending his ~ capital city —*Wall Street Jour.*⟩ **b :** characterized by conflict or controversy ⟨his highly diversified, often ~ experience as an educator — Nat Hentoff⟩

em·battlement \"+\ *n* -S [¹*embattle* + *-ment*] **:** the state of being embattled

em·bour·geoise·ment \əm'bu̇rzh,wäzmənt, äm-, em-, -,mänt, *F* äⁿbu̇rzhwȧzmäⁿ\ *n* -S [F, fr. *embourgeoiser* to make bourgeois (fr. *em-* ¹en- + *bourgeois* bourgeois) + *-ment* ¹-ment] **:** a shift to bourgeois values and practices

embryoid *n* -S [*embryoid,* adj.] **:** a mass of plant or animal tissue that resembles an embryo

emergency medical technician *n* **:** EMT *herein*

emic \'ēmik\ *adj* [phon*emic*] **:** of, relating to, or having characteristics which are significant to the structure of a language or other behavioral system ⟨a phonemic transcription ... is an ~ description of speech — John Algeo⟩ — compare ETIC *herein*

emittance* *n* **:** the energy radiated by the surface of a body per second per unit area

em·pa·na·da \,empə'nädə\ *n* -S [Sp, fr. *empanada* breaded, fem. of *empanado,* past part. of *empanar* to bread, fr. *em-* ¹en- + *pan* bread, fr. L *panis* — more at FOOD] **:** a pastry turnover stuffed esp. with a savory meat filling

empty nester *n* **:** a parent whose children have grown up and moved away from home

EMT \¦ē(¦)em'tē\ *n* -S **:** a person who has undergone a course of special training and is certified to provide basic emergency services (as the bandaging of wounds, the application of splints, and cardiopulmonary resuscitation) before or during transportation to a hospital — called also *emergency medical technician;* compare PARAMEDIC 2 *herein*

emulate* *vt* **:** to imitate (a different computer system) by means of an emulator

emulation* *n* **:** the use of or technique of using an emulator

emulator* *n* **:** a hardware device or a combination of hardware and software that permits one computer to run programs designed for another computer or to process data in the same way as another computer

en·amine \'enə,mēn, e'na,m-\ *n* [⁴*en-* + *amine*] **:** an amine containing the double bond linkage C=C—N

en·cap·su·lant \ən'kapsələnt, en- *also* -syə-\ *n* -S [*encapsulate* + *-ant*] **:** a material used for encapsulating

en·ceph·a·li·to·gen \ən,sefə'līd·əjən, -,jen\ *n* -S [*encephalitogenic*] **:** an encephalitogenic agent (as a virus)

en·ceph·a·lo·myocarditis \en'sefəlō +\ *n* [*encephal-* + *myocarditis*] **:** an acute febrile virus disease characterized by degeneration and inflammation of skeletal and cardiac muscle and lesions of the central nervous system

encounter group *n* **:** a usu. leaderless and unstructured group that seeks to develop the capacity of the individual to openly express human feelings and to form close emotional ties by more or less unrestrained confrontation of individuals — compare T-GROUP

endangered *adj* [fr. past part. of *endanger*] : threatened with extinction ⟨~ species⟩

end around *n* : a football play in which an offensive end comes behind the line of scrimmage to take a handoff and attempts to carry the ball around the opposite flank

end·ar·ter·ec·to·my \ˌen̦därd·ə'rektəmē\ *n* -ES [*endarterium* + *-ectomy*] : surgical removal of the inner layer of an artery when thickened and atheromatous or occluded (as by intimal plaques)

end·exine \"+\ *n* [*end-* + *exine*] : an inner membranous layer of the exine

en·do·cast \'endə̦kast\ *n* [by shortening] : ENDOCRANIAL CAST

en·do·cyt·ic \¦endə¦sid·ək, -¦sīd-·\ *adj* [*end-* + *cyt-* + *-ic*] : of or relating to endocytosis : ENDOCYTOTIC ⟨~ vesicles⟩

en·do·cy·to·sis \ˌendō̦sī'tōsəs\ *n, pl* **endocyto·ses** \-ō̦sēz\ [NL, fr. *end-* + *cyt-* + *-osis*] : incorporation of substances into a cell by phagocytosis or pinocytosis — **en·do·cy·tot·ic** \¦==̦sī¦täd·ik\ *adj*

end–of–day glass \ˌ=='=̦=\ *n* [so called from its resemblance to objects made by glassblowers at the end of the day's work to use up various odds and ends of glass left over] : glass of various colors (as red, blue, green, and white) mixed together

endogenic* *adj* : ENDOGENOUS ⟨~ growth inhibitors⟩

endomorphism* *n* : a homomorphism that maps a mathematical set into itself — compare ISOMORPHISM *herein*

en·do·nuclease \¦endō +\ *n* [*end-* + *nuclease*] : an enzyme that breaks down a nucleotide chain into two or more shorter nucleotide chains by attacking it at points not adjacent to the ends — see RESTRICTION ENZYME *herein;* compare EXONUCLEASE *herein*

en·do·nu·cleo·lyt·ic \¦==̦n(y)üklēō'litik\ *adj* [*end-* + *nucleo-* + *-lytic*] : cleaving a nucleotide chain at an internal point ⟨~ nicks⟩

en·do·peroxide \"+\ *n* [*end-* + *peroxide*] : any of various biosynthetic intermediates in the formation of prostaglandins

en·do·phil·ic \¦endə¦filik\ *adj* [*end-* + *-philic*] : ecologically associated with man and his domestic environment ⟨mosquitoes that are ~ vectors of malaria⟩ — compare EXOPHILIC *herein* — **en·doph·i·ly** \en'däfəlē\ *n* -ES

endoplasmic reticulum *n* : a system of interconnected vesicular and lamellar cytoplasmic membranes that functions esp. in the transport of materials within the cell and that is studded with ribosomes in some places

en·do·radiosonde \¦endō +\ *n* [*end-* + *radiosonde*] : a microelectronic device introduced into the body to record physiological data

en·dor·phin \en'dȯrfən\ *n* [*endo*genous + m*orphine*] : any of a group of proteins with potent analgesic properties that occur naturally in the brain — see BETA-ENDORPHIN *herein;* compare ENKEPHALIN *herein*

en·do·sul·fan \ˌendō'səlfən, -̦fan\ *n* -s [perh. fr. *endr*in + *-o-* + *sulf-* + [3]*-an*] : a brownish crystalline insecticide $C_9H_6Cl_6O_3S$ that is used in the control of numerous crop insects and some mites

en·do·testa \¦endō +\ *n* [*end-* + *testa*] : an inner layer of the testa in various seeds — compare SCLEROTESTA *herein*

endothermy* *n* : physiological regulation of body temperature by metabolic means; *esp* : the property or state of being warm-blooded

endpoint** \'=̦=\ *n* [[1]*end* + *point*] : either of two points or values that mark the ends of a line segment or interval; *also* : a point that marks the end of a ray

en·duro \ən'd(y)u̇(ə)r(̦)ō, en-\ *n* -s [irreg. fr. *endurance*] : a long race (as for automobiles or motorcycles) stressing endurance rather than speed

end user *n* : the ultimate consumer of a finished product

energetics* *n pl but sing in constr* : the total energy relations and transformations of a physical, chemical, or biological system ⟨the ~ of an ecological community⟩

energizer* *n* : ANTIDEPRESSANT *herein*

energy* *n* : usable power; *also* : the resources for producing such power

energy budget *n* : an accounting of the income, use, and loss of energy esp. in an ecosystem ⟨the sun's contribution to the *energy budget* of the earth —M. K. Hubbert⟩

energy efficiency ratio *n, often cap both Es&R* : a number expressing the relative efficiency of an appliance (as a room air-conditioner) that is obtained by dividing the unit's output in BTUs per hour by its energy requirement in watts

en·flur·ane \en'flu̇(ə)r̦ān\ *n* [[2]*en-* + tri*fluoroethane*] : a liquid inhalational general anesthetic $C_3H_2ClF_5O$ prepared from methanol

en·ga·gé \'äŋgä'zhā, ̦eŋ-, *F* äⁿgȧzhā\ *adj* [F, fr. past part. of *engager* to engage, pledge] : committed to or supportive of a cause

english cocker spaniel *n, usu cap E* : any of a breed of spaniels that have square muzzles, wide well-developed noses, and distinctive heads which are ideally half muzzle and half skull with the forehead and skull arched and slightly flattened

English system *n* : the foot-pound-second system of units

en·keph·a·lin \en'kefələn, eŋ-\ *n* -s [NL, fr. *enkephal-*, modif. of *encephal-* + *-in*] : either of two pentapeptides with opiate and analgesic activity that occur naturally in the brain and have a marked affinity for opiate receptors — compare ENDORPHIN

en·tero·bacterium \¦entə(̦)rō +\ *n* [NL, fr. *enter-* + *bacterium*] : any bacterium of the family Enterobacteriaceae — **en·tero·bacterial** \"+\ *adj* — **en·tero·bacteriologist** \"+\ *n*

en·tero·pathogenic \"+\ *adj* [*enter-* + *pathogenic*] : tending to produce disease in the intestinal tract ⟨~ bacteria⟩

en·ter·op·a·thy \ˌentə'räpəthē\ *n* [*enter-* + *-pathy*] : a disease of the intestinal tract

en·tero·virus \¦entərō +\ *n* [NL, fr. *enter-* + *virus*] : any of a group of picornaviruses (as a Coxsackie virus) that typically occur in the gastrointestinal tract but may be involved in respiratory ailments, meningitis, and neurological disorders — **en·tero·viral** \"+\ *adj*

entitlement* *n* : a government program providing benefits to members of a specified group

entrain* *vt* : to determine or modify the phase or period of ⟨circadian rhythms ~*ed* by a light cycle⟩

entry–level \'==̦==\ *adj* : of, relating to, or being at the lowest level of a hierarchy ⟨~ jobs⟩ ⟨an ~ computer system⟩

en·ven·om·ation \ən̦venə'māshən, en̦v-\ *n* -s [*envenom* + *-ation*] : an act or instance of impregnating with a venom (as of a snake or spider); *also* : ENVENOMIZATION *herein*

en·ven·om·iza·tion \-̩mə'zāshən, -(̦)mī'z-\ *n* -s [*envenom* + *-ization*] : a poisoning caused by a bite or sting

environment* *n* **:** an instance of environmental art or theater

environmental* *adj* **:** involving or encompassing the spectator ⟨~ art⟩ ⟨~ theater⟩

environmentalist* *n* **:** one concerned about the quality of the human environment; *specif* **:** a specialist in human ecology

en·zy·mo·log·i·cal \ˌenzəməˈläjəkəl, -ˌzī-\ *adj* [*enzymology* + *ical*] **:** of or relating to enzymology ⟨~ studies⟩

EP* *abbr* European plan

epi·androsterone \ˌepē +\ *n* [*epi-* + *androsterone*] **:** an androsterone derivative $C_{19}H_{30}O_2$ that occurs in normal human urine — called also *isoandrosterone*

epi·con·dy·li·tis \ˌepəˌkändᵊlˈīd·əs, -ˈītəs\ *n* -ES [*epicondyle* + *-itis*] **:** inflammation of an epicondyle or of adjacent tissues — compare TENNIS ELBOW *in the Dict*

epi·fauna \ˌepə, ˌepē +\ *n* [NL, fr. *epi-* + *fauna*] **:** benthic fauna living on the substrate (as a hard sea floor) or on other organisms — compare INFAUNA *herein* — **epi·faunal** \"+\ *adj*

epi·mor·phism \ˌepəˈmȯrˌfizəm\ *n* -S [*epi-* (on) + *homomorphism*] **:** a surjective homomorphism

epi·phyt·ism \ˌepəˈfīˌtizəm\ *n* -S **:** the condition of being epiphytic

episcopal vicar *n* **:** a bishop assigned to the pastoral supervision of a part of a Roman Catholic diocese

epi·some \ˈepəˌsōm\ *n* -S [*epi-* + ³*-some*] **:** a genetic determinant (as the DNA of some bacteriophages) that can replicate either autonomously in bacterial cytoplasm or as an integral part of the chromosomes — compare PLASMID *herein* — **epi·som·al** \ˌepəˈsōməl\ *adj* — **epi·som·al·ly** *adv* — **epi·so·mic** \-ōmik\ *adj*

EPN \ ˌē(ˌ)pēˈen\ *n* -S [ethyl *p*ara-*n*itro-phenyl] **:** an organophosphorous miticide and insecticide $C_{14}H_{14}NO_4PS$ used esp. on cotton and orchard crops that enhances the toxicity of malathion to vertebrates

ep·oxy \əˈpäksē, eˈp-, (ˌ)ēˈp-\ *vt* **ep·ox·ied** *or* **ep·oxyed; epoxied** *or* **epoxyed; ep·oxy·ing; epoxies :** to glue with epoxy

ep·stein–barr virus \ˌepˌstīnˈbär-\ *n, usu cap E&B* [after Michael Anthony *Epstein* and Y. M. *Barr,* 20th cent. Eng. pathologists, its discoverers] **:** a herpesvirus that causes infectious mononucleosis and is associated with Burkitt's lymphoma and nasopharyngeal carcinoma

equal opportunity employer *n* **:** an employer who agrees not to discriminate against any employee or job applicant because of race, color, religion, national origin, sex, physical or mental handicap, or veteran status

equivalence class *n* **:** a set for which a given equivalence relation holds between every pair of elements

equivalence relation *n* **:** a relation (as equality) between elements of a set (as the real numbers) that is symmetric, reflexive, and transitive and for any two elements either holds or does not hold

equivalent* *adj* **1 :** having the same solution set ⟨~ equations⟩ **2 :** related by an equivalence relation

ER *abbr* emergency room

erase* *vt* **:** to delete from a computer storage device

-er·gic \ə(r)jik, ˌərj-\ *adj comb form* [*-ergy* + *-ic*] **:** exhibiting or stimulating activity ⟨syn*ergic*⟩

er·go·met·ric \ˌərgəˈme·trik\ *adj* [*ergometer* + ¹*-ic*] **:** relating to, obtained by, or being an ergometer

er·gon·o·mist \(ˌ)ərˈgänəməst\ *n* -S [*ergonomic* + ¹*-ist*] **:** a specialist in biotechnology

er·o·tol·o·gy \ˌerəˈtäləjē\ *n* -ES [Gk *erōt-, erōs* sexual love + *-logy* — more at EROS] **:** erotic description or literature — **er·o·to·log·i·cal** \ˌerəd·ᵊlˈäjəkəl\ *adj*

er·y·thor·bate \ˌerəˈthȯrˌbāt\ *n* -S [*erythorbic acid* (herein) + *-ate*] **:** a salt of erythorbic acid that is used in foods as an antioxidant

er·y·thor·bic acid \ˌerəˌthȯrbik-\ *n* [prob. fr. *eryth*rose + as*corbic acid*] **:** an optical isomer of ascorbic acid

eryth·ro·leukemia \əˌrithrō +\ *n* [NL, fr. *erythr-* + *leukemia*] **:** a malignant disorder that is marked by proliferation of erythroblastic and myeloblastic tissue and in later stages by leukemia

eryth·ro·poi·e·tin \əˌrithrəˈpȯiətᵊn\ *n* -S [*erythropoietic* + *-in*] **:** a hormonal glycoprotein that is prob. formed in the kidney and stimulates red blood cell formation

es·bat \ˈesˌbat\ *n* -S [OF, esbat, diversion, blow, fr. *esbatre* to divert, amuse, beat, fr. (assumed) VL *exbattuere,* fr. L *ex-* + *battuere* to beat] **:** a meeting of a coven of witches

es·ca·beche \ˌeskəˈbāchā\ *n* -S [Sp, prob. fr. Ar *sakbāj*] **:** fish or chicken fried in oil then marinated in a spicy sauce and served cold

escalate* *vb* ~ *vi* **:** to increase in extent, volume, number, amount, or scope **:** EXPAND ⟨any limited nuclear war would rapidly ~ into full-scale disaster —*Sat. Eve. Post* ⟩ ~ *vt* **:** to increase the extent, volume, number, amount, or scope of

escalation* *n* **:** an increasing in extent, volume, number, amount, or scope — **es·ca·la·to·ry** \ˈeskələˌtōrē, -ˌtȯr-, ÷-kyə-\ *adj*

escapologist* *n* **:** ESCAPE ARTIST

es·cap·ol·o·gy \ˌes(ˌ)kāˈpäləjē, əsˌkā-\ *n* -ES **:** the art or practice of escaping

escudo* *n* **:** a monetary unit of Chile equivalent to $^1/_{1000}$ peso — see MONEY table *in the Dict*

ESL *abbr* English as a second language

ESOP \ˈēˌsäp, ˌēˌes(ˌ)ōˈpē\ *n* -S [*e*mployee *s*tock *o*wnership *p*lan] **:** a program by which a company's stock is acquired by its employees

esoph·a·go·gastric \əˌsäfə(ˌ)gō, ēˌ-+\ *adj* [*esophag-* + *gastric*] **:** of, relating to, involving, or affecting the esophagus and the stomach ⟨~ anastomosis⟩ ⟨~ ulcers⟩

esoph·a·gos·co·py \əˌsäfəˈgäskəpē\ *n* -ES [*esophag-* + *-scopy*] **:** examination of the esophagus by means of an esophagoscope

establishment* *n, often cap* **1 :** a group of social, economic, and political leaders who form a ruling class (as of a nation) ⟨by *them* he meant not the English, but the governing classes, the *Establishment* —A.J.P. Taylor⟩ **2 :** a controlling group ⟨the Welsh literary *Establishment* . . . kept him out of everything —Keidrych Rhys⟩

es·ter·o·lyt·ic \ˌestərōˈlid·ik\ *adj* [*ester* + *-o-* + *-lytic*] **:** of, relating to, carrying out, or being the splitting of an ester into its component alcohol and acid — **es·ter·ol·y·sis** \ˌ==ˈäləsəs\ *n*

estimate* *n* **:** a numerical value obtained from a statistical sample and assigned to a population parameter

estimator* *n* **:** ESTIMATE *herein; also* **:** a statistical function whose value for a sample furnishes an estimate of a population parameter

es·tro·ge·nic·i·ty \ˌestrəjəˈnisəd·ē\ *n* -ES [*estrogenic* + *-ity*] **:** capacity for estrogenic action or effect

ET* *abbr* elapsed time

eta particle *n* [¹*eta*] **:** an uncharged elementary particle with zero spin that has a mass 1074 times the mass of an electron and that decays rapidly into pions or gamma rays

eth·a·cryn·ic acid \\ˌethəˌkrinik-\\ *n* [fr. *eth-* + *acetic* + butyr*yl* + phen*ol*] **:** a potent synthetic diuretic $C_{13}H_{12}Cl_2O_4$ used esp. in the treatment of edema

eth·am·bu·tol \\ethˈambyu̇ˌtȯl, -ˌtōl\\ *n* -s [*eth*ylene + *am*ine + *but*an*ol*] **:** a synthetic drug $C_{10}H_{24}N_2O_2$ used esp. in the treatment of tuberculosis

etha·mi·van \\eˈthaməˌvan, ˌethəˈmīvən\\ *n* -s [di*eth*yl + *ami*de + *van*illic acid] **:** an analeptic drug and central nervous stimulant $C_{12}H_{17}NO_3$ that is related to vanillic acid and is used as a respiratory stimulant for intoxication with central nervous depressants (as barbiturates) and for chronic lung diseases

eth·e·phon \\ˈethəˌfän\\ *n* -s [modif. of chloro*ethyl* phos*phon*ic acid] **:** a synthetic plant growth regulator $C_2H_6ClO_3P$ that induces flowering and abscission by promoting the release of ethylene and has been used to cause early ripening (as of apples on the tree)

ethid·i·um bromide \\eˈthidēəm-\\ *n* [*eth*yl + phenanthr*idinium*] **:** a biological dye that is a phenanthridine derivative used as a trypanocide and to block nucleic acid synthesis (as in mitochondria)

eth·i·on \\ˈethēˌän\\ *n* -s [blend of *eth-* and *thion-*] **:** an organophosphate $C_9H_{22}O_4P_2S_4$ used as a pesticide

eth·i·on·amide \\ˌethēˈänəˌmīd, əˈthīən-, -ˌməd\\ *n* [*eth-* + *thion-* + *amide*] **:** a compound $C_8H_{10}N_2S$ used against mycobacteria (as in tuberculosis and leprosy)

ethiopian orthodox *adj, usu cap E&O* **:** ETHIOPIAN 5

ethnic* *n* **:** a member of an ethnic group; *esp* **:** a member of a minority group who retains the customs, language, or social views of his group

eth·no·methodology \\ˌeth(ˌ)nō+\\ *n* [*ethno-* + *methodology*] **:** a branch of sociology dealing with nonspecialists' commonsense understanding of the structure and organization of society — **eth·no·methodologist** \\"+\\ *n*

eth·no·musicology \\"+\\ *n* [ISV *ethno-* + *musicology*] **:** a study of the music chiefly of non-European cultures esp. in relation to the culture that produces it — **eth·no·musicological** \\"+\\ *adj* — **eth·no·musicologist** \\"+\\ *n*

eth·no·science \\"+\\ *n* [*ethno-* + *science*] **:** the nature lore (as folk taxonomy of plants and animals) of primitive people — **eth·no·scientific** \\"+\\ *adj* — **eth·no·scientist** \\"+\\ *n*

etho·gram \\ˈēthəˌgram\\ *n* -s [*etho*logy + *-gram*] **:** a comprehensive list, inventory, or description of the behavior of an organism

eth·o·sux·i·mide \\ˌethōˈsəksəˌmīd\\ *n* -s [*eth-* + *-suximide* (by shortening and alter. fr. *succinimide*)] **:** an antidepressant drug $C_7H_{11}NO_2$ derived from succinic acid and used to treat epilepsy

et·ic \\ˈed·ik\\ *adj* [phon*etic*] **:** of, relating to, or having linguistic or behavioral characteristics considered without regard to their structural significance ⟨a sound spectrogram is a good example of ~ description —John Algeo⟩ — compare EMIC *herein*

etio·cho·lan·o·lone \\ˌed·ē(ˌ)ōkōˈlanᵊlˌōn *also* ed·ē-\\ *n* [*etio-* + *chol-* + *-ane* + *-ol* + *-one*] **:** a testosterone metabolite $C_{19}H_{30}O_2$ that occurs in urine

etio·pathogenesis \\ˌēd·ēō *also* ˌe\\ +\\ *n* [*etio-* + *pathogenesis*] **:** the cause and development of a disease or abnormal condition

etor·phine \\ēˈtȯrˌfēn, əˈt-, -ȯ(ə)ˌ-\\ *n* -s [perh. fr. *et* her + m*orphine*] **:** a synthetic narcotic drug $C_{25}H_{33}NO_4$ related to morphine but with more potent analgesic properties

ETV *abbr* educational television *herein*

eu·phen·ics \\yüˈfeniks\\ *n pl but sing in constr* [*eu-* + *phen-* (fr. *phenotype*) + *-ics;* after E *genotype: eugenics*] **:** a science that deals with the biological improvement of human beings after birth — **eu·phen·ic** *adj*

eu·ro·bond \\ˈyu̇rō+ˌ\\ *n, usu cap* [*Euro*pe + *bond*] **:** a bond sold outside its country of origin; *esp* **:** one of a U.S. corporation that is sold outside the U.S. and that is denominated and paid for in dollars and yields interest in dollars

euro·centric \\ˌyu̇rō +\\ *adj, usu cap* [*Euro*pe + *-centric*] *chiefly Brit* **:** EUROPOCENTRIC *herein*

euro·communism \\"+\\ *n, usu cap* [*Euro*pean + *communism*] **:** the communism esp. of western European Communist parties that is marked by a willingness to reach power through coalitions and by independence from Soviet leadership — **euro·communist** *n or adj, usu cap*

eu·ro·crat \\ˈyu̇rəˌkrat\\ *n* -s *usu cap* [*Euro*pe + *-crat*] **:** a staff member of the administrative commission of the European Common Market — **eu·ro·crat·ic** \\ˌ==ˈkrad-ik\\ *adj, usu cap*

eu·ro·currency \\ˈyu̇rō+ˌ\\ *n, usu cap* [*Euro*pe + *currency*] **:** moneys (as of the U.S. and Japan) held outside their countries of origin and used in the money markets of Europe

eu·ro·dollar \\"+ˌ\\ *n, usu cap* [*Euro*pe + *dollar*] **:** a U.S. dollar used as Eurocurrency

eu·ro·market \\"+ˌ\\ *n, usu cap* [*Euro*pe + *market*] **:** a money market in Eurocurrencies

eu·ro·po·centric \\yəˌrōpə, ˌyu̇rəpə+\\ *adj, usu cap* [*Europe,* continent + E *-o-* + *-centric*] **:** centered on Europe and the Europeans — **eu·ro·po·cen·trism** \\-ˌsen·trizəm\\ *n* -s *usu cap*

eu·than·a·tize \\yüˈthanəˌtīz\\ *also* **eu·tha·nize** \\ˈyüthəˌnīz\\ *vt* -ED/-ING/-S [fr. Gk *eu-* happy + *thanat*os death + E *-ize*] **:** to subject to euthanasia

EVA *abbr* extravehicular activity

even permutation *n* **:** a permutation that is produced by the successive application of an even number of interchanges of pairs of elements — compare ODD PERMUTATION *herein*

event* *n* **:** a subset of the possible outcomes of a statistical experiment ⟨7 is an ~ in the throwing of two dice⟩

ev·er·glade \\ˈevə(r)ˌglād\\ *n* -s [fr. the *Everglades,* Fla.] **:** a swampy grassland esp. in southern Florida usu. containing sawgrass and at least seasonally covered by slowly moving water — usu. used in pl.

evoked potential *n* **:** recorded electrical activity esp. in the cerebral cortex following stimulation of a peripheral sense receptor

ex·ac·ta \\igˈzaktə, eg-\\ *n* -s [AmSp *quiniela exacta* exact quiniela] **:** PERFECTA *herein*

ex·cess \\ikˈses, ˈekˌses, ekˈses\\ *vt* -ED/-ING/-ES [*excess,* n.] **:** to eliminate the position of ⟨the decline in enrollment has allowed us to ~ about 75 teachers —Stuart Binion⟩

exchange force *n* **:** a force between two elementary particles (as a neutron and a proton) arising from the continuous interchange between them of other particles (as pions)

ex·ci·mer \\ˈeksə(ˌ)mə(r)\\ *n* -s [*exc*ited d*imer*] **:** an aggregate of two atoms or molecules that exists in an excited state

ex·ci·ton \\ˈeksəˌtän, ikˈsīˌ\\ *n* -s [*excit*ation + ²*-on*] **:** a mobile combination of an electron and a hole in an excited crystal (as of a semiconductor) that is produced by the absorption of a photon — **ex·ci·ton·ic** \ˌeksə̇ˈtänik\ *adj*

exclusionary rule *n* **:** a legal rule that bars any unlawfully obtained evidence from being used in court proceedings

exclusive disjunction *n* **:** a compound proposition in logic that consists of two statements and that is true if and only if one and only one of the two statements is true

ex–directory \ˈeks+\ *adj* [L *ex* out of — more at EX-] *Brit* **:** not listed in a telephone directory **:** UNLISTED

executive privilege *n* **:** exemption from legally enforced disclosure of communications within the executive branch of government when such disclosure would adversely affect that branch's functions and decision-making processes

exo·biology \ˈek(ˌ)sō+\ *n* [*exo-* + *biology*] **:** a branch of biology concerned with the search for life outside the earth and its atmosphere and with the effects of extraterrestrial environments on living organisms — **exo·bio·logical** \"+\ *adj* — **exo·biologist** \"+\ *n*

ex·o·cri·nol·o·gy \ˌeksəkrə̇ˈnäləjē, -ˌkrī-, -ˌkrē-\ *n* -ES [*exocrine* + *-o-* + *-logy*] **:** the study of external secretions (as pheromones) that serve an integrative function

exo·cyclic \ˈek(ˌ)sō+\ *adj* [*exo-* + *cyclic*] **:** situated outside of a ring in a chemical structure

exo·cy·to·sis \ˈek(ˌ)sōsīˈtōsə̇s\ *n, pl* **exocyto·ses** \-ōˌsēz\ [NL, *exo-* + *cyt-* + *-osis*] **:** the release of cellular substances (as secretory products) contained in cell vesicles by fusion of the vesicular membrane with the plasma membrane and subsequent release of the contents to the exterior of the cell — **exo·cy·tot·ic** \-sīˈtäd·ik\ *adj*

ex·on \ˈekˌsän\ *n* -s [[1]*ex-* + [1]*-on*] **:** a sequence of nucleotides in DNA or RNA that is expressed as all or part of the polypeptide chain of a protein — compare INTRON *herein* — **ex·on·ic** \ekˈsänik\ *adj*

exo·nuclease \"+\ *n* [*exo-* + *nuclease*] **:** an enzyme that breaks down a nucleic acid by removing nucleotides one by one from the end of a chain — compare ENDONUCLEASE *herein*

exo·nu·cleo·lyt·ic \ˈ==ˌn(y)üklēəˈlid·ik\ *adj* [*exo-* + *nucle-* + *-lytic*] **:** cleaving a nucleotide chain at a point adjacent to one of its ends

exo·nu·mia \ˌeksəˈn(y)ümēə\ *n pl* [NL, fr. *exo-* + E *numismatic* + NL *-ia* [2]-ia] **:** numismatic items (as tokens, medals, or scrip) other than coins and paper money

exo·nu·mist \-mə̇st, ˈ==ˌ==\ *n* -s [*exonumia* (herein) + *-ist*] **1 :** a specialist in exonumia **2 :** a collector of exonumia

exo·phil·ic \ˈeksəˈfilik\ *adj* [*exo-* + *-philic*] **:** ecologically independent of man and his domestic environment ⟨an ~ species of mosquito⟩ — compare ENDOPHILIC *herein* — **ex·oph·i·ly** \ekˈsäfəlē\ *n* -ES

exotic* *adj* **:** of or relating to striptease ⟨~ dancing⟩

exotic* *n* -s **:** a dancer who performs a striptease

ex·pa·tri·a·tism \ekˈspā·trēə·ˌtizəm *also* -rēəd·ˌiz-, *chiefly Brit* -pa-\ *n* -s [*expatriate* + *-ism*] **:** the quality or state of being an expatriate

explosive* *adj* **:** done by the force of a controlled explosion ⟨~ welding⟩ ⟨~ forming of metal parts⟩

exotic shorthair *n, usu cap E&S* **:** any of a breed of stocky short-haired domestic cats developed in the U.S. by crossing the American Shorthair with the Persian

ex·po \ˈek(ˌ)spō\ *n* -s [by shortening] **:** EXPOSITION 3c

ex·po·nence \ikˈspōnən(t)s, ekˈs-, ˈekˌs-\ *n* -s [fr. *exponent* (herein), after such pairs as E *dependent* : *dependence*] **:** the correlation between an abstract linguistic category and its exponents ⟨by moving towards the data within abstractions one is considered to be moving down the scale of ~ —R.H. Robins⟩

exponent* *n* **:** a specific element of a linguistic category ⟨*eat* is an ~ of the class 'verb'⟩

ex·po·nen·ti·a·tion \ˌekspəˌnenchēˈāshən *sometimes* -n(t)sē-\ *n* -s [*exponent* + *-iation* (as in *differentiation*)] **:** INVOLUTION 2

extension* *n* **:** a mathematical set (as a field or group) that includes a given and similar set as a subset

ex·tern·ship \ˈekˌstərnˌship\ *n* [blend of *external* and *internship*] **:** a period of temporary employment for an advanced student in a professional field (as teaching or engineering) for practical experience outside an educational institution

ex·tra·chromosomal \ˈekstrə+\ *adj* [*extra-* + *chromosomal*] **:** situated or controlled by factors outside the chromosomes ⟨~ inheritance⟩ ⟨~ DNA⟩

ex·tra·corporeal \"+\ *adj* [*extra-* + *corporeal*] **:** occurring or based outside the living body ⟨heart surgery employing ~ circulation⟩ — **ex·tra·corporeally** \"+\ *adv*

ex·tra·cranial \"+\ *adj* [*extra-* + *cranial*] **:** situated or occurring outside the cranium ⟨~ arterial occlusion⟩

ex·tra·linguistic \"+\ *adj* [*extra-* + *linguistic*] **:** lying outside the province of linguistics — **ex·tra·linguistically** \"+\ *adv*

ex·tra·mitochondrial \ˈekstrə+\ *adj* [*extra-* + *mitochondrial*] **:** situated or occurring in the cell outside the mitochondria

extraneous* *adj* **:** being a number obtained in solving an equation that is not a solution of the equation ⟨~ roots⟩

extranuclear* *adj* **:** situated outside the nucleus of an atom

ex·traor·di·naire \ikˌstrȯ(r)dᵊnˈe(ə)r, ˌek-, *also* ˌekstrə-ˌȯ(r)d-, *F* ekstr(ȧ)ȯrdēneer\ *adj* [F, extraordinary] **:** markedly exceptional **:** EXTRAORDINARY — used postpositively

ex·tra·position \ˈekstrə +\ *n* [*extra-* + *position*] **:** a transformation in which a sentence constituent is moved to the end of a clause; *esp* **:** one in which a subject that is a sentence which has itself undergone a transformation is so moved and leaves behind the pronoun *it*

ex·tra·renal \"+\ *adj* [*extra-* + *renal*] **:** situated or occurring outside the kidneys ⟨~ action of diuretics⟩

ex·tra·solar \"+\ *adj* [*extra-* + *solar*] **:** originating or existing outside the solar system ⟨~ life⟩

ex·tra·somatic \"+\ *adj* [*extra-* + *somatic*] **:** of, relating to, or being something that exists external to and distinct from the individual human being or the human body

ex·tra·terrestrial \"+\ *n* **:** an extraterrestrial being

ex·tra·vehicular \"+\ *adj* [*extra-* + *vehicular*] **1 :** taking place outside a vehicle (as a spacecraft) ⟨~ activity⟩ **2 :** relating to or used in extravehicular activity ⟨an ~ assignment⟩

eye chart *n* **:** a chart that is read at a fixed distance for purposes of testing sight; *esp* **:** one with rows of letters or objects of decreasing size

eye contact *n* **:** visual contact with another person's eyes

eyeliner \ˈ=ˌ==\ *n* [[1]*eye* + [1]*liner*] **:** makeup used to emphasize the contour of the eyes

eyes only *adj* [fr. expression *for your eyes only*] **:** to be read by only the person addressed

F

f* *abbr* femto- *herein*

fab \ˈfab\ *adj* [by shortening] *chiefly Brit* **:** FABULOUS 3b

fab·ri·ca·ble \ˈfabrəkəbəl\ *adj* [LL *fabricabilis,* fr. L *fabricari* to fabricate — more at FABRIC] **:** capable of being shaped ⟨~ alloys⟩ — **fab·ri·ca·bil·i·ty** \ˌfabrəkəˈbiləd·ē\ *n* -ES

fa·bry's disease \ˈfäbrēz-\ *n, usu cap F* [after Johannes *Fabry* †1930 Ger. dermatologist] **:** a sex-linked inherited disorder of lipid catabolism characterized esp. by renal dysfunction, a rash in the inguinal, scrotal, and umbilical regions, and corneal defects

face fly *n* **:** a European fly of the genus *Musca* (*M. autumnalis*) that is similar to the housefly, is widely established in No. America, and causes distress to livestock by clustering about the face

face–off* *n* **:** a confrontation between opponents to settle an issue

fac·tion \ˈfakshən\ *n* -s [blend of *fact* and *fiction*] **:** literary work based on fact but using the narrative techniques of fiction

fac·tion·al·ize \ˈfakshənᵊlˌīz, -shneˌlīz\ *vt* -ED/-ING/-s **:** to split into factions

factor* *vt* **:** to include or admit as a factor — used with *in* or *into* ⟨~ inflation into our calculations⟩

factor VIII \-ˈāt\ *n* **:** ANTIHEMOPHILIC FACTOR *herein*

factor V \-ˈfīv\ *n* **:** ACCELERATOR GLOBULIN

factor group *n* **:** QUOTIENT GROUP *herein*

fag·got·ry \ˈfagə·trē\ *n* -ES [*faggot* + *-ry*] **:** male homosexuality

fag·goty *also* **fag·got·ty** \ˈfagəd·ē\ *adj* [fr. *faggot* homosexual + ¹*-y*] **:** resembling or suggesting the manner of an effeminate male homosexual — often used disparagingly

fag hag *n, slang* **:** a woman who enjoys the company of male homosexuals

fail* *n* **:** a failure (as by a security dealer) to deliver or receive securities within a prescribed period after a purchase or sale

¹fail–safe \ˈ=ˌ=\ *adj* [from the notion that something fail-safe is safe from failing or safe even if there is some failure] **1 :** incorporating some feature for automatically counteracting the effect of an anticipated possible source of failure **2 :** being or relating to a safeguard that prevents continuing on a bombing mission according to a preconceived plan **3 :** having no chance of failure **:** infallibly problem-free ⟨a written guarantee that your back is in A-1, *fail-safe* condition —Fern Lebo⟩

²fail–safe \"\ *vi* **:** to counteract the effect of a malfunction automatically ~ *vt* **:** to equip with a fail-safe device

fair market value *n* **:** a price at which both buyer and seller are willing to do business

fairness doctrine *n* **:** a tenet of licensed broadcasting that ensures a reasonable opportunity for the airing of conflicting viewpoints on controversial issues of public concern

fake book *n* [³*fake* (to improvise) + *book*] **:** a book that contains the melody lines of popular copyrighted songs without accompanying harmonies and that is published without the permission of the copyright owners

fakelore \ˈ=ˌ=\ *n* [⁵*fake* + *lore* (as in *folklore*)] **:** imitation folklore (as tales or songs) created to pass as genuinely traditional

fa·laf·el \fəˈläfəl\ *or* **fe·laf·el** \"\ *n, pl* **falafel** *or* **felafel** [Ar *falāfil*] **:** a mixture of chick-peas or fava beans and spices (as cumin and coriander) formed into balls or patties and then fried; *also* **:** a sandwich of pita bread filled with falafel

fa·lan·ga \fəˈläŋgə, -aŋ-\ *n* -s [NGk] **:** a method of torture in which the soles of the feet are beaten

fallout* *n* **1 :** an incidental result **:** BY-PRODUCT ⟨the war . . . produced its own literary ~ — a profusion of books —*Newsweek*⟩ **2 :** particulate matter dispersed through the air and landing in a wide distribution

family* *n* **:** a group constituting a unit of a crime syndicate (as the Mafia) and engaging in underworld activities within a defined geographical area

family* *adj* **:** designed or suitable for both children and adults ⟨~ restaurants⟩ ⟨~ movies⟩

family medicine *n* **:** FAMILY PRACTICE *herein*

family planning *n* **:** planning intended to determine the number and spacing of one's children by effective methods of birth control

family practice *n* **:** general medical practice — **family practitioner** *n*

family room *n* **:** a large room designed as a recreation center for members of a family

fan·co·ni's anemia \fänˌkōnēz-, fan-\ *n, usu cap F* [after Guido *Fanconi b*1882 Swiss pediatrician] **:** a rare disease inherited as an autosomal recessive trait that is characterized by progressive hypoplastic pancytopenia, skeletal anomalies (as short stature), and a predisposition to cancer and esp. leukemia

fanconi syndrome *n, usu cap F* [Guido *Fanconi*] **:** a disorder of reabsorption in the proximal convoluted tubules of the kidney that is characterized esp. by the presence of glucose, amino acids, and phosphates in the urine

fan–jet \ˈ=ˌ=\ *n* [¹*fan* + *jet*] **1 :** a jet engine having a ducted fan in its forward end that draws in extra air whose compression and expulsion provide extra thrust **2 :** an airplane powered by a fan-jet engine

fan·tab·u·lous \(ˌ)fanˈtabyələs\ *adj* [blend of *fantastic* + *fabulous*] *slang* **:** marvelously good

fantasy* *n* **:** a coin usu. not intended for circulation as currency and often issued by a dubious authority (as a government-in-exile)

faraday rotation *n, usu cap F* **1 :** optical rotation of a beam of polarized light due to the Faraday effect **2 :** rotation of a beam of polarized microwaves traversing an isotropic medium along the lines of force of a magnetic field

far–out \ˈ=ˈ=\ *adj* [*far out* (adverbial phrase), fr. ME *fer oute,* fr. *fer* far + *out, oute* out] **:** marked by a considerable departure from the conventional or traditional **:** EXTREME ⟨a small, *far-out,* but fervent religious sect — Joseph Alsop⟩ — **far–out** \ˈ=ˈ=\ *n* -s — **far–out·er** \(ˈ)=ˈ==\ *n* -s — **far–out·ness** \(ˈ)=ˈ=nəs\ *n*

far–red \ˈ=ˈ=\ *adj* [²*far* + *red*] **1 :** lying in the part of the infrared spectrum farthest from the red — used of radiations with wavelengths between 30 and about 1000 microns **2 :** lying in the part of the infrared spectrum nearest to the red — used of radiations with wavelengths starting at about .8 micron

fart around *vi* **:** to mess around **:** waste time — often considered vulgar

fastback *n* [[1]*fast* + [1]*back*] **1** \ˈ\ **:** a back roof on a closed passenger automobile sloping in a long unbroken line toward the rear bumper **2** \ˈ\ **:** an automobile having a fastback

fast–breeder reactor \ˈ-\ *n* **:** a breeder reactor that depends on high-energy neutrons to produce fissionable material

fast–food \ˈ\ *adj* **:** specializing in the rapid preparation and service of food (as hamburgers or fried chicken) ⟨a *fast-food* restaurant chain⟩ — **fast food** *n*

fast lane \ˈ\ *n* **:** a way of life marked by fast living and the ready flow of money — used esp in the phrase *life in the fast lane*

fast track \ˈ\ *n* **:** a course leading to rapid advancement or success

fast–track \ˈ\ *adj* **1 :** of, relating to, or moving along a fast track ⟨*fast-track* executives⟩ **2 :** of, relating to, or being a construction procedure in which work on a building begins before designs are completed ⟨*fast-track* designs⟩

fatal *n* -s [*fatal,* adj.] **:** FATALITY 5a

fat city *n, often cap F&C* **:** an extremely comfortable situation or condition of life

fat depot *n* **:** ADIPOSE TISSUE

fate* *n* **:** the expected result of normal development ⟨prospective ~ of embryonic cells⟩

fat farm *n* **:** HEALTH SPA *herein*

faulk·ner·ian \(ˈ)fȯkˌnirēan, -ˌner-\ *adj, usu cap* [William Cuthbert *Faulkner* †1962 Am. novelist + E *-ian*] **:** of, relating to, or suggestive of William Faulkner or his writings

fa·ve·la *also* **fa·vel·la** \fəˈvelə\ *n* -s [Pg *favela*] **:** a settlement of jerry-built shacks lying on the outskirts of a Brazilian city

favorite son* *n* **:** a renowned person (as an artist or celebrity) who is viewed with great favor and affection by the people of his hometown

fax \ˈfaks\ *n* -ES [by shortening and alter.] **:** FACSIMILE 2

FDC* *abbr* fleur de coin *herein*

federal funds *n pl* **:** reserve funds lent overnight by one member bank of the Federal Reserve to another

feed* *n* **:** the process of feeding a television program (as to a local station)

feedback inhibition *n* **:** inhibition of an enzyme controlling an early stage of a series of biochemical reactions by the end product when it reaches a critical concentration

feedthrough \ˈ\ *n* -s **:** a conductor that connects two circuits on opposite sides of a surface

felafel *var of* FALAFEL *herein*

fel·late \ˈfelˌāt, fəˈlāt, *usu* -ād·+V\ *vb* -ED/-ING/-S [L *fellatus,* past part. of *fellare* to suck — more at FELLATIO] *vt* **:** to perform fellatio on ~ *vi* **:** to fellate someone — **fel·la·tor** \ˈfelˌād·ə(r), fəˈlā-\ *n* -s

femme* *n* **:** a lesbian who plays the female role in a homosexual relationship

fem·to- \ˌfem(p)(ˌ)tō\ *comb form* [ISV, fr. Dan or Norw *femten* fifteen (fr. ON *fimmtān*) + *-o-* — more at FIFTEEN] **:** one quadrillionth (10^{-15}) part of ⟨*femto*second⟩

fence–mending \ˈ\ *n* [[1]*fence* + *mending*] **:** the rehabilitating of a deteriorated political relationship

fender bender *n* **:** a minor automobile accident

fen·flur·amine \fenˈflu̇rəˌmēn, -ˌmən\ *n* [*fen-* (alter. of *phen-*) + *flur-* (alter. of *fluor-*) + *amine*] **:** an amphetamine derivative $C_{12}H_{16}F_3N$ used esp. as the hydrochloride salt to suppress appetite in the treatment of obesity

fen·ta·nyl \ˈfentᵊnˌil\ *n* -s [alter. of *phenethyl*] **:** a narcotic analgesic $C_{22}H_{28}N_2O$ with pharmacologic action similar to morphine that is administered esp. as the citrate

fen·thi·on \fenˈthīˌän, -ˌən\ *n* -s [*fen-* (alter. of *phen-*) + *thi-* + *-on*] **:** an organophosphorus insecticide $C_{10}H_{15}O_3PS_2$

fer·mi \ˈfer(ˌ)mē\ *n* -s [after Enrico *Fermi* †1954 Ital. physicist] **:** a unit of length equal to 10^{-13} centimeter

fer·re·dox·in \ˌferəˈdäksən\ *n* -s [L *ferrum* iron + E *redox* + *-in* — more at FARRIER] **:** any of a group of iron-containing plant proteins that function as electron carriers in photosynthetic organisms and in some anaerobic bacteria

ferricyanide* *n* **:** the negative trivalent chemical group $Fe(CN)_6$

ferrocyanide* *n* **:** the negative tetravalent chemical group $Fe(CN)_6$

festival seating *n* **:** a seating arrangement (as in an auditorium) in which unreserved seats are available to the first people to claim them

FET \ˌef(ˌ)ēˈtē\ *n* -S **:** FIELD-EFFECT TRANSISTOR *herein*

FET *abbr* federal excise tax

fetal alcohol syndrome *n* **:** a highly variable group of birth defects including mental retardation, deficient growth, and defects of the skull, face, and brain that tend to occur in the infants of women who consume large amounts of alcohol during pregnancy

fetal hemoglobin *n* **:** a hemoglobin variant that predominates in the blood of a newborn and persists in increased proportions in some forms of anemia (as thalassemia)

fetal position *n* [so called fr. the similar position of the fetus in the womb] **:** a resting position in which the body is curved, the legs and arms are bent and drawn toward the chest, and the head is bowed forward and which is assumed esp. in some forms of psychic regression

fe·tol·o·gy \fēˈtäləjē\ *n* -ES [*feto-* + *-logy*] **:** a branch of medical science concerned with the study and treatment of the fetus in the uterus — **fe·tol·o·gist** \-jəst\ *n* -s

fe·to·protein \ˌfēd·ō, -ē(ˌ)tō +\ *n* [*feto-* + *protein*] **:** any of several fetal antigens present in the adult in some abnormal conditions; *esp* **:** ALPHA-FETOPROTEIN *herein*

fe·tos·co·py \fēd·ˈäskəpē, fēˈtäs-, -pi\ *n* -ES [*feto-* + *-scopy*] **:** examination of the pregnant uterus by means of a fiber-optic tube — **fe·to·scope** \ˈfēd·əˌskōp\ *n*

fettuccine al·fre·do \-(ˌ)alˈfrā(ˌ)dō, -ȧl-, -äl-\ *or* **fettuccine all' alfredo** \-ˌal(ˌ)alˈf-, -ˌȧl(ˌ)ȧl-, -ˌäl(ˌ)äl-\ *n, usu cap Alfredo* [fr. *Alfredo all' Augusteo,* restaurant in Rome, where it originated] **:** a dish consisting of butter, fettuccine, Parmesan cheese, cream, and seasonings

feul·gen \ˈfȯilgən\ *adj, usu cap* **:** of, relating to, utilizing, or staining by the Feulgen reaction ⟨positive *Feulgen* mitochondria⟩

Feyn·man diagram \ˈfīnmən-\ *n* [after Richard *Feynman b*1918 Am. physicist] **:** a diagram of subatomic particle interactions in which lines represent particles and points where lines meet represent interactions

FG *abbr* field goal

fiberfill \'≈,≈\ *n* **:** man-made fibers (as of polyester) used as a filling material (as for cushions)

fiber optics *n pl* **1 :** thin transparent fibers of glass or plastic that are enclosed by material of a lower index of refraction and that transmit light throughout their length by internal reflections; *also* **:** a bundle of such fibers used in an instrument (as for viewing body cavities) **2** *sing in constr* **:** the technique of the use of fiber optics — **fiber–optic** \¦≈¦≈\ *adj*

fi·ber·scope \'fībə(r),skōp\ *n* [*fiber* + *-scope*] **:** a flexible instrument utilizing fiber optics and used esp. in medicine for examination of inaccessible areas (as the stomach)

fi·bo·nac·ci number \'fibə¦nächē-, ,fēb-\ *n, usu cap F* [after Leonardo *Fibonacci* (Leonardo Pisano) †*ab*1250 Ital. mathematician] **:** a number in the infinite sequence 1, 1, 2, 3, 5, 8, 13, . . .of which the first two terms are 1 and 1 and each succeeding term is the sum of the two immediately preceding

fi·branne \¦fī¦bran\ *n* [F, viscose rayon, fr. *fibre*] **:** a fabric made of spun-rayon yarn

fi·brino·peptide \fī¦brinō +\ *n* [*fibrino*gen + *peptide*] **:** any of the vertebrate proteins that are split off from fibrinogen by thrombin during clotting of the blood, comprise two in each species, and exhibit great interspecific variability

fi·bro·cystic \¦fībrə +\ *adj* [*fibr-* + *cystic*] **:** characterized by the presence or development of fibrous tissue and cysts ⟨~ changes in the pancreas —*Lancet*⟩

fi·bro·elas·to·sis \,fī(,)brōə̇,las'tōsə̇s, -ē,las-\ *n* [*fibroelastic* + *-osis*] **:** a condition of the body or one of its organs (as the left ventricle of the heart) characterized by proliferation of fibroelastic tissue

fi·bro·gen·ic \,fībrə'jenik\ *adj* [*fibr-* + *-genic*] **:** promoting the development of fibers ⟨a ~ agent⟩

fiche \'fēsh, *also* 'fish\ *n, pl* **fiche** *also* **fiches** [by shortening] **:** MICROFICHE

fick principle \'fik-\ *n, usu cap F* [after Adolph Eugen *Fick* †1901 Ger. physiologist] **:** a generalization in physiology which states that blood flow is proportional to the difference in concentration of a substance in the blood as it enters and leaves an organ and which is used to determine cardiac output from the difference in oxygen concentration in blood before it enters and after it leaves the lungs and from the rate at which oxygen is consumed

fiddle* *n* [Brit. slang *fiddle* to cheat, fr. ²*fiddle*] **:** SWINDLE

fi·do \'fīd(,)ō\ *n* -s [*f*reaks + *i*rregulars + *d*efects + *o*ddities] **:** a coin having a minting error

fiduciary* *adj* **:** being a mark or set of marks in the reticle of an optical instrument used as a point of reference or for a measure

field* *n* **1 :** a particular area (as a column on a punched card) in which the same type of information is regularly recorded **2 :** a division of a record in computer storage that consists of one or more characters and contains data (as a name or number) to be treated as a unit

field* *vt* **:** to give an impromptu answer or solution to ⟨~*ed* the questions with ease⟩

field–effect transistor \'≈,≈-\ *n* **:** a nonrectifying transistor in which the output current is controlled by a variable electric field

field ion microscope *n* **:** a high-magnification microscope in which an image of the atoms of a metal surface is formed on a fluorescent screen by means of usu. helium ions formed in a high-voltage electric field

field judge *n* **:** a football official whose duties include covering action on kicks and forward passes and timing intermission periods and time-outs

field–test \'≈¦≈\ *vt* **:** to test (as a procedure or product) under conditions of actual use

fièvre bou·ton·neuse \fyeevrᵊbütȯnœ̄œ̄z\ *n* [F] **:** BOUTONNEUSE FEVER

fighting chair *n* **:** a chair attached to the deck of a boat from which a salt-water angler plays a hooked fish

figure–ground \¦≈¦≈\ *adj* [¹*figure* + *ground*] **:** relating to or being the relationships between the parts of a perceptual field which is perceived as divided into a part consisting of figures having form and standing out from a part comprising the background and being relatively formless ⟨an ambiguous diagram in which *figure-ground* relationships are easily perceived as reversed⟩

fil·i·pin \'filə̇pə̇n\ *n* -s [NL, fr. *filip*ensis, species name + *-in*] **:** an antifungal antibiotic $C_{35}H_{58}O_{11}$ produced by a bacterium of the genus *Streptomyces* (*S. filipensis*)

filler* *n* **:** an item of poor quality (as a worn coin) kept in a collection until a better specimen can be found to replace it

filmcard \'≈,≈\ *n* [¹*film* + *card*] **:** MICROFICHE

film noir *n* [F, lit., black film] **:** a type of crime film featuring cynical malevolent characters in a sleazy setting and an ominous atmosphere that is conveyed by shadowy photography and foreboding background music; *also* **:** a film of this type

film·og·ra·phy \fil'mägrəfē, fiu̇'m-\ *n* -ES [¹*film* + *-o-* + *-graphy*] **:** a list of motion pictures featuring the work of a prominent film figure (as an actor or director) or relating to a particular topic

filmscript \'≈¦≈\ *n* [¹*film* + *script*] **:** a script for a motion picture

filmsetting \'≈¦≈\ *n* [¹*film* + *setting*] **:** PHOTOCOMPOSITION — **filmset** \'≈¦≈\ *adj* — **filmset** *vt* — **filmsetter** \'≈¦≈\ *n*

filo *var of* PHYLLO *herein*

finance company* *n* **:** a company that specializes in making loans usu. to individuals

financial service *n* **:** an organization that studies the business situation and security market and makes investment recommendations usu. in a regularly issued publication

finder's fee *n* **:** a fee paid to a financial finder often in the form of a percentage of the sum involved

fine structure *n* **1 :** a multiplet occurring in an atomic spectrum as a result of electron interaction **2 :** microscopic structure of a biological entity or one of its parts esp. as studied in preparations for the electron microscope — **fine structural** *adj*

fine–structure constant \¦≈'≈-\ *n* **:** a dimensionless constant α that is a measure of the strength of electromagnetic interactions of subatomic particles and that has an approximate value of 0.0073 or $^1/_{137}$

fine–tune \¦≈'≈\ *vt* **1 :** to adjust so as to bring to the highest level of performance or efficiency ⟨*fine-tune* a TV set⟩ ⟨*fine-tuning* their policies⟩ **2 :** to stabilize (an economy) by small-scale fiscal and monetary manipulations

finger* *n* **:** BIRD 2 *herein*

finger food *n* **:** a food (as a radish, carrot, or sandwich) that is meant to be eaten with the fingers

finger–popping \'≈,≈\ *adj* [¹*finger* + *popping,* pres. part. of ¹*pop*] **:** characterized by a pronounced beat ⟨*finger-popping,* toe-tapping music⟩

fingerprint* *n* **:** chromatographic, electrophoretic, or spectrographic evidence of the presence or identity of a substance; *esp* **:** the chromatogram or electrophoretogram obtained by cleaving a protein by enzymatic action and subjecting the resulting collection of peptides to two-dimensional chromatography or electrophoresis

fink* *n* **:** one who is disapproved of or is held in contempt

fink out *vi* **1 :** to fail miserably **2 :** to back out **:** cop out

fin·land·iza·tion \\ˌfinləndəˈzāshən, -ˌdīˈz-; (ˌ)finˌlandəˈz-\\ *n* -s *usu cap* [fr. *Finland,* country in northern Europe + *-ization*] **:** a foreign policy of neutrality which makes a non-Communist country susceptible to the influence of the Soviet Union; *also* **:** the conversion to such a policy

firebase \\ˈ=ˌ=\\ *n* [[1]*fire* + *base*] **:** a secured site from which field artillery can lay down interdicting fire

firefight** *n* **:** SKIRMISH 2

fireflood \\ˈ=ˌ=\\ *or* **fireflooding** \\ˈ=ˌ==\\ *n* [[1]*fire* + [1]*flood* or *flooding*] **:** the process of injecting compressed air into a petroleum reservoir and burning some of the oil so as to drive the rest of the oil into producing wells

firmware \\ˈ=ˌ=\\ *n* [[1]*firm* + [4]*ware*] **:** software functions (as a computer program) implemented through a small special-purpose computer memory unit (as a read-only memory)

first blood *n* **1 :** the first drawing of blood in a contest (as boxing) **2 :** an initial advantage over an opponent

first world *n, usu cap F&W* **:** the Western industrialized non-Communist nations

fiscal court *n* **:** the executive agency of a county in some states of the U.S.

fish* *vb* — **fish in troubled waters :** to profit or attempt to profit from unsettled or troubled conditions

fish–eye \\ˈ=ˌ=\\ *adj* [so called fr. the resemblance of the lens to the protruding eye of a fish] **:** being, having, or produced by a wide-angle photographic lens that has a highly curved protruding front, that covers an angle of about 180 degrees, and that gives a circular image with barrel distortion ⟨a *fish-eye* view⟩

fish farm *n* **:** a commercial facility for raising aquatic animals (as fish) for human food — **fish–farm** *vt*

fishnet* *n* **:** a coarse open-mesh fabric

fish protein concentrate *n* **:** FISH FLOUR

five–o'clock shadow *n* [so called fr. the resemblance of a dark beard's stubble to a shadow] **:** the growth of beard present late in the afternoon on the face of a man who has not shaved since morning

fixed–point \\ˈ=ˈ=\\ *adj* **:** involving or being a mathematical notation (as in a decimal system) in which the point separating whole numbers and fractions is fixed — compare FLOATING-POINT *herein*

flack \\ˈflak\\ *vi* -ED/-ING/-S [[3]*flack*] **:** to provide publicity **:** engage in press-agentry

flack·ery \\ˈflak(ə)rē, -ri\\ *n* -ES [[3]*flack* + *-ery*] **:** PUBLICITY, PROMOTION, PRESS-AGENTRY

fla·gel·lin \\fləˈjelən\\ *n* -s [*flagell*um + [1]*-in*] **:** a polymeric protein that is the chief constituent of bacterial flagella and is believed to be responsible for the specificity of their flagellar antigens

flag football *n* **:** a variation of football in which a player must remove a flag attached to a ballcarrier's clothing to stop the play

flagship* *n* **:** the finest, largest, or most important one of a series or group ⟨the company's ~ store⟩

flak* *n* **1 :** abusive criticism ⟨I've taken ~ from newsmen who think I've sold out —Chet Huntley⟩ **2 :** heated discussion **:** OPPOSITION ⟨this modest proposal ran into ~ —Charles MacDonald⟩ **3 :** [3]FLACK

flake* *n* [[2]*flake*] **1 :** one that is flaky **:** SCREWBALL **2** *slang* **:** COCAINE

flakeboard \\ˈ=ˌ=\\ *n* [[2]*flake* + *board*] **:** a composition board made of flakes of wood bonded with synthetic resin

flaky* *also* **flak·ey** *adj* **:** markedly odd or unconventional **:** CRAZY ⟨they used to call me ~ . . . but now that I'm a millionaire they'll be calling me an eccentric —Derek Sanderson⟩

flame–retardant \\ˈ==ˌ==\\ *adj* **:** made or treated so as to resist burning ⟨~ sleepwear⟩

flame stitch *n* **:** a needlepoint stitch that produces a pattern resembling flames

flan·ken \\ˈflaŋkən, -äŋ-\\ *n* -s [prob. fr. Yiddish *flanken;* akin to G *flanke* flank] **:** flank steak boiled in stock with spices and vegetables

flanker* *or* **flanker back** *n* **:** a football player stationed wide of the formation; *esp* **:** an offensive halfback who lines up on the flank slightly behind the line of scrimmage and serves chiefly as a pass receiver

flannel* *n, Brit* **:** flattering or evasive talk; *also* **:** NONSENSE, RUBBISH — **flannel*** *vb, Brit*

flap·pa·ble \\ˈflapəbəl\\ *adj* [[2]*flap* + *-able*] **:** lacking self-assurance and self-control **:** easily upset

flare* *n* **1 :** a short pass in football thrown to a back who is running toward the sideline **2 flares** *pl* **:** trousers that flare toward the bottoms

flash* *vi* **1 :** to expose one's genitals usu. suddenly and briefly in public **2 :** to have a sudden insight — often used with *on* ⟨she just *~ed* on it: for once in her life, she ought to put her own needs right up front —Cyra McFadden⟩

flash* *n* **:** RUSH *herein*

flashback* *n* **:** a brief recurrence of a psychedelic experience

flashcube \\ˈ=ˌ=\\ *n* [[2]*flash* + *cube*] **:** a plastic cube containing four flashbulbs that fits into the top of a camera and revolves after each shot

flashed glass *n* **:** glass in which a very thin layer of colored glass or of a metallic oxide is flashed to clear glass

flasher* *n* **:** an exhibitionist who flashes

flash–forward \\ˈ=ˈ==\\ *n* -s [*flash* (as in [1]*flashback*) + *forward,* adv.] **:** a literary or theatrical technique used esp. in motion pictures and television that involves interruption of the chronological sequence of events by interjection of events or scenes of future occurrence; *also* **:** an instance of a flash-forward

flash photolysis *n* **:** the process of decomposing a chemical with an intense flash of light and observing spectroscopically the transient molecular fragments produced

flash point* *n* **:** TINDERBOX 2

flat* *adj* **:** being or characterized by a horizontal line or tracing without peaks or depressions ⟨a ~ EEG⟩

flavor* *n* **:** a property that distinguishes different types of quarks (as the up, down, strange, charmed, and bottom quarks) and different kinds of leptons (as the electron, muon, and tau)

flea collar *n* **:** a collar for animals that contains insecticide for killing fleas

flea–flicker \\ˈ=ˌ==\\ *n* [[4]*flick* (throw) + *-er*] **:** an offensive play in football that starts out like a running play (as a double reverse) with the ball coming back to the quarterback who then throws a long pass

fleapit \'⸗,⸗\ *n, Brit* **:** a dilapidated building usu. housing a movie theater

fleur de coin \ˌflərdəˈkwaⁿ, -lə̄d-\ *adj* [F *à fleur de coin,* lit., with the bloom of the die] **:** being in the preserved mint condition

flex·a·gon \'fleksəˌgän\ *n* -s [[1]*flex* + *-agon* (as in *hexagon*)] **:** a folded paper figure that can be flexed along its folds to expose various arrangements of its faces

flexor ret·in·ac·u·lum \-ˌretᵊnˈakyələm\ *n* [NL] **:** any of several bands of fascia that overlie and provide channels for tendons esp. of flexor muscles

flex·time \'⸗,⸗\ *or* **flexi·time** \'fleksə̇ˌtīm\ *n* [[1]*flex*ible + *time*] **:** a system that allows employees to choose their own times for starting and finishing work within a broad range of available hours

flick–knife \'⸗,⸗\ *n* [[3]*flick* + *knife*] *Brit* **:** SWITCHBLADE KNIFE

flight attendant *n* **:** a person who attends passengers (as by serving food) on an airplane

flight bag *n* **1 :** a traveling bag usu. with zippered outside compartments for use esp. in air travel; *esp* **:** one that fits under an airplane seat **2 :** a small thin lightweight canvas satchel decorated with the name of an airline

flight jacket *n* [so called fr. its similarity to aviators' jackets of World War II] **:** a zippered leather jacket with front pockets and knitted waistband and wristbands

flip* *vi* **1 :** to lose self-control ⟨when he ~*s* it takes three men to hold him —Eddie Krell⟩ — often used with *out* **2 :** to become extremely enthusiastic ⟨I *flipped* for that man's music —Melissa Hayden⟩

flip chart *n* **:** a series of hinged sheets that can be flipped over the top and out of view in presenting information sequentially

flip–flop \'⸗,⸗\ *n* [fr. the sound made by the soles] **:** a rubber sandal loosely fastened to the foot by means of a thong

flip side *n* [[1]*flip* (to turn over)] **1 :** the reverse and usu. less popular side of a phonograph record **2 :** the reverse or opposite side ⟨the *flip side* of a menu⟩ ⟨part of me is perfectly happy in jeans and sneakers; the *flip side* gets very involved in clothes —Romaine Maloney⟩

flip–top \'⸗ˈ⸗\ *n* **:** a top (as of a can) that is opened by pulling a small tab

flit* *n, slang* **:** a male homosexual

float* *n* **:** the time between a transaction (as the writing of a check or a purchase on credit) and the actual withdrawal from funds to cover it

floater* *n* **:** a bit of optical debris (as a dead cell or a cell fragment) in the vitreous humor or lens that may be perceived as a spot before the eye — usu. used in pl.; see MUSCAE VOLITANTES *in the Dict.*

float fishing *n* **1 :** the practice of fishing from a boat or raft allowed to float down a river **2** *chiefly Brit* **:** the art or practice of fishing usu. with live bait at the end of a line buoyed by a float

floating* *adj* **:** having no fixed value or rate ⟨~ currencies⟩ ⟨~ interest rates⟩

floating decimal *n* **:** a system of decimal point placement in an electronic calculator in which the decimal point is free to move automatically across the display in order to allow the maximum number of decimal places in the readout

floating–point \'⸗⸗ˈ⸗\ *adj* [[2]*floating* + *point*] **:** involving or being a mathematical notation (as scientific notation) in which a quantity is denoted by one number multiplied by a power of the number base — compare FIXED-POINT *herein*

floating point *n* **:** a floating-point system or notation; *also* **:** a point used in such a system or notation

floc·cu·lo·nodular lobe \ˌfläkyə(ˌ)lō+ . . .-\ *n* [fr. *flocculus* + *-o-* + *nodular*] **:** the posterior lobe of the cerebellum that consists of the nodulus and paired lateral flocculi and is concerned with equilibrium

flo·ka·ti \flōˈkätē\ *n* -s [NGk *phlokatē,* fr. *phloko* strand of wool] **:** a hand-woven Greek wool rug with a thick shaggy pile

floor exercise *n* **:** an event in gymnastics competition consisting of various ballet and tumbling movements (as jumps, somersaults, and handstands) performed without apparatus

floor partner *n* **:** a member of a brokerage firm who owns a seat on an exchange and acts as floor broker for his firm

floor–through \'⸗ˈ⸗\ *n* [[1]*floor* + *through*] **:** an apartment that occupies an entire floor of a building

floppy disk *or* **floppy** *also* **floppy diskette** *n* -ES **:** a small flexible plastic disk coated with magnetic material on which data for a computer can be stored

floss *vb* -ED/-ING/-ES *vt* **:** to use dental floss on ⟨the correct way to ~ your teeth⟩ ~ *vi* **:** to use dental floss to clean between the teeth ⟨everyone knows you should brush, but few know they should ~ —Robert Brackett⟩

flour tortilla *n* **:** a tortilla made with wheat flour instead of cornmeal

flower bond *n* **:** a U.S. Treasury bond that may be redeemed at face value before maturity if used in settling federal estate taxes

flower bug *n* **:** any of various small mostly black-and-white predaceous bugs (family Anthocoridae) that frequent flowers and feed on pest insects (as aphids and thrips)

flower child *n* **:** a hippie who wears or displays flowers

flower people *n pl* **:** FLOWER CHILDREN

flu·er·ic \(ˈ)flüˈerik\ *adj* [irreg. fr. L *fluere* to flow + E *-ic* — more at FLUID] **:** FLUIDIC *herein*

flu·er·ics \flüˈeriks\ *n pl but usu sing in constr* [*flueric* (herein) + *-s*] **:** FLUIDICS *herein*

fluidic* *adj* **:** of, relating to, or being a device (as an amplifier or control) that depends for operation on the pressures and flows of a fluid in precisely shaped channels — **fluidic** *n* -s

flu·id·ics \flüˈidiks\ *n pl but usu sing in constr* [[2]*fluid* + *-ics*] **:** the technology of fluidic devices

flu·o·cin·o·lone ac·e·to·nide \ˌflüəˈsinᵊlˌōnˌasəˈtōˌnīd\ *n* [*fluor-* + *cin-* (of unknown origin) + *-ol* + cortis*one* + *acetone* + *-ide*] **:** a glucocorticoid steroid $C_{24}H_{30}F_2O_6$ used esp. as an anti-inflammatory agent in the treatment of skin diseases

flu·o·ro·polymer \ˌflu̇(ə)(ˌ)rō, ˌflōr(ˌ)ō, ˌflȯ(ˌ)rō+\ *n* [*fluor-* + *polymer*] **:** any of various homopolymers or copolymers that consist mainly of fluorine and carbon and that are characterized by chemical inertness, thermal stability, and a low coefficient of friction

flu·o·ro·uracil \"+\ *n* [*fluor-* + *uracil*] **:** a fluorine-containing pyrimidine base $C_4H_3FN_2O_2$ used to treat some kinds of cancer; 5-fluorouracil

flur·az·e·pam \flu̇rˈazəˌpam\ *n* -s [*flur-* (alter. of *fluor-*) + di*azepam* (herein)] **:** a benzodiazepine closely related structurally to diazepam that is used as a hypnotic in the form of its hydrochloride $C_{21}H_{23}ClFN_3O{\cdot}2HCl$ — see DALMANE *herein*

fly* *vi* [[1]*fly*] **1 :** to be high (as on drugs or alcohol) **2 :** to function successfully **:** win popular acceptance ⟨a pure human-rights approach would not ~ —Charles Brydon⟩

fly* *n* **:** a football pass pattern in which the receiver runs straight downfield

fly* *adj* [[3]*fly*] *slang* **:** impressively good, attractive, or stylish ⟨would have to top myself and really come up with something ~ —John Fuqua⟩

fly–off \ˈ=,=\ *n* -s [[1]*fly* + *off*] **:** an exhibition in which competing manufacturers attempt to win government contracts by demonstrating the performance characteristics of their aircraft

FMN \ˌef(ˌ)eˈmen\ *n* -s [*f*lavin *m*ono*n*ucleotide] **:** FLAVIN MONONUCLEOTIDE

foil* *n* **:** HYDROFOIL

fo·late \ˈfō,lāt\ *n* -s [*fol*ic (acid) + [1]*-ate*] **:** FOLIC ACID; *also* **:** a salt or ester of folic acid

folk guitar *n* **:** a flat-topped acoustic guitar

[1]**folk·ie** *also* **folky** \ˈfōkē, -ki\ *n, pl* **folkies** [[2]*folk* + *-ie*] **1 :** a folk singer or musician ⟨a quiet-voiced English ~ —Stephen Holden⟩ **2 :** a fan of folk music ⟨his fans were the sincere, often politically committed . . . ~*s* of the Kennedy years —*Playboy*⟩

[2]**folkie** *or* **folky** \"\ *adj* **:** of or relating to folk music

folk·lor·is·tics \ˌfōk,lōrˈistiks\ *n pl but sing or pl in constr* [*folkloristic* + *-s*] **:** the study of folklore

folk mass *n* **:** a mass in which traditional liturgical music is replaced by folk music

folk–rock \ˈ=,=\ *n* **:** folk songs sung to a rock 'n' roll background — **folk–rock** *adj* — **folk–rocker** \ˈ=,=ə(r)\ *n*

follow–on \ˈ==ˈ=\ *adj* [*follow on,* vb.] **:** being or relating to something (as an object, technique, or event) held to be a second or later generation in the development of an original ⟨a *follow-on* bomber⟩ — **follow–on**** *n*

fondue* *n* **1 :** a dish that consists of small pieces of food (as meat, fruit, or cake) cooked in or dipped into a hot liquid at the table ⟨beef ~⟩ ⟨chocolate ~⟩ **2 :** a chafing dish for fondue

fondue fork *n* **:** a long slender usu. 2-tined fork used in eating or cooking fondue

fon·du·ta \fänˈd(y)üd·ə, -ütə\ *n* -s [Piedmontese, fr. F *fondue* — more at FONDUE] **:** a preparation of melted cheese (as fontina) usu. with milk, butter, egg yolks, and sliced white truffles

food processor *n* **:** an electric appliance that performs many tasks of food preparation (as slicing, shredding, and chopping) with one of a set of interchangeable blades revolving inside a container

food pyramid *n* **:** an ecological hierarchy of food relationships esp. when expressed quantitatively (as in mass, numbers, or energy) in which a chief predator is at the top, each level preys on the next lower level, and usu. green plants are at the bottom

food stamp *n* **:** a government-issued stamp that is sold at little cost or given to low-income persons and is redeemable for food

footpad* *n* **:** a flattish foot on the leg of a spacecraft for distributing weight to minimize sinking into a surface

foreground \ˈ=,=\ *vt* [*foreground,* n.] **:** to place in the foreground **:** EMPHASIZE

foreperson \ˈ=,==\ *n* [*fore-* + *person*] **:** a person of either sex serving in the role of foreman (as of a jury)

forgiving* *adj* **:** providing a margin of error for human performance ⟨~ slopes that make a skier feel as though his skills had miraculously sharpened —C.D. May⟩

format *vt* **formatted; formatted; formatting; formats** [*format,* n.] **:** to arrange (as material to be printed or stored data) in a particular format

formula *adj* [*formula,* n.] *of a racing car* **:** conforming to prescribed specifications of size, weight, and engine displacement and usu. having a long narrow body, open wheels, a single-seat open cockpit, and an engine in the rear

formula investing *n* **:** investing according to a plan (**formula plan**) under which more funds are invested in equity securities when the market is low and more are put into fixed-income securities when the market advances

for·tran \ˈfȯr·,tran\ *n* -s *usu cap F or all cap* [*for*mula *tran*slation] **:** an algebraic and logical language for programming a computer

fortune cookie *n* **:** a thin folded cookie containing a slip of paper on which a fortune, proverb, or humorous statement is printed

forward contract *n* **:** an agreement between a buyer and a seller to conclude the sale of an item at a specified time and at a specified price

found object *n* [trans. of F *objet trouvé*] **:** a natural or discarded object (as a piece of driftwood or junk) found by chance and held to have aesthetic value

found poem *n* **:** a poem consisting of words found in a nonpoetic context (as a product label) and usu. broken into lines that convey a verse rhythm

four–channel \ˈ=ˈ==\ *adj* **:** QUADRAPHONIC *herein*

fou·ri·er transform \ˈfu̇rē,ā-, fu̇rˈyā-\ *n, usu cap F* [after Baron Jean Baptiste Joseph *Fourier* †1830 Fr. geometrician and physicist] **:** a function (as *F(u)*) that under suitable conditions can be obtained from a given function (as *f(x)*) by multiplying by e^{iux} and integrating over all values of *x*

fourplex \ˈfō(ə)r,pleks, -ȯ(ə)r-\ *n* -ES [[1]*four* + *-plex* (as in *duplex*)] **:** a building that contains four separate apartments

fourth market *n* **:** the private market for the sale of securities by institutional investors — compare THIRD MARKET *herein*

fourth wall *n* **:** the opening of the proscenium seen as an imaginary wall between the stage set and the audience of a play

fourth world *n, usu cap F&W* **:** a group of nations esp. in Africa and Asia characterized by extremely low per capita income and an absence of readily exportable natural resources — compare THIRD WORLD *herein*

four–walling \ˈ=ˈ==\ *also* **four–walls contract** \ˈ=ˈ=-\ *n* [fr. the fact that the distributor takes over the entire theater] **:** an arrangement whereby a motion picture distributor rents a theater for the entire run of a film and keeps all the ticket receipts instead of splitting them with the theater owner

fox* *n* **1** *slang* **:** an attractive and stylish young woman **2** *slang* **:** an attractive young man

foxy* *adj* **:** ATTRACTIVE, SEXY ⟨looking incredibly ~ in a feather boa —Cyra McFadden⟩

FPC* *abbr* fish protein concentrate *herein*

frab·jous \ˈfrabjəs\ *adj* [perh. alter. of *fabulous*] **1 :** WONDERFUL **2 :** EXTRAORDINARY — **frab·jous·ly** *adv*

frac·tal \ˈfrakt³l\ *n* -s [*fractional*] **:** any of various extremely crinkly, contorted, or irregular curves, surfaces, shapes, or figures that are assigned fractional dimensions

frag \ˈfrag\ *vt* **fragged; fragged; frag·ging; frags** [*frag,* n.] **:** to deliberately injure or kill (one's military leader) by means of a fragmentation grenade — **frag·ger** *n* -s — **frag·ging** *n* -s

frame* *n* **:** a unit of programmed instruction calling for a response by the student

frameshift \ˈ=,=\ *adj* [²*frame* + ²*shift*] **:** relating to, being, or causing a mutation in which a number of nucleotides not divisible by three is inserted or deleted so that some triplet codons are read incorrectly during genetic translation ⟨~ mutations⟩ ⟨~ mutagens⟩ — **frameshift** *n*

fran·chi·see \ˌfranchəˈzē, -ˌchīˈ-, -raan- *sometimes* -ˈsē\ *n* -s [¹*franchise* + *-ee*] **:** one who is granted a franchise to operate a unit in a chain of business establishments

fran·co–american \ˌfraŋ(ˌ)kō+\ *n, cap F&A* [*Franco-* + *American*] **:** an American of French or esp. French-Canadian descent — **franco–american** *adj, usu cap F&A*

¹fran·co·phone \ˈfraŋkəˌfōn\ *adj, often cap* [F, fr. *franco-* Franco- + Gk *phōnē* voice, speech — more at BAN] **:** having or belonging to a French-speaking population esp. in a country where two or more languages are spoken

²francophone \"\ *n* -s *usu cap* **:** a French-speaking person esp. in a country where two or more languages are spoken

fran·glais \fräⁿˈglā, -äŋˈg-\ *n* -ES *often cap* [F, blend of *français* French and *anglais* English] **:** French marked by a considerable number of borrowings from English

fratricide* *n* **:** the hypothetical destruction of incoming missiles with closely spaced targets (as missile silos) by the effects of the first nuclear warhead to detonate

freak* *n* **1 :** one who uses illicit drugs **2 :** HIPPIE **3 :** an ardent enthusiast ⟨a film ~⟩

freak *vb* [*freak,* n. (herein)] *vi* **1 :** to withdraw from reality and society esp. by taking drugs **2 :** to experience nightmarish hallucinations as a result of taking drugs **:** have a bad trip — often used with *out* **3 a :** to behave irrationally or unconventionally under the influence of drugs — often used with *out* **b :** to lose one's composure — often used with *out* ⟨if I lose my glasses or miss an appointment, I *freak out* —Emmylou Harris⟩ ~ *vt* **1 :** to put under the influence of a psychedelic drug **2 :** to disturb the composure of **:** UPSET — often used with *out* ⟨what he saw *freaked* him out so much that he still gets shaken when he remembers it —*Berkeley Barb*⟩ — **freaked** *or* **freaked–out** *adj*

freak·ery \ˈfrēk(ə)rē\ *n* -ES [¹*freak* + *-ery*] **1 :** FREAKINESS *herein* **2 :** something that is freaky

freak·i·ness \ˈfrēkēnəs, -kin-\ *n* -ES [*freaky* + *-ness*] **:** the quality or state of being freaky

freak·ing *adj* (*or adv*) [alter. of *frigging,* pres. part. of *frig* (copulate)] **:** DAMNED — used as an intensive ⟨it was too ~ much to believe —Chip Crossland⟩

freak–out \ˈ=,=\ *n* -s [*freak,* v. (herein) + *out*] **1 :** a withdrawal from reality esp. by means of drugs **2 a :** a drug-induced state of mind characterized by terrifying hallucinations **:** a bad trip **b :** an irrational act by one that freaks out **3 :** a gathering of hippies **4 :** one who freaks out

free agent *n* **:** a professional athlete who is free to negotiate a contract with any team

free–associate \ˌ==ˈ==ˌ=\ *vi* [back-formation fr. *free association*] **:** to engage in free association

free base *n* **:** cocaine freed from impurities by treatment (as with ether) and heated to produce vapors for inhalation

freebase \ˈ=,=\ *vb* [*free base,* n.] *vi* **:** to prepare or use free base cocaine ~ *vt* **:** to prepare or use (cocaine) as free base

free·bie *or* **free·bee** \ˈfrēbē\ *n* -s [by alter. fr. obs. slang *freeby* gratis, irreg. fr. *free*] **:** something (as a theater ticket) given or received without charge

freedom ride *n, often cap F&R* **:** a ride made by civil rights workers through states of the southern U.S. to ascertain whether public facilities (as bus terminals) are desegregated — **freedom rider** *n, often cap F&R*

free–fire zone \ˌ=ˈ=-\ *n* [¹*free* + *fire*] **:** a combat area where any moving thing is a legitimate target

free–running \ˈ=ˈ==\ *adj* **:** not involving or subjected to entrainment or resetting periodically by an environmental factor (as photoperiod) ⟨a *free-running* circadian rhythm⟩

free safety *n* **:** a safetyman in football who has no specific pass receiver to guard in a man-to-man defense and who usu. helps wherever needed on defense

free university *n* **:** an unaccredited autonomous free institution established within a university by students to present and discuss subjects not usu. dealt with in the academic curriculum

freeze–etch \ˈ=ˈ=\ *adj* **:** of, relating to, or used in freeze-etching

freeze–etched \ˈ=ˈ=\ *adj* **:** having been subjected to or prepared by freeze-etching

freeze–etching \ˈ=,==\ *n* [¹*freeze* + *etching*] **:** preparation of a specimen (as of tissue) for electron microscopic examination by freezing, fracturing along natural structural lines, and preparing a replica (as by simultaneous vapor deposition of carbon and platinum)

freeze–fracture \ˈ=,==\ *also* **freeze–fracturing** *n* [¹*freeze* + *fracture*] **:** FREEZE-ETCHING *herein* — **freeze–fracture** *vt*

freeze–frame \ˈ=,=\ *n* [²*freeze* + ²*frame*] **1 :** a frame of a motion-picture film that is repeated so as to give the illusion of a static picture; *also* **:** a static picture produced from a videodisc or videotape recording **2 :** something like a freeze-frame ⟨exist most vividly in the *freeze-frame* of memory —Gioia Diliberto⟩

fret* *vt* **:** to depress (the strings of a musical instrument) against the frets ~ *vi* **:** to fret the strings of a musical instrument

fried·man·ite \ˈfrēdməˌnīt\ *n* -s *usu cap* [Milton *Friedman* b1912 Am. economist + E ¹*-ite*] **:** a monetarist who adheres to the theory of economist Milton Friedman that economic regulation should be through direct governmental manipulation of the money supply

frijoles re·fri·tos \-(ˌ)rāˈfrē(ˌ)tōz, -ōs\ *n pl* [Sp, lit., refried beans] **:** frijoles cooked with seasonings, fried, then mashed and fried again

Fris·bee \ˈfrizbē\ *trademark* — used for a plastic disk several inches in diameter that is sailed between players by a flip of the wrist

frit·ta·ta \frēˈtäd·ə\ *n* -s [It] **:** an unfolded omelet often containing chopped vegetables or meats

fritted *adj* [²*frit*] **:** being porous glass made of sintered powdered or fiber glass

fritto misto* *n* **:** small pieces of seafood and vegetables that are dipped in batter and fried

frog* *n* **:** a small holder with perforations or spikes that is placed in a bowl or vase to keep cut flowers in position

front–end \ˈ=ˈ=\ *adj* [[1]*front* + *end*] **:** relating to or required at the beginning of an undertaking ⟨take some time for the huge *front-end* investment to be paid off — *Wall Street Jour.*⟩

front end *n* **:** a unit in a computer system devoted to controlling the data communications link between terminals and the main computer (as by routing messages and checking for errors in transmission) and often to preliminary processing of data

front–end load \ˈ=ˌ=-\ *n* [[3]*front* + [1]*end* + [1]*load*] **:** the part of the total load taken out of early payments under a contract plan for the periodic purchase of investment= company shares

front–end loader *n* **:** a usu. wheeled tractor fitted with a wide scoop in front for excavating and loading loose material (as earth or gravel)

fron·te·nis \ˌfrənˈtenəs, (ˈ)frän-\ *n* [AmerSp, blend of Sp *frontón* pelota court and *tenis* tennis, fr. E *tennis* — more at FRONTON] **:** a game of Mexican origin played with rackets and a rubber ball on a 3-walled court

frontlash \ˈ=ˌ=\ *n* -ES [[3]*front* + *-lash* (as in *backlash*)] **:** a counterreaction to a political backlash

front money *n* **:** money that is paid in advance for a promised service or product

frostbelt \ˈ=ˌ=\ *n, often cap* **:** the northern and northeastern states of the U.S. — compare SUNBELT *herein*

frosted* *adj* **:** having undergone frosting ⟨~ hair⟩

frosting* *n* **:** the lightening (as by chemicals) of small strands of hair throughout the entire head to produce a two-tone effect — compare STREAKING *herein*

fruc·to·kinase \ˌfrəktō, ˈfrük-, ˈfrük- +\ *n* [*fructose* + *kinase*] **:** a kinase that catalyzes the transfer of phosphate groups to fructose

fruit jar *n* **:** MASON JAR

fruit leather *n* **:** a sheet of dried pureed fruit

fruit machine *n* [so called fr. the use of pictures of various fruits as symbols to be matched] *Brit* **:** SLOT MACHINE 2

fru·se·mide \ˈfrüsəˌmīd\ *n* -S [by alter.] *chiefly Brit* **:** FUROSEMIDE *herein*

fry bread *n* **:** bread cooked (as by Navajo Indians) by deep frying

fry–up \ˈ=ˌ=\ *n* -S [[1]*fry* + *up*] *Brit* **:** a dish or meal of fried food

FSO \ˌef(ˌ)esˈō\ *abbr or n* -S **:** a foreign service officer

[1]fuck \ˈfək\ *vb* -ED/-ING/-S [of Gmc origin; prob. fr. or akin to D *fokken* to breed (cattle), fr. MD, push, thrust, copulate; akin to Sw dial. *fock* penis] *vi* **1 :** COPULATE — usu. considered obscene; sometimes used in the present participle as an intensive **2 :** to mess around — used with *with;* usu. considered vulgar ~ *vt* **1 :** to engage in coitus with — usu. considered obscene; sometimes used interjectionally with an object (as a pronoun) to express anger, contempt, or disgust **2 :** to deal with unfairly or harshly — usu. considered vulgar

[2]fuck \"\ *n* -S **1 :** an act of copulation — usu. considered obscene **2 :** a sexual partner — usu. considered obscene **3 a :** DAMN 2 — usu. considered vulgar **b** — used esp. with *the* as a meaningless intensive; usu. considered vulgar

fucked–up \ˈ=ˈ=\ *adj* **:** thoroughly confused or disordered — usu. considered vulgar

fuck·er \ˈfəkə(r)\ *n* -S **1 :** one that fucks —usu. considered obscene **2 :** an offensive or disagreeable person — usu. considered vulgar

fuck off *vi* **:** to leave forthwith **:** bug off — usu. used as a command; usu. considered vulgar

fuck over *vt* **:** to take advantage of **:** EXPLOIT — usu. considered vulgar

fuck up *vt* **:** to ruin or spoil esp. through stupidity, ignorance, or carelessness **:** BUNGLE —usu. considered vulgar ~ *vi* **:** to act foolishly or stupidly **:** BLUNDER — usu. considered vulgar

fuckup \ˈ=ˌ=\ *n* -S **1 :** one who fucks up —usu. considered vulgar **2 :** BOTCH, BLUNDER —usu. considered vulgar

fuel cell *n* **:** a device that continuously changes the chemical energy of a fuel (as hydrogen) and an oxidant directly into electrical energy

fueler* *n* **:** a dragster that uses specially blended fuel

fuel injection *n* **:** a system of providing atomized fuel to an internal-combustion engine by spraying a precisely metered amount of fuel into the intake manifold or directly into the cylinder in time for it to be ignited with the compressed air — **fuel–injected** *adj*

full–service \ˈ=ˈ==\ *adj* [[1]*full* + *service*] **:** providing comprehensive service of a particular kind ⟨a *full-service* bank⟩

ful·vic acid \ˌfu̇lvik-, ˌfəl-\ *n* [fr. penicillium *fulv*um, a genus of fungi + *-ic*] **:** a water-soluble substance of low molecular weight derived from humus that combines with lyophilic organic compounds and may serve to inactivate some toxic pollutants in aquatic environments

fu man·chu mustache \ˌfüˌmanˈchü-\ *n, usu cap F & 1st M* [*Fu Manchu,* Chinese villain in stories by "Sax Rohmer" (A. S. Ward †1955)] **:** a heavy mustache with ends that turn down to the chin

fun and games *n pl but sing or pl in constr* **:** light amusement

functor* *n* **1 :** FUNCTION WORD **2 :** a rule defined on two mathematical categories that assigns each object and mapping of one category to an object and mapping of the other in such a way as to preserve certain aspects of structure (as identity mappings, composition of mappings, and isomorphism)

fundamental theorem of algebra : a theorem in algebra: every equation which can be put in the form with zero on one side of the equal-sign and a polynomial of degree greater than or equal to one with real or complex coefficients on the other has at least one root which is a real or complex number

fund–raiser \ˈ=ˌ==\ *n* [[1]*fund* + *raiser*] **1 :** a person employed to raise funds (as for a political campaign or charity) **2 :** an event or campaign organized to raise funds

fun fur *n* **:** relatively inexpensive or synthetic fur for casual wear

funk* *n* **1 :** funky music **2 :** the quality or state of being funky ⟨jeans . . . have lost much of their ~ —Tom Wolfe⟩

funky* *adj* -ER/-EST **1 :** having an earthy unsophisticated style and feeling; *specif* **:** having the style and feeling of early blues ⟨~ piano playing⟩ **2 :** odd or quaint in appearance or style ⟨expected a ~ . . . type, and instead I met this beautiful, gracious lady —Laura Cunningham⟩

funnel cake *n* [so called because the dough is poured through a funnel] **:** a small spiral-shaped cake fried in a skillet

funny car *n* **:** a specialized dragster that has a one-piece molded body resembling the body of a mass-produced car

funny farm *n, slang* **:** an insane asylum

fu·ra·zol·i·done \ˌfyu̇rəˈzäləˌdōn, -zȯl-\ *n* -s [*fur-* + *azole* + *-ide* + *-one*] **:** an antimicrobial drug $C_8H_7N_3O_5$ used against bacteria and some protozoa esp. in infections of the gastrointestinal tract

fu·ro·se·mide \f(y)əˈrōsəˌmīd\ *also* **fur·se·mide** \ˈfərsə-, ˈfə̄sə-\ *n* -s [*fur-* + sulf- + *-emide,* prob. alter. of *amide*] **:** a powerful diuretic $C_{12}H_{11}ClN_2O_5S$ used esp. in the treatment of edema

fu·si·coc·cin \ˌfyüsəˈkäksən\ *n* -s [fr. *fusicoccum* (genus name) + *-in*] **:** a diterpenoid glucoside produced by a pathogenic fungus of the genus *Fusicoccum* (*F. amygdali*) that causes wilting of peach and almond leaves

fu·ton \ˈfüˌtän\ *n, pl* **futons** *also* **futon** [Jap] **:** a mattress filled usu. with cotton that is placed on the floor for use as a bed

future shock *n* **:** the physical and psychological distress suffered by one who is unable to cope with the rapidity of societal and technological changes

futurist* *n* **:** one who studies and predicts the future esp. on the basis of current trends

futurist *adj* [*futurist,* n.] **:** of or relating to futurism or futurists

fu·tur·is·tics \ˌ¦fyüchəˈ¦ristiks\ *n pl but sing in constr* [*futuristic* + *-s*] **:** FUTUROLOGY *herein*

fu·tu·rol·o·gy \ˌfyüchəˈräləjē\ *n* -ES [G *futurologie,* fr. *futur* future + *-o-* + *-logie* -logy] **:** a study that deals with future possibilities based on current trends — **fu·tu·ro·log·i·cal** \ˌ¦fyüchərə-¦läjəkəl\ *adj* — **fu·tu·rol·o·gist** \ˌ==ˈräləjəst\ *n* -s

futz \ˈfəts\ *vi* -ED/-ING/-ES [prob. fr. Yiddish; perh. akin to G *furzen,* E *fart*] *slang* **:** FOOL 1a, c — often used with *around* ⟨~ around without producing any worthwhile music —John Koegel⟩

fuzz tone *or* **fuzz box** *n* **:** an electronic device (as on an electric guitar) which by distorting the sound gives it a fuzzy quality; *also* **:** the sound so produced

FWD* *abbr, often not cap* front-wheel drive

G

g \ˈjē\ *adj, cap* [general] *of a motion picture* **:** of such a nature that persons of all ages may be allowed admission — compare PG *herein,* PG-13 *herein,* R *herein,* X *herein*

g* *abbr, cap* **1** giga- **2** guanine

GABA *abbr* gamma-aminobutyric acid *herein*

ga·ga·ku \gäˈgä(ˌ)kü\ *n, often cap* [Jap, fr. *ga* elegance + *gaku* music] **:** the ancient court music of Japan

gag order *n* **:** a court-imposed ruling barring public disclosure or discussion (as by the press) of evidence relating to an ongoing court case

ga·lac·to·kinase \gəˌlaktō +\ *n* [*galactose* + *kinase*] **:** a kinase that catalyzes the transfer of phosphate groups to galactose

gal·braith·ian \(ˌ)galˌbrāthēən, -thyən\ *adj, usu cap* [John Kenneth *Galbraith* *b*1908 Am. economist + E *-ian*] **:** of or relating to the economic theories or programs of John Kenneth Galbraith

ga·le·ro \gəˈle(ə)r(ˌ)ō\ *n* -s [It, fr. L *galerus, galera* cap of skin worn by certain flamens — more at GALERA] **:** the flat-crowned wide-brimmed tasseled red hat formerly worn by Roman Catholic cardinals — called also *cardinal's hat*

gal friday *n, usu cap F* **:** GIRL FRIDAY

gal·le·ria \ˌgaləˈrēə\ *n* -s [It, gallery, fr. ML *galeria*] **:** a roofed and usu. glass-enclosed promenade or court (as at a shopping mall)

gallium arsenide *n* **:** a synthetic compound GaAs used esp. as a semiconducting material

gallows humor *n* **:** humor that makes fun of very serious or terrifying situations

ga·lois theory \(ˈ)galˌwä-\ *n, usu cap G* [after Evariste *Galois* †1832 Fr. mathematician] **:** a part of the theory of mathematical groups concerned esp. with the conditions under which a solution to a polynomial equation with coefficients in a given mathematical field can be obtained in the field by the repetition of operations and the extraction of nth roots

galvanic skin response *n* **:** a change in the electrical resistance of the skin that is a physiochemical response to a change in emotional state — abbr. *GSR*

ga·may \gaˈmā, ˈgamˌā\ *n* -s *often cap* [after *Gamay,* village in France] **:** a light dry red table wine of California made from the purple grape that is also used for French Beaujolais

game ball* *n* **:** a ball (as a football) presented by the members of a team to a player or coach in recognition of his contribution to the team's victory

game plan *n* [so called fr. the use of a strategy or plan in a game like football] **:** a strategy for achieving an objective

gamma–aminobutyric acid \ˌgaməəˌmē(ˌ)nō, -məˌamə(ˌ)nō + . . .-\ *also* **γ–aminobutyric acid** \"\ *n* [²*gamma* + *amin-* + *butyric acid*] **:** an amino acid $C_4H_9NO_2$ that is a neurotransmitter in the central nervous system — abbr. *GABA*

gamma ray* *n* **:** a high-energy photon

gam·ma–ray astronomy \ˌ==ˌ=-\ *n* **:** astronomy dealing with the properties of celestial bodies deduced from gamma rays they emit

gang bang *n* **:** copulation by several persons in succession with the same passive partner — **gang–bang** \ˈ=ˌ=\ *vb*

gangbuster \ˈ=ˌ==\ *n* [¹*gang* + *buster*] **:** a person and esp. a law officer engaged in the aggressive breakup of organized criminal gangs — **like gangbusters :** with great force or vigor ⟨knows how to just kind of play things cool — instead of coming on *like gangbusters* — Dave Brower⟩; *also* **:** at a great rate ⟨buying foreign wheat *like gangbusters* —*Christian Science Monitor*⟩ — often used as a generalized expression of approval ⟨our defense is playing *like gangbusters* —Joe Theismann⟩

gangbusters *adj or adv* **:** doing very well **:** POPULAR, HOT ⟨in some parts of the country singles are still ~ but in this city they're dead —Perry Ury⟩ ⟨if your company is public and is going ~ —*Esquire*⟩

gan·gle \ˈgaŋgəl, -aiŋ-\ *vi* -ED/-ING/-s [back-formation fr. *gangling*] **:** to walk or move with or as if with a loose-jointed gait **:** move like a gangling person — **gangle** *n* -s

gan·gli·o·si·do·sis \ˌgaŋglēōˌsīˈdōsəs, -ˌsəˈ-\ *n, pl* **gangliosido·ses** \-ōˌsēz\ [*ganglioside* + *-osis*] **:** any of several inherited metabolic diseases (as Tay-Sachs disease) characterized by an enzyme deficiency which causes accumulation of gangliosides in the tissues

gang·sa \ˈgäŋ(ˌ)sä\ *n* -s [Indonesian *gampang gangsa,* fr. *gampang* musical instrument consisting of bars struck by hammers + *gangsa* brass] **:** a Balinese metallophone with bamboo resonators

gang shag *n* [¹*gang* + ⁷*shag*] **:** GANG BANG *herein*

gantry* *n* **:** a movable scaffold with platforms at different levels for use in erecting and servicing rockets before launching

gap junction *n* **:** an area of contact between adjacent cells characterized by modification of the cell membranes for intercellular communication or transfer of low molecular-weight substances — **gap–junctional** \ˌ=ˈ===\ *adj*

garage sale *n* **:** a sale of used household or personal articles (as furniture, tools, or clothing) held on the seller's own premises

ga·ra·gist \gəˈräjəst, -äzhə-; *Brit usu* ˈgaˌräzhəst *or* -äj- *or* ˈgarij-\ *n* -s [¹*garage* + *-ist*] *chiefly Brit* **:** GARAGEMAN

garbage* *n* **:** inaccurate or useless data

gar·bol·o·gist \gärˈbäləjəst, gȧˈb-\ *n* -s [¹*garbage* + *-ologist*] **:** a trash or garbage collector

gar·çon·nière \ˌgärsᵊnˌye(ə)r, -(ˌ)sȯn-\ *n* -s [F, fr. *garçon* boy, bachelor — more at GARÇON] **:** a bachelor apartment

garment bag *n* **:** a traveling bag that folds in half and has a center handle for easy carrying

gar·vey·ism \ˈgärvēˌizəm, ˈgȧv-\ *n* -s *usu cap* [Marcus *Garvey* †1940 Jamaican Black Nationalist + E *-ism*] **:** a 20th century racial and political doctrine advocating black separation and the formation of self-governing black nations in Africa — **gar·vey·ite** \-ēˌīt\ *n* -s *usu cap*

gas* *n, slang* **:** one that is very appealing or enjoyable ⟨the party was a ~⟩

GAS *abbr* general adaptation syndrome

gas chromatograph *n* **:** an instrument used to separate a sample into components in gas chromatography

gas chromatography *n* **:** chromatography in which the sample mixture is vaporized and injected into a stream of carrier gas (as nitrogen or helium) moving through a column containing a stationary phase comprised of a liquid or a particulate solid and is separated into its component compounds according to the affinity of the compounds for the stationary phase — **gas chromatographic** *adj*

gasdynamics \ˌ=(ˌ) =ˈ==\ *n pl but sing in constr* [*gas* + *dynamics*] **:** a branch of dynamics that deals with gaseous fluids including products of combustion and plasmas — **gasdynamic** \ˌ=(ˌ)=ˈ==\ *adj* — **gas·dy·nam·i·cist** \ˌ=(ˌ)dīˈnaməsəst\ *n* -s

gas–guzzler \ˈ=ˌ==\ *n* **:** a usu. large automobile that gets relatively poor mileage — **gas–guzzling** *adj*

gas·ket·ed \ˈgaskəd·əd, -aas-, -ais-\ *adj* [¹*gasket* + *-ed*] **:** furnished with a gasket ⟨a ~ screw-cap can⟩

gas–liquid chromatography \ˌ=ˈ==-\ *n* [¹*gas* + *liquid*] **:** gas chromatography in which the stationary phase is a liquid — **gas–liquid chromatographic** \ˌ=ˈ==-\ *adj*

gas·o·hol \ˈgasəˌhȯl *sometimes* -ˌhäl\ *n* -s [blend of *gasoline* and *alcohol*] **:** a fuel consisting of a blend usu. of 10% ethyl alcohol and 90% gasoline

gastrocolic reflex *n* **:** the occurrence of peristalsis following the entrance of food into the empty stomach

gas·tro·duo·de·nos·to·my \ˌgastrōˌd(y)üəˌdēˈnästəmē, -ˌd(y)ü- ˌädᵊnˈäs-\ *n* -ES [NL, fr. *gastr-* + *duoden-* + ²*-stomy*] **:** surgical formation of a passage between the stomach and the duodenum

gaucherie* *n* **:** gauche quality or behavior ⟨seems now to have lost his early ~ —Peter Evans⟩

gaudy ironstone *n* **:** a polychrome-decorated mid-19th century English ironstone ware

gaussian integer *n, usu cap G* [Karl Friedrich *Gauss* †1855 Ger. mathematician + E *-ian*] **:** a complex number $a + bi$ where a and b are integers and $i = \sqrt{-1}$

gavel–to–gavel \ˈ===ˈ==\ *adj* **:** running from start to finish ⟨*gavel-to-gavel* coverage of a political convention⟩

gay* *n* **:** HOMOSEXUAL

ga·zump \gəˈzəmp\ *vt* -ED/-ING/-s [origin unknown] *Brit* **:** SWINDLE; *specif* **:** to demand a higher price from (the buyer of a house) than that agreed on

GB \(ˈ)jēˈbē\ *n* -s [code name] **:** SARIN

GED *abbr* general educational development

gee–whiz \(ˈ)jēˌ(h)wiz\ *adj* [*gee whiz*] **1 :** designed to arouse wonder or excitement or to amplify the merits or significance of something esp. by the use of clever or sensational language ⟨*gee-whiz* journalism⟩ **2 :** marked by spectacular or astonishing qualities or achievement ⟨*gee-whiz* technology⟩ **3 :** characterized by wide-eyed enthusiasm, excitement, and wonder ⟨a *gee-whiz* approach to politics that wears a little thin —*Business Week*⟩

gel filtration \ˈjel-\ *n* [¹*gel*] **:** chromatography in which the material to be fractionated separates primarily according to molecular size as it moves through a column of a gel and is washed with a solvent so that the fractions appear successively at the end of the column — called also *gel chromatography*

gemini* *n sing, pl* **geminis** *usu cap* **:** one born under the astrological sign Gemini

gem·i·ni·an \ˌjeməˈnīən\ *n* -s *usu cap* [*gemini* + E *-ian*] **:** GEMINI *herein*

ge·müt·lich \gəˈmu̇etlik\ *adj* [G, fr. MHG *gemüetlich,* fr. *gemüete* spirit, heart (fr. *ge-,* perfective, associative, and collective prefix — fr. OHG *gi-* — + *muot* mood, spirit, mind, fr. OHG) + *-lich* -ly, fr. OHG *-lih* — more at MOOD] **:** agreeably pleasant **:** COMFORTABLE ⟨easy, natural and ~ in her writing —*Times Lit. Supp.*⟩

ge·müt·lich·keit \gəˈmu̇etlikˌkīt\ *n* -s [G, fr. *gemütlich* pleasant + *-keit* -hood, fr. MHG, alter. of *-heit,* fr. OHG] **:** CORDIALITY, FRIENDLINESS

gene conversion *n* **:** the production of gametes by a heterozygote esp. in fungi (as of the genera *Saccharomyces, Neurospora,* or *Aspergillus*) in unequal numbers and often in a 3:1 ratio that is thought to occur by selective copying during chromatid replication of one member of the gene pair in preference to the other

gene pool *n* **:** the collection of genes in an interbreeding population that includes each gene at a certain frequency in relation to its alleles **:** the genetic information of a population of interbreeding organisms ⟨the human *gene pool*⟩

general adaptation syndrome *n* **:** the sequence of physiological reactions to prolonged stress that in the classification of Hans Selye includes alarm, resistance, and exhaustion

general obligation bond *n* **:** a municipal bond of which payment of interest and principal is backed by the taxing power and credit of the issuing governmental unit

general term *n* **:** a mathematical expression composed of variables and constants that yields the successive terms of a sequence or series when integers are substituted for one of the variables often denoted by k ⟨x^k is the *general term* of the series $1 + x + x^2 + x^3 + \ldots$⟩

generative grammar *n* **1 :** a description of a language in the form of an ordered set of rules for producing the grammatical sentences of that language **2 :** TRANSFORMATIONAL GRAMMAR *herein*

generative semantics *n pl but usu sing in constr* **:** a description of a language emphasizing a semantic deep structure that is logical in form, that provides syntactic structure, and that is related to surface structure by transformations

generator* *n* **:** a mathematical entity that when subjected to one or more operations yields another mathematical entity or its elements; *specif* **:** GENERATRIX 1

generic* *adj* **:** not limited to a particular application or to use with a particular device ⟨~ computer software⟩

generic* *n* **:** a generic product (as a drug) — usu. used in pl.

gene–splicing \ˈ=ˌ==\ *n* **:** the technique by which recombinant DNA is produced and made to function in an organism

genetic code *n* **:** the biochemical basis of heredity consisting of codons in DNA and RNA that determine the specific amino acid sequence in proteins and that are essentially uniform for the forms of life studied so far — **genetic coding** *n*

genetic counseling *n* **:** medical education of affected individuals and the general public concerning inherited disorders that includes discussion of the probability of producing offspring with a disorder given that it has occurred in a family, techniques of diagnosis, and possibilities for treatment

genetic engineering *n* **:** the directed alteration of genetic material by intervention in genetic processes; *esp* **:** GENE-SPLICING *herein* — **genetic engineer** *n*

genetic map *n* **:** MAP 1 *herein*

genetic marker *n* **:** a usu. dominant gene or trait that serves esp. to identify genes or traits linked with it

genital herpes *or* **genital herpes simplex** *n* **:** HERPES GENITALIS *herein*

ge·noise \zhān'wäz\ *n* -s [F *génoise,* fem. of *génois* of or relating to Genoa, Italy] **:** a light cake of sugar, flour, and stiffly beaten eggs

gen·ta·mi·cin \ˌjentə'mīsᵊn\ *n* -s [alter. of earlier *gentamycin,* fr. *genta-* (prob. irreg. fr. *gentian violet;* fr. the color of the organism from which it is produced) + *mycin*] **:** a broad-spectrum antibiotic mixture that is derived from an actinomycete (*Micromonospora purpurea* or *M. echinospora*) and is extensively used in treating infections esp. of the urinary tract

gentleperson \'≈,≈≈\ *n* **:** a gentleman or lady

gen·tri·fi·ca·tion \ˌjen·trəfə'kāshən\ *n* -s [*gentry* + *-fication*] **:** the immigration of middle-class people into a deteriorating or recently renewed city area; *also* **:** the renewal and rebuilding that accompany such immigration — **gen·tri·fy** \'jentrəfī\ *vt*

geo·corona \ˈjēə+\ *n* [*ge-* + *corona*] **:** the outermost part of the earth's atmosphere consisting primarily of hydrogen

geology* *n* **:** the study of the solid matter of a celestial body

geomagnetic storm *n* **:** MAGNETIC STORM

geometric* *or* **geometrical*** *adj* **:** increasing in a geometric progression ⟨~ population growth⟩

geo·pres·sured \ˈjēōˈpreshərd\ *adj* [*ge-* + *pressured,* fr. past part. of ²*pressure*] **:** being under great pressure from geologic forces ⟨~ methane⟩; *also* **:** of, relating to, or derived from geopressured natural deposits ⟨~ energy⟩

geo·stationary \ˈjē(ˌ)ō +\ *adj* [*ge-* + *stationary*] **:** of, relating to, or being an artificial satellite that travels from west to east at an altitude of over 22,000 miles above the equator and at the same speed as that of the earth's rotation so that the satellite seems to remain in the same place

geo·synchronous \"+\ *adj* [*ge-* + *synchronous*] **:** GEOSTATIONARY *herein* — **geo·synchronously** \"+\ *adv*

geriatric *n* -s [*geriatric,* adj.] **:** an elderly person

german wirehaired pointer *n, usu cap G* **:** any of a German breed of liver or liver and white gundogs with a flat-lying wiry coat composed of hairs one and one-half to two inches in length

germfree \ˈ≈ˈ≈\ *adj* **:** free of microorganisms **:** AXENIC

ge·samt·kunst·werk \gə'zämtˌkunstˌverk\ *n* -s *usu cap* [G, fr. *gesamt* whole, entire + *kunst* art + *werk* work, production] **:** an art work produced by a synthesis of various art forms (as music and drama)

ges·to·sis \jes'tōsəs\ *n, pl* **gesto·ses** \-ōˌsēz\ [NL, fr. *gest*ation + *-osis*] **:** any disorder of pregnancy; *esp* **:** TOXEMIA OF PREGNANCY

get* *vb* — **get it on 1 :** to become enthusiastic, energetic, or excited ⟨when they get with a rock group they just really *get it on* —John Von Ohlen⟩ **2 :** to engage in sexual intercourse — **get it together** *or* **get it all together :** to put things in order **:** get one's act together — **get it up :** to have an erection — **get one's act together 1** *or* **get one's head together :** to put one's life, thoughts, or emotions in order **:** cease to be confused or misdirected **2 :** to begin to function in a skillful or efficient manner ⟨the company finally *got its act together*⟩ — **get one's back up :** to get one's hackles up **:** make one angry, irritated, or annoyed — **get one's rocks off 1 :** to experience orgasm **2 :** to become pleasurably excited — **get on the stick :** to start working energetically on something ⟨worrying what might happen if we didn't *get on the stick* pretty fast —Tim Findley⟩

get off* *vi* **1 :** to get high on a drug — usu. used with *on* ⟨*get off* on heroin⟩ **2 :** to experience orgasm **3 :** to experience great pleasure or satisfaction — usu. used with *on* ⟨*gets off* on the music⟩ ~ *vt* **:** to cause to get off

ge·würz·tra·mi·ner \gəˈvərtsˈtramənər, *Ger* gə'vʊ̈rts-trä-ˌmēnə (r\ *n* -s *often cap* [G, fr. *gewürz* spice + *traminer* of or relating to Tramin (Termeno, Italy)] **:** a light dry Alsatian white wine with a spicy bouquet; *also* **:** a similar wine made elsewhere

ghost·ing \'gōstiŋ\ *n* [fr. gerund of ²*ghost*] **:** GHOST 8c; *also* **:** the formation of ghosts

gi \'gē\ *n* -s [Jap.] **:** a garment worn in practice or exhibition of oriental martial arts (as karate or judo) consisting of loose-fitting pants and a loose jacket held closed by a cloth belt

gig \'gig\ *vi* **gigged; gigged; gigging; gigs** [⁷*gig*] **:** to work as a musician ⟨*gigged* with various bands —*Downbeat*⟩

giga·bit \'jigə, 'gigə +\ *n* [*giga-* + ⁷*bit*] **:** one billion bits

giga·cycle \"+\ *n* [*giga-* + *cycle*] **:** GIGAHERTZ

giga·watt \"+\ *n* [*giga-* + *watt*] **:** a unit of power equal to one billion watts

giggle* *n* **:** one that amuses

GI·GO \'gīˌgō, 'gē-\ *abbr* garbage in, garbage out

gi·ro \'ji(ə)rō, 'zh|, |ē(ˌ)rō *esp Brit* 'jīˌrō\ *n* -s [fr. It *giro* circulation (of currency)] **:** a system of money transfer in Britain and much of Europe that involves a simple transfer of credits from one account to another without money orders or checks

giveback \'≈ˌ≈\ *n* -s **:** a previous gain (as an increase in wages or benefits) given back to management by workers (as in a labor contract) ⟨union workers . . . agreed to ~*s* to avoid layoffs —Lawrence Ingrassia⟩

give–up* *n* [*give up;* fr. the giving up by the first broker of part of the commission to the second] **1 :** a security or commodity market order which one broker executes for a client of a second broker for a share of the commission **2 :** a part of a commission due a broker from a major client (as a mutual fund) that the client directs to be turned over to another broker who has provided special services

glas·phalt \'glaˌsfȯlt\ *n* -s [blend of ¹*glass* and *asphalt*] **:** a mixture of asphalt and crushed glass used to surface roads

glasshouse* *n, Brit* **:** a military prison **:** GUARDHOUSE

gleam·er \'glēmə(r)\ *n* -s [²*gleam* + *-er*] **:** a cosmetic applied to the face or lips to give the appearance of shine or to accent an area (as the cheekbones)

glitch \'glich\ *n* -ES [prob. fr. G *glitschen* to slip, slide, fr. MHG intensive of *glīten* to glide, fr. OHG *glītan* — more at GLIDE] **1 :** an unwanted brief surge of electric power **:** a false or spurious electronic signal **2 a :** MALFUNCTION ⟨a ~ in the fuel cell of a spacecraft⟩ **b :** a minor problem that causes a temporary setback **:** SNAG **3 :** a sudden change in the period of rotation of a neutron star

glit·te·ra·ti \ˌglid·ə'rä|d·(ˌ)ē, ˌglitə-, -'rä|, |(ˌ)tē *also* -'räˌtī\ *n pl* [fr. ²*glitter* + *-ati* (as in *literati*)] **:** BEAUTIFUL PEOPLE *herein*

glitter rock *n* **:** rock music performed by male musicians who are made up to look grotesquely feminine — **glitter rocker** *n*

glitz \'glits\ *n* -ES [fr. Yiddish *glitz* glitter; akin to G *glitzerig* sparkling] **:** extravagant showiness **:** OSTENTATION — **glitzy** \-sē\ *adj* -ER/-EST

global* *adj* **:** of or relating to a celestial body (as the moon)

glogg *or* **glögg** \ˈglüg\ *n* -s [Sw *glögg,* fr. *glödga* to mull; akin to ON *glōth* — more at GLEED] **:** a hot spiced wine and liquor punch

glomus tumor *n* **:** a painful benign tumor that develops by hypertrophy of a glomus

¹glop \ˈgläp\ *n* -s [prob. imit.] **1a :** a thick semiliquid food or mixture of foods that is usu. unappetizing in appearance **b :** a thick sticky liquid **2 :** tasteless or worthless stuff — **glop·py** \-pē\ *adj* -ER/-EST

²glop \"\ *vt* **glopped; glopped; glopping; glops 1 :** to put glop on — often used with *up* ⟨don't ~ up my hamburger with catsup⟩ **2 :** to put (something gloppy) on food ⟨~ blue cheese dressing over the delicate leaves —James Villas⟩

glory hole* *n* **:** a hole made through the partition of adjoining toilet stalls to enable homosexuals to perform fellatio anonymously

gloss* *n* **:** a cosmetic preparation for adding shine and usu. color to the lips

glow plug *n* **:** a heating element in a diesel-engine cylinder to preheat the air and facilitate starting; *also* **:** a similar element for ignition in other internal-combustion engines

glu·can \ˈglü,kan, -ˌkən\ *n* -s [*gluc-* + *-an*] **:** a polysaccharide (as glycogen or cellulose) that is a polymer of glucose

glu·ca·nase \ˈglükə,nās, -āz\ *n* -s [*glucan* (herein) + *-ase*] **:** any of various enzymes that digest glucans

glu·co·cer·e·bro·si·dase \ˌglükō,serəbrōˈsī,dās, -āz\ *n* -s [*glucocerebroside* (herein) + *-ase*] **:** an enzyme of mammalian tissue that catalyzes the hydrolysis of the glucose part of a glucocerebroside and is deficient in patients affected with Gaucher's disease

glu·co·cerebroside \ˌglükō+\ *n* [*gluc-* + *cerebroside*] **:** a lipid composed of a ceramide and glucose that accumulates in the tissues of patients affected with Gaucher's disease

glu·co·gen·ic \ˌglükōˈjenik\ *adj* [*gluc-* + *-genic*] **:** tending to produce a pyruvate residue in metabolism which undergoes conversion to a carbohydrate (as glucose) and is eventually stored as a complex carbohydrate (as glycogen) ⟨~ amino acids⟩

glucosyltransferase \ˌ===ˌ=ˈ==ˌ=\ *n* [*glucosyl* + *transferase*] **:** an enzyme that catalyzes the transfer of a glucosyl group; *esp* **:** one implicated in the formation of dental plaque that catalyzes the formation of glucans

glue–sniffing *n* -s [¹*glue* + *sniffing,* fr. gerund of *sniff,* v.] **:** the deliberate inhalation of volatile organic solvents from plastic glues that may result in symptoms ranging from mild euphoria to disorientation and coma

glu·on \ˈglü,än\ *n* -s [fr. ¹*glue* + *-on*] **:** any of eight hypothetical neutral massless particles thought to bind together quarks to form hadrons (as pions, protons, and neutrons)

glu·tar·aldehyde \ˌglüd·əˈraldə,hīd\ *n* [*glutaryl* + *aldehyde*] **:** a compound $C_5H_8O_2$ that contains two aldehyde groups and is used esp. in leather tanning and in the fixation of biological tissues

glu·teth·i·mide \glüˈtethə,mīd, -ˌməd\ *n* [*glutaryl* + *eth-* + *imide*] **:** a sedative-hypnotic drug $C_{13}H_{15}NO_2$ that induces sleep with less depression of respiration than occurs with comparable doses of barbiturates

gly·co·calyx \ˌglīkō+\ *n* [*glyc-* + *calyx*] **:** a polysaccharide and glycoprotein covering on a cell surface esp. of bacteria

gly·co·ge·no·sis \ˈglīkōjəˈnōsəs\ *n, pl* **glycogeno·ses** \-ō,sēz\ [*glycogen* + *-osis*] **:** any of several metabolic disorders that are characterized esp. by hypoglycemia and abnormal deposits of glycogen and are caused by enzyme deficiencies in glycogen metabolism

gly·cos·ami·no·glycan \ˌglīkōsəˌmē(ˌ)nō, -ōˌsamə(ˌ)nō+\ *n* [*glycose* + *amino-* + *glycan*] **:** MUCOPOLYSACCHARIDE

gly·co·sphingolipid \ˌglīkō+\ *n* [*glyc-* + *sphingolipid*] **:** any of various lipids (as a cerebroside or a ganglioside) which are derivatives of ceramides, do not contain the phosphorus or the extra nitrogenous base of the sphingomyelins, and do contain a carbohydrate (as glucose), and some of which accumulate in disorders of lipid metabolism (as Tay-Sachs disease)

gly·co·syl·a·tion \glī,kōsəˈlāshən\ *n* -s [*glycosyl* + *-ation*] **:** the process of adding glycosyl groups to a protein to form a glycoprotein — **gly·co·syl·ate** \glīˈkōsə,lāt\ *vt* -ED/-ING/-S

glyph* *n* [short for *hieroglyph*] **:** a symbol (as a curved arrow on a road sign) that conveys information nonverbally

gno·to·biology \ˌnōd·ə +\ *n* [Gk *gnōtos* known + E *biology*] **:** GNOTOBIOTICS *herein* — **gno·to·biologist** \"+\ *n*

gno·to·bi·ot·ic \ˌnōd·ə(ˌ)bīˌäd·ik *also* -bēˌä-\ *adj* [Gk *gnōtos* known (fr. *gignōskein* to know) + E *biotic* — more at KNOW, BIOTA] **:** of, relating to, living in, or being a controlled environment containing one or a few kinds of organisms; *also* **:** AXENIC ⟨~ mice⟩ — **gno·to·bi·ote** \ˌnōd·əˈbī,ōt\ *n* -s — **gno·to·bi·ot·i·cal·ly** \ˌnōd·ə(ˌ)bīˌäd·ək(ə)lē *also* -bēˌä-\ *adv*

gno·to·bi·ot·ics \ˈnōd·ə(ˌ)bīˌäd·iks\ *n pl but sing in constr* [*gnoto- biotic* (herein) + *-s*] **:** a biological science concerned with the raising and study of animals under gnotobiotic conditions

go* *vt* **1** *baseball* **:** PITCH ⟨he *went* 7⅓ innings and gave up no runs —D.S. Looney⟩ **2 :** SAY — used chiefly in oral narration of speech ⟨I'm the last person to admit I've achieved anything. . . . But now my friends say it to me, and I ~ "You're right" —Steve Martin⟩ — **go public 1** *of a close corporation* **:** to offer stock for sale to the general public **2 :** to disclose to a much wider audience something not generally known

go* *n* **:** permission to proceed **:** GO-AHEAD ⟨gave the astronauts a ~ for another orbit⟩

go *adj* [¹*go*] **:** functioning properly **:** being in good and ready condition ⟨declared all systems ~⟩

goalmouth \ˈ=ˌ=\ *n* [¹*goal* + ¹*mouth*] **:** the area directly in front of the goal (as in soccer or hockey)

goaltending \ˈ=ˌ==\ *n* -s [¹*goal* + *tending,* fr. gerund of ¹*tend*] **1 :** the act of guarding a goal (as in hockey) **2 :** a violation of the rules that involves touching or deflecting a basketball on its downward path toward the basket or on or within its rim

gö·del's theorem *also* **gödel's incompleteness theorem** \ˈgœdəlz-\ *n, usu cap G* [after Kurt *Gödel* †1978 Am. mathematician] **:** a theorem in advanced logic: in any logical system as complex as or more complex than the arithmetic of the integers there can always be found either a statement which can be shown to be both true and false or a statement whose truth or falsity cannot be deduced from other statements in the system

go down* *vi, slang* **:** to take place **:** HAPPEN ⟨I'll tell you everythin' that *went down* —V.E. Smith⟩ — **go down**

on : to perform fellatio or cunnilingus on — usu. considered vulgar

go·fer *also* **go·pher** \ˈgōfə(r)\ *n* -s [alter. of *go for;* fr. his being required to go for or go after things] **:** an employee whose duties include running errands

go–go \ˈgō(ˌ)gō\ *adj* [a-*go-go* (herein)] **1 :** FASHIONABLE, CHIC ⟨will change the name . . . to something more *go-go* —Al Fleming⟩ **2 a :** of, relating to, or being a discotheque or the music or dances performed there **b :** employed as a featured dancer to entertain patrons esp. in a discotheque or bar ⟨a pretty teenage *go-go* girl dances on top of the pedestal —C.D.B. Bryan⟩ **3 :** marked by spirited or aggressive action or style ⟨playing *go-go* baseball⟩ ⟨the *go-go* U.S. businessman must change his style here, where meetings begin with endless cups of tea — Ray Vicker⟩ **4 a :** relating to, dealing in, or offering popular often speculative investment expected to yield high returns ⟨*go-go* mutual funds⟩ **b :** marked by ready and often speculative investment or fast-paced growth and modernization ⟨losses, then, of three hundred billion dollars . . . such were the bitter fruits of the *go-go* years —John Brooks⟩

go–go boot *n* [*go-go* (herein)] **:** a woman's knee-high boot esp. of patent leather or shiny vinyl with a moderate-to-high heel

gold* *adj* **:** qualifying for a gold record ⟨five . . . recordings are certified ~ —Henry Edwards⟩ — **go gold :** to have enough sales to qualify for a gold record ⟨the album *went gold*⟩

gold·en–ag·er \ˌgōldəˈnājə(r)\ *n* -s [*Golden Age clubs,* organizations for recreational activities of the elderly + E *-er*] **:** an elderly person; *esp* **:** one who has retired

golden–brown alga *n* **:** any alga of the major group Chrysophyta — called also *chrysophyte, golden alga*

golden handshake *n, chiefly Brit* **:** a tidy sum of money given as severance pay esp. to an executive

golden oldie *n* **:** one (as a song, recording, or television show) that was a hit in the past

golden parachute *n* **:** a lump-sum bonus and often other valuable considerations granted to a high executive of a corporation to be paid esp. if the corporation is taken over

gold point* *n* **:** a fixed point on the international temperature scale equal to the melting point of gold or 1064.43°C

gold record *n* **:** a gold phonograph record awarded to a singer or group whose single record has sold at least one million copies or whose album has sold at least 500,000 copies

gold sodium thio·malate \-ˌthīō+\ *n* [*thi-* + *malate*] **:** a gold salt $C_4H_3AuNa_2O_4S{\cdot}H_2O$ used in the treatment of rheumatoid arthritis

golf ball* *n* **:** the spherical printing element of an electric typewriter or printer

golf cart *n* **1 :** a small cart for wheeling a golf bag around a golf course **2 :** a motorized cart for carrying a golfer and his equipment around a golf course

gondola* *n* **:** an enclosed car suspended from a cable and used for transporting passengers; *esp* **:** one used as a ski lift

g₁ phase \(ˈ)jēˈwən-\ *n, usu cap G* **:** the period in the cell cycle from the end of cell division to the beginning of DNA replication — compare G2 PHASE *herein,* M PHASE *herein,* S PHASE *herein*

gong* *n, Brit* **:** MEDAL

gonial angle *n* **:** ANGLE OF THE MANDIBLE

go·ni·ot·o·my \ˌgōnēˈäd·əmē, -ätə-\ *n* -ES [*goni-* + *-tomy*] **:** surgical relief of glaucoma used in some congenital types and achieved by opening Schlemm's canal

gon·o·coc·ce·mia \ˌgänəˌkäkˈsēmēə\ *n* -S [*gonococcus* + *-emia*] **:** the presence of gonococci in the blood — **gon·o·coc·ce·mic** \-mik\ *adj*

go–no–go \ˈgōˈnōˌgō\ *adj* [[1]*go* + [1]*no* + [1]*go*] **1 :** being or relating to a required decision to continue or stop a course of action **2 :** being or relating to a point at which a go-no-go decision must be made

gon·zo \ˈgän(ˌ)zō\ *adj* [prob. fr. It *gonzo* simpleton, perh. fr. It *Borgonzone* Burgundian] **1 :** of or relating to a style of journalism that is a mixture of fact and fiction and is held to be produced under the effect of drugs **2 :** FAR-OUT *herein* **3 :** ZONKED *herein*

good old boy *or* **good ol' boy** *or* **good ole boy** *n* **:** a usu. white Southerner who conforms to the social behavior of his peers

goody–two–shoes \ˌ==ˈ=ˌ=\ *adj or n, often cap G&T&S* [after *Goody Two-Shoes,* heroine of a children's story perh. by Oliver Goldsmith †1774 Brit. author] **:** GOODY-GOODY

goof–off \ˈ=ˌ=\ *n* -s [fr. the verb phrase *goof off*] **:** one who evades work or responsibility

goofy–foot \ˈgüfēˌfu̇t\ *or* **goofy–foot·er** \-u̇d·ə(r)\ *n, pl* **goofy–foots** *or* **goofy–footers :** a surfer who rides a surfboard with the right foot forward

goose* *vt* **:** to increase the activity, speed, power, or intensity of ⟨hired to ~ production in a factory⟩ ⟨the bellows that the pioneers used . . . to ~ recalcitrant fires — John Jobson⟩

gorp \ˈgȯ(ə)rp\ *n* -s [perh. fr. slang *gorp* to eat greedily] **:** a snack consisting usu. of high-energy food (as raisins and nuts)

gospel* *adj* **:** of, relating to, or being religious songs of American origin associated with evangelism and popular devotion and marked by simple melody and harmony and elements of folk songs, spirituals, and occas. jazz ⟨~ singer⟩ — **gospel*** *n*

GPA *abbr* grade point average *herein*

grab* *vt* **:** to seize the attention of **:** IMPRESS, STRIKE ⟨the technique of *grabbing* an audience —Pauline Kael⟩

grade point *n* **:** QUALITY POINT

grade point average *n* **:** the average obtained by dividing the total number of grade points by the total number of credits earned — called also *quality point average*

graft–versus–host *adj* **:** relating to or being the bodily condition that results when cells from a tissue or organ transplant mount an immunologic attack against the cells or tissues of the host

grammar* *n* **:** a system of rules that defines the grammatical structure of a language

gram·mat·i·cal·i·ty \grəˌmad·əˈkaləd·ē\ *n* -ES [*grammatical* + *-ity*] **:** the quality or state of being grammatical

Gram·my \ˈgramē\ *service mark* — used for the annual presentation of a statuette for notable achievement in the recording industry

grandfather *vt* **:** to permit to continue under a grandfather clause ⟨existing personnel would be *~ed* into the present system —*Wall Street Jour.*⟩ ⟨*grandfathered* water rights⟩

grand touring car *n* **:** a usu. 2-passenger coupe

granny dress *n* **:** a long loose-fitting dress usu. with high neck and long sleeves

granny glasses *n pl* **:** spectacles with usu. small oval, round, or square lenses and metal frames

gra·no·la \grə'nōlə\ *n* -s [fr. *Granola,* a trademark] **:** a mixture of rolled oats and other ingredients (as brown sugar, raisins, coconut, and nuts) that is eaten esp. as a breakfast food and health food

grants·man·ship \'gran(t)smən,ship\ *n* [*grants* + *-manship* (herein)] **:** the art of obtaining grants of money (as for research projects) — **grants·man** \-mən\ *n, pl* **grantsmen** \-mən\

granule cell* *n* **:** one of the small neurons of the cortex of the cerebellum and the cerebrum

gra·num \'grānəm\ *n, pl* **gra·na** \-nə\ [NL, fr. L, grain — more at CORN] **:** one of the lamellar stacks of chlorophyll-containing material in plant chloroplasts

graphic* *n* **1 :** a graphic representation displayed by a computer (as on a cathode-ray tube) **2 graphics** *pl but sing or pl in constr* **:** the process whereby a computer displays graphics and an operator can manipulate them (as with a light pen)

graphics tablet *n* **:** a device (as a flat electronic board with an associated stylus) by which graphic data is entered into a computer in a manner similar to drawing

GRAS *abbr* generally recognized as safe

grasp* *vb* — **grasp the nettle :** to take positive and decisive steps to deal with a problem **:** take the bull by the horns

grass* *n* **:** MARIJUANA

grass carp *n* **:** an herbivorous cyprinid fish (*Ctenopharyngodon idella*) of Russia and mainland China that has been introduced elsewhere to control aquatic weeds — called also *white amur*

grasshopper* *n* **:** a cocktail made with crème de menthe, crème de cacao, and usu. light cream

gravitational collapse *n* **:** the tendency of matter to move toward a common center of gravity (as in the formation of galaxies); *esp* **:** the rapid collapse of a star at the end of its life cycle

gravitational interaction *n* **:** a weak fundamental interaction that is hypothesized to occur between elementary particles but that has been observed only on a scale larger than that hypothesized — compare ELECTROMAGNETIC INTERACTION *herein,* STRONG INTERACTION *herein,* WEAK INTERACTION *herein*

gravitational wave *n* **:** a hypothetical wave held to travel at the speed of light and to propagate the gravitational field

grav·i·ton \'gravə̇,tän\ *n* -s [ISV *gravity* + [2]*-on*] **:** a hypothetical particle with zero charge and rest mass that is held to be the quantum of the gravitational field

gravity wave* *n* **:** GRAVITATIONAL WAVE *herein*

grav·lax \'gräv,läks\ *or* **gravlaks** \"\ *n* [Norw *gravlaks,* fr. *grav* buried + *laks* salmon; so called fr. being packed in salt — more at [1]LAX] **:** salmon usu. cured with salt, pepper, dill, and aquavit

gray \'grā\ *n* -s [after Louis Harold *Gray b*1905 Brit. radiobiologist] **:** the mks unit of absorbed dose of ionizing radiation equal to an energy of one joule per kilogram of irradiated material — abbr. *Gy*

gray panther *n, usu cap G&P* [*gray* + *panther* (as in *Black Panther* — herein)] **:** a member of an organization of militant elderly people

greaser* *n* **:** an aggressive swaggering young white male usu. of working-class background

green beret *n, usu cap G&B* [so called fr. the green beret worn as part of the uniform] **:** a member of the U.S. Army Special Forces

green card *n* **:** an identity card attesting the permanent resident status of an alien in the U.S.

green-card·er \ˌ=ˈkärdər, -ˈkȧdə(r\ *n* -s [*green card* + *-er*] **:** a foreign national with permission to work in the U.S.

green-fingered \ˌ=ˈ==\ *adj* [[1]*green* + *fingered*] *chiefly Brit* **:** adept at growing plants

green goddess dressing *n* [fr. *The Green Goddess* (1921) play by William Archer †1924 Scot. dramatist and critic] **:** a green salad dressing consisting of mayonnaise, sour cream, anchovies, chives, parsley, tarragon vinegar, and seasonings

greenhouse effect *n* **:** warming of the lower layers of the atmosphere that tends to increase with increasing atmospheric carbon dioxide and that is caused by conversion of solar radiation into heat in a process involving selective transmission of short wave solar radiation by the atmosphere, its absorption by the earth's surface, and reradiation as infrared which is absorbed and partly reradiated back to the surface by carbon dioxide and water vapor in the air; *also* **:** a comparable warming of the lower layers of the atmosphere of a planet (as Venus) other than the Earth

greening* *n* **:** a restoration of freshness or vigor **:** REVITALIZATION, REJUVENATION

green lacewing *n* **:** a lacewing of the family Chrysopidae **:** GOLDENEYE 2

greenmail \'=,=\ *n* [*green* (money) + *-mail* (as in *blackmail*)] **:** payment by a corporation of a price above market value for shares of stock held by a stockholder threatening a hostile takeover; *also* **:** the demanding of such a payment

green paper *n, often cap G&P, Brit* **:** a government document that discusses proposed approaches to a problem

green revolution *n* **:** the great increase in production of food grains (as rice, wheat, and maize) due to the introduction of high-yielding varieties, to the use of pesticides, and to better management techniques

grem·mie *also* **grem·my** \'gremē, -mi\ *n, pl* **gremmies** [*grem*lin + *-ie*] **:** a young or inexperienced surfer; *esp* **:** one whose behavior is objectionable — called also *gremlin*

grid* *n* **1 :** a network of conductors for the distribution of electric power; *also* **:** a network of radio or television stations **2 :** the starting positions of cars on a racecourse **3 :** a device (as of glass) in a photocomposer on which are located the characters to be exposed as the text is composed **4 :** something resembling a grid esp. in rigidly organized structure

gridlock \'=,=\ *n* -s [*grid* + dead*lock*] **1 :** a traffic jam in which a grid of intersecting streets is so completely congested that no vehicular movement is possible **2 :** a situation resembling gridlock (as in congestion or lack of movement)

gri·ot \'grē(,)ō\ *n* -s [F] **:** any of a class of musician-entertainers of West Africa whose performances include tribal histories and genealogies

grok \'gräk\ *vt* **grokked; grokked; grokking; groks** [coined 1961 in science fiction novel *Stranger in a Strange Land* by Robert A. Heinlein *b*1907 Am. author] **:** to understand profoundly and intuitively **:** establish deep compassionate rapport with ⟨finally they come to ~ each other in their fullness —Bob Singer⟩

groove* *vb* [fr. the phrase *in the groove*] *vt* **1 :** to enjoy appreciatively ⟨~*s* exciting experiences⟩ **2 :** to excite pleasurably ⟨*grooving* their minds with cannabis —Stephen Nemo⟩ ~ *vi* **1 :** to enjoy oneself intensely **:** experience keen pleasure ⟨self-perception that informs you how and when to ~ in your own way —Al Calloway⟩ **2 :** to interact harmoniously ⟨contemporary minds and rock ~ together —Benjamin De Mott⟩

groove* *n* **:** an enjoyable, pleasurable, or exciting experience

gross out *vt* [[1]*gross*] **:** to offend or insult by something gross — **gross–out** \ˈ=ˌ=\ *n*

grot·ty \ˈgrätē, -äd·ē, -i\ *adj* -ER/-EST [alter. (influenced by *rotten*) of *grotesque*] *chiefly Brit* **:** wretchedly shabby **:** of poor quality ⟨but, to some, simply seeing their work in print, however ~, is better than it not appearing at all —John Cotton⟩

ground* *vt* **:** to throw (a football) intentionally to the ground to avoid being tackled for a loss

ground effect* *n* **:** a down force exerted on a racing car by special design features (as winglike airfoils) that enables it to achieve higher speeds through turns before starting to skid — often used in pl.

ground–effect machine \ˈ=ˌ=-\ *n* [so called fr. the support provided by the cushion of air as if the vehicle rode on the ground] **:** an air-cushion vehicle for traveling over land or water

groundout \ˈ=ˌ=\ *n* -s [*grounder* + [3]*out*] **:** a play in baseball in which a batter is put out after hitting a grounder to an infielder

group* *n* **:** a mathematical set that is closed under a binary associative operation and that has an identity element and an inverse for every element

grouper* *n* **:** one of a group of unrelated people who share a rented house (as at the seashore)

group grope *n, slang* **:** a sex orgy

group·ie \ˈgrüpē\ *n* -s [[1]*group* + *-ie*] **1 :** a fan of a rock group; *esp* **:** one who follows the group on tour **2 :** a fan of a celebrity who attends as many of his or her appearances as possible **3 :** an enthusiastic follower or supporter ⟨a political ~⟩ ⟨a fashion ~⟩

group theory *n* **:** a branch of mathematics concerned with finding all mathematical groups and determining their properties — **group theorist** *n*

groupthink \ˈ=ˌ=\ *n* [[1]*group* + *think* (as in *doublethink*)] **:** conformity to group values and ethics

growth* *n* **:** anticipated progressive growth in capital value and income ⟨some investors prefer ~ to immediate income⟩

growth company *n* **:** a company that grows at a greater rate than the economy as a whole

grun·gy \ˈgrənjē\ *adj* -ER/-EST [origin unknown] **:** being in a dirty or uncared-for condition ⟨~ old boots⟩ ⟨~ bars⟩

grunt* *n* **1 :** a U.S. army or marine foot soldier esp. in the Vietnam war **2 :** one who does routine unglamorous work

GSR *abbr* galvanic skin response *herein*

GT \ˌjēˈtē\ *n* -s [grand *t*ouring (car)] **:** GRAND TOURING CAR *herein*

GTP \ˌjē(ˌ)tēˈpē\ *n* -s [guanosine *t*ri*p*hosphate] **:** an energy-rich nucleoside triphosphate analogous to ATP that is composed of guanine linked to ribose and three phosphate groups and is necessary for the formation of peptide bonds during protein synthesis — called also *guanosine triphosphate*

g2 phase \(ˈ)jēˈtü-\ *n, usu cap G* **:** the period in the cell cycle from the completion of DNA replication to the beginning of cell division — compare G1 PHASE *herein,* M PHASE *herein,* S PHASE *herein*

gua·neth·i·dine \gwäˈnethəˌdēn, -ədən\ *n* -s [*guanidine* + *eth-*] **:** a synthetic guanidine derivative $C_{10}H_{22}N_4$ used esp. as the sulfate in treating severe high blood pressure

guanosine mono·phosphate \-ˌmä(ˌ)nō, -ˌmō(ˌ)nō, -nə+\ *n* [*mon-* + *phosphate*] **:** CYCLIC GMP *herein*

guanosine triphosphate *n* **:** GTP *herein*

guanylate cyclase \ˈgwänᵊlˌāt-\ *n* [*guanyl* + *-ate*] **:** an enzyme that catalyzes the formation of cyclic GMP from GTP

guerrilla theater *n* **:** STREET THEATER

guest worker *n* [trans. of G *gastarbeiter*] **:** a foreign laborer working on a temporary basis in an industrialized European country

gu·lag \ˈgüˌläg\ *n* -s *often cap* [Russ *G*lavnoe *U*pravlenie Ispravitel'no-trudovykh *Lag*erei chief administration of corrective labor camps] **1 :** the penal system of the U.S.S.R. consisting of a network of labor camps; *also* **:** such a penal-system in other countries **2 :** LABOR CAMP 1

gull wing door *n* **:** an automobile door that is hinged at the top and resembles an airplane gull wing when open

gun* *n* **:** a long heavy surfboard — called also *big gun* — **under the gun* :** under pressure ⟨I was always *under the gun* to perform —Don Sutton⟩

gunboat diplomacy *n* **:** diplomacy backed by the use or threat of military force ⟨the restraints of nuclear deterrence, and of world public opinion, seem to have ended the effectiveness of *gunboat diplomacy* —H.S. Ashmore⟩

gun lap *n* **:** the final lap of a race in track signaled by the firing of a gun as the leader begins the lap

gunn effect \ˈgən-\ *n, usu cap G* [after J. B. *Gunn* b1928 Brit. physicist] **:** the production of rapid fluctuations of current when the voltage applied to a semiconductor device exceeds a critical value with the result that microwave power is generated

gun patch *n* **:** a patch so placed on a shirt or jacket as to prevent a rifle butt from slipping

gunship \ˈ=ˌ=\ *n* **:** a helicopter or cargo aircraft armed with rockets and machine guns

gus·sy up \ˈgəsēˈəp\ *vt* [origin unknown] **:** to dress up **:** PRETTIFY ⟨women were thought to be more provocative of sinful deliberation if *gussied up* in snaps, bows and frills —Russell Baker⟩

gut *adj* [[1]*gut*] **1 :** arising from one's inmost self **:** VISCERAL ⟨a ~ reaction to the misery he has seen —J.A. Lukas⟩ **2 :** having strong impact or immediate relevance ⟨ordinary voters are likely to be moved by ~ issues. The most important of these is the economy —Anthony Lewis⟩

gut course *n* [[1]*gut;* prob. fr. its being likened in softness to the belly] **:** a course (as in college) that is easily passed

gut·si·ness \ˈgətsēnəs, -sin-\ *n* -ES [*gutsy* + *-ness*] **:** the quality or state of being gutsy

guy* **:** PERSON — used in pl. to refer to the members of a group regardless of sex ⟨saw her and the rest of the ~*s*⟩

gyp·lure \ˈjipˌlu̇(ə)r, -u̇ə\ *n* [*gyp*sy (moth) + *lure*] **:** a synthetic sex attractant used in trapping male gypsy moths

gyp·py tummy \ˈjipē-\ *n* [*gyppy* alter. of *Egyptian;* fr. association of the illness with eating in a foreign country] **:** DIARRHEA

gypsum board *n* **:** PLASTERBOARD

gypsy cab *n* **:** a taxicab licensed only to answer calls; *esp* **:** such a cab that cruises in search of passengers

gy·ro \ˈyē,rō, ˈzhirō\ *n* -s [NGk *gyros* turn; fr. the rotation of the meat on a spit] **:** a sandwich esp. of lamb and beef, tomato, and onion on pita bread

gy·ro·cop·ter \ˈjīrə,käptə(r)\ *n* -s [auto*gyro* + heli*copter*] **:** a usu. one-passenger rotary-wing aircraft that is driven forward by a conventional propeller

H

habituate* *vi* **:** to undergo habituation ⟨~ to a stimulus⟩

habituation* *n* **:** decrease in responsiveness upon repeated exposure to a stimulus

hack·er \ˈhakər\ *n* [*hack* skillful repair of a computer program + *-er*] **:** an expert at programming and solving problems with a computer **:** computer whiz; *also* **:** one who illegally gains access to and sometimes tampers with information in a computer system esp. using a home computer

hacking pocket *n* [so called fr. its use on hacking coats] **:** a slanted coat pocket usu. with a flap

ha·dal \ˈhādᵊl\ *adj* [F, fr. *Hadès* Hades + *-al*] **:** of, relating to, or being the parts of the ocean below 6000 meters

had·ron \ˈhaˌdrän\ *n* -s [ISV *hadr-* + ²*-on*] **:** any of the subatomic particles that are made up of quarks and take part in the strong interaction — **ha·dron·ic** \haˈdränik\ *adj*

haf·nia \ˈhafnēə\ *n* -s [NL, fr. *hafnium* + *-a*] **:** a white refractory crystalline oxide HfO_2 of hafnium

hailer* *n* [short for *loud-hailer*] **:** BULLHORN

hair spray *n* **:** a preparation that is sprayed on the hair to keep it in place

hairweaving \ˈ⸗ˌ⸗⸗\ *n* **:** the process of covering a bald spot with human hair and nylon thread woven into the wearer's own hair — **hairweave** \ˈ⸗ˌ⸗\ *n* — **hair weaver** *n*

ha·la·la *also* **ha·la·lah** \həˈlälə\ *n, pl* **halala** *or* **halalas** [Ar] **1 :** a monetary unit of Saudi Arabia equal to ¹⁄₁₀₀ riyal — see MONEY table *in the Dict* **2 :** a coin representing one halala

half–space \ˈ⸗ˌ⸗\ *n* **:** the part of three-dimensional euclidean space lying on one side of a plane

halfway house* *n* **:** a center for formerly institutionalized individuals (as mental patients or drug addicts) that is designed to facilitate their readjustment to private life

hallucinate* *vt* **:** to perceive or experience as an hallucination

hal·lu·ci·na·tor \həˈlüsᵊnˌād·ər\ *n* -s [LL, fr. *hallucinatus* + *-or*] **:** a person who has hallucinations

halo·carbon \ˈhalə +\ *n* [*hal-* + ¹*carbon*] **:** any of various compounds (as a fluorocarbon) of carbon and one or more halogens and sometimes also hydrogen

halo·cline \ˈhaləˌklīn\ *n* -s [*hal-* + *-cline*] **:** a usu. vertical gradient in salinity

halo·per·i·dol \ˌhalōˈperəˌdòl, -ˌdōl\ *n* -s [*hal-* + *piperidine* + *-ol*] **:** a depressant $C_{21}H_{23}ClFNO_2$ of the central nervous system used esp. as an antipsychotic drug

halo·thane \ˈhaləˌthān\ *n* -s [*halogen* + *ethane*] **:** a nonexplosive inhalational anesthetic $C_2HBrClF_3$

hamate *n* -s [*hamate*, adj.] **:** HAMATUM

hamstring* *or* **hamstring muscle** *n* **:** any of three muscles at the back of the thigh that function to flex and rotate the leg and extend the thigh: **a :** SEMIMEMBRANOSUS **b :** SEMITENDINOSUS **c :** BICEPS b

hand·i·capped \ˈhandēˌkapt, -dəˌ-\ *adj* **:** having a physical or mental disability that substantially limits activity esp. in relation to employment or education

handjob \ˈhanˌjäb\ *n* [¹*hand* + ¹*job*] *slang* **:** an act of stimulating the genitals manually usu. to orgasm

handprint \ˈ⸗ˌ⸗\ *n* **:** an impression of a hand on a surface

hands–on \ˈ⸗¦⸗\ *adj* [*hands-* (as in *hands-off*) + *on*] **:** relating to, being, or providing direct practical experience in the operation or functioning of something ⟨*hands-on* training with a new computer system⟩

hand–wringing \ˈ⸗ˌ⸗⸗\ *n* -s **:** an overwrought expression of concern or guilt

hang* *vt* **:** to throw (a breaking pitch) so that it fails to break properly ~ *vi, of a thrown ball* **:** to fail to break or drop as intended — **hang five :** to ride a surfboard with the weight of the body forward and the toes of one foot turned over the front edge of the board — **hang in there :** to persist in the face of adversity **:** PERSEVERE — **hang loose :** to remain calm and unruffled ⟨decided to *hang loose* and risk it —Cyra McFadden⟩ — **hang ten :** to ride a surfboard with the weight of the body forward and the toes of both feet turned over the front edge of the board — **hang tough :** to persist in the face of adversity

hang glider *n* **:** a kitelike glider from which a harnessed rider hangs while gliding down from a cliff or hill — **hang gliding** *n*

hang–loose \¦⸗¦⸗\ *adj* [fr. *hang loose* (herein)] **:** being highly informal, relaxed, unstructured, or uninhibited

hangtown fry \ˈ⸗ˌ⸗-\ *n, usu cap H & often cap F* [fr. *Hangtown*, nickname for Placerville, California] **:** a scrambled egg dish or omelet containing fried oysters

hang–up* *n* **:** a source of mental or emotional difficulty; *broadly* **:** PROBLEM

ha·ni·wa \ˈhänəˌwä\ *n, pl* **haniwa** [Jap] **:** a large baked clay figure usu. in the form of a hollow cylinder or a crude human figure customarily placed on early Japanese grave mounds

hanky–pank \¦haŋkē¦paŋk\ *n* -s [*hanky-pank*, adj.] **:** any of various carnival games in which contestants may win small prizes for the exercise of simple skills (as dart throwing)

hao \ˈhau̇\ *n, pl* **hao** [native name in Vietnam] **1 :** a monetary unit of Vietnam equal to ¹⁄₁₀ (formerly ¹⁄₁₀₀) dong **2 :** a coin representing one hao

happening* *n* **1 :** an event or series of events designed to evoke a spontaneous audience reaction to sensory, emotional, or spiritual stimuli **2 :** an event that is particularly interesting, entertaining, or important ⟨the hearing is a ~, one of those unique events . . . which will be talked about for years —Douglas Kiker⟩

happy hour *n* **:** a period of time during which the prices of drinks at a bar or lounge are reduced or hors d'oeuvres are served gratis

hap·to·glo·bin \ˈhaptəˌglōbən\ *n* -s [Gk *haptein* to fasten, bind + E *-o-* + hemo*globin* — more at APSIS] **:** any of several carbohydrate-containing serum alpha globulins that can combine with free hemoglobin in the plasma and thereby prevent the loss of iron into the urine

hard* *adj* **1 :** being at once addictive and gravely detrimental to health ⟨such ~ drugs as heroin⟩ **2 :** resistant to biodegradation ⟨~ detergents⟩ ⟨~ pesticides like DDT⟩ **3 :** being, schooled in, or using the methods of one or more branches of mathematics, the life sciences, or the physical sciences ⟨a ~ scientist⟩

hardball* *n* **:** forceful uncompromising methods employed to gain an end ⟨played political ~ to win the nomination⟩

hard copy *n* **:** a copy of textual or graphic information on paper in normal size (as from microfilm or computer storage)

hard–core \ˌ=ˈ=\ *adj* [*hard core*] **1 :** of, relating to, or being persons whose economic position and educational background are substandard and who experience chronic unemployment ⟨the *hard-core* unemployed⟩ **2** *of pornography* **:** containing explicit descriptions of sex acts or scenes of actual sex acts — compare SOFT-CORE *herein*

hard–edge \ˈ=ˌ=\ *adj* **:** of or relating to abstract painting characterized by geometric forms with clearly defined boundaries

hard–edged \ˈ=ˌ=\ *adj* **:** possessing a tough, driving, or sharp quality ⟨*hard-edged* reporting of controversial subjects —Av Westin⟩ ⟨the *hard-edged* cold that clears the air —Leona P. Schecter⟩

hardened* *adj* **:** protected from possible danger from blast or heat by means of concrete or earth or by being situated underground ⟨a ~ missile launching site⟩ ⟨a ~ missile⟩

hard–eyed \ˈ=ˌ=\ *adj* **:** extremely critical and often skeptical ⟨a ~ realist⟩ ⟨~ scrutiny⟩

hardhat** *n* **1 :** a construction worker **2 :** a conservative who is strongly opposed to nonconformists

hard–line \ˈ=ˌ=\ *adj* **:** being, advocating, or pursuing a persistently firm policy or course of action **:** UNYIELDING ⟨a *hard-line* policy toward polluters⟩

hard–lin·er \ˈ=ˈlīnər\ *n* [*hard-line* (herein) + *-er*] **:** one who advocates or pursues a hard-line policy

hard–pressed \ˈ=ˌ=\ *adj* **:** hard put; *esp* **:** being under financial strain

hard rock *n* **:** rock music marked by a heavy jarring beat, high amplification, and usu. frenzied performances — **hard rocker** *n*

hard ticket *n* **:** a reserved seat ticket

hardware* *n* **:** the physical components (as electronic and electrical devices) of a vehicle (as a spacecraft) or an apparatus (as a computer); *broadly* **:** the equipment employed in an activity or undertaking ⟨educational ~⟩

hardwired \ˌ=ˈ=\ *adj* [[1]*hard* + *wired*] **:** implemented in the form of permanent electronic circuits ⟨an instruction repertoire . . . implemented in 400 ~ specifics — *Datamation*⟩

har·dy–wein·berg \ˌhärdēˈwīnˌbərg\ *adj, usu cap H&W* **:** of, relating to, or governed by the Hardy-Weinberg law ⟨*Hardy-Weinberg* equilibrium⟩

hardy–weinberg law *n, usu cap H&W* [after G.H. *Hardy* †1947 Eng. mathematician and W. *Weinberg,* 20th cent. Ger. scientist] **:** a fundamental principle of population genetics: population gene frequencies and population genotype frequencies remain constant from generation to generation if mating is random and if mutation, selection, immigration, and emigration do not occur — called also *Hardy-Weinberg principle*

ha·re krish·na \ˌhärēˈkrishnə\ *n, pl* **hare krishnas** *usu cap H & K* [fr. Hindi *hare* invocation of God + *Krishna* eighth avatar of Vishnu, one of the principal Hindu gods] **:** a member of a religious group dedicated to the worship of the Hindu god Krishna

har·pac·ti·coid \härˈpaktəˌkȯid\ *n* -s [NL *Harpacticoida,* group name, deriv. of Gk *harpaktikos* rapacious] **:** any of an order or suborder (Harpacticoida) of marine or freshwater usu. bottom-dwelling copepods — **harpacticoid** *adj*

har·vey wallbanger \ˌhärvēˈ=ˌ==\ *n, pl* **harvey wallbangers** *usu cap H&W* [origin unknown] **:** a screwdriver with an Italian liqueur floated on top

hash \ˈhash, -aa(ə)sh, -aish\ *n* [by shortening] **:** HASHISH

ha·shi·mo·to's disease \ˌhäshēˈmōd·(ˌ)ōz-, -shiˌ-\ *also* **hashimoto's thyroiditis** *or* **hashimoto's struma** *n, usu cap H* [Hakaru *Hashimoto* †1934 Jap. surgeon] **:** chronic thyroiditis characterized by goiter, thyroid fibrosis, infiltration of thyroid tissue by lymphoid tissue, and the production of autoantibodies that attack the thyroid

hassle* *vb* **~** *vt* **:** to annoy persistently or acutely **:** HARASS

hatchback \ˈ=ˌ=\ *n* **1 :** a back on a closed passenger automobile (as a coupe) having an upward-opening hatch **2 :** an automobile having a hatchback

haul* *vb* — **haul ass** *slang* **:** to move quickly

haute cuisine \ˌ(h)ōt-\ *n* [F, lit., high cuisine] **:** a refined or elaborate style of cooking; *also* **:** food prepared in this style

havana brown *n, usu cap H & B* [[2]*havana* (cigar)] **:** any of a breed of short-haired domestic cats developed in England and having a mahogany-brown coat and chartreuse eyes

ha·var·ti \həˈvärtē\ *n, usu cap* [fr. *Havarti,* place name in Denmark] **:** a semisoft Danish cheese with a mild to sharp flavor

hawaiian shirt *n, usu cap H* **:** a usu. short-sleeved sport shirt with a colorful pattern

hawk* *n* **:** one who takes a militant attitude (as in a dispute) and advocates immediate vigorous action — compare DOVE *herein* — **hawk·ish** *adj* — **hawk·ish·ly** *adv* — **hawk·ish·ness** *n* -ES

haw·thorne effect \ˈhȯˌthȯrn-, -ˌthȯ(ə)n-\ *n, usu cap H* [fr. the *Hawthorne* Works of the Western Electric Co., Cicero, Ill., where its existence was established by experiment] **:** the stimulation to increase output or accomplishment (as in an industrial or educational methods study) that results from the mere fact of being under concerned observation; *also* **:** such an increase in output or accomplishment

hay·lage \ˈhālij\ *n* -s [[2]*hay* + si*lage*] **:** stored forage that is essentially grass silage wilted to 35 to 50 percent moisture

HC* *abbr* hard copy *herein*

head* *n* **1** [short for *pothead* (herein) or *acidhead* (herein)] **:** one who uses a drug (as LSD or marijuana) **2 :** FELLATIO, CUNNILINGUS — usu. used with *give;* often considered vulgar

headcounter \ˈ=ˌ==\ *n* [[1]*head* + *counter*] **:** POLLSTER

head dip *n* **:** a surfing feat in which a surfer squats on the board, leans forward, and dips his head into the wave

header* *n* **1 :** a mounting plate through which electrical terminals pass from a sealed device (as a transistor) **2 :** a fall or dive head foremost **3 :** a shot or pass in soccer made by heading the ball **4 :** HEAD 17a(1)

headhunter* *n* **:** a recruiter of personnel and esp. executives

headliner* *n* **:** HEADLINING

headrest* *n* **:** a resilient pad at the top of the back of an automobile seat esp. for preventing whiplash injury

head restraint *n* **:** HEADREST *herein*

head shop *n* [*head* (herein)] **:** a shop that specializes in articles of interest to drug users

head–to–head \ˌ≈≈ˌ≈\ *adv or adj* **:** in a direct confrontation or encounter usu. between individuals

head trip *n* [[1]*head* + *trip* (herein)] **:** an exploration of one's own emotions and ideas

health food *n* **:** a food promoted as highly conducive to health

health maintenance organization *n* **:** HMO *herein*

health spa *n* **:** a commercial establishment with facilities for assisting its patrons to lose weight — called also *fat farm*

hearing dog *n* **:** a dog trained to alert its deaf or hearing-impaired owner to sounds (as of a telephone, doorbell, or alarm clock)

heat* *n, slang* **:** POLICE

heat island *n* **:** an urban area in which significantly more heat is absorbed and retained than in surrounding areas

heat pipe *n* **:** a closed container in which a continuing cycle of evaporation and condensation of a fluid takes place with the heat being given off at the condenser end and which is more effective in transferring heat than a metallic conductor

heat shield *n* **:** a barrier of ablative material to protect a space capsule from heat on its reentry into the atmosphere

heat sink *n* **:** a substance or device for the absorption or dissipation of unwanted heat (as from a process or an electronic device)

heavy* *adj* **1 :** LONG 11 — usu. used with *on* ⟨~ on creative ideas and light on financial plans —Susan Davis⟩ **2 :** being or playing hard rock **3 :** IMPORTANT, PROMINENT ⟨a ~ star unable to escape his groupies —Garry Wills⟩

heavy* *n* **1 :** someone or something influential, serious, or important **2 :** MUSCLEMAN, THUG

heavy chain *n* **:** either of the two larger of the four polypeptide chains that comprise antibodies — compare LIGHT CHAIN *herein*

heavy metal *n* **:** energetic and highly amplified electronic rock music having a hard beat and usu. an element of the fantastic

heavy weather *n* **:** considerable difficulty **:** HEAVY GOING — often used with *make*

hedge fund *n* [[1]*hedge*] **:** an investing group usu. in the form of a limited partnership that employs speculative techniques (as short selling and leverage) in the hope of obtaining large capital gains

hei·an \ˈheēˈän, ˈhāən\ *adj, usu cap* [Jap, lit., tranquillity] **:** of or relating to a period of Japanese history from the late 8th to the late 12th century

heim·lich maneuver \ˈhīmlik-\ *n, usu cap H* [after Henry J. *Heimlich* *b*1920 Am. surgeon] **:** the manual application of sudden upward pressure on the upper abdomen of a choking victim to force a foreign object from the windpipe

hei·shi *or* **hei·she** \ˈhēshē\ *n* -s [Navajo, lit., shell] **:** a bead made usu. by No. American Indians of disk-shaped shells, turquoise, or coral or of silver tubes

hela cell \ˈhēlə-\ *n, usu cap H & 1st L* [fr. Helen Lane, pseudonym of a cancer victim who donated such cells in 1951] **:** a cell of a continuously cultured strain isolated from a human uterine cervical carcinoma and used in biomedical research esp. to culture viruses

he·lic·i·ty \heˈlisəd·ē, hə-\ *n* -ES [*helic-* + *-ity*] **1 :** the motion of a particle about an axis parallel to its direction of motion **2 :** the component of the spin of a particle in its direction of motion measured in quantum units of spin **3 a :** the quality or state of being helical **b :** the amount or degree of helical curve

heli·pad \ˈ≈≈ˌ≈\ *n* [[2]*heli-* + [1]*pad*] **:** a landing and takeoff surface for helicopters

heli·stop \ˈ≈≈ˌ≈\ *n* [[2]*heli-* + [2]*stop*] **:** HELIPORT

helium–4 \ˌ≈≈≈ˈ≈\ *n* [*helium* + *4*, mass number of the isotope] **:** HELIUM

helium–3 \ˌ≈≈≈ˈ≈\ *n* [*helium* + *3*, mass number of the isotope] **:** the isotope of helium having the mass number three

helper t cell *or* **helper cell** *n, usu cap T* **:** a T cell that assists another T cell or a B cell in responding to a specific antigen or that activates some other kind of cell (as a macrophage) — compare KILLER CELL *herein*, SUPPRESSOR T CELL *herein*

hem·adsorption \ˌhēm +\ *n* [*hem-* + *adsorption*] **:** adherence of red blood cells to the surface of something (as a virus or cell) — **hem·adsorbing** \"+\ *adj*

hemi·cho·lin·ium \ˌhemēkōˈlinēəm, -mək-\ *n* -s [[1]*hemi-* + *choline* + *-ium*] **:** any of several blockers of the parasympathetic nervous system that interfere with the synthesis of acetylcholine

hemi·diaphragm \"+\ *n* [[1]*hemi-* + *diaphragm*] **:** one of the two lateral halves of the diaphragm separating the chest and abdominal cavities in mammals

hem·ing·way·esque \ˌhemiŋˌwāˌesk\ *adj, usu cap* [Ernest Miller *Hemingway* †1961 Am. writer + E [1]*-esque*] **:** of, relating to, or suggestive of Ernest Hemingway or his writings

hemi·pelagic \ˌhemē +\ *adj* [[1]*hemi-* + *pelagic*] **:** of, relating to, or comprising deposits or sediments containing the remains of pelagic organisms and material washed down from land

he·mo·dialysis \ˌhēmō, ˌhemō +\ *n* [*hem-* + *dialysis*] **:** the process of removing blood from an artery (as of a kidney patient) purifying it by dialysis, adding vital substances, and returning it to a vein

he·mo·phil·ic \ˌhēməˈfilik\ *n* [*hemophilic*, adj.] **:** HEMOPHILIAC

hemorrhagic fever *n* **:** any of a diverse group of arthropod-borne virus diseases characterized by a sudden onset, fever, aching, bleeding in the internal organs (as of the gastrointestinal tract), petechiae, and shock

hepatitis A *n* **:** INFECTIOUS HEPATITIS 1

hepatitis B *n* **:** SERUM HEPATITIS

hepatitis B surface antigen *n* **:** an antigen that resembles a virus and is found in the sera esp. of patients with serum hepatitis — called also *Australia antigen*

he·pa·to·biliary \həˌpad·ə, ˌhepəd·ō+\ *adj* [*hepat-* + *biliary*] **:** of, relating to, situated in or near, produced in, or affecting the liver and bile, bile ducts, and gallbladder ⟨~ disease⟩

he·pa·to·cyte \həˈpad·əˌsīt, ˈhepəd·ə-\ *n* -s [*hepat-* + *-cyte*] **:** any of the epithelial parenchymatous cells of the liver that secrete bile

hep·a·top·a·thy \ˌhepəˈtäpəthē\ *n* -ES [*hepat-* + *-pathy*] **:** an abnormal or diseased state of the liver

hep·a·to·tox·ic·i·ty \ˌhepəd·ōˌtäkˈsisəd·ē\ *n* -ES [*hepatotoxic* + *-ity*] **1 :** a state of toxic damage to the liver **2 :** capacity to cause hepatotoxicity

hep·a·to·toxin \ˌhepəd·ō +\ *n* [*hepat-* + *toxin*] **:** a substance toxic to the liver

heritability* *n* **:** the proportion of observed variation in a particular trait (as intelligence) that can be attributed to inherited genetic factors in contrast to environmental ones

he·riz \he'rēz *also* -ēs\ *n* -ES *usu cap* [alter. of *Herīs,* town in Iran] **:** a large Persian rug usu. with a central medallion and angular floral designs in deep colors

her·ma·typ·ic \ˌhərmə'tipik\ *adj* [Gk *herma* prop, reef + E *typ-* (fr. Gk *typtein* to strike, coin) + *-ic* — more at TYPE] **:** building reefs ⟨~ corals⟩

her·mi·tian matrix \hər¦mishən-, er'mēshən-\ *n, usu cap H* [Charles *Hermite* †1901 Fr. mathematician + E *-ian*] **:** a square matrix having the property that each pair of elements comprised of one in the *i*th row and *j*th column and the other in the *j*th row and *i*th column are conjugate complex numbers

herpes gen·i·tal·is \-ˌjenə'taləs\ *n* [NL, lit., genital herpes] **:** herpes simplex of the type typically affecting the genitals — called also *genital herpes*

herpesvirus \¦=(ˌ)=¦==\ *n* [NL, fr. *herpes* + *virus*] **:** any of a group of DNA-containing viruses that replicate in cell nuclei and produce herpes

het·ero \'hed·ə(ˌ)rō\ *adj or n* [by shortening] **:** HETEROSEXUAL

het·ero·atom \¦hed·ərō +\ *n* [*heter-* + *atom*] **:** an atom other than carbon in the ring of a heterocyclic compound

het·ero·duplex \"+\ *n* [*heter-* + *duplex*] **:** a nucleic-acid molecule composed of two chains with each derived from a different parent molecule — **heteroduplex** *adj*

het·ero·junction \"+\ *n* [*heter-* + *junction*] **:** an electrical junction between two different materials (as semiconductors)

heterologous* *adj* **:** characterized by cross-reactivity

het·ero·nym \'hed·ərəˌnim, -ə(ˌ) rōˌn-\ *n* -S [*heter-* + *-onym*] **:** one of two or more homographs that differ in pronunciation and meaning (as a *bass* voice and *bass,* a fish)

het·ero·polysaccharide \¦hed·ərō+\ *n* [*heter-* + *polysaccharide*] **:** a polysaccharide consisting of more than one type of monosaccharide

het·ero·sex \"+\ *n* [by shortening] **:** HETEROSEXUALITY

het·ero·sexism \"+\ *n* [*heter-* + *sexism* (herein)] **:** discrimination or prejudice by heterosexuals against homosexuals — **het·ero·sexist** \"+\ *adj*

heuristic* *n* **:** a heuristic method or procedure

hex \'heks\ *adj or n* [by shortening] **:** HEXADECIMAL *herein*

hexa·decimal \¦heksə +\ *adj* [alter. (influenced by *hexa-*) of *sexadecimal*] **:** of, relating to, utilizing, or being a system of numbers having 16 as a base — **hexadecimal** *n*

hex·os·a·min·i·dase \ˌhekˌsäsə'minəˌdās, -āz\ *n* -S [*hexosamine* + *-ide* + *-ase*] **:** either of two hydrolytic enzymes that catalyze the splitting off of a hexose from a ganglioside and are deficient in some metabolic diseases (as a variant of Tay-Sachs disease)

hickey* *n* **:** a temporary red mark produced in lovemaking by biting and sucking the skin

hidden tax *n* **:** INDIRECT TAX

high–energy \¦=¦===\ *adj* **1 a :** having such speed and kinetic energy as to exhibit relativistic departure from classical laws of motion — used esp. of elementary particles whose velocity has been imparted by an accelerator **b :** of or relating to high-energy particles ⟨a *high-energy* reaction⟩ **2 :** yielding a relatively large amount of energy when undergoing hydrolysis ⟨*high-energy* phosphate bonds in ATP⟩ **3 :** DYNAMIC ⟨*high-energy* music⟩ ⟨a *high-energy* barrage of tales —John Justice⟩

high–energy physics *n* PARTICLE PHYSICS *herein*

highflier* *n* **1 :** a stock whose price rises much more rapidly than the market average **2 :** a company whose stock is a highflier

high hat* *or* **hi–hat** \'=¦=\ *n* **:** a pair of cymbals operated by a foot pedal

high·light·er \'hīˌlīd·ə(r)\ *n* -S **:** a cosmetic for highlighting facial features

1high–rise \'=¦=\ *adj* **1 :** being multistory and equipped with elevators ⟨*high-rise* buildings⟩ **2 :** of, relating to, or characterized by high-rise buildings ⟨a *high-rise* district⟩ **3 a :** of, relating to, or being extra-long bicycle handlebars **b :** being a bicycle equipped with high-rise handlebars

2high–rise \"\ *n* **:** a high-rise building

high–riser \-ə(r)\ *n* -S [1*high-rise* (herein) + 2*-er*] **1 :** HIGH-RISE **2 :** a high-rise bicycle

high tech \'hī'tek\ *n* **1 :** HIGH TECHNOLOGY *herein* **2 :** a style of interior decoration in which industrial products, materials, or designs are appropriated or adapted for use in the home — **high–tech** \'=¦=\ *adj*

high technology *n* **:** technology involving the production or use of advanced or sophisticated methods or devices esp. in the fields of electronics and computers

hi·jack \'hīˌjak\ *n* -S [*hijack,* v.] **:** an instance of hijacking

hil·bert space \'hilbərt-\ *n, usu cap H* [after David *Hilbert* †1943 Ger. mathematician] **:** a vector space for which a scalar product is defined and in which every Cauchy sequence composed of elements in the space converges to a limit in the space

himalayan* *n, usu cap* **:** any of a breed of domestic cats developed by crossing the Persian and the Siamese and having the stocky build and long thick coat of the former and the blue eyes and coat pattern of the latter

hindu–arabic \¦==¦===\ *adj, usu cap H&A* **:** relating to, being, or composed of Arabic numerals

hip* *n* [8*hip*] **:** HIPNESS *herein*

hip–huggers \'=ˌ==\ *n pl* **:** low-slung usu. close-fitting trousers that rest on the hips

hip·ness \'hipnəs\ *n* -ES [8*hip* + *-ness*] **:** the quality or state of being hip

hip·pie *or* **hip·py** \'hipē\ *n, pl* **hippies** [8*hip* + *-ie*] **:** a young person who rejects the mores of established society and adheres to a nonviolent ethic; *broadly* **:** a long-haired unconventionally dressed young person — **hip·pie·dom** \-pēdəm, -pid-\ *n* -S

hip–pocket \¦=¦==\ *adj* [2*hip* + *pocket*] **:** of small size or scope

hip·ster·ism \'hipstəˌrizəm\ *n* -S [*hipster* + *-ism*] **1 :** HIPNESS *herein* **2 :** the way of life characteristic of hipsters

hire* *n* **:** a newly hired worker

his·pan·ic \(')hi¦spanik\ *n* -S *usu cap* [*hispanic,* adj.] **:** an American of Spanish or esp. Latin American descent

his·ti·di·ne·mia \'histədə'nēmēə\ *n* -S [*histidine* + *-emia*] **:** a recessive autosomal metabolic defect that results in an excess amount of histidine in the blood and urine due to a deficiency of histidase and is characterized by speech defects and mild mental retardation — **his·ti·di·ne·mic** \ˌ=='=mik\ *adj*

his·to·compatibility \¦hi(ˌ)stō +\ *n* [*hist-* + *compatibility*] **:** a state of mutual tolerance between tissues that allows them to be grafted effectively — see MAJOR HISTOCOMPATIBILITY COMPLEX *herein* — **his·to·compatible** \"+\ *adj*

histocompatibility antigen *n* **:** any of the antigenic glycoproteins on the surface membranes of cells that enable the body's immune system to recognize a cell as native or foreign and that are determined by the major histocompatibility complex

his·to·incompatibility \"+\ n [*hist-* + *incompatibility*] **:** a state of mutual intolerance between tissues (as of a fetus and its mother or a graft and its host) that normally leads to reaction against or rejection of one by the other — **his·to·incompatible** \"+\ *adj*

his·to·physiological \"+\ *or* **his·to·physiologic** \"+\ *adj* [*histophysiology* + *-ical*] **:** of or relating to histophysiology

hit* *vb* — **hit the fan :** to have a major usu. undesirable impact

hit* *n* **1 :** a single dose of a narcotic drug **2 :** a premeditated murder usu. committed by a member of a crime syndicate

hitch·cock·ian \(ˈ)hich¦käkēən, -kyən\ *adj, usu cap* [Alfred Joseph *Hitchcock* †1980 Am. (Eng.-born) motion-picture director + E *-ian*] **:** of, relating to, or suggestive of the cinematic style or technique of Alfred Hitchcock

hit list \ˈ=,=\ *n* [*hit* (herein)] **:** a list esp. of persons or programs to be opposed or eliminated

hit man *n* [*hit* (herein)] **1 :** a professional assassin who works for a crime syndicate **2 :** HATCHET MAN

hive off* *vb* ~ *vt* **:** to separate from a group

HLA \¦ā(,)chel'ā\ *adj* [*h*uman *l*eukocyte *a*ntigen] **:** of, relating to, or being histocompatibility antigens or the major histocompatibility complex in man ⟨~ antigens⟩ ⟨~ typing⟩ — often used with a letter to designate a genetic locus and a number to designate an allele at the locus or the antigen of the major histocompatibility complex corresponding to the locus and allele

HMO \,ā(,)chem'ō\ *n* -s [*h*ealth *m*aintenance *o*rganization] **:** an organization that provides health care to voluntarily enrolled individuals and families in a particular geographic area by member physicians with limited referral to outside specialists and that is financed by fixed periodic payments determined in advance

hmong \ˈməŋ\ *n, pl* **hmong** *cap* [Miao, lit., free-roaming] **:** MIAO

hoa·gie *also* **hoa·gy** \ˈhōgē\ *n, pl* **hoagies** [origin unknown] **:** GRINDER 6

hobo* *also* **hobo bag** *n* **:** a large shoulder bag shaped like a pouch

ho·dad \ˈhō,dad\ *n* -s [perh. alter. of *hodag*] **:** a nonsurfer who frequents surfing beaches and pretends to be a surfer

hoi·sin sauce \¦hȯi¦s(h)in-\ *n* [Chin (Cant) seafood, fr. *hoi* sea + *sin* fresh] **:** a thick reddish sauce of soybeans, spices, and garlic used in oriental cookery

hold* *n* **:** a delay in a countdown (as in launching a missile) — **on hold 1 :** into or in a state of interruption during a telephone call that occurs when one party switches to another line without disconnecting the other party **2 :** into or in a state or period of indefinite suspension ⟨put our plans *on hold*⟩

holding pattern *n* **1 :** a usu. oval course flown (as over an airport) by aircraft awaiting clearance to land **2 :** a state of waiting or suspended activity

ho·lid·ic \hä'lidik, hō'-\ *adj* [*hol-* + *-idic* (as in *meridic* — herein)] **:** having the active constituents chemically defined ⟨~ diets⟩ — compare MERIDIC, OLIGIDIC *herein*

holism* *n* **:** a holistic study or method of treatment

holistic* *adj* **:** relating to or concerned with wholes or with complete systems rather than with the analysis of, treatment of, or dissection into parts ⟨~ medicine⟩ ⟨~ ecology⟩

hol·ler·ith \ˈhälə,rith\ *n* -s *usu cap* [after Herman *Hollerith* †1929 Am. engineer] **:** a code for representing alphanumeric information on punch cards — called also *Hollerith code*

hollerith card *n, usu cap H* **:** PUNCH CARD

holocaust* *n* **1 :** a great slaughter; *specif, often cap* **:** a genocidal slaughter (as of European Jews by the Nazis during World War II) **2 :** DISASTER ⟨turn an ordinary matrimonial civil war into an explosive do-or-die end-of-the-world ~ —J. A. Ornstein⟩ — **holo·caus·tal** \¦hälə¦kȯstᵊl, ¦hōl- *also* ¦hȯl- *or* -¦käst-\ *adj*

ho·lo·gram \ˈhälə,gram, ˈhōl-\ *n* -s [*hol-* + *-gram*] **:** a three-dimensional picture that is made on a photographic film or plate without the use of a camera, that consists of an interference pattern produced by a split coherent beam of radiation and esp. light, and that for viewing is usu. illuminated with coherent light from behind

ho·lo·graph \-af\ *n* -s [*hol-* + *-graph*] **:** HOLOGRAM *herein*

ho·log·ra·phy \həˈlägrəfē, hō-\ *n* -ES [*hol-* + *-graphy*] **:** the process of making or using a hologram — **holograph** *vt* -ED/-ING/-S — **ho·log·ra·pher** \hōˈlägrəfər\ *n* — **ho·lo·graph·ic** \,==¦=ik\ *adj* — **ho·lo·graph·i·cal·ly** \-k(ə)lē\ *adv*

ho·lo·mor·phic \,hōləˈmȯrfik, ,häl-\ *adj* [*hol-* + *-morphic*] **:** being a single-valued function of a complex variable that is differentiable at every point of its domain of definition

homebuilt \ˈ=¦=\ *adj* **:** HOMEMADE 1

home computer *n* **:** a small inexpensive microcomputer

home free *adv* **:** in a comfortable situation usu. after considerable effort

homeland* *n* **:** a state or area set aside to be a state for a people of a particular national, cultural, or racial origin ⟨black ~s in South Africa⟩

home screen *n* **:** TELEVISION

home stand *n* **:** a series of consecutive baseball games played at a team's home field

homestay \ˈ=¦=\ *n* [¹*home* + ⁴*stay*] **:** a period during which a visiting foreign student lives in the home of a host family

hom·i·ni·za·tion \,hämənəˈzāshən, -,nī'-\ *n* -s [F *hominisation*] **1 :** the evolutionary development of human characteristics that differentiate man from his primate ancestors **2 :** the process of altering the environment and adapting it to the uses of human beings

hom·i·nized \¦hämə,nīzd\ *adj* [*homin-* + *-ize* + *-ed*] **:** characterized by hominization

hommos *var of* HUMMUS *herein*

ho·mo·cys·ti·nu·ria \,hōmə,sistəˈn(y)u̇rēə, ,häm-\ *n* [*homocystine* + *-uria*] **:** a metabolic disorder inherited as a recessive autosomal trait, caused by deficiency of an enzyme important in the metabolism of homocystine with resulting accumulation of homocystine in the body and its excretion in the urine, and characterized typically by mental retardation, dislocation of the crystalline lenses, and cardiovascular and skeletal involvement

ho·moe·ol·og·ous \,hōmēˈäləgəs, ,häm-\ *adj* [*home-* + homo*logous*] **:** of similar genic constitution — used of chromosomes believed to have been completely homologous in an ancestral form — **ho·moeo·logue** *or* **ho·moeo·log** \ˈ==ə,lȯg, -,läg\ *n* -s

homogeneity* *n* **:** the state of having identical distribution functions or values ⟨a test for ~ of variances⟩

ho·mo ha·bi·lis \¦hō(,)mōˈhabələs\ *n, usu cap 1st H* [NL, fr. L *homo* man + *habilis* skillful, handy — more at

HOMAGE, ABLE] : an extinct primate that is known from eastern African fossil remains associated with crude tools, is believed to have flourished some two million years ago, and is variously interpreted as the earliest true man or an australopithecine

homomorphism* *n* : a mapping of a mathematical set (as a group, ring, or vector space) on which one or more operations are defined into or onto another set or itself on which one or more corresponding operations are defined in such a way that the result obtained by applying the operations to elements of the first set is mapped onto the result obtained by applying the corresponding operations to their respective images in the second set and such that if there is a unit element in the first set it is mapped onto the unit element of the second set

ho·mo·phile \ˈhōmə͵fīl\ *adj* [*homo*sexual + [2]*-phil*] : GAY 8 — **homophile** *n* -s

ho·mo·phobia \ˌhōmə, -mō +\ *n* [*homo*sexual + *phobia*] : irrational fear or hatred of homosexuality or homosexuals — **ho·mo·phobic** \"+\ *adj*

homopolar* *adj* : having the conductors cut lines of unidirectional flux between poles of a magnet ⟨a ~ generator⟩

ho·mo·sex \"+\ *n* [by shortening] : HOMOSEXUALITY

hon·cho \ˈhän(͵)chō\ *n* -s [Jap *hanchō* squad leader, fr. *han* squad + *chō* head, chief] : BOSS, LEADER; *also* : HOTSHOT ⟨every other slick guitar ~ in the city was looking to jam with you —Tim Cahill⟩

honest broker *n* : a neutral mediator

honey bucket *n* : a bucket for collecting human excrement

honey wagon *n* **1** : a vehicle for transporting human excrement **2** : a portable outdoor toilet

hon·ky *or* **hon·kie** *also* **hon·key** \ˈhȯŋkē, ˈhäŋ-, -ki\ *n, pl* **honkies** [origin unknown] : a white man — usu. used disparagingly

hook* *n* : a device esp. in music or writing that catches the attention ⟨trick is to find some sonic ~ that will galvanize dancers on the floor —*Newsweek*⟩

hook, line and sinker *adv* : without hesitation or reservation : COMPLETELY

hook up* *vi* : to become associates esp. in a working or social relationship ⟨moved here and *hooked up* with three musicians from the city —Robert Palmer⟩

hoot* *n* : something or someone amusing

hootch *or* **hooch** \ˈhüch\ *n* [prob. fr. Jap *uchi* house] : a thatched hut esp. in Vietnam; *broadly* : HOUSE, DWELLING, BARRACKS

hoo·ver \ˈhüvə(r)\ *vb* -ED/-ING/-s [fr. *Hoover,* a trademark] *vt, Brit* : to clean with or as if with a vacuum cleaner ~ *vi, Brit* : [3]VACUUM *vi* 2

hopefully* *adv* : it is hoped ⟨procedures which would ~ lead to the resolution of the . . . issue —*Amer. Assoc. of Univ. Prof. Bull.*⟩

horse's ass *n* : a stupid or incompetent person : BLOCKHEAD — often considered vulgar

ho scale \(ˈ)āˌchō-\ *n, usu cap H&O* [so called fr. its fitness for rails of HO gage] : a scale of 3.5 millimeters to one foot used esp. for model toys (as automobiles or trains)

hospice* *n* : a facility or program designed to provide a caring environment for supplying the physical and emotional needs of the terminally ill

hospitality suite *n* : a room or suite esp. in a hotel set aside as a place for socializing usu. in connection with a business meeting or convention

host plant *n* : a plant upon which an organism (as an insect or mildew) lodges and subsists

hot* *adj* : being full of detail and information and requiring little or no involvement of the listener, viewer, or reader ⟨a ~ medium like radio —H.M. McLuhan⟩

hot* *n* **hots** *pl* : strong sexual desire — used with *the* ⟨about a young girl . . . with the ~*s* for gypsy-dark men —H.C. Veit⟩

hot comb *n* : a metal comb usu. electrically heated for straightening or styling the hair

hot damn *interj* — usu. used to express pleasant surprise ⟨*hot damn,* that was a good audience out there —Steve Miller⟩

hot dog* *n* : one that hotdogs; *also* : SHOW-OFF

hot·dog \ˈhät͵dȯg *sometimes* -däg\ *vi* **hot·dogged; hot·dogged; hot·dog·ging; hot·dogs** [prob. fr. [2]*hot dog*] : to perform in a conspicuous or often ostentatious manner; *esp* : to perform fancy stunts and maneuvers (as when surfing or skiing) — **hot·dog·ger** *n* -s — **hotdog·ging** *n* -s

hotel china *n* [so called fr. its capacity to withstand the hard use typically met with in hotels] : a high-fired well-vitrified American ceramic ware approaching hard-paste porcelain in composition

hot line *n* **1** : a direct line of communication between heads of government (as of the U.S. and the U.S.S.R.) **2** : a usu. toll-free telephone service available to the public for some specific purpose: as **a** : one by which callers can talk confidentially about personal problems to a sympathetic listener ⟨a suicide *hot line*⟩ **b** : one by which callers can obtain free advice ⟨a legal *hot line*⟩ ⟨a grammar *hot line*⟩ **c** : one by which a citizen can report illegal activities (as to a government agency)

hot pants* *n pl* : very short shorts

hot shit *n* : HOTSHOT; *also* : HOT STUFF — usu. considered vulgar

hot shoe *n* : a receptacle on a camera that provides a point of attachment and electrical contact for an electronic flash lamp

hot tub *n* : a large usu. wooden tub filled with hot water in which bathers soak and usu. socialize

hot–wire \ˈ=ˌ=\ *vt* : to short-circuit the wires of (an automotive vehicle or its ignition system) in order to start the engine without using a key

househusband \ˈ=ˌ==\ *n* [[1]*house* + *husband*] : a husband who does housekeeping usu. while his wife earns the family income

house nigger *n* : UNCLE TOM — used disparagingly

house sitter *n* : a person who occupies a dwelling to provide security and maintenance while the tenant is away — **house–sit** \ˈ=ˌ=\ *vi* — **house–sitting** \ˈ=ˌ==\ *n*

HTLV \ˌāchˌtēˌelˈvē\ *n* -s [*h*uman *T*-cell *l*eukemia *v*irus] : any of several retroviruses that include one causing AIDS — often used with a number or Roman numeral to indicate the type; called also *human T-cell leukemia virus*

hub·ble constant \ˌhəbəl-\ *n, usu cap H* [after Edwin P. *Hubble* †1953 Am. astronomer] : a proportionality constant indicative of the rate of expansion of the universe that is used in relating the apparent velocity of recession of a distant galaxy and its distance so that a greater rate of recession indicates a greater distance

hu·go \ˈ(h)yügō\ *n* -s *usu cap* [after *Hugo* Gernsback †1967 Am. (Luxembourg-born) author, inventor, and publisher] : any of several trophies awarded annually by a professional organization for notable achievement in science-fiction writing

human ecology* *n* **:** the ecology of man and of human communities and populations esp. as concerned with preservation of environmental quality (as of air or water) through proper application of conservation and civil engineering practices

human t–cell leukemia virus *n, usu cap T* **:** HTLV

hum·mus \'həməs\ *also* **hom·mos** \'həm-, 'häm-\ *n* [Ar *ḥummuṣ* chick-pea] **:** a paste of pureed chick-peas usu. mixed with sesame oil or sesame paste and eaten as a dip or sandwich spread

hu·mon·gous \(h)yü'məŋəs, -'mäŋ-\ *or* **hu·mun·gous** \-'məŋ\ *adj* [alter. of *huge* + *monstrous*] *slang* **:** extremely large **:** HUGE

hundreds digit *n* **:** HUNDRED 4

hundreds place *n* **:** the place three to the left of the decimal point in a number expressed in the Arabic system of notation

hung \'həŋ\ *adj* [fr. past part. of [1]*hang*] **:** having a large penis

hunger* *n* — **from hunger :** very bad **:** PATHETIC ⟨they were strictly patchwork and strictly *from hunger* —A. J. Daley⟩

hung up* *adj* **1 :** having a hang-up **:** ANXIOUS ⟨don't know why women have to be so *hung up* about age —Pauline Kael⟩ **2 :** being much involved with: as **a :** INFATUATED ⟨they get *hung up* on some fellow here —Jeff Brown⟩ **b :** ENTHUSIASTIC ⟨people who are *hung up* on French Provincial —Walter Goodman⟩ **c :** PREOCCUPIED ⟨*hung up* on winning⟩

hunk* *n* **:** an attractive well-built man

huntboard \'=,=\ *n* [from its use at hunt breakfasts] **:** a piece of furniture similar to a sideboard but usu. taller, smaller, and simpler

hunting* *n* **1 :** a periodic variation in speed of a synchronous electrical machine from that of the true synchronous speed **2 :** a self-induced and undesirable oscillation of a variable above and below the desired value in an automatic control system **3 :** a continuous attempt by an automatically controlled system to find a desired equilibrium condition

hutzpah *or* **hutzpa** *var of* CHUTZPAH *herein*

hwyl \'hüil\ *n* -s [W] *Brit* **:** FERVOR, EXCITEMENT

hyaline membrane disease *n* **:** a respiratory disease of unknown cause that occurs in newborn premature infants and is characterized by deficiency of the surfactant coating the inner surface of the lungs, by failure of the lungs to expand and contract properly during breathing with resulting collapse, and by the accumulation of a protein-containing film lining the alveoli and their ducts — called also *respiratory distress syndrome*

hybrid* *n* **:** something (as a power plant, vehicle, or electronic circuit) that has two different types of components performing essentially the same function — **hybrid*** *adj*

hybrid computer *n* **:** a computer system consisting of a combination of analog and digital computer systems

hybridoma \,hī(,)brid'ōmə\ *n* -s [*hybrid* + *-oma*] **:** a hybrid cell produced by the fusion of an antibody-producing lymphocyte with a tumor cell and used to continuously culture a specific antibody of a single molecular species

hy·dra·tase \'hīdrə·,tās, -,drād·,ās, -āz\ *n* -s [*hydrate* + *-ase*] **:** any of several lyases that catalyze the hydration or dehydration of a carbon-oxygen bond

hy·dro·acoustic \¦hī(,)drō+\ *adj* [*hydr-* + *acoustic*] **1 :** of or relating to the production of acoustic energy from the flow of fluids under pressure **2 :** of or relating to the transmission of sound in water

hy·dro·biologist \"+\ *n* -s [*hydrobiology* + [1]*-ist*] **:** a specialist in hydrobiology

hy·dro·chlo·ro·thi·a·zide \,hīdrə,klōrə'thīə,zīd\ *n* [*hydr-* + *chlor-* + *thiazide* (herein)] **:** a diuretic and antihypertensive drug $C_7H_8ClN_3O_4S_2$

hy·dro·crack \¦hī(,)drō +\ *vt* [*hydr-* + *crack*] **:** to crack (hydrocarbons) in the presence of hydrogen

hy·dro·cracker \"+\ *n* **:** an apparatus for hydrocracking

hy·dro·dy·nam·i·cist \,hīdrōdī'naməsə̇st\ *n* -s [*hydrodynamics* + *-ist*] **:** one who specializes in hydrodynamics

hydrofoil* *n* **:** a motorboat equipped with hydrofoils

hy·dro·gasification \¦hīdrō+\ *n* [*hydr-* + *gasification*] **:** the process of reacting hydrogen or a mixture of steam and hydrogen with coal at high temperature and high pressure so that the carbon in the coal reacts directly or indirectly to produce methane used for fuel — **hy·dro·gasifier** \"+\ *n*

hy·dro·magnetic \"+\ *adj* [*hydr-* + *magnetic*] **:** MAGNETOHYDRODYNAMIC

hy·dro·magnetics \"+\ *n pl but sing in constr* [*hydr-* + *magnetics*] **:** MAGNETOHYDRODYNAMICS

hydromagnetic wave *n* **:** a wave in an electrically conducting fluid (as a plasma) in a magnetic field

hy·dro·naut \'hīdrə,nȯt, -nät\ *n* -s [*hydr-* + *-naut* (as in *astronaut*)] **:** a member of the crew of a deep-sea vehicle (as a bathyscaphe) other than a submarine

hy·dro·nau·tics \(')hīdrə¦nȯd·iks\ *n pl but sing in constr* [*hydr-* + *-nautics* (as in *aeronautics*)] **:** the science of constructing and operating marine craft and instruments designed to explore the ocean environment

hy·dron·ic \hī'dränik\ *adj* [*hydr-* + *-onic* (as in *electronic*)] **:** of, relating to, or being a system of heating or cooling that involves transfer of heat by a circulating fluid (as water or vapor) in a closed system of pipes — **hy·dron·i·cal·ly** \-nə̇k(ə)lē\ *adv*

hy·dron·ics \-niks\ *n pl but usu sing in constr* [*hydronic* (herein) + *-s*] **:** a hydronic system

hydroplane* *vi, of a vehicle or tire* **:** to ride supported by a film of water on a wet surface when a critical speed is reached with a resultant loss of directional stability and braking effectiveness

hy·dro·skimmer \'hīdrō+,\ *n* [*hydr-* + *skimmer*] **:** an air-cushion vehicle for use over water

hy·dro·space \"+,\ *n* [*hydr-* + *space*] **:** the regions beneath the surface of the ocean

hy·dro·treat \"+,\ *vt* [*hydr-* + *treat*] **:** to subject to hydrogenation ⟨~ lube oil⟩ — **hy·dro·treat·er** *n*

hy·dro·trope \'hīdrə·,trōp\ *n* -s [back-formation fr. *hydrotropic*] **:** a hydrotropic substance

hy·droxo·cobalamin \hī¦dräksə, -(,)sō+\ *n* [*hydroxo-* + *cobalamin*] **:** a member $C_{62}H_{89}CoN_{13}O_{15}P$ of the vitamin B_{12} group used in treating and preventing B_{12} deficiency

hy·drox·y·lase \hī'dräksə,lās, -,lāz\ *n* -s [*hydroxyl* + *-ase*] **:** any of a group of enzymes that catalyze oxidation reactions in which one of the two atoms of molecular oxygen is incorporated into the substrate and the other is used to oxidize NADH or NADPH

hy·droxy·lysine \hī¦dräksə̇+\ *n* [*hydroxy-* + *lysine*] **:** an amino acid $C_6H_{14}N_2O_3$ that is found esp. in collagen

hy·droxy·urea \(¦)hī,dräksē+\ *n* [*hydroxy-* + *urea*] **:** an antineoplastic drug $CH_4N_2O_2$ used to treat some forms of leukemia

hype* *n* **1 :** DECEPTION, PUT-ON ⟨had come upon some way I could work a ~ on the penal authorities — Malcolm X⟩ **2 :** promotional advertising esp. of an extravagant or contrived kind

hype *vt* -ED/-ING/-S [*hype,* n. (herein)] **1 :** to put on **:** MISLEAD, DECEIVE **2 a :** STIMULATE, JAZZ 2a — usu. used with *up* ⟨his assignment is to ~ up the crowd —J.S. Radosta⟩ **b :** INCREASE ⟨tried to ~ sales by enticing offers⟩ **3 :** PROMOTE, PUBLICIZE ⟨~ youth-oriented products to young people —Nancy McCarthy⟩ — **hyped-up** \ˌhīpˌdəp\ *adj*

hy·per \ˈhīpə(r)\ *adj* [back-formation from *hyperactive*] **:** HIGH-STRUNG, EXCITABLE; *also* **:** extremely active

hyper-* *prefix* **:** that is or exists in a space of more than three dimensions ⟨*hyper*cube⟩ ⟨*hyper*space⟩

hyperactive *n* [*hyperactive,* adj.] **:** a hyperactive person

hy·per·aldosteronism \ˌhīpər+\ *n* [*hyper-* + *aldosteronism* (herein)] **:** ALDOSTERONISM *herein*

hy·per·alimentation \"+\ *n* [*hyper-* + *alimentation*] **:** the intravenous administration of nutrients esp. to patients who cannot ingest food through the alimentary tract

hyperbaric* *adj* **:** of, relating to, or utilizing greater than normal pressure esp. of oxygen ⟨~ medicine⟩ ⟨~ chamber⟩ — **hy·per·bar·i·cal·ly** \ˌhīpə(r)ˌbarə̇k(ə)lē\ *adv*

hyperbolic* *adj* **:** of, relating to, or being a space in which more than one line parallel to a given line passes through a point ⟨~ geometry⟩

hy·per·charge \ˈhīpə(r) +ˌ\ *n* [*hyper-* + *charge*] **:** a quantum characteristic of a closely related group of strongly interacting particles represented by a number equal to twice the average value of the electric charge of the group

hy·per·complex \ˌhīpə(r)+\ *adj* [*hyper-* + *complex*] **:** of, relating to, or being a general form of number that can be expressed as a vector of *n* dimensions in the form $x_1e_1 + x_2e_2 + \ldots + x_ne_n$ where the coefficients $x_1, x_2, \ldots x_n$ range over a given number field and $e_1 = (e, 0, 0, \ldots 0)$, $e_2 = (0, e, 0, \ldots 0)$, $\ldots$ $e_n = (0, 0, \ldots e)$ where *e* is the multiplicative identity of the field ⟨~ variable⟩

hy·per·diploid \"+\ *adj* [*hyper-* + *diploid*] **:** having slightly more than the diploid number of chromosomes — **hy·per·diploidy** \"+\ *n*

hy·per·excitability \"+\ *n* [*hyper-* + *excitability*] **:** the state or condition of being unusually or excessively excitable — **hy·per·excitable** \"+\ *adj*

hy·per·extend \"+\ *vt* [*hyper-* + *extend*] **:** to extend so that the angle between bones of a joint is greater than normal — **hy·per·extension** \"+\ *n*

hy·per·fine structure \"+ . . . -\ *n* [*hyper-* + ³*fine*] **:** a fine structure multiplet occurring in an atomic spectrum that is due to interaction between electrons and nuclear spin

hypergeometric distribution *n* **:** a probability function of the form

$$f(x) = \frac{\binom{M}{x}\binom{N-M}{n-x}}{\binom{N}{n}} \text{ where } \binom{M}{x} = \frac{M!}{x!(M-x)!}$$

that gives the probability of obtaining exactly *x* elements of one kind and *n–x* elements of another if *n* elements are chosen at random without replacement from a finite population containing *N* elements of which *M* are of the first kind and *N–M* are of the second kind

hy·per·inflation \ˌhīpər+\ *n* [*hyper-* + *inflation*] **:** inflation at a very high rate (as in Germany after World War I)

hy·per·ka·le·mia \ˌhīpə(r)ˌkāˈlēmēə\ *n* -S [NL, fr. *hyper-* + E *kalium* + NL *-emia*] **:** the presence of an abnormally high concentration of potassium in the blood

hy·per·lip·id·emia \ˌhīpə(r)ˌlipə̇ˈdēmēə\ *n* -S [NL, fr. ISV *hyper-* + *lipid* + *-emia*] **:** HYPERLIPEMIA — **hy·per·lip·id·emic** \-mik\ *adj*

hy·per·li·po·pro·tein·emia \ˌ==ˌlīpəˌprōˌtēˈnēmēə, -ˌlip- *also* -ˌprōd·ēə̇ˈn-\ *n* -S [NL, fr. *hyper-* + E *lipoprotein* + NL *-emia*] **:** the presence of excess lipoprotein in the blood

hy·per·market \ˈhīpə(r) +ˌ\ *n* [*hyper-* + *market*] *Brit* **:** a very large department store that includes a supermarket

hy·per·pha·gic \ˌ==ˈfājik\ *adj* [*hyperphagia* + ¹*-ic*] **:** relating to or affected with hyperphagia ⟨~ rats⟩

hy·per·polarize \ˌhīpə(r)+\ *vb* [*hyper-* + *polarize*] *vt* **:** to produce an increase in potential difference across (a biological membrane) or across the membrane of (a nerve cell) ~ *vi* **:** to undergo or produce an increase in potential difference across something — **hy·per·polarization** \"+\ *n*

hy·per·sexual \"+\ *adj* [*hyper-* + *sexual*] **:** characterized by excessive sexual arousal or overindulgence in sexual activity — **hy·per·sexuality** \"+\ *n*

hy·per·tri·glyc·er·i·de·mia \ˌhīpə(r)ˌtrīˌglisəˌrīˈdēmēə\ *n* -S [NL, fr. *hyper-* + E *triglyceride* + NL *-emia*] **:** the presence of an excess of triglycerides in the blood — **hy·per·tri·gly·cer·i·de·mic** \-mik\ *adj*

hy·per·velocity \"+\ *n* [*hyper-* + *velocity*] **:** a high or relatively high velocity; *esp* **:** one greater than 10,000 feet per second

hy·per·ventilate \"+\ *vb* [*hyper-* + *ventilate*] *vi* **:** to undergo hyperventilation ⟨some swimmers ~⟩ ~ *vt* **:** to subject to hyperventilation ⟨he *hyperventilated* his lungs by deep breathing⟩

hyp·no·therapist \ˌhipnō +\ *n* [*hypnotherapy* + *-ist*] **:** a specialist in hypnotherapy

hypodermis* *n* **:** SUPERFICIAL FASCIA

hy·po·diploid \ˌhīpō+\ *adj* [*hypo-* + *diploid*] **:** having slightly fewer than the diploid number of chromosomes — **hy·po·diploidy** \"+\ *n*

hy·po·gam·ma·glob·u·li·ne·mia \ˌhīpəˌgaməˌgläbyələ̇ˈnēmēə, -pō-\ *n* -S [NL, fr. *hypo-* + E *gamma globulin* + NL *-emia*] **:** a deficiency of gamma globulins and esp. immunoglobulins in the blood; *also* **:** a state of immunological deficiency characterized by this — **hypo·gam·ma·glob·u·li·ne·mic** \-mik\ *adj*

hy·po·ther·mic \ˌhīpəˌthərmik, -thəm-\ *adj* [*hypothermia* + ¹*-ic*] **:** relating to, utilizing, or characterized by hypothermia

hy·pox·emic \ˌhīˌpäkˈsēmik\ *adj* [*hypoxemia* + ¹*-ic*] **:** relating to, characterized by, or affected with hypoxemia

I

ibi·zan hound \i¦bēzən-, ē¦vēthən-\ *n, usu cap I* [*Ibiza,* island in the Balearic group] **:** any of a breed of slender agile medium-sized hunting dogs developed in the Balearic islands

ibu·pro·fen \ˌībyü'prōfən, -ˌfen, -ˌfēn\ *n* -s [fr. *iso-* + *bu*tyl- + *pro*pionic acid + *fen* (alter. of *phenyl*)] **:** an anti-inflammatory drug $C_{13}H_{18}O_2$ used esp. to relieve the symptoms of rheumatoid arthritis and degenerative arthritis

IC \ˌī'sē\ *n* -s **:** INTEGRATED CIRCUIT *herein*

ice* *n* **:** an undercover premium paid to a theater employee for choice theater tickets

ice* *vt* **1 :** to shoot (an ice hockey puck) the length of the rink and beyond the opponents' goal line **2** *slang* **:** KILL

ice–cream chair *n* [so called fr. its use in ice-cream parlors] **:** a small armless chair with a circular seat for use at a table

ice·kha·na \'īsˌkänə, -kan-, -kȧn-, ˌ=ˈ==\ *n* -s [[1]*ice* + gym*khana*] **:** an automobile gymkhana held on a frozen lake or river

ice lolly *n, Brit* **:** a confection made of flavored and colored water frozen on a stick

ice–out \'=ˌ=\ *n* -s [[1]*ice* + [1]*out*] **:** the disappearance of ice from the surface of a body of water (as a lake) as a result of thawing

icing* *n* **:** an addition that is not essential but adds to the interest or appeal of the main item or event — often used in the phrase *icing on the cake*

ICU *abbr* intensive care unit

ID \ˌī'dē\ *n* -s [*id*entification] **:** STATION BREAK

idem·po·tent \¦īdəm¦pōtᵊnt, ī'dempəd·ənt\ *adj* [ISV *idem-* same (fr. L *idem*) + L *potent-, potens* having power — more at IDENTITY, POTENT] **:** relating to or being a mathematical quantity which when applied to itself under a given binary operation (as multiplication) equals itself; *also* **:** relating to or being an operation under which a mathematical quantity is idempotent — **idem·po·ten·cy** \-ənsē, -ᵊnsē\ *n* — **idempotent** *n* -s

identification parade *n, Brit* **:** a line of persons arranged by the police esp. for the identification of a suspected criminal by a victim or an eyewitness

Iden·ti–Kit \ī'dentəˌkit\ *trademark* — used for a method of creating a picture (as of the face of a person wanted by police) by combining several separate images (as of different features)

iden·ti·kit \"\ *adj, sometimes cap* [fr. *Identi-Kit,* a trademark] *chiefly Brit* **:** produced by or as if by the routine assembly of stock materials **:** lacking variety or individuality **:** PREFABRICATED, STEREOTYPED ⟨an ~ novel⟩

identity crisis *n* **:** personal psychosocial conflict esp. in adolescence that involves confusion about one's social role and often a sense of loss of the continuity of one's personality; *broadly* **:** a state of confusion or uncertainty about one's role, function, or goals ⟨both weeklies now seem involved in a sort of middle-aged, corporate *identity crisis* —Dan Wakefield⟩

identity function *n* **:** a function (as $f(x)$) that is everywhere equal in value to the value of its independent variable (as x)

identity matrix *n* **:** a square matrix with numeral 1's along the principal diagonal and 0's elsewhere

ideo·phone \'idēəˌfōn *also* 'īd-\ *n* -s [*ideo-* + *-phone*] **:** an onomatopoeic element functioning as part of a distinct word class esp. in African languages

idiot light *n* **:** a colored light (as on an automobile instrument panel) designed to give a warning (as of low oil pressure)

id·io·type \'idēəˌtīp\ *n* [*idio-* + *type*] **:** the molecular structure and conformation of an immunoglobulin that confers its antigenic specificity — compare ALLOTYPE *herein,* ISOTYPE *herein* — **id·io·typ·ic** \¦===ˈtipik\ *adj*

IDP *abbr* **1** inosine diphosphate **2** integrated data processing **3** international driving permit

iff \'if\ *conj* [alter. of *if*] **:** if and only if ⟨two lines that are not vertical are parallel ~ they have equal slopes⟩

ig·nim·brite \'ignəmˌbrīt\ *n* -s [G *ignimbrit,* fr. L *ign*is + *imbr-* (fr. *imber* rain, rain shower) + G *-it* [1]-ite (mineral)] **:** a hard rock formed by solidification of chiefly fine deposits of volcanic ash

ike·ba·na \ˌikə'bänə, ˌēk-, -kē'-\ *n* -s [Jap, fr. *ikeru* to keep alive, arrange + *hana* flower] **:** the Japanese art of flower arranging that emphasizes form and balance

il·legal \(ˈ)i(l), ə+\ *n* -s **:** an illegal immigrant

il·locutionary \ˌi(l)+\ *adj* [[2]*in-* + *locutionary* (herein)] **:** of, relating to, or being an act (as informing, warning, or predicting) performed by a speaker in the course of making an utterance — compare LOCUTIONARY *herein,* PERLOCUTIONARY *herein* — **il·locution** \ˌi(l)+\ *n* -s

illuminate* *vt* **:** to subject to radiation

IM* *abbr* **1** intermodulation distortion **2** individual medley

image* *n* **1 :** a set of values of a mathematical function (as a homomorphism) that corresponds to a particular subset of the domain **2 :** a popular conception (as of a person, institution, or nation) projected esp. through the mass media ⟨promoting a corporate ~ of brotherly love and concern —R.C. Buck⟩

im·bal·anced \(ˈ)im¦balən(t)st\ *adj* [*imbalance* + *-ed*] **:** not balanced; *esp* **:** having a disproportionately large number of members of one racial or ethnic group ⟨~ schools⟩

imip·ra·mine \ə'miprəˌmēn\ *n* [*imi*d- + *pro*pyl + *amine*] **:** a tricyclic antidepressant drug $C_{19}H_{24}N_2$ administered esp. as the hydrochloride

im·mit·tance \i'mitᵊn(t)s\ *n* -s [*im*pedance + ad*mittance*] **:** ADMITTANCE; *also* **:** IMPEDANCE — used of transmission lines, networks, and measuring instruments

immune response *n* **:** a bodily response to an antigen that involves the interaction of the antigen with lymphocytes to induce the formation of antibodies and lymphocytes capable of reacting with it and rendering it harmless

immune system *n* **:** the bodily system that protects the body from foreign substances, cells, and tissues by producing the immune response and that includes esp. the thymus, spleen, lymph nodes, special deposits of lymphoid tissue (as in the gastrointestinal tract and bone marrow), lymphocytes including the B cells and T cells, and immunoglobulins including all known antibodies

im·mu·no·adsorbent \ˌimyənō, əˌmyünō+\ *n* [*immuno-* + *adsorbent*] : IMMUNOSORBENT *herein* — **immunoadsorbent** *adj*

im·mu·no·assay \"+\ *n* [*immuno-* + *assay*] : the determination of the presence, absence, or quantity of a substance (as a protein) through its capacity to act as an antigen — **immunoassay** *vt* — **im·mu·no·assayable** \"+\ *adj*

im·mu·no·competence \"+\ *n* [*immuno-* + *competence*] : the capacity for a normal immune response ⟨altered the ~ of the lymphocytes⟩ — **im·mu·no·competent** \"+\ *adj*

im·mu·no·compromised \"+\ *adj* [*immuno-* + *compromised*] : having the immune system impaired or weakened (as by drugs or illness)

im·mu·no·cyte \ˈimyənəˌsīt\ *n* -s [*immuno-* + *-cyte*] : a cell (as a lymphocyte) that has an immunologic function

im·mu·no·cytochemistry \ˌimyənō, əˌmyünō+\ *n* [*immuno-* + *cytochemistry*] : the biochemistry of cellular immunology — **im·mu·no·cytochemical** \"+\ *adj*

im·mu·no·deficiency \"+\ *n* [*immuno-* + *deficiency*] : inability to produce a normal complement of antibodies or immunologically sensitized T cells esp. in response to specific antigens — see AIDS *herein* — **im·mu·no·deficient** \"+\ *adj*

im·mu·no·depression \"+\ *n* [*immuno-* + *depression*] : IMMUNOSUPPRESSION *herein* — **im·mu·no·depressant** \"+\ *n* — **im·mu·no·depressive** \"+\ *adj*

im·mu·no·diagnosis \"+\ *n* [*immuno-* + *diagnosis*] : diagnosis (as of cancer) by immunological methods — **im·mu·no·diagnostic** \"+\ *adj*

im·mu·no·diffusion \"+\ *n* [*immuno-* + *diffusion*] : any of several techniques for obtaining a precipitate between an antibody and its specific antigen by suspending one in a gel and letting the other migrate through it from a well or by letting both antibody and antigen migrate through the gel from separate wells to form an area of precipitation

im·mu·no·electrophoresis \"+\ *n, pl* **immunoelectrophore·ses** \-ē(ˌ)sēz\ [*immuno-* + *electrophoresis*] : electrophoretic separation of proteins followed by identification by the formation of precipitates through specific immunologic reactions — **im·mu·no·electrophoretic** \"+\ *adj* — **im·mu·no·electrophoretically** \"+\ *adv*

im·mu·no·fluorescence \"+\ *n* [*immuno-* + *fluorescence*] : the labeling of antigens or antibodies with fluorescent dyes for the purpose of demonstrating the presence of corresponding antibodies or antigens in a tissue preparation or a smear

im·mu·no·geneticist \"+\ *n* [*immunogenetics* + *-ist*] : a specialist in immunogenetics

im·mu·no·globulin \"+\ *n* [*immuno-* + *globulin*] : any of the vertebrate serum proteins that are made up of light chains and heavy chains usu. linked by disulfide bonds and include all known antibodies

im·mu·no·hematology \"+\ *n* [*immuno-* + *hematology*] : a branch of immunology that deals with the immunologic properties of blood — **im·mu·no·hematologic** \"+\ *or* **im·mu·no·hematological** \"+\ *adj* — **im·mu·no·hematologist** \"+\ *n*

im·mu·no·histochemical \"+\ *adj* [*immuno-* + *histochemical*] : of or relating to the application of histochemical and immunologic methods to chemical analysis of living cells and tissues — **im·mu·no·histochemically** \"+\ *adv* — **im·mu·no·histochemistry** \"+\ *n*

im·mu·no·histology \ˌimyənō, əˌmyünō +\ *n* [*immuno-* + *histology*] : a branch of immunology that deals with the application of immunologic methods to histology — **im·mu·no·histological** \"+\ *also* **im·mu·no·histologic** \"+\ *adj* — **im·mu·no·histologically** \"+\ *adv*

im·mu·no·pathology \"+\ *n* [*immuno-* + *pathology*] : a branch of medicine that deals with immune responses associated with disease — **im·mu·no·pathologic** \"+\ *or* **im·mu·no·pathological** \"+\ *adj* — **im·mu·no·pathologist** \"+\ *n*

im·mu·no·pharmacology \"+\ *n* [*immuno-* + *pharmacology*] **1** : a branch of pharmacology concerned with the application of immunological techniques and theory to the study of the effects of drugs esp. on the immune system **2** : the immunological effects and significance of a particular drug (as morphine) — **im·mu·no·pharmacologist** \"+\ *n*

im·mu·no·precipitation \"+\ *n* [*immuno-* + *precipitation*] : precipitation of a complex of an antibody and its specific antigen — **im·mu·no·precipitate** \"+\ *n* — **im·mu·no·precipitate** \"+\ *vt*

im·mu·no·prophylaxis \"+\ *n* [*immuno-* + *prophylaxis*] : the prevention of disease by the production of active or passive immunity

im·mu·no·reactive \"+\ *adj* [*immuno-* + *reactive*] : reacting to particular antigens or haptens ⟨~ lymphocytes⟩ — **im·mu·no·reactivity** \"+\ *n*

im·mu·no·sorbent \"+\ *n* [*immuno-* + *sorbent*] : a preparation of a specific antibody chemically combined with an insoluble substance (as cellulose) that is used to selectively remove its specific antigen from solution; *also* : a similar preparation of an antigen used to remove its specific antibody from solution — **im·mu·no·sorbent** \"+\ *adj*

im·mu·no·suppression \"+\ *n* [*immuno-* + *suppression*] : suppression (as by drugs) of natural immune responses — **im·mu·no·suppress** \"+\ *vt* — **im·mu·no·suppressant** \"+\ *n or adj* — **im·mu·no·suppressive** \"+\ *adj*

im·mu·no·therapeutic \"+\ *adj* [*immuno-* + *therapeutic*] : of, relating to, or characterized by immunotherapy ⟨~ techniques for treating cancer⟩

impact* *vt* : to have an adverse effect on ⟨imports of stainless steel products continued to ~ . . . profits — *Annual Report Armco Steel Corp.*⟩ ~ *vi* : to have an adverse effect

impacted* *adj* : deeply entrenched : not easily changed or removed ⟨the ~ cynicism about most things American —W.F. Buckley *b*1925⟩

impacted area *n* : an area in which a large number of public school students are from families living or working on nontaxable federal property

implicit differentiation *n* : the process of finding the derivative of a dependent variable in an implicit function by differentiating each term separately, by expressing the derivative of the dependent variable as a symbol, and by solving the resulting expression for the symbol

implode* *vi* **1** : to undergo violent compression **2** : to collapse inward as if from external pressure; *also* : to become greatly reduced as if from collapsing ~ *vt* : to cause to implode

implosion* *n* : an inward collapse; *also* : a reduction or compaction as if from external pressure ⟨a population ~⟩

imported fire ant *n* : either of two So. American fire ants of the genus *Solenopsis* (*S. invicta* and *S. richteri*) that are pests of agricultural and medical importance in parts of the southeastern U.S.

impressionist* *n* **:** an entertainer who does impressions of noted personalities

imprint* *n* **:** the name under which a publisher issues books

imu \'ēmü\ *n* -s [Hawaiian] **:** a Hawaiian cooking pit in which hot stones bake the food

in* *adj* **1 :** keenly aware of and responsive to what is new and smart ⟨the ~ crowd⟩ **2 :** extremely fashionable ⟨the ~ place to go⟩ — **in–ness** \'innə̇s\ *n* -ES

-in \ˌin\ *n comb form* -s [[2]*in* (as in *sit-in*)] **1 :** organized public protest by means of or in favor of **:** demonstration ⟨teach-*in*⟩ ⟨love-*in*⟩ **2 :** public group activity ⟨swim-*in*⟩

in–and–out* *adj* **:** characterized by purchase and sale of the same security within a short period ⟨*in-and-out* trading⟩

inbounds \ˈ≡ˌ≡\ *adj* **:** of or relating to putting a basketball in play by passing it onto the court from out of bounds ⟨~ pass⟩

inc* *abbr* incomplete

in·ca·pac·i·tant \ˌinkəˈpasətənt, -sәd·ə-\ *n* -s [*incapacitate* + *-ant*] **:** a chemical or biological agent (as tear gas) used to temporarily incapacitate people or animals

incomplete* *adj, of insect metamorphosis* **:** having no pupal stage between the immature stages and the adult with the young insect usu. resembling the adult — compare COMPLETE 1 *herein*

inconsistent* *adj* **:** not satisfiable by the same set of values for the unknowns ⟨~ equations⟩ ⟨~ inequalities⟩

in·cre·men·tal·ism \ˌiŋkrəˈmentᵊlˌizəm, ˌink-\ *n* -s [*incremental* + *-ism*] **:** a policy or advocacy of a policy of political or social change in small increments — **in·cre·men·tal·ist** \-ᵊlə̇st\ *n* -s

independent* *adj* **1 :** having linear independence ⟨an ~ set of vectors⟩ **2 :** having the property that the joint probability (as of events or samples) or the joint probability density function (as of random variables) equals the product of the probabilities or probability density functions of separate occurrence

independent assortment *n* **:** formation of random combinations of chromosomes in meiosis and of genes on different pairs of homologous chromosomes by the passage at random of one of each diploid pair of homologous chromosomes into each gamete independently of each other pair

in–depth \ˈ≡ˌ≡\ *adj* [[1]*in* + *depth*] **:** COMPREHENSIVE, THOROUGH ⟨an *in-depth* study⟩

in·dex·ation \ˌinˌdekˈsāshən\ *n* -s [[2]*index* + *-ation*] **:** a system of economic control in which certain variables (as wages and interest) are tied to a cost-of-living index so that both rise or fall at the same rate and the detrimental effect of inflation is theoretically eliminated — called also *indexing*

index fund *n* **:** a portfolio made up primarily of stocks listed on a standard index of stock market performance

indicator* *n* **:** any of a group of statistical values (as level of employment and change in the price of industrial raw materials) that taken together give an indication of the health of the economy — see COINCIDENT, LAGGING INDICATOR, LEADING INDICATOR *herein*

individual retirement account *n* **:** a savings account in which a person may deposit up to a stipulated amount each year with the deposits deductible from taxable income and both deposits and interest taxable after the person's retirement

in·do·cyanine green \ˈində+ . . . -\ *n* [[2]*ind-* + *cyanine*] **:** a green tricarbocyanine dye $C_{43}H_{47}N_2NaO_6S_2$ used esp. in testing liver blood flow and cardiac output

indoleamine \ˈ≡ˌ≡ˈ≡(ˌ)≡, ˈ≡ˌ≡≡ˈ≡\ *n* [*indole* + *amine*] **:** any of various indole derivatives (as serotonin or tryptamine) that contain an amine group

in·do·meth·a·cin \ˌindōˈmethəsə̇n\ *n* -s [*indo+ meth-* + *acetic acid* + *-in*] **:** a nonsteroid anti-inflammatory antipyretic analgesic drug $C_{19}H_{16}ClNO_4$ used esp. in the treatment of rheumatoid arthritis

inducer* *n* **:** a substance capable of activating a structural gene by combining with and inactivating a genetic repressor

industrial action *n, Brit* **:** JOB ACTION *herein*

industrial archaeology *n* **:** the study of the buildings, machinery, and equipment of the industrial revolution — **industrial archaeologist** *n*

industrial–revenue bond \≡ˈ≡≡≡ˈ≡≡ˌ≡-\ *n* **:** a revenue bond issued to provide industrial facilities for lease and dependent on the lease revenue for amortization and interest payments

inertial platform *n* **:** an assemblage of devices used in inertial guidance together with the mounting

inertial space *n* **:** a part of space away from the earth assumed to have fixed coordinates so that the trajectory of an object (as a spacecraft or missile) may be calculated in relation to it

in·fan·ti·lize \ˈinfəntᵊlˌīz *sometimes* inˈfantᵊl-\ *vt* -ED/-ING/-S [*infantile* + *-ize*] **1 :** to make or keep infantile **2 :** to treat as if infantile — **in·fan·ti·li·za·tion** \ˌinfantᵊlə̇ˈzāshən, -ᵊlˌīˈz- *sometimes* inˌfantᵊl-\ *n* -s

in·fauna \ˈin+ˌ\ *n* [NL, fr. *in-* [2]in- + *fauna*] **:** benthic fauna living in the substrate and esp. in a soft sea bottom — compare EPIFAUNA *herein* — **in·faunal** \"+\ *adj* — **in·faunally** \"+\ *adv*

infectious bovine rhi·no·tracheitis \-ˈrī(ˌ)nō +\ *n* [NL *rhinotracheitis,* fr. *rhin-* + *tracheitis*] **:** a disease of cattle caused by a virus serologically related to human herpesvirus and characterized by inflammation and ulceration of the nasal cavities and trachea

in–flight \(ˌ)≡ˈ≡\ *adj* [fr. the phrase *in flight*] **1 :** made or carried out while in flight ⟨*in-flight* calculations⟩ **2 :** provided for use or enjoyment while in flight ⟨*in-flight* movies⟩

in·flu·en·tial \ˌinˌflüˈenchəl\ *n* -s [*influential,* adj.] **:** one that has great influence

in·for·mat·ics \ˌinfə(r)ˈmad·iks\ *n pl but sing in constr* [ISV *information* + *-ics*] *chiefly Brit* **:** INFORMATION SCIENCE *herein*

information* *n* **:** the attribute inherent in and communicated by one of two or more alternative sequences or arrangements of something (as nucleotides in DNA or binary digits in a computer program) that produce specific effects

information retrieval *n* **:** the techniques of storing and recovering and often disseminating recorded information esp. through the use of a computerized system

information science *n* **:** the collection, classification, storage, retrieval, and dissemination of recorded knowledge treated both as a pure and as an applied science — **information scientist** *n*

informed consent *n* **:** consent to surgery by a patient or to participation in a medical experiment by a subject after achieving an understanding of what is involved

in·fra·sound \ˈinfrə+ˌ\ *n* [*infra-* + [3]*sound*] **:** a wave phenomenon of the same physical nature as sound but with frequencies below the range of human hearing

inhalation therapy *n* **:** the therapeutic use of inhaled gases and esp. oxygen (as in the treatment of respiratory disease) — **inhalation therapist** *n*

in–house \ˈ;=ˈ=\ *adj* [[1]*in* + [1]*house*] **:** existing, originating, or carried on within a group or organization or its facilities **:** not outside ⟨*in-house* training⟩ ⟨an *in-house* publication⟩ ⟨a company's *in-house* staff⟩ — **in–house** *adv*

ini·tial·ism \əˈnishəˌlizəm\ *n* -s [[2]*initial* + *-ism*] **:** an acronym formed from initial letters; *esp* **:** one (as *RPG*) that is pronounced as separate letters

ini·tial·ize \-ˌlīz\ *vt* -ED/-ING/-S [[1]*initial* + *-ize*] **:** to set to a starting state, position, or value ⟨~ a computer program counter⟩ ⟨~ a diskette⟩ — **ini·tial·iza·tion** \əˌnish(ə)ləˈzāshən\ *n*

initial teaching alphabet *n* [so called because it is used only in the initial stages of teaching reading] **:** a 44-symbol alphabet designed esp. for children who are learning to read English

in·jec·tant \inˈjektənt\ *n* -s [*inject* + *-ant*] **:** a substance that is injected into something

injection* *n* **1 a :** the placing of an artificial satellite or a spacecraft into an orbit or on a trajectory — called also *insertion* **b :** the time or place at which injection occurs **2 :** a mathematical function that is a one-to-one mapping — compare BIJECTION *herein*, SURJECTION *herein*

in·jec·tive \inˈjektiv, -ēv\ *adj* [*inject* + *-ive*] **:** being a one-to-one mathematical function

injector razor *n* **:** a safety razor with a narrow single-edged blade that is forced into place by a blade dispenser

in–joke \ˈ=ˌ=\ *n* [*in* (herein) + *joke*] **:** a joke for or about a select group of people

in–kind \ˈ;=ˈ=\ *adj* **:** consisting of something (as goods or commodities) other than money ⟨*in-kind* relief such as food and health care —D.E. Rosenbaum⟩

in–line \(ˈ;)=ˈ;=\ *adj (or adv)* [*in line*] **:** having the parts or units arranged in a straight line; *also* **:** being so arranged

inner city *n* **:** the usu. older and more densely populated central section of a city — **inner–city** \ˈ;==ˈ;==\ *adj*

inner space *n* **1 :** space at or near the earth's surface and esp. under the sea **2 :** one's inner self

in·numeracy \(ˈ)in +\ *n* [*in-* + *numeracy* (herein)] *Brit* **:** the state of being innumerate

in·numerate \"+\ *adj* [fr. *innumeracy* (herein); after such pairs as E *illiteracy: illiterate*] *Brit* **:** marked by ignorance of mathematics and the scientific approach — **innumerate** *n* -s *Brit*

input \ˈinˌpu̇t, *usu* d·+V\ *vt* **in·put·ted** *or* **input; in·put·ted** *or* **input; in·put·ting; in·puts** [*input*, n.] **:** to enter (as data) into a computer or data processing system

insertion* *n* **:** INJECTION 1 *herein*

in–service* *adj* **:** of, relating to, or being one that is fully employed ⟨*in-service* teachers⟩ ⟨*in-service* police officers⟩

inside* *adv* **:** in prison

instant* *adj* **:** produced or occurring with or as if with extreme rapidity and ease ⟨what the technology of communications now offers us — ~ knowledge on the one hand, and ~ boredom . . . on the other —Arlene Croce⟩ ⟨there are always lots of chicks around for ~ sex —Barbara A. Bannon⟩

in·stant·ize \ˈinstənˌtīz\ *vt* -ED/-ING/-S **:** to make (a food product) instant ⟨*instantized* nonfat milk⟩

instant replay *n* **:** a videotape recording of an action (as a play in football) that can be played back (as in slow motion) immediately after the action has been completed

instruction* *n* **:** a code that tells a computer to perform a particular operation

instrumental* *adj* **:** OPERANT 2 ⟨~ learning⟩ ⟨~ conditioning⟩

in·su·li·no·ma \ˌin(t)sələˈnōmə\ *n, pl* **insulinomas** \-məz\ *or* **insulinoma·ta** \-məd·ə\ [NL, fr. ISV *insulin* + NL *-oma*] **:** a usu. benign insulin-secreting tumor of the islets of Langerhans

in·sur·ance \ənˈshu̇r(ə)n(t)s, *chiefly in southern U.S.* ˈinˌ=(=)\ *adj* **:** being a score (as a run or goal) that adds to a team's lead so that the opponents cannot tie the game with their next score

integral domain *n* **:** a mathematical ring in which multiplication is commutative, which has a multiplicative identity element, and which contains no pair of nonzero elements whose product is zero

integrated circuit *n* **:** a tiny complex of electronic components (as transistors, resistors, and capacitors) and their interconnections produced in or on a single small slice of material (as silicon) — called also *chip, microchip* — **integrated circuitry** *n*

in·te·gro·differential \ˌ;intə̇(ˌ)grō *also* inˌ;teg-\ *adj* [[1]*integral* + *-o-* + *differential*] **:** involving both mathematical integration and differentiation ⟨~ equations⟩

intelligent* *adj* **1 :** guided or controlled by a computer; *esp* **:** using a built-in microprocessor for automatic operation, for processing of input data, or for achieving greater versatility ⟨an ~ terminal⟩ — compare DUMB *herein* **2 :** capable of producing printed material from electronic signals ⟨an ~ office copier⟩

intensive care *adj* **:** having special medical facilities, services, and monitoring devices to meet the needs of gravely ill patients ⟨an *intensive care* unit⟩ — **intensive care** *n*

interactive* *adj* **:** of, relating to, or being a two-way electronic communication system (as a telephone, cable television, or a computer) that involves a user's orders (as for information or merchandise) or responses (as to a poll) — **interactively** *adv*

interception* *n* **:** an intercepted forward pass

in·ter·crural \ˌ;intə(r) +\ *adj* [*inter-* + *crural*] **:** situated or taking place between two crura and esp. in the region of the groin ⟨~ intercourse⟩

in·ter·ethnic \"+\ *adj* [*inter-* + *ethnic*] **:** existing or occurring between ethnic groups

interface* *n* **1 :** the place at which two independent systems meet and act upon or communicate with each other ⟨the ~ between engineering and science⟩ ⟨the man-machine ~⟩; *broadly* **:** an area in which diverse things interact on each other ⟨~ between the known and unknown⟩ **2 :** the means by which interaction or communication is achieved at an interface ⟨an ~ between a computer and a typesetting machine⟩

interface *vt* **1 :** to connect by means of an interface ⟨~ a machine with a computer⟩ **2 :** to serve as an interface for ~ *vi* **1 :** to become interfaced ⟨a system that ~*s* with a computer⟩ **2 :** to interact or coordinate harmoniously ⟨the computer technicians . . . ~ with the flight controllers —H.S.F. Cooper, Jr.⟩

in·ter·fer·on \ˌintə(r)ˈfi(ə)ˌrän\ *n* -s [*interference* + [1]*-on*] **:** any of a group of heat-stable soluble basic antiviral glycoproteins of low molecular weight produced usu. by cells exposed to the action of a virus, sometimes to the action of another intracellular parasite (as a brucella), or experimentally to the action of some chemicals

in·ter·generational \¦intə(r)+\ *adj* [*inter-* + *generational*] **:** existing or occurring between generations ⟨~ conflicts⟩

in·ter·individual \"+\ *adj* [*inter-* + *individual*] **:** involving or taking place between individuals ⟨~ conflicts⟩

in·ter·laboratory \"+\ *adj* [*inter-* + *laboratory*] **:** of, relating to, or engaged in by more than one laboratory

interleave* *vt* **:** to arrange in or as if in alternate layers

in·ter·leu·kin \ˌintə(r)ˈlükən\ *n* -s [*inter-* (as in *interferon*) + *leuk-* + *-in*] **:** any of several compounds of low molecular weight that are produced by lymphocytes or monocytes and that function esp. in regulation of the immune system and esp. cell-mediated immunity

interlock* *n* **1 :** a stretchable fabric made on a circular knitting machine and consisting of two ribbed fabrics joined by interlocking **2 :** a garment made of interlock

1in·ter·media \¦intə(r) +\ *adj* [*inter-* + *media*] **:** involving the simultaneous use of several media

2intermedia \"\ *n* -s [*intermedia,* adj. (herein)] **:** an art form involving the simultaneous use of several media

intermediate* *n* **:** an automobile larger than a compact but smaller than a full-sized automobile

in·ter·mod·al \¦intə(r)¦mōdᵊl\ *adj* [*inter-* + 1*mode* + *-al*] **1 :** being or involving transportation by more than one form of carrier during a single journey **2 :** used for intermodal transportation

interpreter* *n* **:** a computer program that translates an instruction into machine language and executes it before going to the next instruction

in·ter·ro·bang *also* **in·tera·bang** \inˈterəˌbaŋ\ *n* -s [*interrogation* (*point*) + *bang* (printers' slang for *exclamation point*)] **:** a punctuation mark ‽ designed for use esp. at the end of an exclamatory rhetorical question

interrogate* *vt* **:** to give or send out a signal to (as a transponder or computer) for triggering an appropriate response

interrupt *n* [*interrupt,* v.] **:** a feature of a computer that permits the execution of one program to be interrupted in order to execute another; *also* **:** the interruption itself

in·ter·sensory \¦intə(r) +\ *adj* [*inter-* + *sensory*] **:** involving two or more sensory systems ⟨~ factors in memory loss⟩

in·ter·state \ˈintə(r)+ˌ\ *n, often cap* [*inter-* + *state*] **:** any of a system of highways connecting most major U.S. cities

in·ter·stimulus \¦intə(r)+\ *adj* [*inter-* + *stimulus*] **:** of, relating to, or being the interval between the presentation of two discrete stimuli

in·ter·stock \ˈintə(r)+ˌ\ *n* [*inter-* + 1*stock*] **:** a piece inserted between scion and stock in grafting (as to allow union of incompatible varieties or to induce dwarfing)

in·ter·term \"+ˌ\ *n* [*inter-* + *term*] **:** INTERSESSION

interview* *n* **:** a person who is interviewed ⟨he was our ~ that morning —Sally Quinn⟩

interview* *vi* **:** to have an interview (as with a prospective employer) ⟨one of my law school classmates ~*ed* with a . . . law firm in 1967 —Lana Borsook⟩

into* *prep* **:** involved with or interested in ⟨her two children . . . are both ~ art —*New York*⟩

intra-aortic balloon counterpulsation \¦==ˈ=-\ *n* **:** counterpulsation in which circulatory assistance is provided by a balloon inserted in the thoracic aorta which is inflated during diastole and deflated just before systole

in·tra-arterial \¦in·trə, ¦in·(ˌ)trä +\ *adj* [*intra-* + *arterial*] **:** situated or occurring within, administered into, or involving entry by way of an artery ⟨*intra-arterial* chemotherapy⟩ ⟨an *intra-arterial* catheter⟩ — **in·tra-arterially** \"+\ *adv*

in·tra-articular \"+\ *adj* [*intra-* + *articular*] **:** situated within, occurring within, or administered by entry into a joint

in·tra·cardiac \"+\ *also* **in·tra·car·di·al** \¦=(ˌ)=-¦kärdēəl\ *adj* [*intracardiac* fr. *intra-* + *cardiac; intracardial* fr. *intra-* + *cardi-* + *-al*] **:** situated or occurring within, introduced into, or involving entry into the heart ⟨~ surgery⟩ ⟨an ~ catheter⟩ — **in·tra·car·di·al·ly** \-ēəlē\ *adv*

in·tra·day \¦==ˌ=\ *adj* [*intra-* + *day*] **:** occurring in the course of a single day ⟨the market showed wide ~ fluctuations⟩

intradermal test *n* **:** a test for immunity or hypersensitivity made by injecting a minute amount of diluted antigen into the skin

in·tra·galactic \¦in·trə, ¦in·(ˌ)trä +\ *adj* [*intra-* + *galactic*] **:** situated or occurring within the confines of a single galaxy

in·tra·gastric \"+\ *adj* [*intra-* + *gastric*] **:** situated or occurring within the stomach ⟨~ intubation⟩ — **in·tra·gas·tri·cal·ly** \-k(ə)lē\ *adv*

in·tra·governmental \"+\ *adj* [*intra-* + *governmental*] **:** occurring or existing between different branches or departments of government ⟨~ cooperation⟩ ⟨~ competition⟩

in·tra·operative \"+\ *adj* [*intra-* + *operative*] **:** occurring, carried out, or encountered in the course of surgery ⟨~ radiation⟩ ⟨~ infarction⟩ — **in·tra·operatively** \"+\ *adv*

in·tra·personal \"+\ *adj* [*intra-* + *personal*] **:** occurring within the individual mind or self ⟨~ concerns of the aged⟩

in·tra·population \"+\ *adj* [*intra-* + *population*] **:** occurring within or taking place between members of a population ⟨~ allografts⟩

intrauterine device *n* **:** a device (as a spiral of plastic or a ring of stainless steel) inserted and left in the uterus to prevent effective conception — called also *intrauterine contraceptive device, IUD*

in·tra·vascular \¦in·trə, ¦in·(ˌ)trä +\ *adj* [ISV *intra-* + *vascular*] **:** situated in, occurring in, or administered by entry into a blood vessel ⟨~ thrombosis⟩ ⟨an ~ injection⟩ — **in·tra·vascularly** \"+\ *adv*

in·tro·gres·sant \ˌin·trəˈgresᵊnt, -trō-\ *n* -s [*introgression* + 1*-ant*] **:** an individual resulting from and exhibiting evidence of introgression — **introgressant** *adj*

in·tron \ˈinˌträn\ *n* -s [*intragenic region*] **:** a polynucleotide sequence in a nucleic acid that does not code information for protein synthesis and is removed before translation of messenger RNA — compare EXON *herein*

invasive* *adj* **:** involving entry into the living body (as by incision or by insertion of an instrument) ⟨~ diagnostic techniques⟩

inverse* *n* **:** a set element that is related to another element in such a way that the result of applying a given binary operation to them is an identity element of the set — see ADDITIVE INVERSE *herein,* MULTIPLICATIVE INVERSE *herein*

inversely* *adv* **:** in the manner of inverse variation

inversely proportional *adj* **:** related by inverse variation

inverse variation *n* **1 :** mathematical relationship between two variables which can be expressed by an equation in which the product of two variables is equal to a constant **2 :** an equation or function expressing inverse variation — compare DIRECT VARIATION 2 *herein*

investment letter stock *n* **:** LETTER STOCK *herein*

I/O *abbr* input/output

ion–exchange chromatography \ˈ≈≈ˈ≈-\ *n* **:** chromatography in which the separation and deposition of components in the liquid phase is achieved by differences in their rate of migration through a column, layer, or impregnated paper containing an ion-exchange material and by the exchange of ions in solution for those of like charge in the ion-exchange material

ion·o·mer \īˈänəmə(r)\ *n* -s [*ion* + *-o-* + poly*mer*] **:** any of a class of tough synthetic ethylene-based thermoplastic resins consisting of a copolymer containing cross-links formed by ionic bonds

ion·ophore \īˈänə+ˌ\ *n* -s [*ion* + *-o-* + *-phore*] **:** a compound that facilitates transmission of an ion (as of calcium) across a lipid barrier (as in a cell membrane) by combining with the ion or by increasing the permeability of the barrier to it

ion·o·sonde \īˈänəˌsänd\ *n* [ISV *iono*sphere + *sonde*] **:** a device for determining and recording the heights of ionized layers in the ionosphere by shortwaves reflected from them

ion propulsion *n* **:** propulsion of a body by the forces resulting from the rearward discharge of a stream of ionized particles

ion rocket *n* **:** ION ENGINE

IRA \ˌī(ˌ)ärˈā *also* ˈīrə\ *abbr or n* -s individual retirement account *herein*

ir·i·dol·o·gy \ˌi(ə)rəˈdäləjē, -ji\ *n* -ES [*irid-* + *-logy*] **:** the study of the iris of the eye for indications of bodily health and disease — **ir·i·dol·o·gist** \-əjə̇st\ *n* -s

iron maiden *n, sometimes cap I&M* **:** a supposed medieval instrument of torture consisting of an iron frame in human form hinged to admit a victim who was impaled on the spiked interior as the frame closed

irreducible* *adj* **:** incapable of being factored into polynomials of lower degree with coefficients in some given field (as the rational numbers) or integral domain (as the integers) ⟨~ polynomials⟩ ⟨an ~ equation⟩ — **irreducibility*** *n*

ISBN *abbr* International Standard Book Number

iso·androsterone \ˌ¦ī(ˌ)sō *also* ¦ī(ˌ)zō+\ *n* [*iso-* + *androsterone*] **:** EPIANDROSTERONE *herein*

iso·car·box·az·id \¦≈≈ˌkärˈbäksəzə̇d\ *n* -s [*iso-* + *carb-* + *ox-* + *az-* + *-id*] **:** a hydrazide monoamine oxidase inhibitor $C_{12}H_{13}N_3O_2$ used as an antidepressant drug

iso·enzyme \¦īsō *also* ¦īzō +\ *n* [*is-* + *enzyme*] **:** any of two or more chemically distinct but functionally similar enzymes — **iso·enzymatic** \"+\ *or* **iso·enzymic** \"+\ *adj*

iso·ge·ne·ic \ˌīsōjəˈnēik *also* ˌīzō-\ *adj* [*is-* + *-geneic* (as in *syngeneic*)] **:** SYNGENEIC *herein* ⟨an ~ graft⟩

iso·la·to \ˌīsəˈläd·ō *also* ˌīzə-\ *n* -ES [It, adj., isolated — more at ISOLATED] **:** one who is physically or spiritually isolated from his fellowman

iso·met·rics \ˌīsəˈme·triks *also* ˌīzə-\ *n pl but sing or pl in constr* [[1]*isometric* + *-s*] **:** exercise or a system of exercises involving isometric contraction of muscles

isom·e·try \īˈsäməˌtrē\ *n* -ES [*is-* + *-metry*] **:** a mapping of a metric space onto another or onto itself so that the distance between any two points in the original space is the same as the distance between their images in the second space ⟨rotation and translation are *isometries* of the plane⟩

isomorphic* *adj* **:** related by an isomorphism ⟨~ mathematical rings⟩ — **iso·mor·phi·cal·ly** \¦≈(ˌ)≈ˈ≈≈(≈)≈\ *adv*

isomorphism* *n* -s **:** a one-to-one correspondence between two mathematical sets; *esp* **:** a homomorphism that is one-to-one — compare ENDOMORPHISM *herein*

isopycnic* *adj* **:** being or produced by a technique (as centrifugation) in which the components of a mixture are separated on the basis of differences in density

isosceles* *adj, of a trapezoid* **:** having the two nonparallel sides equal

iso·spin \ˈīsəˌspin *also* ˈīzə-\ *n* [*iso*topic *spin* (herein)] **:** a quantum characteristic of a group of closely related subatomic particles (as a proton and a neutron) handled mathematically like ordinary spin with the possible orientations in a hypothetical space specifying the number of particles of differing electric charge comprising the group

isotopic spin *n* **:** ISOSPIN *herein*

isotype* *n* **:** any of the categories of immunoglobulins determined by their physicochemical properties (as molecular weight) and antigenic characteristics that occur in all individuals of a species — compare ALLOTYPE *herein*, IDIOTYPE *herein* — **isotypic*** *adj*

iso·zyme \ˈīsəˌzīm *also* ˈīzə-\ *n* -s [*is-* + *-zyme*] **:** ISOENZYME *herein* — **iso·zy·mic** \¦īsə¦zīmik *also* ¦īzə-\ *adj*

ITA *abbr* initial teaching alphabet *herein*

italian sandwich *n, usu cap I* **:** GRINDER 6

iteration* *n* **1 :** a procedure in which repetition of a sequence of operations yields results successively closer to a desired result **2 :** the repetition of a sequence of computer instructions a specified number of times or until a condition is met — compare RECURSION 2 *herein* **3 :** one execution of a sequence of operations or instructions in an iteration

iterative* *adj* **:** relating to or being an iteration

IUD \ˌīyüˈdē, ˌīˌyü-\ *abbr or n* -s intrauterine device *herein*

J

jackboot* *n* **:** the spirit or policy of militarism or totalitarianism ⟨hurried to completion under threat of Hitler's ~ —*Commonweal*⟩

jackbooted* *adj* **:** ruthlessly and violently oppressive ⟨~ militarism⟩

Ja·cuz·zi \jə'küzē, ja-\ *trademark* — used for a whirlpool bath and a recreational bathing tub or pool

jam* *n* **:** a round in roller derby in which a jammer from each team attempts to circle the course and pass members of the opposing team in order to score points

jammer* *n* **:** a player on a roller derby team who attempts to score during a jam

Jams \'jamz\ *trademark* — used for knee-length loose-fitting swim trunks

japanese bobtail *n, usu cap J&B* **1 :** a breed of short-haired domestic cats that originated in Japan and is characterized by a short stumpy tail resembling a pompom and a coat often marked with solid patches of black, white, and red **2 :** a cat of the Japanese Bobtail breed

japanese quail *n, usu cap J* **:** any of a subspecies (*Coturnix coturnix japonica*) of Old World quail from China and Japan used extensively in laboratory research

ja·pa·nol·o·gist \ˌjapə'näləjəst, jəˌpa'n-\ *n* -s *usu cap* [fr. *Japan* + *-logy* + *-ist*] **:** a specialist in the study of Japan and the Japanese

jap·lish \'japlish\ *n, usu cap* [*Jap*anese + Eng*lish*] **:** Japanese marked by a considerable number of borrowings from English

ja·po·nais·erie \zhäˌpónez(ə)'rē\ *n* -s [F, fr. *japonais* Japanese + *-erie* -ery] **:** a style of art reflecting Japanese qualities or motifs; *also* **:** a work of art in this style

jawbone *vt* [*jawbone,* n.] **:** to talk to or about in order to gain some end

jawboning *n* -s [fr. gerund of *jawbone* (herein)] **:** the use of public appeals (as by a president) to influence the actions esp. of business and labor leaders; *broadly* **:** the use of spoken persuasion

Jaws of Life *trademark* — used for a hydraulic tool that is used esp. to free victims trapped inside wrecked motor vehicles

jay* *n* **:** a marijuana cigarette **:** JOINT

jazz* *n* **:** similar but unspecified things **:** STUFF ⟨I *love* sailing . . . that wind, and the waves, and all that ~ —John Updike⟩

jazz–rock \'=ˌ=\ *n* **:** a blend of jazz and rock music

jesus freak *n, usu cap J & often cap F* [after *Jesus* Christ] **:** a member of a fundamentalist youth group whose life-style includes communal living, Bible study, street preaching, and abstinence from illicit drugs

jet boat *n* **:** a boat propelled by an engine which expels a powerful jet of water

jet lag *n* **:** a condition that is characterized by various psychological and physiological effects (as fatigue and irritability), occurs following long flight through several time zones, and prob. results from disruption of circadian rhythms in the human body — called also *jet fatigue* — **jet–lagged** *adj*

jet set *n* [so called fr. the fact that jet-setters frequently travel by jet] **:** an international social group of wealthy individuals who frequent fashionable resorts — **jet-set·ter** \'jetˌsed·ə(r)\ *n*

Jet·way \'jetˌwā\ *trademark* — used for a telescoping bridge ramp for loading and unloading passengers between an aircraft and a terminal building

jewish princess *n, usu cap J* **:** a daughter of a well-to-do American Jewish family — called also *Jewish American princess;* usu. used disparagingly

jim·mies \'jimēz, -iz\ *n pl* [origin unknown] **:** tiny rod-shaped bits of variously flavored candy often sprinkled on ice cream and pastry **:** SPRINKLES

jive \'jīv\ *adj* [*jive,* n.] *slang* **:** MISLEADING, DECEITFUL, PHONY ⟨if you are late getting to heaven, you will give Saint Peter some ~ excuse —Langston Hughes⟩

job action *n* **:** a temporary action (as a slowdown) by workers as a protest and means toward forcing compliance with demands

job bank *n* **:** a usu. computerized job listing or placement service for the unemployed

job–hopping \'=ˌ==\ *n* -s **:** the practice of moving (as for immediate financial gain) from job to job — **job–hopper** \'=ˌ==\ *n*

jock* *n* [so called fr. the wearing of jockstraps by male athletes] **:** ATHLETE; *esp* **:** a school or college athlete

Jock·ey \'jäkē, -ki\ *trademark* — used for briefs for men

jogging *n* -s [fr. gerund of *jog*] **:** running at a slow even pace esp. for exercise

john* *n, often cap* **:** a prostitute's client

john birch·er \'jän'-\ *n, usu cap J&B* **:** BIRCHER *herein*

join* *n* **:** UNION 1 *herein*

joint* *n* **1** *slang* **:** PRISON **2 :** PENIS — usu. considered vulgar

joint* *adj* **:** being a function of or involving two or more variables and esp. random variables ⟨a ~ probability density function⟩

jo·mon \'jōˌmän\ *adj, often cap* [Jap *jōmon* straw rope pattern; fr. the characteristic method of forming designs on pottery of the period] **:** of, relating to, or typical of a Japanese neolithic cultural period extending from about the 5th or 4th millennium B.C. or earlier to about 200 B.C. and characterized esp. by elaborately ornamented hand-formed unglazed pottery (**Jomon ware**)

jones \'jōnz\ *n* -ES [prob. fr. the name *Jones*] **1** *slang* **:** HABIT, ADDICTION; *esp* **:** addiction to heroin **2** *slang* **:** HEROIN

jordan curve theorem *n, usu cap J* **:** a fundamental theorem of topology: every simple closed curve divides the plane into two regions and is the common boundary between them

jo·seph·son effect \'jōzəfsən- *also* -ōsə-\ *n, usu cap J* [after B.D. *Josephson,* 20th cent. Eng. physicist] **:** the movement of electron pairs through a thin insulator separating two superconductors carrying low current that can be stopped by raising the current in the superconductors above a certain level or by the application of an external voltage

jo·seph·son junction \ˈjōzəfsən- *also* -ōsə-\ *n, usu cap 1st J* [B.D. *Josephson*] **:** an electronic fast-switching device that consists of two layers of superconducting metal separated by a thin layer of insulator and that makes use of the Josephson effect

jou·al \zhü'äl, -'äl\ *n* -s *often cap* [CanF, fr. Joual *joual* horse, fr. F *cheval*] **:** a French patois spoken esp. by uneducated French Canadians

joystick* *n* **:** a manual control for any of various devices (as a computer display) that resembles an airplane's joystick esp. in being capable of motion in two or more directions

jpn *abbr, usu cap* Japan; Japanese

j/psi particle \'jā'sī-\ *n, usu cap J* **:** an unstable neutral fundamental particle of the meson family that has a mass about 6000 times the mass of an electron, has an unusually long lifetime, and is thought to consist of a charmed quark and antiquark pair — called also *J particle, psi particle*

ju·do·ist \'jü(,)dōəst, -üdəwə-\ *n* -s [*judo* + *-ist*] **:** one who is trained or skilled in judo

jug band *n* **:** a band using usu. crude or improvised instruments (as jugs, washboards, and kazoos) to play blues, jazz, and folk music

juice* *n* **1** *slang* **:** LIQUOR **2** *slang* **:** exorbitant interest exacted of a borrower under the threat of violence **3** *slang* **:** INFLUENCE, PULL, CLOUT ⟨a cop may go out of his way to prove that your ~ doesn't influence him — George Frazier⟩ **4 :** a motivating, inspiring, or enabling force or factor ⟨when the creative ~*s* were running high —Eudora Welty⟩

juicer* *n* [*juice* (herein) + *-er*] *slang* **:** a heavy or habitual drinker of alcoholic beverages

juke* *vb* ~ *vi* **:** to juke someone (as in football or basketball) ~ *vt* **:** to fake out of position (as in football)

jump* *vi* **:** to go from one sequence of instructions in a computer program to another ⟨~ to a subroutine⟩

jump* *n* **:** a transfer from one sequence of instructions in a computer program to a different sequence ⟨conditional ~⟩

jump cut *n* **:** a discontinuity or acceleration in the action of a filmed scene brought about by removal of medial portions of the shot — **jump–cut** \'=,=\ *vb*

jumper* *n* **:** JUMP SHOT 3

jumping–jack** \'==,=\ *n* **:** a conditioning exercise performed while standing by jumping from a position with the feet together and arms at the sides to a position with legs spread and hands touching overhead and then to the original position — called also *side-straddle hop*

jumpsuit** \'=,=\ *n* **:** a one-piece garment consisting of a blouse or shirt with attached trousers or shorts

jun \'jün\ *n, pl* **jun** [Korean] **1 :** a monetary unit of No. Korea equal to 1/100 won — see MONEY table *in the Dict* **2 :** a coin or note representing one jun

junk art *n* **:** three-dimensional art made from discarded material (as of metal, mortar, glass, or wood) — **junk artist** *n*

junk food *n* **1 :** food high in calories but low in nutritional value **2 :** something appealing or enjoyable but of little or no real value ⟨the ultimate in *junk food* for young minds —Cleveland Amory⟩

junkie* *n* **:** a person who derives great pleasure from or is dependent on something ⟨sports ~*s*⟩ ⟨computer ~*s*⟩ ⟨an ideal book for opera fans and glitter ~*s* —Anthony Burgess⟩

ju·ri·me·tri·cian \,jürəmə·'trishən\ *n* -s [*jurimetrics* (herein) + [1]*-an*] **:** a specialist in jurimetrics

ju·ri·met·rics \,jürə'me·triks\ *n pl but usu sing in constr* [L *juri-, jus* law + E *-metrics* (as in *econometrics*) — more at JUST] **:** the application of scientific methods to legal problems

ju·ris doctor \'jürəs-\ *n, usu cap J & D* [NL, fr. L, doctor of law] **:** a degree equivalent to bachelor of laws

jury* *n* **:** one (as the public or test results) that will decide — used esp. in the phrase *the jury is (still) out* ⟨on the question of how well it works, the ~ is still out —Martin Mayer⟩

jury–rig \'==,=\ *vt* [back-formation fr. *jury-rigged*] **:** to erect, construct, or arrange in a makeshift fashion

ju·va·bi·one \,jüvə'bī,ōn\ *n* -s [*ju*venile + NL *Abies* (genus name of balsam fir, in which the substance is found) + hormone] **:** PAPER FACTOR *herein*

juvenile hormone *n* **:** an insect hormone that is secreted by the corpora allata, inhibits maturation to the imago, controls maturation of eggs and yolk deposition in the imago, and has been used experimentally to control pest insects by disrupting their life cycles

ju·ve·nil·ize \'jüvənᵊl,īz, -vnəl-\ *vt* -ED/-ING/-S [*juvenile* + *-ize*] **:** to restrain from normal development and maturation **:** prolong the immaturity of ⟨chemicals that ~ insect larvae⟩ — **ju·ve·nil·iza·tion** \,jüvənᵊlə'zāshən, -vnəl-, -ᵊl,ī'z-\ *n* -s

jux·ta·glomerular \'jəkstə+\ *adj* [*juxta-* + *glomerular*] **:** situated near a kidney glomerulus ⟨~ cells⟩

K

k* *n* [*kilo-*] **1 :** THOUSAND ⟨a salary of $14*K*⟩ **2** [fr. the fact that 1024 (2^{10}) is the power of 2 closest to 1000] **:** a unit of computer storage capacity equal to 1024 bytes ⟨a computer memory of 64*K*⟩

k \ˈkā\ *abbr or n* -s *usu cap* [struck] strikeout

k* *abbr* kindergarten

kaf·ka·esque \ˌ¦käfkə¦esk, ¦kaf-\ *adj, usu cap* [Franz *Kafka* †1924 Austrian writer + E *-esque*] **:** of, relating to, or suggestive of Franz Kafka or his writings

kai·nic acid \ˌkīnik-, ˌkān-\ *n* [fr. Gk *kainos* new + E *-ic*] **:** the neurotoxic active principle $C_{10}H_{15}NO_4$ from a dried red alga (*Digenia simplex*) used as an ascaricide

ka·lim·ba \kəˈlimbə, kä-\ *n* -s [of African origin; akin to Bemba *akalimba* zanza, Kimbundu *marimba* xylophone] **:** an African thumb piano derived from the zanza

kal·li·din \ˈkalədən\ *n* -s [G, fr. *kalli*krein + *-d-* (prob. fr. *dekapeptid* peptide having 10 amino acids, fr. *deka-* + *peptid* peptide) + *-in*] **:** either of two vasodilator kinins formed from blood plasma globulin by the action of kallikrein: **a :** BRADYKININ *herein* **b :** one that has the same amino acid sequence as bradykinin with a terminal lysine added

kal·li·kre·in \ˌkaləˈkrēən, kəˈlik-\ *n* -s [G, fr. *kalli-* calli- + pan*kre*as pancreas (fr. Gk) + *-in;* prob. fr. its therapeutic use in pancreatic disorders] **:** a hypotensive proteinase that liberates kinins from blood plasma proteins and is used therapeutically for vasodilation

ka·na·my·cin \ˌkanəˈmīsᵊn, ˌkän-\ *n* -s [NL *kanamyceticus* (specific epithet of *Streptomyces kanamyceticus*) + E *-in*] **:** a broad-spectrum antibiotic from a Japanese soil actinomycete of the genus *Streptomyces* (*S. kanamyceticus*)

kangaroo pocket *n* **:** a large front pocket (as in a winter jacket)

ka·on \ˈkāˌän\ *n* -s [ISV *ka* (fr. *K-meson* — herein) + ²*-on*] **:** an unstable meson of cosmic radiation or produced in high-energy particle collisions with its charged forms being 966.3 times more massive than the electron and its neutral form being 974.6 times more massive than the electron

ka·po·si's sarcoma \ka¦pōs(h)ēz-, ¦kapəs(h)ēz-\ *n, usu cap K* [Moritz *Kaposi* †1902 Hungarian dermatologist] **:** a disease prob. of viral origin affecting esp. the skin and mucous membranes, characterized esp. by the formation of reddish-brown or bluish tumorous plaques on the lower extremities, and formerly limited primarily to elderly men in whom it followed a benign course but now being a major and sometimes fatal disease associated with immunodeficient individuals with AIDS

ka·ra·tsu ware \kəˈrät(ˌ)sü-\ *n, usu cap K* [fr. *Karatsu,* city in Japan] **:** a Japanese ceramic ware traditionally made from about the 16th century at Karatsu on Kyushu island that is probably the earliest glazed Japanese ceramic ware, includes both earthenware and stoneware, and comprises chiefly vessels for chanoyu

karma* *n* **:** VIBRATION 4

kart \ˈkärt\ *n* -s [prob. fr. *GoKart,* a trademark] **:** a miniature motorcar used esp. for racing

kart·ing \ˈkärd·iŋ\ *n* -s [*kart* (herein) + *-ing*] **:** the sport of racing miniature motorcars

kar·yo·gram \ˈkarēəˌgram\ *n* [ISV *kary-* + *-gram*] **:** KARYOTYPE; *esp* **:** a diagrammatic representation of the chromosome complement of an organism

kb *abbr* kilobase *herein*

kbar *abbr* kilobar *herein*

keeper* *n* **:** an offensive football play in which the quarterback runs with the ball

kel·vin \ˈkelvən\ *n* -s [*Kelvin,* adj.] **:** a unit of temperature equal to 1/273.16 of the Kelvin scale temperature of the triple point of water

ken·ya·pi·the·cus \ˌkenyəˈpithəkəs, ˌkēn-, -pəˈthēk-\ *n* [NL, fr. *Kenya,* country in Africa + *-pithecus*] **1** *cap* **:** a genus of ancient prehuman African primates that is held to belong to the human ancestral line and is sometimes included in the genus *Ramapithecus* **2** -ES *usu cap* **:** a primate of the genus *Kenyapithecus*

keogh plan \ˈkē(ˌ)ō-\ *n, usu cap K* [after Eugene James *Keogh* b1907 Am. politician] **:** an individual retirement account for the self-employed — called also *Keogh*

ke·rat·in·o·cyte \kəˈrat(ᵊ)nəˌsīt\ *n* -s [NL, fr. *keratin* + *-o-* + *-cyte*] **:** an epidermal cell that produces keratin

ker·a·to·conus \¦kerəd·ō¦kōnəs\ *n* -ES [NL, fr. *kerat-* + L *conus* cone] **:** cone-shaped protrusion of the cornea

ker·a·top·a·thy \ˌkerəˈtäpəthē\ *n* -ES [ISV *kerat-* + *-pathy*] **:** any noninflammatory disease of the eye

keratosis fol·li·cu·lar·is \-ˌfäləkyə¦lerəs\ *n* [NL *follicularis,* fr. L *folliculus* small sac (dim. of *follis* bag) + L *-aris* -ar] **:** DARIER'S DISEASE *herein*

kernel* *n* **:** a subset of the elements of one set (as a group) that a function (as a homomorphism) maps onto an identity element of another set

kernel sentence *also* **kernel*** *n* **:** a sentence (as "John is big" or "John has a book") exemplifying in a language one of a very small group of the grammatically simplest sentence types or patterns (as noun phrase + be + adjective phrase or noun phrase + verb + noun phrase) which in transformational grammar are the basic stock from which all sentences in that language are derived and in terms of which they can all ultimately be described

ke·to·glu·ta·rate \ˌked·ō(ˌ)glüˈtäˌrāt\ *n* -s [*ketoglutaric* (acid) + ¹*-ate*] **:** a salt or ester of ketoglutaric acid

key* *vi* **:** to observe the position or movement of an opposing player in football in order to anticipate the play — usu. used with *on* ⟨the middle linebacker was ~*ing* on the halfback⟩

key \ˈkē\ *n* -s [by shortening and alter. of *kilo*] *slang* **:** a kilogram esp. of marijuana or heroin

keyboard* *n* **:** a small usu. portable musical instrument that is played by means of a keyboard like that of a piano and that produces a variety of sounds electronically — **keyboard·ist** *n* -s

key club *n* [so called because each member is provided with a key to the premises] **:** an informal private club serving liquor and providing entertainment

keypad \ˈ=ˌ=\ *n* [¹*key* + *pad*] **:** a small often hand-held keyboard

keyset \ˈ=ˌ=\ *n* [¹*key* + ³*set*] **:** KEYBOARD 2

keystroke \ˈ=ˌ=\ *n* [¹*key* + *stroke*] **:** the act or an instance of depressing a key on a keyboard — **keystroke** *vb*

khoum \'küm, 'k̲üm\ *n* -s [native name in Mauritania] **1** : a monetary unit of Mauritania equal to 1/5 ouguiya — see MONEY table *in the Dict* **2** : a coin representing one khoum

kick* *vb* — **kick ass** : to use bluntly forceful or coercive measures in order to achieve a desired end

kick out* *vi* : to turn a surfboard around and drive it over the top of a wave by pushing down on the rear of the board with the foot

kicky* *adj* : providing a kick or thrill ⟨~ violent scenes —Pauline Kael⟩ — often used as a generalized term of approval ⟨~ clothes⟩

kid·nap·ee \ˌkidˌna'pē\ *n* -s [[1]*kidnap* + *-ee*] : a person who has been kidnapped

kid·vid \'kid'vid\ *n* -s [[1]*kid* + *video*] : television programs for children

killer cell *also* **killer t cell** *n, usu cap T* : a T cell that functions in cell-mediated immunity by destroying a cell (as a tumor cell) having a specific antigenic molecule on its surface by causing lysis of the cell or by releasing a nonspecific toxin — compare HELPER T CELL *herein*, SUPPRESSOR T CELL *herein*

ki·lo·bar \'kēlə, 'kilə +ˌ\ *n* [ISV *kilo-* + [7]*bar*] : a unit of pressure equal to 1000 bars — abbr. *kbar*

ki·lo·base \"+ˌ\ *n* [ISV *kilo-* + *-base*] : a unit of measure of the length of a nucleic-acid chain (as of DNA or RNA) that equals one thousand base pairs

ki·lo·baud \" +ˌ\ *n* [ISV *kilo-* + *baud* (herein)] : 1000 baud

ki·lo·bit \" +ˌ\ *n* [ISV *kilo-* + [2]*bit*] **1** : 1000 bits **2** : 1024 bits

ki·lo·byte \"+ˌ\ *n* [ISV *kilo-* + *byte* (herein)] : 1024 bytes

ki·lo·joule \"+ˌ\ *n* [ISV *kilo-* + *joule*] : 1000 joules

kilo·megacycle \'kilə+\ *n* [ISV *kilo-* + *megacycle*] : GIGAHERTZ

ki·lo·oer·sted \'kēlō, 'kilō +\ *n* [ISV *kilo-* + *oersted*] : 1000 oersteds

ki·lo·pascal \"+\ *n* [ISV *kilo-* + *pascal* (herein)] : 1000 pascals

ki·lo·rad \'kēlō, 'kilō +ˌ\ *n* [ISV *kilo-* + *rad*] : 1000 rads

ki·na \'kēnə\ *n, pl* **kina** *also* **kinas** [native name in Papua New Guinea, orig. a kind of seashell] **1** : the basic monetary unit of Papua New Guinea — see MONEY table *in the Dict* **2** : a coin or note representing one kina

kinetic art *n* : art in which movement (as of a motor-driven part or a changing electronic image) is a basic element — **kinetic artist** *n*

ki·net·i·cism \kə'ned·əˌsizəm, kī'-\ *n* -s [*kinetic* (*art*) + *-ism*] : KINETIC ART *herein*

ki·net·i·cist \-ˌsə̇st\ *n* -s [*kinetic* + *-ist*] **1** : a specialist in kinetics **2** : KINETIC ARTIST *herein*

ki·ne·tin \'kīnətə̇n\ *n* -s [*kinet-* + *-in*] : a cytokinin $C_{10}H_9N_5O$ that increases mitosis and callus formation

ki·neto·some \kə'ned·əˌsōm, kī'-\ *n* -s [*kinet-* + [3]*-some*] : BASAL BODY 1

kingside \'=ˌ=\ *n* : the side of a chessboard containing the file on which both kings sit at the beginning of the game

ki·nin \'kīnə̇n\ *n* -s [Gk *kinein* to move, stimulate + E *-in* — more at HIGHT] **1** : any of various polypeptide hormones that are formed locally in the tissues and have their chief effect on smooth muscle **2** : CYTOKININ *herein*

ki·ni·nase \'kīnəˌnās, -āz\ *n* -s [*kinin* (herein) + *-ase*] : an enzyme in blood that destroys a kinin

ki·nin·o·gen \kī'ninəjə̇n\ *n* -s [*kinin* (herein) + *-o-* + *-gen*] : an inactive precursor of a kinin — **ki·nin·o·gen·ic** \(ˌ)=ˌ==ˌjenik\ *adj*

kinky* *adj* **1** : relating to, having, or appealing to bizarre or unconventional tastes esp. in sex ⟨every ~ weirdo thing you want to do —Philip Roth⟩; *also* : being sexually deviant ⟨a ~ baron in leg irons, begging for another spanking —Diana Davenport⟩ **2** : OUTLANDISH, FAR-OUT *herein* ⟨~ clothes⟩ — **kinkiness** *n*

kir \'ki(ə)r\ *n* -s *often cap* [after Felix *Kir* †1968 Fr. clergyman and politician] : a drink made of dry white wine and crème de cassis

kir·li·an photography \ˌki(ə)rlēən-\ *n, usu cap K* [Semyon D. *Kirlian* and Valentina K. *Kirlian fl*1939 Soviet inventors] : a process in which an image is obtained by application of a high-frequency electrical field to an object (as a leaf or metal coin) so that it radiates a characteristic pattern of luminescence that is recorded on photographic film

ki·run·di \kə'ründē\ *n, usu cap* : the Bantu language of the central African republic of Burundi

kiss-and-tell \'==ˌ=\ *adj* : telling details of private matters ⟨*kiss-and-tell* autobiographies⟩

kissing disease *n* [so called fr. the belief that it is frequently transmitted by kissing] : INFECTIOUS MONONUCLEOSIS

kiss of life **1** *Brit* : artificial respiration by the mouth-to-mouth method **2** *Brit* : something that restores vitality

kis·wa·hi·li \(ˌ)kiˌswä'hēlē\ *n, usu cap* : SWAHILI 2

kitchen-sink \ˌ==ˌ=\ *adj, chiefly Brit* : portraying or emphasizing the squalid aspects of modern life ⟨the *kitchen-sink* realism of contemporary British drama —*Current Biog.*⟩

kiwifruit \'kēwēˌ-\ *n* [*kiwi*, nickname for New Zealanders; fr. the fact that it was first established as a commercial crop in New Zealand] : the fruit of the Chinese gooseberry — called also *kiwi*

klick \'klik\ *n* -s [by shortening & alter.] *slang* : KILOMETER

kline·fel·ter's syndrome \'klīnˌfeltə(r)(z)-\ *also* **klinefelter syndrome** *n, usu cap K* [after Harry F. *Klinefelter b*1912 Am. physician] : an abnormal condition in a male characterized by two X and one Y chromosomes, infertility, and smallness of the testicles

kludge *or* **kluge** \'klüj\ *n* -s [origin unknown] : a system and esp. a computer system made up of components that are poorly matched or were orig. intended for some other use

klutz \'kləts\ *n* -ES [Yiddish *klotz, klutz*, fr. G *klotz*, lit., wooden block, fr. MHG *kloz* lumpy mass — more at CLOT] : a clumsy and awkward person — **klutzy** *adj* -ER/-EST

k-meson \'kā+\ *n, usu cap K* [[1]*K* + *meson*] : KAON *herein*

knee-jerk \'=(ˌ)=\ *adj* [*knee jerk*] : readily predictable : AUTOMATIC ⟨*knee-jerk* reactions⟩; *also* : reacting in a readily predictable way ⟨*knee-jerk* liberals⟩

knock off* *vt* **1** : to make a knockoff of ⟨*knocks off* popular dress designs⟩ **2** : to make knockoffs of the designs of ⟨*knock off* a well-known designer⟩

knockoff** \'=ˌ=\ *n* : a copy that sells for less than the original; *broadly* : a copy or imitation of someone or something popular or succecssful

knuckle sandwich *n, slang* : a punch in the mouth

ko·bo \'kō,bō\ *n, pl* **kobo** [alter. of *copper*] **1 :** a monetary unit of Nigeria equal to $^{1}/_{100}$ naira — see MONEY table *in the Dict* **2 :** a coin representing one kobo

kook \'kük\ *n* -s [by shortening and alter. fr. *cuckoo*] **:** one whose ideas or actions are eccentric, fantastic, or insane

kooky *also* **kook·ie** \'kükē\ *adj* **kook·i·er; kook·i·est** [*kook* (herein) + [1]*-y* or *-ie,* alter. (influenced by *-ie*) of [1]*-y*] **:** having the characteristics of a kook **:** CRAZY, OFFBEAT — **kook·i·ly** *adv* — **kook·i·ness** *n* -ES

ko·ra \'kōr(,)ä, 'kór-, -rə\ *n* -s [native name in Senegal] **:** a 21-string musical instrument of African origin that resembles a lute

ko·rat \kō'rät\ *n, usu cap* [fr. *Khorat* plateau, Thailand, where the breed originated] **:** any of a breed of short-haired domestic cats that originated in Thailand and are characterized by a heart-shaped face, a silver-blue coat, and green eyes

kovsh \'kóvsh\ *n, pl* **kov·shi** \-shē\ [Russ, scoop, ladle] **:** a low boat-shaped drinking vessel with a long handle at one end

k particle *n, usu cap K* [[1]*K*] **:** KAON *herein*

krad \'kā,rad\ *n, pl* **krad** *also* **krads** [*kilorad*] **:** KILORAD *herein*

krem·lin·ol·o·gy \,kremlə'näləjē\ *n* -ES *usu cap* [*Kremlin* + *-o-* + *-logy*] **:** the study of the policies and practices of the Soviet Russian government — **krem·lin·olog·i·cal** \¦kremlənᵊl¦äjəkəl\ *adj, usu cap* — **krem·lin·ol·o·gist** \,==ˈ==jəst\ *n* -s *usu cap*

krewe \'krü\ *n* -s [alter. of *crew*] **:** a private organization staging festivities (as parades and balls) during Mardi Gras in New Orleans

kro·neck·er delta \¦krō,nekə(r)-\ *n, usu cap K* [after Leopold *Kronecker* †1891 Ger. mathematician] **:** a function of two variables that is 1 when the variables have the same value and is 0 when they have different values

kru·ger·rand \'krügə,rand, *in So. Afr. usu* -,ránd *or* -,ránt *or* -,ränt\ *n, usu cap* [S.J.P. *Kruger* †1904 So. African statesman + *rand* (herein)] **:** a one-ounce gold coin of the Republic of So. Africa

ku·do \'k(y)üd(,)ō\ *n, pl* **kudos** [back-formation fr. *kudos* (taken as a pl.)] **1 :** AWARD, HONOR ⟨a score of honorary degrees and . . . other ~*s* —*Time*⟩ **2 :** COMPLIMENT, TRIBUTE ⟨to all three should go some kind of special ~ for refusing to succumb —Al Hine⟩

kun·da·li·ni \,kündᵊl'ēnē, -dä'lē-\ *n* -s *often cap* [Skt *kuṇḍalinī,* fr. fem. of *kuṇḍalin* circular, coiled, fr. *kuṇḍala* ring] **:** the yogic life-force that is held to lie coiled at the base of the spine until it is aroused and sent to the head to trigger enlightenment

kung fu \,kəŋ'fü, ,kúŋ-\ *n* [Chin dial.; akin to Chin (Pek) *ch'üan*[2] *fa*[3], lit., boxing principles] **:** any of various Chinese arts of self-defense resembling karate

ku·ru \'kü(,)rü\ *n* -s [native name in New Guinea, lit., trembling] **:** a fatal disease of the nervous system that is caused by a slow virus, resembles scrapie in sheep, and occurs among tribesmen in eastern New Guinea

ku·ta·ni \kú'tänē\ *or* **kutani ware** *n* -s *usu cap K* [fr. *Kutani,* village in Japan] **:** a Japanese porcelain orig. produced in and about the village of Kutani on Honshu island beginning in the mid-17th century and esteemed for originality of design and coloring

[1]**kvetch** \'kvech, 'kfe-, kə'vech\ *vi* -ED/-ING/-ES [Yiddish *kvetchen,* lit., to squeeze] **:** to complain habitually **:** GRIPE ⟨~*es* constantly about being 33 years old —H.F. Waters⟩

[2]**kvetch** \"\ *n* -ES [Yiddish, complainer, fr. *kvetch* pinch; akin to G *quetschen* to bruise] **1 :** an habitual complainer **2 :** COMPLAINT

kwa·cha \'kwächə\ *n, pl* **kwacha** [native name in Zambia, lit., dawn] **1 :** the basic monetary unit of Malawi and Zambia — see MONEY table *in the Dict* **2 :** a note representing one kwacha

kwan·za \'kwänzə\ *n, pl* **kwanza** *or* **kwanzas** [perh. fr. Swahili *kwanza* first] **1 :** the basic monetary unit of Angola — see MONEY table *in the Dict* **2 :** a coin or note representing one kwanza **3** *usu cap* **:** an Afro-American festival held late in December

KWIC \'kwik\ *n* -s [*key word in context*] **:** a computer-generated index alphabetized on a keyword that appears within a portion of its context

L

la·bano·ta·tion \ˌlābənō'tāshən, ˌlab-; ləˌbän(ˌ)nō-\ *n, usu cap* [fr. Rudolf von *Laban* †1958 Czech dance theorist + *notation*] **:** LABAN SYSTEM

labor–intensive \ˌ⸗⸗ˈ⸗⸗\ *adj* [¹*labor* + *intensive*] **:** having high labor costs per unit of output; *esp* **:** requiring greater expenditure on labor than in capital

lab·y·rin·thec·to·my \ˌlabə(ˌ)rin'thektəmē\ *n* -ES [*labyrinth* + *-ectomy*] **:** surgical removal of the labyrinth of the ear

la·combe \lə'kōm\ *n* [fr. *Lacombe* Experiment Station, Lacombe, Alta., Canada, where the breed was developed] **1** *usu cap* **:** a breed of white bacon-type swine developed in Canada from Landrace, Chester White, and Berkshire stock **2** -s *often cap* **:** an animal of the Lacombe breed

lactate dehydrogenase *n* **:** any of a group of isoenzymes that catalyze reversibily the conversion of pyruvic acid to lactic acid, are found esp. in the liver, kidneys, striated muscle, and the myocardium, and tend to accumulate in the body when these organs or tissues are diseased or injured

lactic dehydrogenase *n* **:** LACTATE DEHYDROGENASE *herein*

lac·to·peroxidase \ˌlak(ˌ)tō+\ *n* [*lact-* + *peroxidase*] **:** a peroxidase that is found in milk and saliva and is used to catalyze the iodination of tyrosine-containing proteins (as thyroglobulin)

la·e·trile \'lāəˌtril, - -trəl\ *n* -s *often cap* [fr. *laevorotarynitrile* (fr. *laev-* + *rotary* + *nitrile*)] **:** a drug derived from apricot pits that contains amygdalin and has been used in the treatment of cancer although of unproved effectiveness

laf·fer curve \'lafər-\ *n, usu cap L* [Arthur *Laffer b*1940 Am. economist] **:** a diagram shaped like a normal curve that is intended to show the relationship between tax rates and tax revenues

lagging indicator *n* **:** an economic indicator (as spending on new plants and equipment) that more often than not maintains an existent trend for some time after the state of the economy has turned onto an opposite trend — called also *lagger*

laid–back \ˌ⸗ˈ⸗\ *adj* **:** having a relaxed style or character ⟨*laid-back* music⟩ ⟨a *laid-back* attitude⟩

la·maze \lə'mäz\ *adj, usu cap* [fr. Fernand *Lamaze* †1957 Fr. obstetrician] **:** relating to or being a method of childbirth that involves psychological and physical preparation by the mother in order to suppress pain and facilitate delivery without drugs

lambda* *or* **lambda particle** *n* **:** an uncharged unstable subatomic particle that has a mass 2183 times that of an electron and decays typically into a nucleon and a pion

lame* *adj, slang* **:** not being in the know **:** SQUARE

lame \'lām\ *n* -s *slang* **:** a person who is not in the know

LAN *abbr or n* -s local area network *herein*

lander* *n* **:** one that lands; *esp* **:** a space vehicle that is designed to land on a celestial body (as the moon or a planet)

landmark* *n* **:** a structure (as a building) of unusual historical and usu. aesthetic interest; *esp* **:** one that is officially designated and set aside for preservation

lane cake *n* [perh. fr. the name *Lane*] **:** a white layer cake with a rich filling usu. containing whiskey or wine, pecans, coconut, raisins, and candied fruit

lan·gous·tine \ˌlaŋgə'stēn, läⁿgüstēn\ *also* **lan·gos·ti·no** \ˌlaŋgə'stēnō\ *n, pl* **langoustines** *also* **langostinos** [*langoustine,* fr. F, dim. of *langouste; langostino,* fr. Sp, dim of *langosta* spiny lobster, locust, fr. (assumed) VL *lacusta* — more at LOCUST] **:** a large prawn

language* *n* **:** MACHINE LANGUAGE *herein*

lan·tian man \ˈlanˌtyan-\ *also* **lan–t'ien man** \-ˌtyen-\ *n, usu cap L* [fr. *Lant'ien,* district in Shensi province, China] **:** an extinct man known from parts of a skull excavated in China and now classified with various other extinct men as a member of the genus *Homo* (*H. erectus*)

lap·a·ro·scope \'lap(ə)rəˌskōp\ *n* [ISV *laparo-* (fr. Gk. *lapara* flank, fr. *laparos* slack, loose) + *-scope*] **:** a long slender optical instrument for insertion through the abdominal wall that is used to visualize the interior of the peritoneal cavity

lap·a·ros·co·py \ˌlapə'räskəpē\ *n* -ES [ISV *laparo-* + *-scopy*] **1 :** visual examination of the interior of the abdomen by means of a laparoscope **2 :** an operation involving laparoscopy; *esp* **:** one for sterilization of the female or for removal of ova that involves use of a laparoscope to guide surgical procedures within the abdomen — **lap·a·ro·scop·ic** \-ərə'skäpik\ *adj* — **lap·a·ros·co·pist** \-ə'räskəpəst\ *n* -s

lap belt *n* **:** a seat belt that fastens across the lap

la·place transform \lə'pläs-, -las-\ *n, usu cap L* [after Pierre Simon de *Laplace* †1827 Fr. astronomer and mathematician] **:** a transformation of a function $f(x)$ into the function

$$g(t) = \int_0^\infty e^{-xt} f(x)dx$$

that is useful esp. in reducing the solution of an ordinary linear differential equation with constant coefficients to the solution of a polynomial equation

large–scale integration \ˈ⸗ˈ⸗-\ *n* **:** the process of placing a large number (as hundreds) of circuits on a small semiconductor chip — abbr. *LSI*

lase \'lāz\ *vi* -ED/-ING/-s [back-formation fr. *laser*] **:** to emit coherent light

laser disc *n* **:** OPTICAL DISC *herein; esp* **:** one used in a video game

l–as·par·a·gi·nase \ˈelaˈsparəjəˌnās, -āz\ *n* -s *usu cap L* [*L-* (levorotatory) + *asparagine* + *-ase*] **:** an enzyme that breaks down the physiologically commoner form of asparagine, is obtained esp. from bacteria, and is used esp. to treat leukemia

las·sa fever \ˌlasə-\ *n, usu cap L* [fr. *Lassa,* village in Nigeria] **:** a virus disease esp. of Africa that is characterized by a high fever, headaches, mouth ulcers, muscle aches, small hemorrhages under the skin, heart and kidney failure, and a high mortality rate

last hurrah *n* [*The Last Hurrah* (1956) by Edwin O'Connor †1968 Am. novelist] **:** a last effort or attempt ⟨his unsuccessful Senate run was his *last hurrah* — R.W. Daly⟩

latchkey child *n* **:** a young child of working parents who spends part of the day at home unsupervised

latent root *n* **:** an eigenvalue of a matrix

lateral condyle *n* **:** a condyle on the outer side of the lower extremity of the femur; *also* **:** a corresponding eminence on the upper part of the tibia that articulates with the lateral condyle of the femur — compare MEDIAL CONDYLE *herein*

lateral thinking *n* **:** thinking that is not deductive

lath·y·rit·ic \ˌlathəˈrid·ik\ *adj* [*lathy*rism + *-itic*] **:** of, relating to, affected with, or characteristic of lathyrism ⟨~ rats⟩

lath·y·ro·gen \ˈlathərəˌjen, -jən\ *n* -s [*lathyr*ism + *-o-* + *-gen*] **:** any of a group of nucleophilic compounds that tend to cause lathyrism and inhibit collagen cross-linking — **lath·y·ro·gen·ic** \ˌ≈≈≈ˈjenik\ *adj*

la·tic·i·fer \lāˈtisəfə(r)\ *n* -s [ISV *latici-* (fr. NL *latic-, latex*) + *-fer*] **:** a plant cell or vessel that contains latex

latin americanist *n, usu cap L&A* **:** a specialist in Latin American civilization

lattice* *n* **:** a mathematical set that has some elements ordered and that is such that for any two elements there exists a greatest element in the subset of all elements less than or equal to both and a least element in the subset of all elements greater than or equal to both

laugher* *n* **:** something (as a game or contest) that is easily won or handled

launch vehicle *n* **:** a rocket used to launch a satellite or spacecraft

launder* *vt* **:** to cause (as illegally obtained money) to appear legitimate by using an outside party to conceal the true source

laundry list *n* [so called fr. the listing of articles of clothing sent to a laundry] **:** a usu. long list of items ⟨the *laundry list* of new consumer-protection bills —N.C. Miller⟩

lavaliere microphone *n* **:** a small microphone hung around the neck of the user

law of parsimony* **:** OCKHAM'S RAZOR

law·ren·cium \lòˈren(t)sēəm, lə'-, -nch(ē)əm\ *n* -s [NL, fr. Ernest O. *Lawrence* †1958 Am. physicist + NL *-ium*] **:** a short-lived radioactive element of atomic number 103 that is produced artificially from californium — symbol *Lr;* see ELEMENT table *in the Dict*

layabout \ˈ≈≈ˌ≈\ *n* -s [fr. the phrase *lay about,* nonstandard alter. of *lie about*] *chiefly Brit* **:** IDLER 1

lay–by* *n* **:** the final operation (as a last cultivating) in the growing of a field crop

layer* *vt* **:** to wear (clothes) in layers ~ *vi* **:** to form out of superimposed layers

layperson \ˈ≈ˌ≈≈\ *n* **:** LAYMAN

lazy eye *n* [so called fr. the fact that a person suffering from this condition uses only one eye] **:** AMBLYOPIA; *also* **:** an eye affected with amblyopia

lazy eye blindness *n* **:** AMBLYOPIA

LCD \ˌel(ˌ)sēˈdē\ *n* -s [*l*iquid *c*rystal *d*isplay] **:** a constantly operating display (as of the time in a digital watch) that consists of segments of a liquid crystal whose reflectivity varies according to the voltage applied to them

l cell *n, usu cap L* **:** a fibroblast cell of a strain isolated from mice and used esp. in virus research

LDC \ˌel(ˌ)dēˈsē\ *abbr or n* -s **:** a less developed country

LDH *abbr* lactate dehydrogenase; lactic dehydrogenase

l–do·pa \(ˈ)elˈdōpə\ *n, usu cap L* [*l-* + *dopa*] **:** the levorotatory form of dopa found esp. in broad beans or prepared synthetically and used in treating Parkinson's disease

leading indicator *n* **:** an economic indicator (as the level of corporate profits or of stock prices) that more often than not shows a change in direction before a corresponding change in the state of the economy — called also *leader*

leaf·let \ˈlēflət, *usu* -əd·+V\ *vb* **leafleted** *or* **leafletted; leafleted** *or* **leafletted; leafleting** *or* **leafletting; leaflets** [*leaflet,* n.] *vi* **:** to pass out leaflets ~ *vt* **:** to pass out leaflets to — **leaf·le·teer** \ˌlēfləˈti(ə)r\ *n* -s

leaky* *adj* **:** relating to or being a mutant gene that changes the structure of the protein and esp. an enzyme that it determines so that some but not all of its biological activity is lost; *also* **:** being such a protein with subnormal activity

lean* *vb* — **lean on :** to apply pressure to **:** COERCE

learning curve *n* **:** PRACTICE CURVE; *esp* **:** one that graphs the decline in unit costs with cumulative output

leash law *n* **:** a usu. municipal ordinance requiring dogs to be restrained when not confined to their owners' property

[1]lech \ˈlech\ *n* -ES [by shortening] **1 :** [2]LETCH **2 :** LECHER

[2]lech \"\ *vi* -ED/-ING/-ES [[1]*lech* (herein)] **:** to experience sexual desire

LED \ˌel(ˌ)ēˈdē, ˈled\ *n* -s [*l*ight-*e*mitting *d*iode] **:** a semiconductor diode that emits light when subjected to an applied voltage and that is usu. used in an electronic display (as for a pocket calculator or a digital watch)

left field* *n* **:** a position far from the mainstream (as of prevailing opinion)

legal pad *n* **:** a writing tablet of usu. $8^1/_2$ by 14 inch ruled yellow paper

le·gion·el·la \ˌlējəˈnelə\ *n, cap* [NL, fr. E *legion*naire + NL *-ella*] **:** a genus of gram-negative rod-shaped bacteria that includes the causative agent (*L. pneumophila*) of Legionnaires' disease

legionnaires'disease *also* **legionnaire's disease** *n, usu cap L* [so called fr. its first recognized occurrence during the 1976 American Legion convention] **:** a lobar pneumonia caused by a bacterium of the genus *Legionella* (*L. pneumophila*)

leish·man–don·o·van body \ˌlīshmənˈdänəvən-, -ˈdən-\ *n, usu cap L&D* [fr. Sir William B. *Leishman* †1926 Eng. army surgeon & Charles *Donovan* †1951 Irish physician] **:** a protozoan of the genus *Leishmania* (esp. *L. donovani*) in its nonmotile stage that is found esp. in cells of the skin, spleen, and liver of individuals affected with leishmaniasis and esp. kala-azar — compare DONOVAN BODY *in the Dict*

leisure suit *n* **:** a suit consisting of a shirt jacket and matching trousers for informal wear

lek·var \ˈlekˌvär, -ˌvá(r\ *n* -s [Hung] **:** a prune butter used as a pastry filling

LEM \ˈlem\ *abbr or n* -s lunar excursion module *herein*

lem·ma·tize \ˈleməˌtīz, -ədˌīz\ *vt* -ED/-ING/-s [fr. *lemmata,* pl. of [1]*lemma* + *-ize*] **:** to sort (words in a corpus) in order to group with a lemma all its variant and inflected forms — **lem·ma·ti·za·tion** \ˌleməd·əˈzāshən, -əˌtīˈz-\ *n* -s

leo* *n, usu cap* **:** one born under the astrological sign Leo

le·one \lēˈōn\ *n, pl* **leones** *or* **leone** [fr. Sierra *Leone,* Africa] **1 :** the basic monetary unit of Sierra Leone — see MONEY table *in the Dict* **2 :** a note representing one leone

le·oni·an \lēˈōnēən\ *n* -s *usu cap* [fr. *leon-,* alter. (perh. influenced by *leonine*) of *Leo* + *-ian*] **:** LEO *herein*

leo·nid \ˈlēənəd\ *n, pl* **leo·nids** *or* **le·on·i·des** \lēˈänə̇ˌdēz\ *usu cap* [L *Leon-, Leo,* a constellation, lit., lion + E [1]*-id;* fr. their appearing to radiate from a point in the constellation Leo] **:** any of the meteors in a meteor shower occurring every year about November 14

lep·ton·ic \(ˈ)lepˈtänik\ *adj* [*lepton* + *-ic*] **:** of, relating to, or producing a lepton ⟨∼ decay of a hyperon⟩

lep·to·spire \ˈleptəˌspī(ə)r, -īə\ *n* -s [by alter.] **:** LEPTOSPIRA 2

lesch–ny·han syndrome \ˈleshˈnīən-\ *also* **lesch–nyhan disease** *n, usu cap L&N* [after Michael *Lesch* *b*1939 Am. cardiologist and W.L. *Nyhan* *b*1926 Am. pediatrician] **:** a rare and usu. fatal genetic disorder of male children that is transmitted as a recessive trait linked to the X chromosome and that is characterized by hyperuricemia, mental retardation, spasticity, compulsive biting of the lips and fingers, and a deficiency of an enzyme that conserves hypoxanthine in the body by limiting its conversion to uric acid

lesion *vt* -ED/-ING/-S [*lesion,* n.] **:** to produce lesions in

let* *vb* — **let it all hang out :** to reveal one's true feelings **:** act without dissimulation — **let the chips fall where they may :** to act knowing that the consequences may prove to be undesirable or disadvantageous

letter bomb *n* **:** an explosive device concealed in an envelope and mailed to the intended victim

letterform \ˈ==ˌ=\ *n* **:** the shape of a letter of an alphabet esp. from the standpoint of design or development

letter quality *n* [[1]*letter* (missive)] **:** printing produced by a computer printer in solid letters similar to or clearer than those produced by a conventional typewriter

let·ter·set \ˈ==ˌset\ *n* -s [*letter*press + off*set*] **:** DRY OFFSET

letter stock *n* [so called fr. the letter signed by the purchaser stating that the stock is acquired for investment and not for public sale] **:** restricted and unregistered stock that may not be sold to the general public without undergoing registration

leu·ke·mic \lüˈkēmik\ *n* -s [*leukem*ia + [2]*-ic*] **:** a person suffering from leukemia

leu·ko·dys·tro·phy \ˌlükōˈdistrəfē\ *n* [*leuc-* + *dystrophy*] **:** any of several genetically determined diseases characterized by progressive degeneration of the white matter of the brain

leu·ko·tri·ene \ˌlükōˈtrīˌēn\ *n* -s [*leuko*cyte + *-triene;* fr. the discovery of the substances in leukocytes] **:** any of a group of substances related to the prostaglandins that are generated in basophils, mast cells, macrophages, and human lung tissue from polysaturated fatty acids and esp. arachidonic acid by lipoxygenase-catalyzed oxygenation and that participate in allergic responses (as bronchoconstriction in asthma)

lev·al·lor·phan \ˌlevəˈlȯrˌfan, -fən\ *n* -s [*lev-* + *all*yl + *morph*ine + [3]*-an*] **:** a drug $C_{19}H_{25}NO$ related to morphine that is used to counteract morphine poisoning

level of significance : the probability of rejecting the null hypothesis in a statistical test when it is true — called also *significance level*

leverage* *n* **1 a :** borrowed money or its use to supplement capital or to increase the earning power of a relatively small investment **b :** the ability of a small investment to produce a large return ⟨∼ is so great with any options strategy that . . . this portfolio can double in just a few months —M.G. Ansbacher⟩ **c :** the advantage gained by using leverage ⟨it gave business healthy ∼: business could do more with less of its own money — Chris Welles⟩ **2 :** the ratio of debt to equity ⟨three other critical performance measures: return on assets, ∼, and return on equity —*Business Week*⟩

leverage *vt* -ED/-ING/-S [*leverage,* n.] **:** to provide (as a corporation) or supplement (as money) with leverage ⟨has stretched and *leveraged* capital —*Fortune*⟩; *also* **:** to enhance as if by supplying with financial leverage ⟨who use tools to ∼ personal capabilities to the limit —*advt*⟩

lever·aged \ˈlev(ə)rijd, ˈlēv-\ *adj* **1 :** having a high proportion of debt relative to equity ⟨mismanaged, unwisely ∼, and highly illiquid corporations —N.A. Bailey⟩ **2** *of the purchase of a company* **:** made with borrowed money that is secured by the assets of the company bought ⟨a ∼ buyout⟩

levo·do·pa \ˈlevəˌdōpə\ *n* **:** L-DOPA *herein*

lex·i·cal·iza·tion \ˌleksə̇kələˈzāshən\ *n* -s [*lexical* + *-ization*] **1 :** the realization of a meaning in a single word or morpheme of a language rather than in a grammatical construction **2 :** the treatment of a formerly freely composed, grammatically regular, and semantically transparent phrase or inflected form as a formally or semantically idiomatic expression — **lex·i·cal·ize** \ˈ===ˌlīz\ *vt* -ED/-ING/-S

lex·is \ˈleksə̇s\ *n, pl* **lex·es** \-kˌsēz\ [Gk, speech, word — more at LEXICON] **:** VOCABULARY, WORD-STOCK

lib \ˈlib\ *n* -s [by shortening] **:** LIBERATION *herein*

lib·ber \ˈlibə(r)\ *n* -s [*lib* (herein) + [2]*-er*] **:** one who advocates liberation ⟨a women's ∼⟩

liberation* *n* **:** a movement seeking equal rights and status for a group ⟨women's ∼⟩

libra* *n, usu cap* **:** one born under the astrological sign Libra

li·bran \ˈlēbrən, ˈlīb-\ *n* -s *usu cap* [*libra* + E *-an*] **:** LIBRA *herein*

Lib·ri·um \ˈlibrēəm\ *trademark* — used for a preparation of chlordiazepoxide

licensed practical nurse *n* **:** a person trained and licensed (as by a state) to provide routine care for the sick —abbr. *LPN*

licensed vocational nurse *n* **:** a licensed practical nurse authorized by license to practice in California or Texas —abbr. *LVN*

li·cen·te \lə̇ˈsentē\ *n, pl* **licente** *or* **li·cen·ti** \-tē\ [native name in Lesotho] **:** a unit equal to $^{1}/_{100}$ loti — see MONEY table *in the Dict*

lid* *n* **:** an ounce of marijuana

li·dar \ˈlīˌdär\ *n* -s [*l*ight + ra*dar*] **:** a device or system for locating an object that is similar in operation to radar but emits pulsed laser light instead of microwaves

lie algebra \ˈlē-\ *n, usu cap L* [after Sophus *Lie* †1899 Norw. mathematician] **:** a linear algebra which has the multiplicative operation denoted by [,] and is bilinear such that

$$[aA + bB, C] = a[A,C] + b[B,C] \quad \text{and} \quad [A, aB + bC] = a[A,B] + b[A,C]$$

and satisfies the conditions that

$$[A,A] = 0 \quad \text{and} \quad [[A,B],C] + [[B,C],A] + [[C,A],B] = 0$$

where *A, B, C* are any vectors in the vector space and *a, b, c* are scalars from the associated field

lie group *n, usu cap L* [Sophus *Lie*] **:** a topological group for which the coordinates of the product of two elements are functions of the coordinates of the elements themselves and the coordinates of the inverse of an element are functions of the coordinates of the element itself and for which all derivatives of these functions exist and are continuous

life list *n* **:** a record kept of all birds sighted and identified by a birder

lifer* *n* **1 :** a career member of the armed forces **2 :** a person who has made a life-long commitment (as to a way of life)

life science *n* **:** a branch of science (as biology, medicine, anthropology, or sociology) that deals with living organisms and life processes — usu. used in pl. — **life scientist** *n*

life–support system \ˈ≈ˌ≈-\ *n* **:** a system that provides all or some of the items (as oxygen, food, water, control of temperature and pressure, disposition of carbon dioxide and body wastes) necessary for maintaining life or health: as **a :** one used to maintain the health of a person or animal in outer space, underwater, or in a mine **b :** one used to maintain the life of an injured or ill person unable to maintain certain physiological processes without artificial support **c :** BIOSPHERE 1

lifting body *n* **:** a maneuverable rocket-propelled wingless vehicle that is capable of travel in aerospace or in the earth's atmosphere where its lift is derived from its shape and that can be landed on the ground

li·gase \ˈlīˌgās, -ˌgāz\ *n* -s [ISV *lig-* (fr. L. *ligare* to bind, tie) + *-ase* — more at LIGATURE] **:** SYNTHETASE

light* *also* **lite** *adj* **:** made with a lower calorie content or with less of some ingredient (as salt or fat) than usual ⟨~ beer⟩ ⟨~ oleomargarine⟩ ⟨~ salad dressing⟩

light–adapt·ed \ˈ≈ˌ≈\ *adj* **:** adjusted for vision in bright light **:** having undergone light adaptation

light chain *n* **:** either of the two smaller of the four polypeptide chains that are subunits of antibodies — compare HEAVY CHAIN *herein*

light–day \ˈ≈ˌ≈\ *n* **:** a unit of length in astronomy equal to the distance that light travels in one day in a vacuum

light–emitting diode \ˈ≈ˌ≈-\ *n* **:** LED *herein*

light guide *n* **:** fiber optics used esp. for telecommunication with light waves

light–hour \ˈ≈ˌ≈\ *n* **:** a unit of length in astronomy equal to the distance that light travels in one hour in a vacuum

light pen *n* **:** a pen-shaped device for a computer that when held to a point on a video screen allows the computer to sense the pen's position and that is used for direct input of data

light pipe *n* **:** fiber optics or a solid transparent plastic rod used for transmitting light

light pollution *n* **:** artificial skylight (as from city lights) that interferes with astronomical observations

light reaction *n* **:** the phase of photosynthesis that requires the presence of light and that involves photophosphorylation

light show *n* **:** a kaleidoscopic display of colored lights, slides, and films

light water *n* **:** WATER 1a — compare HEAVY WATER *in the Dict*

light–year* *n* **:** a very great distance — usu. used in pl. to emphasize contrast ⟨only minutes from downtown, it is *light-years* away from the bustle of modern Japan — George O'Brien⟩

lig·no·caine \ˈlignəˌkān\ *n* -s [*lign-* + *-caine*] **:** LIDOCAINE

like \(ˌ)līk\ *interj* [[5]*like*] — used chiefly in informal speech as a meaningless expletive or intensifier or to lessen the emphasis of a preceding or following word or phrase ⟨I'm ~ the straightest member of my family —Huey Lewis⟩

li·ku·ta \ləˈküd·ə, (ˈ)lēˌk-\ *n, pl* **ma·ku·ta** \(ˈ)mäˌk-\ [of Niger-Congo origin; prob. akin to obs. Nupe *kuta* stone] **1 :** a monetary unit of Zaire equal to $^1/_{100}$ zaire — see MONEY table *in the Dict* **2 :** a coin representing one likuta

li·lan·geni \ˌlē(ˌ)läŋˈ(g)enē\ *n, pl* **ema·lan·geni** \ˌemə(ˌ)läŋˈ(g)enē\ [native name in Swaziland] **1 :** the basic monetary unit of Swaziland — see MONEY table *in the Dict* **2 :** a coin or note representing one lilangeni

limbic* *adj* **:** of, relating to, or being the limbic system of the brain

limbic system *n* **:** a group of subcortical structures (as the hypothalamus, the hippocampus, and the amygdala) of the brain that are concerned esp. with emotion and motivation

lim·bo \ˈlim(ˌ)bō\ *n* -s [native name in West Indies] **:** a West Indian acrobatic dance orig. for men that involves bending over backward and passing under a horizontal pole which is lowered slightly for each successive pass

limit point *n* **:** a point that is related to a set of points in such a way that every neighborhood of the point no matter how small contains another point belonging to the set — called also *point of accumulation*

limo \ˈlim(ˌ)ō\ *n* -s [by shortening] **:** LIMOUSINE

lim·ou·sin \ˈliməˌzēn, ˌ≈ˈ≈, *F* lēmüzaⁿ\ *n, usu cap* [F, of or relating to Limoges, France] **1 :** a French breed of medium-sized yellow-red cattle bred esp. for meat **2** -s **:** an animal of the Limousin breed

limp·en \ˈlimpən\ *vi* -ED/-ING/-S [[3]*limp* + [2]*-en*] **:** to become limp ⟨~*ed* instantly and fell —Carson McCullers⟩

limp–wristed \ˈ≈ˌristəd\ *adj* [[1]*limp* + *wrist* + *-ed*] **1 :** EFFEMINATE **2 :** WEAK, FLABBY

lin·ac \ˈlinˌak\ *n* -s [*lin*ear *ac*celerator] **:** LINEAR ACCELERATOR

lin·co·my·cin \ˌliŋkəˈmīsᵊn\ *n* -s [*linco-* (fr. *Streptomyces lincolinensis,* a streptomyces) + *-mycin*] **:** an antibiotic $C_{18}H_{34}N_2O_6S$ obtained from an actinomycete of the genus *Streptomyces* (*S. lincolnensis*) and found effective esp. against cocci

line* *n* **1 :** any circuit in an electronic communication system **2 :** a telephone connection ⟨tried to get a ~⟩; *also* **:** an individual telephone extension ⟨a call on ~ 2⟩ **3 :** any of the successive horizontal rows of picture elements on a television screen — **on line 1 :** in or into operation ⟨base load generating plants take about ten years to bring *on line* —*Resources*⟩ **2 :** in line

linear* *adj* **1 :** composed of simply drawn lines with little attempt at pictorial representation ⟨~ script⟩ **2 a :** relating to, concerned with, or influenced by the sequential structure of the printed line ⟨~ learning patterns⟩ **b :** arranged or presented in a logical or temporal sequence ⟨~ procedures⟩ ⟨the march of events is strictly ~ — Robert Towers⟩

linear A *n, usu cap L* **:** a linear form of writing used in Crete from the 18th to the 15th centuries B.C.

linear algebra *n* **1 :** a branch of mathematics that is concerned with mathematical structures closed under the operation of addition and scalar multiplication and with their applications and that includes the theory of systems of linear equations, matrices, determinants, vector spaces, and linear transformations **2 :** a mathematical ring which is also a vector space with scalars from an associated field and whose multiplicative operation is such that $(aA)(bB) = (ab)(AB)$ where a and b are scalars and A and B are vectors — called also *algebra*

linear alkylate sulfonate *n* **:** a biodegradable salt of sulfonic acid used in detergents as a surface-active agent
linear B *n, usu cap L* **:** a linear form of writing employing syllabic characters and used at Knossos on Crete and on the Greek mainland from the 15th to the 12th centuries B.C. for documents in the Mycenaean language
linear combination *n* **:** a mathematical entity (as $4x + 5y + 6z$) which is composed of sums and differences of elements (as variables, matrices, or functions) whose coefficients are not all zero
linear dependence *n* **:** the property of one set (as of matrices or vectors) of having at least one linear combination of its elements equal to zero when the coefficients are taken from another given set and at least one of the coefficients is not equal to zero — **linearly dependent** *adj*
linear independence *n* **:** the property of one set (as of matrices or vectors) of having no linear combination of its elements equal to zero when the coefficients are taken from another given set unless the coefficient of each element is zero — **linearly independent** *adj*
linear motor *n* **:** a motor that produces thrust in a straight line by direct induction rather than with the use of gears
linear space *n* **:** VECTOR SPACE *herein*
linear transformation *n* **1 :** a transformation in which the new variables are linear functions of the old variables **2 :** a function that maps the vectors of one vector space onto the vectors of the same or another vector space with the same field of scalars in such a way that the image of the sum of two vectors equals the sum of their images and the image of a scalar product equals the product of the scalar and the image of the vector
line judge *n* **:** a football linesman whose duties include keeping track of the official time for the game
line printer *n* **:** a high-speed printing device (as for a computer) that prints each line as a unit rather than character by character — **line printing** *n*
line score *n* **:** a score of a baseball game giving the runs, hits, and errors made by each team
lineup* *n* **:** a television programming schedule
lin·gui·ne \liŋ'gwēnē, -(ˌ)nā\ *also* **lin·gui·ni** \-nē, -ni\ *n* -s [It, pl. of *linguina,* dim. of *lingua* tongue, fr. L — more at TONGUE] **:** thin flat pasta in long solid strings
link* *n* **:** an identifier attached to an element (as an index term) in a system in order to indicate or permit connection with other similarly identified elements
linked* *adj* **:** having or provided with links
lin·u·ron \'linyəˌrän\ *n* -s [*lin-* (of unknown origin) + *urea* + [1]*-on*] **:** a selective herbicide $C_9H_{10}O_2Cl_2N_2$ used esp. to control weeds in crops of soybeans or carrots
lip cell *n* **:** one of the narrow thin-walled cells of the sporangia in some ferns that mark the point at which dehiscence begins
li·pid·ic \lə'pidik\ *adj* [ISV, fr. *lipid* + [1]*-ic*] **:** of or relating to lipids
li·po·polysaccharide \ˌlīpō, ˌlipō +\ *n* [ISV *lip-* + *polysaccharide*] **:** a large molecule consisting of lipids and sugars joined by chemical bonds
li·po·some \'lipəˌsōm, 'lip-\ *n* -s [*lip-* + *-some*] **:** an artificial vesicle composed of one or more concentric phospholipid bilayers — **li·po·so·mal** \ˌ==ˌsōməl\ *adj*
li·po·tro·pin \ˌlipə'trōpən, ˌlī-\ *n* -s [*lipotropic* + *-in*] **:** either of two protein hormones of the anterior part of the pituitary gland that function in the mobilization of fat reserves; *esp* **:** BETA-LIPOTROPIN *herein*
li·pox·y·gen·ase \ˌlip'äksəjəˌnās, ˌlīp-, -ˌnāz\ *n* -s [*lip-* + *oxygen* + *-ase*] **:** LIPOXIDASE
lip·pes loop \'lipəs-, -pēz-\ *n, usu cap 1st L* [after Jack *Lippes* b1924 Am. physician] **:** an S-shaped plastic intrauterine contraceptive device
lip–synch *or* **lip–sync** *vt* **:** to pretend to sing or say in synchronization with something recorded ~ *vi* **:** to lip-synch something
lip·tau·er \'lipˌtau̇(ə)r, -au̇ə(r\ *n* -s *usu cap* [G, fr. *Liptau* Liptow, Hungary] **1 :** a soft Hungarian cheese **2 :** a cheese spread of Liptauer and seasonings (as paprika); *also* **:** an imitation of this made with cream cheese or cottage cheese
liquid chromatography *n* **:** chromatography in which the mobile phase is a liquid
liquid crystal display *n* **:** LCD *herein*
lit–crit \ˌlit'krit\ *n* -s [*lit*erary *cri*ticism] **:** literary criticism
lite *var of* LIGHT *herein*
literary executor *n* **:** a person entrusted with the management of the papers and unpublished works of a deceased author
litmus test *n* **:** a test in which a single indicator (as an attitude, event, or fact) is decisive
litterbag \'==ˌ=\ *n* [[1]*litter* + *bag*] **:** a bag used (as in an automobile) for refuse disposal
little man *n* **:** the ordinary individual **:** COMMON MAN
live \'līv\ *adv* **:** at the actual time of occurrence **:** during or at a live performance ⟨the sessions were carried ~ in their entirety by the public television station —Peter Binzen⟩
live–in \'=ˌ=\ *adj* **1 :** living in one's place of employment ⟨a *live-in* maid⟩ **2 :** involving or involved with cohabitation ⟨a *live-in* relationship⟩ ⟨a *live-in* partner⟩
living will *n* **:** a document in which the signer requests to be allowed to die rather than be kept alive by artificial means in the event of becoming disabled beyond a reasonable expectation of recovery
LM* *abbr or n* -s lunar module *herein*
LNG *abbr* liquefied natural gas
load* *n* **:** the decrease in capacity for survival of the average individual in a population due to the presence of deleterious genes in the gene pool
load* *vt* **:** to copy (as a program or data) esp. from an external storage device (as a disk drive) into a computer's memory
loader* *n* **:** a computer program that loads a program and readies it for execution
loadmaster \'=ˌ==\ *n* [[1]*load* + *master*] **:** a crew member of a transport aircraft who is in charge of the cargo
local area network *n* **:** a network of personal computers in a small area (as an office) that are linked by cable, can communicate directly with other devices in the network, and can share resources
locked–in* *adj* **:** unable or unwilling to shift invested funds because of the tax effect of realizing capital gains
locus coe·ru·le·us *also* **locus ce·ru·le·us** \ˌlōkə(s)si'rülēəs\ *n* [NL, lit., dark blue place, fr. L *caeruleus, coeruleus* dark blue, prob. fr. *caelum* sky] **:** a blue area of the brain stem with many norepinephrine-containing neurons
lo·cu·tion·ary \lō'kyüsh(ə)ˌnerē\ *adj* [*locution* + *-ary*] **:** of or relating to the physical act of saying something considered apart from the statement's effect or intention — compare ILLOCUTIONARY *herein,* PERLOCUTIONARY *herein*

logic* *n* **:** the fundamental principles and applications of truth tables and of the interconnection of circuit elements and gating necessary for computation in a computer; *also* **:** the circuits themselves

lognormal \(ˈ)ˌ=ˈ==\ *adj* [[4]*log* + *normal*] **:** relating to or being a normal distribution that is the distribution of the logarithm of a random variable; *also* **:** relating to or being such a random variable — **lognormality** \ˌ=(ˌ)=ˈ===\ *n* — **lognormally** \(ˈ)=ˈ===\ *adv*

loll·er \ˈlälə(r)\ *n* -s [[1]*loll* + *-er*] **:** one that lolls around

lonely hearts *adj* **:** of or relating to lonely people who are seeking companions or spouses ⟨*lonely hearts* club⟩

long-term* *adj* **:** generated by assets held for longer than six months ⟨*long-term* capital gains⟩

look-alike \ˈ==ˌ=\ *n* -s [[1]*look* + *alike*] **:** one that looks like another **:** DOUBLE — **look-alike** \"\ *adj*

look-in* *n* **:** a quick pass in football to a receiver running diagonally toward the center of the field

lookup \ˈ=ˌ=\ *n* -s [*look up*] **:** the process or an instance of looking something up; *esp* **:** the process in which a computer matches data with material stored in memory (as in a table)

loop* *n* **1 :** a series of instructions (as for a computer) that is repeated usu. until a terminating condition is reached **2 :** INTRAUTERINE DEVICE *herein; esp* **:** LIPPES LOOP *herein*

loosey-goosey \ˌlüsēˌgüsē\ *adj* [fr. the phrase *loose as a goose*] **:** notably loose or relaxed **:** not tense

lo·rentz force \(ˌ)lōrˈents-, (ˌ)lȯr-\ *n, usu cap L* [after Hendrik A. *Lorentz* †1928 Du. physicist] **:** the force exerted on a moving charged particle in electric and magnetic fields

LOS *abbr* **1** line of scrimmage **2** line of sight

loser* *n* **:** one who is incompetent or unable to succeed ⟨believes that any woman unmarried after the age of twenty-two is a ~ —Lyn Tornabene⟩; *also* **:** something doomed to fail or disappoint ⟨the breaded and fried veal cutlet Milanese . . . had to be a ~ —Mimi Sheraton⟩

lo·ti \ˈlōtē\ *n, pl* **ma·lo·ti** \məˈlōtē\ [native name in Lesotho] **:** the basic monetary unit of Lesotho — see MONEY table *in the Dict*

lou geh·rig's disease \ˌlüˈge(ə)rigz-\ *n, usu cap L&G* [after *Lou Gehrig* †1941 Am. baseball player who died of this disease] **:** AMYOTROPHIC LATERAL SCLEROSIS *herein*

love beads *n pl* **:** a necklace of beads; *esp* **:** beads worn as a symbol of love and peace

lovebug \ˈ=ˌ=\ *n* [so called fr. the fact that it is usually seen copulating] **:** a small black bibionid fly (*Plecia nearctica*) with a red thorax that is often a nuisance esp. while copulating along highways in states of the U.S. bordering the Gulf of Mexico

love-in \ˈ=ˌ=\ *n* -s [[2]*love* + *-in* (herein)] **:** a gathering of people for the expression of mutual love

lowball \ˈ=ˌ=\ *vt* **:** to give (a customer) a deceptively low price or cost estimate that one has no intention of honoring; *also* **:** to make (as a cost estimate) deliberately and misleadingly low — **lowball** *n*

low blow* *n* **:** an unprincipled attack

lowest terms *n pl* **:** the form of a fraction in which the numerator and denominator have no factor in common except 1 ⟨reduce a fraction to *lowest terms*⟩

low-rise \ˈ=ˈ=\ *adj* [*low* + *-rise* (as in *high-rise* — herein)] **1 :** being one or two stories and not equipped with elevators ⟨a *low-rise* building⟩ **2** *of trousers* **:** having a low waist and usu. close-fitting

low-tech \ˈ=ˈ=\ *adj* **:** not relating to or characterized by high technology **:** technologically unsophisticated ⟨*low-tech* industries⟩

LPM *abbr, often not cap* lines per minute

LPN \ˌel(ˌ)pēˈen\ *n* -s **:** LICENSED PRACTICAL NURSE *herein*

Lr *symbol* lawrencium *herein*

LSI \ˌelˌesˈī\ *abbr or n* -s **1 :** LARGE-SCALE INTEGRATION *herein* **2 :** an integrated circuit (as for a computer) employing large-scale integration

LSM* *abbr* letter-sorting machine

lu·ba·vitch·er \ˈlübəˌvichə(r), lüˈbäˌv-\ *n* -s *usu cap* [Yiddish, fr. *Lubavitch*, lit., city of love, Jewish town in Russia + *-er* -er] **:** a member of a Hasidic sect founded by Schneour Zalman of Lyady in the late 18th century — **lubavitcher** \"\ *adj, usu cap*

luddite* *n, usu cap* **:** one who is opposed to change and esp. to technological change

lu·dic \ˈlüdik\ *adj* [F *ludique*, fr L *ludus* play] **:** of, relating to, or characterized by play **:** PLAYFUL ⟨~ behavior⟩ ⟨a ~ novel⟩

lu·mi·nar·ia \ˌlüməˈnerēə\ *n* -s [Sp, decorative light, fr. L *lumenarium* light, torch, fr. *lumen* light + *-arius* -ary] **:** a traditional Mexican Christmas lantern consisting of a brown paper bag with a lighted candle inside

lump* *n, Brit* **:** nonunion construction workers who work as self-employed subcontractors ⟨~ labour⟩

lump·ec·to·my \ˌləmˈpektəmē\ *n* -ES [*lump* + ISV *-ectomy*] **:** excision of a breast tumor with a limited amount of associated tissue

lum·pen \ˈlu̇mpən, ˈləm-\ *n, pl* **lumpen** *or* **lumpens :** a member of the crude and uneducated lowest class of society

lunar excursion module *or* **lunar module** *n* **:** a space vehicle module designed to carry astronauts from the command module to the surface of the moon and back

lu·nar·naut \ˈlünə(r)ˌnȯt, -ˌnärˌn-, -ät\ *n* [fr. *lunar* + *-naut* (as in *astronaut*)] **:** an astronaut who explores the moon

lunch* *n* —**out to lunch** *slang* **:** out of touch with reality

luteinizing hormone-releasing hormone *also* **luteinizing hormone-releasing factor** *n* **:** a hormone secreted by the hypothalamus that stimulates the pituitary gland to release luteinizing hormone

LVN \ˌel(ˌ)vēˈen\ *n* -s **:** LICENSED VOCATIONAL NURSE *herein*

lwei \ləˈwā\ *n, pl* **lwei** *also* **lweis** [native name in Angola] **1 :** a monetary unit of Angola equal to $^{1}/_{100}$ kwanza — see MONEY table *in the Dict* **2 :** a coin representing one lwei

ly·ase \ˈlīˌās, -āz\ *n* -s [Gk *lyein* to loosen, release + E *-ase* — more at LOSE] **:** an enzyme (as a decarboxylase) that forms double bonds by removing groups from a substrate other than by hydrolysis or that adds groups to double bonds

lyme disease \ˈlīm-\ *n, usu cap L* [*Lyme*, Connecticut, where it was first reported] **:** an acute inflammatory disease caused by a spirochete transmitted by the bite of a tick of the genus *Ixodes* (*I. dammini*)

lym·phan·gi·og·ra·phy \ˌlimˌfanjēˈägrəfē\ *n* -ES [*lymphangi-* + *-graphy*] **:** X-ray depiction of lymph vessels and lymph nodes after use of a radiopaque material — called also *lymphography* — **lym·phan·gio·gram** \limˈfanjēəˌgram\ *n* — **lym·phan·gio·graph·ic** \=ˈ==əˈgrafik, ˌ=ˌ===ˈ==\ *adj*

lym·pho·blast·oid \¦lim(p)fə¦bla,stȯid\ *adj* [*lymphoblast* + *-oid*] **:** resembling a lymphoblast

lym·pho·gran·u·lo·ma·tous \,lim(p)fə,granyə'lōməd·-əs\ *adj* [NL *lymphogranulomat-, lymphogranuloma* + E *-ous*] **:** of, relating to, or characterized by lymphogranulomas

lym·phog·ra·phy \lim'fägrəfē\ *n* -ES [*lymph-* + *-graphy*] **:** LYMPHANGIOGRAPHY *herein* — **lym·pho·gram** \'lim(p)fə,gram\ *n* — **lym·pho·graph·ic** \¦==¦grafik\ *adj*

lym·pho·kine \'lim(p)fə,kīn\ *n* -s [NL, fr. *lymph-* + Gk *kinein* to move, arouse] **:** any of various substances (as interferon) of low molecular weight that are not immunoglobulins, are secreted by T cells in response to stimulation by antigens, and have a role (as the activation of macrophages or the enhancement or inhibition of antibody production) in cell-mediated immunity

lym·pho·proliferative \¦lim(p)fə+\ *adj* [*lymph-* + *proliferative*] **:** of or relating to the proliferation of lymphoid tissue ⟨a ~ response⟩ ⟨~ abnormalities⟩

lym·pho·reticular \"+\ *adj* [*lymph-* + *reticular*] **:** RETICULOENDOTHELIAL ⟨~ neoplasms⟩

lym·pho·sarcomatous \"+\ *adj* [NL *lymphosarcomat-, lymphosarcoma* + E *-ous*] **:** being, affected with, or characterized by lymphosarcomas ⟨large ~ masses⟩ ⟨~ cows⟩

ly·oph·i·liz·er \(,)lī'äfə'līzə(r)\ *n* -s [*lyophilize* + [2]*-er*] **:** a device used to carry out the process of freeze-drying

ly·si·metric \¦līsə +\ *adj* [*lysimeter* + [1]*-ic*] **:** relating to or involving the use of a lysimeter ⟨~ observations⟩

lysogen* *n* **:** a lysogenic bacterium or bacterial strain

lysogenic* *adj* **:** TEMPERATE 1f ⟨~ viruses⟩

ly·sog·e·nize \lī'säjə,nīz\ *vt* -ED/-ING/-s [*lysogen* (herein) + *-ize*] **:** to make lysogenic — **ly·sog·e·ni·za·tion** \-,säjənə'zāshən, -,nī-\ *n* -s

ly·sog·e·ny \lī'säjənē\ *n* -ES [*lys-* + *-geny*] **:** the state of being lysogenic

ly·so·some \'līsə,sōm\ *n* -s [ISV *lys-* + [3]*-some;* orig. formed in F] **:** a saclike cellular organelle that contains various hydrolytic enzymes — **ly·so·som·al** \¦līsə¦sōməl\ *adj* — **ly·so·som·al·ly** \,==¦=əlē\ *adv*

ly·so·staph·in \,līsə'stafən\ *n* -s [*lys-* + *staph* + *-in*] **:** an antimicrobial enzyme that is obtained from a strain of staphylococcus and is effective against other staphylococci

M

ma–and–pa \ˌ⸗⸗ˈ⸗\ *adj* **:** MOM-AND-POP *herein*

MABE *abbr* master of agricultural business and economics

mace \ˈmās\ *vt* -ED/-ING/-S **:** to attack with the liquid Mace

Mace \ˈmās\ *trademark* — used for a temporarily disabling liquid that when sprayed in the face of a person (as a rioter) causes tears, dizziness, immobilization, and sometimes nausea

machine language *n* **1 :** the set of numeric codes usu. in binary form used to represent operations and data in a machine (as a computer) **2 :** ASSEMBLY LANGUAGE

machine–readable \⸗ˈ⸗ˌ⸗⸗⸗\ *adj* **:** directly usable by a computer

machine translation *n* **:** automatic translation from one language to another

ma·chis·mo \mäˈchē|z(ˌ)mō, mə-, -ˈkē|, -ˈki|, -ˈchi|, |s(-\ *n* -s [MexSp, fr. Sp *macho* male + *-ismo* -ism] **1 :** a strong sense of masculine pride **:** an exaggerated masculinity **2 :** an exaggerated or exhilarating sense of power or strength ⟨museums which flaunt their directorial ~ —*Time*⟩

[1]**ma·cho** \ˈmä(ˌ)chō\ *adj* [Sp, male, fr. L *masculus* — more at MALE] **:** having or showing machismo **:** aggressively virile ⟨all their ~ swagger and bravado —Burr Snider⟩

[2]**macho** \"\ *n* -s **1 :** MACHISMO *herein* **2 :** one who exhibits machismo

mack·man \ˈmakˌman, -ˌmən\ *n, pl* **mack·men** \-ˌmen, -ˌmən\ [[2]*mack* + *man*] *slang* **:** PIMP, MACK

mac·lau·rin's series \məˈklȯrən(z)-\ *n, usu cap M* [after Colin *Maclaurin* †1746 Scot. mathematician] **:** a Taylor's series of the form

$$f(x) = f(0) + \frac{f'(0)}{1!}x + \frac{f''(0)}{2!}x^2 + \ldots + \frac{f^{(n)}(0)}{n!}x^n + \ldots$$

in which the expansion is about the reference point zero — called also *Maclaurin series*

mc·lu·han·esque \məˌklüəˈnesk\ *adj, usu cap M&L* [Herbert Marshall *McLuhan* † 1980 Canad. educator + E *-esque*] **:** of, relating to, or suggestive of Marshall McLuhan or his theories

mac·ro \ˈmak(ˌ)rō\ *n* -s [short for *macroinstruction* (herein)] **:** a single computer instruction that stands for a sequence of operations

mac·ro·aggregate \ˌmakrō+\ *n* [*macr-* + *aggregate*] **:** a relatively large particle (as of soil or a protein) — **mac·ro·aggregated** \"+\ *adj*

mac·ro·benthos \"+\ *n* [*macr-* + *benthos*] **:** the relatively large organisms living on or in the bottom of bodies of water — **mac·ro·benthic** \"+\ *adj*

macrobiotic* *adj* **:** of, relating to, or being an extremely restricted diet (as one containing chiefly whole grains) that is usu. undertaken by its advocates to promote health and well-being although it may be deficient in essential nutrients (as fats)

macrobiotics* *n pl but sing in constr* **:** a macrobiotic dietary system

mac·ro·globulin \ˌmakrō +\ *n* [ISV *macr-* + *globulin*] **:** a highly polymerized globulin of high molecular weight

mac·ro·glob·u·lin·emia \ˌmakrōˌgläbyələˈnēmēə\ *n* -s [NL, fr. ISV *macroglobulin* + NL *-emia*] **:** a disorder characterized by increased blood serum viscosity and by macroglobulins in the serum — **mac·ro·glob·u·lin·emic** \-nēmik\ *adj*

mac·ro·instruction \ˌmakrō +\ *n* [*macr-* + *instruction*] **:** MACRO *herein*

mac·ro·invertebrate \"+\ *n* [*macr-* + *invertebrate*] **:** any of various invertebrate macroorganisms (as a crayfish or stonefly)

macro lens *n* **:** a camera lens designed to focus at very short distances with up to life-size magnification of the image

mac·ro·lide \ˈmakrəˌlīd\ *n* -s [*macro*cyclic + *l*actone + *-ide*] **:** any of several antibiotics that contain a macrocyclic lactone ring and are produced by actinomycetes of the genus *Streptomyces*

mac·ro·organism \ˌmakrō+\ *n* [*macr-* + *organism*] **:** an organism large enough to be seen by the normal unaided human eye — compare MICROORGANISM *in the Dict*

MAD* *abbr* mutual assured destruction

mafia* *n, often cap* **:** a group of people of similar interests or backgrounds prominent in a particular field or enterprise ⟨as the little guy in the world of broadcasting, he throws down the gauntlet to the network *Mafia* —Stanley Marcus⟩

ma·fi·o·so \ˌmäfēˈō(ˌ)sō, -af-, -)zō\ *n, pl* **mafio·si** \-sē, -zē\ *also* **mafiosos** *often cap* [It, fr. *mafioso,* adj., belonging to the Mafia, fr. *Mafia* + *-oso* -ous, fr. L *-osus*] **:** a member of the Mafia or a mafia

magazine* *n* **:** a radio or television program presenting usu. several short segments on a variety of topics

magic bullet *n* **:** a substance or therapy capable of destroying pathogenic agents (as bacteria or cancer cells) without deleterious side effects

magic number *n* **1 :** one of a set of numbers for which an atomic nucleus exhibits a high degree of stability when either the proton or neutron count is equal to the number **2 :** a number that represents a combination of wins for a leader (as in a baseball pennant race) and losses for a contender which mathematically guarantees the leader's winning the championship

mag·i·cube \ˈmajəˌkyüb\ *n* [blend of [2]*magic* and [1]*cube*] **:** a flashcube that for its firing depends only on the mechanical ignition of a primer within the device

magnetic* *n* **:** a magnetic substance

magnetic bottle *n* **:** a magnetic field for confining plasma for experiments in nuclear fusion

magnetic bubble *n* **:** a tiny magnetized cylindrical volume that is formed in a thin amorphous or crystalline magnetic material, can be moved by a magnetic field, and can be used with other like volumes to represent a bit of information (as in a computer)

magnetic core *n* **1 :** CORE 1i **2 :** CORE 1 *herein*

magnetic disk *n* **:** DISK 1 *herein*

mag·ne·to·cardiograph \magˌnēd·ō, -ed·-+\ *n* [*magnet-* + *cardiograph*] **:** an instrument for recording the changes in the magnetic field around the heart that is used to supplement information given by an electrocardiograph — **mag·ne·to·cardiogram** \"+\ *n* — **mag·ne·to·cardiographic** \"+\ *adj* — **mag·ne·to·cardi·ography** \"+\ *n*

mag·ne·to·fluiddynamic \mag¦nēd·ō¦==¦==, -ned--\ *adj* [*magnet-* + [2]*fluid* + [1]*dynamic*] **:** MAGNETOHYDRODYNAMIC — **mag·ne·to·fluiddynamics** \-,==ˈ==\ *n pl but sing or pl in constr*

mag·ne·to·gasdynamics \-,==ˈ==\ *n pl but sing in constr* [*magnet-* + *gas* + *dynamics*] **:** MAGNETOHYDRODYNAMICS — **mag·ne·to·gasdynamic** \-¦==¦==\ *adj*

mag·ne·to·pause \magˈnēd·ə,pȯz, -ed-\ *n* [*magnetosphere* (herein) + *pause*] **:** the outer boundary of a magnetosphere

mag·ne·to·plasmadynamic \mag¦nēd·ō,==¦==\ *adj* [*magnet-* + *plasma* + [1]*dynamic*] **:** MAGNETOHYDRODYNAMIC — **mag·ne·to·plasmadynamics** \-,==ˈ==\ *n pl but sing or pl in constr*

mag·ne·to·sphere \magˈnēd·ə, -ed·ə +,\ *n* [*magnet-* + *sphere*] **:** a region of space that surrounds a celestial object (as the earth or a star) and is dominated by the object's magnetic field so that charged particles are trapped in it — **mag·ne·to·spheric** \=¦==+\ *adj*

mag·ne·to·tail \"+\ *n* [*magnet-* + *tail*] **:** the region of the magnetosphere that is swept back by the solar wind so that it extends from a planet (as the earth) in the direction away from the sun

magnet school *n* **:** a school with superior facilities and staff designed to attract pupils from all segments of the community

mag·non \ˈmag,nän\ *n* -s [[1]*magn*etic + [2]*-on*] **:** SPIN WAVE *herein*

magpie* *n* **:** one who collects indiscriminately

mah·ler·ian \mäˈlerēən, -ˈlir-\ *adj, usu cap* [Gustav *Mahler* †1911 Austrian composer + E *-ian*] **:** of, relating to, or suggestive of Gustav Mahler or his music

mail cover *n* **:** a postal monitoring and recording of information about all mail going to a designated addressee

Mail·gram \ˈmā(ə)l¦gram, -aa(ə)m\ *trademark* — used for a message sent by wire to a post office which delivers it to the addressee

mainframe *or* **mainframe computer** \ˈ=¦=\ *n* [[2]*main* + *frame*] **:** a computer with its cabinet and internal circuits; *also* **:** a large fast computer that can handle multiple tasks concurrently

mainline \¦=,=\ *adj* [*main line,* n.] **1 :** being part of an established group ⟨~ churches⟩ **2 :** MAINSTREAM *herein*

[1]**mainstream** \¦=,=\ *adj* [*mainstream,* n.] **:** having, reflecting, or being compatible with the prevailing attitudes and values of a society or group ⟨a strictly ~ Christian, Victorian approach toward marriage and morality — Gerda Lerner⟩

[2]**mainstream** \ˈ=,=\ *vt* **:** to place (as a handicapped child) in conventional school classes — **main·stream·ing** \ˈ=,==\ *n* -s

mai tai \ˈmī¦tī\ *n, pl* **mai tais** [Tahitian *maitai* good] **:** a cocktail made with rum, curaçao, orgeat, lime, and fruit juices, shaken with shaved ice, and often garnished with fruit

majolica* *n* **:** a 19th century earthenware modeled in naturalistic shapes and glazed in bright colors

major histocompatibility complex *n* **:** a group of genes that function esp. in determining the histocompatibility antigens found on cell surfaces and that in man comprise the alleles occurring at four loci on the short arm of chromosome 6 — abbr. *MHC*

major-medical \¦==¦===\ *adj* **:** of, relating to, or being a form of insurance designed to pay all or part of the medical bills of major illnesses usu. after deduction of a fixed initial sum

make* *vb* — **make it 1 :** to be successful ⟨trying to *make it* as writer-in-residence at the university — Gershon Legman⟩ **2 :** to have sexual intercourse ⟨one young couple who would . . . *make it* in a rear seat — Thomas Pynchon⟩ **3 :** to be satisfactory or pleasing **:** make the grade ⟨southern cities, with their . . . climates, don't *make it* for me —Bill AuCoin⟩ — **make waves :** to disturb the status quo ⟨unimaginative, traditional career man who does not *make waves* —Henry Trewhitt⟩

make out* *vi* **1 :** to engage in sexual intercourse **2 :** NECK 1

makuta *pl* of LIKUTA *herein*

mal·apportioned \¦mal+\ *adj* [[1]*mal-* + *apportioned,* past part. of *apportion*] **:** characterized by an inequitable or unsuitable apportioning of representatives to a legislative body ⟨one of the country's most ~ legislatures. Eight percent of the population controlled a majority of the Senate seats —*N.Y. Times*⟩

mal·apportionment \"+\ *n* [[1]*mal-* + *apportionment*] **:** the state of being malapportioned

mal·i·bu board \ˈmalə̇,bü-\ *n, usu cap M* [fr. *Malibu* Beach, California] **:** a lightweight surfboard 9 to 10 feet long

ma·lic \ˈmalə̇k, ˈmāl-\ *adj* **:** involved in and esp. catalyzing a reaction in which malic acid participates ⟨~ dehydrogenase⟩

mall* *n* **:** SHOPPING MALL *herein*

ma·lo·lactic \¦malō, ¦mālō+\ *adj* [[2]*mal-* + *lactic*] **:** relating to or involved in the bacterial conversion of malic acid to lactic acid in wine ⟨~ fermentation⟩

maloti *pl of* LOTI *herein*

MALS *abbr* master of arts in library science

mam·mo·gram \ˈmamə,gram\ *n* [[2]*mamma* + *-o-* + *-gram*] **:** a photograph of the breasts made by X rays

mam·mog·ra·phy \maˈmägrəfē\ *n* -ES [[2]*mamma* + *-o-* + *-graphy*] **:** X-ray examination of the breasts (as for early detection of cancer) — **mam·mo·graph·ic** \,maməˈgrafik\ *adj*

man* *n, usu cap* **1 :** POLICE ⟨when I heard the siren, I knew it was the *Man* —*Amer. Speech*⟩ **2 :** the white establishment **:** white society ⟨surprise that any black man . . . should take on so about the *Man* —Peter Goldman⟩

mandate* *vt* **:** to make mandatory **:** ORDER ⟨this . . . verdict *mandating* school desegregation —M. L. Abramson⟩; *also* **:** DIRECT, REQUIRE ⟨people are not *mandated* to wreck their own economic system —Norman Cousins⟩

man·eb \ˈma,neb\ *n* -s [*man*ganese + *e*thylene + *b*is-] **:** a carbamate agricultural fungicide $C_4H_6MnN_2S_4$

man·hat·tan·iza·tion \,man,hat(ᵊ)nə̇ˈzāshən, -n,īˈzā-\ *n* -s *usu cap* [fr. *Manhattan,* borough of New York + *-ization*] **:** congestion of an urban area by tall buildings

ma·ni·cot·ti \,manə̇ˈkäd·ē\ *n, pl* **manicotti** [It, lit., muff, fr. *manica* sleeve, fr. L — more at MANCHE] **:** tubular pasta shells stuffed with ricotta

manifold* *n* **1 :** a mathematical set **2 :** a topological space such that every point has a neighborhood which is homeomorphic to the interior of a sphere in euclidean space of the same number of dimensions

-man·ship \mən,ship\ *n suffix* -s [sports*manship*] **:** art or practice of maneuvering to gain a tactical advantage ⟨games*manship*⟩

many–valued \¦==¦==\ *adj* **:** MULTIPLE-VALUED *herein*

mao \ˈmau̇\ *adj, usu cap* [after *Mao* Tse-tung *b*1893 Chin. communist leader] **:** having a long narrow cut and a mandarin collar — usu. used of a jacket

MAO *abbr* monoamine oxidase *herein*

mao·ism \ˈmau̇,izəm\ *n* -s *usu cap* [*Mao* Tse-tung + E *-ism*] **:** the theory and practice of Marxism-Leninism developed in China chiefly by Mao Tse-tung — **mao·ist** \ˈmau̇əst\ *n or adj, usu cap*

mao–tai \ˈmau̇ˈdī, -ˈtī\ *n* [fr. *Mao-Tai,* town in China] **:** a strong Chinese liquor made from sorghum

map* *n* **1 :** the arrangement of genes on a chromosome — called also *genetic map* **2 :** FUNCTION 6

map* *vt* **:** to locate (a gene) on a chromosome ⟨mutants which have been genetically *mapped* ⟩ ~ *vi, of a gene* **:** to be located ⟨a repressor ~*s* near the corresponding structural gene⟩

MAP* *abbr* modified American plan

map·ping \ˈmapiŋ\ *n* -s [fr. gerund of [2]*map*] **:** FUNCTION 6

mar·ag·ing steel \¦mär,ājiŋ-\ *n* [*mar*tensite + *aging*] **:** a strong tough low-carbon martensitic steel containing up to 25 percent nickel and hardening precipitates formed by aging

mar·ek's disease \ˈmarəks-, ˈmer-\ *n, usu cap M* [after J. *Marek* †1952 Ger. veterinarian] **:** a cancerous disease of poultry that is characterized esp. by proliferation of lymphoid cells and is caused by a virus resembling a herpesvirus

mar·fan's syndrome *or* **mar·fan syndrome** \¦mär-,fan-\ *n, usu cap M* [after Antonin Bernard Jean *Marfan* †1942 Fr. pediatrician] **:** a hereditary disorder characterized by abnormal elongation of the long bones and often by ocular and circulatory defects

mar·ga·ri·ta \,märgəˈrēd·ə, -ētə\ *n* -s [MexSp, prob. fr. the name *Margarita* Margaret] **:** a cocktail consisting of tequila, lime or lemon juice, and an orange-flavored liqueur

marginal* *adj* **:** relating to or being a function of a random variable that is obtained from a function of several random variables by integrating or summing over all possible values of the other variables ⟨a ~ probability function⟩

mari·culture \ˈmarə +,\ *n* [*mari-* + *culture*] **:** the cultivation of marine organisms by exploiting their natural environment — **mari·culturist** \¦marə +\ *n*

mar·i·na·ra \,marəˈnarə, ,merəˈnerə, -när-\ *adj* [It (*alla*)-*marinara* in sailor style, fr. *marinara,* fem. of *marinaro,* of sailors, fr. *marino* marine — more at MARINATE] **:** made with tomatoes, onion, garlic, and spices ⟨~ sauce⟩; *also* **:** served with marinara sauce ⟨spaghetti ~⟩

mark* *n* [G — more at [3]*mark*] **:** the basic monetary unit of East Germany — see MONEY table *in the Dict*

marker* *or* **marker gene** *n* **:** GENETIC MARKER *herein*

market* *n* **1 :** the available supply of or potential demand for specified goods or services ⟨the labor ~⟩ ⟨has captured more than two-thirds of the cleaning-agent ~ —Barry Commoner⟩ **2 :** a specified category of potential buyers ⟨youth ~⟩

mar·ko·vi·an \märˈkōvēən\ *or* **mar·kov** \ˈmär,kȯf, -ȯv\ *also* **mar·koff** \-ȯf\ *adj, usu cap* [*Markov* (*process*) + E *-ian*] **:** of, relating to, or resembling a Markov process or Markov chain esp. by having probabilities defined in terms of transition from the possible existing states to other states ⟨*Markovian* models⟩

markov process *also* **markoff process** *n, usu cap M* [after Andrei Andreevich *Markov*] **:** a stochastic process (as Brownian movement) that resembles a Markov chain except that the states are continuous; *also* **:** MARKOV CHAIN

markup* *n* **:** the putting of a bill into final form by a U.S. congressional committee; *also* **:** the session at which this is done

martial art *n* **:** one of several arts of combat (as karate, judo, or kung fu) of oriental origin that are widely practiced as sport — **martial artist** *n*

mar·tin lu·ther king day *R* ,märtᵊn,lüthərˈkiŋ-, *—R* ,mȧtᵊn- ,lüthəˈk-\ *n, usu cap M&L&K&D* [*Martin Luther King* †1968, Am. civil rights leader] **:** January 15 observed as a legal holiday in some states of the U.S.

mary gre·go·ry \-ˈgreg(ə)rē, -rāg-\ *n, usu cap M&G* [after *Mary Gregory,* thought to have been a late 19th cent. Am. glass painter] **:** colored glassware of a popular 19th century style marked by white enamel decoration usu. including figures of children

mary jane *n, usu cap M&J* [by folk etymology (influenced by Sp *Juana* Jane)] *slang* **:** MARIJUANA

mas·con \ˈmas,kän\ *n* -s [[2]*mass* + *con*centration] **:** one of the concentrations of large mass under the surface of the moon's maria whose gravitational effect is held to cause perturbations of the paths of spacecraft orbiting the moon

mas·cu·lin·ist \ˈmaskyələnəst, -,lin-\ *n* -s [*masculine* + *-ist*] **:** an advocate of male superiority or dominance **:** male chauvinist

mash* *n, Brit* **:** mashed potatoes

mask* *n* **:** an opaque material used to shield selected parts of a photosensitive surface during deposition or etching (as in producing an integrated circuit)

massage* *vt* **1 :** to treat flatteringly **:** BLANDISH ⟨be attentive, ~ my ego, advise me —Sally Quinn⟩ **2 :** to alter to suit one's purpose **:** work over **:** MODIFY ⟨computers to collect and rapidly ~ vast amounts of data —A.L. Robinson⟩

mass·cult \ˈmas,kəlt\ *n* -s [*mass cult*ure] **:** the artistic and intellectual culture associated with and disseminated through the mass media **:** mass culture

mass·less \ˈmasləs\ *adj* [[2]*mass* + *-less*] **:** having no mass ⟨~ particles⟩ — **mass·less·ness** *n* -ES

mass of the resurrection *usu cap M&R* **:** a mass for the dead in which the celebrant wears white vestments to symbolize the joyous resurrection of the dead

mass spectrometry *or* **mass spectroscopy** *n* **:** the use of the mass spectrometer — **mass spectrometric** *adj*

master* *n* **:** an original record (as a film, sound recording, or videotape) from which copies can be produced

master* *vt* **:** to produce a master of (as a sound recording)

master class *n* **:** a seminar for advanced students (as of music or dance) conducted by a master

mas·to·cy·to·ma \,mastə,sīˈtōmə\ *n, pl* **mas-tocytomas** *or* **mastocyto·ma·ta** \-ōməd·ə, -ətə\ [*mastocyte* + *-oma*] **:** a tumorous mass produced by proliferation of mast cells

MAT* *abbr* master of arts in teaching

matching *adj* **:** provided to supplement by matching funds provided by the recipient ⟨~ funds⟩ ⟨a ~ grant⟩

matchup \'≍,≍\ *n* -s [²*match* + *up*] : ¹MATCH 1, 2

maternity *adj* [*maternity,* n.] **1** : designed for wear during pregnancy ⟨a ~ dress⟩ **2** : effective for the period close to and including childbirth ⟨~ leave⟩

mathematical biology *n* : a branch of biology concerned with the construction of mathematical models to describe and solve biological problems — **mathematical biologist** *n*

ma·tri·focal \ˌma·trə, ˌmā-+\ *adj* [*matr-* + *focal*] : MATRICENTRIC

matrix algebra *n* : generalized algebra that deals with the operations and relations among matrices

matrix sentence *n* : that one of a pair of sentences joined by means of a transformation that keeps its essential external structure and syntactic status ⟨in "the book that I want is gone", "the book is gone" is the *matrix sentence*⟩

mature* *adj* : having achieved a low but stable growth rate ⟨~ businesses⟩ ⟨~ products⟩ ⟨~ markets⟩

maul* *n* : a tool like a sledgehammer with one wedge-shaped end that is used to split wood

ma·ven *also* **ma·vin** *or* **may·vin** \'māvən\ *n* -s [Yiddish *meyvn,* fr. LHeb *mēbhīn,* perh. fr. Heb *mēbhī* one who has brought in] : one who is experienced or knowledgeable : EXPERT; *also* : FREAK 3 *herein*

maxi \'maksē\ *n* -s [*maxi-* (herein)] : a long skirt or coat that usu. extends to the ankle — called also respectively *maxiskirt, maxicoat*

maxi- \'maksē, -si\ *comb form* [fr. *maximum,* after E *minimum: mini-* (herein)] **1** : extra long ⟨*maxi*-dress⟩ ⟨*maxi*-kilt⟩ **2** : extra large ⟨*maxi*-sculpture⟩ ⟨*maxi*-problems⟩

max·il·lo·facial \makˌsi(ˌ)lō +\ *adj* [*maxill-* + *facial*] : of, relating to, treating, or affecting the maxilla and the face

maxi·min \'maksə̇ˌmin\ *n* -s [*maxi*mum + *min*imum] : the maximum of a set of minima; *esp* : the largest of a set of minimum possible gains each of which occurs in the least advantageous outcome of a strategy followed by a participant in a situation governed by the theory of games — compare MINIMAX *herein* — **maximin** *adj*

maximum likelihood *n* : a statistical method for estimating population parameters (as the mean and variance) from sample data that selects as estimates those parameter values maximizing the probability of obtaining the observed data

ma·yo \'mā(ˌ)ō\ *n* -s [by shortening] : MAYONNAISE

MBD *abbr* minimal brain dysfunction *herein*

mbi·ra \em'birə, əm-, -bēr-\ *n* -s [native word in southern Africa; of Bantu origin] : an African musical instrument that consists of a gourd resonator, a wooden box, and a varying number of tuned metal or wooden strips that vibrate when plucked with the thumb or fingers

MCS *abbr* **1** master of commercial science **2** master of computer science **3** missile control system

mean value theorem *n* **1** : a theorem in differential calculus: if a function of one variable is continuous on a closed interval and differentiable on the interval minus its endpoints there is at least one point where the derivative of the function is equal to the slope of the line joining the endpoints of the curve representing the function on the interval **2** : a theorem in integral calculus: if a function of one variable is continuous on a closed interval and differentiable on the interval minus its endpoints, there is at least one point in the interval where the product of the value of the function and the length of the interval is equal to the integral of the function over the interval

meat* *n* : PENIS — usu. considered vulgar

meat-and-potatoes \ˌ≍≍≍ˌ≍≍\ *adj* **1** : of fundamental importance : BASIC ⟨the *meat-and-potatoes* problems of everyday living and loving —D.J. Heckman⟩ **2** : PRACTICAL, EVERYDAY

meat and potatoes \"+\ *n pl but sing or pl in constr* : a main object of interest : ESSENCE, MEAT 6

mec·a·myl·amine \ˌmekə'miləˌmēn, -ˌmən\ *n* -s [*me*thyl + *c*amphane + *amine*] : a drug that in the hydrochloride $C_{11}H_{21}N{\cdot}HCl$ is used orally as a ganglionic blocking agent to effect a rapid lowering of severely elevated blood pressure

mechanical bank *also* **mechanical*** *n* : a toy bank in which operation of a lever activates a mechanism that goes through some amusing or absurd routine and deposits a coin

mech·a·no·chemical \ˌmekənō+\ *adj* [*mechan-* + *chemical*] : relating to or being chemistry that deals with the conversion of chemical energy into mechanical work (as in the contraction of a muscle) — **mech·a·no·chemically** \"+\ *adv* — **mech·a·no·chemistry** \"+\ *n*

mech·a·no·receptor \ˌmekə(ˌ)nō +\ *n* [*mechan-* + *receptor*] : a neural end organ (as a tactile receptor) that responds to a mechanical stimulus (as a change in pressure) — **mech·a·no·reception** \"+\ *n* — **mech·a·no·receptive** \"+\ *adj*

mech·lor·eth·amine \ˌmeˌklōr'ethəˌmēn, -lȯr-, -ˌmən\ *n* [*me*thyl + *chloroeth*yl + *amine*] : a nitrogen mustard $C_5H_{11}Cl_2N$ used as an insect chemosterilant, as a war gas, and in palliative treatment of some neoplastic diseases

mec·li·zine \'meklə̇ˌzēn\ *n* -s [*me*thyl + *c*h*l*or- + *-izine* (alter. of *azine*)] : a drug $C_{25}H_{27}ClN_2$ used usu. in the form of its hydrochloride to treat nausea and vertigo

med·fly \'medˌflī\ *n, often cap* [*Med*iterranean + *fly*] : MEDITERRANEAN FRUIT FLY

media event *n* : a publicity event staged for coverage by the news media

me·dia·ge·nic \ˌmēdēə'jenik *also* -jēn-\ *adj* [*media,* pl. of *medium* + *-genic*] : likely to appeal to the audiences of the mass media and esp. television ⟨~ politicians⟩

medial condyle *n* : a condyle on the inner side of the lower extremity of the femur; *also* : a corresponding eminence on the upper part of the tibia that articulates with the medial condyle of the femur — compare LATERAL CONDYLE *herein*

median* *n* **1** : a vertical line that divides the histogram of a frequency distribution into two parts of equal area **2** : a value of a random variable for which all greater values make the distribution function greater than one half and all lesser values make it less than one half

median eminence *n* : a raised area in the floor of the third ventricle of the brain produced by the infundibulum of the hypothalamus

med·ic·aid \'medə̇ˌkād, -dē-\ *n, often cap* [*medic*al + *aid*] : a program of medical aid designed for those unable to afford regular medical service and financed by the state and federal governments

medi·care \'medə̇-, -dē +ˌ\ *n, often cap* [blend of *medical* and *care*] : a government program of medical care esp. for the aged

me·di·og·ra·phy \ˌmēdēˈägrəfē, -fi\ *n* -ES [*medium* + *-o-* + *-graphy*] **:** a list of multimedia materials on a given subject

me·droxy·progesterone acetate \meˌdräksē+ . . .-\ *n* [fr. *medr-*, alter. of *methylhydroxyl* containing a methyl and hydroxyl group + *oxy-* + *progesterone*] **:** a synthetic steroid progestational hormone $C_{24}H_{34}O_4$ that is a derivative of progesterone and is used in oral and parenteral contraceptives

me·dul·lin \məˈdələn, me-; ˈmedᵊl-, ˈmejəl-\ *n* -s [NL *medulla* + E *-in;* fr. its isolation from the medulla of the kidney] **:** a renal prostaglandin effective in reducing blood pressure

mef·e·nam·ic acid \ˌmefəˌnamik-\ *n* [di*m*ethyl + *fen-* (by shortening and alter. fr. *phenyl*) + *am*inobenzo*ic acid*] **:** a drug $C_{15}H_{15}NO_2$ used as an anti-inflammatory

mega·bar \ˈmegə +ˌ\ *n* [ISV *mega-* + [7]*bar*] **:** a unit of pressure equal to one million bars

mega·bit \"+ˌ\ *n* [*mega-* + [7]*bit*] **:** one million bits

mega·buck \"+ˌ\ *n* [*mega-* + [1]*buck*] **:** one million dollars; *also* **:** money in millions — usu. used in pl.

mega·byte \"+ˌ\ *n* [*mega-* + *byte* (herein); fr. the fact that 1,048,576 (2^{20}) is the power of 2 closest to one million] **:** 1,048,576 bytes

mega·death \"+ˌ\ *n* [*mega-* + *death*] **:** one million deaths — usu. used as a unit in reference to nuclear warfare

mega·dose \"+ˌ\ *n* [*mega-* + *dose*] **:** a large dose (as of a vitamin)

mega·machine \"+ˌ\ *n* [*mega-* + *machine*] **:** a social system that functions impersonally like a gigantic machine

mega·rad \"+ˌ\ *n* [*mega-* + [3]*rad*] **:** one million rads

mega·structure \"+ˌ\ *n* [*mega-* + *structure*] **:** a very large multistory building or complex of buildings

mega·unit \"+ˌ\ *n* [*mega-* + *unit*] **:** one million units

mega·vitamin \ˌmegə+\ *adj* [*mega-* + *vitamin*] **:** relating to or consisting of very large doses of vitamins ⟨~ therapy⟩

mega·vitamins \ˈmegə+ˌ\ *n pl* [*mega-* + *vitamins*] **:** a large quantity of vitamins

me·gil·lah *also* **me·gil·la** \məˈgilə\ *n* -s [Yiddish *megillah* rigmarole, fr. Heb *mĕgillāh* scroll (used esp. of the Book of Esther, the whole of which is read aloud during Purim)] *slang* **:** a long involved story or account ⟨the whole ~⟩ ⟨he'd had a lot of stuff patented over the years, but people had robbed him or swiped his ideas; the usual inventor's ~ —Alexander King⟩

meio·fauna \ˈmīō +\ *n* [ISV *meio-* + *fauna*] **:** the mesofauna of the benthos — **meio·faunal** \ˌmīō +ˌ\ *adj*

melanocyte–stimulating hormone \ˌ≈≈ˌ≈ˌ≈≈ˌ≈≈-, ≈ˌ≈-\ *n* **:** either of two vertebrate hormones of the pituitary gland that darken the skin by stimulating melanin dispersion in pigment-containing cells — abbr. *MSH*; called also *melanophore-stimulating hormone*

mel·a·no·some \ˈmelənōˌsōm\ *n* -s [*melan-* + [3]*-some*] **:** a melanin-producing granule in a melanocyte

mel·a·to·nin \ˌmeləˌtōnən\ *n* -s [prob. fr. *mela*nocyte + sero*tonin;* fr. its power to lighten melanocytes] **:** a vertebrate hormone of the pineal gland that produces lightening of the skin by causing contraction of melanophores in pigment-containing cells and that plays a role in sexual development and maturation by inhibiting gonadal development and the estrous cycle

meld \ˈmeld\ *n* -s [[3]*meld*] **:** BLEND, MIXTURE

Mel·lo·tron \ˈmeləˌträn\ *trademark* — used for an electronic keyboard instrument programmed to produce the tape-recorded sounds usu. of orchestral instruments

mellow* *adj* **1** *slang* **:** EXCELLENT, APPEALING, FINE ⟨at first the gig looked ~: $300 for two shows and a supposedly hip crowd —Mark Jacobson⟩ **2 :** feeling relaxed and good from smoking marijuana

mel·pha·lan \ˈmelfəˌlan\ *n* -s [prob. fr. *me*thano*l* + *ph*enyl*alan*ine] **:** an antineoplastic drug $C_{13}H_{18}Cl_2N_2O_2$ that is a derivative of nitrogen mustard and is used esp. in the treatment of multiple myeloma

meltdown* *n* **:** the melting of the core of a nuclear reactor

mem·bran·al \ˌmemˌbrānᵊl\ *adj* [*membran-* + [1]*-al*] **:** relating to or characteristic of cellular membranes

memory* *n* **:** capacity for storing information ⟨a computer with 16K words of ~⟩

memory lane *n* **:** an imaginary path through the nostalgically remembered past — usu. used in such phrases as *a walk down memory lane*

men·a·zon \ˈmenəˌzän\ *n* -s [perh. fr. di*me*thyl + diami*no-* + tri*az*ine + thi*on*ate] **:** an organophosphate insecticide $C_6H_{12}N_5O_2PS_2$ used esp. against parasitic insects of warm-blooded animals

me·nin·go·encephalitic \məˌniŋ(ˌ)gō, -in(ˌ)jō +\ *adj* [*menin- goencephalitis* + [1]*-ic*] **:** relating to or characteristic of meningoencephalitis ⟨~ lesions⟩

menopause* *n* **:** MALE MENOPAUSE — **menopausal*** *adj*

meno·taxis \ˌmenə +\ *n* [NL, fr. [2]*meno-* + *taxis*] **:** a taxis involving a constant reaction (as movement at a constant angle to a light source) but not a simple movement toward or away from the directing stimulus

mensch \ˈmench, ˈmensh\ *n* -ES [Yiddish, fr. G, man, human being] **:** a person of integrity and honor

menu* *n* **:** a list shown on the display of a computer from which a user can select the operation the computer is to perform

mer·cap·to·ethanol \(ˌ)mərˌkaptō+\ *n* [*mercapt-* + *ethanol*] **:** a reducing agent $HSCH_2CH_2OH$ used to break disulfide bonds in proteins (as for the destruction of their physiological activity)

mercy killing *n* **:** EUTHANASIA

me·rid·ic \məˈridik\ *adj* [Gk *merid-*, *meris* part + E *-ic;* akin to Gk *meros* part — more at MERIT] **:** having some but not all active constituents chemically defined ⟨insects reared on a ~ diet⟩ — compare HOLIDIC *herein*, OLIGIDIC *herein*

mer·i·toc·ra·cy \ˌmerəˈtäkrəsē\ *n* -ES [[1]*merit* + *-cracy*] **1 :** a system in which the talented are chosen and moved ahead on the basis of their achievement **2 a :** leadership by the talented **b :** MERITOCRATS *herein* — **mer·it·o·crat·ic** \ˌmerəd·əˌkrad·ik\ *adj*

mer·it·o·crat \ˈmerəd·ōˌkrat\ *n* -s [[1]*merit* + *-crat*] **:** one who advances through a meritocratic system

mer·lot \me(ə)rˈlō\ *n* -s *often cap* [F] **:** a dry red varietal wine made from a widely grown grape orig. used in the Bordeaux region of France for blending

mero·myosin \ˌmerə+\ *n* [[3]*mer-* + *myosin*] **:** either of two structural subunits of myosin obtained esp. by tryptic digestion

mesial* *adj* **:** of, relating to, or being the surface of a tooth that is next to the tooth in front of it or that is closest to the middle of the front of the jaw — compare DISTAL *herein*, PROXIMAL *herein* — **me·si·al·ly*** \-ə-lē\ *adv*

meso·pelagic \ˌme|zō, ˌmē|, |sō +\ *adj* [*mes-* + *pelagic*] **:** of, relating to, or inhabiting oceanic depths from about 600 to 3000 feet ⟨~ fish⟩

me·so·scale \"+\ *adj* [*mes-* + ⁷*scale*] **:** of or relating to a meteorological phenomenon approximately 1 to 100 kilometers in horizontal extent ⟨~ cloud pattern⟩ ⟨~ wind circulation⟩

mesosome* *n* **:** an organelle of bacteria that appears in electron micrographs as an invagination of the plasma membrane and is a site of localization of respiratory enzymes

messenger* *n* **:** MESSENGER RNA *herein*

messenger RNA *n* **:** an RNA that carries the code for a particular protein from the nuclear DNA to a ribosome in the cytoplasm and acts as a template for the formation of that protein — compare TRANSFER RNA *herein*

mess over *vt, slang* **:** to treat harshly or unfairly **:** ABUSE

mes·tra·nol \ˈmestrəˌnȯl, -ˌnōl\ *n* -s [*meth-* + *estr*ogen + pregn*ane* + *-ol*] **:** a synthetic estrogen $C_{21}H_{26}O_2$ used in oral contraceptives

meta·centric \ˌmed·ə+\ *n* -s **:** a metacentric chromosome

me·tal·lic \məˈtalik\ *n* -s [*metallic,* adj.] **:** a fiber or yarn made of or coated with metal; *also* **:** a fabric made of this

met·al·lide \ˈmed·ᵊlˌīd, -etᵊl-\ *vt* -ED/-ING/-s [obs. *metallide,* n., a binary compound of metals, fr. *metall-* + ¹*-ide*] **:** to diffuse (atoms of a metal or metalloid) into the surface of a metal by electrolysis in order to impart a desired surface property (as hardness) to the bulk metal

me·tal·lo·enzyme \mə·ˌtalō+\ *n* [*metall-* + *enzyme*] **:** an enzyme consisting of a protein linked with a specific metal

me·tal·lo·protein \"+\ *n* [*metall-* + *protein*] **:** a conjugated protein in which the prosthetic group is a metal

me·tal·lo·thio·nein \mə·ˌtalōˈthīəˌnēn\ *n* -s [*metall-* + *thionein,* a protein] **:** a metal-binding protein involved in the storage of copper in the liver

metal–oxide semiconductor \ˌ=ˌ=ˌ=-\ *n* **:** a semiconductor device (as a diode or a capacitor) in which a metallic oxide (as silicon dioxide) serves as an insulating layer

metameric* *adj* **:** of, relating to, or being color metamers ⟨a ~ pair⟩ — **metamerism***n*

meta·ram·i·nol \ˌmed·əˈraməˌnȯl, -ˌnōl\ *n* -s [perh. fr. *meta-* + hydroxy- + *amin-* + *-ol*] **:** a sympathomimetic drug $C_9H_{13}NO_2$ used esp. as a vasoconstrictor

meta·rhodopsin \ˌmed·ə+\ *n* [*meta-* + *rhodopsin*] **:** either of two intermediate compounds formed in the bleaching of rhodopsin by light

me·te·or·oi·dal \ˌmēd·ēəˌrȯidᵊl\ *adj* [*meteoroid* + *-al*] **:** of or relating to meteoroids

me·te·pa \məˈtēpə, meˈ-\ *n* -s [*me*thyl + *tepa* (herein)] **:** an insect chemosterilant $C_9H_{18}N_3OP$ that is a methyl derivative of tepa

meter maid *n* **:** a female member of a police force who is assigned to write tickets for parking violations

meth·a·pyr·i·lene \ˌmethəˈpirəˌlēn *also* -ˈpīr-\ *n* -s [di*methyl* + *pyri*dinyl + *-ene*] **:** an antihistamine drug $C_{14}H_{19}N_3S$ widely used in the form of its fumarate or hydrochloride as a mild sedative in proprietary sleep-inducing drugs

metha·qua·lone \ˌmethəˈkwāˌlōn, meˈthakwəˌlōn\ *n* -s [*meth*yl + *quina*zo*l*ine + *-one*] **:** a sedative and hypnotic drug $C_{16}H_{14}N_2O$ that is not a barbiturate but is habit-forming and subject to abuse — see QUAALUDE *herein*

Meth·e·drine \ˈmethəˌdrēn, -ˌdrən\ *trademark* — used for a preparation of methamphetamine

meth·i·cil·lin \ˌmethəˈsilən\ *n* -s [*meth-* + pen*icillin*] **:** a semisynthetic penicillin $C_{17}H_{19}N_2O_6NaS$ esp. effective against penicillinase-producing staphylococci

me·thi·ma·zole \meˈthīməˌzōl, məˈ-\ *n* -s [*meth*yl + *imi*d*azole*] **:** a drug $C_4H_6N_2S$ used to inhibit activity of the thyroid gland

method* *n, usu cap* **:** a dramatic technique by which an actor seeks to gain complete identification with the inner personality of the character being portrayed

method of fluxions : DIFFERENTIAL CALCULUS

meth·o·trex·ate \ˌmethə·ˈtrekˌsāt, -sət\ *n* -s [*meth-* + *-trex-* (arbitrary infix) + *-ate*] **:** a toxic anticancer drug $C_{20}H_{22}N_8O_5$ that is an analogue of folic acid and an antimetabolite

me·thox·amine \meˈthäksəˌmēn, -ˌmən\ *n* [fr. *meth*yl + *ox-* + *amine*] **:** a sympathomimetic amine $C_{11}H_{17}NO_3$ used in the form of its hydrochloride esp. to raise or maintain blood pressure (as during surgery) by its vasoconstrictor effects

me·thoxy·flu·rane \meˌthäksēˈflu̇(ə)rˌān\ *n* -s [*meth-* + *oxy-* + *fluor-* + eth*ane*] **:** a potent nonexplosive inhalational general anesthetic $C_3H_4Cl_2F_2O$ administered as a vapor

meths \ˈmeths\ *n pl but sing in constr* [contr. of *methylated spirits*] *Brit* **:** methylated spirits esp. as an illicit beverage

meth·yl·ase \ˈmethəˌlās, -āz\ *n* -s [*methyl* + *-ase*] **:** an enzyme that catalyzes methylation (as of RNA or DNA)

methyldopa \ˌ=ˌ=ˌ=\ *n* [*methyl* + *dopa*] **:** a drug $C_{10}H_{13}NO_4$ used to lower blood pressure

methylmercury \ˌ=ˌ=ˌ=\ *n* [*methyl* + *mercury*] **:** any of various toxic compounds of mercury containing the complex CH_3Hg — that enter the environment as pollutants formed as industrial by-products or pesticide residues, tend to accumulate in living organisms (as fish) esp. in food chains, are rapidly and easily absorbed through the human intestinal wall, and cause neurological dysfunction in man — see MINAMATA DISEASE *herein*

methyl parathion *n* **:** a potent synthetic organophosphate insecticide $C_8H_{10}NO_5PS$ that is more toxic than parathion

meth·yl·phe·ni·date \ˌmethəlˈfenəˌdāt, -ˈfēn-\ *n* -s [*methyl* + *phen*yl + piper*id*ine + acet*ate*] **:** a mild stimulant $C_{14}H_{19}NO_2$ of the central nervous system that is an analogue of amphetamine and is used in the form of its hydrochloride to treat narcolepsy and hyperkinetic behavior disorders in children — see RITALIN *herein*

methylprednisolone \ˌ=ˌ=ˌ=ˌ=\ *n* [*methyl* + *prednisolone*] **:** a glucocorticoid $C_{22}H_{30}O_5$ that is a derivative of prednisolone and is used as an anti-inflammatory agent; *also* **:** any of several of its salts (as an acetate) used similarly

methyltransferase \ˌ=ˌ=ˌ=ˌ=\ *n* [*methyl* + *transferase*] **:** any of several transferases that promote transfer of a methyl group from one compound to another

meth·y·ser·gide \ˌmethəˈsərˌjīd\ *n* -s [*methyl* + ly*serg*ic acid + am*ide*] **:** a serotonin antagonist $C_{21}H_{27}N_3O_2$ used as its maleate esp. in the treatment and prevention of migraine headaches

met·i·cal \ˈmetəkəl, ˌmetəˈkal\ *n* -s [Ar *mithqāl* — more at MISKAL] **:** the basic monetary unit of Mozambique — see MONEY table *in the Dict*

met·o·clo·pra·mide \ˌmed·əˈklōprəˌmīd\ *n* -s [*met*hoxy + *chlor-* + *-pr-* (perh. arbitrary infix) + *amide*] **:** an antiemetic drug $C_{14}H_{22}ClN_3O_2$ administered as the hydrochloride

me–too* *adj* **:** similar or identical to an established product (as a drug) with no significant advantage over it

metric* *n* **:** a mathematical function that associates with each pair of elements of a set a real nonnegative number constituting their distance and satisfying the conditions that the number is zero only if the two elements are identical, the number is the same regardless of the order in which the two elements are taken, and the number associated with one pair of elements plus that associated with one member of the pair and a third element is equal to or greater than the number associated with the other member of the pair and the third element

met·ri·cate \\'me·trə̇,kāt\\ *vt* -ED/-ING/-S [2*metric* + 4*-ate*] *Brit* **:** METRICIZE *herein*

met·ri·ca·tion \\,me·trə̇'kāshən\\ *n* -S [2*metric* + *-ation*] **:** the act or process of metricizing

metricize* *vt* **:** to change into or express in the metric system

metric space *n* **:** a mathematical set for which a metric is defined for any pair of elements

1**met·ro** \\'me·(,)trō\\ *n* -S [fr. the phrase *metropolitan government*] **:** a metropolitan regional government

2**metro** \\"\\ *adj* **:** METROPOLITAN 5

met·ro·ni·da·zole \\,me·trə'nīdə,zōl\\ *n* [*me*thyl + *-tron-* (prob. fr. *nitro*) + imi*de* + *azole*] **:** a drug $C_6H_9N_3O_3$ used esp. in treating vaginal trichomoniasis

me·tyr·a·pone \\mə'tirə,pōn\\ *n* -S [perh. fr. *methyl* + *-rapone* (perh. alter. of *propanone*)] **:** a metabolic hormone $C_{14}H_{14}N_2O$ that inhibits biosynthesis of cortisol and corticosterone and is used to test for normal functioning of the pituitary gland

me·val·o·nate \\mə'valə,nāt\\ *n* -S [fr. *mevalon*ic acid + 4*-ate*] **:** a salt of mevalonic acid

MHC *abbr* major histocompatibility complex *herein*

MIA \\,e(,)mī'ā\\ *n* -S [*m*issing *i*n *a*ction] **:** a member of the armed forces whose whereabouts following a combat mission are unknown and whose death cannot be established beyond reasonable doubt

mi·chae·lis constant \\mī¦kāləs-, mə̇-\\ *n, usu cap M* [after Leonor *Michaelis* †1949 Am. biochemist] **:** a constant that is a measure of the kinetics of an enzyme reaction and that is equivalent to the concentration of substrate at which the reaction takes place at one half its maximum rate

mick·ey–mouse \\¦mikē¦maùs, -ki-\\ *vt* -ED/-ING/-S [fr. *Mickey Mouse,* a trademark] **:** to provide (a film) with accompanying music that closely describes or mimics the action

1**mickey mouse** *adj, usu cap both Ms* [fr. *Mickey Mouse,* a trademark used for a cartoon character] **1 :** lacking importance **:** INSIGNIFICANT ⟨switch to *Mickey Mouse* courses, where you don't work too hard —Willie Cager⟩ **2 :** annoyingly petty ⟨*Mickey Mouse* regulations⟩ **3 :** being or performing insipid or corny popular music

2**mickey mouse** *n, usu cap both Ms* **:** something that is Mickey Mouse ⟨eliminating the *Mickey Mouse* from the soldier's routine —L.J. Binder⟩

MICR *abbr* magnetic ink character recognition

micro* *n* **1 :** MICROCOMPUTER *herein* **2 :** MICROPROCESSOR *herein*

micro* *adj* **:** concerned with individuals, small units, or small quantities; *also* **:** involving minute quantities or variations

mi·cro·algae \\¦mīkrō+\\ *n pl* [*micr-* + *algae*] **:** algae (as diatoms or chlorellas) not visible to the unaided eye — **mi·cro·algal** \\"+\\ *adj*

mi·cro·anatomical \\"+\\ *adj* [*microanatomy* + *-ical*] **:** HISTOLOGICAL

mi·cro·an·gi·op·a·thy \\¦==,anjē'äpəthē\\ *n* -ES [*micr-* + *angi-* + *-pathy*] **:** a disease of very fine blood vessels ⟨thrombotic ~⟩ — **mi·cro·an·gi·o·path·ic** \\-jēə'pathik\\ *adj*

mi·cro·beam \\'mīkrō+,\\ *n* [*micr-* + *beam*] **:** a beam of radiation of small cross section ⟨a focused laser ~⟩ ⟨a ~ of electrons⟩

micro·body \\"+,\\ *n* [*micr-* + *body*] **:** PEROXISOME *herein*

mi·cro·capsule \\¦mīkrō+\\ *n* [*micr-* + *capsule*] **:** a tiny capsule containing material (as an adhesive or a medicine) that is released when the capsule is broken, melted, or dissolved

mi·cro·chip \\"+,\\ *n* [*micr-* + *chip*] **:** INTEGRATED CIRCUIT *herein*

mi·cro·circuit \\"+,\\ *n* [*micr-* + *circuit*] **:** a compact electronic circuit **:** INTEGRATED CIRCUIT *herein* — **mi·cro·circuitry** \\"+\\ *n*

mi·cro·circulation \\¦mīkrō +\\ *n* [*micr-* + *circulation*] **1 :** the part of the circulatory system made up of very fine channels (as capillaries or venules) **2 :** circulation through very fine channels — **mi·cro·circulatory** \\"+\\ *adj*

mi·cro·coccal \\"+\\ *adj* [*micrococcus* + 1*-al*] **:** relating to or characteristic of micrococci ⟨~ enzymes⟩

mi·cro·code \\"+,\\ *n* [*micr-* + *code*] **:** microinstructions esp. for a microprocessor

mi·cro·computer \\¦mīkrō+\\ *n* [*micr-* + *computer*] **1 :** a very small computer; *esp* **:** one built around a microprocessor **2 :** MICROPROCESSOR *herein*

mi·cro·culture \\'==+,\\ *n* [*micr-* + *culture*] **1 :** the culture of a small group of human beings with limited perspective **2 :** a microscopic culture of cells or organisms — **mi·cro·cultural** \\¦mīkrō +\\ *adj*

mi·cro·distribution \\¦mīkrō+\\ *n* [*micr-* + *distribution*] **:** the precise distribution of one or more kinds of organisms in a microhabitat or in part of an ecosystem ⟨~ of soil mites⟩

mi·cro·dot \\'==+,\\ *n* [*micr-* + *dot*] **1 :** a photographic reproduction of printed matter reduced to the size of a dot for ease or security of transmittal **2 :** a very small pill or capsule of LSD

mi·cro·earthquake \\¦==+\\ *n* [*micr-* + *earthquake*] **:** an earthquake of low intensity; *esp* **:** one of magnitude of less than 3 on the Richter scale

mi·cro·ecology \\"+\\ *n* [*micr-* + *ecology*] **:** ecology of all or part of a small community (as a microhabitat or a housing development) — **mi·cro·ecological** \\"+\\ *adj*

mi·cro·economic \\"+\\ *adj* [*micr-* + *economic*] **:** of or relating to microeconomics ⟨~ theory⟩

mi·cro·electronics \\¦mīkrō+\\ *n pl* [*micr-* + *electronics*] **1** *sing in constr* **:** a branch of electronics that deals with the miniaturization of electronic circuits and components **2 :** devices, equipment, or circuits produced using the methods of microelectronics — **mi·cro·electronic** \\"+\\ *adj*

mi·cro·emulsion \\"+\\ *n* [*micr-* + *emulsion*] **:** an emulsion in which the dispersed phase is in the form of very small droplets usu. produced and maintained with the aid of surfactants and having diameters of from 50 to 500 angstroms

mi·cro·encapsulate \\"+\\ *vt* [*micr-* + *encapsulate*] **:** to enclose in a microcapsule ⟨*microencapsulated* aspirin⟩ — **mi·cro·encapsulation** \\"+\\ *n*

mi·cro·filament \"+\ *n* [*micr-* + *filament*] **:** any of the minute protein filaments that are widely distributed in the cytoplasm of eukaryotic cells, help maintain their structural framework, and play a role in the movement of cell components

mi·cro·floppy *or* **microfloppy disk** \"+\ *n* [*micr-* + *floppy* (herein)] **:** a floppy disk smaller than 5¼ inches in diameter

mi·cro·fluorometry \"+\ *n* [*micr-* + *fluorometry*] **:** the detection and measurement of the fluorescence produced by minute quantities of materials (as in cells) — **mi·cro·fluorometer** \"+\ *n* — **mi·cro·fluorometric** \"+\ *adj*

mi·cro·form* \ˈmīkrə+ˌ\ *n* **1 :** a process or medium for reproducing printed matter in a much reduced size **2 a :** matter reproduced by microform **b :** MICROCOPY

mi·cro·fungus \ˌ==+\ *n* [*micr-* + *fungus*] **:** a fungus (as a mold) with a microscopic fruiting body — **mi·cro·fun·gal** \"+\ *adj*

mi·cro·gauss \ˈmīkrō+ˌ\ *n* [ISV, fr. *micr-* + *gauss*] **:** one millionth of a gauss

mi·cro·graphics \ˌmīkrə+\ *n pl but sing in constr* [*micr-* + *graphics,* pl. of ²*graphic*] **:** the industry concerned with the manufacture and sale of graphic material in microform; *also* **:** the production of graphic material in microform — **mi·cro·graphic** \"+\ *adj*

mi·cro·heterogeneity \ˌmīkrō +\ *n* [*micr-* + *heterogeneity*] **:** a variation in the chemical structure of a substance (as the amino acid sequence of a protein) that does not produce a major change in its properties

mi·cro·image \ˈmīkrō+ˌ\ *n* [*micr-* + *image*] **:** an image (as on a microfilm) that is of greatly reduced size

mi·cro·inject \ˌmīkrō +\ *vt* [*micr-* + *inject*] **:** to subject to or use in microinjection

mi·cro·instruction \ˌmīkrō+\ *n* [*micr-* + *instruction*] **:** a computer instruction that activates the circuits necessary to perform a single machine operation usu. as part of the execution of a machine-language instruction

mi·cro·machining \"+\ *n* -s [*micr-* + *machining,* gerund of ²*machine*] **:** the removing (as in drilling, planing, or shaping) of small amounts of material (as metal) by action other than that of a sharp-edged tool ⟨~ done with an electron beam⟩

micrometeorite* *n* **:** a meteoritic particle of very small size — **mi·cro·meteoritic** \ˌmīkrō+\ *adj*

mi·cro·meteoroid \ˌmīkrō+\ *n* [*micr-* + *meteoroid*] **:** MICROMETEORITE *herein*

mi·cro·miniature \"+\ *adj* [*micr-* + *miniature*] **1 :** MICROMINIATURIZED *herein* **2 :** suitable for use with microminiaturized parts

mi·cro·miniaturization \"+\ *n* [*micr-* + *miniaturization*] **:** the process of producing microminiaturized things

mi·cro·miniaturized \"+\ *adj* [*micr-* + *miniaturized*] **:** reduced to or produced in a very small size and esp. in a size smaller than one considered miniature ⟨~ electronic circuit⟩

mi·cro·module \"+\ *n* [*micr-* + *module*] **:** a microminiaturized module

mi·cro·morphology \"+\ *n* [*micr-* + *morphology*] **1 :** MICROSTRUCTURE — used esp. with reference to soils **2 :** minute morphological detail esp. as determined by electron microscopy; *also* **:** the study of such detail — **mi·cro·morphologic** \"+\ *or* **mi·cro·morphological** \"+\ *adj* — **mi·cro·morphologically** \"+\ *adv*

mi·cro·population \"+\ *n* [*micr-* + *population*] **1 :** a population of microorganisms **2 :** the population of organisms within a small area

mi·cro·prism \"+\ *n* [*micr-* + *prism*] **:** a usu. circular area on the focusing screen of a camera that is made up of tiny prisms and causes the image in the viewfinder to blur if the subject is not in focus

mi·cro·probe \ˈmīkrə+ˌ\ *n* [*micr-* + *probe*] **:** a device for microanalysis that operates by exciting radiation in a minute area or volume of material so that the composition may be determined from the emission spectrum

mi·cro·processor \ˌmīkrō+\ *n* [*micr-* + *processor* (herein)] **:** a computer processor contained on an IC chip; *also* **:** such a processor along with memory and associated circuits on a chip

mi·cro·programming \"+\ *n* [*micr-* + *programming,* gerund of ²*program*] **:** the use of routines stored in memory rather than specialized circuits for controlling a device (as a computer) — **mi·cro·program** \"+\ *n or vt*

mi·cro·publication \"+\ *n* [*micr-* + *publication*] **1 :** MICROPUBLISHING *herein* **2 :** something published in microform

mi·cro·publishing \"+\ *n* [*micr-* + *publishing*] **:** the publishing of new or previously published material in microform — **mi·cro·publish** \"+\ *vt* — **mi·cro·publisher** \"+\ *n*

mi·cro·puncture \"+\ *n* [*micr-* + *puncture*] **:** an extremely small puncture ⟨a ~ of the nephron⟩

mi·cro·quake \ˈ==+ˌ\ *n* [*micr-* + *quake*] **:** MICROEARTHQUAKE *herein*

mi·cro·spo·ran·gi·ate \ˌ==spəˌranjēə̇t\ *adj* [*microsporangium* + ³*-ate*] **:** bearing or being microsporangia

mi·cro·state \ˈmīkrō+ˌ\ *n* [*micr-* + *state*] **:** an independent nation that is extremely small in area and population

mi·cro·surgery \ˌmīkrō+\ *n* [*micr-* + *surgery*] **:** minute dissection or manipulation (as by a micromanipulator or laser beam) of living structures (as cells) for surgical or experimental purposes — **mi·cro·surgeon** \"+\ *n* — **mi·cro·surgical** \"+\ *adj* — **mi·cro·surgically** \"+\ *adv*

mi·cro·teaching \ˈ==+ˌ\ *n* [*micr-* + *teaching*] **:** practice teaching in which a student teacher's teaching of a small class for a short time is videotaped for subsequent evaluation

mi·cro·tektite \ˌmīkrō+\ *n* [*micr-* + *tektite*] **:** a minute tektite one millimeter or less in diameter found esp. in sediments on the ocean floor

mi·cro·text \ˈ==+ˌ\ *n* [*micr-* + *text*] **:** text in microform

mi·cro·tubule \ˌmīkrō+\ *n* [*micr-* + *tubule*] **:** any of the minute cylindrical structures in cells that are widely distributed in protoplasm and are made up of protein subunits — **mi·cro·tubular** \"+\ *adj*

mi·cro·vascular \"+\ *adj* [*micr-* + *vascular*] **:** of, relating to, or constituting the part of the circulatory system made up of minute vessels (as venules or capillaries) that average less than 0.3 millimeter in diameter — **mi·cro·vasculature** \"+\ *n*

mi·cro·vessel \"+\ *n* [*micr-* + *vessel*] **:** a blood vessel (as a capillary, arteriole, or venule) of the microcirculatory system

mi·cro·villus \"+\ *n* [NL, fr. *micr-* + *villus*] **:** a microscopic projection of a tissue, cell, or cell organelle; *esp* **:** any of the fingerlike outward projections of some cell surfaces — **mi·cro·vil·lar** \ˌ==ˌvilər\ *adj* — **mi·cro·vil·lous** \-ləs\ *adj*

microwave* *or* **microwave oven** *n* **:** an oven in which food is cooked by the heat produced as a result of microwave penetration of the food

microwave* *vt* **:** to cook or heat in a microwave oven

midcourse \ˈ=,=\ *adj* [*midcourse, n.,* fr. [1]*mid* + *course*] **:** being or relating to the part of a course (as of spacecraft) that is between the initial and final phases — **midcourse** \ˈ=ˈ=\ *n*

mid·cult \ˈmid,kəlt\ *n* -s [*mid*dlebrow *cult*ure] **:** the artistic and intellectual culture that is neither highbrow culture nor lowbrow culture **:** middlebrow culture

middle america *n, often cap M & cap A* **:** the middle-class segment of the U.S. population; *esp* **:** the traditional or conservative element of the middle class — **middle american** *n, often cap M & cap A*

middle–of–the–road·ism \,====ˈrōd,izəm\ *n* -s [*middle-of-the-road* + *-ism*] **:** a middle-of-the-road policy or attitude

midi \ˈmidē\ *n* -s [[1]*mid* + *-i* (as in *mini* — herein)] **:** a dress, skirt, or coat that usu. extends to the mid-calf — called also respectively *midi dress, midi skirt, midi coat*

mid–life crisis \ˈ=ˈ=-\ *n* **:** a period of emotional turmoil in middle age caused by the realization that one is no longer young and characterized esp. by a strong desire for change

mid·size \ˈmid,sīz\ *adj* **:** of intermediate size ⟨a ~ car⟩

mike* *vt* **:** to supply with a microphone ⟨~ a singer⟩

mil* *n* **:** THOUSAND ⟨found a salinity of 38.4 per ~⟩

milanese* *adj, usu cap* **:** coated with flour or bread crumbs, often seasoned with cheese, and sautéed ⟨veal cutlet *Milanese*⟩

mil·i·tar·ia \,miləˈterēə\ *n pl* [*military* + [2]*-ia*] **:** military objects (as firearms and uniforms) of historical value or interest

military collar *n* **:** a wide double-pointed collar that lies flat and open esp. on a double-breasted coat

millimicro- *comb form* [*milli-* + *micr-*] **:** [2]NANO-

mil·li·osmol \ˌmilēˌäz,mōl, -ˌäs-\ *n* [*milli-* + *osmol*] **:** one thousandth of an osmol

mil·li·radian \ˌmilə+\ *n* [ISV *milli-* + *radian*] **:** one thousandth of a radian

mil·li·rem \"+\ *n* [*milli-* + *rem*] **:** one thousandth of a rem

mim·eo \ˈmimē,ō\ *n* -s [short for *mimeographed*] **:** a mimeographed publication

mim–mem \ˈmimˈmem\ *adj* [*mim*icry + *mem*orization] **:** of, relating to, or being a drill pattern in which students repeat usu. in chorus a foreign language phrase supplied by their instructor

mina·mata disease \,minəˈmätə-\ *n, usu cap M* [fr. *Minamata,* town in Japan where it was first recognized] **:** a toxic neuropathy caused by the ingestion of methylmercury compounds (as in contaminated seafood) and characterized by impairment of cerebral functions, constriction of the visual field, and progressive weakening of muscles

mi·nau·dière \mēnōdyeer\ *n* -s [F, affected, coquettish, fr. *minauder* to simper, smirk, fr. OF *mine* appearance] **:** a small decorative case for cosmetics or jewelry

mind–bending \ˈ=,==\ *adj* **:** MIND-BLOWING *herein*

mind–blowing \ˈ=ˈ==\ *adj* **1 :** PSYCHEDELIC 1b *herein* **2 :** MIND-BOGGLING *herein* — **mindblower** \ˈ=ˈ=(=)\ *n*

mind–bog·gling \ˈ=,==\ *adj* **:** mentally or emotionally exciting **:** OVERWHELMING

mind–expanding \ˈ==,===\ *adj* **:** PSYCHEDELIC 1a *herein*

minefield* *n* **:** something resembling a minefield; *esp* **:** a situation or area having many dangers or requiring extreme caution

[1]**mini** \ˈminē, -ni\ *n* -s [*mini-* (herein)] **:** one that is small of its kind: as **a :** MINICAR **b :** MINISKIRT *herein* **c :** MINICOMPUTER *herein*

[2]**mini** \"\ *adj* **:** very small **:** MINIATURE

mini- *comb form* [*mini*ature] **:** very small **:** miniature

miniature pinscher *n* **:** a toy dog that suggests a small Doberman pinscher and measures 10 to 12½ inches in height at the withers

miniature schnauzer *n* **:** a schnauzer of a breed that is 12 to 14 inches in height and is classified as a terrier

mini·bike \ˈminē, -nə+,\ *n* [*mini-* (herein) + *bike*] **:** a small one-passenger motorcycle having a low frame and elevated handlebars — **mini·biker** \"+\ *n*

mini·bus \"+\ *n* [*mini-* (herein) + *bus*] **:** a small bus

mini·cab \"+\ *n* [*mini-* (herein) + *cab*] **:** a small car used as a taxicab

Mini·cam \ˈminē,kam\ *trademark* — used for a portable television camera

mini·computer \ˌminē, -nə+\ *n* [*mini-* (herein) + *computer*] **:** a computer that is intermediate between a mainframe and a microcomputer in size, speed, and capacity, that can support time-sharing, and that is often dedicated to a single application

mini·floppy \"+\ *n* [*mini-* (herein) + *floppy* (herein)] **:** a floppy disk that is 5¼ inches in diameter

minimal* *adj, often cap* **:** of, relating to, or being minimal art

minimal art *n* **:** abstract art (as painting or sculpture) consisting primarily of simple geometric forms executed in an impersonal style — **minimal artist** *n*

minimal brain dysfunction *n* **:** a syndrome of learning and behavioral problems that is not caused by any serious underlying physical or mental disorder and is characterized esp. by difficulty in sustaining attention, by impulsive behavior (as in speaking out of turn), and usu. by hyperactivity — abbr. *MBD*; called also *minimal brain damage, minimal cerebral dysfunction*

min·i·mal·ism \ˈminəmə,lizəm\ *n* [*minimal* + *-ism*] **1 :** MINIMAL ART *herein* **2 :** a style or technique (as in music or design) that is characterized by the use of few and simple elements — **min·i·mal·ist** \-ləst\ *n or adj*

min·i·mal·ity \,minəˈmaləd·ē, -ətē, -i\ *n* -ES [*minimal* + *-ity*] **:** the state or quality of being minimal

[1]**mini·max** \ˈminə,maks, -nē,m-\ *n* -ES [*mini*mum + *max*imum] **:** the minimum of a set of maxima; *esp* **:** the smallest of a set of maximum possible losses each of which occurs in the most unfavorable outcome of a strategy followed by a participant in a situation governed by the theory of games — compare MAXIMIN *herein*

[2]**minimax** \"\ *adj* **:** of, relating to, or based on a minimax, the minimax principle, or the minimax theorem

minimax principle *n* **:** a principle of choice for a decision problem: one should choose the action which minimizes the loss that he stands to suffer even under the worst circumstances

minimax theorem *n* **:** a theorem in the theory of games: the lowest maximum expected loss equals the highest minimum expected gain

minimum* *n* **:** the lowest speed allowed on a highway

mini·park \ˌminē, -ni+\ *n* [*mini-* (herein) + *park*] **:** a small city park

mini·recession \"+\ *n* [*mini-* (herein) + *recession*] **:** a brief economic downturn of minor proportions

mini·series \"+\ *n* [*mini-* (herein) + *series*] **:** a television production of a story presented in sequential episodes

mini·ski \'minē, -nə+,\ *n* [*mini-* (herein) + *ski*] **1 :** a short ski worn esp. by beginners **2 :** a miniature ski worn by a skibobber

mini·skirt \¦minē, -ni+\ *n* [*mini-* (herein) + *skirt*] **:** a short skirt or dress that usu. extends to the mid-thigh — called also *minidress* \"+\

mini·state \"+,\ *n* [*mini-* (herein) + *state*] **:** MICROSTATE *herein*

mini·sub \"+,\ *n* [*mini-* (herein) + [4]*sub*] **:** a very small submarine used esp. in research (as on the ocean bottom)

min·ke whale *also* **min·ke** \'miŋkə-\ *n* [Norw *minkehval* fr. *minke* lesser, smaller + *hval* whale] **:** a small whalebone whale of the genus *Balaenoptera* (*B. acutorostrata*)

minnesota multiphasic personality inventory *n, usu cap both Ms&P&I* [fr. the University of *Minnesota,* where it was developed] **:** a test of personal and social adjustment based on a complex scaling of the answers to an elaborate true or false test

minority* *n* **:** a member of a minority group

MIPS *abbr* million instructions per second

miracle fruit *n* **:** MIRACULOUS FRUIT 2a; *also* **:** its fruit

mi·rex \'mī,reks\ *n* -ES [prob. fr. pis*mire* + *ex*terminator] **:** an organochlorine insecticide $C_{10}Cl_{12}$ formerly used esp. against ants that is a suspected carcinogen

[1]**MIRV** \'mərv\ *n* -s [*m*ultiple *i*ndependently targeted *r*eentry *v*ehicle] **:** a missile with two or more warheads that are designed to reenter the atmosphere on the way to separate enemy targets; *also* **:** any of the warheads of such a missile

[2]**MIRV** \"\ *vb, past or past part* **MIRVed;** *pres part* **MIRV·ing** [*MIRV,* n. (herein)] *vt* **:** to equip with MIRV warheads ⟨both sides would ~ their submarine-borne missiles —Stewart Alsop⟩ ~ *vi* **:** to arm one's forces with MIRVs

mis·allocation \¦mis+\ *n* [[1]*mis-* + *allocation*] **:** faulty or improper allocation

mis·communication \"+\ *n* [[1]*mis-* + *communication*] **:** failure to communicate clearly

mis·diagnose \(¦)mis+\ *vt* [[1]*mis-* + *diagnose*] **:** to diagnose incorrectly — **mis·diagnosis** \¦mis+\ *n*

mis·orient \"+\ *vt* [[1]*mis-* + *orient*] **:** to orient improperly or incorrectly — **mis·orientation** \"+\ *n*

mis·sense \'mis,sen(t)s\ *n* -s [[1]*mis-* + *-sense* (as in *nonsense*)] **:** genetic mutation involving alteration of one or more codons so that different amino acids are determined — compare NONSENSE *herein*

missionary position *n* [perh. so called fr. the insistence of some missionaries that the traditional Western coital position is the only acceptable one] **:** a coital position in which the female lies on her back with the male on top and with his face opposite hers

mist* *n* **:** a drink of alcoholic liquor (as Scotch) served over cracked ice and garnished with a twist of lemon peel

mister charlie *n, usu cap M&C* **:** MR. CHARLIE *herein* — usu. used disparagingly

mith·ra·my·cin \,mithrə'mīsᵊn\ *n* -s [*mithra-* (of unknown origin) + *-mycin*] **:** an antineoplastic antibiotic $C_{52}H_{76}O_{24}$ produced by two bacteria of the genus *Streptomyces* (*S. argillaceus* and *S. tanashiensis*)

mi·to·gen \'mīd·əjən\ *n* -s [*mit-* + *-gen*] **:** a substance that induces mitosis

mi·to·genesis \¦mīd·ō, ¦mitō +\ *n* [*mit-* + *genesis*] **:** the production of cell mitosis

mi·to·gen·ic \¦mīd·ə¦jenik\ *adj* [*mit-* + *-genic*] **:** MITOGENETIC — **mi·to·ge·nic·i·ty** \,mīd·əjə'nisəd·ē\ *n* -ES

mi·to·my·cin \,mīd·ə'mīsᵊn\ *n* -s [prob. fr. ISV *mit-* + *-mycin*] **:** a complex of antibiotic substances which is produced by a Japanese streptomyces (*Streptomyces caespitosus*) and one form of which acts directly on DNA and shows promise as an anticancer agent

mi·to·spore \'mīd·ə +,\ *n* [*mit-* + *spore*] **:** a haploid or diploid spore produced by mitosis

mit·tel·eu·ro·pa \¦mid·ᵊlyü'rōpə, *G* ¦mitəlȯi¦rōpə\ *adj, usu cap* [G, central Europe, fr. *mittel* middle + *Europa* Europe] **:** of or from central Europe **:** of the kind or style prevalent in central Europe

mix* *vt* **:** to produce (as a phonograph record) by electronically combining or adjusting sounds from more than one source

mix* *n* **1 :** a commercially prepared nonalcoholic mixture of ingredients for a mixed drink ⟨mai tai ~⟩ **2 :** the combination or adjustment of sounds from different sources in a phonograph record or tape ⟨a record with a good ~⟩

mixed–media \'=¦===\ *adj* [*mixed* + *media,* pl. of *medium*] **:** MULTIMEDIA *herein*

mixed media *n* **:** MULTIMEDIA *herein*

MLD *abbr* median lethal dose

MMPI *abbr* Minnesota Multiphasic Personality Inventory *herein*

MMT \,em(,)em'tē\ *n* [*m*ethylcyclopentadienyl *m*anganese *t*ricarbonyl] **:** an organometallic compound $CH_3C_5H_4Mn(CO)_3$ added to a motor fuel to increase the octane number

MNC \,em(,)en'sē\ *n* -s [*m*ulti*n*ational *c*orporation] **:** MULTINATIONAL *herein*

mobile home *n* **:** a trailer that is used as a permanent dwelling, is usu. connected to utilities, and is designed without a permanent foundation — compare MOTOR HOME *herein*

[1]**mod** \'mäd\ *adj, often cap* [short for *modern*] **:** MODERN; *esp* **:** bold, free, and unconventional in style or dress

[2]**mod** \"\ *n* -s *often cap* **:** one who wears mod clothes

[3]**mod** \"\ *prep* [by shortening] **:** MODULO

[4]**mod** \"\ *n* -s [short for *module* (herein)] **:** a class period in a modular schedule

model* *n* **1 :** a system of postulates, data, and inferences pre-sented as a mathematical description of an entity or state of affairs **2 :** VERSION, EQUIVALENT

model* *vt* **:** to produce a representation or simulation of ⟨using a computer to ~ a problem⟩

mo·dem \'mō,dem\ *n* -s [*mo*dulator + *dem*odulator] **:** a device that converts signals from one form to a form compatible with another kind of equipment

modesty panel *n* **:** a panel designed to conceal the legs of a person sitting esp. at a desk or table

modified american plan *n, usu cap A* **:** a hotel rate whereby guests are charged a fixed sum (as by the day or week) for room, breakfast, and lunch or dinner

modular* *adj* **:** of or relating to a school schedule in which subjects pertinent to more than one course are covered in common class sessions

modular arithmetic *n* **:** arithmetic that deals with whole numbers where the numbers are replaced by their remainders after division by a fixed number ⟨5 hours after 10 o'clock is 3 o'clock because clocks follow a *modular arithmetic* with modulus 12⟩

mod·u·lar·i·ty \ˌmäjəˈlarəd·ē, -ler-\ *n* -ES [*modular* + *-ity*] **1 :** the use of discrete functional units in building an electronic or mechanical system **2 :** a feature of a computer language that allows programs to be composed of modules

mod·u·lar·ized \ˈmäjələˌrīzd\ *adj* [*modular* + *-ize* + *-ed*] **:** constructed of modules ⟨~ electronic equipment⟩

module* *n* **1 :** any in a series of standardized units for use together: as **a :** a unit of furniture or architecture **b :** an educational or instructional unit which covers a single subject or a discrete part of a broad subject **2 :** an assembly of components that are packaged or mounted together and constitute a functional unit for an electronic or mechanical system ⟨a ~ for a computer⟩ **3 :** an independent unit that constitutes a part of the total structure of a space vehicle ⟨a propulsion ~⟩ **4 a :** a subset of an additive group that is also a group under addition **b :** a mathematical set that is a commutative group under addition and that is closed under multiplication which is distributive from the left or right or both by elements of a ring and for which $a(bx) = (ab)x$ or $(xb)a = x(ba)$ or both where a and b are elements of the ring and x belongs to the set **5 :** a usu. semi-independent routine in a computer program that usu. corresponds to one step in the solution of the problem the program was designed to solve

modulus* *n* **1 :** the factor by which a logarithm of a number to one base is multiplied to obtain the logarithm of the number to a new base **2 :** the number of different numbers used in a system of modular arithmetic

mogul \ˈmōgəl\ *n* -s [prob. of Scand origin; akin to Norw dial. *muge* heap, fr. ON *mūgi* — more at MOW] **:** a bump in a ski run

mois·tur·ize \ˈmȯischəˌrīz\ *vt* -ED/-ING/-s [*moisture* + *-ize*] **:** to add moisture to ⟨~ the air⟩ — **moisturizer** *n* -s

moldy fig *n* **1 :** a person who prefers the traditional form of a kind of music (as jazz) **2 :** one that is old-fashioned

mole* *n* **:** a spy who establishes a cover long before beginning espionage and who usu. has reached a responsible position in the organization being spied on

molecular mass *n* **:** MOLECULAR WEIGHT

mom-and-pop \ˌ==ˈ=\ *adj* **:** being a small owner-operated business ⟨a *mom-and-pop* candy store⟩

moment of truth **1 :** the final sword thrust in a bullfight **2 :** a moment of crisis on whose outcome much or everything depends ⟨the lift-off of a . . . space vehicle with three men aboard is an awesome *moment of truth* —R.A. Petrone⟩

mon·e·ta·rism \ˈmänətəˌrizəm, ˈmən-, *also* ˈmōn-\ *n* -s [*monetary* + *-ism*] **:** QUANTITY THEORY — **mon·e·ta·rist** \-rəst, -ˌrist\ *n* -s

money* *n* — **on the money :** exactly right or accurate

mon·go \ˈmäŋ(ˌ)gō\ *n, pl* **mongo** [Mongolian] **1 :** a monetary unit of Outer Mongolia equal to $^1/_{100}$ tugrik **2 :** a coin representing one mongo

mongolian gerbil *n, usu cap M* **:** a gerbil of the genus *Meriones* (*M. unguiculatus*) of Mongolia and northern China that has an external resemblance to a rat, has a high capacity for temperature regulation, and is used as an experimental laboratory animal

monitor* *n* **:** software or hardware that monitors the operation of a system and esp. a computer system

[1]mono \ˈmä(ˌ)nō *also* ˈmō(ˌ)-\ *adj* [by shortening] **:** MONOPHONIC 3 ⟨a ~ phonograph record⟩

[2]mono *n* -s **1 :** a mono phonograph record **2 :** mono reproduction

[3]mono *n* -s [by shortening] **:** MONONUCLEOSIS

monoamine* *n* **:** PRIMARY AMINE; *esp* **:** one (as serotonin or norepinephrine) that is functionally important in neural transmission

monoamine oxidase *n* **:** an enzyme that deaminates mono-amines and that functions in the nervous system by breaking down monoamine neurotransmitters oxidatively

mono·am·i·ner·gic \ˌmänōˌaməˈnərjik, ˌmōn-\ *adj* [*monoamine* (herein) + *erg-* + *-ic*] **:** liberating or involving monoamines (as serotonin or norepinephrine) in neural transmission ⟨~ neurons⟩

mono·cha·sial \ˌmänəˈkāzh(ē)əl, ˌmōn-, -zēəl\ *adj* [*monocha- si*um + [1]*al*] **:** of, relating to, or being a monochasium

monochrome* *adj* **:** BLACK-AND-WHITE 4b

[1]mono·clo·nal \ˌmänəˈklōnᵊl, ˌmōn-\ *adj* [*mon-* + *clone* + *-al*] **:** produced by, being, or composed of cells derived from a single cell ⟨~ antibodies⟩ ⟨a ~ tumor⟩; *esp* **:** relating to or being an antibody derived from a single cell in large quantities for use against a specific antigen (as a cancer cell)

[2]monoclonal *n* -s **:** a monoclonal antibody

mono·contaminate \ˌmän(ˌ)ō, ˌmōn-, -nə+\ *vt* **:** to infect (a germ-free organism) with one kind of pathogen — **mono·contamination** \"+\ *n*

mono·crystal \ˌmän(ˌ)ō, ˌmōn-, -nə+\ *n* [*mon-* + *crystal*] **:** a single crystal — **monocrystal** *adj* — **monocrystalline** \"+\ *adj*

mono·functional \"+\ *adj* [*mon-* + *functional*] **:** of, relating to, or being a compound with one highly reactive site in a molecule (as in polymerization) ⟨formaldehyde is a ~ reagent⟩

mono·germ \ˌ=(ˌ)=ˌjərm, -jəm\ *adj* [prob. fr. *mon-* + *germinate*] **:** producing or being a fruit that gives rise to a single plant ⟨a ~ variety of sugar beet⟩ — compare MULTIGERM *herein*

mono·hull \"+\ *n* [*mon-* + *hull*] **:** a vessel (as a sailboat) with a single hull

mono·ki·ni \ˌmänəˈkēnē\ *n* -s [*mon-* + *-kini* (as in *bikini*)] **1 :** a topless bikini **2 :** extremely brief shorts for men — **mono·ki·nied** \-nēd\ *adj*

monolithic* *adj* **1 :** formed from a single crystal ⟨a ~ silicon chip⟩ **2 :** produced in or on a monolithic chip ⟨a ~ circuit⟩ **3 :** consisting of or utilizing a monolithic circuit or circuits

mono·oxygenase \ˌmän(ˌ)ō, ˌmōn-, -nə+\ *n* [*mon-* + *oxygenase* (herein)] **:** any of several oxygenases that bring about the incorporation of one atom of molecular oxygen into a substrate

monoploid* *adj* **:** having or being the basic haploid number of chromosomes in a polyploid series of organisms

mono·pole \ˈmänəˌpōl, ˈmōn-\ *n* [*mon-* + [4]*pole*] **1 :** a single positive or negative electrical charge; *also* **:** a hypothetical north or south magnetic pole existing alone **2 :** a radio antenna in the form of a single often straight radiating element

mono·sexual \ˌmä(ˌ)nō, ˌmō(ˌ)- +\ *adj* [*mon-* + *sexual*] **1 :** being or relating to a male or a female rather than a bisexual **2 :** composed of or intended for individuals of one sex ⟨~ schools⟩ — **mono·sexuality** \"+\ *n*

monosome* *n* **:** a single ribosome

mono·specific *adj* **:** specific for a single antigen or receptor site on an antigen — **mono·specificity** \"+\ *n*

monster* *n* **:** a roving football linebacker who plays in no set position — called also *monster back, monster man*

montagnard* *n, often cap* **:** a member of a people inhabiting a highland region in southern Vietnam bordering on Cambodia — **montagnard** *adj, often cap*

mon·te car·lo \ˌmäntēˈkär(ˌ)lō-, -tə̇ˈk-\ *adj, usu cap M&C* [fr. *Monte Carlo,* Monaco, city noted for its gambling casino] **:** of, relating to, or involving the use of random sampling techniques and often the use of computer simulation to obtain approximate solutions to mathematical or physical problems esp. in terms of a range of values each of which has a calculated probability of being the solution ⟨*Monte Carlo* methods⟩ ⟨*Monte Carlo* calculations⟩

mon·te·zu·ma's revenge \ˌ¦mäntə¦züməz-\ *n, usu cap M* [after *Montezuma* II †1520 last Aztec ruler of Mexico] **:** diarrhea contracted in Mexico esp. by tourists

mon·uron \ˈmänyəˌrän, ˈmōn-\ *n* -s [*mon-* + *urea* + [1]*-on*] **:** a persistent herbicide $C_9H_{11}ClN_2O$ used esp. to control mixed broad-leaved weeds

mood ring *n* **:** a ring with a stone made of crystals that change color in response to minute variations in body temperature

Moog \ˈmōg, ˈmüg\ *trademark* — used for a music synthesizer

moon* *n, slang* **:** the naked buttocks; *also* **:** an act of exposing the naked buttocks — **moon*** *vt, slang*

mooncraft \ˈ=ˌ=\ *n* [*moon* + *craft*] **:** MOONSHIP *herein*

moonflight \ˈ=ˌ=\ *n* [*moon* + *flight*] **:** a flight to the moon

moon·ie \ˈmünē\ *n* -s *usu cap* [after Sun Myung *Moon* *b*1920 Korean religious leader + E *-ie*] **:** a member of the Unification Church founded by Sun Myung Moon

moon·ing \ˈmüniŋ\ *n* -s [*moon* (herein) + [3]*-ing*] **:** the practice of exposing one's buttocks (as through the window of a moving vehicle) as a prank

moonport \ˈ=ˌ=\ *n* [[1]*moon* + *port* (harbor)] **:** a facility for launching spacecraft to the moon

moonship \ˈ=ˌ=\ *n* [[1]*moon* + *ship*] **:** spacecraft for travel to the moon

moonshot \ˈ=ˌ=\ *or* **moon shoot** \ˈ=ˌ=\ *n* [*moon* + [1]*shot* or [2]*shoot*] **:** the act or an instance of launching a spacecraft on a course to the moon

moonwalk \ˈ=ˌ=\ *n* [[1]*moon* + *walk*] **:** an instance of walking on the moon — **moonwalker** \ˈ=ˌ==\ *n*

mo·ped \ˈmōˌped\ *n* -s [Sw, fr. *mo*tor motor + *ped*al pedal] **:** a lightweight low-powered motorbike that can be pedaled

MOR *abbr* middle of the road

morning–after pill \ˌ==ˈ==-\ *n* [so called fr. its being taken after rather than before intercourse] **:** an oral drug that interferes with pregnancy by blocking implantation of a fertilized egg in the human uterus

morph \ˈmȯ(ə)rf, ˈmȯ(ə)f\ *n* -s [Gk *morphē* form — more at FORM] **1 :** a local population of a species that consists of interbreeding organisms and is distinguishable from other populations by morphology or behavior though capable of interbreeding with them **2 :** a phenotypic variant of a species

morph- *or* **morpho-*** *comb form* **:** form and ⟨*morpho*functional⟩

mor·phac·tin \mȯrˈfaktə̇n\ *n* -s [prob. fr. *morph-* + *act-* (fr. L *actus* motion) + *-in* — more at ACT] **:** any of several synthetic fluorine-containing compounds that tend to produce morphological changes and suppress growth in plants

mor·pho·gen \ˈmȯrfəjən, -ˌjen\ *n* -s [*morph-* + *-gen*] **:** a diffusible chemical substance that exerts control over morphogenesis esp. by forming a gradient in concentration

mor·pho·physiological \ˌ¦mȯr(ˌ)fō +\ *adj* [*morph-* + *physiological*] **:** of, relating to, or concerned with biological interrelationships between form and function — **mor·pho·physiology** \"+\ *n*

MOS *abbr* metal-oxide semiconductor

möss·bau·er effect \ˈmə(r)sˌbau̇(ə)r-, ˈməs-, ˈmœs-, ˈmȯs-\ *n, usu cap M* [after Rudolph L. *Mössbauer* *b*1929 Ger. physicist] **:** the emission and absorption of gamma rays without recoil by various radioactive nuclei embedded in solids — compare NUCLEAR RESONANCE *herein*

mössbauer spectroscopy \¦=ˌ=(=)-\ *n, usu cap M* **:** spectroscopy that utilizes the Mössbauer effect

mos·tac·cio·li \ˌmȯstätˈchōlē\ *n* -s [It, lit., moustaches, fr. It *mostaccio* moustache — more at MOUSTACHE] **:** a pasta in the form of a short tube with oblique ends

mother* *n* [by shortening] **:** MOTHERFUCKER *herein* — usu. used as a generalized term of abuse

motherfucker \ˈ==¦==\ *n* [[1]*mother* + *fucker* (herein)] **:** one that is formidable, contemptible, or offensive — usu. considered obscene; usu. used as a generalized term of abuse — **motherfucking** \¦==¦==\ *adj*

mo·to·cross \ˈmōd·ōˌkrȯs\ *n* -ES [*motor* + *cross*-country] **:** a motorcycle race on a tight closed course over natural terrain that includes steep hills, sharp turns, and often mud

motor home *n* **:** an automotive vehicle built on a truck or bus chassis and equipped as a self-contained traveling home — compare MOBILE HOME *herein*

motor inn *or* **motor hotel** *n* **:** a usu. multistory urban motel

mous·sa·ka \müˈsäkə, ˈmüˌs-, ˌmüsäˈkä\ *n* -s [NGk *mousakas*] **:** a dish of ground meat (as lamb) and sliced eggplant or potatoes often topped with a seasoned sauce

mouth hook *n* **:** one of a pair of hooked larval mouthparts of some two-winged flies that function as jaws

mover and shaker *n, pl* **movers and shakers :** a person who is active and influential in some field of endeavor

mov·i·ola \ˌmüvēˈōlə\ *n* -s [fr. *Moviola,* a trademark] **:** a device for editing motion-picture film and synchronizing the sound

mox·i·bus·tion \ˌ¦mäksə̇¦bəschən\ *n* -s [*moxa* + *-i-* + *-bustion* (as in *combustion*)] **:** medical use of a moxa

MPA *abbr* master of public administration

MPH* *abbr* master of public health

m phase *n, usu cap M* **:** the period in the cell cycle during which cell division takes place — called also *D phase;* compare G1 PHASE *herein,* G2 PHASE *herein,* S PHASE *herein*

mr. charlie \-ˈchärlē, -ȧl-, -i\ *n, usu cap M&C* [*Charlie,* fr. *Charles,* proper name] **:** a white man **:** white people — usu. used disparagingly

mri·dan·ga \mrēˈdəŋgə, ˌmərē-\ *or* **mri·dan·gam** \-gəm\ *n* -s [Skt *mṛdaṅga,* prob. of imit. origin] **:** a drum of India that is shaped like an elongated barrel and has tuned heads of different diameters

mRNA \ˌ¦emˌär(ˌ)enˈā\ *n* -s [*messenger RNA* (herein)] **:** MESSENGER RNA *herein*

mr. right *n, usu cap M & Right* [[1]*right*] **:** a man who would make the perfect husband

ms. \(ˈ)miz *sometimes* (ˈ)mis\ *n, usu cap* [prob. blend of *miss* and *Mrs.*] — used instead of *Miss* or *Mrs.* (as when the marital status of a woman is unknown or irrelevant) ⟨*Ms.* Mary Smith⟩

MSG* *abbr* master sergeant

MSH *abbr* melanocyte-stimulating hormone *herein*

m16 \ˌemsikˈstēn\ *or* **m16 rifle** *n* -s *usu cap M* [model *16*] **:** a .223 caliber (5.56 mm.) gas-operated magazine-fed automatic or semiautomatic rifle used by U.S. troops since the mid 1960s

MSLS *abbr* master of science in library science

MSW *abbr* master of social work

mu·co·ciliary \ˌmyükō+\ *adj* [*muc-* + *ciliary*] **:** of, relating to, or involving cilia of the mucous membranes of the mammalian respiratory system ⟨~ transport in the lung⟩

mu·co·peptide \ˌmyükō +\ *n* [*muco-* + *peptide*] **:** PEPTIDOGLYCAN *herein*

mu·co·poly·sac·cha·ri·do·sis \ˌmyükōˌpälēˌsakə(ˌ)rīˈdōsəs\ *n, pl* **mucopolysaccharido·ses** \-ōˌsēz\ [NL, fr. *mucopolysaccharide* + *-osis*] **:** any of a group of genetically determined disorders of mucopolysaccharide metabolism that are characterized by the accumulation of mucopolysaccharides in the tissues and their excretion in the urine

MUF *abbr* material unaccounted for

mug·gee \ˌməgˈē\ *n* -s [⁶*mug* + *-ee*] **:** a person who is mugged

mug's game *n* [¹*mug* (fool)] **:** a profitless or futile activity

mu·ja·hid·een \müˌjahiˈdēn, mu̇ˌjä-\ *n pl* [Ar, pl. of *mujāhid*] **:** Islamic guerrilla fighters esp. in the Middle East

mule* *n, slang* **:** a person who smuggles or delivers illicit drugs

mul·ti·band \ˌməltə̇, -tē, -ˌtī +\ *adj* [*multi-* + *band*] **:** of, relating to, or operable on two or more bands (as of frequencies or wavelengths) ⟨a ~ radio⟩

mul·ti·center \"+\ *adj* [*multi-* + *center*] **:** involving more than one medical or research institution ⟨a ~ clinical study⟩

mul·ti·centric \"+\ *adj* [*multi-* + *-centric*] **:** having multiple centers of origin ⟨a ~ tumor⟩ — **mul·ti·cen·trically** \"+\ *adv* — **mul·ti·centricity** \"+\ *n*

mul·ti·chain \"+\ *adj* [*multi-* + *chain*] **:** containing more than one chain ⟨~ proteins⟩

mul·ti·company \"+\ *n* [*multi-* + *company*] **:** a large corporate enterprise with interests in two or more separate industries

mul·ti·enzyme \"+\ *adj* [*multi-* + *enzyme*] **:** composed of or involving two or more enzymes or subunits similar to enzymes esp. when they have related functions in a biosynthetic pathway

multifactorial* *or* **mul·ti·factor** \"+\ *adj* **:** having, involving, or produced by a variety of elements or causes ⟨a ~ study⟩

mul·ti·focal \"+\ *adj* [*multi-* + *focal*] **1 :** having more than one focal length ⟨~ lenses⟩ **2 :** arising from or occurring in more than one focus or location ⟨~ convulsions⟩

mul·ti·function *or* **mul·ti·functional** \"+\ *adj* [*multi-* + *function* or *functional*] **:** having or performing more than one function

mul·ti·germ \"+\ *adj* [prob. fr. *multi-* + *germ*inate] **:** producing or being a fruit cluster capable of giving rise to several plants ⟨a ~ variety of sugar beet⟩ — compare MONOGERM *herein*

mul·ti·grade \"+\ *adj* [*multi-* + *grade*] *of motor oil* **:** characterized by a range of viscosities that permits use in either high or low temperatures

mul·ti·hull \"+\ *n* [*multi-* + *hull*] **:** a vessel (as a catamaran) with two or more hulls usu. joined by a common deck

mul·ti–industry \"+\ *adj* [*multi-* + *industry*] **:** active in or concerned with two or more separate industries

mul·ti·layered \"+\ *or* **mul·ti·layer*** \"+\ *adj* [*multi-* + *layered* or *layer*] **:** having or involving several distinct layers, strata, or levels — **multilayer*** *n*

mul·ti·market \" +\ *adj* [*multi-* + *market*] **:** MULTI-INDUSTRY *herein*

¹mul·ti·media \"+\ *adj* [*multi-* + *media,* pl. of ¹*medium*] **:** using, involving, or encompassing several media

²multimedia \"\ *n pl but sing or pl in constr* **:** communication, entertainment, or art in which several media are employed

mul·ti·nation \ˌməltə̇, -tē, -ˌtī +\ *adj* [*multi-* + *nation*] **:** MULTINATIONAL 1 *herein*

¹mul·ti·national \"+\ *adj* [*multi-* + *national*] **1 a :** of, relating to, or involving more than two nations ⟨a ~ nuclear force⟩ **b :** having divisions in more than two countries ⟨a ~ corporation⟩ **2 :** of or relating to more than two nationalities ⟨a ~ society⟩

²mul·ti·national \"+\ *n* **:** a multinational corporation

mul·ti·nationalism \"+\ *n* [¹*multinational* (herein) + *-ism*] **:** the establishment or operation of multinational corporations

mul·ti·party \"+\ *adj* [*multi-* + *party*] **:** of, relating to, or involving more than two political parties

multiple* *n* **1 :** something containing or consisting of more than one or two units of a kind **2 :** a mass-produced work of art **3 :** a number that expresses the price-earnings ratio of a stock **:** PRICE-EARNINGS MULTIPLE *herein*

multiple regression *n* **:** regression in which one variable is estimated by the use of more than one other variable

multiple store *n, chiefly Brit* **:** CHAIN STORE

multiplet* *n* **1 :** any of two or more atomic, molecular, or nuclear quantum states that are usu. close together in energy and that arise from different relative orientations of angular momenta **2 :** a group of spectral frequencies arising from transitions to or from a multiplet quantum state **3 :** a group of elementary particles different in charge but similar in other properties (as mass)

multiple–valued \ˈ===ˈ==\ *adj* **:** having at least one and sometimes more of the values of the range associated with each value of the domain — compare SINGLE-VALUED *in the Dict*

multiplication sign *n* **:** a symbol used to indicate multiplication: **a :** TIMES SIGN *herein* **b :** DOT 2c(2)

multiplicative identity *n* **:** an identity element (as 1 in the group of rational numbers without 0 under the operation of multiplication) that in a given mathematical system leaves unchanged any element by which it is multiplied

multiplicative inverse *n* **:** an element of a mathematical set that when multiplied by a given element yields the identity element — called also *reciprocal*

multiplicity* *n* **:** the number of times a root of an equation or zero of a function occurs when there is more than one root or zero

multiplier effect *n* **:** the effect of a relatively minor factor in precipitating a great change; *esp* **:** the effect of a relatively small change in one economic factor (as rate of saving or level of consumer credit) in inducing a disproportionate increase or decrease in another (as gross national product)

mul·ti·ply \ˈmәltә,plī\ *n* -ES [*multiply,* v.] **:** an instance of multiplication performed by a computer; *also* **:** the means for performing multiplication

mul·ti·potential \¦mәltә̇, -tē, -,tī +\ *adj* [*multi-* + *potential*] **:** having the potential of becoming any of several mature cell types ⟨~ stem cell⟩

mul·ti·processing \"+\ *n* [*multi-* + *processing,* gerund of ²*process*] **:** the processing of several computer programs at the same time esp. by a computer system with several processors sharing a single memory — **mul·ti·proces·sor** \"+\ *n*

mul·ti·programming \"+\ *n* [*multi-* + *programming*] **:** the technique of utilizing several interleaved programs concurrently in a single computer system — **mul·ti·pro·grammed** \"+\ *adj*

mul·ti·pronged \"+\ *adj* [*multi-* + *pronged*] **1 :** having several prongs ⟨~ fishing spears⟩ **2 :** having several distinct aspects or elements ⟨a ~ attack on the problem⟩

mul·ti·resistant \"+\ *adj* [*multi-* + *resistant*] **:** biologically resistant to several toxic agents ⟨~ falciparum malaria⟩ — **mul·ti·resistance** \"+\ *n*

mul·ti·sensory \"+\ *adj* [*multi-* + *sensory*] **:** relating to, having, or involving perception by several senses ⟨~ experience⟩

mul·ti·spectral \"+\ *adj* [*multi-* + *spectral*] **:** of or relating to two or more ranges of frequencies or wavelengths in the electromagnetic spectrum

mul·ti·variable \"+\ *adj* [*multi-* + *variable*] **:** MULTIVARIATE

mul·ti·ver·si·ty \¦mәltә̇¦vәrsәd·ē, -tē¦v-, -stē\ *n* -ES [*multi-* + *-versity* (as in *university*)] **:** a very large university with many component schools, colleges, or divisions, with widely diverse functions, and with a large staff engaged in activities other than instruction and esp. in administration

mun·chies \ˈmәnchēz\ *n pl* [¹*munch* + *-ie* + *-s*] **1 :** light snack foods **2 :** hunger pangs; *esp* **:** hunger pangs induced by the use of marijuana

munch·kin \ˈmәnchkә̇n\ *n* -s [name of diminutive creatures in *The Wonderful Wizard of Oz* (1900), children's book by L. Frank Baum †1919 Am. writer, prob. fr. *munch* + *-kin*] **:** one that is small and charming or weak

mu·ni·cip·io \,myünә̇ˈsipēō\ *n* -s [Sp] **:** a chiefly rural territorial unit of local government in many Latin American countries that includes several villages or barrios

mu·on·ium \m(y)üˈōnēәm, -ˈän-\ *n* -s [*muon* + *-ium*] **:** a short-lived quasi-atom consisting of an electron and a positive muon

mu·ram·ic acid \myu̇,ramә̇k-\ *n* [*mur-* (fr. L *murus* wall) + glucos*amide* + *-ic*] **:** an amino sugar $C_9H_{17}NO_7$ that is a lactic acid derivative of glucosamine and is found esp. in bacterial cell walls and in blue-green algae

mu·rein \ˈmyu̇rēәn, ˈmyu̇(ә)r,ēn\ *n* -s [*mur*amic acid (herein) + *-ein*] **:** PEPTIDOGLYCAN *herein*

mur·phy \ˈmәrfē\ *or* **murphy game** *n, usu cap M* [fr. the name *Murphy*] **:** a confidence game and esp. one in which the victim believes he is paying for sex

murphy's law \¦mәrfēz-, ¦mәf-, ¦mәif-\ *n, usu cap M&L* [prob. after E.A. *Murphy,* 20th cent. Am. engineer] **:** an observation: anything that can go wrong will go wrong ⟨it has been established that computers are followers of *Murphy's Law* —P.H. Dorn⟩

mus·ca·det \,mәskәˈdā, *F* mu̅e̅skȧde\ *n* -s *often cap* [F, fr. Prov, muscadet grape, fr. *musc* musk scent — more at MUSK] **:** a dry white wine from the Loire valley of France

muscle car *n* **:** any of a group of American-made 2-door sports coupes of various makes with powerful engines that are designed for high-performance driving

muslim* *n, usu cap* **:** BLACK MUSLIM *herein*

mu·ta·ge·nic·ity \,myüd·әjә̇ˈnisәd·ē\ *n* -ES [*mutagenic* + *-ity*] **:** the capacity to induce mutations

mu·ta·gen·ize \ˈmyüd·әjә,nīz\ *vt* -ED/-ING/-S [*mutagen* + *-ize*] **:** MUTATE

mu·ta·ro·tase \,myüd·әˈrō,tās, -āz\ *n* -S [*mutarot*ation + *-ase*] **:** an isomerase found esp. in mammalian tissues that catalyzes the interconversion of anomeric forms of some sugars

mu·ta·tor gene \¦myü,tād·ә(r)-\ *also* **mutator** \ˈ=,==, =ˈ==\ *n* -S [L *mutator* one that changes, fr. *mutatus,* past part. of *mutare* to change + *-or* — more at MISS] **:** a gene that increases the rate of mutation of one or more other genes

mutually exclusive *adj* **:** being related such that each excludes or precludes the other ⟨*mutually exclusive* events⟩; *also* **:** INCOMPATIBLE ⟨their outlooks were not *mutually exclusive*⟩

Mu·zak \ˈmyü,zak\ *trademark* — used for recorded background music that is transmitted by wire to the loudspeaker of a subscriber (as an office or restaurant)

MV* *abbr* main verb

MVP *abbr* most valuable player

MY *abbr, often not cap* million years

my·co·phile \ˈmīkō,fīl\ *n* -s [*myc-* + *-phile*] **:** a person whose hobby is hunting wild edible mushrooms

my·co·plasma \¦mīkō +\ *n, pl* **my·co·plasmas** *or* **my·co·plasmata** \"+\ **:** PLEUROPNEUMONIA-LIKE ORGANISM — **my·co·plasmal** \"+\ *adj*

my·co·toxin \"+\ *n* [*myc-* + *toxin*] **:** a poisonous substance produced by a fungus and esp. a mold — compare AFLATOXIN *herein* — **my·co·toxic** \"+\ *adj* — **my·co·toxicity** \"+\ *n* — **my·co·toxicosis** \"+\ *n*

myelocytic leukemia *n* **:** MYELOGENOUS LEUKEMIA

my·elo·fibrosis \¦mīәlō +\ *n* [NL, fr. *myel-* + *fibrosis*] **:** an anemic condition in which bone marrow becomes fibrotic and the liver and spleen usu. exhibit development of blood cell precursors — **my·elo·fibrotic** \"+\ *adj*

my·elo·peroxidase \"+\ *n* [*myel-* + *peroxidase*] **:** a peroxidase of phagocytic cells (as polymorphonuclear leukocytes) that is held to assist in bactericidal activity by catalyzing the oxidation of ionic halogen to free halogen

my·e·lo·proliferative \"+\ *adj* [*myel-* + *proliferative*] **:** of, relating to, or being a disorder (as leukemia) marked by excessive proliferation of bone marrow elements and esp. blood cell precursors

My·lar \ˈmī,lär\ *trademark* — used for a polyester film

myo·electric \¦mīō +\ *also* **myo·electrical** \"+\ *adj* [*my-* + *electric*] **:** of, relating to, or utilizing electricity generated by muscle ⟨a ~ prosthesis⟩ — **myo·electrically** \"+\ *adv*

myo·filament \"+\ *n* [*my-* + *filament*] **:** one of the individual filaments of actin or myosin that make up a myofibril

myotube \"+\ *n* [*my-* + *tube*] **:** a developmental stage of a muscle fiber composed of a syncytium formed by fusion of myoblasts

myxo·virus \¦miksə +\ *n* [NL, fr. *myx-* + *virus;* fr. its affinity for certain mucins] **:** any of a group of rather large RNA-containing viruses that includes the influenza viruses — **myxo·viral** \"+\ *adj*

N

n* *abbr* ²nano-
NA* *abbr* not available
nab·o·kov·ian \ˌnabəˈkōvēən, -ˈkȯv-, -ˈkȯfēən\ *adj, usu cap* [Vladimir Vladimirovich *Nabokov* †1977 Am. (Russ.-born) novelist & poet + E *-ian*] **:** of, relating to, or suggestive of Vladimir Nabokov or his writings
nacho \ˈnäch(ˌ)ō\ *n* -s [perh. fr. Sp *nacho* flat-nosed] **:** a tortilla chip topped with cheese and a savory substance (as chili peppers or refried beans) and broiled
NAD \ˌe(ˌ)nāˈdē\ *n* -s [*n*icotinamide *a*denine *d*inucleotide] **:** DIPHOSPHOPYRIDINE NUCLEOTIDE
na·der·ism \ˈnādəˌrizəm\ *n* -s *usu cap* [after Ralph *Nader* *b*1934 Am. consumer advocate] **:** the promotion of consumer interests esp. by public outcry against dangerous or defective goods
NADH \ˌeˌnā(ˌ)dēˈāch\ *n* -s [*h*ydrogen] **:** the reduced form of NAD
NADP \ˌeˌnā(ˌ)dēˈpē\ *n* -s [*n*icotinamide *a*denine *d*inucleotide *p*hosphate] **:** TRIPHOSPHOPYRIDINE NUCLEOTIDE
NADPH \ˌeˌnāˌdē(ˌ)pēˈāch\ *n* -s **:** the reduced form of NADP
naf·cil·lin \ˌnafˌsilən\ *n* -s [*naf-* (alter. of *naphth-*) + peni*cillin*] **:** a semisynthetic penicillin $C_{21}H_{22}N_2O_5S$ that is resistant to penicillinase and is used esp. in the form of its sodium salt as an antibiotic
nai·ra \ˈnī(ə)rə\ *n* -s [alter. of *Nigeria,* country in West Africa] **1 :** the basic monetary unit of Nigeria — see MONEY table *in the Dict* **2 :** a coin or note representing one naira
naïve* *adj* **1 :** not previously subjected to experimentation or to a particular experimental situation ⟨experimentally ~ rats⟩; *also* **:** not having previously used a particular drug (as marijuana) **2 :** PRIMITIVE 4d
naked* *adj* **:** not backed by the writer's ownership of the commodity contract or security ⟨selling ~ options⟩
na·led \ˈnāˌled\ *n* -s [origin unknown] **:** a short-lived insecticide $C_4H_7Br_2Cl_2O_4P$ of relatively low toxicity to warm-blooded animals that is used esp. to control crop pests and mosquitoes
na·li·dix·ic acid \ˌnāləˌdiksik-\ *n* [perh. fr. *na*phthyr*idi*ne ($C_8H_6N_2$ — fr. *naphth-* + *pyridine*) + carbo*x*yl*ic acid*] **:** an antibacterial agent $C_{12}H_{12}N_2O_3$ that is used esp. in the treatment of genitourinary infections
nal·ox·one \nalˈäkˌsōn\ *n* -s [*N-al*lyl + hydr*ox*y- + *-one*] **:** a potent antagonist $C_{19}H_{21}NO_4$ of narcotic drugs and esp. morphine that is administered esp. as the hydrochloride
nal·trex·one \nalˈtrekˌsōn\ *n* -s [*N-al*lyl + *-trex-* (as in *methotrexate*) + *-one*] **:** a narcotic antagonist $C_{20}H_{23}NO_4$
name of the game : the essential or intrinsic quality or nature of a situation **:** the fundamental goal of an activity ⟨the American businessman is taught early that profits are the *name of the game* —Frank Gibney⟩
¹na·mib·i·an \nəˈmibēən\ *adj, usu cap* [fr. *Namibia* (formerly South-West Africa), country in southwest Africa, fr. *Namib,* desert on the southwest coast of Africa + *-an*] **:** of or relating to Namibia or its inhabitants
²namibian \"\ *n* -s *cap* **:** a native or inhabitant of Namibia

NAND \ˈnand, ˈnaa(ə)nd\ *n* [*n*ot *AND*] **:** a computer logic circuit that produces an output which is the inverse of that of an AND circuit
nan·no·fossil \ˌnanō +\ *n* [*nann-* + *fossil*] **:** a fossil of nannoplankton
nano·meter \ˌnanō +\ *n* [ISV ²*nano-* + ⁴*meter*] **:** one billionth of a meter — abbr. *nm*
nano·second \"+\ *n* [ISV ²*nano-* + ⁴*second*] **:** one billionth of a second — abbr. *nanosec, nsec*
nan·tua sauce \nän(n)ˈtwä-\ *n, usu cap N* [fr. *Nantua,* France] **:** a cream sauce flavored with shellfish (as crayfish or lobster)
nap* *n* -s [⁷*nap*] *Brit* **:** a pick or recommendation as a good bet to win a contest (as a horse race); *also* **:** one named in a nap
¹nap \ˈnap\ *vt* **napped; napped; napping; naps** [*nap,* n. (herein)] *Brit* **:** to pick or single out (as a race horse) in a nap
²nap \"\ *vt* **napped; napped; napping; naps** [by shortening fr. F *napper* to cover meat in a sauce] **:** to pour or spread a sauce over (a prepared dish)
na·prox·en \nəˈpräksən\ *n* -s [*na*phtha + *pro*pionic acid + *ox-* + *-en* (arbitrary suffix)] **:** an anti-inflammatory analgesic antipyretic drug $C_{14}H_{14}O_3$ used esp. to treat arthritis
narc *or* **nark** \ˈnärk\ *n* -s [short for *narcotics agent*] **:** one (as a government agent) who investigates narcotics violations
narcotic* *n* **:** a drug (as marijuana or LSD) subject to restriction similar to that of addictive narcotics whether in fact physiologically narcotic and addictive or not
narrowcast \ˈ==ˌ=\ *vi* [¹*narrow* + *cast*] **:** to aim a broadcast at a narrowly defined area or audience
na·so·gastric \ˌnāzō +\ *adj* [*nas-* + *gastric*] **:** of, relating to, being, or performed by intubation of the stomach by way of the nasal passages ⟨a ~ tube⟩ ⟨~ suction⟩
na·ta·lism \ˈnātᵊlˌizəm\ *n* -s [fr. *natalist* (fr. F *nataliste*), after such pairs as *Communist* : *Communism*] **:** an attitude or policy favoring or encouraging population growth — **na·ta·list** \-ᵊləst\ *n* -s
natch \ˈnach\ *adv* [by shortening & alter.] *slang* **:** of course **:** NATURALLY
national seashore *n, sometimes cap N&S* **:** an area of seacoast maintained by the federal government as a preserve for the natural environment and wildlife and as a public recreation area
native american* *adj, usu cap N&A* **1 :** of or relating to Native Americans **2 :** of American Indian descent
native american* *n, cap N&A* **:** AMERICAN INDIAN
na·tri·ure·sis \ˌnā·trē(y)əˌrēsəs, ˌna-\ *also* **na·tru·re·sis** \-trə- ˌrē-\ *n* [NL, fr. *natr*ium or *natr-* + *uresis*] **:** excessive loss of cations and esp. sodium in the urine — **na·tri·uret·ic** \-trē(y)əˌred- ik\ *adj or n*
natural* *adj* **1 :** relating to or being natural food **2 :** AFRO *herein* — **natural** *n*
natural food *n* **:** food that has undergone minimal processing and contains no preservatives or artificial additives
natural gas* *n* **:** gas manufactured from organic matter (as coal)

natural language* *n* **:** the language of ordinary speaking and writing — distinguished from *machine language, herein*

natural scientist *n* **:** a specialist in natural science

nature trail *n* **:** a trail (as through a woods) usu. with natural features identified for better enjoyment or study of nature

Nau·ga·hyde \'nógə,hīd, 'näg-\ *trademark* — used for vinyl-coated fabrics

NEB *abbr* New English Bible

neb·bish \'nebish\ *n* -ES [Yiddish *nebach, nebech* poor thing (used interjectionally), of Slav origin; akin to Czech *nebohy* wretched, Pol *nieboże* poor creature] **:** a timid, meek, or ineffectual person — **neb·bishy** \-ē\ *adj*

neck* *n* **:** the part of a tooth between the crown and the root

needle* *n* **:** a teasing or gibing remark

needleleaf \'==,=\ *adj* **:** populated with trees having leaves that are needles ⟨~ evergreen forests⟩; *also* **:** having leaves that are needles ⟨~ trees⟩

negative income tax *n* **:** a system of federal subsidy payments to families with incomes below a stipulated level proposed as a substitute for or supplement to welfare payments

negative option *n* **:** a provision in a mail-order contract (as of a book club) that requires the customer either to return a refusal card within a specified time or to accept the current selection

negative transfer *n* **:** the impeding of learning or performance in a situation by the carry-over of learned responses from another situation — compare INTERFERENCE 9, TRANSFER 6b

ne·gri·tude \'nēgrə,tüd, 'neg-, -rə·,tyüd\ *n* -s [F *négritude,* fr. *nègre* Negro + *-i-* + *-tude* (fr. MF) — more at NEGRESS, -TUDE] **1 :** a consciousness of and pride in the cultural and physical aspects of the African heritage **2 :** the state of being a Negro

ne·gro·ness \'=(,)=nəs\ *n, usu cap* [*Negro* + *-ness*] **:** the quality or state of being Negro **:** NEGRITUDE

ne·gro·ni \nə'grōnē\ *n* -s *often cap* [prob. fr. the name *Negroni*] **:** a cocktail consisting of sweet vermouth, bitters, and gin

neh·ru \'ne(ə)r(,)ü, 'nā(,)rü\ *adj, usu cap* [after Jawaharlal *Nehru* †1964 Indian nationalist] **:** MAO *herein*

[1]nelly* *or* **nel·lie** \'nelē\ *n, pl* **nellies :** an effeminate homosexual — **not on your nelly** *sometimes cap 2d N* [perh. fr. the phrase *not on your Nelly Duff,* rhyming slang for Brit slang *puff* breath, life] *Brit* **:** certainly not

[2]nelly *or* **nellie** \"\ *adj* [[1]*nelly,* n. (herein)] **:** conspicuously effeminate

neo·colonialism \¦nē(,)ō +\ *n* [*ne-* + *colonialism*] **:** the economic and political policies by which a Great Power indirectly maintains or extends its influence over other areas or peoples — **neo·colonial** \"+\ *adj* — **neo·colonialist** \"+\ *n or adj*

neo·conservative \"+\ *n* [*ne-* + *conservative*] **:** a former liberal espousing political conservatism — **neo·con·servatism** \"+\ *n* — **neoconservative** *adj*

neo·cortical \"+\ *adj* [*ne-* + *cortical*] **:** of or relating to the neocortex

neo–dada \"+\ *n, usu cap D* [*ne-* + *Dada*] **:** an anti-art movement esp. of the late 1950s and the 1960s based on tenets similar to those of Dada but having more interest in the object than Dada claimed to have; *broadly* **:** JUNK ART *herein* — **neo–dadaism** \"+\ *n, usu cap D* — **neo–dadaist** \"+\ *adj or n, usu cap D*

neo·na·tol·o·gy \,nēōnā'täləjē\ *n* -ES [*neonate* + *-ology*] **:** a branch of medicine concerned with the care, development, and diseases of newborn infants — **neo·na·tol·o·gist** \-jəst\ *n* -s

neo·phil·ia \,nēō'filēə\ *n* -s [*ne-* + *-philia*] **:** love of or enthusiasm for what is new or novel

neo·phil·i·ac \-'filē,ak\ *n* -s [fr. *neophilia* (herein), after such pairs as *necrophilia*: *necrophiliac*] **:** one who has or expresses neophilia

neo·ri·can \¦nēō¦rēkən\ *n* -s *cap* [*ne-* + Puerto *Rican*] **:** a Puerto Rican who lives on the U.S. mainland or who has lived there but has returned to Puerto Rico

neo·vascularization \¦nē(,)ō+\ *n* [*ne-* + *vascularization*] **:** vascularization esp. in abnormal quantity (as in some conditions of the retina) or in abnormal tissue (as a tumor)

ne·phrit·o·gen·ic \nə,frid·ə'jenik, ,nefrid·ō'-\ *adj* [*nephritis* + *-o-* + *-genic*] **:** causing nephritis ⟨~ types of streptococci⟩

ne·phros·to·my \nə'frästəmē, ne-\ *n* -ES [NL, fr. *nephr-* + [2]*-stomy*] **:** the surgical formation of an opening between a kidney pelvis and the outside of the body

nephrotic syndrome *n* **:** an abnormal condition that is marked by deficiency of albumin in the blood and its excretion in the urine due to altered permeability of the glomerular basement membranes (as by a toxic chemical agent)

nerd \'nərd, 'nə̄d, 'nəid\ *n* -s [perh. alter. (influenced by *nerts* and *turd*) of earlier *nard* wimp] *slang* **:** an unpleasant, unattractive, unstylish, or insignificant person — **nerdy** \-dē\ *adj* -ER/-EST

nerf \'nərf, 'nə̄f, 'nəif\ *vt* -ED/-ING/-s [origin unknown] **:** to bump (another car) in an automobile race

nerf bar *or* **nerfing bar** *n* [fr. *nerf* (herein)] **:** a usu. tubular steel bumper on some racing cars to keep wheels from touching when cars bump during a race

nerve growth factor *n* **:** a protein that promotes development of the sensory and sympathetic nervous systems and is required for maintenance of sympathetic neurons — abbr. *NGF*

nest·ed \'nestəd\ *adj* [fr. past part of [2]*nest*] **:** forming a sequence or hierarchy with each member contained in or containing the next ⟨~ subroutines in computer programming⟩

network* *n* **:** a system of computers, terminals, and data bases connected by communications lines

net·work·ing \'=,==\ *n* -s **1 :** the exchange of information or services among individuals, groups, or institutions **2 :** the process of establishing or using a computer network

neur·amin·i·dase \,n(y)ùrə'minə,dās, -āz\ *n* -s [*neuraminic* acid + *-idase* (as in *glucosidase*)] **:** a glycosidase that splits mucoproteins by breaking a glucoside link and occurs esp. in influenza viruses as an antigen

neu·ris·tor \n(y)ù'ristə(r)\ *n* -s [*neuron* + *transistor;* fr. its functioning like a neuron and not requiring the use of transistors] **:** a usu. electronic device along which a signal propagates with uniform velocity and without attenuation

neu·ro·active \¦n(y)ùrō, -ù- +\ *adj* [*neur-* + [1]*active*] **:** stimulating neural tissue ⟨~ substances⟩

neu·ro·biology \"+\ *n* [*neur-* + *biology*] **:** a branch of the life sciences that deals with the anatomy, physiology, and pathology of the nervous system — **neu·ro·biological** \"+\ *adj* — **neu·ro·biologically** \"+\ *adv* — **neu·ro·biologist** \"+\ *n*

neu·ro·chemistry \"+\ *n* [*neur-* + *chemistry*] **1 :** the study of the chemical makeup and activities of nervous tissue **2 :** chemical processes and phenomena related to the nervous system — **neu·ro·chemical** \"+\ *adj or n* — **neu·ro·chemist** \"+\ *n*

neuroendocrine* *adj* **:** of, relating to, or functioning in neurosecretion

neu·ro·endocrinology \¦n(y)ürō, -ü- +\ *n* [*neur-* + *endocrinology*] **:** a branch of the life sciences dealing with neurosecretion and the physiological interaction between the central nervous system and the endocrine system — **neu·ro·endocrinological** \"+\ *adj* — **neu·ro·endocrinologist** \"+\ *n*

neurofibrillary tangle *n* **:** an abnormality of the cytoplasm of the pyramidal cells of the hippocampus and neurons of the cerebral cortex that occurs esp. in Alzheimer's disease and appears under the light microscope after impregnation and staining with silver as arrays of parallel thick coarse argentophil fibers

neu·ro·genesis \"+\ *n* [*neur-* + *genesis*] **:** development of nerves, nervous tissue, or the nervous system

neu·ro·he·mal organ *also* **neu·ro·hae·mal organ** \ˌn(y)ürōˌhēməl-, -ü-\ *n* [*neur-* + *hem-* + *-al*] **:** an organ (as a corpus cardiacum of an insect) that releases stored neurosecretory substances into the blood

neu·ro·hypophyseal *or* **neu·ro·hypophysial** \¦n(y)üro, -ü- +\ *adj* [*neur-* + *hypophyseal*] **:** of, relating to, or secreted by the neurohypophysis ⟨~ hormones⟩

neu·ro·lept·analgesia \¦n(y)ürōˌlept, -ü- +\ *or* **neu·ro·lep·to·analgesia** \ˌn(y)ürō¦leptō, -ü- +\ *n* [NL, fr. ISV *neurolept-* or *neurolepto-* (fr. *neuroleptic* — herein) + *analgesic* + NL *-ia* (as in *analgesia*)] **:** joint administration of a tranquilizing drug and an analgesic esp. for relief of surgical pain — **neu·ro·lept·analgesic** \¦n(y)ürōˌlept, -ü- +\ *adj*

neu·ro·lep·tic \ˌn(y)ürō'leptik, -ü-\ *n* -s [ISV *neur-* + psycho*leptic;* orig. formed as F *neuroleptique*] **:** TRANQUILIZER 2 — **neuroleptic** \¦==¦==\ *adj*

neu·ro·peptide \"+\ *n* [*neur-* + *peptide*] **:** an endogenous peptide (as an endorphin or enkephalin) that influences neural activity or functioning

neu·ro·pharmacology \"+\ *n* [*neur-* + *pharmacology*] **1 :** a branch of medical science dealing with the action of drugs on and in the nervous system **2 :** the properties and reactions of a drug on and in the nervous system ⟨the ~ of lithium⟩ — **neu·ro·pharmacological** \"+\ *also* **neu·ro·pharmacologic** \"+\ *adj* — **neu·ro·pharmacologist** \"+\ *n*

neu·ro·phy·sin \ˌn(y)ürō'fīsən, -ür-, -'fiz-\ *n* -s [*neur-* + *physin* (fr. Gk *physis* natural constitution + E *-in*)] **:** any of several brain hormones that bind with and carry either oxytocin or vasopressin

neu·ro·psychic \¦n(y)ürō, -ü-+\ *also* **neu·ro·psychical** \"+\ *adj* [*neur-* + *psychic* or *psychical*] **:** of or relating to both the mind and the nervous system as affecting mental processes

neu·ro·radiology \"+\ *n* [*neur-* + *radiology*] **:** radiology of the nervous system — **neu·ro·radiological** \"+\ *also* **neu·ro·radiologic** \"+\ *adj* — **neu·ro·radiologist** \"+\ *n*

neu·ro·science \"+\ *n* [*neur-* + *science*] **:** a branch (as neurology or neurophysiology) of the life sciences that deals with the anatomy, physiology, biochemistry, or molecular biology of nerves and nervous tissue and esp. with their relation to behavior and learning — **neu·ro·scientist** \"+\ *n*

neu·ro·sensory \"+\ *adj* [*neur-* + *sensory*] **:** of or relating to afferent nerves ⟨~ control of feeding behavior⟩

neu·ros·po·ra \n(y)ü'räspərə\ *n* -s **:** a fungus of the genus *Neurospora*

neu·ro·transmission \¦n(y)ürō, -ü-+\ *n* [*neur-* + *transmission*] **:** the transmission of nerve impulses across a synapse

neu·ro·transmitter \"+\ *n* [*neur-* + *transmitter*] **:** a chemical substance (as norepinephrine or acetylcholine) that transmits nerve impulses across a synapse

neu·ter·cane \'n(y)üd·ə(r)ˌkān\ *n* -s [L *neuter* neither + E *-cane* (as in hurricane); from the difficulty of classifying it as either hurricane or frontal storm] **:** a subtropical cyclone that is usu. less than 100 miles in diameter and that draws energy from sources common to both the hurricane and the frontal cyclone

neutral current *n* **:** a weak nuclear interaction between a lepton (as a neutrino) and a hadron (as a neutron) in which the electric charges of the particles remain unchanged

neutron bomb *n* **:** a nuclear warhead designed to produce lethal neutrons but less blast and fire damage than other nuclear bombs

neutron star *n* [so called fr. the hypothesis that their cores are composed entirely of neutrons] **:** a hypothetical dense celestial object that consists primarily of closely packed neutrons and that results from the collapse of a much larger stellar body

never–never land* *n* **:** an exotic place ⟨a *never-never land* of poodles and chauffeurs —Kathryn Livingston⟩; *also* **:** an absurd or indeterminate situation ⟨was capital disappearing into an unproductive *never-never land*? —Gregg Easterbrook⟩

new drug *n* **:** a drug that has not been declared safe and effective by qualified experts under the conditions prescribed, recommended, or suggested in the label and that may be a new chemical formula or an established drug prescribed for use in a new way

new economics *n pl but usu sing in constr* **:** an economic concept that is a logical extension of Keynesianism and that holds that appropriate fiscal and monetary maneuvering can maintain healthy economic growth and prosperity indefinitely

new guard *n, sometimes cap N&G* **:** a group of persons who have recently gained prominence or power in a particular field (as politics or business); *also* **:** a group of persons united in an effort to change the status quo

new journalism *n, usu cap N&J* **:** journalism that features the author's subjective responses to people and events and that often employs the techniques of fiction — **new journalist** *n, usu cap N&J*

new left *n, usu cap N&L* **:** a political movement originating esp. among students in the 1960s, favoring confrontational tactics, often breaking with traditional leftist ideologies, and associated esp. with antiwar, antinuclear, feminist, and ecological issues — **new leftist** *n, often cap N&L*

new math *or* **new mathematics** *n* **:** mathematics based on set theory esp. as taught in elementary and secondary school

new right *n, usu cap N&R* **:** a U.S. political movement originating esp. among southern and western Protestant fundamentalists, opposing esp. liberal ideology, and concerned with issues esp. of church and state, gun ownership, pornography, and abortion

newspeak \ˈ=,=\ *n, often cap* [*Newspeak,* a language "designed to diminish the range of thought" in the novel *Nineteen Eighty-Four* (1949) by George Orwell †1950 Eng. author, fr. [1]*new* + [2]*speak*] **:** propagandistic language characterized by euphemism, circumlocution, and the inversion of customary meanings

newsperson \ˈ=,==\ *n* [[1]*news* + *person*] **:** REPORTER c

new town* *n* **:** an urban development comprising a small to medium-size city with a broad range of housing and planned industrial, commercial, and recreational facilities

new wave *n, often cap N&W* [trans. of F *nouvelle vague*] **1 :** a cinematic movement that is characterized by improvisation, abstraction, and subjective symbolism and that often makes use of experimental photographic techniques **2 :** a new movement in a particular field (as art or cooking) ⟨young chefs who call themselves the *New Wave* —R.A. Sokolov⟩ **3 :** rock music characterized by cohesive ensemble playing rather than extended solos and usu. lyrics which express anger and social discontent — **new waver** *n, often cap N&W*

nexus* *n* **:** a point of focus or intersection **:** CENTER ⟨"one little spot on earth" that has served as the ~ of three great religions —John J. O'Connor⟩

ng *abbr* nanogram

n–galaxy *n, usu cap N* [fr. *n*uclear + *galaxy*] **:** a galaxy that has a brilliant starlike nucleus surrounded by a much fainter halo or extension

NGF *abbr* nerve growth factor *herein*

NGU *abbr* nongonococcal urethritis

ngul·trum \enˈgu̇ltrəm, eŋˈ-\ *n, pl* **ngultrums** *also* **ngultrum** [native name in Bhutan] **1 :** the basic monetary unit of Bhutan — see MONEY table *in the Dict* **2 :** a coin or note representing one ngultrum

ngwee \enˈgwē, eŋˈ-\ *n, pl* **ngwee** [native name in Zambia, lit., bright] **1 :** a monetary unit of Zambia equal to $^1/_{100}$ kwacha — see MONEY table *in the Dict* **2 :** a coin representing one ngwee

ni·al·amide \nīˈalə,mīd, -,məd\ *n* [*ni*cotinic acid + *amyl* + *am- ide*] **:** a synthetic antidepressant drug $C_{16}H_{18}N_4O_2$ that is an inhibitor of monoamine oxidase

nick* *vt* **:** to produce a nick in (DNA or RNA)

nick* *n* **1** *slang Brit* **:** JAIL; *also* **:** POLICE STATION **2 :** a break in a strand of DNA or RNA

nickel* *n* **1** *slang* **:** five dollars **2** *or* **nickel bag** *slang* **:** a packet containing five dollars worth of an illicit drug (as marijuana) **3 :** one's own expense ⟨all the exploration is on our ~ —Thomas Kruzshak⟩ — often used in phrases like *it's your nickel*

[1]**nickel–and–dime** *adj* **1 :** involving or offering only a small amount of money ⟨*nickel-and-dime* insurance claims⟩ ⟨*nickel-and-dime* jobs⟩ **2 :** SMALL-TIME ⟨*nickel-and-dime* dealers⟩

[2]**nickel–and–dime** *vt* **nickeled–and–dimed** *or* **nickel–and–dimed; nickeled–and–dimes** *or* **nickel–and–dimed; nickeling–and–diming** *or* **nickel–and–diming; nickels–and–dimes** *or* **nickel–and–dimes :** to impair, weaken, or defeat piecemeal (as through a series of small incursions or excessive attention to minor details) ⟨*nickeled-and-dimed* the Democrats to defeat . . . upstate —*Pittsburgh (Pa.) Press*⟩; *also* **:** to pester, impoverish, or reduce by small sums ⟨prove their mettle by *nickel-and-diming* your budget —W.G. McDonald⟩ ⟨wanted to *nickel-and-dime* its customers to death —J.C. Dvorak⟩

nicotinamide adenine dinucleotide *n* **:** DIPHOSPHOPYRIDINE NUCLEOTIDE

nicotinamide adenine dinucleotide phosphate *n* **:** TRIPHOSPHOPYRIDINE NUCLEOTIDE

nigger* *n* **:** a member of a socially disadvantaged class of persons ⟨it's time for somebody to lead all of America's ~*s* . . . all the people who feel left out of the political process —Ron Dellums⟩

nig·gle \ˈnigəl\ *n* -s [*niggle,* v.] *chiefly Brit* **:** a trifling doubt, objection, or complaint

nightglow \ˈ=,=\ *n* [*night* + air*glow*] **:** airglow seen at night

nightside* *n* **:** the side of a celestial body not in daylight

nig–nog \ˈnigˈnȯg, -ˈnäg\ *n* -s [redupl. of *nig*] *Brit* **:** NEGRO — usu. used disparagingly

ni·gro·striatal \ˌnīgrō, ˌnig-+\ *adj* [fr. substantia *nigra* + *-o-* + *striatal*] **:** of, relating to, or joining the corpus striatum and the substantia nigra ⟨the ~ dopamine pathway degenerates in Parkinson's disease —S.H. Snyder *et al*⟩

-nik \(ˌ)nik\ *n suffix* -s [Yiddish, fr. Pol & Russ] **:** one connected with or characterized by being ⟨peace*nik*⟩ ⟨neat*nik*⟩

nil·po·tent \ˌnil+\ *adj* [L *nil* nothing + *potent-, potens* having power — more at POTENT] **:** equal to zero when raised to some power — **nil·potency** \"+\ *n* — **nil·potent** \"+\ *n*

nine–to–fiver \ˌ==ˈfīvə(r)\ *n* **:** a person who works at a job with regular daytime hours

nit \ˈnit\ *n* -s [ISV, fr. L *nitēre* to shine — more at NEAT] **:** a unit of brightness equal to one candle per square meter of cross section perpendicular to the rays

ni·ti·nol \ˈnītᵊn,ȯl, -,ōl\ *n* -s [fr. *Ni* + *Ti* + *-nol* (fr. *N*aval *O*rdnance *L*aboratory, where the alloy was created)] **:** a nonmagnetic alloy of titanium and nickel that after being deformed returns to its original shape upon being reheated

nit·pick \ˈnit,pik\ *vb* -ED/-ING/-S [back-formation fr. *nit-picking* (herein)] *vi* **:** to engage in nit-picking ~ *vt* **:** to criticize by nitpicking — **nit·pick·er** *n* -s

nit–picking \ˈ=,==\ *n* -s [[1]*nit* + *picking,* gerund of [1]*pick*] **:** minute and usu. petty criticism

ni·tro·fu·ran·to·in \ˌnī·(ˌ)trōfyəˈrantəwən\ *n* -s [*nitrofuran* + hydan*toin*] **:** a nitrofuran derivative $C_8H_6N_4O_5$ that is a broad-spectrum antimicrobial agent used esp. in treating urinary tract infections

ni·tro·ge·nase \ˌnī·ˈträjə,nās, ˈnī·trəj-, -āz\ *n* -s [*nitrogen* + *-ase*] **:** an iron- and molybdenum-containing enzyme of various nitrogen-fixing microorganisms (as some bacteria and blue-green algae) that catalyzes the reduction of molecular nitrogen to ammonia

nitrogen narcosis *n* **:** a state of euphoria and exhilaration that occurs when nitrogen in normal air enters the bloodstream at approximately seven times atmospheric pressure (as in deep-water diving) — called also *rapture of the deep*

ni·tro·so·dimethylamine \nī·ˌtrō(ˌ)sō+\ *n* [*nitros-* + *dimethylamine*] **:** DIMETHYLNITROSAMINE *herein*

ni·tro·so·guanidine \"+\ *n* [*nitros-* + *guanidine*] **:** an explosive compound CH_4N_4O often used as a mutagen in biological research

ni·tro·so·urea \"+\ *n* [*nitros-* + *urea*] **:** any of a group of lipid-soluble drugs that function as alkylating agents, have the ability to enter the central nervous system, and are effective in the treatment of some brain tumors and meningeal leukemias

nit·ty–grit·ty \ˌnid-ēˌgrid-ē\ *n* [origin unknown] **:** what is essential or basic **:** specific practical details ⟨getting down to the *nitty-gritty*⟩ — **nitty–gritty** *adj*

Nix·ie \ˈniksē\ *trademark* — used for an electronic indicator tube

nm *abbr* nanometer *herein*

NMR *abbr* nuclear magnetic resonance *herein*

nobble* *vt, Brit* **:** to get hold of **:** CATCH, NAB

nod* *n* **:** a drowsy stupefied state caused by or as if by the use of narcotic drugs — used esp. in the phrase *on the nod*

node* *n* **1 :** VERTEX 1a(2) **2 :** a receiving or transmitting station (as a computer terminal) in an electronic communications network

nod out *vi* **:** to pass out or fall asleep ⟨parks lined with winos and junkies *nodding out* —Tony Kornheiser⟩

no–fault \ˈ=ˌ=\ *adj* **1 :** of, relating to, or being a motor vehicle insurance plan under which an accident victim is compensated usu. up to a stipulated limit for actual losses (as medical bills and lost wages) but not for nuisance claims (as of pain or suffering) by his own insurance company regardless of who is responsible for the accident **2 :** of, relating to, or being a divorce law according to which neither party is held responsible for the breakdown of the marriage **3 :** being such that individuals are not held responsible for harmful acts or for personal shortcomings ⟨we established a *no-fault* society, a guilt-free age — Eugene Kennedy⟩

no–frills \ˈ=ˌ=\ *adj* **:** offering or providing only the essentials **:** not fancy, elaborate, or luxurious ⟨*no-frills* flights⟩

noise* *n* **1 :** electromagnetic radiation (as light or radio waves) that is composed of several frequencies and that involves random changes in frequency or amplitude **2 :** something that attracts attention ⟨Utah makes big ~ this year —*Ski*⟩ ⟨the play . . . will make little ~ in the world —Brendan Gill⟩ **3 :** something spoken or uttered ⟨when he responded, gave him supportive ~*s:* "Outasight" —Judson Jerome⟩ ⟨made some encouraging ~*s* about Britain's good standing in Arab eyes —William Hardcastle⟩ **4 :** irrelevant or meaningless output (as from a computer or instrument) occurring along with desired information

noise pollution *n* **:** environmental pollution consisting of annoying or harmful noise (as of automobiles or jet airplanes)

no–knock \ˈ=ˌ=\ *adj* **:** of, relating to, or being the entry by police into private premises without knocking and without identifying themselves (as to make an arrest) — **no–knock** *n*

no–load \ˈ=ˌ=\ *adj* **:** charging no sales commission ⟨*no-load* mutual funds⟩ — **no–load** \ˈ=ˌ=\ *n*

nominal* *adj* **:** being according to plan **:** falling within a range of acceptable planned limits **:** SATISFACTORY ⟨everything was ~ during the spacecraft launch⟩ ⟨the satellite had a ~ orbit⟩

nominal* *n* **1 :** a linguistic form (as English *boy* or *he*) that inflects for number or case or for both **2 :** a word or word group functioning as a noun normally functions

nom·i·nal·iza·tion \ˌnämənᵊləˈzāshən, -mnəl-\ *n* -s [²*nominal* + *-ization*] **:** the process or result of forming a noun phrase from a clause — **nominalize*** *vt*

non·addicting \ˌnän *sometimes* ˌnən +\ *adj* **:** not causing addiction ⟨~ painkillers⟩

non·additive \"+\ *adj* [¹*non-* + *additive*] **1 :** not having a numerical value equal to the sum of values for the component parts **2 :** of, relating to, or being a genic effect that is not additive — **nonadditivity** \"+\ *n*

non·aligned \"+\ *adj* [¹*non-* + *aligned,* past part. of *align*] **:** not allied with other nations and esp. with either the Communist or the non-Communist blocs

non·alignment \"+\ *n* **:** the condition of a state or government that is nonaligned

non·book \ˈnän *sometimes* ˈnən +ˌ\ *n* **:** a book that has little literary merit or factual information and is often a compilation (as of pictures or press clippings)

non·candidate \"+\ *n* **:** one who is not a candidate; *esp* **:** one who has declared himself not a candidate for a particular political office — **non·candidacy** \"+\ *n*

non·carcinogenic \"+\ *adj* **:** not producing or inciting cancer

non·chromosomal \ˌnän *sometimes* ˌnən +\ *adj* **1 :** not situated on a chromosome ⟨~ DNA⟩ **2 :** not involving chromosomes ⟨~ mutations⟩

non·constant \"+\ *adj* **:** not constant; *esp* **:** having a range that includes more than one value ⟨a ~ function⟩

non·crossover \(ˈ)=+\ *adj* **:** having or being chromosomes that have not participated in genetic crossing-over ⟨~ offspring⟩

non·dairy \ˌnän *sometimes* ˌnən +\ *adj* [*non-* + *dairy*] **:** containing no milk or milk products ⟨~ coffee lightener⟩

non·degree \"+\ *adj* [*non-* + *degree*] **:** not being, leading to, or required for an academic degree ⟨~ program⟩ ⟨~ courses⟩

non·destructive \"+\ *adj* **:** not destructive; *specif* **:** not causing destruction of material being investigated or treated ⟨~ testing of metal⟩ — **non·destructively** \"+\ *adv*

non·diabetic \"+\ *adj* **:** not affected with diabetes — **non·diabetic** \"+\ *n*

non·diapausing \"+\ *adj* **1 :** not having a diapause **2 :** not being in a state of diapause

non·discrimination \"+\ *n* **:** the absence or avoidance of discrimination — **non·discriminatory** \"+\ *adj*

non·dividing \"+\ *adj* **:** not undergoing cell division

non·drinker \(ˈ)=+\ *n* [*non-* + *drinker*] **:** one who abstains from alcoholic beverages

non·drinking \ˌnän *sometimes* ˌnən +\ *adj* [*non-* + ²*drinking*] **:** abstaining from alcoholic beverages ⟨a ~ family⟩

non·empty \"+\ *adj* **:** not empty; *specif* **:** containing at least one element ⟨~ sets⟩

non·enzymatic \"+\ *or* **non·enzymic** \"+\ *also* **non·enzyme** \"+\ *adj* **:** not involving the action of enzymes ⟨~ cleavage of protein⟩ — **nonenzymatically** \"+\ *adv*

non·event \ˈ=+\ *n* **1 a :** an event that fails to take place or to satisfy expectations **b :** a highly publicized event of little intrinsic interest **2 :** an occurrence that is officially ignored

nonfiction novel *n* **:** a book-length factual narrative written in the style of a novel

non·fluency \ˌnän *sometimes* ˌnən +\ *n* **1 :** lack of fluency **2 :** an instance of nonfluency — **non·fluent** \"+\ *adj*

non·gonococcal \"+\ *adj* [*non-* + *gonococcal*] **:** not caused by the gonococcus ⟨~ urethritis⟩

non·graded \"+\ *adj* **:** having no grade levels ⟨~ schools⟩

non·green \"+\ *adj* **:** not green; *specif* **:** containing no chlorophyll ⟨fungi and other ~ saprophytes⟩

non·hero \ˈ=+ˌ\ *n* **:** ANTI-HERO *herein*

non·hibernating \(ˈ)⸗+\ *adj* **1 :** not being in hibernation **2 :** not capable of hibernation ⟨a ~ strain of hamster⟩

non·histone \(ˈ)⸗+\ *adj* [*non-* + *histone*] **:** rich in aromatic amino acids and esp. tryptophan ⟨~ proteins⟩

non·host \ˈ⸗+ˌ\ *n* [*non-* + [3]*host*] **:** a plant that is not attacked or parasitized by a particular organism

non·identical \ˌnän *sometimes* ˌnən +\ *adj* [*non-* + *identical*] **1 :** DIFFERENT **2 :** FRATERNAL 2

non·impact \"+\ *adj* [[1]*non-* + *impact*] **:** of or relating to a printing process in which the printing element does not strike the paper ⟨a ~ printer⟩

non·insecticidal \"+\ *adj* **1 :** lacking an insecticidal action **2 :** not involving the use of an insecticide

non·invasive \"+\ *adj* [*non-* + *invasive*] **1 :** not tending to spread; *specif* **:** not tending to infiltrate and destroy healthy tissue ⟨~ cancer of the bladder⟩ **2** *of a diagnostic procedure in medicine* **:** not involving penetration (as by surgery) of body tissue — **non·invasively** \"+\ *adv*

non·judgmental \"+\ *adj* **:** avoiding judgments based on one's personal and esp. moral standards ⟨~ counseling on birth control and abortion —*N.Y. Times*⟩

non·negative \"+\ *adj* **1 :** being either positive or zero ⟨a ~ integer⟩ **2 :** taking on nonnegative values ⟨a ~ function⟩

non·neoplastic \"+\ *adj* [[1]*non-* + *neoplastic*] **:** not being or not caused by neoplasms ⟨~ diseases⟩

non·nuclear \"+\ *adj* **1 :** not producing or involving a nuclear explosion ⟨a ~ bomb⟩ ⟨a ~ mining blast⟩ **2 :** not operating by or involving atomic energy ⟨a ~ propulsion system⟩ **3 :** not having developed or not having the atom bomb ⟨a ~ country⟩ **4 :** not involving the use of atom bombs ⟨~ war⟩

no–no \ˈnōˌnō\ *n, pl* **no–no's** *or* **no–nos :** something that is unacceptable or forbidden

non–oil \ˌnän *sometimes* ˌnən +\ *adj* [*non-* + *oil*] **:** being a net importer of petroleum or petroleum products ⟨*non⸗oil* nations⟩

non·persistent \"+\ *adj* **:** not persistent: as **a :** decomposed rapidly by environmental action ⟨~ insecticides⟩ **b :** capable of being transmitted by a vector for only a relatively short time ⟨~ viruses⟩

non·person \ˈ⸗+ˌ\ *n* **:** a person who is regarded as nonexistent: as **a :** UNPERSON *herein* **b :** one having no social or legal status

non·polluting \ˌnän *sometimes* ˌnən +\ *adj* **:** causing little or no pollution ⟨a freely available, ~, renewable source of energy — sunlight —Barry Commoner⟩

non·positive* *adj* **1 :** being either negative or zero ⟨a ~ integer⟩ **2 :** taking on nonpositive values ⟨a ~ function⟩

non·proliferation \"+\ *adj* [*non-* + *proliferation*] **:** providing for the stoppage of proliferation esp. of nuclear weapons ⟨a ~ treaty⟩ — **nonproliferation** *n*

non·psychotic \"+\ *adj* **:** not psychotic

non·recombinant \"+\ *adj* **:** not exhibiting the results of genetic recombination ⟨~ progeny⟩

non·reduction \"+\ *n* **:** the failure of homologous chromosomes to break apart into separate sets in the reduction division of meiosis with the result that some gametes have the diploid number of chromosomes

non·reproductive \"+\ *adj* **:** not reproducing; *esp* **:** not capable of reproducing — **nonreproductive** *n*

non·sedimentable \"+\ *adj* **:** not capable of being sedimented under specified conditions (as of centrifugation) ⟨~ RNA⟩

non·self \"+\ *n* [[1]*non-* + *self*] **:** material that is foreign to the body of an organism

nonsense* *n* **:** genetic information consisting of one or more codons that do not code for any amino acid and usu. cause termination of the molecular chain in protein synthesis — compare MISSENSE *herein*

nonsense* *adj* **:** consisting of one or more codons that are genetic nonsense

non·sexist \ˌnän *sometimes* ˌnən +\ *adj* [*non-* + *sexist* (herein)] **:** not biased or discriminating against persons on the basis of sex; *esp* **:** not discriminating against women

nonsignificant* *adj* **:** having or yielding a value lying within limits between which variation is attributed to chance ⟨a ~ statistical test⟩ — **non·significantly** \ˌ⸗+\ *adv*

non·starter \"+\ *n* **1 :** one that does not start **2 :** someone or something that is not productive or effective ⟨his son has been, in politics a ~ —Anthony Lejeune⟩

non·steroidal *also* **non·steroid** \ˌnän *sometimes* ˌnən +\ *adj* **:** of, relating to, or being a compound and esp. a drug that is not a steroid — **nonsteroid** *n*

non·stick \"+\ *adj* [*non-* + *stick*] **:** allowing of easy removal of cooked food particles ⟨a ~ coating on a frying pan⟩

non·system \(ˈ) ⸗+\ *n* [*non-* + *system*] **:** a system that lacks effective organization

non·target \ˌnän *sometimes* ˌnən +\ *adj* [*non-* + *target*] **:** not being the intended object of action by a particular agent

non·terminating \"+\ *adj* **:** not terminating or ending; *esp* **:** being a decimal for which there is no place to the right of the decimal point such that all places farther to the right contain 0

non·title \"+\ *adj* [*non-* + *title*] **:** of, relating to, or being an athletic contest in which a title is not at stake

non·trivial \"+\ *adj* **1 :** not trivial **2 :** having the value of at least one variable or term not equal to zero

non–U \"+\ *adj* [[1]*non-* + *U* (herein)] **:** not belonging to or characteristic of the upper classes ⟨a *non-U* word⟩

non·vanishing \"+\ *adj* **:** not zero or becoming zero

non·vector \(ˈ)⸗+\ *n* [*non-* + *vector*] **:** an organism (as an insect) that does not transmit a particular pathogen (as a virus)

non·vocoid \"+\ *n* [[1]*non-* + *vocoid*] **:** CONTOID *herein*

non·voter \"+\ *n* [*non-* + *voter*] **:** one that does not vote

noo·sphere \ˈnōə +ˌ\ *n* [ISV *noo-* + *sphere;* prob. orig. formed as Russian *noosfera*] **:** the sphere of human consciousness and mental activity esp. in regard to its influence on the biosphere and in relation to evolution

NOR \ˈnȯ(ə)r\ *n* [not *OR*] **:** a computer logic circuit that produces an output that is the inverse of that of an OR circuit

nor·adrenergic \ˌnȯ(ə)r+\ *adj* [*noradren*aline + *-ergic* (as in *adrenergic*)] **:** liberating, activated by, or involving norepinephrine in the transmission of nerve impulses ⟨~ synapses⟩ — compare ADRENERGIC *in the Dict,* CHOLINERGIC *in the Dict*

nordic* *adj, usu cap* **:** of, relating to, or being competitive ski events consisting of ski jumping and cross-country racing — compare ALPINE *herein*

nor·eth·in·drone \nȯˈrethənˌdrōn\ *n* -s [*nor-* + *ethin*yl + *-dr-* (perh. fr. *androgen*) + testoster*one*] **:** a synthetic progestational hormone $C_{20}H_{26}O_2$ used in oral contraceptives often in the form of its acetate

nor·ethisterone \ˌnȯ(ə)r+\ *n* [*nor-* + *ethisterone*] *chiefly Brit* : NORETHINDRONE *herein*

nor·ethyn·o·drel \ˌnȯrə'thinəˌdrel\ *n* -s [*nor-* + *ethynyl* + *-o-* + *-dr-*) (perh. fr. *androgen*) + *-el* (perh. alter. of [3]*-al*)] : a progesterone derivative $C_{20}H_{26}O_2$ used in oral contraceptives and clinically in the treatment of abnormal uterine bleeding and the control of menstruation

norm* *n* **1 :** a real-valued nonnegative function defined on a vector space and satisfying the conditions that the function is zero if and only if the vector is zero, the function of the product of a scalar and a vector is equal to the product of the absolute value of the scalar and the function of the vector, and that the function of the sum of two vectors is less than or equal to the sum of the functions of the two vectors; *specif* **:** the square root of the sum of the squares of the absolute values of the elements of a matrix or of the components of a vector **2 :** the greatest distance between two successive points of a set of points that partition an interval into smaller intervals

normal* *adj* **1** *of a subgroup* **:** having the property that every coset produced by operating on the left with a given element is equal to the coset produced by operating on the right with the same element **2 :** relating to, involving, or being a normal curve or normal distribution ⟨~ approximation to the binomial distribution⟩ **3** *of a matrix* **:** having the property of commutativity under multiplication by the transpose of a matrix each of whose elements is a conjugate complex number with respect to the corresponding element of the given matrix

normal divisor *n* **:** a normal subgroup

normalize* *vt* **1 :** to make mathematically or statistically normal **2 :** to bring or restore (as relations between countries) to a normal condition — **nor·mal·iz·a·ble** \-ˌlī-zə-bəl\ *adj*

normalizer* *n* **1 :** a subgroup consisting of those elements of a group for which the group operation with regard to a given element is commutative **2 :** the set of elements of a group for which the group operation with regard to every element of a given subgroup is commutative

normal orthogonal *adj* **:** ORTHONORMAL *herein*

normed \'nȯ(ə)rmd\ *adj* [*norm* (herein) + [1]*-ed*] **:** being a mathematical entity upon which a norm is defined ⟨a ~ vector space⟩

nor·mo·ther·mia \ˌnȯrmə'thərmēə\ *n* -s [NL, fr. *norm-* + *-ther- mia*] **:** normal body temperature — **nor·mo·ther·mic** \ˌ⁼⁼ˈ⁼mik\ *adj*

northern corn rootworm *n* **:** a corn rootworm of the genus *Diabrotica* (*D. longicornis*) often destructive to maize in the northern parts of the central and eastern U.S.

nor·trip·ty·line \nȯr'triptəˌlēn\ *n* -s [*nor*mal + *tript-* (alter. of *trypt-* — as in *tryptophan*) + *-yl* + [2]*-ine*] **:** a tricyclic antidepressant $C_{19}H_{21}N$

noseguard \'⁼ˌ⁼\ *n* [so called because he plays nose-to-nose against the offensive center] **:** a defensive lineman in football who plays opposite the offensive center

nose job *n* **:** RHINOPLASTY

nose–ride \'⁼ˌ⁼\ *vi* **:** to ride or perform stunts on the nose of a surfboard — **nose–rider** \'⁼ˌ⁼⁼\ *n*

nose tackle *n* **:** a noseguard esp. in a 3-man defensive line

[1]**nosh** \'näsh\ *vb* -ED/-ING/-ES [Yiddish *nashn,* fr. MHG *naschen* to eat on the sly] *vi* **:** to eat a snack ~ *vt* **:** CHEW, MUNCH — **nosh·er** \-shə(r)\ *n* -s

[2]**nosh** \"\ *n* -ES **1 :** a light snack **2** *chiefly Brit* **a :** MEAL **b :** FOOD

no–show* *n* **1 :** a person who buys a ticket (as to a sporting event) but does not attend; *broadly* **:** a person who is expected but does not show up **2 :** failure to show up ⟨was fired . . . for too many *no-shows* —Mary Vespa⟩

nosh–up \'⁼ˌ⁼\ *n* -s [[2]*nosh* (herein) + *up*] *chiefly Brit* **:** a meal and esp. a large or elaborate meal

nos·tal·gist \nə'staljəst, nä'-\ *n* -s [*nostalgia* + *-ist*] **:** a person fond of the objects and style of the past

NOT \'nät\ *n* [*not*] **:** a logical operator that produces a statement that is the inverse of an input statement

notchback \'⁼ˌ⁼\ *n* [[1]*notch* + [1]*back*] **1 :** a back on a closed passenger automobile having a distinct deck — compare FASTBACK *herein* **2 :** an automobile having a notchback

not–for–profit \ˌ⁼⁼'⁼⁼\ *adj* **:** NONPROFIT ⟨a *not-for-profit* organization⟩

not·geld \'nōtˌgeld, 'nät-, *G* 'nōtˌgelt\ *n* -s [G, emergency money, fr. *not* necessity + *geld* money — more at NEED, GOLD] **:** necessity money used in Germany and some eastern European states esp. after World War I

no–till \(ˈ)nō'til\ *n* **:** NO-TILLAGE *herein*

no–till·age \-əj, -ēj\ *n* **:** a system of farming that consists of planting a narrow slit trench without tillage and with the use of herbicides to suppress weeds

nou·velle cuisine \nü'vel-\ *n* [F, lit., new cooking] **:** a form of French cuisine that uses little flour or fat and stresses light sauces and the use of fresh seasonal produce

nou·velle vague \(ˌ)nüˌvel'väg, -ȧg\ *n* [F, lit., new wave, fr. *nouvelle* (fem. of *nouveau* new, fr. L *novellus*) + *vague* wave, fr. OF *wage,* fr. ON *vāgr;* akin to OE *wǣg* wave, *wegan* to move — more at NOVELLA, WAY] **:** NEW WAVE 1, 2 *herein*

NOW account \'nau̇-\ *n* [*n*egotiable *o*rder of *w*ithdrawal] **:** a savings account on which checks may be drawn

no way** \'⁼'⁼\ *adv* — used interjectionally to express emphatic negation

no–win \'⁼'⁼\ *adj* **:** not likely to give victory, success, or satisfaction **:** that cannot be won ⟨a *no-win* situation⟩ ⟨a *no-win* war⟩

nsec *abbr* nanosecond *herein*

nuclear force *n* **1 :** the powerful force between nucleons that holds atomic nuclei together **2 :** STRONG INTERACTION *herein*

nuclear magnetic resonance *n* **1 :** the magnetic resonance of an atomic nucleus **2 :** chemical analysis that uses nuclear magnetic resonance esp. to study molecular structure — abbr. *NMR*

nuclear resonance *n* **1 :** the resonance absorption of a gamma ray by a nucleus identical to the nucleus that emitted the gamma ray — compare MÖSSBAUER EFFECT *herein* **2 :** RESONANCE 1a *herein*

nu·cleo·capsid \ˌn(y)üklēō +\ *n* [*nucle-* + *capsid* (herein)] **:** the nucleic acid and surrounding protein coat of a virus

nu·cleo·genesis \"+\ *n* [*nucle-* + *genesis*] **:** NUCLEOSYNTHESIS *herein*

nu·cle·o·lo·ne·ma \n(y)üˌklēələ'nēmə\ *also* **nu·cle·o·lo·neme** \-'klēələˌnēm\ *n* -s [NL *nucleolonema* fr. *nucleolus* + *-o-* + Gk *nēma* thread — more at NEEDLE] **:** a filamentous network consisting of small granules in some nucleoli

nucleon* *n* **:** a hypothetical single entity with one-half unit of isospin capable of manifesting itself as either a proton or a neutron and of making transitions between these two states

nu·cleo·phile \ˈn(y)üklēō,fīl\ *n* -s [*nucle-* + [1]*-phil*] **:** a nucleophilic substance (as an electron-donating reagent)

nu·cleo·some \ˈ≈≈,sōm\ *n* -s [ISV *nucle-* + *-some*] **:** any of the repeating globular subunits of chromatin that consist of a complex of DNA and histone and are thought to be present only during interphase — **nu·cleo·so·mal** \ˌ≈≈ˈsōməl\ *adj*

nu·cleo·synthesis \ˌn(y)üklēō +\ *n* [NL, fr. *nucle-* + *synthesis*] **:** the production of a chemical element from hydrogen nuclei (as in stellar evolution) — **nu·cleo·syn·thetic** \"+\ *adj*

nu·cleo·ti·dyl·transferase \ˌn(y)üklēəˌtīdᵊl+\ *n* [*nucleotide* + *-yl* + *transferase*] **:** any of several enzymes that catalyze the transfer of a nucleotide residue from one compound to another

[1]nud·ie \ˈn(y)üdē\ *n* -s [[1]*nude* + *-ie*] **1 :** SKIN FLICK *herein* **2 :** a publication that features photographs of nudes

[2]nudie \"\ *adj* **:** featuring nudes ⟨~ films⟩ ⟨~ magazines⟩

[1]nuke \ˈn(y)ük\ *n* -s [by shortening & alter.] **1 :** a nuclear weapon **2 :** a nuclear-powered electric generating station

[2]nuke \"\ *vt* -ED/-ING/-S **:** to attack or destroy with nuclear weapons

null* *adj* **1 :** having zero as a limit ⟨~ sequence⟩ **2** *of a matrix* **:** having all elements equal to zero

nullity* *n* **:** the number of elements in a basis of a null-space

null-space \ˈ≈,≈\ *n* **:** a subspace of a vector space consisting of vectors that under a given linear transformation are mapped to zero

number crunching *n* **:** the performance of long complex often repetitive mathematical calculations — **number cruncher** *n*

number line *n* **:** a line of infinite extent whose points correspond to the real numbers according to their distance in a positive or negative direction from a point arbitrarily taken as zero

nu·mer·ate \ˈn(y)ümərət\ *adj* [L *numerus* number + E *-ate* (as in *literate*) — more at NIMBLE] **:** marked by the capacity for quantitative thought and expression — **nu·mer·a·cy** \-rəsē\ *n* -ES

nu·mer·ic \n(y)u̇ˈmerik\ *n* -s [*numeric,* adj.] **:** NUMBER, NUMERAL

numerical analysis *n* **:** the study of quantitative approximations to the solutions of mathematical problems including consideration of the errors and bounds to the errors involved

numerical control *n* **:** automatic control (as of a machine tool) by a digital computer — **numerically controlled** *adj*

numerical taxonomy *n* **:** taxonomy that applies the quantitative measurement of many characters to the determination of taxa and to the construction of diagrams indicating systematic relationships — **numerical taxonomic** *adj* — **numerical taxonomist** *n*

nu·me·ro uno \ˌn(y)ümə(ˌ)rōˈü(ˌ)nō\ *n or adj* [It or Sp] **:** NUMBER ONE

nun·cha·ku \ˈnən,chək, nünˈchäk(ˌ)ü\ *n* -s [Jap] **:** a weapon of Japanese origin that consists of two hardwood sticks joined at their ends by a short length of rawhide, cord, or chain

nurd *var of* NERD

nur·tur·ance \ˈnərchərən(t)s\ *n* -s [[2]*nurture* + *-ance*] **:** affectionate care and attention — **nur·tur·ant** \-rənt\ *adj*

nut* *n* **1 :** a large sum of money **2** *slang* **:** a bribe given to a policeman

nuts-and-bolts \ˌ≈≈ˈ≈\ *adj* **:** of, relating to, or dealing with specific practical details ⟨*nuts-and-bolts* aspects of the job⟩

nuts and bolts *n pl* **1 :** the working parts or elements **2 :** the practical workings of a machine or enterprise as opposed to theoretical considerations or speculative possibilities

ny·norsk \ˈn(y)üˈnu̇(ə)rsk, ˈnue̅ˈ-\ *n* -s *usu cap* [Norw, lit., new Norwegian, fr. *ny* new (fr. ON *nȳr*) + *norsk* Norwegian — more at NEW, NORSK1] **:** LANDSMÅL

O

obie \ˈōbē\ *n* -s *usu cap* [*O.B.,* abbr. for *off-Broadway* (herein)] **:** any of several prizes awarded annually by a newspaper for excellence in off-Broadway theater

object language *n* **:** TARGET LANGUAGE *herein*

ob·jet trou·vé \ˌȯbˌzhā(ˌ)trüˈvā\ *n, pl* **objets trouvés** *same*\ [F, lit., found object] **:** FOUND OBJECT *herein*

ocea·naut \ˈōshəˌnȯt, -nät\ *n* -s [blend of *ocean* and *-naut* (as in *aquanaut* — herein)] **:** AQUANAUT *herein*

ocean engineering *n* **:** engineering that deals with the application of design, construction, and maintenance principles and techniques to the ocean environment

ocean·ol·o·gist \ˌōshəˈnäləjəst\ *n* [*oceanology* + [1]*-ist*] **:** OCEANOGRAPHER

och·ra·toxin \ˌōkrə+\ *n* [NL *ochraceus* (specific epithet of *Aspergillis ochraceus*) + E *toxin*] **:** a mycotoxin produced by a fungus of the genus *Aspergillus* (*A. ochraceus*)

OCR *abbr* optical character reader; optical character recognition

oc·ta·peptide \ˌäktə +\ *n* [*octa-* + *peptide*] **:** a protein fragment or molecule (as oxytocin or vasopressin) that consists of eight amino acids linked in a polypeptide chain

oc·to·pamine \äkˈtōpəˌmēn, -ˌmən\ *n* [NL, fr. *octopus* + *amine*] **:** an adrenergic biogenic amine $C_8H_{11}NO_2$ that has been implicated as a neurotransmitter

oc·to·thorp \ˈäktōˌthȯrp\ *n* -s [*octo-* + *thorp,* of unknown origin; fr. the eight points on its circumference] **:** the symbol #

oc·u·lar·ist \ˈäkyələrəst\ *n* -s [[2]*ocular* + *-ist*] **:** a person who makes and fits artificial eyes

[1]**OD** \ˌōˈdē\ *n* -s [*overdose*] **1 :** an overdose of a narcotic **2 :** one who has taken an overdose of a narcotic

[2]**OD** \"\ *vi* **OD'd** *or* **ODed; OD'd** *or* **ODed; OD'ing; OD's 1 :** to become ill or die from an OD **2 :** to have or experience too much of something — used with *on* ⟨*OD* on television⟩

odd–lot·ter \ˈädˈläd·ə(r)\ *n* -s [*odd lot* + *-er*] **:** a speculator or an investor who habitually buys and sells stock in less than round lots

odd permutation *n* **:** a permutation that is produced by the successive application of an odd number of interchanges of pairs of elements — compare EVEN PERMUTATION *herein*

odont·o·log·i·cal \(ˌ)ōˌdäntᵊlˈäjəkəl\ *adj* [*odontology* + *-ical*] **:** of or relating to odontology

oem \ˌōˌēˈem\ *n* -s *usu cap* [*o*riginal *e*quipment *m*anufacturer] **:** one that produces complex equipment (as a computer system) from components usu. bought from other manufacturers

off* *vt, slang* **:** KILL, MURDER ⟨~*ed* over 20 souls, none of them with a machine gun —Molly Ivins⟩

off broadway *n, often cap O & usu cap B* [so called fr. its usu. being produced in smaller theaters outside of the Broadway theatrical district] **:** a part of the New York professional theater stressing fundamental and artistic values and formerly engaging in experimentation — **off–broadway** \¦=¦==\ *adj or adv, often cap O & usu cap B*

off–camera \¦=¦=(=)=\ *adv or adj* **1 :** out of the range of a motion-picture or television camera ⟨chided me *off-camera* during a commercial break —W.H. Manville⟩ **2 :** in private life

offering price* *n* **:** the price at which an open-end mutual fund is sold consisting of its asset value usu. plus a specified load

of·fi·ci·a·lis \əˌfishēˈäləs, -ˈal-\ *n, pl* **of·fi·ci·a·les** \-ˈä(ˌ)lās, -ˈa(ˌ)lēz\ [NL, fr. ML, official — more at OFFICIAL] **:** the presiding judge of the matrimonial court of a Roman Catholic diocese

off–line* \ˈ=¦=\ *adj* **:** not connected to or served by a system and esp. a computer or telecommunications system; *also* **:** done independently of a system ⟨*off-line* computer storage⟩ — **off–line** *adv*

off–off–broadway \(ˈ)=ˈ=ˌ=ˌ=\ *n, often cap both Os & usu cap B* [so called fr. its relation to off-Broadway being analogous to the relation of off-Broadway to Broadway] **:** an avant-garde theatrical movement in New York that stresses untraditional techniques and radical experimentation — **off–off–broadway** *adj or adv, often cap both Os & usu cap B*

off–price \ˈ=¦=\ *adj* **:** of, relating to, selling, or being discounted merchandise ⟨an *off-price* store⟩ ⟨*off-price* apparel⟩

off–putting \ˈ=ˌ==\ *adj* **:** that puts one off **:** REPELLENT, DISAGREEABLE ⟨anything new is always *off-putting* and upsetting —Dwight Macdonald⟩

off–road \ˈ=¦=\ *adj* **:** of, relating to, or being a vehicle designed esp. to operate away from public roads

offshore fund *n* **:** an investment fund based outside the U.S., not subject to registration with the Security and Exchange Commission, and barred by law from selling its shares within the U.S.

off–speed \¦=¦=\ *adj* **:** being slower than usual or expected ⟨throwing *off-speed* pitches⟩

off–the–peg \ˌ==¦=\ *adj, chiefly Brit* **:** READY-MADE ⟨*off-the-peg* clothes —*The People*⟩

off–the–rack \ˌ==¦=\ *adj* **:** READY-MADE ⟨*off-the-rack* suits⟩

off–the–shelf \ˌ==¦=\ *adj* **:** available as a stock item **:** not specially designed or custom-made

off–the–wall \ˌ==¦=\ *adj* **:** highly unusual **:** BIZARRE ⟨an *off-the-wall* sense of humor⟩

offtrack \¦=¦=\ *adj or adv* **:** situated or occurring away from a racetrack ⟨~ bookies⟩; *esp* **:** relating to or being pari-mutuel betting that is carried on away from the racetrack

OJT *abbr* on-the-job training

ok·to·ber·fest \äkˈtōbə(r)ˌfest\ *n* -s *usu cap* [G, fr. *Oktober* October + *fest* festival] **:** a fall festival usu. featuring beer drinking

old lady* *n* **:** GIRL FRIEND; *esp* **:** one with whom a man cohabits

old man* *n* **:** BOYFRIEND; *esp* **:** one with whom a woman cohabits

old–money \¦=ˌ==\ *adj* **:** possessing wealth that has been inherited through several generations

ole·an·do·my·cin \ˌōlēˌandəˈmīsᵊn\ *n* -s [prob. fr. *oleander* + *-o-* + *-mycin*] **:** an antibiotic $C_{35}H_{61}NO_{12}$ produced by a bacterium of the genus *Streptomyces* (*S. antibioticus*)

o level *n, usu cap O* **:** the earlier and less advanced of two standardized British examinations of achievement in a secondary school subject; *also* **:** the level of education required to pass an O level examination — called also *Ordinary level;* compare A LEVEL *herein*

ol·i·gid·ic \ˌälə'gidik, ˌōl-, -'ji-\ *adj* [*olig-* + *-idic* (as in *meridic* — herein)] **:** having the active constituents with the exception of water undefined chemically ⟨~ growth medium⟩ — compare HOLIDIC *herein,* MERIDIC *herein*

oligo·mer \ō'ligəmə(r), ə'l-\ *n* -s [*olig-* + *-mer*] **:** a polymer or polymer intermediate that contains relatively few structural units — **oligo·mer·ic** \ˌ=ˌ==ˌmerik, ˌäləgōˌm-, -mir-\ *adj* — **oligo·mer·iza·tion** \=ˌ==ˌmerə'zāshən, -mir-\ *n* -s

oli·go·my·cin \ˌäligō'mīsᵊn, ˌōli-\ *n* -s [*olig-* + *-mycin*] **:** any of several antibiotic substances produced by a streptomyces (of a species similar to *Streptomyces diastatochromogenes*) and used esp. in biochemical research to inhibit oxidative phosphorylation

ol·i·go·nucleotide \ˌäləgō, əˌligə +\ *n* [*olig-* + *nucleotide*] **:** a chain of usu. from 2 to 10 nucleotides

olin·go \ō'liŋˌgō\ *n* -s [AmerSp, howling monkey] **:** any of a genus (*Bassaricyon*) of long-tailed slender-bodied carnivores of Central and So. America that are related to the raccoon

om·buds·man \'ämˌbu̇dzmən, 'ȯm-, -(ˌ)bəd-, äm'b-, ȯm'b-, -ˌman\ *n, pl* **ombuds·men** \-mən, -ˌmen\ [Sw, lit., representative, commissioner, fr. ON *umbothsmathr,* fr. *umboth* commission (fr. *um* around + *bjōtha* to command) + *mathr* man — more at EMBER DAY, BID, MAN] **1 :** a government official (as in Sweden or New Zealand) appointed to receive and investigate complaints made by individuals against abuses or capricious acts of public officials **2 :** one that investigates complaints (as from students or customers), reports findings, and helps to achieve equitable settlements — **om·buds·man·ship** \-ˌmənˌship\ *n*

om·buds·woman \-zˌwu̇mən\ *n, pl* **om·buds·women** \-zˌwimən\ [*ombuds-* (as in *ombudsman*) + *woman*] **:** a female ombudsman

omega* *n* **1** *or* **omega particle :** a negatively charged elementary particle that has a mass 3280 times the mass of an electron and that is an unstable baryon decaying into a xi and a pion with an average lifetime of about 10^{-10} second **2** *or* **omega meson :** a very short-lived unstable meson with mass 1532 times the mass of an electron

om·ni·focal \ˌämnə, -nē +\ *adj* [*omn-* + *focal*] **:** of, relating to, or being a bifocal eyeglass that is so ground as to permit smooth transition from one correction to the other

on–air \ˌ=ˌ=\ *adj* [¹*on* + *air*] **:** appearing, used, or done on a radio or television broadcast

onboard \ˌ=ˌ=\ *adj* [*on board*] **:** carried within or occurring aboard a vehicle (as a satellite or spacecraft) ⟨an ~ computer⟩

on–camera \ˌ=ˌ=(=)=\ *adv or adj* **:** within the range of a motion-picture or television camera ⟨read their lines *on-camera*⟩

on·co·gene \'äŋkəˌjēn\ *n* [¹*onco-* + *gene*] **:** a gene having the potential to cause a normal cell to become cancerous

on·co·genesis \ˌäŋkō +\ *n* [NL, fr. ¹*onco-* + *genesis*] **:** the induction or formation of tumors

on·co·ge·nic·i·ty \ˌäŋkōjə'nisəd·ē\ *n* -ES [¹*onco-* + *-genic* + *-ity*] **:** the capacity to induce or form tumors

on·cor·na·virus \än'kȯrnə, äŋ-+\ *n* [*onco-* + *RNA* + *virus*] **:** any of a group of RNA-containing viruses that produce tumors

one–lin·er \ˌ='līnə(r)\ *n* **:** a very succinct joke or witticism

one–night stand* *n* **:** a sexual encounter limited to a single occasion

one–off \ˌ=ˌ=\ *adj* [¹*one* + *off*] *Brit* **:** limited to a single time, occasion, or instance **:** ONE-SHOT — **one–off** \"\ *n, Brit*

¹**one–on–one** \ˌ==ˌ=\ *adj or adv* **1 :** playing directly against a single opposing player **2 :** involving a direct encounter between one person and another

²**one–on–one** \ˌ=='=\ *n* **:** a game or an aspect of a game which pits one offensive player against a single defender; *esp* **:** an informal basketball game between two players who alternate at offense and defense

one–tailed \ˌ=ˌ=\ *also* **one–tail** *adj* **:** being a statistical test for which the critical region consists of all values of the test statistic greater than a given value or less than a given value but not both — compare TWO-TAILED *herein*

one–time pad \ˌ=ˌ=-\ *n* [¹*one* + ¹*time* + ¹*pad;* prob. fr. its original form's being a pad of keys whose sheets were torn off and discarded after a single use] **:** a random-number additive or mixed keying sequence to be used for a single coded message and then destroyed

one–up \ˌ='=\ *vt* **one–upped; one–upped; one–upping; one–ups** [back-formation fr. *one-upmanship*] **:** to practice one-upmanship on

one–world·ism \ˌ='wər(ə)lˌdizəm, -'wəl-\ *n* -s [¹*one* + *world* + *-ism*] **:** a belief in world government

onion dome *n* **:** a dome (as of a church) having the general shape of an onion — **onion–domed** *adj*

on–line \ˌ=ˌ=\ *adj* [¹*on* + ³*line*] **:** connected to, served by, or available through a system and esp. a computer or telecommunications system ⟨an *on-line* data base⟩; *also* **:** done while connected to a system ⟨*on-line* computer storage⟩ — **on–line** *adv*

on–screen \ˌ='=\ *adv or adj* **:** in a motion picture or a television program

on–the–job \ˌ==ˌ=\ *adj* **:** of, relating to, or being something (as training or experience) learned, gained, or done while working at a job and often under supervision

on–the–scene \ˌ==ˌ=\ *adj* **:** being at the place of an action or occurrence ⟨an *on-the-scene* witness⟩

onto* *prep* — used as a function word which precedes a word or phrase denoting a set each element of which is the image of at least one element of another set

on·to \'ȯn(ˌ)tü, 'än-\ *adj* [*onto,* prep. (herein)] **:** mapping elements in such a way that every element in one set is the image of at least one element in another set ⟨a function that is one-to-one and ~⟩ — see SURJECTION *herein*

OOB \ˌōˌō'bē\ *n* -s [off-off-*B*roadway (herein)] **:** OFF-OFF-BROADWAY *herein*

op \'äp\ *or* **op art** *n* -s [by shortening] **:** OPTICAL ART *herein* — **op artist** *n*

op–ed page \ˌäpˌed-\ *n* [*op*posite + *ed*itorial] **:** the page opposite the editorial page of a newspaper that features by-lined articles (as by columnists) reflecting individual points of view

open* *adj* **1 :** being a mathematical interval that contains neither of its endpoints **2 :** being a set each point of which has a neighborhood all of whose points are contained in the set **3 :** being a universe in which the force of gravity from the mass contained in the universe is insufficient to halt the universe's expansion

open admission *n, pl* **open admissions** *usu sing in constr* **:** OPEN ENROLLMENT 2 *herein*
open bar *n* **:** a bar (as at a wedding reception) at which drinks are served free — compare CASH BAR *herein*
open classroom *n* **1 :** an informal flexible system of elementary education in which open discussions and individualized activities replace the traditional subject-centered studies **2 :** a classroom in an open classroom system
open dating *n* **:** the marking of perishable food products with a clearly readable date indicating when the food was packaged or the last date on which it should be sold or used
open enrollment *n* **1 :** the voluntary enrollment of a student in a public school other than the one he is assigned to on the basis of his residence **2 :** enrollment on demand as a student in an institution of higher learning irrespective of formal qualifications
open–heart \ˌ≈ˈ≈\ *adj* **:** of, relating to, or performed on a heart temporarily relieved of circulatory function and laid open for inspection and treatment ⟨*open-heart* surgery⟩
open loop *n* **:** a control system for an operation or process in which there is no self-correcting action
open marriage *n* **:** a marriage in which the partners agree to let each other have sexual partners outside the marriage
open season *n* **:** a time during which someone or something is the object of strong and continued attack or criticism
open sentence *n* **:** a statement (as in mathematics) that contains at least one blank or unknown and that becomes true or false when the blank is filled or a quantity is substituted for the unknown
operand* *n* -s **:** the part of a computer instruction that indicates the quantities to be operated on; *also* **:** one of these quantities
operating system *n* **:** software that controls the operation of a computer and directs the processing of the user's programs (as by assigning storage space in memory and controlling input and output functions)
operation* *n* **:** a single step performed by a computer in the execution of a program
op·er·a·tion·al·is·tic \ˌäpəˌrāshnəlˈistik, -shənᵊl-\ *adj* [*operationalist* + [1]*-ic*] **:** of or relating to operationalism
op·er·a·tion·al·ize \ˌäpəˈrāshnəlˌīz, -shənᵊl-\ *vt* -ED/-ING/-S [*operational* + *-ize*] **:** to make operational ⟨~ a program⟩ — **op·er·a·tion·al·iza·tion** \äp(ə)ˌrāshnəl-əˈzāshən, -shənᵊl-, -(ᵊ)l(ˌ)īz-\ *n* -s
op·er·a·tion·ist \ˌäpəˈrāsh(ə)nəst\ *n* -s [*operation* + *-ist*] **:** OPERATIONALIST
operator* *or* **operator gene** *n* **:** a chromosomal region that triggers formation of messenger RNA by one or more nearby structural genes and is itself subject to inhibition by a genetic repressor — compare OPERON *herein*
op·er·on \ˈäpəˌrän\ *n* -s [ISV *operator* + *-on* (herein); prob. orig. formed in F] **:** the closely linked combination of an operator and the structural genes it regulates
opi·oid \ˈōpēˌȯid\ *adj* [[2]*opiate* + *-oid*] **1 :** possessing some properties characteristic of opiate narcotics but not derived from opium **2 :** of, involving, or induced by an opioid substance or an opioid peptide
opioid peptide \"...-\ *also* **opioid** *n* -s **:** any of a group of endogenous neural polypeptides (as an endorphin or enkephalin) that bind esp. to opiate receptors and mimic some of the pharmacological properties of opiates
op·son·iza·tion \ˌäpsənəˈzāshən, -ˌnīˈz-\ *n* -s [*opson-* + *-ization*] **:** the process of opsonizing
optical* *adj* **1 :** of, relating to, or being objects that emit light in the visible range of frequencies ⟨an ~ galaxy⟩ ⟨~ astronomy⟩ **2 a :** of, relating to, or utilizing light or lasers ⟨~ microscopy⟩ **b :** involving the use of light-sensitive devices to acquire information for a computer ⟨~ character recognition⟩ **3 :** of or relating to optical art
optical art *n* **:** nonobjective art characterized by the use of straight or curved lines or geometric patterns often for an illusory effect (as of perspective or motion)
optical disc *n* **:** a disc with a plastic coating on which information (as music or visual images) is recorded digitally as tiny pits and which is read using a laser
optical fiber *n* **:** a single fiber-optic strand
optic tectum *n* **:** the visual projection area of fish and amphibians homologous to the mammalian superior colliculus; *also* **:** SUPERIOR COLLICULUS
op·to·electronics \ˈäp(ˌ)tō +\ *n pl but sing in constr* [*optical* + *-o-* + *electronics*] **:** a branch of electronics that deals with devices for emitting, modulating, transmitting, and sensing light — **op·to·electronic** \"+\ *adj*
OR \ˈȯ(ə)r, ˈȯ(ə)\ *n* -s [[1]*or*] **:** a logical operator equivalent to the sentential connective *or* ⟨~ gate in a computer⟩
OR* *abbr* operations research
or·a·cy \ˈōrəsē, ˈȯr-, ˈär-\ *n* -ES [[1]*oral* + *-acy* (as in *literacy*)] **:** the capacity for producing and understanding spoken language
oral history *n* **1 :** tape-recorded historical information obtained in interviews concerning personal experiences and recollections; *also* **:** the study of such information **2 :** a written work based on oral history — **oral historian** *n*
order* *n* **1 :** the number of elements in a finite mathematical group **2 :** a class of mutually exclusive linguistic forms any and only one of which may occur in a fixed definable position in the permitted sequence of items forming a word
ordered* *adj* **:** having elements succeeding or arranged according to a rule: as **a :** having the property that every pair of different elements is related by a transitive relationship that is not symmetric **b :** having the elements labeled by ordinal numbers ⟨an ~ triple has a first, second, and third element⟩
ordinal number* *n* **:** a number assigned to an ordered set that designates both the order of its elements and its cardinal number
ordinary level *n, usu cap O* **:** O LEVEL *herein*
or·ga·no \ˈȯrgə(ˌ)nō, ȯrˈga(-\ *adj* [*organo-*] **:** of, relating to, or being a chemical compound composed of an organic group bonded to an inorganic element or group
or·gano·chlorine \ȯrˈganə, ˌȯrgənō +\ *adj* [*organ-* + [2]*chlorine*] **:** of, relating to, or belonging to the chlorinated hydrocarbon pesticides (as aldrin, DDT, or dieldrin) — **organochlorine** *n*
or·ga·nol·o·gy \ˌȯrgəˈnäləjē, ˌȯ(ə)g-\ *n* -ES [[1]*organ* + *-o-* + *-logy*] **:** the study of the structure, history, and use of musical instruments — **or·ga·nol·o·gist** \-jəst\ *n* -s
or·gano·phosphate \"+\ *n* [*organ-* + *phosphate*] **:** an organophosphorus pesticide — **organophosphate** *adj*
or·gano·phosphorus \"+\ *also* **or·gano·phosphor·ous** \"+\ *adj* [*organ-* + *phosphorus* or *phosphorous*] **:** of, relating to, or being a phosphorus-containing organic compound and esp. a pesticide (as malathion) that acts by inhibiting cholinesterase — **organophosphorus** *n*

oriental shorthair *n, usu cap O&S* **:** any of a breed of slender short-haired domestic cats resembling the Siamese in conformation but having a solid-colored coat in a wide range of colors

ori·en·teer·ing \ˌōrēən·ˈti(ə)riŋ, -ē(ˌ)en-\ *n* -s [prob. modif. (influenced by *-eer*) of Sw *orientering,* fr. *orientera* to orient, fr. F *orienter*] **:** a cross-country race in which each participant uses a map and compass to navigate his way between checkpoints along an unfamiliar course

oro·so·mucoid \ˌ¦ȯrəsōˈmyüˌkȯid\ *n* [Gk *oros* whey + E *-o-* + ²*mucoid*] **:** a mucoprotein found in blood and in nephrotic urine

orthodromic* *adj* **:** of, relating to, or inducing nerve impulses along an axon in the normal direction — compare ANTIDROMIC *in the Dict* — **or·tho·drom·i·cal·ly** \ˌ¦ȯrthə¦drämək(ə)lē\ *adv*

orthogonal* *adj* **1 :** having a sum of products or an integral that is zero or sometimes one under specified conditions: as **a** *of real-valued functions* **:** having the integral of the product of each pair of functions over a specific interval equal to zero **b** *of vectors* **:** having the scalar product equal to zero **c** *of a square matrix* **:** having the sum of products of corresponding elements in any two rows or any two columns equal to one if the rows or columns are the same and equal to zero otherwise **:** having a transpose with which the product equals the identity matrix **2** *of a linear transformation* **:** having a matrix that is orthogonal **:** preserving length and distance **3 :** composed of mutually orthogonal elements ⟨an ~ basis of a vector space⟩

or·thog·o·nal·iza·tion \ȯ(r)ˌthägənᵊlə̇ˈzāshən, -gnəl-, -(ᵊ)lˌīˈz-\ *n* -s [*orthogonalize* + *-ation*] **:** the replacement of a set of vectors by a linearly equivalent set of orthogonal vectors

or·tho·molecular \ˌ¦ȯ(r)thə +\ *adj* [*orth-* + *molecular*] **:** relating to, based on, using, or being a theory according to which disease and esp. mental illness may be cured by restoring the optimum amounts of substances normally present in the body ⟨~ therapy⟩

or·tho·normal \"+\ *adj* [*orth-* + *normal*] **1** *of real-valued functions* **:** orthogonal with the integral of the square of each function over a specified interval equal to one **2 :** being or composed of orthogonal elements of unit length ⟨~ basis of a vector space⟩

¹or·thot·ic \ȯrˈthäd·ik\ *adj* **1 :** of or relating to orthotics ⟨~ research⟩ **2 :** designed for the support of weak or ineffective joints or muscles ⟨~ devices⟩

²orthotic *n* -s **:** an orthotic support or brace

or·thot·ics \ȯrˈthäd·iks\ *n pl but sing in constr* [fr. Gk *orthōsis* straightening; after such pairs as E *prosthesis: prosthetics* — more at ORTHOSIS] **:** a branch of mechanical and medical science dealing with the support and bracing of weak or ineffective joints or muscles — **or·tho·tist** \ˈȯrthətə̇st\ *n* -s

orthotropic* *adj* **1 :** being, having, or relating to properties (as strength, stiffness, and elasticity) that are symmetric about two or three mutually perpendicular planes ⟨a piece of straight-grained wood is an ~ material⟩ **2** *of a bridge* **:** designed so that the roadway serves as an orthotropic structural member **:** constructed with a steel-plate deck as an integral part of the support structure

or·vie·to \ȯrˈvyā(ˌ)tō, -yed·ō\ *n* -s *usu cap* [*Orvieto,* city in central Italy] **:** a usu. dry Italian white wine

or·well·ian \ȯrˈwelēən\ *adj, usu cap* [George *Orwell* (pseudonym of Eric Blair †1950 Eng. writer) + E *-ian*] **:** of, relating to, or suggestive of George Orwell or his writings; *esp* **:** relating to or suggestive of his novel *1984*

or·zo \ˈȯrd(ˌ)zō\ *n* -s [It, perh. fr. *orzo* barley] **:** rice-shaped pasta

osculating circle *n* **:** a circle which is tangent to a curve at a given point, which lies in the limiting plane determined by the tangent to the curve and a point moving along the curve to the point of tangency, which has its center situated on the normal to the curve at the given point and, also, on the concave side of the projection of the curve onto the limiting plane, and which has a radius equal to the radius of curvature

os·mol \ˈäzˌmōl, ˈäˌsmōl\ *n* -s [blend of *osmosis* and *mol*] **:** a standard unit of osmotic pressure based on a one molal concentration of an ion in a solution

os·mo·lal·ity \ˌäzməˈlaləd·ē, ˌäsm-\ *n* -ES [*osmol* + *-al* + *-ity*] **:** the concentration of an osmotic solution esp. when measured in osmols or milliosmols per 1000 grams of solvent — **os·mo·lal** \äzˈmōləl, äsˈ-\ *adj*

os·mo·lar·i·ty \ˌäzməˈlarəd·ē, ˌäsm-\ *n* -ES [*osmol* + *-ar* + *-ity*] **:** the concentration of an osmotic solution esp. when measured in osmols or milliosmols per liter of solution — **os·mo·lar** \äzˈmōlər, äsˈ-\ *adj*

osmotic shock *n* **:** a rapid change in the osmotic pressure (as by transfer to a medium of different concentration) affecting a living system

os·so bu·co *also* **os·so buc·co** \ˌōsōˈbü(ˌ)kō\ *n* [It *ossobuco* marrowbone] **:** a dish of veal shanks braised with vegetables, white wine, and seasoned stock

osteogenic sarcoma *n* **:** OSTEOSARCOMA

os·te·on \ˈästēˌän\ *n* -s [Gk, bone] **:** HAVERSIAN SYSTEM

ost·mark \ˈōstˌmärk, ˈäs-\ *n* -s [G, lit., East mark] **:** the mark of East Germany — see MONEY table *in the Dict*

os·to·my \ˈästəmē\ *n* -ES [col*ostomy*] **:** an operation (as a colostomy) to create an artificial passage for bodily elimination

OTB* *abbr* offtrack betting

OTC *abbr* over-the-counter

oto·toxic \ˌ¦ōd·ə +\ *adj* [*ot-* + *toxic*] **:** producing, involving, or being adverse effects on organs or nerves involved in hearing or balance — **oto·toxicity** \"+\ *n*

ou·gui·ya \üˈg(w)ē(y)ə\ *n, pl* **ouguiya** *or* **ouguiyas** [native name in Mauritania] **1 :** the basic monetary unit of Mauritania — see MONEY table *in the Dict* **2 :** a coin or note representing one ouguiya

out* *adj* **:** not approved of or accepted by those who are keenly aware of and responsive to what is new and smart **:** not in

out–front \ˈ=ˈ=\ *adj* [¹*out* + *front*] **:** FRANK, OPEN, UNABASHED

out–of–sight \ˌ==ˈ=\ *adj, slang* **:** WONDERFUL

out–of–stat·er \ˌ¦==¦stād·ə(r), -ātə-\ *n* -s [fr. the phrase *out of state* + *-er*] **1 :** a visitor from another state **2 :** a person whose legal domicile is in one state but who lives for an extended time in another state (as to attend college)

out–of–town·er \-¦taünə(r)\ *n* -s [fr. the phrase *out of town* + *-er*] **:** a visitor from out of town

outplacement \ˈ=ˌ==\ *n* [¹*out* + *placement*] **:** the process of easing unwanted or unneeded executives out of a company by providing them company-paid assistance in finding new jobs

outreach* *n* **:** the extending of services or activities beyond current or conventional limits; *also* **:** the extent of such services or activities

outside* *adj* **:** made or done from the outside or from a distance

outsourcing \'aůt,sōrsiŋ, -,sȯ(r)s-\ *n* -s [3*out* + *source* + 3-*ing*] **:** the procurement by a corporation from outside and esp. foreign or nonunion suppliers of parts it formerly manufactured

ovals of cas·si·ni \-kə'sēnē, -ka-, -kå-\ *usu cap C* [after G. D. *Cassini* †1712 Fr. astronomer] **:** a curve that is the locus of points of the vertex of a triangle whose opposite side is fixed and the product of whose adjacent sides is a constant and that has the equation $[(x+a)^2+y^2][(x-a)^2+y^2]-k4=0$ where k is the constant and a is one half the length of the fixed side

ovenproof \'==,=\ *adj* [*oven* + *proof*] **:** capable of withstanding the heat normally produced in a kitchen oven ⟨~ glass⟩

over·achiev·er \'==ə'chēvə(r)\ *n* -s [1*over* + *achieve* + -*er*] **:** one who achieves success over and above a standard or expected level — **overachieve** \'==='=\ *vi*

overbook \'=='=\ *vb* [1*over* + 2*book*] *vt* **:** to issue reservations for (as an airplane flight) in excess of the space available ~ *vi* **:** to issue reservations in excess of the space available

overdominance \,=='===\ *n* [3*over* + *dominance*] **:** the property of having a heterozygote that produces a phenotype more extreme or better adapted than that of the homozygote — **overdominant** \'=='===\ *adj*

1**overdub** \'=='=\ *vt* [1*over* + *dub*] **:** to transfer (recorded sound) onto a recording that bears sound recorded earlier in order to produce a combined effect

2**overdub** *n* **1 :** the act or an instance of overdubbing **2 :** recorded sound that is overdubbed ⟨vocal ~*s*⟩

overfatigue \'==='=\ *n* [1*over* + *fatigue*] **:** excessive fatigue esp. when carried beyond the recuperative capacity of the individual

overground \'==,=\ *n* -s [2*over* + *ground*] **:** ESTABLISHMENT *herein* ⟨the underground medium as it grows often takes on the characteristics of the ~ —R. J. Glessing⟩ ⟨~ press⟩

overhang* *n* **:** an excess of something that is left over and not easily disposed of ⟨inventory ~⟩ ⟨an ~ of unemployment⟩

overkill \'==,=\ *n* [*overkill*, v. (herein) fr. 1*over* + 1*kill*] **1 :** the capability of destroying an enemy or target with a nuclear force larger than is required **2 :** an excess of something (as a quantity or an action) beyond what is required or suitable for a particular purpose ⟨promotional ~⟩ ⟨an ~ in weaponry⟩ **3 :** killing in excess of what is intended or required — **overkill** \'==,=, ,=='=\ *vb*

overnight* *n* **:** an overnight stay

overnutrition \'==='==\ *n* [3*over* + *nutrition*] **:** excessive food intake esp. when viewed as a factor in pathology

overprescribe \'==='=\ *vb* [1*over* + *prescribe*] *vi* **:** to prescribe excessive or unnecessary medication ~ *vt* **:** to prescribe (medication) unnecessarily or to excess

overrespond \'==='=\ *vi* [1*over* + *respond*] **:** OVERREACT

overshoot \'==,=\ *n* [*overshoot*, v.] **:** the action or an instance of overshooting; *esp* **:** a going beyond an intended point

oversteer \'=='=\ *n* [3*over* + 4*steer*] **:** the tendency of an automobile to steer into a sharper turn than the driver intends sometimes with the result that the vehicle's rear end swings to the outside; *also* **:** the action or an instance of oversteer

over–the–transom \'==='==\ *adj* **:** offered without prior arrangement esp. for publication ⟨an *over-the-transom* manuscript⟩

overwinter \'=='==\ *adj* [2*over* + 1*winter*] **:** occurring during the period spanning the winter ⟨~ mortality of small game⟩

overwithhold \'==='=\ *vt* [1*over* + *withhold*] **:** to deduct a greater amount of (money) from an employee's pay for withholding tax than the employee is legally required to pay

ovon·ics \ō'väniks\ *n pl but usu sing in constr, usu cap* [*Ov*shinsky effect (herein) + electr*onics*] **:** a branch of electronics that deals with applications of the Ovshinsky effect — **ovonic** *adj, often cap*

ov·shin·sky effect \äv'shin(t)skē-, ōv-\ *n, usu cap O* [after Stanford R. *Ovshinsky b*1923 Am. inventor] **:** the change from an electrically nonconducting state to a semiconducting state shown by glasses of special composition upon application of a certain minimum voltage

OW* *abbr* one way

ox·a·cil·lin \'äksə'silən\ *n* -s [is*oxa*zole + peni*cillin*] **:** a semisynthetic penicillin that is esp. effective in the control of infections caused by penicillin-resistant staphylococci

ox·az·e·pam \äk'sazə,pam\ *n* -s [hydr*oxy*- + di*azepam* (herein)] **:** a tranquilizing drug $C_{15}H_{11}ClN_2O_2$

ox·bridge \'äksbrij\ *adj, usu cap* [*Ox*ford University, England + Cam*bridge* University, England] **:** of, relating to, or characteristic of Oxford and Cambridge universities — compare PLATEGLASS *herein*, REDBRICK *herein*

oxidative phosphorylation *n* **:** the synthesis of ATP by phosphorylation of ADP for which energy is obtained by electron transport and which takes place in the mitochondria during aerobic respiration

oxo·trem·o·rine \,äksō'tremə,rēn, -,rən\ *n* -s [1*ox*- + 1*tremor* + 2-*ine*] **:** a cholinergic agent $C_{12}H_{18}N_2O$ that induces tremors and is used to screen drugs for activity against Parkinson's disease

oxy·acid \'äksē +\ *n* [2*oxy*- + *acid*] **:** an acid (as sulfuric acid) that contains oxygen — called also *oxygen acid*

ox·y·gen·ase \'äksəjə,nās, -,nāz\ *n* -s [*oxygen* + -*ase*] **:** an enzyme that catalyzes the reaction of an organic compound with molecular oxygen

oxygen cycle *n* **:** the cycle whereby atmospheric oxygen is converted to carbon dioxide in animal respiration and regenerated by green plants in photosynthesis

oxygen demand *n* **:** BIOCHEMICAL OXYGEN DEMAND

oxy·phen·bu·ta·zone \,äksē,fen'byüd·ə,zōn, -ütə-\ *n* -s [2*oxy*- + *phenylbutazone*] **:** a phenylbutazone derivative $C_{19}H_{20}N_2O_3$ used for its anti-inflammatory, analgesic, and antipyretic effects

oxy·some \'äksə,sōm\ *n* -s [2*oxy*- + 3-*some*] **:** one of the structural units of mitochondrial cristae that are observed by the electron microscope usu. as spheres or stalked spheres and that are prob. sites of fundamental energy-producing reactions

oysters rocke·fel·ler \-'räk(ə),felə(r)\ *n pl, usu cap R* [after John Davison *Rockefeller* †1937 Am. oil magnate] **:** a dish of oysters baked with chopped spinach and a seasoned sauce

ozonesonde \'=,=,=\ *n* [*ozone* + *sonde*] **:** a balloon-borne instrument that measures the concentration of ozone at various altitudes and broadcasts the data by radio

P

p* *abbr* pico-

p* *symbol* **1** momentum of a particle **2** *often cap* the probability of obtaining a result as great as or greater than the observed result in a statistical test if the null hypothesis is true

pa* *abbr, usu cap* pascal *herein*

PA* *abbr* physician's assistant

pa·'anga \pä-'äŋ(g)ə\ *n, pl* **pa'anga** [Tongan, lit., seed] **1 :** the basic monetary unit of Tonga — see MONEY table *in the Dict* **2 :** a coin or note representing one pa'anga

PAC \'pak, 'pē¦ā'sē\ *abbr or n* -s [*p*olitical *a*ction *c*ommittee] **:** a group formed (as by a corporation, an industry, a union, or an issue-oriented organization) to raise and contribute money to the campaigns of candidates likely to advance the group's interests

pace car *n* **:** an automobile that leads the field of competitors through a pace lap but does not participate in the race

pace lap *n* **:** a lap of an auto racecourse by the entire field of competitors before the start of a race to allow the engines to warm up and to permit a flying start

packet* *n* **:** a short fixed-length section of data that is transmitted as a unit in an electronic communications network

pad* *n* **1 :** frictional material that presses against the disks in a disk brake **2 :** a horizontal concrete surface (as for parking a mobile home) — **on the pad** *of a police officer* **:** receiving money in exchange for ignoring illegal activities **:** taking graft

paddle* *n* **:** a small hand-held remote control device; *esp* **:** such a device having a dial used to control linear movement of a visual cue (as a cursor) on a computer display screen

page* *n* **1 :** a sizable subdivision of computer memory; *also* **:** a block of information that fills a page and can be transferred as a unit between the internal and external storage of a computer **2 :** the usu. textual information displayed at one time on a video screen

page* *vi* **:** to proceed through matter displayed on a video screen as if turning pages

pager* *n* **:** BEEPER *herein*

pail·lard \pī'yär *also* -ärd\ *n* -s [origin unknown] **:** a piece of beef or veal usu. pounded thin and grilled

pair–bond \'=,=\ *n* **:** an exclusive union with one mate at any one time **:** a monogamous relationship — **pair–bonding** \'=,==\ *n*

paired–associate learning \¦==¦=(=)=-\ *n* **:** the learning of items (as syllables, digits, or words) in pairs so that one member of the pair evokes recall of the other

pak \'pak, 'päk, 'pák\ *n* -s *cap* [by shortening] **:** PAKISTANI — sometimes taken to be offensive

paki \'páki, 'pak-, -ē\ *n* -s *cap* [short for *Pakistani*] *chiefly Brit* **:** a Pakistani immigrant — usu. used disparagingly

palazzo pants *n pl* **:** extremely wide-legged pants for women

pa·leo·bio·geography \¦pālēō,bīō +, *chiefly Brit* ¦pal-\ *n* [*pale-* + *bi-* + *geography*] **:** a science that deals with the geographical distribution of plants and animals of former geological epochs — **pa·leo·bio·geographical** \"+\ *adj*

pa·leo·climate \¦pālēō, *chiefly Brit* ¦palēō +\ *n* [*pale-* + *climate*] **:** the climate during a past geological age

pa·leo·environment \"+\ *n* [*pale-* + *environment*] **:** an environment of a past geological age — **pa·leo·environmental** \"+\ *adj*

pa·leo·magnetism \"+\ *n* [*pale-* + *magnetism*] **1 :** the intensity and direction of residual magnetization in ancient rocks **2 :** a study that deals with paleomagnetism — **pa·leo·magnetic** \"+\ *adj* — **pa·leo·magnetically** \"+\ *adv* — **pa·leo·magnetist** \"+\ *n*

pa·leo·temperature \"+\ *n* [*pale-* + *temperature*] **:** the temperature (as of the ocean) during a past geological age

palestinian* *n, cap* **:** a usu. Muslim or Christian member of an Arab people living in what was formerly Palestine

pal·i·mo·ny \'palə,mōnē\ *n* -ES [blend of *pal* and *alimony*] **:** a court-ordered allowance paid by one member of a couple formerly living together out of wedlock to the other

palimpsest* *n* **:** something having usu. diverse layers or aspects apparent beneath the surface ⟨Egypt has many pasts — the country is a cultural ~ with many layers of civilization —Willis Barnstone⟩

pal·yno·morph \'palənə,mórf, -,mó(ə)f\ *n* -s [fr. *palyn-* (as in *palynology*) + *-o-* + *-morph*] **:** a microscopic fossil composed esp. of pollen or spores

pan–africanism \¦pan +\ *n, usu cap P&A* **:** a movement for the political union of all the African nations — **pan–african** \"+\ *adj, usu cap P&A* — **pan–africanist** \"+\ *n or adj, usu cap P&A*

panama red *n, usu cap P&R* **:** marijuana of a reddish tint that is of Panamanian origin and is held to be very potent

pan·chres·ton \pan'krestən, -,tän\ *n* -s [Gk *panchrēston* panacea, fr. neut. of *panchrēstos* good for all work, fr. *pan-* + *chrēstos* good — more at CHRESTOMATHY] **:** a broadly inclusive thesis that is intended to cover all possible variations within an area of concern and that in practice usu. proves to be an unacceptable oversimplification

pan·cu·ro·ni·um bromide \,pankyə'rōnēəm-\ *or* **pancuronium** *n* -s [perh. fr. *pan-* + *-cur-* (prob. as in *tubocurarine*) + *-onium*] **:** a neuromuscular blocking agent $C_{35}H_{60}Br_2N_2O_4$ used as a skeletal muscle relaxant

panda car *n, sometimes cap P* [so called fr. its black and white coloration] *Brit* **:** a police patrol car

P and H *abbr, usu not cap* postage and handling

pan·encephalitis \¦pan +\ *n* [NL, fr. *pan-* + *encephalitis*] **:** inflammation of the brain affecting both white and gray matter — see SUBACUTE SCLEROSING PANENCEPHALITIS *herein*

pan·gram \'pangrəm, -aŋg-, -,gram\ *n* -s [*pan-* + Gk *grammat-, gramma* letter — more at GRAM] **:** a short sentence containing all 26 letters of the English alphabet — **pan·gram·mat·ic** \¦pangrə¦mad·ik, -aŋg-\ *adj*

pannier* *n* **:** a usu. double pack or basket hung over the rear wheel of a vehicle (as a bicycle)

pantdress \'=,=\ *n* [[4]*pant* + *dress*] **1 :** a garment having a divided skirt **:** CULOTTE 2 **2 :** a dress worn over matching shorts

panther* *n, usu cap* **:** BLACK PANTHER *herein*

pantsuit *or* **pants suit** \'≈,≈\ *n* [[4]*pant* or *pants* + *suit*] **:** a woman's ensemble consisting usu. of a long jacket and tailored pants of the same material — **pantsuited** *or* **pants-suited** *adj*

panty hose *also* **panti·hose** \'pantē,hōz\ *n* **:** a one-piece undergarment for women consisting of hosiery combined with a panty — usu. pl. in constr.

panty raid *n* **:** a raid on a women's dormitory by male college students to obtain panties as trophies

panty stockings *n pl* **:** PANTY HOSE *herein*

papanicolaou smear *n, usu cap P* [after George N. *Papanicolaou* †1962 Am. medical scientist] **:** PAPANICOLAOU TEST

pa·pa·raz·zo \,päpə'rät(,)sō\ *n, pl* **paparaz·zi** \-sē\ [It, fr. It dial., a buzzing insect] **:** a free-lance photographer who aggressively pursues celebrities in order to take candid photographs

paper factor *n* **:** a substance orig. isolated from pulpwood of the balsam fir that is a selectively effective insecticide with activity like that of juvenile hormone — called also *juvabione*

paper gold *n* **:** SDRS *herein*

paper–train \'≈,≈\ *vt* **:** to train (as a dog) to defecate and urinate on paper in the house

pa·po·va·vi·rus \pə'pōvə,vīrəs\ *n* [*pa*pilloma + *po*lyoma + *va*cuolation + *virus*] **:** any of a group of viruses that have a capsid with 42 protuberances resembling knobs and that are associated with or are responsible for various neoplasms (as some warts) of mammals

pap smear *also* **pap test** \'pap-\ *n, usu cap P* [*pap* short for *Papanicolaou*] **:** PAPANICOLAOU TEST

paradigm* *n* **:** a philosophical and theoretical framework of a scientific school or discipline within which theories, laws, and generalizations and the experiments performed in support of them are formulated — **paradigmatic*** *adj*

par·a·dor \,pärä'thȯr\ *n* -s [Sp, akin to Sp *parar* stop, prepare, fr. L *parare* prepare — more at PARE] **:** a usu. government-operated hostelry found esp. in Spain

paradoxical sleep *n* **:** REM SLEEP *herein*

para·foil \'parə,fȯil\ *n* [*para*chute + *-foil* (as in *airfoil*)] **:** a self-inflating fabric device that resembles a parachute, behaves in flight like an airplane wing, is maneuverable, is capable of landing a payload at slow speed, and can be launched from the ground in a high wind like a kite

para·glider \'parə +,\ *n* [*para*chute + *glider*] **:** a triangular device on a spacecraft or rocket that consists of two flexible sections, that resembles a kite, and that is deployed when needed for guiding and landing a spacecraft after reentry or for recovering a launching rocket

para·influenza virus \¦parə + . . .-\ *also* **parainfluenza** *n* [[1]*para-* + *influenza*] **:** any of several myxoviruses associated with or responsible for some respiratory infections in children

para·journalism \"+\ *n* [[1]*para-* + *journalism*] **:** NEW JOURNALISM *herein* — **para·journalist** \"+\ *n* — **para·journalistic** \"+\ *adj*

para·language \'parə +,\ *n* [[1]*para-* + *language*] **:** optional vocal effects (as tone of voice) that accompany or modify the phonemes of an utterance and may communicate meaning

para·legal \"+\ *adj* [[1]*para-* + *legal*] **:** of, relating to, or being a paraprofessional who assists a lawyer — **paralegal** *n* -s

para·linguistics \¦parə +\ *n pl but usu sing in constr* [[1]*para-* + *linguistics*] **:** the study of paralanguage — **para·linguistic** \"+\ *adj*

parallel* *adj* **1 :** arranged in parallel ⟨a ~ processor⟩ **2 :** relating to or being a connection in a computer system in which the bits of a byte are transmitted over separate channels at the same time

parallel* *n* **:** an arrangement or state that permits several operations or tasks to be performed simultaneously rather than consecutively

paramagnetic resonance *n* **:** ELECTRON SPIN RESONANCE *herein*

para·medic \¦parə+\ *also* **para·medical** \"+\ *n* [[1]*para-* + *medic, medical*] **1 :** one who works in a health field in an auxiliary capacity to a physician (as by treating common complaints, taking X rays, or giving injections) **2 :** a person who has undergone an extensive course of special training and is certified to provide a wide range of emergency services (as defibrillation and the intravenous administration of drugs) before or during transportation to a hospital — compare EMT *herein*

parameter* *n* **1 :** any of a set of physical properties whose values determine the characteristics or behavior of a system ⟨~*s* of the atmosphere such as temperature, pressure, and density⟩ **2 :** something represented by a parameter; *broadly* **:** CHARACTERISTIC, ELEMENT, FACTOR ⟨political dissent as a ~ of modern life⟩ **3 :** LIMIT, BOUNDARY ⟨working within established ~*s*⟩

pa·ram·e·ter·ize \pə'ramədə,rīz, 'pram-\ *or* **pa·ram·e·trize** \-mə·,trīz\ *vt* -ED/-ING/-S [*parameter* + *-ize*] **:** to express in terms of parameters — **pa·ram·e·ter·iza·tion** \-,ramədərə'zāshən, ,pram-, -mə·trə-, -,ī'z-\ *or* **pa·ram·e·tri·za·tion** \-mə·trə-\ *n* -s

parametric amplifier *n* **:** a high-frequency amplifier whose operation is based on time variations in a parameter (as reactance) and which converts the energy at the frequency of an alternating current into energy at the input signal frequency in such a way as to amplify the signal

parametric equation *n* **:** any of a set of equations that express the coordinates of the points of a curve as functions of one parameter or that express the coordinates of the points of a surface as functions of two parameters

para·myosin \¦parə +\ *n* [[1]*para-* + *myosin*] **:** a fibrous protein that is found in molluscan muscle

para·myxovirus \"+\ *n* [[1]*para-* + *myxovirus* (herein)] **:** any of a group of RNA-containing viruses (as the mumps and measles viruses) that are larger than the related myxoviruses

paranoid* *adj* **:** extremely or unreasonably fearful

para·professional \"+\ *n* [[1]*para-* + *professional*] **:** a trained aide who assists a professional person (as a teacher or physician) — **para·professional** \"+\ *adj*

para·protein \"+\ *n* [[1]*para-* + *protein*] **:** any of various abnormal serum globulins with unique physical and electrophoretic characteristics

para·quat \'parə,kwät\ *n* [[1]*para-* + *quat*ernary] **:** an herbicide containing a salt of a cation $C_{12}H_{14}N_2$ that is used esp. as a weed killer

para·sexual \¦parə +\ *adj* [[1]*para-* + *sexual*] **:** relating to or being reproduction that results in recombination of genes from different individuals but does not involve meiosis and formation of a zygote by fertilization as in sexual reproduction ⟨the ~ cycle in some fungi⟩ — **parasexuality*** *n*

para·ventricular nucleus \ˌparə+ . . .-\ *n* [[1]*para-* + *ventricular*] **:** a nucleus in the hypothalamus that produces vasopressin and esp. oxytocin and that innervates the neurohypophysis

para·wing \ˈparə +ˌ\ *n* [*para*chute + *wing*] **:** PARAGLIDER *herein*

par·ent·ing \ˈpa(a)rəntiŋ, ˈper-\ *n* -s [fr. gerund of [2]*parent*] **:** the raising of a child by its parents ⟨felt ~ was his wife's job more than his —Virginia Satir⟩

par·gy·line \ˈpärjəˌlēn\ *n* [pro*pargyl* + [2]*-ine*] **:** a monoamine oxidase inhibitor $C_{11}H_{13}N$ that is used as the hydrochloride as an antihypertensive and antidepressant agent

parietal* *n* **parietals** *pl* **:** the regulations governing the visiting privileges of members of the opposite sex in campus dormitories

parity* *n* **1 a :** the property of an integer with respect to being odd or even ⟨3 and 7 have the same ~⟩ **b** (1) **:** the state of being odd or even used as the basis of a method of detecting errors in binary-coded data (2) **:** PARITY BIT *herein* **2 :** the property of oddness or evenness of a wave function in quantum mechanics **3 :** the symmetry of behavior in an interaction of a physical entity (as a subatomic particle) with that of its mirror image

parity bit *n* **:** a bit added to an array of bits (as on magnetic tape) to provide parity

parking orbit *n* **:** an orbit of a spacecraft from which the spacecraft or another vehicle may be launched on a new trajectory

par·kin·son's law \ˌpärkənsənz-, ˌpȧk-\ *n, usu cap P&L* [after C. Northcote *Parkinson b*1909 Eng. historian] **1 :** an observation in office organization: the number of subordinates increases at a fixed rate regardless of the amount of work produced **2 :** an observation in office organization: work expands so as to fill the time available for its completion

par·o·mo·my·cin \ˌparəmōˈmīsᵊn\ *n* -s [*paromo-* (fr. Gk *paromois* closely resembling) + *-mycin*] **:** a broad-spectrum antibiotic $C_{23}H_{45}N_5O_{14}$ that is obtained from a bacterium of the genus *Streptomyces* (*S. rimosus* subspecies *paromomycinus*) and is used against intestinal amebiasis esp. in the form of its sulfate

par·so·ni·an \pärˈsōnēən, pȧˈs-\ *adj, usu cap* [Talcott *Parsons* †1979 Am. sociologist + E *-ian*] **:** of or relating to the sociological theories of Talcott Parsons

parsons table *n, usu cap P* [prob. fr. the name *Parsons*] **:** a usu. rectangular table having straight legs that form the four corners

partially ordered *adj* **:** having some or all mathematical elements connected by a relation that is transitive and antisymmetric

partial product *n* **:** a product obtained by multiplying a multiplicand by one digit of a multiplier with more than one digit

particleboard \ˈ⸗⸗⸗ˌ⸗\ *n* **:** a composition board made of very small pieces of wood bonded together (as with a synthetic resin)

particle physics *n* **:** a branch of physics dealing with the constitution, properties, and interactions of subatomic particles esp. as revealed in experiments using particle accelerators — called also *high-energy physics* — **particle physicist** *n*

partition* *n* **1 :** any of the expressions that for a given positive integer consist of a sum of positive integers equal to the given integer ⟨1 +2 +3 is a ~ of 6⟩ **2 :** the separation of a set (as the points of a line) into subsets such that every element belongs to one set and no two subsets have an element in common — **partition*** *vt*

par·ton \ˈpärˌtän\ *n* -s [[1]*part* + [2]*-on*] **:** a hypothetical particle (as a quark or a gluon) that is held to be a constituent of hadrons

party poop·er \-ˌpüpə(r)\ *n* [[7]*poop* + [2]*-er*] **:** one who refuses to join in the fun at a party; *broadly* **:** one who refuses to go along with everyone else

parv·albumin \ˌpärv, ˌpȧv+\ *n* [*parv-* + *albumin*] **:** a small calcium-binding protein in vertebrate skeletal muscle

par·vo·virus \ˌpärvō, ˌpȧvō+\ *n* [*parv-* + *virus*] **1 :** any of a group of small DNA-containing viruses that are thought to include the virus causing infectious hepatitis **2 :** a highly contagious febrile disease of dogs that is caused by a parvovirus which may be a mutated form of the virus causing panleukopenia in cats and is marked by loss of appetite, lethargy, often bloody diarrhea and vomiting, and sometimes death

par·y·lene \ˈparəˌlēn\ *n* -s [contr. of *paraxylene*] **:** any of several thermoplastic crystalline materials that are polymers of paraxylene and are used esp. as electrical insulation coating

pas·cal \pasˈkal, pȧskȧl\ *n* -s [after Blaise *Pascal* †1662 Fr. scientist and philosopher] **1 :** a unit of pressure in the mks system equivalent to one newton per square meter **2** *usu cap P or all cap* **:** a computer programming language developed from Algol and designed to process both numerical and textual data

pas de deux* *n* **:** an intricate relationship or activity involving two parties or things ⟨every play written for the stage is . . . a *pas de deux* between language and action —Hilton Kramer⟩

pass–fail \ˈ⸗ˈ⸗\ *n* **:** a system of grading whereby the grades "pass" and "fail" replace the traditional letter grades — **pass–fail** *adj*

passivate* *vt* **:** to protect (as a solid-state device) against contamination by coating or surface treatment — **passivation*** *n*

passive* *adj* **1 :** not involving expenditure of chemical energy ⟨~ transport across a cell membrane⟩ **2 a :** exhibiting no gain or control — used of an electronic device (as a capacitor or resistor) **b :** operating solely by means of the power of an input signal ⟨a ~ communication satellite that reflects television signals⟩ **c :** relating to the detection of or to orientation by means of an object through its emission of energy **3 :** of, relating to, or making direct use of the sun's heat usu. without the intervention of mechanical devices ⟨~ technique⟩ ⟨~ building design⟩

passive immunization *n* **:** the process of conferring passive immunity

passive restraint *n* **:** a restraint (as an air bag or self-locking seat belt) that acts automatically to protect an automobile passenger during a crash

pasteurization* *n* **:** partial sterilization of perishable food products (as fruit or fish) with radiation (as gamma rays)

past·ies \ˈpāstēz\ *n pl* [[2]*paste* + *-ie*] **:** small round coverings for a woman's nipples worn esp. by a stripteaser

pas·ti·na \päˈstēnə\ *n* -s [It dim. of *pasta*] **:** very small bits of pasta used esp. in soup or broth

pas·tis \pȧstēs\ *n* [F] **:** a French liqueur flavored with aniseed

pata·physics \ˌpad·ə +\ *n pl but sing in constr* [F *pataphysique*] **:** intricate and whimsical nonsense intended as a parody of science — **pata·physical** \"+\ *adj* — **pata·physician** \"+\ *n*

patch* *n* **:** a minor usu. temporary correction or modification in a computer program

patch* *vt* **1 :** to make a patch in (a computer program) **2 :** to connect (as circuits) by a patch cord

patchboard \ˈ=,=\ *n* **:** a plugboard in which circuits are interconnected by patch cords

patch panel *n* **:** PATCHBOARD *herein*

path* *n* **:** a sequence of arcs in a network that can be traced continuously without retracing any arc

patho·biology \¦pathō +\ *n* [*path-* + *biology*] **:** PATHOLOGY 1, 2a

patho·morphology \"+\ *n* [*path-* + *morphology*] **:** morphology of abnormal conditions — **patho·morphological** \"+\ *or* **patho·morphologic** \"+\ *adj*

pa·tri·focal \¦pa·trə, ¦pā·- +\ *adj* [*patr-* + *focal*] **:** PATRICENTRIC

patterning* *n* **:** physiotherapy designed to improve malfunctioning nervous control by means of feedback from muscular activity imposed by an outside source or induced by other muscles

pat·zer \ˈpätsə(r), ˈpat-\ *n* -s [G *patzer* blunderer, fr. *patzen* to blunder] **:** an inept chess player

pau·piette \pōˈpyet, -ˌpēˈet\ *n* -s [F] **:** a thin slice of meat or fish wrapped around a filling (as of forcemeat)

pay* *vb* — **pay one's dues** *also* **pay dues** **1 :** to experience life's hardships **:** earn a right or position through experience, suffering, or hard work **2 :** to suffer the consequences of or penalty for an act

pay–cable \ˈ=ˈ==\ *n* **:** pay-TV in which programs are sent through a cable television system to customers provided with a special signal decoder — compare SUBSCRIPTION TV *herein*

payload* *n* **:** the load that is carried by a spacecraft and that consists of things (as passengers or instruments) which relate directly to the purpose of the flight as opposed to things (as fuel) which are necessary for operation; *also* **:** the weight of such a load

payout ratio *n* **:** a ratio relating dividend payout of a company to its earnings or cash flow

pay television *n* **:** PAY-TV *herein*

pay–TV \ˈ=(ˌ)=¦=\ *n* **:** a service providing special noncommercial television programming (as recent movies or entertainment specials) by means of a scrambled signal over the air or through a cable system to subscribers who are provided with a signal decoding device — compare PAY=CABLE *herein*, SUBSCRIPTION TV *herein*

pazazz *var of* PIZZAZZ *herein*

PBB \¦pē¦bēˈbē\ *n* -s [*polybrominated biphenyl*] **:** POLYBROMINATED BIPHENYL *herein*

PC* *abbr* **1** personal computer *herein* **2** professional corporation *herein*

PCB \¦pē¦sēˈbē\ *n* -s [*polychlorinated biphenyl*] **:** POLYCHLORINATED BIPHENYL *herein*

PCP \¦pē¦sēˈpē\ *n* -s **1** [prob. fr. *phenyl cyclohexyl piperidine*] **:** PHENCYCLIDINE *herein* **2 :** PENTACHLOROPHENOL

PCV valve \¦pē¦sēˈvē-\ *n* [*positive crankcase ventilation*] **:** an automotive-emission control valve that recirculates gases (as from blow-by) through the combustion chambers to permit more complete combustion

PE* *abbr* physical education

peaceful coexistence *n* **:** a living together in peace rather than in constant hostility

peace·nik \ˈpē(ˌ)snik\ *n* -s [*peace* + *-nik* (herein)] **:** an opponent of war; *specif* **:** one who participates in antiwar demonstrations

peace sign *n* **:** a sign made by holding the palm outward and forming a V with the index and middle fingers and used to indicate the desire for peace or as a greeting or farewell

peace symbol *n* **:** the symbol ☮ used to signify peace

peaches–and–cream \¦===¦=\ *adj* **:** of, relating to, or having a smooth wholesome complexion

pearl* *vi, of a surfboard* **:** to make a nose dive into the trough of a wave

peatland \ˈ=,=\ *n* **:** land rich in peat

peck's bad boy \¦peks-\ *n, usu cap P* [fr. the book *Peck's Bad Boy and his Pa* (1883) by George Wilbur Peck †1916 Am. journalist, humorist, and politician] **:** one whose bad behavior is a source of embarrassment or annoyance

pedal steel *or* **pedal steel guitar** *n* **:** a box-shaped musical instrument with legs that has usu. 10 strings which are plucked with metal finger picks and of which the pitch may be adjusted either by sliding a steel bar along them or by using foot pedals to change their tension — compare HAWAIIAN GUITAR *in the Dict*

pedestrianize* *vb* ~ *vt* **:** to convert into a walkway or mall — **pe·des·tri·an·iza·tion** \pə,destrēənəˈzāshən, -ˌnīˈz-\ *n* -s

pe·do·phile \ˈpēdə,fīl\ *n* -s [back-formation fr. *pedophilia*] **:** a person affected with pedophilia

peek–a–boo** \¦==,=\ *adj* **:** of, relating to, or being a document retrieval system in which desired documents are identified by light shining through matching holes in index cards

peel* *vi* **:** to break away from a group or formation — often used with *off*

Peg–Board \ˈ=,=\ *trademark* — used for material (as fiberboard) with evenly spaced holes into which hooks may be inserted for the storage or display of articles

peking duck* *n, usu cap P* **:** a Chinese dish consisting of roasted duck meat and strips of crispy duck skin topped with scallions and sauce and wrapped in thin pancakes

pe·king·ol·o·gy \ˌpē(ˌ)kiŋˈäləjē\ *n* -ES *usu cap* [*Peking*, capital of Communist China + *-o-* + *-logy*] **:** the study of the policies and practices of Communist China — **pe·king·ol·o·gist** \-jəst\ *n* -s *usu cap*

pel·o·ton \ˈpelə,tän, *F* plôtōⁿ\ *or* **peloton glass** *n* [prob. fr. F *peloton* ball, ball of string] **:** a European ornamental glass often with a variegated metallized and satinized surface and usu. overlaid with strands of contrasting color

pelvic inflammatory disease *n* **:** inflammation of the female genital tract that occurs esp. as a result of a sexually transmitted disease, tends to occur more frequently in individuals using IUDs, and is a leading cause of sterility in women — abbr. *PID*

pem·o·line \ˈpemə,lēn, -ˌlən\ *n* -s [perh. fr. *phenyl* + *imino* + oxazo*lidinone*, a derivative of oxazolidine, fr. *oxazolidine* + *-one*] **:** a synthetic organic drug $C_9H_8N_2O_2$ that is usu. mixed with magnesium hydroxide, is a mild stimulant of the central nervous system, and is used experimentally to improve memory

pen·ta·gastrin \¦pentə +\ *n* [*penta*peptide (herein) + *gastrin*] **:** a pentapeptide $C_{37}H_{49}N_7O_9S$ that stimulates gastric acid secretion

pen·ta·peptide \¦pentə +\ *n* [*penta-* + *peptide*] **:** a polypeptide that contains five amino acid residues

pen·taz·o·cine \pen'tazə,sēn, -ˌsən\ *n* -s [*penta-* + *-azocine* (as in *phenazocine* — herein)] **:** an analgesic drug $C_{19}H_{27}NO$ that is less addictive than morphine

pen·to·barbitone \ˌpentō +\ *n* [*penta-* + *-o-* + *barbitone*] *Brit* **:** PENTOBARBITAL

people mover *n* **:** any of various rapid-transit systems (as of moving sidewalks or automated driverless cars) for shuttling people (as within an airport or to and from it)

people's republic *n, often cap P&R* **:** a republic organized and controlled by a national Communist Party

pepper steak *n* **1 :** thin-sliced steak cooked with green peppers, onions, tomatoes, and soy sauce **2 :** STEAK AU POIVRE *herein*

pep·tid·er·gic \ˌpeptīd'ərjik\ *adj* [*peptide* + *erg-* (fr. Gk *ergon* work) + *-ic* — more at WORK] **:** being, relating to, releasing, or activated by neurotransmitters that are short-chain peptides

pep·ti·do·glycan \ˌpep,tīdō+\ *n* [*peptide* + *-o-* + *glycan*] **:** a polymer that is composed of polysaccharide and peptide chains and is found esp. in bacterial cell walls — called also *mucopeptide, murein*

percentile* *n* **:** a value on a scale of one hundred that indicates the percent of a distribution that is equal to or below it (as in performance) ⟨a score in the 95th ~ is a score equal to or better than 95 percent of the scores⟩

per·cia·tel·li \ˌperchə'te(l)lē, ˌpər-\ *n* -s [It] **:** long tubular pasta slightly larger than spaghetti

pe·re·on·ite \pə'rēə,nīt\ *n* -s [*pereon* (var. of *pereion*) + [1]*-ite*] **:** any of the segments of a pereion

per·fec·ta \pə(r)'fektə\ *n* -s [AmerSp *quiniela perfecta* perfect quiniela] **:** a betting pool in which the bettor must pick the first and second finishers in a specified race or contest in the correct order — called also *exacta*

performance* *n* **:** linguistic behavior — compare COMPETENCE 2 *herein*

per·for·ma·tive \pər'fȯrməd·iv\ *n* -s [*perform* + *-ative* (as in [2]*imperative*)] **:** an expression that serves to effect a transaction or that constitutes the performance of the specified act by virtue of its utterance — **performative** *adj*

peri·apsis \ˌperē +\ *n, pl* **periapsides** [NL, fr. *peri-* + *apsis*] **:** the apsis nearest the center of attraction **:** the low point in an orbit — compare APOAPSIS *herein*

peri·cardio·centesis \ˌperə̇ˌkärdēō+\ *n* [NL, fr. *pericardi-* + *centesis*] **:** surgical puncture of the pericardium esp. to aspirate pericardial fluid

peri·cyn·thi·on \ˌperəˌsin(t)thēən\ *n* -s [NL, fr. *peri-* + *Cynthia,* goddess of the moon (fr. Gk *Kynthia*) + *-on* (as in *aphelion*)] **:** PERILUNE *herein*

peri·lune \'perə,lün\ *n* -s [*peri-* + L *luna* moon — more at LUNAR] **:** the point in the path of a body orbiting the moon that is nearest to the center of the moon

peri·nuclear \ˌperə̇+\ *adj* [*peri-* + *nuclear*] **:** situated around or surrounding the nucleus of a cell ⟨~ structures⟩

peripheral* *adj* **:** AUXILIARY, SUPPLEMENTARY ⟨~ equipment⟩; *also* **:** of or relating to computer peripherals

peripheral *n* -s **:** a device connected to a computer to provide communication (as input and output) or auxiliary functions (as additional storage)

peripheral nervous system *n* **:** the part of the nervous system that is outside the central nervous system and comprises the cranial nerves excepting the optic nerve, the spinal nerves, and the autonomic nervous system

peristaltic pump *n* **:** a pump in which fluid is forced along by waves of contraction produced mechanically on flexible tubing

pe·ri·tus \pə'rēd·əs\ *n, pl* **peri·ti** \-ēd·ē, -ē,tē\ [NL, fr. L *peritus,* adj., skilled, experienced — more at PERITE] **:** an expert (as in theology or canon law) who advises and assists the hierarchy (as in the drafting of schemata) at a Vatican council

peri·ventricular \ˌperə̇ +\ *adj* [*peri-* + *ventricular*] **:** situated or occurring around a ventricle esp. of the brain ⟨~ white matter⟩

per·locutionary \ˌpər, ˌpə̄+\ *adj* [*per-* + *locutionary* (herein)] **:** of or relating to an act (as persuading, frightening, or annoying) performed by a speaker upon a listener by means of an utterance — compare ILLOCUTIONARY *herein,* LOCUTIONARY *herein* — **per·locution** \"+\ *n* -s

[1]perm \'pərm, 'pə̄m, 'pəim\ *vt* -ED/-ING/-S [[2]*perm*] **:** to give (hair) a permanent wave

[2]perm \'pə̄m, 'pərm\ *n* -s [short for *permutation*] *Brit* **:** an arrangement of all possible combinations of a selected number of competitors for wagering on predicted winners (as in a football pool) or the order of finish (as in a horse race)

[3]perm \"\ *vt, Brit* **:** to select for a betting perm

permanent press *n* **1 :** the process of treating a fabric with a chemical (as a resin) and heat for setting the shape and for improving resistance to wrinkles **2 :** material treated by permanent press **3 :** the condition of material treated by permanent press — **permanent-press** *adj*

per·me·ase \'pərmē,ās, -āz\ *n* -s [ISV *perme-* (fr. *permeate*) + *-ase*] **:** an enzyme that catalyzes the transport of another substance across a cell membrane

permutation group *n* **:** a group of which the elements are permutations and in which the product of two permutations is a permutation whose effect is the same as the successive application of the first two

per·oxi·some \pə'räksə̇,sōm\ *n* -s [*peroxi*de + [3]*-some*] **:** a cytoplasmic cell organelle containing enzymes for the production and decomposition of hydrogen peroxide — **per·oxi·som·al** \-ˌräksə̇'sōməl\ *adj*

per·phe·na·zine \(ˌ)pər'fēnə,zēn, -'fen-\ *n* -s [blend of *piperazine* and *phen-*] **:** a phenothiazine tranquilizer $C_{21}H_{26}ClN_3OS$ that is used to control tension, anxiety, and agitation esp. in psychotic conditions

persistent* *adj* **1 :** degraded only slowly by the environment ⟨~ pesticides⟩ **2 :** remaining infective for a relatively long time in a vector after an initial period of incubation ⟨~ viruses⟩

personal computer *n* **:** MICROCOMPUTER 1 *herein*

personality inventory *n* **:** any of several tests that attempt to characterize the personality of an individual by objective scoring of replies to numerous questions concerning his own behavior and attitudes — compare MINNESOTA MULTIPHASIC PERSONALITY INVENTORY *herein*

personal tax *n* **:** DIRECT TAX

personhood \'==,=\ *n* [*person* + *-hood*] **:** the fact or state of being a person ⟨we recognize them as rights. They are the privileges of ~ —Willard Gaylin & Marc Lappé⟩; *esp* **:** one's distinctive personal identity ⟨the brave, awkward attempts made . . . to assert their pride and ~ — Dotson Rader⟩

PERT \'pərt\ *n* -s [*p*rogram *e*valuation and *r*eview *t*echnique] **:** a technique for planning, scheduling, and monitoring a complex project esp. by graphically displaying the separate tasks and showing how they are interconnected

pe·se·wa \pə'säwə\ *n* -s [native name in Ghana] **1 :** a monetary unit of Ghana equal to 1/100 cedi — see MONEY table *in the Dict* **2 :** a coin representing one pesewa

PET *abbr* positron-emission tomography *herein*

peter principle *n, usu cap both Ps* [after Laurence Johnston *Peter b*1919 Am. (Canad.-born) educator, its formulator] **:** an observation: in a hierarchy every employee tends to rise to the level of his or her incompetence

petit bourgeois *adj* [*petit bourgeois,* n.] **:** of, relating to, or characteristic of the petite bourgeoisie

petite si·rah \-sə'rä\ *n, pl* **petite sirahs** *often cap P&S* [modif. of F *petite syrah,* fr. *petite* small + *syrah,* alter. of *chiraz,* type of grape, lit., Shīrāz, town in Iran famed for wine] **:** a dry red varietal wine made esp. in California

pet·nap·ping \'pet,napiŋ\ *n* -s [[1]*pet* + *-napping* (as in *kidnapping*)] **:** the act of stealing a pet (as a cat or dog) usu. for profit

pet·ro·dollar \ˌpe·trō+\ *adj* [*petrodollars* (herein)] **:** of, relating to, or involving petrodollars

pet·ro·dollars \"+\ *n pl* [*petro*leum + *dollars*] **:** foreign exchange obtained by petroleum-exporting countries through sales abroad; *esp* **:** the part in excess of domestic needs that constitutes a pool of potential foreign investment

pet·ro·politics \"+\ *n pl* [*petro*leum + *politics*] **:** the strategy of controlling petroleum sales as a way of achieving international political goals

petting zoo *n* **:** a collection of farm animals (as baby goats) or gentle exotic animals (as llamas) for children to pet and feed

PF* *abbr, usu not cap* personal foul

pg* *abbr* picogram *herein*

PG \ˌpē'jē\ *adj* [parental guidance] *of a motion picture* **:** of such a nature that persons of all ages may be allowed admission but parental guidance is suggested — compare G *herein,* PG-13 *herein,* R *herein,* X *herein*

PG* *abbr* prostaglandin *herein*

PG–13 \ˌ=ˈ=,=ˈ=\ *adj, of a motion picture* **:** of such a nature that persons of all ages may be admitted but parental guidance is suggested esp. for children under 13 — compare G *herein,* PG *herein,* R *herein,* X *herein*

phago·some \'fagə,sōm\ *n* -s [*phag-* + [3]*-some*] **:** a membrane-surrounded vesicle that encloses materials taken into the cell by endocytosis

phallic* *adj* **:** of, relating to, or being the stage of psychosexual development in psychoanalytic theory during which a child becomes interested in his own sexual organs — **phal·li·cal·ly** \'falik(ə)lē\ *adv*

phantasmagoria* *n* **:** a bizarre or fantastic combination, collection, or assemblage

phar·ma·co·genetics \ˌfärməkō +\ *n pl but sing in constr* [ISV *pharmaco-* + *genetics*] **:** the study of the interrelation of hereditary constitution and variation in response to drugs — **phar·ma·co·genetic** \"+\ *adj*

phar·ma·co·kinetics \"+\ *n pl but sing in constr* [ISV *pharmaco-* + *kinetics*] **1 :** the study of the bodily absorption, distribution, metabolism, and excretion of drugs **2 :** the characteristic interactions of a drug and the body in terms of its absorption, distribution, metabolism, and excretion — **phar·ma·co·kinetic** \"+\ *adj*

phasedown \'=,=\ *n* -s [*phase* + *down*] **:** a gradual reduction (as in size or operation) **:** a slowing down by phases

phaseout \'=,=\ *n* -s [*phase out*] **:** a gradual stopping of operations or production **:** a closing down by phases

phe·naz·o·cine \fə'nazə,sēn, -sən\ *n* -s [*phen-* + *-azocine* (perh. irreg. fr. [2]*azoic* + *-ine*)] **:** a drug $C_{22}H_{27}NO$ related to morphine that has greater pain-relieving and slighter narcotic effect

phen·cy·cli·dine \(ˈ)fen'siklə,dēn, -'sīk-, -ˌdən\ *n* -s [*phen-* + *cycl-* + *-idin*] **:** a piperidine derivative $C_{17}H_{25}N$ used medicinally as an anesthetic and sometimes illicitly as a psychedelic drug to induce vivid mental imagery — called also *angel dust, PCP*

phen·el·zine \'fenᵊl,zēn\ *n* -s [*phen-* + *ethyl* + *hydrazine*] **:** a monoamine oxidase inhibitor $C_8H_{12}N_2$ used esp. as an antidepressant drug

phe·neth·i·cil·lin \fəˌnethəˌsilən\ *n* -s [*phen-* + *eth-* + *penicillin*] **:** a synthetic penicillin administered orally and used esp. in the treatment of less severe infections caused by bacteria that do not produce penicillinase

phe·net·ic \fə'ned·ik\ *adj* [*pheno*type + *-etic* (as in *genetic*)] **:** of, relating to, or being classificatory systems and procedures that are based on overall similarity usu. of many characters without regard to the evolutionary history of the organisms involved — compare CLADISTIC *herein*

phe·net·ics \-iks\ *n pl but sing in constr* **:** biological systematics based on phenetic relationships — **phe·net·i·cist** \-d·əsəst\ *n* -s

phen·met·ra·zine \(ˈ)fen'me·trə,zēn\ *n* -s [*phen*yl + *me*thyl + te*tra-* + oxa*zine*] **:** a sympathomimetic stimulant $C_{11}H_{15}NO$ used in the form of its hydrochloride as an appetite suppressant

phe·no·gram \'fēnə,gram\ *n* [*phen-* + *-gram*] **:** a branching diagrammatic tree used in biological classification to illustrate phenetic relationships — compare CLADOGRAM

phenothiazine* *n* **:** any of various phenothiazine derivatives (as chlorpromazine) that are used as tranquilizing agents esp. in the treatment of schizophrenia

phe·noxy·ben·za·mine \fəˌnäksēˌbenzə,mēn\ *n* [ISV *phen-* + [2]*oxy-* + *benz-* + *amine*] **:** a drug $C_{18}H_{22}ClNO$ that blocks the activity of alpha-receptors and is used in the form of its hydrochloride esp. to produce peripheral vasodilatation

phen·tol·amine \fen'tälə,mēn, -ˌmən\ *n* [*phen-* + *tol*uidine + *amine*] **:** an adrenergic blocking agent $C_{17}H_{19}N_3O$ that is used esp. in the diagnosis of hypertension due to pheochromocytoma

phenyl·eth·yl·amine \ˌ== +\ *n* [*phenyl* + *ethylamine*] **:** a neurotransmitter $C_8H_{11}N$ that is an amine resembling amphetamine in structure and pharmacological properties; *also* **:** any of various derivatives of phenylethylamine

phe·ren·ta·sin \fə'rentəzən, -əsən\ *n* -s [Gk *pherein* to carry + *entasis* tension, stretching + E *-in*] **:** a pressor amine present in the blood in severe hypertension

pher·o·mone \'ferə,mōn\ *n* -s [ISV *phero-* (fr. Gk *pherein* to carry) + *-mone* (as in *hormone*); orig. formed as G *pheromon;* fr. its conveying information from one individual to another — more at BEAR] **:** a chemical substance that is produced by an animal and serves as a specific stimulus to other individuals of the same species for one or more behavioral responses — **pher·o·mon·al** \ˌferə'mōnᵊl\ *adj* — **pher·o·mo·nal·ly** \-ᵊlē\ *adv*

phil·lips curve \ˌfiləps-\ *n, usu cap P* [after A.W.H. *Phillips b*1914 Brit. economist] **:** a graphic representation of the relation between inflation and unemployment which indicates that as the rate of either increases that of the other declines

phil·lu·men·ist \fə'lümənəst\ *n* -s [*phil-* + L *lumen* light + E *-ist*] **:** one who collects matchbooks or matchbox labels

phle·bol·o·gy \flə'bäləjē\ *n* -ES [ISV *phleb-* + *-logy*] **:** a branch of medicine concerned with the veins — **phle·bol·o·gist** \-jəst\ *n* -s

phone–in \'⸗,⸗\ *adj* [[2]*phone* + *in*] **:** CALL-IN *herein*

pho·no·cardiograph \¦fōnə +\ *n* [*phon-* + *cardiograph*] **:** a recording instrument used in phonocardiography

pho·no·cardiographic \"+\ *also* **pho·no·car·dio·graph·i·cal** \"+¦⸗⸗¦grafəkəl\ *adj* [*phonocardiograph* (herein) + *-ic, -ical*] **:** of, relating to, or involving phonocardiography or a phonocardiogram — **pho·no·car·di·o·graph·i·cal·ly** \"+¦⸗⸗¦⸗k(ə)lē\ *adv*

pho·no·record \'fōnō +,\ *n* [*phono*graph + *record*] **:** a phonograph record

pho·no·tac·tics \,fōnə'taktiks\ *n pl but sing in constr* [*phon-* + *tactics*] **:** the area of phonology concerned with the analysis and description of the permitted phoneme sequences of a language — **pho·no·tac·tic** \¦⸗⸗¦tik\ *adj*

phor·ate \'fō(ə)r,āt, 'fȯ(-\ *n* -s [phos*phor-* + thion*ate*] **:** a very toxic organophosphate systemic insecticide $C_7H_{17}O_2PS_3$ that is used esp. to treat seeds

phos·pham·i·don \fäs'famə,dän\ *n* -s [*phosph-* + *amid-* + [1]*-on*] **:** a contact and systemic organophosphorus insecticide and miticide $C_{10}H_{19}ClNO_5P$

phosphate* *n* **:** a trivalent anion PO^{3-}_4 derived from phosphoric acid H_3PO_4

phosphatidylcholine \¦⸗⸗¦⸗⸗¦⸗,⸗, ⸗¦⸗⸗¦⸗,⸗\ *n* [*phosphatidyl* + *choline*] **:** LECITHIN

phosphatidylethanolamine \¦⸗⸗¦⸗⸗,⸗⸗¦⸗⸗,⸗, ⸗¦⸗⸗,-\ *n* [*phosphatidyl* + *ethanolamine*] **:** [2]CEPHALIN

phos·pho·enol·pyr·uvate \¦fäs,fōə,nȯlpī'rü,vāt, -,nōl-, -,pī(ə)r-'yü-\ *n* -s [*phosphoenolpyruv*ic (acid) + [1]*-ate*] **:** a salt or ester of phosphoenolpyruvic acid

phos·pho·fruc·to·kinase \¦fäs(,)fō,frəktō, -frük-, -frük- +\ *n* [*phosph-* + *fructose* + *kinase*] **:** an enzyme that functions in carbohydrate metabolism and esp. in glycolysis by catalyzing the transfer of a second phosphate (as from ATP) to fructose

phos·pho·glyceraldehyde \¦fäs(,)fō +\ *n* [*phosph-* + *glyceraldehyde*] **:** a phosphate of glyceraldehyde $C_3H_5O_3(H_2PO_3)$ that is formed esp. in anaerobic metabolism of carbohydrates by the splitting of a diphosphate of fructose

phos·pho·kinase \"+\ *n* [*phosph-* + *kinase*] **:** KINASE 2

phos·pho·pyruvate \"+\ *n* [*phosph-* + *pyruvate*] **:** PHOSPHOENOLPYRUVATE *herein*

phos·pho·rylcho·line \¦⸗⸗'⸗⸗\ *n* [*phosphoryl* + *choline*] **:** a hapten used medicinally in the form of its chloride $C_5H_{15}ClNO_4P$ to treat hepatobiliary dysfunction

phos·pho·transferase \¦fäs(,)fō +\ *n* [*phosph-* + *transferase*] **:** any of several enzymes that catalyze the transfer of phosphorus-containing groups from one compound to another

pho·to·autotroph \¦fōd·ō +\ *n* [*phot-* + *autotroph*] **:** a photoautotrophic organism

pho·to·biologist \¦fōd·(,)ō +\ *n* [*phot-* + *biologist*] **:** a specialist in photobiology

[1]**pho·to·chro·mic** \¦fōd·ə¦krōmik\ *adj* [*phot-* + *chrom-* + *-ic*] **1 :** capable of changing color on exposure to radiant energy (as light) ⟨~ glass⟩ ⟨~ proteins⟩ **2 :** of, relating to, or utilizing the change of color shown by a photochromic substance ⟨a ~ process⟩ — **pho·to·chro·mism** \-,mizəm\ *n* -s

[2]**photochromic** \"\ *n* -s **:** a photochromic substance — usu. used in pl.

pho·to·coagulation \¦fōd·ō +\ *n* [*phot-* + *coagulation*] **:** a surgical process of coagulating tissue by means of a precisely oriented high-energy light source — **pho·to·coagulator** \"+\ *n*

pho·to·degradable \"+\ *adj* [*phot-* + *degradable* (herein)] **:** subject to photodegradation ⟨~ plastics⟩

pho·to·diode \"+\ *n* [*phot-* + *diode*] **:** a semiconductor device for detecting and measuring radiant energy (as light) by means of its conversion into an electric current

photo–essay \¦⸗⸗¦⸗,⸗\ *n* **:** a photographic presentation usu. dealing with its subject from a personal point of view

pho·to·fabrication \¦fōd·,ō +\ *n* [*phot-* + *fabrication*] **:** a process for manufacturing components (as microcircuits) in which a design is photographed, reduced, and chemically etched on a surface (as of a semiconductor)

pho·to·induced \"+\ *adj* [*phot-* + *induced,* past part. of *induce*] **:** induced by the action of light

pho·to·isomerization \"+\ *n* [*phot-* + *isomerization*] **:** the light-initiated process of change from one isomeric form of a compound, radical, or ion to another

photolithography* *n* **:** a process involving the photographic transfer of a pattern to a surface for etching

pho·to·morphogenesis \"+\ *n* [NL, fr. *phot-* + *morphogenesis*] **:** plant morphogenesis controlled by radiant energy (as light) — **pho·to·morphogenic** \"+\ *adj*

photoperiod* *n* **:** PHOTOPHASE 2 *herein*

pho·to·phase \'fōd·ō,fāz\ *n* [*phot-* + *phase*] **1 :** LIGHT REACTION *herein* **2 :** the light period of a photoperiodic cycle of light and dark

pho·to·phosphorylation \¦fōd·ō +\ *n* [*phot-* + *phosphorylation*] **:** the synthesis of ATP from ADP and phosphate that occurs in a plant using radiant energy absorbed during photosynthesis

pho·to·pigment \"+\ *n* [*phot-* + *pigment*] **:** a pigment (as chlorophyll or a compound in the retina) that undergoes a physical or chemical change under the action of light

pho·to·plate \'fōd·ō+,\ *n* [*phot-* + *plate*] **:** a photographic plate

pho·to·polarimeter \¦fōd·ō+\ *n* [*phot-* + *polarimeter*] **:** an instrument used to measure the intensity and polarization of reflected light (as from clouds enveloping a planet)

pho·to·polymer \"+\ *n* [*phot-* + *polymer*] **:** a photosensitive plastic used esp. in the manufacture of printing plates

pho·to·reactivation \"+\ *n* [*phot-* + *reactivation*] **:** repair of DNA (as of a bacterium) esp. by a light-dependent enzymatic reaction after damage by ultraviolet irradiation — **pho·to·reactivating** \"+\ *adj*

pho·to–realism \¦fōd·ō+\ *n* [*phot-* (photographic) + *realism*] **:** realism in painting characterized by extremely meticulous depiction of detail — **pho·to–realist** \"+\ *n or adj*

pho·to·reduce \"+\ *vt* [*phot-* + *reduce*] **1 :** to cause to undergo chemical photoreduction **2 :** to reduce photographically

pho·to·resist \"+\ *n* [*phot-* + *resist*] **:** a photosensitive resin that loses its resistance to chemical etching when exposed to radiation and is used esp. in the transference of a circuit pattern to a semiconductor chip during the production of an integrated circuit

pho·to·respiration \"+\ *n* [*phot-* + *respiration*] **:** oxidation involving production of carbon dioxide during photosynthesis

pho·to·scan \'fōd·ō +,\ *n* [*photoscan,* v. (herein), fr. *phot-* + [1]*scan*] **:** a photographic representation of variation in tissue state (as of the kidney) determined by gamma ray emission from an injected radioactive substance — **photo·scan** *vb* — **pho·to·scanner** \"+,\ *n*

pho·to·system \"+,\ *n* [*phot-* + *system*] **:** either of two photochemical reactions occurring in chloroplasts: **a :** one that proceeds best in long wavelength light — called also *photosystem I* \-'wən\ **b :** one that proceeds best in short wavelength light — called also *photosystem II* \-'tü\

pho·to·toxic \¦fōd·ō+\ *adj* [*phot-* + *toxic*] **1** *of a substance ingested or brought into contact with skin* **:** rendering the skin susceptible to damage (as sunburn or blisters) upon exposure to light and esp. ultraviolet light **2 :** induced by a phototoxic substance ⟨a ~ response⟩ — **pho·to·toxicity** \"+\ *n*

phrase marker *n* **:** a representation of the immediate constituent structure of a linguistic construction

phrase structure *n* **:** the arrangement of the constituents of a sentence

phyl·lo \'fē(,)lō, 'fī(-\ *n* -s [modif. of NGk *phyllon* leaf, sheet (of pastry); akin to L *folium* leaf — more at BLADE] **:** extremely thin pastry dough that is layered to produce a flaky pastry

phys ed \¦fiz'ed\ *n* [by shortening] **:** PHYSICAL EDUCATION

physical* *adj* **:** characterized by esp. rugged and forceful physical activity **:** ROUGH ⟨a ~ hockey game⟩

physician's assistant *or* **physician assistant** *n* **:** a person who has received special training and is certified to provide basic medical services usu. under the supervision of a licensed physician — abbr. *PA*

phy·tane \'fī,tān\ *n* -s [*phyt-* + *-ane*] **:** an isoprenoid hydrocarbon $C_{20}H_{42}$ that is found esp. associated with fossilized plant remains from the Precambrian and later eras

phy·to·alexin \¦fīd·ō +\ *n* [*phyt-* + *alexin*] **:** an antimicrobial chemical substance produced by a plant to combat infection by a pathogen (as a fungus)

phy·to·chemical \"+\ *adj* [*phyt-* + *chemical*] **:** of, relating to, or being phytochemistry — **phy·to·chemi·cally** \"+\ *adv*

phy·to·chemistry \"+\ *n* [*phyt-* + *chemistry*] **:** the chemistry of plants, plant processes, and plant products — **phy·to·chemist** \"+\ *n*

phy·to·chrome \'fīd·ə,krōm\ *n* -s [*phyt-* + *-chrome*] **:** any of a group of chromoproteins that are present in traces in many plants and that play a role in initiating floral and developmental processes when activated by red or far-red radiation

phy·to·hemagglutinin *also* **phy·to·haemagglutinin** \¦fīd·ō +\ *n* [*phyt-* + *hemagglutinin*] **:** a proteinaceous hemagglutinin of plant origin used esp. to induce mitosis (as in lymphocytes)

phy·to·sanitary \"+\ *adj* [*phyt-* + *sanitary*] **:** of, relating to, or being measures for the control of plant diseases esp. in agricultural crops ⟨~ treatments⟩ ⟨a ~ commission⟩

phy·to·tron \'fīd·ə,trän\ *n* -s [*phyt-* + *-tron* (as in *cyclotron*)] **:** a laboratory with facilities for growing plants under various combinations of strictly controlled environmental conditions

PI* *abbr* programmed instruction *herein*

pia·get·ian \pyä'zhāən, ,pēə'jetēən\ *adj, usu cap* [Jean *Piaget* †1980 Swiss psychologist + E *-ian*] **:** of, relating to, or dealing with Jean Piaget or his writings, theories, or methods

piano bar *n* **:** a cocktail bar that features live piano music

pic·ca·ta \pə'käd·ə, -ätə\ *n* -s [It *piccata* fried meat interlarded with bacon, fr. *piccare* to prick] **:** thin slices of meat (as veal) sautéed and served in a lemon and butter sauce

pick* *n* **:** a comb with long widely spaced teeth used to give height to a hairstyle

picker* *n* **:** a person who locates and purchases antiques and collectibles for resale to dealers

pick off* *vt* **:** INTERCEPT ⟨*picked off* a pass⟩

pick up* *vb* — **pick up on 1 a :** UNDERSTAND, APPRECIATE **b :** to become aware of **:** NOTICE **2 :** to adopt as one's own

pi·clo·ram \'pikl ə,ram, 'pīk-\ *n* -s [*pic*oline + *chlor-* + *amine*] **:** a systemic herbicide $C_6H_3Cl_3N_2O_2$ that breaks down only very slowly in the soil

pi·co·farad \¦pēkō +\ *n* [ISV *pico-* + *farad*] **:** one trillionth of a farad

pi·co·gram \"+\ *n* [ISV *pico-* + *gram*] **:** one trillionth of a gram

pi·co·mole \"+\ *n* [*pico-* + *mole*] **:** one trillionth of a mole

pi·cor·na·virus \pə¦kȯrnə +\ *n* [*pico-* + *RNA* + *virus*] **:** any of a group of RNA-containing viruses that includes the enteroviruses and rhinoviruses

pi·co·second \¦pēkō +\ *n* [ISV *pico-* + *second*] **:** one trillionth of a second

PID *abbr* pelvic inflammatory disease *herein*

piece* *n* — **piece of the action :** a share in activity or profit

piece of cake : something easily done **:** CINCH, BREEZE

piece·wise \'pēs,wīz\ *adv* [[1]*piece* + *-wise*] **:** with respect to a number of discrete intervals, sets, or pieces

pig* *n* **:** POLICEMAN — usu. used disparagingly

piggyback* *adj* **1 :** of, relating to, or being something (as a capsule or package) carried into space as an extra load by a vehicle (as a spacecraft or rocket) **2 :** of, relating to, or being a radio or television commercial that is presented in addition to other commercials during one commercial break **3 :** SUPPLEMENTAL, ADDITIONAL — **piggyback***adv*

piggyback* *vt* **:** to set up or cause to function in conjunction with something larger or more important ⟨school bus drivers' union is ~*ing* its demand for recognition . . . on the teachers' strike —*New Orleans (La.) Times-Picayune*⟩ **~** *vi* **:** to function or be carried as if on the back of another

pig out *vi, slang* **:** to eat greedily **:** GORGE — **pig–out** *n* -s

pil·i·pi·no \,pilə'pē(,)nō\ *n, usu cap* [Pilipino, fr. Sp *Filipino* Philippine] **:** the Tagalog-based official language of the Republic of the Philippines

pill* *n, often cap* **:** an oral contraceptive — usu. used with *the*

pillhead \'=,=\ *n* [[4]*pill* + *head*] **:** a person who takes pills or capsules (as of amphetamines) for nonmedicinal reasons

pillow talk *n* **:** intimate conversation between lovers in bed

pill pool *n* [[4]*pill;* fr. the drawing of small numbered balls from a bottle to determine order of play] **:** KELLY POOL

pilot* *n* **1 :** a television show produced as a sample of a proposed series **2 :** PILOT BURNER

pimpmobile \ˈpimpmō͵bēl, -mə͵- *sometimes* -͵bil\ *n* -S [[1]*pimp* + *mobile*] **:** an ostentatious customized luxury car that is used by a pimp or looks as if it would be used by a pimp

pi·ña co·la·da \ˌpēnyəkōˈlädə\ *n* [Sp, lit., strained pineapple] **:** a tall iced drink made of rum, coconut cream, and pineapple juice

pi·ne·a·lec·to·mize \͵pinēəˈlektə͵mīz, ͵pī-\ *vt* -ED/-ING/-S [*pinealectomy* (herein) + *-ize*] **:** to perform a pinealectomy on

pi·ne·a·lec·to·my \-təmē\ *n* -ES [NL, fr. *pineal* body + *-ectomy*] **:** surgical removal of the pineal body

ping-pong \ˈ=ˌ=\ *vb* -ED/-ING/-S [fr. *Ping-Pong*, a trademark] **:** SHIFT, BOUNCE ⟨the issue was *ping-ponged* back and forth⟩

pinholder \ˈ=͵==\ *n* **:** a flower holder that consists of a substantial base topped with projecting pins

pink-collar \ˈ=ˌ==\ *adj* **:** of, relating to, or constituting a class of employees in occupations (as nursing or clerical jobs) traditionally held by women

pi·no·cy·tot·ic \ˌpinō(͵)sīˈtäd·ik, ˌpīn-, -͵səˈt-\ *or* **pi·no·cyt·ic** \ˌ==ˈsid·ik\ *adj* [*pinocytosis* + [1]*-otic* or [1]*-ic*] **:** of, relating to, or being pinocytosis — **pi·no·cy·tot·i·cal·ly** \-ək(ə)lē\ *adv*

pinta \ˈpīntə\ *n* -S [*pint* + *-a* (as in *cuppa* — herein)] *Brit* **:** a pint of milk

pinteresque \ˌpintəˈresk\ *adj, usu cap* [Harold *Pinter* *b*1930 Eng. dramatist + *-esque*] **:** of, relating to, or characteristic of the writings of Harold Pinter

pin·yin \ˈpinˈyin\ *n* -S *often cap* [Chin (Pek) *p'in*[1] *yin*[1] to spell phonetically, fr. *p'in*[1] to arrange + *yin*[1] sound, pronunciation] **:** a system for romanizing Chinese ideograms

pi·sce·an \ˈpīsēən *also* ˈpis-\ *n* -S *usu cap* [*Pisces* + *-an*] **:** PISCES *herein*

pisces* *n, usu cap* **:** one born under the astrological sign Pisces

pi·sci·cide \ˈpīsə͵sīd, ˈpisə-, ˈpiskə-\ *n* -S [*pisci-* + *-cide*] **:** a substance used to kill fish — **pi·sci·ci·dal** \ˈ==ˌsīdᵊl\ *adj*

piss·er \ˈpisə(r)\ *n* -S [[1]*piss* + *-er*] **:** one that is inferior, difficult, or unpleasant — sometimes considered vulgar

piss off *vi, Brit* **:** to leave forthwith **:** get out — usu. used as a command; sometimes considered vulgar ~ *vt* **:** ANGER, IRRITATE — sometimes considered vulgar

pis·tou \pēstü\ *n* -S [F] **:** a vegetable soup served with a puree of garlic, herbs, oil, and cheese and often tomatoes

pit* *n* **pits** *pl* **:** something or someone that is the worst — used with *the*

pi·ta \ˈpēd·ə, -ētə\ *n* -S [NGk *pita* pie, cake] **:** a thin flat bread that can be separated easily into two layers

pit stop *n* **1 :** a stop at a pit during an automobile race **2 a :** a stop for fuel, food, rest, or relief (as during a trip) **b** (1) **:** a place where a pit stop can be made (2) **:** an establishment providing food or drink

pivot* \ˈpivət\ *n* **:** an offensive player position in basketball that is occupied by a player (as a center) who usu. faces away from the basket to relay passes, shoot, or provide a screen for teammates

pivotman \ˈ==(͵)=\ *n, pl* **pivotmen** [*pivot* (herein) + *man*] **:** one who plays the pivot; *specif* **:** a center on a basketball team

pix·el \ˈpiksəl, -͵sel\ *n* -S [fr. [2]*pix* + *el*ement] **1 :** any of the numerous small discrete elements that together constitute an image (as on a television screen) **2 :** any of the detecting elements of a charge-coupled device used as an optical sensor

piz·zazz *or* **pi·zazz** *also* **pa·zazz** \pəˈzaz\ *n* -ES [origin unknown] **:** the quality of being exciting or attractive: as **a :** GLAMOUR, APPEAL ⟨bemoans the lack of color and provocative ~ in today's stars —Vernon Scott⟩ **b :** SPIRIT, VITALITY ⟨we had four numbers with ~ and the rest of the show died around them —Gower Champion⟩

pk* *abbr* pike

PKU *abbr* phenylketonuria

placebo effect *n* **:** improvement in the condition of a sick person that occurs in response to treatment but cannot be considered due to the specific treatment used

place value *n* **:** the value of the location of a digit in a numeral ⟨in 425 the location of the digit 2 has a *place value* of ten

[1]**planeside** \ˈ=͵=\ *n* [[4]*plane* + [1]*side*] **:** the area adjacent to an airplane ⟨speaking briefly at ~ —*Christian Science Monitor*⟩

[2]**planeside** \ˌ=͵=\ *adj* **:** engaged in or made at planeside ⟨paused first for a ~ interview —*Time*⟩ ⟨his ~ remark —*Newsweek*⟩

plan·e·tol·o·gy \͵planəˈtäləjē\ *n* -ES [*planet* + *-o-* + *-logy*] **:** a science that deals with the condensed matter (as the planets, natural satellites, comets, and meteorites) of the solar system — **plan·e·to·log·i·cal** \-͵tᵊlˈäjəkəl\ *adj* — **plan·e·tol·o·gist** \-ˈtäləjəst\ *n* -S

plaque* *n* **:** a clear area in a bacterial culture produced by destruction of cells by a virus

plasma jet *n* **1 :** a stream of very hot gaseous plasma; *also* **:** a device for producing such a stream **2** *or* **plasma engine :** a rocket engine designed to derive thrust from the discharge of a magnetically accelerated plasma

plasmapause \ˈ==͵=\ *n* [*plasma* + *pause*] **:** the outer boundary of a plasmasphere

plasmasphere \ˈ==͵=\ *n* [*plasma* + *sphere*] **:** a region of a planet's atmosphere containing electrons and highly ionized particles that rotate with the planet

plasma torch *n* **:** a device that heats a gas by electrical means to form a plasma for high-temperature operations (as melting metal)

plas·mid \ˈplazməd\ *n* -S [*plasma* + [4]*-id*] **:** an extrachromosomal ring of DNA that replicates autonomously and is found esp. in bacteria — compare EPISOME *herein*

plas·mon \ˈplaz͵män\ *n* -S [*plasma* + [2]*-on*] **:** a quantum of energy that propagates through a plasma as a result of charge density fluctuation

plastic* *adj* **:** not genuine or sincere **:** ARTIFICIAL ⟨the ~ age, the era of the sham and the bogus —Logan Gourlay⟩

plastic* *n* **:** credit cards used for payment ⟨the bill was £17.00, the banks were closed, and they don't take ~ —David Coombs⟩

plas·to·cyanin \ˌplastō+\ *n* [*plasto-* + *cyanin*] **:** a copper-containing protein that acts as an intermediary in photosynthetic electron transport

plas·to·quinone \"+\ *n* [*plasto-* + *quinone*] **:** any of a group of substances that occur mostly in plant chloroplasts, consist of paraquinone with two methyl substituents and a side chain of one or more isoprene units, are related to vitamin K, and play a role in photosynthetic phosphorylation

plate* *n* **1 :** LICENSE PLATE **2 :** a schedule of work to be done **3 :** any of the large movable segments into which

the earth's crust is divided according to the theory of plate tectonics
plate* *vt* [fr. the crossing of home plate by the scoring runner] **:** to cause (as a run) to score in baseball
plated amberina *n* **:** an ornamental glass consisting of an amberina casing over a fiery opalescent or white lining
plateglass \ˌ=ˈ=\ *adj, usu cap* [fr. *plate glass,* n.] **:** of, relating to, or being the British universities founded in the latter half of the twentieth century — compare OXBRIDGE *herein,* REDBRICK *herein*
platemaker \ˈ=ˌ==\ *n* [¹*plate* + *maker*] **:** a machine for making printing plates and esp. offset printing plates — **platemaking** \ˈ=ˌ==\ *n*
plate tectonics *n pl but sing in constr* **:** a theory that the lithosphere of the earth is divided into a small number of plates which float on and travel independently over the mantle and that much of the earth's seismic activity occurs at the boundaries of these plates as a result of frictional interaction; *also* **:** the process and dynamics of plate movement — **plate–tectonic** \ˌ=ˌ=ˈ==\ *adj*
platform tennis *n* **:** a variation of paddle tennis that is played on a platform enclosed by a wire fence
platinum* *adj* **:** relating to or being a record album that has sold at least one million copies — **go platinum :** to sell one million copies
platoon* *n* **:** two or more players (as in baseball) who alternate playing the same position
platoon* *vt* **:** to alternate (one player) with another player in the same position ⟨if I can't play him every day, I'll ~ him in left field —Leo Durocher⟩ **~** *vi* **1 :** to alternate with another player in the same position **2 :** to use alternate players at the same position
play* *vt* **1 :** to catch or pick up (a batted ball) **:** FIELD ⟨~*ed* the ball bare-handed⟩ **2 :** to direct the course of (as a ball) **:** HIT ⟨~*ed* a wedge shot to the green⟩; *also* **:** to cause (a ball or puck) to rebound ⟨~*ed* the ball off the backboard⟩ — **play by ear :** to deal with (as a situation) without previous planning or instructions — **play games :** to try to hide the truth from someone by deceptive means — **play one's cards :** to act with the means available to one
play–action pass \ˌ=ˈ==-\ *n* **:** a pass play in football in which the quarterback fakes a hand-off before passing the ball
playbook* *n* **:** a notebook containing diagramed football plays
playdate \ˈ=ˌ=\ *n* [¹*play* + *date*] **:** a scheduled showing of a production (as a movie)
playlist \ˈ=ˌ=\ *n* **:** a list of recordings to be played on the air by a radio station
plaza* *n* **:** an open area often featuring pedestrian walkways and shops and usu. located near urban buildings
plea bargaining *n* **:** the negotiation of an agreement between a prosecutor and a defendant whereby the defendant is permitted to plead guilty to a reduced charge — **plea–bargain** \ˈ=ˈ==\ *vi* — **plea bargain** *n*
PL/1 \ˌpēˌelˈwən\ *n* -s [*p*rogramming *l*anguage (version) *1*] **:** a general-purpose language for programming a computer
plot* *vi* **:** to be located by means of coordinates ⟨the data ~ at a single point⟩
plug* *vb* — **plug into :** to connect or become connected to by or as if by means of a plug ⟨the entire school is *plugged into* a . . . computer system —Patricia Linden⟩ ⟨pay up to $100 a month to *plug into* these agencies —Elliott McCleary⟩
plug·ola \ˌpləˈgōlə\ *n* -s [¹*plug* + pay*ola*] **:** incidental advertising on radio or television that is not purchased like regular advertising
plume* *n* **:** a hypothetical column of molten rock rising continuously from the earth's lower mantle that is held to be the driving force in plate movement in plate tectonics
plus* *prep* **:** BESIDES — not often in formal use ⟨~ which, we were traveling in an area exposed to few blacks —Linda Harris⟩
¹plus *adv* **:** BESIDES — not often in formal use ⟨hang around it because it's an open building with no lock on the door. *Plus* they go in there to hang out, out of the cold —Barbara Lamont⟩
²plus *conj* **:** AND — not often in formal use ⟨if you want to make a super investment, ~ you don't happen to be rich —*advt*⟩
p marker \ˈ=ˌ==\ *n, usu cap P* [*P,* symbol for *phrase*] **:** PHRASE MARKER *herein*
pocket* *n* **:** an area formed by blockers from which a football quarterback attempts to pass
pocket bread *n* **:** PITA *herein*
pod* *n* **:** a detachable compartment (as for personnel, a power unit, or an instrument) on a spacecraft
po–faced \ˈpōˌfāst\ *adj* [origin unknown] *chiefly Brit* **:** having an assumed solemn, serious, or earnest expression or manner **:** piously or hypocritically solemn
po·go·noph·o·ran \ˌpōgəˈnäfərən\ *n* -s [*Pogonophora* + ¹*-an*] **:** any marine worm belonging to the phylum or class Pogonophora — **pogonophoran** *adj*
point* *n* **points** *pl* **1 :** a percentage of the face value of a loan often added as a placement fee or service charge **2 :** credit accruing from creating a good impression — usu. used in pl. ⟨he gets ~*s* for courage —Sally Quinn⟩
point estimate *n* **:** the single value assigned to a parameter in point estimation
point estimation *n* **:** estimation in which a single value is assigned to a parameter
point man* *n* **:** a soldier who goes ahead of a patrol; *broadly* **:** anyone who is in the forefront ⟨establishing himself as *point man* for the new Republican foreign policy —R.L. Strout⟩
point of accumulation : LIMIT POINT *herein*
point of no return **1 :** the point in the flight of an aircraft beyond which the remaining fuel will be insufficient for a return to the starting point with the result that the craft must proceed **2 :** a critical point (as in development or a course of action) at which turning back or reversal is not possible
point–of–sale *also* **point–of–sales** \ˌ==ˈ=\ *adj* **:** of or relating to the place (as a check-out counter) where an item is purchased ⟨*point-of-sale* advertising⟩ ⟨electronic *point-of-sale* terminals⟩
point set *n* **:** a collection of points in geometry or topology
point set topology *n* **:** a branch of topology concerned with the properties and theory of topological spaces and metric spaces developed with emphasis on set theory
point–slope form \ˌ=ˈ=-\ *n* **:** the equation of a straight line in the form $y - y_1 = m(x - x_1)$ where m is the slope of the line and (x_1, y_1) are the coordinates of a given point on the line — compare SLOPE-INTERCEPT FORM *herein*
point spread *n* **:** the number of points by which a person who sets odds expects a favorite (as a football or basketball team) to defeat an underdog
pois·son distribution \pwäˈsōⁿ-\ *n, usu cap P* [after Siméon D. *Poisson* †1840 Fr. mathematician] **:** a proba-

bility density function that is often used as a mathematical model of the number of outcomes (as traffic accidents, atomic disintegrations, or organisms) obtained in a suitable interval of time and space, that has the mean equal to the variance, that is used as an approximation to the binomial distribution, and that has the form

$$f(x) = \frac{e^{-\mu}\mu^x}{x!}$$

where μ is the mean and x takes on nonnegative integral values

polar* *adj* **1 a :** passing over a planet's north and south poles ⟨a satellite in a ~ orbit⟩ **b :** traveling in a polar orbit ⟨a ~ satellite⟩ **2 :** of, relating to, or expressed in polar coordinates ⟨~ equations⟩; *also* **:** of or relating to a polar coordinate system

pole* *or* **pole position** *n* [¹*pole*] **:** the front-row position nearest the infield in the starting lineup of an automobile race

pole* *n* [⁴*pole*] **:** the point of origin of two tangents to a conic section that determine a polar

pole lamp *n* **:** a lamp that consists of a pole to which light fixtures are attached and that usu. extends from floor to ceiling

po·le·mol·ogy \(ˌ)pōlə'mäləjē\ *n* -ES [Gk *polemos* war + E *-logy* — more at POLEMIC] **:** the study of war

police procedural *n, pl* **police procedurals :** a mystery story written from the point of view of the police investigating the crime

po·lio·virus \¦pōlē(ˌ)ō +\ *n* [NL, fr. *polio*myelitis + *virus*] **:** an enterovirus that occurs in several antigenically distinct forms and is the causative agent of human poliomyelitis

po·lit·i·ci·za·tion \pəˌlid·əsə'zāshən\ *n* -s [*politicize* + *-ation*] **:** the act or process of politicizing ⟨the ~ of art is typical of totalitarian tyranny —B.W. Garfield⟩

poll* *vt* **:** to test (as several computer terminals sharing a single line) in sequence for messages to be transmitted

po·loi·dal \pō'lȯidᵊl\ *adj* [⁴*pole* + *-oid* + *-al*] **:** relating to or being a magnetic field that extends between the poles of a magnetic body (as the earth) into surrounding space

po·lo·nia \pə'lōnēə\ *n* -s *cap* [ML, Poland] **:** people of Polish descent living outside Poland

poly \'pälē\ *n* -s [short for *polymer*] **:** a polymerized plastic or something made of this; *esp* **:** a polyester fiber, fabric, or garment

poly(A) \¦pälē'ā\ *n* -s [*poly-* + *a*denylic acid] **:** RNA or a segment of RNA that is composed of a polynucleotide chain consisting only of adenine-containing nucleotides and that codes for polylysine when functioning as messenger RNA in protein synthesis

poly·acrylamide \¦pälē +\ *n* [*poly-* + *acrylamide*] **:** a polyamide $(-CH_2CHCONH_2-)_x$ of acrylic acid

polyacrylamide gel *n* **:** hydrated polyacrylamide that is used esp. for electrophoresis

poly·ad·e·nyl·ate \¦pälēˌadᵊn'ilˌāt\ *n* -s [*polyadenylic* acid (herein) + *-ate*] **:** POLY(A) *herein* — **poly·ad·e·nyl·ated** \-ˌātəd\ *adj* — **poly·ad·e·nyl·a·tion** \-nil'āshən\ *n* -s

poly·adenylic acid \"+ . . .-\ *n* [*poly-* + *adenylic acid*] **:** POLY(A) *herein*

poly·alcohol \"+\ *n* [ISV *poly-* + *alcohol*] **:** an alcohol (as ethylene glycol) that contains more than one hydroxyl group

poly·brominated biphenyl \¦pälē, -lə +\ *n* [*poly-* + *brominated*] **:** any of several compounds that are closely related to polychlorinated biphenyls in environmental toxicity and in structure except that various hydrogen atoms are replaced by bromine — called also *PBB*

poly·carbonate \¦pälē, -lə +\ *n* [*poly-* + *carbonate*] **:** any of various tough thermoplastics characterized by high impact strength and high softening temperature

poly·cen·trism \ˌpälē'sen·ˌtrizəm, -lə-\ *n* -s [ISV *poly-* + *-centric* + *-ism;* prob. orig. formed in It] **:** the existence of a plurality of centers of Communist thought and leadership — **poly·cen·trist** \-ˌtrəst\ *n or adj*

poly·chlorinated biphenyl \¦pälē, -lə + . . .-\ *n* [*poly-* + *chlorinated,* past part. of *chlorinate*] **:** any of several compounds that are produced by replacing hydrogen atoms in biphenyl with chlorine, have various industrial applications, and are poisonous environmental pollutants which tend to accumulate in animal tissues

polychromatic* *adj* **:** being or relating to radiation that is composed of more than one wavelength

poly·cistronic \¦pälē, -lə +\ *adj* [*poly-* + *cistronic* (herein)] **:** containing the genetic information of a number of cistrons

poly·clo·nal \¦pälē¦klōnᵊl, -lə¦k-\ *adj* [*poly-* + *clone* + *-al*] **:** produced by or being cells derived from two or more cells of different ancestry or genetic constitution ⟨~ antibody synthesis⟩

poly·cytidylic acid \¦pälē, -lə+\ *n* [*poly-* + *cytidylic acid*] **:** RNA or a segment of RNA that is composed of a polynucleotide chain consisting entirely of cytosine-containing nucleotides and that codes for a polypeptide chain consisting of proline residues when functioning as messenger RNA in protein synthesis — see POLY I:C *herein*

poly·ether \¦pälē +\ *n* [*poly-* + *ether*] **:** any of a group of polymers in which the repeating unit contains a carbon-oxygen bond derived esp. from an aldehyde or an epoxide and which are used esp. in the manufacture of plastic foams

po·lyg·ra·pher \pə'ligrəfər, 'pälēˌgrafər, -ləˌ-, -ráf-\ *n* -s **:** POLYGRAPHIST

poly I:C \ˌpälēˌī'sē\ *or* **poly I·poly C** \ˌpälē'īˌpälē'sē\ *n* [*poly-* + *i*nosinic acid + *poly-* + *c*ytidylic acid] **:** a synthetic 2-stranded RNA composed of one strand of polyinosinic acid and one strand of polycytidylic acid that induces interferon formation and has been used experimentally as an anticancer and antiviral agent

poly·imide \¦pälē +\ *n* [*poly-* + *imide*] **:** any of a class of polymeric synthetic resins resistant to high temperatures, wear, and corrosion and used esp. for coatings and films

poly·inosinic acid \"+ . . .-\ *n* [*poly-* + *inosinic acid*] **:** RNA or a segment of RNA that is composed of a polynucleotide chain consisting entirely of inosinic-acid residues — see POLY I:C *herein*

poly·lysine \"+\ *n* [*poly-* + *lysine*] **:** a protein whose polypeptide chain consists entirely of lysine residues

poly·mer·ase \'pälәməˌrās, -āz, pə'lim-\ *n* -s [*polymer* + *-ase*] **:** any of several enzymes that catalyze the formation of DNA or RNA from precursor substances in the presence of preexisting DNA or RNA acting as a template

poly·oma *or* **poly·oma virus** \ˌpälē'ōmə-\ *n* -s [NL *polyoma,* fr. *poly-* + *-oma*] **:** a papovavirus of rodents that is associated with various kinds of tumors

poly·ribosome \¦pälē, -lə+\ *n* [*poly-* + *ribosome* (herein)] **:** a cluster of ribosomes held together by a molecule of messenger RNA and forming the site of protein synthesis — **poly·ribosomal** \"+\ *adj*

poly·some \'pälē,sōm, -lə̇-\ *n* -s [*poly-* + ribo*some* (herein)] : POLYRIBOSOME *herein*

poly·sorbate \¦pälē, -lə̇ +\ *n* [*poly-* + *sorbate*] : any of several emulsifiers used in preparing some pharmaceuticals and foods

poly·synaptic \"+\ *adj* [*poly-* + *synaptic*] : involving two or more synapses in the central nervous system ⟨~ reflexes⟩ — **poly·synaptically** \"+\ *adv*

poly(U) *n* -s [*poly-* + *u*ridylic acid] : POLYURIDYLIC ACID *herein*

poly·unsaturated \¦pälē +\ *adj* [*poly-* + *unsaturated*] *of a fat or oil* : rich in unsaturated bonds — **poly·unsaturate** \"+\ *n*

poly·uridylic acid \"+ . . .-\ *n* [*poly-* + *uridylic acid*] : RNA or a segment of RNA that is composed of a polynucleotide chain consisting entirely of uracil-containing nucleotides and that codes for a polypeptide chain consisting of phenylalanine residues when functioning as messenger RNA in protein synthesis

pom \'päm\ *n* -s *usu cap* [*pom*my] *Austral* : a British person : POMMY — usu. used disparagingly

pong \'päŋ\ *n* -s [origin unknown] *Brit* : ODOR; *esp* : an unpleasant odor — **pong** *vi* -ED/-ING/-S

pony car *n* [so called fr. the fact that the trade names of several such cars come from the names of breeds of small horses] : one of a group of 2-door hardtops of different makes that are similar in sporty styling, high performance characteristics, and price range

pon·zi scheme *also* **ponzi** \'pänzē-\ *n, usu cap P* [after Charles A. *Ponzi* †1949 Am. (Ital.-born) swindler] : an investment swindle in which some early investors are paid off with the money put up by later ones in order to encourage more and bigger risks

-poo \,pü\ *suffix* [origin unknown] — used as a disparaging diminutive ⟨cutesy-*poo*⟩ ⟨drinki*poo*⟩

poof \'püf, 'pu̇f\ *also* **poove** \'püv, 'pu̇v\ *n* -s [prob. alter. of ²*puff*] *Brit* : HOMOSEXUAL

poof·ter *also* **poof·tah** \'püftə, 'pu̇f-\ *n* -s [alter. of *poof* (herein)] *Brit* : POOF *herein*

poo–poo \'pü,pü\ *n* -s [redupl. of ²*poop*] *slang* : EXCREMENT

poorboy \'≈,≈\ *n* [fr. the phrase *poor boy;* prob. fr. its resemblance esp. in fit to the sort of outgrown sweater a poor child might wear] : a close-fitting ribbed sweater

poor–mouth \'≈,mau̇th, -t͟h\ *vb* [*poor mouth*] *vi* : to plead poverty as a defense or excuse ⟨usually *poor-mouths* when it's his turn to contribute⟩ ~ *vt* : to speak disparagingly of

pop* *n* [¹*pop*] — **a pop** : for each one : APIECE ⟨tickets at $5 *a pop* —Bob McCoy⟩

pop* *vt* : to take (drugs) orally or by injection ⟨he ~*s* vitamins . . . the way some cowboys gobble jelly beans —P.A. Witteman⟩ ~ *vi* : PAY ⟨the house ~*s* for every third beer —Studs Terkel⟩

pop* *adj* **1** : POPULAR ⟨~ fiction⟩; *esp* : of or relating to the popular culture disseminated through the mass media ⟨~ psychology⟩ **2** : of or relating to pop art

pop* *n* [⁶*pop*] **1** : pop music **2** : POP ART *herein* **3** : pop culture

pop art *n* : art in which commonplace objects (as road signs, hamburgers, comic strips, or soup cans) are used as subjects and often physically incorporated in the work — **pop artist** *n*

popper* *n, slang* : a vial of amyl nitrite esp. when illicitly used as an aphrodisiac

pop·ster \'päpstə(r)\ *n* -s [*pop* (herein) + *-ster*] : a practitioner of pop

pop–top \¦≈,≈\ *adj* [¹*pop* + ¹*top*] : having a closure that can be popped open without use of an opening device ⟨a *pop-top* can⟩ — **pop–top** \'≈'≈\ *n*

population explosion *n* : a pyramiding of numbers of a biological population; *esp* : the recent great increase in human numbers resulting from both increased survival and exponential population growth

population genetics *n pl but sing in constr* : a branch of genetics concerned with gene frequencies and genotype frequencies in populations and considering esp. randomness of mating, immigration, emigration, mutation, and selection — see HARDY-WEINBERG LAW *herein*

pop wine *n* : an inexpensive sweet wine and esp. a fruit wine or a fruit-flavored wine

pork belly *n* : an uncured side of pork

porn \'pȯ(ə)rn, 'pȯ(ə)n\ *or* **por·no** \'pȯr(,)nō, 'pȯ(ə)(-\ *n* -s [by shortening] : PORNOGRAPHY — **porn** *or* **porno** *adj*

pornography* *n* **1** : material (as a book) that is pornographic **2** : the depiction or portrayal of acts in a sensational manner so as to arouse (as by lurid details) a quick intense emotional reaction ⟨the ~ of violence⟩

porny \'pȯrnē, 'pȯ(ə)n-, -ni\ *adj* -ER/-EST [*porn* (herein) + ¹*-y*] : PORNOGRAPHIC

po·ro·mer·ic \¦pōrə¦merik, ¦pȯr-\ *n* -s [*poro-* + poly*meric*] : any of a class of tough porous synthetic materials used as a substitute for leather (as in shoe uppers)

portable* *adj* : able to be used on any computer without modification ⟨~ software⟩

POS *abbr* point-of-sale *herein*

posi·grade \'päzə,grād\ *adj* [*posi*tive + *-grade* (as in *retrograde*)] : relating to, using, or being an auxiliary rocket that imparts additional thrust to a spacecraft in the direction of motion

posit* *vt* : to propose as an explanation : SUGGEST

positional notation *n* : a system of expressing numbers in which the digits are arranged in succession, the position of each digit has a place value, and the number is equal to the sum of the products of each digit by its place value

position paper *n* : a detailed report that recommends a course of action on a particular issue

positive definite *adj* **1** : having a positive value of all values of the constituent variables ⟨*positive definite* quadratic forms⟩ **2** *of a matrix* : having the characteristic roots real and positive

positron–emission tomography \¦≈≈,≈≈¦≈≈-\ *n* : tomography in which an in vivo, noninvasive, cross-sectional image of regional metabolism is obtained by a usu. color-coded CRT representation of the distribution of gamma radiation given off in the collision of electrons in cells with positrons emitted by radionuclides incorporated into metabolic substances — abbr. *PET*

post·code \'≈¦≈\ *n* : a code (as of numbers and letters) used similarly to the zip code esp. in the United Kingdom and Australia

post–determiner \'pōs(t) +\ *n* [*post-* + *determiner*] : a limiting noun modifier (as *first* or *few*) characterized by occurrence after the determiner in a noun phrase

pos·ter·iza·tion \,pōstərə̇'zāshən, -rī'z-\ *n* -s [²*poster* + *-ization*] : the obtaining of posterlike reproductions having solid tones or colors and little detail from photographs or other continuous-tone originals by means of separation negatives — **pos·ter·ize** \ˈpōstə,rīz\ *vb* -ED/-ING/-S

post·industrial \ˈpōst +\ *adj* [*post-* + *industrial*] **:** coming after the predominance of large-scale industry ⟨a ~ society⟩

post·irradiation \¦pōst+\ *adj* [*post-* + *irradiation*] **:** occurring after irradiation ⟨mutations in ~ cell divisions⟩

post·literate \"+\ *adj* [*post-* + *literate*] **:** relating to or occurring after the introduction of the electronic media

post·marital \¦pōs(t)+\ *adj* [*post-* + *marital*] **:** occurring after a marriage has been terminated

post·modern \"+\ *adj* [*post-* + *modern*] **:** of or relating to any of several artistic movements that are reactions against the philosophy and practices of modern arts or literature

post·production \"+\ *n* [*post-* + *production*] **:** the operations (as editing or scoring) following filming by which a motion picture or television show is readied for public presentation

post·test \ˈpōs(t) +,\ *n* [*post-* + *test*] **:** a test given to students after the completion of an instructional program to measure their achievement and the effectiveness of the program

post·transcriptional \¦pōs(t)+\ *adj* [*post-* + *transcriptional*] **:** occurring, acting, or existing after genetic transcription

post·transfusion \"+\ *adj* [*post-* + *transfusion*] **1 :** caused by transfused blood ⟨malpractice suits for ~ hepatitis⟩ **2 :** occurring after blood transfusion ⟨induction of ~ shock⟩

post·translational \"+\ *adj* [*post-* + *translational*] **:** occurring or existing after genetic translation

post·treatment \(ˈ)pōs(t) +¦\ *adj* [*post-* + *treatment*] **:** relating to, typical of, or occurring in the stage following treatment ⟨~ examinations⟩ — **posttreatment** *adv*

potassium–argon \¦=¦==¦=\ *adj* **:** of, relating to, or being a method of dating archaeological or geological materials based on the radioactive decay of potassium to argon in a specimen

potential* *n* **:** POTENTIAL DIFFERENCE

pothead \ˈ=,=\ *n* [¹*pot* + *head*] **:** one who smokes marijuana

pot sticker *n* **:** a crescent-shaped dumpling filled usu. with pork, steamed, and then fried, and usu. served as an appetizer

pouil·ly–fuis·sé \pü'yēfwʸē'sā\ *n* -s [fr. Solutré-*Pouilly* and *Fuissé*, Fr. villages] **:** a dry white Burgundy

powder–puff \¦==,=\ *adj* **:** of, relating to, or being a competitive activity or event for women ⟨she played *powder-puff* football —*Sports Illustrated*⟩

power* *n* **:** the probability of rejecting the null hypothesis in a statistical test when a particular alternative hypothesis is true

power broker *n* **:** a person (as in politics) able to exert strong influence through control of votes or individuals

power function *n* **1 :** a function of a parameter under statistical test whose value for a particular value of the parameter is the probability of rejecting the null hypothesis if that value of the parameter is true **2 :** a function (as $f(x) = ax^k$) that equals the product of a constant and a power of the independent variable

powerlifting \ˈ==,==\ *n* **:** weight lifting in which lifters compete in the squat, bench press, and dead lift — **powerlifter** \ˈ==,==\ *n*

power series *n* **:** an infinite series whose terms are successive integral powers of a variable multiplied by constants

power structure *n* **1 :** a group of persons having control of an organization **:** ESTABLISHMENT **2 :** the hierarchical interrelationships existing within a controlling group

power sweep *n* **:** an end run in football in which one or more linemen pull out and run interference for the ballcarrier

poxvirus \ˈ=¦==\ *n* [¹*pox* + *virus*] **:** any of a group of relatively large round, brick-shaped, or ovoid animal viruses (as the causative agent of smallpox) that have a fluffy appearance caused by a covering of tubules and threads

PPLO \¦pē(,)pē,elˈō\ *n, pl* **PPLO** [*p*leuro*p*neumonia-*l*ike *o*rganism] **:** MYCOPLASMA

pre·agricultural \¦prē +\ *adj* [*pre-* + *agricultural*] **:** existing or occurring before the practice of agriculture

pre·biological \"+\ *also* **pre·biologic** \"+\ *adj* [*pre-* + *biologic*] **:** of, relating to, or being chemical or environmental precursors of the origin of life ⟨~ molecules⟩ ⟨~ chemical evolution⟩

pre·biotic \"+\ *adj* [*pre-* + ¹*biotic*] **:** PREBIOLOGICAL *herein*

pre·calculus \"+\ *adj* [*pre-* + *calculus*] **:** relating to or being mathematical prerequisites for the study of calculus ⟨~ mathematics⟩ — **precalculus** *n*

pre·capillary \(ˈ)prē +\ *adj* [*pre-* + *capillary*] **:** being on the arterial side of and immediately adjacent to a capillary

precision* *n* **1 :** the accuracy (as in binary or decimal places) with which a number can be represented usu. expressed in terms of the number of computer words available for representation ⟨double ~ arithmetic permits the representation of an expression by two computer words⟩ **2 :** RELEVANCE *herein*

pre·coital \(ˈ)prē +\ *adj* [*pre-* + *coital*] **:** occurring before coitus

pre·conference \ˈprē +,\ *n* [*pre-* + *conference*] **:** a conference held before the start of another conference or convention

pre·copulatory \(ˈ)prē +\ *adj* [*pre-* + *copulatory*] **:** preceding copulation ⟨~ behavior⟩

pre·determiner \¦prē +\ *n* [*pre-* + *determiner*] **:** a limiting noun modifier (as *both* or *all*) characterized by occurrence before the determiner in a noun phrase

pre·diabetes \"+\ *n* [*pre-* + *diabetes*] **:** an inapparent abnormal state that precedes the development of clinically evident diabetes — **pre·diabetic** \"+\ *adj or n*

predominantly* *adv* **:** for the most part **:** MAINLY ⟨a ~ middle-class neighborhood⟩

pre·emergent \"+\ *adj* [*pre-* + *emergent*] **:** PREEMERGENCE

preempt* *vt* **1 :** to take the place of **:** take precedence over ⟨the busing issue has ~*ed* discussion of more basic problems —William Serrin⟩ **2 :** to gain a commanding or preeminent place in ⟨lost the 1970 congressional race . . . but ran so well that he ~*ed* the Democratic field for a rematch two years later —R. M. Williams⟩

preemptive* *adj* **:** marked by the seizing of the initiative; *specif* **:** being or relating to a first military strike made to gain an advantage when a strike by the enemy is believed imminent — compare PREVENTIVE *in the Dict*

pre–engineered \¦prē +\ *adj* [*pre-* + *engineered*, past part. of *engineer*] **:** constructed of or employing prefabricated modules

preg·gers \ˈpregə(r)z\ *adj* [by alter.] *chiefly Brit* **:** PREGNANT — used as a predicate adjective

prehistoric* *adj* **:** of or relating to a language in a period of its development from which contemporary records of its actual sounds and forms have not been preserved

prehistory* *n* **:** the prehistoric period of man's evolution

pre·implantation \ˌprē +\ *adj* [*pre-* + *implantation*] **:** of, involving, or being an embryo before uterine implantation

pre·incubation \"+\ *n* [*pre-* + *incubation*] **:** incubation (as of a biochemical) prior to a process (as a reaction) — **pre·incubate** \"+\ *vt*

prelate nul·li·us \-nüˈlēəs\ *n, pl* **prelates nullius** [part translation of NL *praelatus nullius dioecesis* prelate of no diocese] **:** a Roman Catholic prelate having ordinary jurisdiction over a district independent of any diocese

pre·launch \ˈprē +\ *adj* [*pre-* + [2]*launch*] **:** preparing for or preliminary to launch (as of a spacecraft)

pre·meiotic \"+\ *adj* [*pre-* + *meiotic*] **:** of, occurring in, or typical of a stage prior to meiosis ⟨~ DNA synthesis⟩ ⟨~ tissue⟩

premenstrual syndrome *n* **:** a varying constellation of symptoms manifested by some women prior to menstruation that may include emotional instability, irritability, insomnia, fatigue, anxiety, depression, headache, edema, and abdominal pain

pre·oviposition \"+\ *adj* [*pre-* + *oviposition*] **:** of, relating to, or being the period before oviposition of the first eggs by an adult female (as of an insect)

pre–owned \ˌ=ˈ=\ *adj* [*pre-* + *owned*] **:** SECONDHAND, USED ⟨a *pre-owned* luxury car⟩

pre·plant \ˈ=ˌ=, ˌ=ˌ=\ *also* **pre·planting** \ˈ=ˌ==, ˌ=ˌ==\ *adj* [*pre-* + [2]*plant* or [1]*planting*] **:** occurring or used before planting a crop

[1]**prep·py** *or* **prep·pie** \ˈprepē\ *n, pl* **preppies** [*prep* + *-y* or *-ie* one associated with] **1 :** a student at or a graduate of a preparatory school **2 :** a person deemed to dress or behave like a preppy

[2]**preppy** *or* **preppie** *adj* -ER/-EST **1 :** relating to, characteristic of, or being a preppy **2 :** relating to or being a style of dress characterized esp. by classic clothing and neat appearance — **prep·pi·ly** \ˈprepəlē\ *adv* — **prep·pi·ness** \ˈprepēnəs, -pin-\ *n*

pre·preg \ˈprēˌpreg\ *n* -s [*pre-* + im*preg*nated] **:** a reinforcing or molding material (as paper or glass cloth) impregnated with a synthetic resin before use

pre·process \(ˈ)prē +\ *vt* [*pre-* + *process*] **:** to do preliminary processing of (as data) — **pre·processor** \"+\ *n*

[1]**preproduction** \ˌprē +\ *adj* [*pre-* + *production*] **:** involving, existing, or taking place in the period before production begins ⟨~ planning⟩; *esp* **:** relating to or being a prototype ⟨~ models⟩

[2]**preproduction** \"+\ *n* **:** the period in the development of a play or motion picture prior to staging or filming that usu. involves casting, hiring production crews, constructing sets, and finding a suitable theater or location for filming

pre·program \ˌprē +\ *vt* [*pre-* + *program*] **:** to program in advance of some anticipated use

pre·punch \(ˈ)prē +\ *vt* [*pre-* + *punch*] **:** to punch in advance of some anticipated use

pre·quel \ˈprēkwəl\ *n* -s [*pre-* + *-quel* (as in *sequel*)] **:** a literary or dramatic work whose story precedes that of an earlier work

pre·screen \(ˈ)prē +\ *vt* [*pre-* + *screen*] **1 :** to screen beforehand ⟨~ schoolchildren for potential learning and behavior problems —Robert Reinhold⟩ **2 :** to view (as a television show) before public release

pres·en·tism \ˈprezənˌtizəm\ *n* -s [[4]*present* + *-ism*] **:** an outlook dominated by present-day attitudes and experiences

[1]**pre·soak** \(ˈ)prē +\ *vt* [*pre-* + *soak*] **:** to soak beforehand

[2]**presoak** \ˈ=ˌ=\ *n* **1 :** a cleaning agent used in presoaking clothes **2 :** an instance of presoaking

pre·sort \(ˈ)prē +\ *vt* [*pre-* + *sort*] **:** to sort (outgoing mail) by zip code usu. before delivery to a post office

press* *vb* — **press the flesh :** to greet and shake hands with people esp. while campaigning for political office

press kit *n* **:** a collection of promotional material for distribution to the press

press secretary *n* **:** a person officially in charge of press relations for a usu. prominent public figure

pre·stress \ˈprē +\ *n* [*prestress,* v.] **1 :** the process of prestressing **2 :** the stresses introduced in prestress **3 :** the condition of being prestressed

pre·synaptic \ˌprē +\ *adj* [*pre-* + *synaptic*] **:** situated or occurring just before a nerve synapse ⟨a ~ nerve ending⟩ ⟨~ inhibition⟩ — **pre·synaptically** \"+\ *adv*

pre·tax \(ˈ)prē +\ *adj* [*pre-* + [2]*tax*] **:** existing before provision for taxes ⟨~ earnings⟩

[1]**pre·teen** \ˌprē +\ *adj* [*pre-* + [3]*teen*] **1 :** relating to or produced for children younger than 13 ⟨~ fashions⟩ **2 :** being younger than 13 ⟨~ youngsters⟩

[2]**preteen** \"+\ *n* **:** a boy or girl not yet 13 years old

pre·treatment \(ˈ)prē +\ *adj* [*pre-* + *treatment*] **:** occurring in or typical of the period prior to treatment

prevent defense \ˈprēˌventˈ=ˌ=; ˌprēˈvent-, -prəˈ-, *also* -ˌ=ˈ=\ *n* **:** a football defense in which linebackers and backs play deeper than usual in order to prevent the completion of a long pass

preventive detention* *n* **:** imprisonment without the right to bail of an arrested person awaiting trial for a felony who is considered dangerous to society

pre·writing \ˈprē+,\ *n* **:** the formulation and organization of ideas preparatory to writing

price–earnings ratio \ˈ=ˈ==-\ *n* **:** a measure of the value of a common stock determined as the ratio of its market price to its earnings per share and usu. expressed as a simple numeral **(price–earnings multiple)**

primal scream therapy *or* **primal therapy** *or* **primal scream** *n* **:** psychotherapy in which the patient recalls and reenacts a particularly disturbing past experience and expresses normally repressed anger or frustration esp. through spontaneous and unrestrained screams, hysteria, or violence

primary* *adj* **1 :** of, relating to, or being the amino acid sequence in proteins ⟨~ protein structure⟩ **2 :** of, relating to, involving, or derived from primary meristem ⟨~ tissue⟩ ⟨~ growth⟩ **3 :** of, relating to, or involved in the production of organic substances by green plants ⟨~ productivity⟩

primary care *also* **primary health care** *n* **:** health care provided by a medical professional with whom a patient has initial contact and by whom the patient may be referred to a specialist

primary consumer *n* **:** a plant-eating organism **:** HERBIVORE

primary derivative *n* **:** a word (as *telegram*) whose immediate constituents are bound forms

primary structure *n* **:** sculpture in the idiom of minimal art — **primary struc·tur·ist** \-ˌstrəkchərəst, -ksh(ə)rəst\ *n*

primary tooth *n* **:** MILK TOOTH

pri·ma·to·log·i·cal \ˌprīməd-ᵊlˈäjəkəl\ *adj* [*primatology* + *-ical*] **:** of or relating to primatology ⟨~ research⟩

primer* *n* **:** a molecule (as of DNA) whose presence is required for formation of more molecules of the same kind

prime rate *n* **:** an interest rate formally announced by a bank as the lowest normally available at a particular time to its most creditworthy customers

prime time *n* **:** the evening period generally from 7 to 11 p.m. during which television has its largest number of viewers — **prime–time** \ˈ=ˌ=\ *adj*

pri·mi·done \ˈprīməˌdōn\ *n* -s [alter. of *pyrimid*inedi*one* (chemical name)] **:** an anticonvulsant phenobarbital derivative $C_{12}H_{14}N_2O_2$ used esp. to control epileptic seizures

principal diagonal *n* **:** the diagonal in a square matrix that runs from upper left to lower right

principial* *adj* **:** of, relating to, or based on principle

print out *vt* [²*print* + ¹*out*] **:** to make a printout of

printout \ˈ=ˌ=\ *n* -s [*print out,* v. (herein)] **:** a printed record produced automatically (as by a computer)

printwheel \ˈ=ˌ=\ *n* **:** DAISY WHEEL *herein*

pri·or·i·tize \ˌprīˈȯrəˌtīz, ˈprīər-\ *vt* -ED/-ING/-S [*priority* + *-ize*] **:** to list or rate (as projects or goals) in order of priority — **pri·or·i·ti·za·tion** \ˌ=ˈ==tiˈzāshən, ˈ===ti-\ *n* -s

pri·va·tism \ˈprīvəˌtizəm\ *n* -s [¹*private* + *-ism*] **:** the attitude of being uncommitted to or avoiding involvement in anything beyond one's immediate interests — **pri·va·tis·tic** \ˌ==ˈtistik\ *adj*

pro·abortion \(ˌ)prō +\ *adj* **:** favoring the legalization of abortion — **pro·abortionist** \"+\ *n*

pro·active \(ˈ)prō +\ *adj* [L *pro-* forward (fr. *pro* before, for) + E *active* — more at FOR] **1 :** relating to, caused by, or being interference between previous learning and the recall or performance of later learning ⟨~ inhibition of memory⟩ **2 :** acting in anticipation of future problems or needs ⟨a ~ company⟩

probability density *n* **:** PROBABILITY DENSITY FUNCTION; *also* **:** a particular value of a probability density function

probability distribution *n* **:** PROBABILITY FUNCTION; *also* **:** PROBABILITY DENSITY FUNCTION 2

probe* *n* **:** a device (as an ultrasound generator) or a substance (as DNA in genetic research) used to obtain specific information for diagnostic or experimental purposes

pro·ben·e·cid \prōˈbenəsəd\ *n* -s [*pro*pyl + *ben*zoic + connective *-e-* + a*cid*] **:** a drug $C_{13}H_{19}NO_4S$ that acts on renal tubular function and is used to increase the concentration of some drugs (as penicillin) in the blood by inhibiting their excretion and to increase the excretion of urates in gout

prob·lem·at·ic \ˌpräbləˈmad·ik\ *n* -s [*problematic,* adj.] **:** something that is problematic **:** a problematic aspect or concern ⟨~*s* of womanhood, of men and women together —Stephen Koch⟩

pro bono \ˌprōˈbōnō\ *adj* [L *pro bono publico* for the public good] **:** donated esp. for the public good ⟨*pro bono* legal work⟩

pro·busing \ˈprō+ˈ\ *adj* [²*pro-* + *busing* (herein)] **:** favoring busing as a means of establishing racial balance in the schools

pro·car·ba·zine \prōˈkärbəˌzēn, -ȧb-, -əˌzən\ *n* -s [²*pro-* + *carb-* + *azine*] **:** an antineoplastic drug $C_{12}H_{19}N_3O$ that is a monoamine oxidase inhibitor used as the hydrochloride esp. in the palliative treatment of Hodgkin's disease

pro·ce·dur·al \prəˈsējərəl\ *n* -s [*procedural,* adj.] **:** POLICE PROCEDURAL *herein*

procedure* *n* **:** a series of instructions that has a name by which it can be called into action and that is usu. part of a computer program

pro·cess·ible *or* **pro·cess·able** \ˈpräˌsesəbəl, ˈprō-, -ˌsəs-\ *adj* **:** suitable for processing **:** capable of being processed — **pro·cess·ibil·i·ty** *or* **pro·cess·abil·i·ty** \ˌ=(ˌ)=əˈbiləd·ē, -ətē\ *n*

processor* *n* **1 a :** COMPUTER **b :** the part of a computer system that operates on data — called also *central processing unit* **2 :** a computer program (as a compiler) that puts another program into a form acceptable to the computer

pro–choice \ˌ=ˈ=\ *adj* **:** PROABORTION *herein* — **pro–choic·er** \ˌprōˈchȯisər\ *n* -s

pro·coagulant \ˌprō+\ *adj* [¹*pro-* + *coagulant*] **:** promoting the coagulation of blood ⟨~ activity⟩ — **procoagulant** *n*

producer* *n* **:** any of various organisms (as a green plant) which produce their own organic compounds from simple precursors (as carbon dioxide and inorganic nitrogen) and many of which are food sources for other organisms — compare CONSUMER *herein*

productivity* *n* **:** rate of production esp. of food by the utilization of solar energy by producer organisms

professional corporation *n* **:** a corporation organized by one or more licensed individuals (as a doctor, lawyer, dentist, or physical therapist) esp. for the purpose of providing professional services and obtaining tax advantages

profile* *n* **:** degree or level of public exposure ⟨trying to keep a low ~⟩ ⟨a job with a high ~⟩

pro·ges·to·gen *also* **pro·ges·ta·gen** \prōˈjestəjən, -ˌjen\ *n* -s [*progest*ational + *-ogen* (as in *estrogen*) or *-agen* (by alter.)] **:** any of several progestational steroids (as progesterone) — **pro·ges·to·gen·ic** \prōˌjestəˈjenik, -ēk\ *adj*

pro·grade \ˈprōˌgrād\ *adj* [L *pro-* forward + E *-grade* (as in *retrograde*)] **:** having or being a direction of rotation or revolution that is counterclockwise as viewed from the north pole of the sky or a planet

program* *n* **:** a sequence of coded instructions that is part of an organism ⟨the animal does have a ~ of reactions to stimuli arising in its external and internal worlds —W. G. Van der Kloot⟩

program* *vt* **1 :** to code in an organism's program ⟨the death of cells and the destruction of tissues, organs, and organ systems are *programmed* as normal morphogenetic events in the development of multicellular organisms —J. W. Saunders, Jr.⟩ **2 :** to provide with a biological program ⟨cells *programmed* to synthesize hemoglobin⟩ **3 :** to direct or predetermine as if by computer programming; *esp* **:** to direct or predetermine the thinking or behavior of ⟨those who . . . *programmed* him to kill —Jim Hougan⟩ ⟨children are *programmed* into violence —Lisa A. Richette⟩

¹pro·gram·ma·ble *also* **pro·gram·able** \ˌprōˌgraməbəl\ *adj* [²*program* + *-able*] **:** capable of being programmed ⟨a ~ calculator⟩ — **pro·gram·ma·bil·i·ty** \ˌ=ˌ==ˈbiləd·ē\ *n* -ES

[2]**programmable** \"\ *n* -s **:** a programmable calculator
programmed instruction *n* **:** instruction through information given in small steps with each requiring a correct response by the learner before going on to the next step
programmer* *or* **pro·gram·er** *n* **:** one that prepares an instructional program
programming* *or* **programing*** *n* **1 :** the process of instructing or learning by means of an instructional program **2 :** the process of preparing an instructional program
progressive rock *n* **:** rock music characterized by relatively complex phrasings and improvisations and intended for a sophisticated audience
pro·insulin \(ˈ)prō+\ *n* [[1]*pro-* + *insulin*] **:** a single-chain pancreatic polypeptide precursor of insulin that gives rise to the double chain of insulin by loss of the middle part of the molecule
projection* *n* **:** the process or technique of reproducing a spatial object upon a plane or curved surface or a line by projecting its points; *also* **:** a graph or figure so formed
pro·kary·ote *also* **pro·cary·ote** \(ˈ)prōˈkarē,ōt\ *n* -s [*pro-* + *kary-* + *-ote* (as in *zygote*)] **:** a cellular organism (as a bacterium or a blue-green alga) that does not have a distinct nucleus — compare EUCARYOTE *in the Dict* — **pro·kary·otic** *also* **pro·cary·otic** \(ˌ)≐ˌ≐ˈäd·ik\ *adj*
pro–life \ˈprōˈlīf\ *adj* [[2]*pro-* + *life*] **:** ANTIABORTION *herein* — **pro–lif·er** \ˈ≐ˈ≐ə(r)\ *n*
[1]**pro·mo** \ˈprō(ˌ)mō\ *adj* [by shortening] **:** PROMOTIONAL ⟨~ leaflets⟩
[2]**promo** \"\ *n* -s **:** a promotional announcement, film, recording, blurb, or appearance
promotor* *n* **:** the region of a genetic operon where transcription is initiated by binding with an appropriate polymerase
pro·nase \ˈprō,nās, -āz\ *n* -s [perh. fr. *protein* + *-ase*] **:** a protease from an actinomycete of the genus *Streptomyces* (*S. griseus*)
pro·neth·a·lol \prōˈnethə,lȯl, -ōl\ *n* -s [*pro*pyl + ami*ne* + *meth*yl + naphth*a*lene + methan*ol*] **:** a drug $C_{15}H_{19}NO$ that is a beta-adrenergic blocking agent
pro·nom·i·nal·iza·tion \prō,nämənələˈzāshən, prə,-\ *n* -s [*pronominal* + *-ization*] **:** the process or fact of using a pronoun instead of another sentence constituent (as a noun or noun phrase) — **pro·nom·i·nal·ize** \prōˈnämənə,līz, prəˈ-\ *vb* -ED/-ING/-S
pro·nuclear \(ˈ)prō+\ *adj* [[2]*pro-* + *nuclear*] **:** advocating the use of nuclear-powered generating stations
proof* *vt* **:** to activate (yeast) by mixing with water and sometimes sugar or milk
pro·pa·nil \ˈprōpə,nil\ *n* -s [*prop-* + *anil*ide] **:** an herbicide $C_9H_9Cl_2NO$ used esp. to control weeds in rice fields
prophase* *n* **:** the initial stage of meiosis in which the chromosomes become visible, homologous pairs of chromosomes undergo synapsis and become shortened and thickened, individual chromosomes become visibly double as paired chromatids, chiasmata occur, and the nuclear membrane disappears — compare DIAKINESIS *in the Dict,* DIPLOTENE *in the Dict,* LEPTOTENE *in the Dict,* PACHYTENE *in the Dict,* ZYGOTENE *in the Dict*
pro·pio·phe·none \ˌprōpēōˈfē,nōn, -ˈfen,ōn\ *n* -s [ISV *propio-* + *phen*yl + *-one*] **:** a flowery-smelling compound $C_9H_{10}O$ used in perfumes and in the synthesis of pharmaceuticals (as ephedrine) and organic compounds
pro·poxy·phene \prōˈpäksə̇,fēn\ *n* -s [*propi-* + *oxy-* + *phene* (alter. of *phenyl*)] **:** an analgesic $C_{22}H_{29}NO_2$ structurally related to methadone but less addicting that is administered in the form of its hydrochloride — called also *dextropropoxyphene*
pro·pran·o·lol \prōˈpranə,lȯl, -,lōl\ *n* -s [prob. alter. of earlier *propanolol,* fr. *propanol* + *-ol*] **:** a beta-blocker $C_{16}H_{21}NO_2$ used in the form of its hydrochloride in the treatment of abnormal heart rhythms and angina pectoris
pros·e·cu·to·ri·al \ˌpräsəkyüˈtōrēəl, -ˈtȯr-\ *adj* [*prosecutory* + *-al*] **:** of, relating to, or being a prosecutor or prosecution
pross \ˈpräs\ *also* **pros·sie** \ˈpräsē, -si\ *or* **pros·tie** *or* **pros·ty** \ˈprästē, -ti\ *n, pl* **prosses** *also* **prossies** *or* **prosties** [by shortening & alter.] *slang* **:** PROSTITUTE
pros·ta·glan·din \ˌprästəˈglandə̇n\ *n* -s [ISV *prosta*te *gland* + *-in;* fr. its occurrence in the sexual glands of mammals] **:** any of various oxygenated unsaturated cyclic fatty acids of animals that may perform a variety of hormonelike actions (as in controlling blood pressure or smooth muscle contraction)
pro·tein·oid \ˈprō,tē,nȯid, ˈprōtᵊn,ȯid, ˈprōd·ēə,nȯid\ *n* -s [*protein* + [1]*-oid*] **:** any of various polypeptides which can be obtained by suitable polymerization of mixtures of amino acids and some of which may represent an early stage in the evolution of proteins
proteo·glycan \ˌprōd·ēō +\ *n* [ISV *prote-* + *glycan*] **:** any of a class of glycoproteins of high molecular weight that are found in the extracellular matrix of connective tissue, are made up mostly of carbohydrate consisting of various polysaccharide side chains linked to a protein, and resemble polysaccharides rather than proteins in their properties
protestant ethic *n, usu cap P* **:** an ethic that stresses the virtue of hard work, thrift, and self-discipline
pro·the·tel·ic \ˌprōthəˈtelik\ *adj* [*prothetely* + [1]*-ic*] **:** of, relating to, or characterized by prothetely ⟨a ~ larva⟩
prothoracic gland *n* **:** one of a pair of thoracic endocrine organs in some insects that control molting
protocol* *n* **:** a set of conventions governing the treatment and esp. the formatting of data in an electronic communications system
pro·to–oncogene \ˌprōd·ō +\ *n* [*prot-* + *oncogene*] **:** a gene having the potential for change into an active oncogene
pro·to·porcelain \ˌprōd·(ˌ)ō +\ *n* [*prot-* + *porcelain;* prob. trans. of G *urporzellan*] **:** a porcelaneous ware lacking some of the qualities of a true porcelain; *specif* **:** a hard-fired gray kaolinic Chinese stoneware known since Han times
protract* *vt* **:** to extend forward or outward ⟨the mandible is *~ed* and retracted in chewing⟩
pro·vi·ral \ˌprōˌvīrəl\ *adj* [*provir*us + [1]*-al*] **:** of, relating to, or being a provirus ⟨~ DNA⟩
pro·vo \ˈprō(ˌ)vō\ *n* -s *usu cap* [by shortening & alter. fr. *provisional* (wing), name of the faction] **:** a member of the extremist faction of the Irish Republican Army
prox·e·mics \präkˈsēmiks\ *n pl but sing in constr* [*proximity* + *-emics* (as in *phonemics*)] **:** the study of the nature, degree, and effect of the spatial separation individuals naturally maintain (as in various social and interpersonal situations) and of how this separation relates to environmental and cultural factors
proximal* *adj* **:** of, relating to, or being the mesial and distal surfaces of a tooth — **prox·i·mal·ly*** \-mə-lē\ *adv*
pseud \ˈsüd\ *n* -s [short for *pseudo-intellectual*] *Brit* **:** a person who is affectedly intellectual

pseu·do·cholinesterase \ˈsüdō +\ *n* [*pseud-* + *cholinesterase*] **:** CHOLINESTERASE

pseudo–event \ˈsüdō +\ *n* [*pseud-* + *event*] **:** an event (as a press conference) that is designed primarily to attract attention

pseu·do·random \"+\ *adj* [*pseud-* + *random*] **:** being or involving entities (as numbers) that are selected by a definite computational process (as one involving a computer) but that satisfy one or more standard tests for statistical randomness

pseu·do·uridine \"+\ *n* [ISV *pseud-* + *uridine*] **:** a nucleoside $C_9H_{12}O_6N_2$ that is a uracil derivative incorporated as a structural component into transfer RNA

psi* *or* **psi particle** *n* **:** J/PSI PARTICLE *herein*

psi·lo·cin \ˈsīləsən\ *n* -s [NL *Psilocybe mexicana,* fungus from which it is obtained + E *-in*] **:** a hallucinogenic tertiary amine $C_{12}H_{16}N_2O$ obtained from a fungus *(Psilocybe mexicana)*

psi·lo·cy·bin \ˌsīləˈsībən\ *n* -s [NL *Psilocybe mexicana,* fungus from which it is obtained + E *-in*] **:** a hallucinogenic indole $C_{12}H_{17}N_2O_4P$ obtained from a fungus *(Psilocybe mexicana)*

psi·lo·phyt·ic \ˌsīləˈfid·ik\ *adj* [*psilophyte* + [1]*-ic*] **:** of, relating to, or being plants of the order Psilophytales

pso·ra·len \ˈsōrələn, ˈsȯr-\ *n* -s [modif. of *psorlea*] **:** a substance $C_{11}H_6O_3$ found in some plants that photosensitizes mammalian skin and has been used in treating psoriasis; *also* **:** any of various derivatives of psoralen having similar properties

psych* *also* **psyche** \ˈsīk\ *vt* -ED/-ING/-S **1 :** to make (oneself) psychologically ready for performance — usu. used with *up* ⟨~*ed* himself up for the race⟩ **2 :** to make psychologically uneasy **:** INTIMIDATE, SCARE ⟨pressure doesn't ~ me —Jerry Quarry⟩ — often used with *out*

psych *also* **psyche** \"\ *n* -s **:** the state of being psyched up ⟨spoiled his ~ for the race —Patricia N. Warren⟩; *also* **:** PSYCH-OUT *herein*

psy·che·de·lia \ˌsīkəˈdēlyə\ *n* [NL, fr. E *psychedelic* (herein) + L *-ia* -y] **:** the world of people, phenomena, or items associated with psychedelic drugs

[1]**psy·che·del·ic** \ˌsīkəˌdelik *also* -dēl-\ *n* -s **1 :** a psychedelic drug (as LSD) **2 a :** a user or an advocate of psychedelic drugs **b :** a person with psychedelic social and cultural interests and orientation

[2]**psychedelic** *adj* [Gk *psychē* soul + *dēloun* to show, reveal (fr. *dēlos* evident) + E *-ic* — more at PSYCHE, ADEL-] **1 a :** of, relating to, or being drugs (as LSD) capable of producing abnormal psychic effects (as hallucinations) and sometimes psychic states resembling mental illness **b :** produced by or associated with the use of psychedelic drugs ⟨a ~ experience⟩ **2 a :** imitating, suggesting, or reproducing the effects (as distorted or bizarre images or sounds) of psychedelic drugs ⟨~ art⟩ **b** (1) **:** very bright in color ⟨ferryboats soon will take on a ~ look, with an overall coat of international orange and touches of red and yellow —*N. Y. Times*⟩ (2) *of colors* **:** FLUORESCENT **3 :** of or relating to the culture associated with psychedelic drugs ⟨a year ago we couldn't even begin to sell '60s ~ stuff —Paul Glynn⟩ — **psy·che·del·i·cal·ly** \-lək(ə)lē\ *adv*

psychic energizer *n* **:** ANTIDEPRESSANT *herein*

psy·cho·active \ˌsīkō +\ *adj* [*psych-* + *active*] **:** affecting the mind or behavior ⟨~ drugs⟩

psy·cho·babble \ˈsīkōˌbabəl\ *n* [*psych-* + *babble*] **:** a predominantly metaphorical language for expressing one's feelings that resembles the hippie argot of the 1960s and is held to be prevalent esp. in California

psy·cho·biography \ˌsī(ˌ)kō +\ *n* [*psych-* + *biography*] **:** a character analysis **:** PSYCHOGRAPH 4 — **psy·cho·bi·ographer** \"+\ *n* — **psy·cho·biographical** \"+\ *adj*

psy·cho·chemical \ˌsīkō +\ *n* [*psych-* + *chemical*] **:** a psychoactive chemical — **psychochemical** *adj*

psy·cho·history \"+\ *n* [*psych-* + *history*] **:** an analysis of an historical person or issue by psychoanalytic methods — **psy·cho·historian** \"+\ *n* — **psy·cho·his·torical** \"+\ *adj*

psy·cho·pharmaceutical \ˌsīkō +\ *n* [*psych-* + *pharmaceutical*] **:** a drug having an effect on the mental state of a person

psy·cho·pharmacologist \"+\ *n* [*psych-* + *pharmacologist*] **:** a specialist in psychopharmacology

psy·cho·quack \ˈsīkō +ˌ\ *n* [*psych-* + [3]*quack*] **:** an unqualified psychologist or psychiatrist — **psy·cho·quackery** \ˌsīkō +\ *n*

psy·cho·surgeon \ˌsīkō +\ *n* [*psych-* + *surgeon*] **:** a surgeon specializing in psychosurgery

psy·chot·o·gen \sīˈkäd·əjən\ *n* -s [*psychotic* + *-o-* + *-gen*] **:** a chemical agent (as a drug) that induces a psychotic state — **psy·choto·gen·ic** \(ˌ)sīˌkäd·əˌjenik\ *adj*

psy·choto·mimetic \sīˌkäd·ō +\ *adj* [*psychotic* + *-o-* + *mimetic*] **:** of, relating to, or involving psychotic alteration of behavior and personality ⟨~ drugs⟩ — **psychotomimetic** *n* -s — **psychoto·mimetically** \"+\ *adv*

psy·cho·toxic \ˌsīkə +\ *adj* [*psych-* + *toxic*] **:** of, relating to, or being an habituating drug (as amphetamine) which is not a true narcotic but the abuse of which may be correlated with deleterious personality and behavioral changes

psych–out \ˈ=ˌ=\ *n* -s [fr. the verb phrase *psych out,* fr. *psych* (herein)] **:** an act or an instance of psyching out ⟨in a *psych-out* you always make a show of confidence, while you work to undermine the confidence of your competition —Don Schollander & Duke Savage⟩

PTO* *abbr* **1** parent-teacher organization **2** power take-off

PTV *abbr* public television *herein*

public access *n* **:** the provision of access by the public to television broadcasting facilities (as a cable TV channel) for the presentation of programs

public television *n* **:** television that provides cultural, informational, and instructional programs for the public and that does not promote the sale of a product or service but does identify the donors of program funds **:** noncommercial television

puff* *n* **:** an enlarged region of a chromosome that is associated with intensely active genes involved in RNA synthesis

pu·gil stick \ˈpyüjəl-\ *n* [*pugilism*] **:** a heavy pole with padded ends used in training in the armed services to simulate bayonet fighting

puka* *n* **:** a small white perforated shell found along beaches esp. in Hawaii and used to make necklaces

pu·la \ˈp(y)ülə\ *n, pl* **pula** [native name in Botswana] **1 :** the basic monetary unit of Botswana — see MONEY table *in the Dict* **2 :** a coin or note representing one pula

pull* *vi* **1** *of an offensive lineman in football* **:** to move back from the line of scrimmage toward one flank to provide blocking for a ballcarrier **2 :** to work together to achieve a goal ⟨~*ing* with them to get the bill passed⟩ —

pull one's coat *slang* **:** to provide information — **pull out all the stops :** to use all one's resources without restraint — **pull the rug from under** *or* **pull the rug out from under :** to remove support or assistance from

pull date *n* **:** a date stamped on perishable products (as baked goods or dairy products) after which they should not be sold

pullman* *n, often cap* **:** a large suitcase

pullman* *adj, sometimes cap* **:** being long and square-shaped ⟨a ~ loaf of bread⟩

pul·sar \'pəl,sär\ *n* -s [*pulse* + *-ar* (as in *quasar* — herein)] **:** a celestial source of pulsating electromagnetic radiation (as radio waves) marked by a short relatively constant interval (as .033 second) between pulses that is held to be a rotating neutron star

pulse* *n* **:** a dose of a substance esp. when applied over a short period of time ⟨~*s* of colchicine applied to the cells⟩

pump* *n* **1 :** electromagnetic radiation for pumping atoms or molecules **2 :** the process of pumping atoms or molecules **3 :** a mechanism (as the sodium pump) for pumping atoms, ions, or molecules

pump* *vt* **1 :** to transport (as ions) against a concentration gradient by the expenditure of energy **2 a :** to raise (atoms or molecules) to a higher energy level by exposure to usu. electromagnetic radiation at one of the resonant frequencies so that reemission may occur at another frequency resulting in amplification or sustained oscillation **b :** to expose (as a laser, semiconductor, or crystal) to radiation in the process of pumping — **pump iron :** to lift weights esp. for exercise or bodybuilding

pumped storage *n* **:** a hydroelectric system in which electricity is generated during periods of greatest consumption by the use of water that has been pumped into a reservoir at a higher altitude during periods of low consumption

punch out *vt* **:** to beat up

punch–out \'=,=\ *n* -s [*punch out* (herein)] **:** FISTFIGHT

punctuated equilibrium *n* **1 :** a lineage of evolutionary descent characterized by long periods of stability in characteristics of the organism and short periods of rapid change during which new forms appear esp. from small subpopulations of the ancestral form in restricted parts of its geographic range **2** *or* **punctuated equilibrium theory :** a theory or model of evolution emphasizing punctuated equilibria

pun·ji \'pənjē\ *n* -s *often attrib* [Vietnamese] **:** a sharpened stick usu. of bamboo set in the grouond esp. in Vietnam as an antipersonnel weapon ⟨~ stick⟩ ⟨~ trap⟩

punk* *n* **1 :** PUNK ROCK *herein* **2 :** a punk rock musician **3 :** one who affects punk styles — **punky** \'pəŋkē\ *adj* -ER/-EST

punk* *adj* **1 :** of or relating to punk rock **2 :** relating to or being the styles (as of dress or hair) inspired by punk rock

punk rock *n* **:** a form of new-wave rock music characterized by extreme and often deliberately offensive expressions of alienation and social discontent — **punk rocker** *n*

puppy dog *n* **:** a domestic dog; *esp* **:** one having the lovable attributes of a puppy

purse crab* *n* **:** any of the family Leucosiidae of crabs characterized by a granular carapace and long claws and by an adult female having the abdomen formed into a hemispherical cup that snaps shut against the sternum to form a brood chamber for the eggs; *esp* **:** one (*Persephona mediterranea*) that occurs in shallow water along the Atlantic coast of Mexico and of the U.S. as far north as New Jersey

pushdown \'=,=\ *n* -s [fr. the verb phrase *push down*] **:** a store of data (as in a computer) from which the item stored last must be the first retrieved — called also *pushdown list, pushdown stack*

pushout \'=,=\ *n* -s [[1]*push* + *out*] **:** one who is dismissed (as from a school or job)

pussycat* *n* **:** one that is weak, compliant, or amiable **:** SOFTY

put* *vb* — **put the make on :** to make sexual advances toward — **put the screws on** *also* **put the screws to :** to exert extreme pressure on ⟨*put the screws on* the small farmers to sell out⟩

put down* *vt* **1 a :** BELITTLE, DISPARAGE ⟨many writers want to *put down* not only their interviewers but their critics —Melvin Maddocks⟩ **b :** DISAPPROVE, CRITICIZE ⟨*put down* for the way he dressed⟩ **2 :** DEFLATE, SQUELCH ⟨a legendary step-parent: rigid, oppressive, untrue, ever ready to *put down* the honest feeling and sound thought that arise within the individual —R.B. Heilman⟩

put–down \'=,=\ *n* -s [*put down* (herein)] **:** an act or instance of putting down; *esp* **:** a deflating remark

put–on* *n* **:** an instance of putting someone on ⟨the question might be serious or just a *put-on*⟩; *also* **:** PARODY, SPOOF ⟨a kind of *put-on* of every pretentious film ever made —C.A. Ridley⟩

putz \'pəts\ *n* -ES [Yiddish; perh. akin to G *putz* plaster, adornment] **1** *slang* **:** PENIS **2** *slang* **:** a stupid, foolish, or ineffectual person **:** JERK

py·re·throid \pī'rē,thrȯid, -'re,-\ *n* -s [*pyrethr*in + [1]*-oid*] **:** any of various synthetic compounds related to and resembling in insecticidal properties the pyrethrins — **pyrethroid** *adj*

py·ri·meth·amine \,pirə'methə,mēn, ,pīr-\ *n* [*pyrim*idine + *eth*yl + *amine*] **:** a folic acid antagonist $C_{12}H_{13}ClN_4$ used in the treatment of malaria and of toxoplasmosis

Q

qi·vi·ut \ˈkēvēət, -vē,üt\ *n* -s [Esk] : the wool of the undercoat of the musk-ox

QSO \,kyü(,)eˈsō\ *n* -s [*q*uasi-*s*tellar *o*bject (herein)] : QUASI-STELLAR OBJECT *herein*

Quaa·lude \ˈkwā,lüd\ *trademark* — used for methaqualone

[1]**quad** \ˈkwäd\ *n* -s [by shortening] : QUADRAPHONICS *herein*

[2]**quad** \"\ *adj* [by shortening] : QUADRAPHONIC *herein*

[3]**quad** \"\ *n* -s [short for *quadrillion*] : a unit of energy equal to one quadrillion British thermal units

qua·dran·tid \kwäˈdrantəd\ *n* -s *usu cap* [NL *Quadrant-, Quadrans (Muralis)* mural quadrant, a group of stars in the constellation Draco from which the shower appears to radiate + E [1]*-id*] : any of the meteors in a meteor shower that occurs each year about January 3

quad·ra·phon·ic *also* **quad·ri·phon·ic** \,kwädrəˈfänik\ *adj* [*quadra-* (alter. of *quadri-*) + *phonic*] : of, relating to, or using four channels for the transmission, recording, or reproduction of sound

quad·ra·phon·ics *or* **quad·ri·phon·ics** \-niks\ *n pl but sing or pl in constr* [*quadraphonic* (herein) + *-s*] : quadraphonic sound

quadratic form *n* : a homogeneous polynomial of the second degree ⟨$x^2 + 5xy + y^2$ is a *quadratic form*⟩

quality circle *n* : a group of employees who volunteer to meet regularly to discuss and propose solutions to problems (as of quality or productivity) in the workplace

quality point average *n* : GRADE POINT AVERAGE *herein*

quan·go \ˈkwaŋ,gō\ *n* -s [*qua*si *n*on*g*overnmental *o*rganization] *chiefly Brit* : a partly autonomous regulatory agency; *esp* : one in Britain organized outside the civil service but financed and appointed by the government

quan·ta·some \ˈkwäntə,sōm\ *n* -s [prob. fr. *quanta,* pl. of *quantum* + [3]*-some*] : one of the chlorophyll-containing spheroids found in the grana of chloroplasts

quantifier* *n* : one that quantifies; *esp* : a person who quantifies data, an activity, or a field of study (as history)

quantum chromodynamics *n pl but sing in constr* : a theory of fundamental particles based on the assumption that quarks are distinguished by differences in color and are held together (as in hadrons) by an exchange of gluons

quantum electronics *n pl but sing in constr* : a branch of physics that deals with the interaction of radiation with discrete energy levels in substances (as in a maser or laser)

quantum jump* *or* **quantum leap** *n* : an abrupt and usu. significant change or increase

quark \ˈkwärk, -wȯr-\ *n* -s [coined by Murray Gell-Mann *b*1929 Am. physicist] : any of several elementary particles that are postulated to come in pairs (as of the up and down varieties) of similar mass with one member having a charge of $+2/3$ and the other a charge of $-1/3$ and are held to make up hadrons

quartz heater *n* : a portable electric radiant heater that has heating elements sealed in quartz-glass tubes in front of a reflective backing

quartz–iodine lamp \ˈ=ˈ===-\ *n* : an incandescent lamp that has a quartz bulb and a tungsten filament and that contains iodine which reacts with the vaporized tungsten to prevent excessive blackening of the bulb

qua·sar \ˈkwā,zär *also* -,sär\ *n* -s [*quas*i-stell*ar* radio source (herein)] : any of various celestial objects that resemble stars but are apparently far more distant and emit copious quantities of radiation usu. as bright blue and ultraviolet light and powerful radio waves

quasiparticle \ˈ=(,)=ˈ===\ *n* [[2]*quasi* + *particle*] : a composite entity (as a vibration in a solid) that is analogous in its behavior to a single particle

quasi–stellar object \ˈ=(,)=,==-\ *n* : QUASAR *herein*

quasi–stellar radio source \ˈ=(,)=ˈ==-\ *n* [*quasi-stellar* fr. [1]*quasi* + *stellar*] : QUASAR *herein*

quas·qui·centennial \ˈkwäskwē, -kwə +\ *n* [fr. L *quadrans* quarter, after L *semis* half: E *sesquicentennial* — more at QUADRANT, SESQUI-] : a 125th anniversary — **quasquicentennial** *adj*

queenside \ˈ=,=\ *n* : the side of the chessboard containing the file on which both queens sit at the beginning of the game

queen–size \ˈ=,=\ *adj* **1** : having dimensions of approximately 60 inches by 80 inches — used of a bed **2** : of a size that fits a queen-size bed ⟨a *queen-size* bedspread⟩

queen substance *n* : a pheromone secreted by queen bees and consumed by worker bees inhibiting the development of their ovaries; *also* : the same or a similar substance secreted by termites

queue* *n* : a sequence of messages or jobs held in auxiliary storage awaiting transmission or processing

queue* *vt* : to send to or place in a queue

queuing theory *n* : the mathematical and statistical theory of queues and waiting lines (as in heavy traffic or in the use of telephone circuits)

quiche lor·raine \-ləˈrān, -lȯ-, -lōˈ-\ *n, often cap L* [after *Lorraine,* region of western Europe] : a quiche containing cheese and crisp bacon bits

quick and dirty *adj* : expedient and effective but not without flaws or unwanted side effects ⟨a *quick and dirty* solution to the problem⟩

quick fix *n* : an expedient often inadequate solution to a problem

quick kick *n* : a punt in football made on first, second, or third down from a running or passing formation and designed to take the opposing team by surprise

quick opener *n* : an offensive play in football in which a back takes a direct handoff and runs straight to a hole in the line

qui·nu·cli·di·nyl ben·zi·late \kwəˈn(y)ükləˈdēnᵊl-ˈbenzə,lāt\ *n* -s [*quinuclidine* + *-yl* + *benzil* + *-ate*] : BZ *herein*

quotient group *n* : a group whose elements are the cosets of a normal subgroup of a given group — called also *factor group*

quotient ring *n* : a ring whose elements are the cosets of an ideal in a given ring

QWER·TY *or* **QWERTY keyboard** \ˈkwərd·ē-\ *n, often not cap* [fr. the first six letters in the second row of the keyboard] : a standard typewriter keyboard

R

r *adj, cap* [restricted] *of a motion picture* **:** of such a nature that admission is restricted to persons over a specified age (as 17) or to younger persons who are accompanied by a parent or guardian — compare G *herein,* PG *herein,* PG-13 *herein,* X *herein*

r* *abbr* **1** repeat **2** rerun

rabbit* *n* **:** a runner in a long-distance race who sets a fast pace in the first part of the race

rab·bit \ˈrabət, *usu* -əd·+V\ *vi* -ED/-ING/-S [fr. *rabbit-and-pork,* rhyming slang for *talk*] *Brit* **:** to talk idly or incessantly — often used with *on* ⟨look at the way we go ~*ing* on about our wonderful system of justice —*The People*⟩

rabbit ears *n pl* **:** an indoor dipole television antenna consisting of two usu. extensible rods connected to a base to form a V shape

race walking *n* **:** racing at a fast walk in track-and-field competition with each competitor required to maintain continuous foot contact with the ground and to keep the supporting leg straight — **race walker** *n*

rack car* *n* **:** a railroad flatcar equipped with a 2-level or 3-level framework for transporting motor vehicles

rac·lette \raˈklet\ *n* -S [F, lit., scraper, fr. F *racler* to scrape — more at RASE] **:** a dish of Swiss origin consisting of melted cheese traditionally served with tiny boiled potatoes and sour pickles; *also* **:** a firm cheese suitable for use in this dish

racquetball \ˈ==,=\ *n* **:** a game similar to handball played on a 4-walled court with a short-handled racket and a ball larger than a handball

radar astronomy *n* **:** astronomy dealing with investigations of celestial bodies in the solar system by analyzing radar waves directed toward and reflected from the object being studied

radar telescope *n* **:** a radar transmitter-receiver with an antenna for use in radar astronomy

radial* *n* **:** RADIAL TIRE *herein*

radial ker·a·tot·o·my \-,kerəˈtäd·əmē\ *n* -ES [ISV *kerat-* + *-tomy*] **:** multiple incision of the cornea forming a series of slits in a radial pattern resembling the spokes of a wheel that is performed to correct myopia

radially symmetrical *adj* **:** of, relating to, or characterized by radial symmetry

radial tire *or* **radial–ply tire** *n* **:** a pneumatic tire in which the ply cords that extend to the beads are laid at right angles to the center line of the tread

radical chic *n* **:** the fashion among socially prominent people of hobnobbing with social inferiors who are usu. left-wing political activists; *broadly* **:** fashionable and usu. superficial left-wing radicalism — **radical–chic** \ˌ===ˈ=\ *adj*

ra·dic·chio \raˈdikēō\ *n* -S [It, lit., chicory] **:** a chicory of a red variety with variegated leaves that is used as a salad green

ra·di·esthesia \ˌrādē +\ *n* [NL, fr. L *radius* ray + NL *esthesia* — more at RAY] **1 :** sensitiveness held to enable a person with the aid of divining rod or pendulum to detect things (as the presence of underground water, the nature of an illness, or the guilt of a suspected person); *also* **:** DOWSING, DIVINING **2 :** a study that deals with radiesthesia

radiocarbon dating *n* **:** CARBON DATING *herein*

ra·dio·chromatogram \ˌrādē(,)ō+\ *n* [*radio-* + *chromatogram*] **:** a chromatogram revealing one or more radioactive substances

ra·dio·chromatography \"+\ *n* [*radio-* + *chromatography*] **:** the process of making a quantitative or qualitative determination of a radioisotope-labeled substance by measuring the radioactivity of the appropriate zone or spot in the chromatogram — **ra·dio·chromatographic** \"+\ *adj*

ra·dio·ecology \"+\ *n* [*radio-* + *ecology*] **:** the study of the effects of radiation and radioactive substances on ecological communities — **ra·dio·ecological** \"+\ *adj* — **ra·dio·ecologist** \"+\ *n*

radio galaxy *n* **:** a galaxy that is a strong source of radio waves

ra·dio·immunoassay \ˈrādē,ō +\ *n* [*radio-* + *immunoassay* (herein)] **:** immunoassay of a substance (as insulin) that has been radioactively labeled — **ra·dio·immunoassayable** \"+\ *adj*

ra·dio·immunological \"+\ *also* **ra·dio·immunologic** \"+\ *adj* [*radio-* + *immunological* or *immunologic*] **:** of, relating to, or involving radioimmunoassay ⟨~ detection of a hormone⟩

ra·dio·iodinated \"+\ *adj* [*radio-* + *iodinated,* past part. of *iodinate*] **:** treated or labeled with radioactive iodine — **ra·dio·io·dination** \"+\ *n*

ra·dio·isotopic \ˌrādē(,)ō +\ *adj* [*radioisotope* + *-ic*] **:** of, relating to, or being a radioisotope ⟨~ techniques⟩ — **ra·dio·isotopically** \"+\ *adv*

ra·dio·label \"+\ *vt* [*radio-* + *label*] **:** to label with a radioactive atom or substance

ra·dio·pharmaceutical \"+\ *n* [*radio-* + [2]*pharmaceutical*] **:** a radioactive drug used for diagnostic or therapeutic purposes — **radiopharmaceutical** *adj*

ra·dio·protective \"+\ *adj* [*radio-* + *protective*] **:** serving to protect or aiding in protecting against the injurious effect of radiations ⟨~ drugs⟩ — **ra·dio·protection** \"+\ *n*

ra·dio·protector \"+\ *also* **ra·dio·pro·tec·tor·ant** \ˌrādē(,)ōprəˌtekt(ə)rənt\ *n* [*radio-* + *protector* or *protectorant* (fr. *protector* + *-ant*)] **:** a radioprotective chemical agent

ra·dio·resistance \ˌrādē(,)ō+\ *n* [*radio-* + *resistance*] **:** resistance (as of a cell or organism) to the effects of radiant energy — **ra·dio·resistant** \"+\ *adj*

ra·dio·sensitizer \"+\ *n* [*radio-* + *sensitizer*] **:** a substance or condition capable of increasing the radiosensitivity of a cell or tissue — **ra·dio·sensitization** \"+\ *n* — **ra·dio·sensitizing** \"+\ *adj*

ra·dio·sterilized \"+\ *adj* [*radio-* + *sterilized*] **:** sterilized by irradiation (as with X rays or gamma rays) ⟨~ mosquitoes⟩ ⟨~ syringes⟩ — **ra·dio·sterilization** \"+\ *n*

ra·dio·telemetry \"+\ *n* [*radio-* + *telemetry* (herein)] **1 :** TELEMETRY 1 *herein* **2 :** BIOTELEMETRY *herein* — **ra·dio·telemetric** \"+\ *adj*

ra·dio–ulna \"+\ *n* [NL, fr. *radius* (fr. L) + *-o-* + *ulna*] **:** a single bone in the forelimb of an amphibian (as a frog) that represents fusion of the separate radius and ulna of higher forms

Rag·doll \'rag,däl, -,dȯl\ *trademark* — used for a breed of domestic cats

ragtop \'=,=\ *n* [¹*rag* + *top*] **:** a convertible automobile

rail* *n* **:** a specialized drag-racing vehicle with very large wide tires in the rear and tiny bicycle tires in the front and with a chassis that consists essentially of two long braced rails

rainbow* *or* **rainbow pill** *n, slang* **:** a drug in a tablet or capsule of several colors; *esp* **:** a combination of the sodium derivatives of amobarbital and secobarbital in a blue and red capsule

rain date *n* **:** an alternative date set aside for use if a scheduled outdoor event must be postponed because of rain

rainsuit \'=,=\ *n* [¹*rain* + *suit*] **:** a suit of waterproof material consisting of pants and a usu. hooded jacket for wear in the rain usu. over ordinary clothes

raised ranch *n* **:** BI-LEVEL *herein*

rallymaster \'==,==\ *n* [²*rally* + *master*] **:** one who organizes and conducts an automobile rally

ralph \'ralf, 'raůf\ *vb* -ED/-ING/-S [imit.] *slang* **:** VOMIT

RAM \'ram\ *abbr or n* -S random-access memory *herein*

rancher* *n* **:** RANCH HOUSE 2

ranch·ette \,ran'chet\ *n* -S [²*ranch* + *-ette*] **:** a small ranch

rand \'rand, *in So. Afr. usu* 'rȧnd *or* 'rȧnt *or* 'ränt\ *n, pl* **rand** *or* **rands** [fr. the *Rand* (*Witwatersrand*), gold= producing district in So. Africa] **1 a :** the basic monetary unit of the Republic of So. Africa established in 1961 — see MONEY table *in the Dict* **b :** the former basic monetary unit of Lesotho **2 :** a coin or note representing one rand

R and B *abbr or n* rhythm and blues *herein*

R and D *abbr or n* **:** research and development

random–access \',==',=,=\ *adj* **:** permitting access (as to stored information) in any order the user desires ⟨*random-access* capability of a videodisc player⟩

random–access memory *n* **:** a computer memory that provides the main internal storage available to the user for programs and data — called also *RAM*; compare READ-ONLY MEMORY

ran·dom·iz·er \'randə,mīzə(r)\ *n* -S [*randomize* + ²*-er*] **:** a device or procedure used for randomization

rank* *n* **1 :** the number of linearly independent rows in a matrix **2 :** FACE CORD

¹rap \'rap\ *n* -S [perh. by shortening & alter. fr. *repartee*] **1 :** TALK, CONVERSATION **2 a :** a rhythmic chanting often in unison of usu. rhymed couplets to a musical accompaniment **b :** a piece so performed

²rap \"\ *vi* **rapped; rapped; rapping; raps :** to talk freely and frankly ⟨at the corner bar *rapping* — *Newsweek*⟩ — **rap·per** *n* -S

rapid eye movement *n* **:** rapid conjugate movement of the eyes associated esp. with REM sleep

rapid eye movement sleep *n* **:** REM SLEEP *herein*

rap sheet *n* **:** a police arrest record esp. for an individual

rapture of the deep : NITROGEN NARCOSIS *herein*

ra·schel \(')rä'shel\ *n* -S **:** a fabric made by raschel knitting

ras·ta \'rastə\ *also* **ras·ta·man** \-mən, -,man\ *n, pl* **rastas** *also* **ras·ta·men** \-mən, -,men\ *usu cap* [*rasta* by shortening; *rastaman* fr. *rasta* + *man*] **:** RASTAFARIAN *herein*

ras·ta·fa·ri·an \,rastə'farēən, -'fer-\ *n* -S *usu cap* [*Ras Tafari*, name before coronation of Haile Selassie †1975 Ethiopian emperor + E *-an*] **:** an adherent of Rastafarianism

ras·ta·fa·ri·an·ism \-ə,nizəm\ *n* -S *cap* [*Rastafarian* (herein) + *-ism*] **:** a religious cult among black Jamaicans that teaches the eventual redemption of blacks and their return to Africa, employs the ritualistic use of marijuana, forbids the cutting of hair, and venerates Haile Selassie as a god

raster* *n* **:** a pattern for scanning an area from side to side in lines from top to bottom ⟨an electron beam in a cathode-ray tube scans the phosphor screen in a ~⟩

rate of change : a value that results from dividing the change of a function of a variable by the change in the variable ⟨velocity is the *rate of change* of distance with respect to time⟩

rat fink *n* **:** FINK *herein*

ratio *vt* -ED/-ING/-S [*ratio*, n.] **:** to compare esp. numerically or quantitatively with another value or set of values **:** express in a ratio

rational* *adj* **:** relating to, consisting of, or being one or more rational numbers

rat's ass *n* **:** a minimum amount or degree of care or interest **:** HOOT, DAMN — usu. used in the phrase *don't give a rat's ass;* often considered vulgar

raunch \'rȯnch, 'rän-\ *n* -ES [back-formation fr. *raunchy*] **:** VULGARITY, LEWDNESS

rave–up \'=,=\ *n* -S [¹*rave* + *up*] *Brit* **:** a wild party **:** BASH

raw bar *n* **:** a restaurant that features raw shellfish usu. served at a counter

ray·naud's phenomenon \(')rā¦nōz-\ *also* **raynaud's syndrome** *n, usu cap R* [Maurice *Raynaud* †1881 Fr. physician] **:** the symptoms associated with Raynaud's disease

RBE *abbr* relative biological effectiveness *herein*

read* *vt* **1 :** to sense the meaning of (information) in recorded and coded form (as in storage) **:** acquire (information) from storage — used of a computer or data processor **2 :** to read the coded information on (as tape or a punch card) **3 :** to cause to be read and transferred to storage ⟨~ the contents of a punch card into memory⟩

read* *n* **:** something that is read ⟨an old-fashioned good ~, bursting with characters and drama and emotion — Jane Clapperton⟩

read–only memory \',=',==-\ *n* **:** a usu. small computer memory containing special-purpose information that cannot be altered — called also *ROM*; compare RANDOM-ACCESS MEMORY *herein*

readout* *n* **1 :** the process of reading **2 a :** the process of removing information from an automatic device (as an electronic computer) and displaying it in an understandable form **b :** the information removed from such a device and displayed or recorded (as by magnetic tape or printing device) **c :** an electronic device that presents information in visual form **3 :** the radio transmission of data or pictures from a space vehicle either immediately upon acquisition or later by playback of a tape recording

readymade** *n* -S **:** an artifact (as a comb or a pair of ice tongs) selected and displayed as a work of art

re·aggregate \(')rē +\ *vb* [*re-* + *aggregate*] *vt* **:** to cause to re-form into an aggregate or whole ~ *vi* **:** to re-form into an aggregate or whole ⟨the cells *reaggregated* into organized tissue⟩ — **re·aggregate** \"+\ *n* — **re·ag·gregation** \"+\ *n*

real* *adj* **:** REAL-VALUED *herein* ⟨functions of a ~ variable⟩

real time *n* **:** the actual time during which something takes place ⟨here's how it looked in *real time* and in slow motion —J.W. Chancellor⟩ — **real–time** *adj*

real–valued \ˈ=ˌ==\ *adj* **:** taking on only real numbers for values

rear–end \ˌ=ˈ=\ *vt* **:** to crash into the back of (as an automobile)

re·branch \(ˈ)rē +\ *vi* [*re-* + *branch*] **:** to form secondary branches

recall* *n* **1 :** a public call by a manufacturer for the return of a product that may be defective or contaminated **2 :** the ability (as of an information retrieval system) to retrieve stored material

recamier** *n* [so called fr. its appearance in a well-known portrait of Mme. Récamier by Jacques-Louis David †1825 Fr. painter] **:** a usu. backless couch with a high curved headrest and low footrest

re·canalization \(ˌ)rē +\ *n* [*re-* + *canalization*] **:** the process of reuniting an interrupted channel of a bodily tube (as a vas deferens) — **re·canalize** \(ˈ)rē+\ *vt*

rechargeable \(ˈ)rēˌchärjəbəl, -āj-\ *adj* [*recharge* + *-able*] **:** capable of being recharged ⟨~ batteries⟩

re·charter \(ˈ)rē +\ *vt* [*re-* + *charter*] **:** to grant a new charter to ⟨~*ed* the national bank⟩ — **recharter** *n*

reciprocal* *n* **:** MULTIPLICATIVE INVERSE *herein*

re·cla·ma \rəˈklämə\ *vi* -ED/-ING/-S [perh. fr. L *reclamare* to contradict loudly] **:** to request the reconsideration of a decision or a change in policy — used esp. in the military

re·clos·able \(ˈ)rēˈklōzəbəl\ *adj* [*re-* + *close* + *-able*] **:** capable of being tightly closed again after opening

recombinant DNA *n* **:** DNA prepared in the laboratory by breaking up and splicing together DNA from several different species of organisms

reconciliation* *n* **:** the Roman Catholic sacrament of penance

record* *n* **:** a collection of related items of information (as in a data base) treated as a unit

recreational vehicle *n* **:** a vehicle (as a motor home or trailer) equipped for use in camping — called also *RV*

recursion* *n* **1 :** the determination of a succession of elements (as numbers or functions) by operation on one or more preceding elements according to a recursive definition — compare FIBONACCI NUMBER *herein* **2 :** the solution of a problem by means of a procedure that uses a copy of itself as one of its steps so that the problem is simplified with each execution of the procedure until a simplest case is reached for which the solution has been defined and the basic solution is applied to complete the solutions of the more complex versions — compare ITERATION 2 *herein*

re·cur·sive \rəˈkərsiv, rēˈ-, -ˈkəs-\ *adj* [²*recursion* + *-ive*] **1 :** of, relating to, or involving recursion **2 :** of, relating to, or being a procedure that can repeat itself indefinitely or until a specified condition is met ⟨a ~ rule in a grammar⟩ — **recursively** *adv* — **recursiveness** *n* -ES

re·cycle* *vt* **1 :** to process (as liquid body waste, glass, or cans) in order to regain material for human use **2 :** to adapt to a new use **:** ALTER, TRANSFORM ⟨~ recent real events into prime time entertainment —Karl Meyer⟩ **3 :** to bring back **:** REUSE, REPEAT ⟨a light, chatty tribute that ~*s* a number of good anecdotes —Larry McMurtry⟩ **4 :** to make ready for reuse **:** RESTORE ⟨the move to ~ unused gas stations —Robert Frausto⟩ **5 :** to reuse (money) by investing esp. in an area or enterprise that will allow the investment to return as new profits ⟨*recycle* petrodollars⟩ ~ *vi* **1 :** to stop the counting and return to an earlier point in a countdown **2 :** to return to an original condition so that operation can begin again — used of an electronic device — **re·cy·cla·ble** \(ˈ)rēˈsīk(ə)ləbəl\ *adj* — **re·cycler** \"+\ *n* -s

recycle* *n* **:** the process of recycling

red* *n* **reds** *pl, also* **red devils** *slang* **:** red drug capsules containing the sodium salt of secobarbital

redbrick \ˈ=ˌ=\ *adj, sometimes cap* [*red* + *brick*] **1 :** built of red brick **2 :** of, relating to, or being the British universities founded in modern times — compare OXBRIDGE *herein,* PLATEGLASS *herein*

re·describe \ˌrē +\ *vt* [*re-* + *describe*] **:** to describe anew or again; *esp* **:** to give a new and more complete description to (a biological taxon)

re·description \"+\ *n* [*re-* + *description*] **:** a new and more complete description esp. of a biological taxon

red–eye* *n* **1 :** the phenomenon of a subject's eyes appearing red in color flash photography **2 :** a late night or overnight flight

red flag *n* **:** something that attracts usu. irritated attention

red guard *n, usu cap R&G* [¹*red* (communist) + *guard*] **:** a member of a teenage activist organization in China serving the Maoist cause

re·dis·tri·bu·tion·ist \(ˈ)rēˌdistrəˌbyüsh(ə)nəst\ *n* -s [*redistribution* + *-ist*] **:** WELFARE STATER

redline* *vi* **:** to withhold home-loan funds or insurance from neighborhoods considered poor economic risks ~ *vt* **:** to discriminate against in housing or insurance — **redlining** *n*

redline \ˈ=ˌ=\ *n* [*red* + *line*] **:** a recommended safety limit **:** the fastest, farthest, or highest point or degree considered safe; *also* **:** the red line which marks this point on a gauge

redshirt* *n* [so called fr. the red jersey commonly worn by such a player in practice scrimmages against the regulars] **:** a college athlete who is kept out of varsity competition for a year in order to extend the period of his eligibility — **redshirt** \ˈ=ˌ=\ *vb* — **redshirting** \ˈ=ˌ==\ *n*

reductionism* *n* **:** the attempt to explain all biological processes by the same explanations (as by physical laws) that chemists and physicists use to interpret inanimate matter; *also* **:** the theory that complete reductionism is possible — **reductionist*** *n*

redundancy* *n, chiefly Brit* **:** dismissed from a job esp. by layoff or early retirement

redundant* *adj* **1 :** serving as a duplicate for preventing failure of an entire system (as a spacecraft) upon failure of a single component **2** *Brit* **:** being out of work **:** laid off **:** DISCHARGED ⟨he appeared in successive shows . . . before being made ~ —*The Guardian* (*London*)⟩

re·dux \(ˈ)rēˌdəks\ *adj* [L, lit., brought back, returned, fr. L *reducere* to bring back, fr. *re-* re- + *ducere* lead — more at TOW] **:** brought back — used postpositively

reel–to–reel \ˌ==ˈ=\ *adj* **:** of, relating to, or utilizing magnetic tape that requires threading on a take-up reel

reference* *vt* **:** to refer to ⟨a variable in a computer program *references* a location in memory⟩; *also* **:** to cite as a reference ⟨a frequently *referenced* study⟩

reflection* *n* **1 :** a transformation of a figure in which each point is replaced by a point symmetric with respect to a line **2 :** a transformation that involves reflection in more than one axis of a rectangular coordinate system

re·fried beans \(ˈ)rē + . . . -\ *n pl* [trans. of Sp *frijoles refritos*] **:** FRIJOLES REFRITOS *herein*

re·fuse·nik *or* **re·fus·nik** \rəˈfyüz,nik, rē-\ *n* [¹*refuse* + *-nik* (herein), part trans. of Russ *otkaznik*, fr. *otkaz* refusal] **:** a Soviet scientist who has been refused permission to emigrate

reg·gae \ˈrā(,)gā, ˈre-; ˈregē\ *n* -s [origin unknown] **:** popular music of Jamaican origin that combines indigenous styles with elements of rock 'n' roll and soul music and is performed at moderate tempos with the accent on the offbeat

region* *n* **:** an open connected set together with none, some, or all of the points on its boundary

re·gion·al \ˈrējənᵊl, -jnəl\ *n* -s **:** something or someone regional

register* *n* **1 :** a device in a computer or calculator for storing small amounts of data; *esp* **:** one in which data can be both stored and operated on **2 :** a variety of a language that is appropriate to a particular subject or occasion

regression analysis *n* **:** the use of mathematical and statistical techniques to estimate one variable from another esp. by the application of regression coefficients, regression curves, regression equations, or regression lines to empirical data

regulatory gene *or* **regulator gene** *n* **:** a gene controlling the production of a genetic repressor

re·hab \ˈrē,hab\ *n* -s *often attrib* [by shortening] **1 :** REHABILITATION **2 :** a rehabilitated building or dwelling — **rehab** *vt* **rehabbed; rehabbed; rehab·bing; rehabs** — **re·hab·ber** *n* -s

re·industrialization \(ˈ)rē +\ *n* [*re-* + *industrialization*] **:** a policy of stimulating economic growth esp. through government aid to revitalize and modernize aging industries and encourage growth of new ones — **re·industrialize** \"+\ *vb*

reinforce* *vb* ~ *vt* **:** to stimulate with a reinforcer following a correct or desired performance — **re·in·force·able** \,rēənˈfō(ə)rsəbəl, -ȯ(ə)r-, -ōəs-, -ȯ(ə)s-\ *adj*

reinforcer* *n* **:** a stimulus (as a reward or the removal of discomfort) that is effective esp. in operant conditioning because it regularly follows a desired response

re·insertion \(ˈ)rē +\ *n* [*re-* + *insertion*] **:** the action of reinserting something

rejection* *n* **:** the immunological process of sloughing off foreign tissue or an organ (as a transplant) by the recipient organism

rejective art *n* **:** MINIMAL ART *herein*

relative biological effectiveness *n* **:** the relative capacity of a particular ionizing radiation to produce a response in a biological system — abbr. *RBE*

relatively prime *adj, of integers* **:** having no common factors except +1 and −1 ⟨12 and 25 are *relatively prime*⟩

relativistic* *adj* **1 :** moving at or being a velocity that is a significant fraction of the speed of light so that effects predicted by the theory of relativity become evident ⟨a ~ electron⟩ **2 :** of or relating to a relativistic particle

released time* *n* **:** time off from regular duties (as teaching) granted for a specific activity (as research or committee work)

relevance* *n* **1 :** the ability (as of an information retrieval system) to retrieve material that satisfies the needs of the user **2 :** practical esp. social applicability **:** PERTINENCE

relocate* *vi* **:** to move to a new location

reluctant dragon *n* **:** a leader (as a politician or military officer) who avoids confrontation or conflict

REM \,är(,)ēˈem, ˈrem\ *n* -s [*r*apid *e*ye *m*ovement] **:** RAPID EYE MOVEMENT *herein*

re·master \(ˈ)rē +\ *vt* [*re-* + *master*] **:** to create a new master of esp. by altering or enhancing the sound quality of an older recording

remote* *adj* **:** acting, acted on, or controlled indirectly or from a distance ⟨time-sharing and other ~ computing services —*GT&E Annual Report*⟩; *also* **:** relating to the acquisition of information about a distant object (as by radar or photography) without coming into physical contact with it ⟨~ sensing instruments⟩

rem sleep *n, usu cap R&E&M* **:** a state of sleep that recurs cyclically several times during a normal period of sleep and that is characterized by increased neuronal activity of the forebrain and midbrain, by depressed muscle tone, and esp. in man by dreaming, rapid eye movements, and vascular congestion of the sex organs — called also *paradoxical sleep, rapid eye movement sleep*

renewable* *adj* **:** capable of being replaced by natural ecological cycles or sound management practices

ren·min·bi \ˈrenˈminˈbē\ *n pl* [Chin *ren²min²* (fr. *ren²* human + *min²* people) people's + *bi⁴* currency] **:** the currency of the People's Republic of China consisting of yuan

re·no·gram \ˈrēnə,gram\ *n* [*reno-* + *-gram*] **:** a photographic depiction of the course of renal excretion of a radioactively labeled substance — **re·no·graph·ic** \,==ˈgrafik\ *adj* — **re·nog·ra·phy** \rēˈnägrəfē, rə̇ˈ-\ *n* -ES

re·no·vascular \ˌrēnō +\ *adj* [*reno-* + *vascular*] **:** of, relating to, or involving the blood vessels of the kidneys

rent strike *n* **:** a refusal by a group of tenants to pay rent (as in protest against poor service)

reo·vi·rus \ˌrēōˌvīrəs\ *n* [*r*espiratory *e*nteric *o*rphan *virus*] **:** any of a group of rather large, widely distributed, and possibly tumorigenic viruses with double-stranded RNA

repertoire* *n* **:** a list or supply of capabilities ⟨the instruction ~ of a computer⟩

re·plantation \ˌrē +\ *n* [*replant* + *-ation*] **:** reattachment or reinsertion of a bodily part (as a limb or tooth) after separation from the body — **replant*** *vt*

rep·li·ca·ble \ˈreplə̇kəbəl\ *adj* [LL *replicabilis* worth repeating, fr. *replicare* to repeat, reply + L *-abilis* -able — more at REPLY] **:** capable of replication ⟨~ experimental results⟩

rep·li·case \ˈreplə̇,kās, -āz\ *n* -s [*replic*ation + *-ase*] **:** a polymerase that promotes synthesis of a particular RNA in the presence of a template of RNA — called also *RNA replicase*

replicate* *vi* **:** to undergo replication **:** produce a replica of itself

replicate* *n* **:** something (as a gene, DNA, or a cell) produced by replication

rep·li·ca·tive \ˈreplə̇,kād·iv\ *adj* [¹*replicate* + ¹*-ive*] **:** of, relating to, involved in, or characterized by replication

rep·li·con \ˈreplə̇,kän\ *n* -s [*replic*ate + ²*-on*] **:** a linear or circular section of DNA or RNA which replicates sequentially as a unit

re·po \ˈrē(,)pō\ *n* -s [by shortening & alter.] **:** REPURCHASE AGREEMENT

re·polarization \ˌrē+\ *n* [*re-* + *polarization*] **:** polarization of a muscle fiber, cell, or membrane following depolarization — **re·polarize** \"+\ *vb*

repress* *vt* **:** to inactivate (a gene or formation of a gene product) by allosteric combination at a DNA binding site

re·press·ible \rə̇ˈpresəbəl\ *adj* [[1]*repress* + *-able*] **:** capable of being repressed — **re·press·ibil·i·ty** \-ˌpresəˈbiləd·ē\ *n* -ES

repressor* *n* **:** a protein that is determined by a regulatory gene and that inhibits the function of a genetic operator

re·pro \ˈrē(ˌ)prō\ *n* -s [by shortening] **:** REPRODUCTION

re·process \(ˈ)rē+\ *vt* [*re-* + *process*] **:** to subject to a special process or treatment in preparation for reuse; *specif* **:** to extract uranium and plutonium from (the spent fuel rods of a nuclear reactor) for use again as fuel

re·program \(ˌ)rē +\ *vb* [*re-* + *program*] *vt* **:** to program anew; *esp* **:** to write new programs for (as a computer) ~ *vi* **:** to rewrite a computer program

re·prog·ra·phy \rə̇ˈprägrəfē, rēˈp-\ *n* -ES [ISV *reproduction* + *-graphy*] **:** the facsimile reproduction (as by photocopying) of graphic matter (as books or documents) — **re·prog·ra·pher** \-fə(r)\ *n* -s — **re·pro·graph·ic** \ˈrēprəˈgrafik, ˈrep-, -ēk\ *adj* — **re·pro·graph·ics** \-iks, -ēks\ *n pl but sing in constr*

re–refine \ˈrē +\ *vt* [*re-* + *refine*] **:** to refine (used motor oil) in order to produce a clean usable lubricant — **re–refiner** \"+\ *n*

re·segregation \(ˈ)rē +\ *n* [*re-* + *segregation*] **:** a return (as of a school) to a state of segregation after a period of desegregation

re·ser·pi·nized \rə̇ˈsərpə̇ˌnīzd, rē-\ *adj* [*reserpine* + *-ize* + *-ed*] **:** treated or medicated with reserpine or a reserpine derivative — **re·ser·pin·iza·tion** \-ˌsərpə̇nəˈzāshən, -ˌnīˈz-\ *n* -s

reserve* *n* **:** the lowest price that a seller agrees to accept for an item offered at auction

reserve clause *n* **:** a clause formerly common in contracts of professional athletes reserving for the club the exclusive right automatically to renew the contract and binding the athlete to the club for his entire playing career or until traded or released

re·sid \rə̇ˈzid\ *n* [by shortening] **:** RESIDUAL OIL *herein*

residence* *n* **:** the persistence of a substance that is suspended or dissolved in a medium ⟨the ~ time of a pollutant⟩

residual* *n* **:** a payment (as to an actor or writer) for each rerun esp. of a commercial

residual oil *n* **:** fuel oil that remains after the removal of valuable distillates (as gasoline) from petroleum and that is used esp. by industry — called also *resid*

residual security *n* **:** common stock or a security convertible into common stock

residue* *n* **:** the remainder after subtracting a multiple of a modulus from an integer or a power of the integer that can appear as the second of the two terms in an appropriate congruence

residue class *n* **:** the set of elements (as integers) that leave the same remainder when divided by a given modulus

resilience* *n* **:** an ability to recover from or adjust easily to misfortune or change

resistance* *n* **:** RESISTANCE LEVEL *herein*

resistance level *or* **resistance area** *n* **:** a price level on a rising market at which a security resists further advance due to increased attractiveness of the price to potential sellers

resonance* *n* **1 a :** the enhancement of an atomic, nuclear, or particle reaction or a scattering event by excitation of internal motion in the system **b :** MAGNETIC RESONANCE **2 :** an extremely short-lived elementary particle **3 :** the synchronous relationship involving gravitation that exists between orbital periods of two celestial bodies (as moons) that orbit a third (as a planet)

respiratory distress syndrome *n* **:** HYALINE MEMBRANE DISEASE *herein*

res·pi·ro·met·ric \ˌrespərōˈme·trik, rə̇ˌspīrəˈ-\ *adj* [*respirometry* + [1]*-ic*] **:** of or relating to respirometry or to the use of a respirometer ⟨~ studies⟩

respondent* *n* **:** a reflex that occurs in response to a specific external stimulus ⟨the knee jerk is a typical ~⟩

respondent* *adj* **:** relating to or being behavior or responses to a stimulus that are followed by a reward ⟨~ conditioning⟩ — compare OPERANT 2 *in the Dict*

res·sen·ti·ment \rəˌsäⁿtēˈmäⁿ\ *n* -s [G, fr. F, resentment — more at RESENTMENT] **:** deep-seated resentment, frustration, and hostility accompanied by a sense of being powerless to express these feelings directly

restriction enzyme *also* **restriction endonuclease** *n* **:** any of various enzymes that break double-stranded DNA into fragments at specific sites in the interior of the molecule

re·tard \ˈrēˌtärd, rə̇ˈtärd\ *n* -s [by shortening] **:** RETARDATE

reticent* *adj* **:** RELUCTANT, HESITANT

ret·i·nal \ˈretᵊnˌal, -ˌȯl\ *n* -s [[2]*retin-* + [3]*-al*] **:** a yellowish to orange aldehyde $C_{20}H_{28}O$ derived from vitamin A that in combination with proteins forms the visual pigments of the retinal rods and cones

retinitis pig·men·to·sa \-ˌpigmənˈtōsə, -(ˌ)men-, -ōzə\ *n* [NL, fem. of *pigmentosus* pigmented, fr. L *pigmentum* pigment + *-osus* -ose] **:** any of several hereditary progressive degenerative diseases of the eye marked by night blindness in the early stages, atrophy and pigment changes in the retina, constriction of the visual field, and eventual blindness

ret·i·nol \ˈretᵊnˌȯl, -ˌōl\ *n* -s [[2]*retin-* + [2]*-ol;* fr. its being the source of retinal] **:** VITAMIN A_1

ret·i·no·tec·tal \ˌretᵊnōˈtektəl\ *adj* [*retin-* + *tectum* + *-al*] **:** of, relating to, or being the nerve fibers connecting the retina and the tectum of the midbrain ⟨~ pathways⟩

retro \ˈre·trō\ *adj* [F *rétro,* short for *rétrospective* retrospective] **:** of, relating to, or being the styles or esp. the fashions of the past (as the 1930s or 1950s)

ret·ro–engine \ˈre·trō *sometimes* -ē- +ˌ\ *n* [*retro-* + *engine*] **:** a rocket engine on a spacecraft that produces thrust in the direction opposite to that of the motion of the spacecraft

ret·ro·fire \"+\ *vb* [*retro-* + [2]*fire*] *vi, of a retro-engine or retro-rocket* **:** to become ignited ~ *vt* **:** to cause to retrofire — **retrofire** *n*

ret·ro·fit \"+\ *vt* [*retrofit,* n.] **:** to furnish (as a computer, airplane, or building) with new parts or equipment not available, considered necessary, or in place at the time of manufacture or construction

retrograde* *adj* **:** being or relating to the rotation of a satellite in a direction opposite to that of the body being orbited

ret·ro·pack \ˈre·trō *sometimes* -ē- +ˌ\ *n* [*retro-* + *pack*] **:** a system of retro-rockets on a spacecraft

ret·ro·reflection \ˌre·trō *sometimes* -ē- +\ *n* [*retro-* + *reflection*] **:** the action or use of a retroreflector

ret·ro·reflector \"+\ *n* [*retro-* + *reflector*] **:** a device that reflects radiation (as light) so that the paths of the rays are parallel to those of the incident rays

ret·ro·virus \"+\ *n* [*retro-* + *virus*] **:** any of a group of RNA-containing viruses (as the Rous sarcoma virus and the HTLV causing AIDS) that produce reverse transcriptase by means of which DNA is formed using their RNA as a template and incorporated into the genome of infected cells and that include numerous viruses causing tumors in animals including man — **ret·ro·viral** \"+\ *adj*

reu·ben sandwich \ˌrübən- *in rapid speech also* ˌrüb-ᵊm-\ *n, usu cap R* [fr. the name *Reuben*] **:** a grilled sandwich consisting of corned beef, Swiss cheese, and sauerkraut usu. on rye bread

re·uptake \(ˈ)rē +\ *n* [*re-* + *uptake*] **:** the reabsorption by a neuron of a neurotransmitter following the transmission of a nerve impulse across a synapse

re·vanch·ism \rəˈvänˌshizəm\ *n* -s [*revanche* + *-ism*] **:** REVANCHE ⟨a policy of nationalistic ~ —Bernard Fall⟩

re·vascularization \(ˌ)rē +\ *n* [*re-* + *vascularization*] **:** a surgical procedure for the provision of a new, additional, or augmented blood supply to a body part or organ

revenue sharing *n* **:** the dispensing of a portion of federal tax revenue to state and local governments to assist in meeting their monetary needs

re·verb \rəˈvərb, ˈrē-,, -vəb, -vəib\ *n* -s [short for *reverberation*] **:** an electronically produced echo effect in recorded music; *also* **:** a device for producing reverb

reverse discrimination *n* **:** discrimination against whites or males (as in employment or education)

reverse engineer *vt* **:** to disassemble and examine or analyze in detail (as a product or device) to discover the concepts involved in manufacture usu. in order to produce something similar — **reverse engineering** *n*

reverse osmosis *n* **:** the flow of fresh water through a semipermeable membrane when pressure is applied to a solution (as seawater) on one side of it

reverse tran·scrip·tase \-ˌtranˈskrip(ˌ)tās, -āz\ *n* [*transcription* (herein) + *-ase*] **:** a polymerase that catalyzes the formation of DNA using RNA as a template and that is found in many tumor-producing viruses (as the retroviruses) containing RNA

re·ver·tant \rəˈvərtᵊnt, rēˈ-, -vət-\ *n* -s [¹*revert* + ¹*-ant*] **:** a mutant gene, individual, or strain that regains a former capability (as the production of a particular protein) by undergoing further mutation ⟨yeast ~*s*⟩ — **revertant** *adj*

revolving door* *n* **:** a revolving-door system or process

revolving-door \=ˌ=ˈ=\ *adj* **:** characterized by a repeated succession or exchange of places or conditions ⟨two years of *revolving-door* governments —Tom Buckley⟩

reward* *n* **:** a stimulus administered to an organism following a correct or desired response that increases the probability of occurrence of the response — **reward*** *vt*

rex* *n* **:** any domestic cat of the Cornish rex or Devon rex breeds

reye's syndrome \ˌrīz- *also* ˌrāz-\ *also* **reye syndrome** \ˌrī- *also* ˌrā-\ *n, usu cap R* [R. D. K. *Reye* †1977 Australian pathologist] **:** an often fatal encephalopathy esp. of childhood characterized by fever, vomiting, fatty infiltration of the liver, and swelling of the kidneys and brain

R factor *n* [resistance] **:** a group of genes present in some bacteria that provide a basis for resistance to antibiotics and can be transferred from cell to cell by conjugation

rhab·do·virus \ˌrabdō+\ *n* [*rhabd-* + *virus*] **:** any of a group of RNA-containing rod- or bullet-shaped viruses found in plants and animals and including the causative agents of rabies and vesicular stomatitis

rheology* *n* **:** the ability to flow or be deformed

rheumatoid factor *n* **:** an autoantibody of high molecular weight that is usu. present in rheumatoid arthritis

rhi·no·tracheitis \ˌrīnō+\ *n* [NL, fr. *rhin-* + *tracheitis*] **:** inflammation of the nasal cavities and trachea; *esp* **:** a disease of the upper respiratory system in cats that is characterized by sneezing, conjunctivitis with discharge, and nasal discharges and that affects esp. young kittens — see INFECTIOUS BOVINE RHINOTRACHEITIS *herein*

rhi·no·virus \"+\ *n* [NL, fr. *rhin-* + *virus*] **:** any of a group of picornaviruses that are related to the enteroviruses and associated with upper respiratory tract disorders

RHIP *abbr* rank has its privileges

rho* *or* **rho particle** *n* **:** a very short-lived unstable meson with mass 1490 times the mass of an electron

rhythm and blues *n* **:** blues orig. performed by black musicians for a black audience and marked by a strong simple beat and often an electronically amplified accompaniment

RIA *abbr* radioimmunoassay *herein*

rial* *n* **1 :** the basic monetary unit of the Yemen Arab Republic — see MONEY table *in the Dict* **2 :** a coin representing one rial

ri·bo·nucleoside \ˌrī(ˌ)bō +\ *n* [*ribose* + *nucleoside*] **:** a nucleoside that contains ribose

ri·bo·nucleotide \"+\ *n* [*ribose* + *nucleotide*] **:** a nucleotide that contains ribose and occurs esp. as a constituent of RNA

ribosomal RNA *n* **:** RNA that is a fundamental structural element of the ribosome

ri·bo·some \ˈrībəˌsōm\ *n* -s [*ribo*nucleic acid + ³*-some*] **:** any of the RNA-rich cytoplasmic granules that are sites of protein synthesis — **ri·bo·som·al** \ˌ==ˈsōməl\ *adj*

rib-tickler \ˈ=ˌ=(=)=\ *n* **:** something that provokes laughter

rich·ter scale \ˌriktə(r)-\ *n, usu cap R* [after Charles F. *Richter* *b*1900 Am. seismologist] **:** an open-ended logarithmic scale for expressing the magnitude of a seismic disturbance (as an earthquake) in terms of the energy dissipated in it with 1.5 indicating the smallest earthquake that can be felt, 4.5 an earthquake causing slight damage, and 8.5 a very devastating earthquake

ricky-tick \ˌrikēˈtik\ *n* [imit.] **:** sweet jazz of a style reminiscent of the 1920s — **ricky-ticky** \-tikē\ *adj*

ride* *vb* — **ride shotgun 1 :** to guard someone or something while in transit **2 :** to ride in the front passenger seat of a motor vehicle

ridership *n* [*rider* + *-ship*] **:** the number of persons who ride a particular system of public transportation

rie·mann integral \ˌrēˌmän-, -ˌmən-\ *n, usu cap R* [after G.F.B. *Reimann* †1866 Ger. mathematician] **:** a definite integral defined as the limit of sums found by partitioning the interval comprising the domain of definition into subintervals, by finding the sum of products each of which consists of the width of a subinterval multiplied by the value of the function at some point in it, and by letting the maximum width of the subintervals approach zero

rif·am·pin \'rif,ampən\ *or* **rif·am·pi·cin** \(')rif'ampəsən\ *n* -s [*rif*amycin (from which it is derived) + *ampicillin* (which it resembles in efficacy)] **:** a semisynthetic antibiotic $C_{43}H_{58}N_4O_{12}$ that acts against some viruses and bacteria esp. by inhibiting RNA synthesis

rif·a·my·cin \,rifə'mīsᵊn\ *n* -s [alter. of earlier *rifomycin*, fr. *rif-* (fr. *r*eplication *i*nhibiting *f*ungus) + *-o-* + *-mycin*] **:** any of several antibiotics that are derived from a bacterium of the genus *Streptomyces* (*S. mediterranei*)

righteous* *adj, slang* **:** GENUINE

right on *interj* — used to express agreement or to give encouragement

right–on \ˌ≐'≐\ *adj* **1 :** exactly correct **2 :** attuned to the spirit of the times

right–to–life \ˌ≐≐'≐\ *adj* **:** opposed to abortion — **right–to–lif·er** \-'līfər\ *n*

right–to–work law \ˌ≐≐'≐-\ *n* **:** any of various state laws banning the closed shop and the union shop

righty \'rīd·ē\ *n* -ES [*right* + *-y*] **:** RIGHT-HANDER

ring·git \'riŋgət\ *n* -s [native name in Malaysia] **1 :** the basic monetary unit of Malaysia — see MONEY table *in the Dict* **2 :** a coin or note representing one ringgit

[1]**rin·ky–dink** \ˌriŋkēˌdiŋk\ *adj* [origin unknown] **1 :** OLD-FASHIONED **2 :** SMALL-TIME

[2]**rinky–dink** \"\ *n* **1 :** one that is rinky-dink **2 :** RICKY-TICK *herein*

rin·ky–tink \ˌ≐≐ˌtiŋk\ *n* [by alter.] **:** RICKY-TICK *herein* — **rin·ky–tin·ky** \ˌ≐≐ˌtiŋkē\ *adj*

rio·ja \rē'ō(,)hä\ *n* -s *often cap* [La *Rioja*, district of Spain] **:** a wine from the Rioja district

ripe* *adj* **1 :** SMELLY, STINKING **2 :** sexually or scatalogically suggestive ⟨*riper* video fiction for adults —Les Brown⟩

rip off *vt* **1 :** ROB ⟨he *ripped off* a guy for ten grand —G.V. Higgins⟩; *also* **:** STEAL ⟨$5-million worth of goods *ripped off* at various merchandise-loading . . . spots —*New York*⟩ **2 :** to exploit esp. financially **:** CHEAT ⟨being *ripped off* by . . . bakers who give us zero nutritional value for our money —Mary Daniels⟩

rip–off \'≐ˌ≐\ *n* -s **1 :** an act or an instance of stealing **:** THEFT ⟨site of a famous gem theft, among other *rip-offs* —R.R. Lingeman⟩; *also* **:** an instance of financial exploitation **:** GYP ⟨don't waste your money on this book . . . it's a *rip-off* —Peter Stollery⟩ **2 :** something (as a story or motion picture) that is obviously based on or imitative of something else ⟨this kaleidoscopic fantasy, a *rip-off* on everything from spy novels to the Oedipus complex —Barbara A. Bannon⟩

ripple effect *n* **:** a spreading, pervasive, and usu. unintentional effect or influence ⟨the whole industry would be forced to close down, which would have a *ripple effect* on other industries —Joe Klein⟩ — compare DOMINO EFFECT *herein*

ripstop \'≐ˌ≐\ *adj* [[3]*rip* + *stop*] **:** of or relating to a fabric that is woven with a double thread at regular intervals so that small tears do not spread ⟨~ nylon⟩

rise·time \'rīz +,\ *n* [[2]*rise-* + *time*] **:** the time required for a pulse or signal (as on an oscilloscope) to increase from one specified value (as 10 percent) of its amplitude to another (as 90 percent)

ris·to·ce·tin \ˌristəˌsētᵊn\ *n* -s [origin unknown] **:** either of two antibiotics or a mixture of both produced by an actinomycete of the genus *Nocardia* (*N. lurida*)

Ri·tal·in \'ritələn\ *trademark* — used for methylphenidate

river blindness *n* **:** ONCHOCERCIASIS

RNA polymerase *n* **:** an enzyme that promotes the synthesis of RNA using DNA or RNA as a template

RNA replicase *n* **:** REPLICASE *herein*

RNase \ˌä'renˌās, -āz\ *or* **RNAase** \ˌä(ˌ)re'nāˌās, -ˌāz\ *n* -s [*RNA* + *-ase*] **:** RIBONUCLEASE

roadholding \'≐ˌ≐≐\ *n* [[1]*road* + *holding*] *chiefly Brit* **:** the qualities of an automobile that tend to make it hold the road

road·ie \'rōdē\ *n* -s [[1]*road* + *-ie*] **1 :** one who manages the activities of entertainers on the road — called also *road manager* **2 :** one who works (as by moving heavy equipment) for traveling entertainers

road racing *n* **:** racing (as in automobiles or on motorcycles) over public roads or over a closed course designed to simulate public roads (as with left and right turns, sharp corners, and hills)

rob·ert·so·ni·an \ˌräbə(r)t'sōnēən\ *adj, usu cap* [prob. after W. *Robertson* fl1916 Am. physician] **:** relating to or being a reciprocal translocation that takes place between two acrocentric chromosomes, between two metacentric chromosomes having one arm of each composed of heterochromatin, or between two chromosomes including one of each kind, that involves a break close to the centromere in one and just to the other side of the centromere in the other, and that is sometimes a mechanism in evolution for the reduction of chromosome number

ro·bot·ics \rō'bäd·iks\ *n pl but sing in constr* [*robot* + *-ics*] **:** technology dealing with the design, construction, and operation of robots in automation

rock·a·bil·ly \'räkəˌbilē\ *n* -ES [*rock* + *-a-* (as in *rockaby* and *hootananny*) + hill*billy*] **:** pop music marked by features of rock and country and western styles

rocker* *n* **:** a rock performer, song, or enthusiast

ro·la·mite \'rōləˌmīt\ *n* -s [*roll* + *-amite*, of unknown origin] **:** a nearly frictionless elementary mechanism consisting of two or more rollers inserted in the loops of a flexible metal or plastic band with the band acting to turn the rollers whose movement can be directed to perform various functions

role model *n* **:** a person whose behavior in a particular role is imitated by others

role–play \'≐ˌ≐\ *vb* [*role* + *play*] *vt* **:** to act out ⟨students were asked to *role-play* the thoughts and feelings of each character —R. G. Lambert⟩ ~ *vi* **:** to play a role

rolf·ing \'ròlfiŋ *also* 'rôf-\ *n* -s *sometimes cap* [Ida *Rolf* †1979 Am. biochemist and physiotherapist + E *-ing*] **:** a method of systematically massaging the deep muscles that is intended to serve as both physical and emotional therapy — **rolf** \'ròlf *also* rôf\ *vt* -ED/-ING/-S — **rolf·er** \'ròlfər *also* 'rôf-\ *n* -s

roll* *n* — **on a roll** **1 :** in the midst of a series of successes **:** on a hot streak **2** — used with a modifier to indicate momemtum of a specified kind ⟨swept the . . . doubleheader, 8-3 and 7-1, and, *on a* wild *roll* now, knocked out eighteen hits the next afternoon —Roger Angell⟩ ⟨we've been *on a* bad *roll* —Henry Catto⟩

roll bar *n* **:** an overhead metal bar on an automobile designed to protect an occupant in case of a turnover

roll cage *n* **:** a protective framework of metal bars encasing the driver of a racing car

roller hockey *n* **:** a variation of ice hockey played on roller skates

rolle's theorem \'ròlz-, 'rōlz-\ *n, usu cap R* [after Michel *Rolle* †1719 Fr. mathematician] **:** a theorem in mathematics: if a curve is continuous, crosses the x-axis at two points, and has a single tangent at every point between the two intercepts, its tangent is parallel to the x-axis at some point between the intercepts

roll out* *vi* **:** to run toward one flank usu. parallel to the line of scrimmage esp. before throwing a pass ⟨the quarterback would either hand off to the fullback or fake to him and *roll out* —Arthur Sampson⟩ ~ *vt* **:** to introduce (as a new product) esp. for widespread sale to the public

rollout** *n* **1 :** a football play in which the quarterback rolls out **2 :** the broad public introduction of a new product or service

roll over* *vt* **1 :** to renegotiate the terms of (a financial agreement) **2 :** to place (invested funds) in a new investment of the same kind **:** REINVEST ⟨*roll over* IRA funds⟩

rollover \ˈ=ˌ==\ *n* -s [*roll over* (herein)] **1 :** an act or instance of rolling over **2 :** an accident (as of a motor vehicle) in which the vehicle rolls over

ROM *abbr or n* -s read-only memory *herein*

root canal* *n* **:** a dental operation to save a tooth by removing the contents of its root canal and filling the cavity with a protective substance

ror·schach \ˈrȯ(ə)r-ˌshäk\ *adj, usu cap* **:** of, relating to, used in connection with, or resulting from the Rorschach test

rose* *n* **:** a plane curve which consists of three or more loops meeting at the origin and whose equation in polar coordinates is of the form $\rho = a \sin n\theta$ or $\rho = a \cos n\theta$ where n is an integer greater than 1

rose medallion *n* **:** a chiefly 19th century enamel-decorated Chinese porcelain with medallions of oriental figures surrounded and separated by panels of flowers and butterflies

rosette* *n* **:** a rose-shaped cluster of cells

rotator cuff *n* **:** a supporting and strengthening structure of the shoulder joint that is made up of part of its capsule blended with tendons of the subscapularis, infraspinatus, supraspinatus, and teres minor muscles as they pass to the capsule or across it to insert on the humerus

ro·ta·vi·rus \ˈrōd·əˌvīrəs\ *n* [L *rota* wheel + *virus*] **:** an RNA-containing virus with a double-layered capsid and a wheel-like appearance that causes diarrhea esp. in infants

rough trade *n* **:** male homosexuals who are or affect to be rugged and potentially violent; *also* **:** a homosexual of this sort

rouille \rüy\ *n* -s [F, lit., rust] **:** a peppery garlic sauce of Mediterranean French origin usu. served with fish soups and stews

round file *n* **:** WASTEBASKET

RP *abbr* received pronunciation

RPG \ˌärˌpēˈjē\ *n* -s [*r*eport *p*rogram *g*enerator] **:** a computer language that generates programs from the user's specifications esp. to produce business reports

rRNA \ˈärˌärˌenˌā\ *n* -s **:** RIBOSOMAL RNA *herein*

rub* *vb* — **rub one's nose in :** to bring forcefully or repeatedly to one's attention ⟨the satirist's business is to *rub our noses in* the mess, without relief —R.B. Heilman⟩

rubber–chicken circuit \ˌ==ˈ==-\ *n* **:** a series of social gatherings (as dinners) before which a traveling celebrity (as a campaigning politician) gives speeches

rub·bish \ˈrəbish\ *vt* -ED/-ING/-ES [*rubbish,* n.] *chiefly Austral* **:** to express disapproval of **:** DISPARAGE ⟨generally ~*ed* the other side's manifesto —William Hardcastle⟩

rub off *vi* **:** to become transferred — usu. used with *on* ⟨the decorum in [his] narrative voice surely appealed to my grandmother; perhaps she hoped that some of it might *rub off* on me —John Irving⟩

rub–off \ˈ=ˌ=\ *n* -s [*rub off* (herein)] **:** an instance or result of rubbing off

rubout \ˈ=ˌ=\ *n* -s [*rub out*] **:** an act or instance of rubbing someone or something out

ru·go·la \ˈrügələ\ *n* -s [alter. of *arugula* (herein)] **:** GARDEN ROCKET 1

ru·ma·ki *also* **ra·ma·ki** \rəˈmäkē\ *n* -s [origin unknown] **:** a cooked appetizer consisting of pieces of usu. marinated chicken liver wrapped together with sliced water chestnuts in bacon slices

runaway* *adj* **:** operating out of control ⟨a ~ oil well⟩ ⟨a ~ car⟩

running dog *n* [trans. of Chin (Pek) *tsou²kou³* hunting dog, lackey, lit., running dog, fr. *tsou³* to go, walk, run + *kou³* dog] **:** one who does someone else's bidding **:** LACKEY ⟨charge the missionaries with being *running dogs* for the imperialistic foreign powers —*Living Age*⟩

run–up* *n, chiefly Brit* **:** a period immediately preceding an action or event

rush* *n* **1 :** the immediate pleasurable feeling produced by a drug (as heroin or amphetamine) — called also *flash* **2 :** a feeling of pleasure or euphoria **:** THRILL, BANG, KICK

RV \ˌärˈvē\ *abbr or n* -s recreational vehicle *herein*

r–value \ˈ=ˌ=(ˌ)=\ *n, usu cap R* [prob. fr. thermal *r*esistance] **:** a measure of the ability of a substance or combination of substances (as building material or insulation) to retard the flow of heat with higher numbers indicating better insulating properties

rya \ˈrēə, ˈrīə\ *n* -s [fr. *Rya,* village in southwest Sweden] **:** a Scandinavian handwoven rug with a deep resilient comparatively flat pile; *also* **:** the weave typical of this rug

S

s* *abbr* siemens *herein*

saccade* *n* **:** a small rapid jerky movement of the eye esp. as it jumps from fixation on one point to another (as in reading)

sacred mushroom *n* **:** any of various New World hallucinogenic fungi (as of the genus *Psilocybe*) used esp. in some Indian ceremonies

saddled prominent *n* [so called fr. the hump or prominence on the back of the larva] **:** a notodontid moth (*Heterocampa guttivitta*) whose larva is a serious defoliator of hardwood trees in the eastern and midwestern U.S.

safari jacket *n* **:** a belted shirt jacket with bellows pockets

safari park *n* **:** a large open reserve stocked with usu. big-game animals (as lions) that visitors driving through can observe in natural surroundings

safari suit *n* **:** a safari jacket with matching pants

safe house *n* **:** a place where one may take refuge or engage in secret activities

safety net *n* **:** something (as a government program or a prudent precaution) that provides security against misfortune or difficulty

sag·it·tar·ian \ˌsajəˈta(a)rēən\ *n* -s *usu cap* [*Sagittarius* + E *-an*] **:** SAGITTARIUS *herein*

sagittarius* *n, usu cap* **:** one born under the astrological sign Sagittarius

sa·hel \ˈsähəl; səˈhā(ə)l, -ˈhē(ə)l\ *n* -s *usu cap* [F, fr. Ar. *sāḥil* coast, shore] **:** a savanna or steppe region bordering a desert and esp. the Sahara desert — **sa·hel·ian** \-ˈhālēən, -ˈhēl-\ *adj, usu cap*

sailboard \ˈ=ˌ=\ *n* **:** a small flat sailboat resembling a surfboard

sai·min \ˈsīˈmin\ *n* -s [prob. fr. Chin (Cantonese) *saì mìn,* lit., fine noodles] **:** an Hawaiian noodle soup

saint emi·lion \ˌsaⁿtāmēˈlyōⁿ\ *n, pl* **saint emilions** *same*\ *usu cap S&E* [*Saint-Émilion,* village in southwestern France] **:** a red Bordeaux wine

salad bar *n* **:** a self-service counter (as in a restaurant) featuring an array of salad makings and dressings

sal·bu·ta·mol \salˈbyüd·əˌmȯl, -ütə-, -ōl\ *n* -s [*sal*icyl- + *but*yl + *am*ino + *-ol*] **:** a xylene derivative $C_{13}H_{21}NO_3$ used as a bronchodilator

sal·sa \ˈsȯlsə, ˈsäl-\ *n* -s [Sp, lit., sauce] **1 :** popular music of Latin American origin that has absorbed characteristics of rhythm and blues, jazz, and rock **2 :** a spicy sauce of tomatoes, onions, and hot peppers

sal·tim·boc·ca \ˌsȯltimˈbä(k)kə, -ˈbȯ(-\ *n* -s [It] **:** scallops of veal prepared with sage, slices of ham, and sometimes cheese and served with a wine sauce

sal·uret·ic \ˌsalyəˈred·ik\ *n* -s [L *sal* salt + E di*uretic* — more at SALT] **:** a drug that facilitates the urinary excretion of salt and esp. of sodium ion — **saluretic** \ˌ==ˈ==\ *adj* — **sal·u·ret·i·cal·ly** \-ˈred·ək(ə)lē\ *adv*

SAM \ˈsam, ˌe(ˌ)sāˈem\ *n* -s **:** SURFACE-TO-AIR MISSILE *herein*

sam·bo \ˈsam(ˌ)bō, ˈsäm-\ *n* -s [Russ, fr. *sam*ozashchita *bez or*u-zhiya self-defense without weapons] **:** an international style of wrestling employing judo techniques

sa·miz·dat \ˈsämēzˌdät\ *n* -s [Russ, fr. *sam* self + *izdat*el'stvo publisher, fr. *izdat'* to publish, fr. *iz* out, from + *dat'* to give; akin to L *dare* to give — more at DATE] **:** the system in the U.S.S.R. by which government-suppressed literature is clandestinely printed and distributed; *also* **:** such literature

sampling distribution *n* **:** the distribution of a statistic (as a sample mean)

san·cerre \säⁿser\ *n* -s *usu cap* [fr. *Sancerre,* France] **:** a white wine from the Loire valley of France

san·da ware \ˈsandə-, ˈsän-\ *n, usu cap S* [fr. *Sanda,* city in western Honshu, Japan, where it originated] **:** a Japanese pottery and esp. porcelain ware produced since the late 17th century and noted for its celadons

san·di·nis·ta \ˌsandəˈnēstə, ˌsän-\ *or* **san·di·nist** \ˈsandənəst\ *n* -s *usu cap* [after Augusto César *Sandino* †1933 Nicaraguan rebel leader] **:** a member of a military and political coalition taking power in Nicaragua in 1979

S and L \ˌ==ˈ=\ *n* **:** SAVINGS AND LOAN ASSOCIATION

S and M *abbr* sadism and masochism; sadist and masochist

sandwich coin *n* **:** a clad coin

sandwich shop *n* **:** LUNCHEONETTE

san·gria \saŋˈgrēə, san-, säŋ-, sän-\ *n* -s [Sp *sangría,* lit., bleeding — more at SANGAREE] **:** a punch made of red wine, fruit juice, sugar, and usu. brandy, sliced fruit, and soda water

sanitize* *vt* **:** to make more acceptable by removing unpleasant or undesired features ⟨~ a document⟩

san·te·ria \ˌsanteˈrēə, ˌsän-\ *n* -s *usu cap* [AmerSp *santería,* fr. Sp *santero* seller of religious images, fr. *santo* saint] **:** a religion in which the gods of an African tribal religion are identified with Roman Catholic saints

sapir–whorf hypothesis \səˌpi(ə)rˈ(h)wȯ(ə)rf-\ *n, usu cap S&W* [after Edward *Sapir* †1939 and Benjamin Lee *Whorf* †1941 Am. anthropologists] **:** WHORFIAN HYPOTHESIS *herein*

sa·ran·gi \ˈsärənˌgē, -əŋˌg-\ *n* -s [Skt *sāraṅgī*] **:** a stringed musical instrument of India that is played with a bow and that has a tone similar to that of the viola

SASE *abbr* self-addressed stamped envelope

sas·quatch \ˈsasˌkwach, -äch\ *n* -ES *usu cap* [Salish *se'sxac* wild men] **:** a hairy manlike creature reported to exist in the northwestern U.S. and western Canada and said to be a primate between 6 and 15 feet tall — called also *bigfoot*

satellite* *n* **:** a usu. independent urban community situated on the outskirts of a large city

satellite DNA *n* **:** a DNA fraction differing in density from most of an organism's DNA as determined by centrifugation that apparently consists of repetitive nucleotide sequences, does not undergo transcription, and is found in some organisms (as the mouse) esp. in centromeric regions

sat·is·fice \ˈsad·əˌsfīs\ *vi* -ED/-ING/-S [E dial., lit., satisfy] **:** to pursue the minimum satisfactory condition or outcome — **sat·is·fic·er** \-sər\ *n* -s

saturated diving *n* **:** SATURATION DIVING *herein* — **saturated diver** *n*

saturation diving *n* **:** diving in which a person remains underwater at a certain depth breathing a mixture of gases under pressure until his body becomes saturated with the gases so that decompression time remains the same regardless of how long he remains at that depth — **saturation dive** *n*

saturday night special *n, usu cap 1st S* **:** a cheap easily concealed handgun

sau·vi·gnon blanc \ˌsōvēˌnyōⁿ'bläⁿ, -äŋk\ *n, pl* **sauvignon blancs** \-äⁿ, -äŋks\ *often cap S&B* [F, white sauvignon (variety of grape)] **:** a dry white California wine made from a grape orig. grown in Bordeaux and the Loire valley

saxi·toxin \ˈsaksə +\ *n* [NL *Saxidomus giganteus,* species of butter clam from which it is isolated + E *toxin*] **:** a potent nonprotein poison $C_{10}H_{17}N_7O_4{\cdot}2HCl$ that originates in dinoflagellates of the genus *Gonyaulax* found in red tides and that sometimes occurs in and renders toxic normally edible mollusks which feed on them

SBN *abbr* Standard Book Number

scag \'skag, -aa(ə)g, -aig\ *or* **skag*** *n* -s [prob. fr. ²*skag*] *slang* **:** HEROIN

scalar* *adj* **:** of or relating to a scalar or scalar product

scaler* *n* **:** a dental instrument for removing tartar from teeth

sca·lop·pi·ne \ˌskälə'pēnē, ˌskal-\ *var of* SCALLOPINI

¹scam \'skam, -aa(ə)m, -aim\ *n* -s [origin unknown] **:** a confidence scheme in which an established business is taken over, merchandise is purchased on credit and quickly sold, and then the business is abandoned or bankruptcy is declared; *broadly* **:** a fraudulent or deceptive practice ⟨insurance swindles, credit-card rackets, and practically every ~ devised by man —Joe Flaherty⟩

²scam \"\ *vt* **scammed; scammed; scamming; scams** *slang* **:** DECEIVE, DEFRAUD ⟨~*s* his senile grandmother out of $3 million —Jane Clapperton⟩ — **scam·mer** \-ə(r)\ *n* -s *slang*

scam·pi \'skampē\ *n, pl* **scampi** [It, pl. of *scampo* Norway lobster] **:** SHRIMP; *esp* **:** large shrimp prepared with a garlic-flavored sauce

scan* *vt* **:** to make a scan of (as a human body)

scan* *n* **1 a :** a depiction (as a photograph) of the distribution of radioactive material in something (as a body organ) **b :** an image of a bodily part produced by combining (as by computer) radiographic data obtained from several angles or sections **2 :** TRACE 5c

scanner* *n* **:** a device (as a CAT scanner) for making scans of the human body

scanning electron micrograph *n* **:** a micrograph made by scanning electron microscopy

scanning electron microscope *n* **:** an electron microscope in which a beam of focused electrons moves across the object with the secondary electrons produced by the object and the electrons scattered by the object being collected to form a three-dimensional image on a cathode-ray tube — called also *scanning microscope;* compare TRANSMISSION ELECTRON MICROSCOPE *herein* — **scanning electron microscopy** *n*

scarf \'skärf, 'skȧf\ *vt* -ED/-ING/-S [perh. alter. of ³*scoff*] **:** to eat or consume esp. rapidly or greedily

scattering matrix *n* **:** S MATRIX *herein*

scenario* *n* **:** a sequence of events esp. when imagined; *esp* **:** an account or synopsis of a projected course of action or events ⟨had drawn up a number of possible ~*s* in which nuclear weapons would be used —Martin Mayer⟩

scene* *n* **:** a sphere of activity **:** a way of life ⟨the social ~⟩

schizophrenia* *n* **:** the presence of mutually contradictory or antagonistic parts or qualities

schizy *or* **schiz·zy** \'skitsē\ *adj* [*schiz*oid + ¹-*y*] **:** SCHIZOID

schlepp* *or* **schlep** *or* **shlep** *vi* **schlepped** *or* **shlepped; schlepped** *or* **shlepped; schlepping** *or* **shlepping; schleps** *or* **shleps :** to proceed or move slowly, tediously, or awkwardly

schlepp *or* **schlep** *or* **shlep** \'shlep\ *or* **schlep·per** *or* **shlep·per** \-epə(r)\ *n* -s [Yiddish *shlep, shleper,* fr. *shlepen* to drag, pull, jerk — more at SCHLEPP, V.] **:** an awkward or incompetent person **:** JERK

schlock \'shläk\ *also* **schlocky** \-ē\ *or* **shlock** \'shläk\ *or* **shlocky** \-ē\ *adj* [Yiddish *shlak,* lit., blow, apoplectic stroke, curse, fr. MHG *slag, slac,* fr. OHG *slag,* fr. *slahan* to strike — more at SLAY] **:** of low quality or little worth ⟨~ books⟩ ⟨~ merchandise⟩ — **schlock** *n* -s

schlock·meis·ter \'shläkˌmīstə(r)\ *n* -s [*schlock* (herein) + G *meister* master] **:** one who makes or sells schlock products

schmear *or* **schmeer** *also* **shmear** \'shmi(ə)r, -iə(r\ *n* -s [Yiddish *shmir* smear, fr. *shmiren* to smear, fr. MHG *smiren, smirwen,* fr. OHG *smirwen* — more at SMEAR] **:** an aggregate of related things ⟨the whole ~⟩

schmuck *or* **shmuck** \'shmək\ *n* -s [Yiddish *shmok* penis, fool, fr. G *schmuck* adornment, fr. MLG *smuck;* akin to OE *smoc* smock — more at SMOCK] **:** a stupid, naïve, or foolish person **:** JERK; *also* **:** one who is mean or nasty

schtick *var of* SHTICK *herein*

schussboomer \'=ˌ==\ *n* [¹*schuss* + ¹*boomer*] **:** one who skis usu. straight downhill at high speed

schwarz·schild radius \'shwȯrtˌshild-, 's(h)wȯrts-ˌchīld-; 'shvärtˌshilt-\ *n, usu cap S* [after Karl *Schwarzschild* †1916 Ger. astronomer] **:** the radius of the spherical volume at which a given mass (as of a star) in collapse becomes a black hole

SCID *abbr* severe combined immunodeficiency *herein*

sci–fi \ˈsīˈfī\ *adj* [*sci*ence *fi*ction] **:** of, relating to, or being science fiction ⟨*sci-fi* writers⟩ ⟨*sci-fi* stories⟩

scin·ti·scan \'sintəˌskan\ *n* [*scinti*llation + *scan*] **:** a two-dimensional representation of radioisotope radiation from a bodily organ (as the spleen or kidney) — **scin·ti·scan·ning** \-iŋ\ *n*

scle·ro·testa \ˈsklirō, -lerō +\ *n* [NL, fr. *scler-* + *testa*] **:** the middle stony layer of the testa in various seeds — compare ENDOTESTA *herein* — **scle·ro·tes·tal** \-ˈtestᵊl\ *adj*

score* *n, slang* **:** a purchase or sale of narcotics

score* *vt* **1 :** to have sexual relations with ⟨adventuress who . . . ~*s* the dude and splits —Elizabeth Ashley⟩ **2 :** to be successful in obtaining ⟨should be able to ~ a ham sandwich —Glenn O'Brien⟩ **~** *vi* **:** to succeed in having sexual relations ⟨college roommates who . . . ~ with the same girl —L. H. Lapham⟩

scorpio* *n* -s *usu cap* **:** one born under the astrological sign Scorpio

scorpion* *n, usu cap* **:** SCORPIO *herein*

scotch egg *n, usu cap S* **:** a hard-boiled egg wrapped in sausage meat, covered with bread crumbs, and fried

scottish fold *n, usu cap S&F* **:** any of a breed of short-haired domestic cats having ears folded over at the top that originated in Scotland as a spontaneous mutation

scouse \'skau̇s\ *n* -s *cap* [back-formation fr. *Scouser* (herein)] **1 :** SCOUSER *herein* **2 :** a dialect of English spoken in Liverpool

scous·er \'skau̇sə(r)\ *n* -s *cap* [*scouse* (in the Dict.) + *-er;* fr. the popularity of lobscouse in Liverpool] **:** a native or inhabitant of Liverpool

scramble* *vi, of a football quarterback* **:** to run with the ball after the pass protection breaks down

scramble* *n* **:** a motorcycle race over a rough hilly course

scram·jet \'skram͵jet\ *n* [supersonic combustion *ramjet*] **:** a ramjet airplane engine in which thrust is produced by burning fuel in a supersonic airstream after the airplane has attained supersonic speed by other means of propulsion

scratch* *adj* **:** made from scratch **:** made with basic ingredients

scratchpad** *n* **:** a small fast auxiliary computer memory

screening test *n* **:** a preliminary or abridged test intended to eliminate the less probable members of an experimental series

screw up* *vb* ~ *vt* **1 :** BUNGLE, BOTCH **2 :** to cause to act or function in a crazy or confused way **:** CONFOUND, DISTURB ~ *vi* **:** to botch an activity or undertaking

screw–up \'=͵=\ *n* -s [*screw up* (herein)] **1 :** one who screws up **2 :** BLUNDER

scrimshander* *n* **:** a person who makes scrimshaw

scripture cake *n, usu cap S* **:** a fruitcake whose recipe refers to biblical passages where the ingredients are mentioned

scroll* *vt* **:** to cause (text or graphics on a display screen) to move vertically or horizontally usu. one line or column at a time as if by unrolling a scroll ~ *vi* **1 :** to move text or graphics across a display screen **2** *of text or graphics* **:** to move across a screen

scrum* *n, Brit* **:** MADHOUSE 2

scuba diver *n* **:** one who swims under water with the aid of scuba gear — **scuba dive** *vi*

scuffle* *vi* **:** to struggle (as by working odd jobs) to get by

scumbag \'=͵=\ *n* [¹*scum* + *bag*] **1** *slang* **:** CONDOM **2** *slang* **:** a dirty or unpleasant person — used as a generalized term of abuse

scut work *n* [perh. fr. E slang *scut* junior intern] **:** routine and often menial work

scuz·zy \'skəzē\ *adj* -ER/-EST [perh. alter. of *disgusting*] *slang* **:** NASTY, SQUALID

SDRs \͵es(͵)dē'ärz, -'äz\ *n pl* [special *d*rawing *r*ights] **:** an international means of exchange created under the auspices of the International Monetary Fund for use by governments in settling their international indebtedness

SE* *abbr* standard English

sea–grant college \'=͵=-\ *n* **:** an institution of higher learning that receives federal grants for research in oceanography

seat* *n* **:** a precise or accurate contact between parts or surfaces

secondary* *or* **secondary offering** *n* **:** SECONDARY DISTRIBUTION

secondary derivative *n* **:** a word (as *teacher*) whose immediate constituents are a free form and a bound form

secondary recovery *n* **:** the process of obtaining oil (as by waterflood) from a well that has stopped producing

second–strike \¦==¦=\ *adj* [¹*second* + *strike*] **:** being or relating to a weapons system capable of surviving a nuclear attack and then striking enemy targets

second world *n, often cap S&W* **:** the Communist nations as a political and economic bloc

security blanket *n* **1 :** a blanket carried by a child as a protection against anxiety **2 :** a usu. familiar object or person whose presence dispels anxiety

sedimentation coefficient *n* **:** a measure of the rate at which a molecule (as a protein) suspended in a colloidal solution sediments in an ultracentrifuge usu. expressed in svedbergs

seed money *n* **:** money used for setting up a new enterprise

see–through \¦=͵=\ *adj* [¹*see* + *through*] **:** TRANSLUCENT, TRANSPARENT — **see–through** \'=¦=\ *n* -s

sel·e·nod·e·sy \͵selə'nädəsē\ *n* -ES [*selen-* + *-odesy* (as in *geodesy*)] **:** a branch of physical science that deals with determination of the shape and size of the moon and of the exact positions of points on it and with variations of lunar gravity — **sel·e·no·det·ic** \¦selənō¦ded·ik\ *adj*

self–actualize \¦='==(=)͵=\ *vi* **:** to realize fully one's potential — **self–actualization** \¦=͵==(=)='==\ *n* — **self–actualizer** \¦='==(=)͵==\ *n* -s

self–assembly \¦==¦==\ *n* [*self-* + *assembly*] **:** the process by which a complex macromolecule (as collagen) or a supramolecular system (as a virus) spontaneously assembles itself from its components

self–concept \'='=͵=\ *n* **:** the mental image one has of oneself

self–dealing \'='==\ *n* **:** financial dealing that is not at arm's length; *esp* **:** borrowing from or lending to a company by a controlling individual primarily to his own advantage

self–destruct \¦==¦=\ *vi* **:** to destroy itself — **self–destruct** \"\ *adj*

self–fulfilling \¦==¦==\ *adj* **:** becoming real or true by virtue of having been predicted or assumed ⟨a ~ prophecy⟩

self–medication \¦=͵==¦==\ *n* **:** medication of oneself

self–paced \¦=¦=\ *adj* **:** designed to permit the student or subject to learn or proceed at his or her own pace

self–perception \¦==¦==\ *n* [*self-* + *perception*] **:** perception of oneself; *esp* **:** SELF-CONCEPT *herein*

self–recognition \¦=͵=='==\ *n* **1 :** recognition of one's own self **2 :** the process by which the immune system of an organism learns to distinguish between the body's own chemicals, cells, and tissues and intruders from the outside — compare SELF-TOLERANCE *herein*

self–referential \¦=͵==¦==\ *adj* **:** referring to itself; *esp* **:** concerned with the mental attitudes and creative processes that brought it into existence

self–replicating \¦='==͵==\ *adj* **:** reproducing itself autonomously — **self–replication** \¦=͵==¦==\ *n*

self–reproducing \¦=(͵)=='==\ *adj* **:** SELF-REPLICATING *herein*

self–serve \¦='=\ *adj* **:** permitting self-service

self–stick \¦='=\ *adj* **:** capable of adhering to a surface by application of pressure without the addition of moisture

self–stimulation \¦=͵=='==\ *n* **:** stimulation of oneself as a result of one's own activity or behavior ⟨electrical *self=stimulation* of the brain in rats⟩ — **self–stimulatory** \¦=¦===͵==\ *adj*

self–tolerance \¦='===\ *n* **:** the physiological state that exists in an organism when its immune system has lost the capacity to attack and destroy its own bodily constituents — compare SELF-RECOGNITION 2 *herein*

self–worth \¦='=\ *n* **:** SELF-ESTEEM

selling climax *n* **:** a sharp decline in stock prices for a short time on very heavy trading volume followed by a rally

semi–antique \ˌsemē, -ˌmī +\ *adj, of a carpet or rug* **:** being approximately 50 to 100 years old; *broadly* **:** being of a quality sufficient to become antique and having had some use but not yet old enough to be considered an antique — **semi–antique** *n*

semi·automated \ˌsemē, -ˌmī, -ˌmi+\ *adj* [*semi-* + *automated,* past part. of *automate*] **:** partly automated

semi·axis \"+\ *n* [*semi-* + *axis*] **:** a line segment that has one endpoint at the center of a geometric figure (as an ellipse) and that forms half of an axis

semi·comatose \ˌsemē, -ˌmī, -ˌmə +\ *adj* [*semi-* + *comatose*] **:** lethargic and disoriented but not completely comatose

semi·conservative \"+\ *adj* [*semi-* + *conservative*] **:** relating to or being replication (as of DNA) in which the original separates into parts each of which is incorporated into a new whole and serves as a template for the formation of the missing parts — **semi·conservatively** *adv*

semi·dwarf \"+\ *adj* [*semi-* + *dwarf*] **:** of or being a plant of a variety that is undersized but larger than a dwarf ⟨∼ wheats⟩ — **semidwarf** *n*

semi·group \ˈsemē, -mə +ˌ-\ *n* [*semi-* + *group*] **:** a mathematical set that is closed under an associative binary operation

semi·lethal \ˌsemē, -ˌmī, -ˌmə +\ *n* [*semi-* + *lethal*] **:** a mutation that in the homozygous condition produces more than 50 percent mortality but not complete mortality — **semilethal** *adj*

semi·nat·u·ral \"+\ *adj* [*semi-* + *natural*] **:** modified by human influence but retaining many natural features

sen* *n* [fr. ²*sen*] **:** a monetary unit of Malaysia equivalent to $^{1}/_{100}$ ringgit — see MONEY table *in the Dict*

send up* *vt* **:** to make fun of **:** SATIRIZE, PARODY

send–up \ˈ≐ˌ≐\ *n* -s [*send up* (herein)] **:** SATIRE, PARODY

sene \ˈsenē\ *n, pl* **sene** *or* **senes** [Samoan, fr. E *cent*] **1 :** a monetary unit of Western Samoa equivalent to $^{1}/_{100}$ tala — see MONEY table *in the Dict* **2 :** a coin representing one sene

sen·gi \ˈseŋgē\ *n, pl* **sengi** [native name in the Congo] **:** a monetary unit of Zaire equal to $^{1}/_{100}$ likuta or $^{1}/_{10,000}$ zaire

senior citizen *n* **:** an elderly person; *esp* **:** one who has retired

sen·i·ti \ˈsenətē\ *n, pl* **seniti** [Tongan, modif. of E *cent*] **1 :** a monetary unit of Tonga equal to $^{1}/_{100}$ pa'anga — see MONEY table *in the Dict* **2 :** a coin representing one seniti

sen·ryu \ˈsenrē(ˌ)ü\ *n, pl* **senryu** [Jap] **:** a 3-line unrhymed Japanese poem structurally similar to haiku but treating human nature usu. in an ironic or satiric vein

sensitivity training *n* **:** training in a small interacting group that is designed to increase each individual's awareness of his own feelings and the feelings of others and to enhance interpersonal relations through the exploration of the behavior, needs, and responses of the individuals making up the group

sen·so·ri·neural \ˌsen(t)s(ə)rē +\ *adj* [*sensory* + *neural*] **:** of, relating to, or involving the aspects of sense perception mediated by nerves ⟨∼ hearing loss⟩

sen·ti \ˈsentē\ *n, pl* **senti** [Swahili, modif. of E *cent*] **:** the cent of Tanzania

sen·ti·mo \ˈsentəˌmō\ *n* -s [Pilipino, fr. Sp. *céntimo* — more at CENTIMO] **1 :** a monetary unit of the Republic of the Philippines equal to $^{1}/_{100}$ peso **:** CENTAVO — see MONEY table *in the Dict* **2 :** a coin representing one sentimo

sequence* *vt* **:** to determine the sequence of chemical constituents (as amino-acid residues) in

sequential *n* -s [*sequential,* adj.] **:** an oral contraceptive in which the pills taken during approximately the first three weeks contain only estrogen and those taken during the rest of the cycle contain both estrogen and progestogen

serial* *adj* **:** relating to or being a connection in a computer system in which the bits of a byte are transmitted sequentially over a single wire

se·ri·al·ism \ˈsirēəˌlizəm, ˈsēr-\ *n* -s [¹*serial* + *-ism*] **:** serial music; *also* **:** the theory or practice of composing serial music

serial section *n* **:** any of a series of sections cut in sequence by a microtome from a prepared specimen (as of tissue) — **serially sectioned** *adj* — **serial sectioning** *n*

se·ro·conversion \ˌsi(ˌ)rō *sometimes* ˌse(-+\ *n* [*sero-* + *conversion*] **:** the production of antibodies in response to an antigen administered as a vaccine

se·ro·epidemiologic \"+\ *or* **se·ro·epidemiological** \"+\ *adj* [*sero-* + *epidemiologic* or *epidemiological*] **:** of, relating to, or being epidemiologic investigations involving the identification of antibodies to specific antigens in populations of individuals — **se·ro·epidemiology** \"+\ *n*

se·ro·group \"+\ *n* [*sero-* + *group*] **:** a group of serotypes having one or more antigens in common

se·ro·to·ner·gic \ˌsirətəˈnərjik\ *also* **se·ro·to·nin·er·gic** \ˌsirəˌtōnəˈnərjik, -ˌtän-\ *adj* [*serotonin* + *-ergic* (herein)] **:** liberating, activated by, or involving serotonin in the transmission of nerve impulses ⟨∼ pathways⟩

se·ro·type \ˈsirəˌtīp, ˈser-\ *vt* [*sero-* + *type*] **:** to determine the serotype of

service break *n* **:** a game won on an opponent's serve (as in tennis)

service module *n* **:** a space vehicle module containing propellant tanks, fuel cells, and the main rocket engine

session man *n* **:** a studio musician who backs up a performer at a recording session

set back *n* **:** an offensive back in football who usu. lines up behind the quarterback

setback* *n* **:** an automatic scheduled adjustment to a lower temperature setting of a thermostat

se·to ware \ˈsāˌtō-, ˈse-\ *also* **seto** *n* -s *usu cap S* [fr. *Seto,* city in central Honshu, Japan, where it originated] **:** a Japanese ceramic ware traditionally produced since the 10th century comprising in its earlier period earthenwares often based on contemporaneous Chinese and Korean porcelains, later high-fired stonewares sometimes with notable brown, black, yellow, or celadon glazes, and from the end of the 18th century chiefly porcelain often decorated with underglaze blue

severe combined immunodeficiency *or* **severe combined immune deficiency** *n* **:** a rare congenital disorder of the immune system that is characterized by inability to produce a normal complement of antibodies and of T cells and that results usu. in early death — abbr. *SCID*

Sev·in \ˈsevən\ *trademark* — used for an insecticide consisting of a preparation of carbaryl

sex* *n* **:** GENITALIA

sex chromatin *n* **:** BARR BODY *herein*

sexi·decimal \ˌseksə̇, -ksē +\ *adj* [*sex-* + *-decimal* (as in *duodecimal*)] **:** HEXADECIMAL *herein*

sex·ism \ˈsekˌsizəm\ *n* -s [[1]*sex* + *-ism* (as in *racism*)] **1 :** prejudice or discrimination based on sex; *esp* **:** discrimination against women **2 :** behavior, conditions, or attitudes that foster stereotypes of social roles based on sex — **sex·ist** \ˈseksə̇st\ *adj or n*

sex kitten *n* **:** a woman with conspicuous sex appeal

sex object *n* **:** a person regarded as an object of sexual interest

sex·ploi·ta·tion \ˌsekˌsplȯiˈtāshən\ *n* [blend of *sex* and *exploitation*] **:** the exploitation of sex in the media and esp. in film

sex symbol *n* **:** a person noted for conspicuous sex appeal

sexually transmitted disease *n* **:** a disease usu. transmitted by direct sexual contact **:** VENEREAL DISEASE — called also *STD*

sexy* *adj* **:** strongly attractive or interesting ⟨colorless benefits, ~ only to economists —Howard Felsher⟩

sey·fert galaxy \ˌsēfə(r)t-, ˌsī-\ *n, usu cap S* [after Carl K. *Seyfert* †1960 Am. astronomer] **:** any of a class of spiral galaxies that have small compact bright nuclei exhibiting variability in light intensity, emission of radio waves, and spectra which indicate hot gases in rapid motion

shade* *n* **shades** *pl* **:** SUNGLASSES

shadow mask *n* **:** a metal plate in a color television tube that contains minute apertures permitting passage of the electron beam to specific phosphors on the screen during a scan

shakeout** *n* **:** a sharp break in a particular industry that usu. follows overproduction or excessive competition and tends to force out weaker producers

sha·ku·ha·chi \ˌshäkəˈhächē\ *n, pl* **shakuhachi** [Jap] **:** a Japanese bamboo flute

sham·a·teur·ism \ˈshaməˌtərˌizəm, -əd·əˌri-, -əˌt(y)u̇(ə)rˌi-, -əˌchu̇(ə)rˌi-, -əchəˌri-\ *n* -s [blend of [3]*sham* and *amateurism*] **:** the practice of treating certain athletes as amateurs so that they will be eligible for amateur competition while subsidizing them with illegal payments or with excessive expense money

shape* *vt* **:** to modify (behavior) by rewarding changes that tend toward a desired response

shatter cone *n* **:** a conical fragment of rock that has striations radiating from the apex and that is formed by high pressure (as from volcanism or meteorite impact)

sha·zam \shəˈzam, -ˈzaa(ə)m\ *interj* [incantation used by the comic-strip hero Captain Marvel, fr. *S*olomon, *H*ercules, *A*tlas, *Z*eus, *A*chilles, and *M*ercury, on whom he called] — used to indicate an instantaneous transformation or appearance

shell* *n* **1 :** a plain usu. sleeveless overblouse **2** *or* **shell company :** a business that exists without assets or independent operation as a legal entity through which another company can conduct certain dealings

shell* *vt* **:** to score heavily against (as a pitcher in baseball)

shell–shocked \ˈ=ˌ=\ *adj* **:** mentally confused, upset, or exhausted as a result of excessive stress

shi·at·su \shēˈät(ˌ)sü\ *n* -s *often cap* [short for Jap *shiatsuryōhō*, lit., finger-pressure therapy, fr. *shi* finger + *atsu-* pressure + *ryōhō* treatment] **:** a massage with the fingers applied to those specific areas of the body used in acupuncture — called also *acupressure*

shield law *n* **:** a law that protects journalists from forced disclosure of confidential news sources

shift* *n* **1 :** a movement of bits in a computer register a specified number of places to the right or left **2 :** the act or an instance of depressing the shift key (as on a typewriter)

shih tzu \ˈshēdˈzü, -ˈzu̇\ *n, pl* **shih tzus** *usu cap S&T* [Chin (Pek) *shih*[1] *tzŭ*[3] *kou*[3] Pekingese dog, fr. *shih*[1] lion + *tzŭ*[3] son + *kou*[3] dog] **:** any of an old Chinese breed of dogs that have a square short unwrinkled muzzle, short muscular legs, and massive amounts of long dense hair

shilingi \ˈshiliŋgē\ *n, pl* **shilingi** [Swahili, fr. E *shilling*] **:** the shilling of Tanzania

ship* *n* **:** SPACECRAFT

shirtdress \ˈ=ˌ=\ *n* **:** a dress that is patterned after a shirt and has buttons down the front and a collar

shirt–jac \ˈ=ˌjak\ *n* -s [by shortening] **:** SHIRT JACKET *herein*

shirt jacket *n* **:** a jacket having an open shirtlike collar and usu. long sleeves with cuffs **:** a shirt designed to be worn over another shirt or blouse

shirt suit *n* **:** a clothing ensemble consisting of a shirt or shirt jacket and matching pants

shirt·waist·er \ˈ=ˌwāstə(r)\ *n* -s [*shirtwaist* + *-er*] *Brit* **:** a shirtwaist dress **:** SHIRTDRESS *herein*

shit* *n* **:** any of several intoxicating or narcotic drugs; *esp* **:** HEROIN — usu. considered vulgar

shithead \ˈ=ˌ=\ *n* [[2]*shit* + *head*] **:** a contemptible person — usu. considered vulgar

shitkicker \ˈ=ˌ==\ *n* [[2]*shit* + *kicker*] **1** *slang* **:** an unsophisticated person from a rural area **2** *slang* **:** a fan or performer of country and western music

shit·less \ˈshitlə̇s\ *adv* [[2]*shit* + *-less*] **:** to an extreme degree — used as an intensive ⟨scared ~⟩; usu. considered vulgar

shlep, shlepper *var of* SCHLEPP *herein*

shlock *var of* SCHLOCK *herein*

shmear *var of* SCHMEAR *herein*

shmuck *var of* SCHMUCK *herein*

shoot* *vt* **:** to inject (an illicit drug) esp. into the bloodstream — **shoot from the hip :** to act or speak hastily without consideration of the consequences — **shoot the curl** *or* **shoot the tube :** to surf into or through the curl of a wave — **shoot the pier :** to surf between the pilings of an ocean pier

shoot down* *vt* **1 :** to put an end to **:** make ineffective or void **:** DEFEAT **2 :** DEFLATE, RIDICULE; *also* **:** REPROVE **3 :** to expose weakness or inaccuracy in **:** DISCREDIT ⟨*shoot down* a theory⟩

shoot–'em–up \ˈ==ˌ=\ *n* -s **:** a movie or television show with much shooting and killing

shoot–out* *n* **:** a sharp struggle between adversaries ⟨a corporate *shoot-out*⟩

shopper* *n* **:** a usu. free paper carrying advertising and sometimes local news

shopping bag *n* **:** a bag (as of strong paper or plastic) that has handles and is intended for carrying purchases

shopping–bag lady \ˈ==ˌ=-\ *n* **:** BAG LADY *herein*

shopping mall *n* **1 :** a pedestrian mall lined with shops **2 :** a large usu. suburban building or group of buildings containing various shops with associated passageways

short* *adj* **:** near the end of one's tour of duty

short* *vt* **:** to sell (as stocks) short

short fuse *n* **:** a tendency to get angry quickly **:** a quick temper

shortlist \'=,=\ *n* [[1]*short* + *list*] *Brit* **:** a list of candidates for final consideration (as for a position or a prize)

short-list \(')=¦=\ *vt* [*shortlist* (herein)] *Brit* **:** to place on a shortlist

short position* *n* **:** the market position of a trader who has made but not yet covered a short sale

short-term* *adj* **:** generated by assets held six months or less

shot* *n* **:** an act, instance, or result of hitting: **a :** BLOW ⟨the boxer took a hard ~ to the body⟩ **b :** a hard-hit baseball ⟨a three-run ~ over the left-field wall⟩

shotgun* *n* **:** an offensive football formation in which the quarterback plays a few yards behind the line of scrimmage and the other backs are scattered as flankers or slotbacks

shotmaking \'=,==\ *n* -s **:** the ability to make accurate or successful shots (as in golf or basketball)

shoulder belt *or* **shoulder harness** *n* **:** an automobile safety belt worn across the torso and over the shoulder

show-and-tell \¦==¦=\ *n* **1 :** a classroom exercise in which children display an item and talk about it **2 :** a public display or demonstration

showboat* *n* **:** one who tries to attract attention by conspicuous behavior

showboat *vi* [*showboat*, n. (herein)] **:** to show off

shrink* *n* **1** [short for *headshrinker*] **:** HEADSHRINKER 2 **2 :** a woman's short usu. sleeveless sweater often worn over a long-sleeved blouse or sweater

shrink-wrap \'=¦=\ *vt* [[1]*shrink* + *wrap*] **:** to wrap (as a book or meat) in tough clear plastic film that is then shrunk (as by heating) to form a tightly fitting package — **shrink-wrap** \'=,=\ *n*

shtick *or* **schtick** *also* **shtik** \'shtik\ *n* -s [Yiddish *shtik*, lit., piece, fr. MHG *stücke*, fr. OHG *stucki* — more at STOCK] **1 :** a show-business routine, gimmick, or gag **:** BIT **2 :** one's special trait, interest, or activity **:** BAG *herein*, THING *herein*

[1]**shuck** \'shək\ *n* -s [origin unknown] **:** a wily deception **:** SHAM

[2]**shuck** \"\ *vi* **:** to talk or act deceptively ~ *vt* **:** DECEIVE, TRICK

shun·pik·er \'shən,pīkə(r)\ *n* -s [*shunpike* + [2]*-er*] **:** one who engages in shunpiking

shun·pik·ing \-kiŋ\ *n* -s [*shunpike* + [3]*-ing*] **:** the practice of avoiding superhighways esp. for the pleasure of driving on back roads — **shunpike** \'=¦=\ *vi*

shunt* *n* **:** a minor collision in auto racing

shuttle* *n* **:** SPACE SHUTTLE *herein*

shuttle diplomacy *n* **:** negotiations esp. between nations carried on by an intermediary who shuttles back and forth between the disputants

SI [*F Système International d'Unités*] *abbr* International System of Units

sick·ie *also* **sick·ee** \'sikē\ *n* -s **:** a person who is morally or mentally sick

sicko \'sik(,)ō\ *n* -s [*sick* + [1]*-o*] **:** SICKIE *herein*

sick-out \'=,=\ *n* -s **:** an organized absence from work by workers on the pretext of sickness in order to apply pressure to management without an actual strike

sidedress \'=,=\ *n* **1 :** plant nutrients used to side-dress a crop **2 :** the act or process of side-dressing a crop

side-straddle hop \'=,==-\ *n* **:** JUMPING-JACK *herein*

SIDS *abbr* sudden infant death syndrome *herein*

sie·mens \'sēmənz, 'zē-\ *n, pl* **siemens** [after Werner von *Siemens* †1892 Ger. electrical engineer and inventor] **:** a unit of conductance in the mks system equivalent to one ampere per volt

sigma* *or* **sigma particle** *n* **:** an unstable subatomic particle of the baryon family existing in positive, negative, and neutral charge states with masses respectively 2328, 2343, and 2333 times the mass of an electron

sigma factor *n* **:** a detachable polypeptide subunit of RNA polymerase that is held to determine the genetic material which undergoes transcription

sign* *n* **:** SIGN LANGUAGE

sign·age \'sīnij\ *n* -s [[1]*sign* + *-age*] **:** signs (as of identification, warning, or direction) or a system or design of such signs

significance level *n* **:** LEVEL OF SIGNIFICANCE *herein*

signifier* *n* **:** one who engages in signifying

sig·ni·fy·ing \'signə̇,fīiŋ\ *n* -s [fr. gerund of *signify*] **:** a good-natured needling or goading esp. among urban blacks by means of indirect gibes and clever often preposterous put-downs; *also* **:** DOZENS *herein*

sign·ing \'sīniŋ\ *n* -s [gerund of *sign*] **1 :** SIGNAGE *herein* ⟨highway ~⟩ **2 :** SIGN LANGUAGE

sign off* *vi* **:** to approve or acknowledge something by or as if by a signature — used with *on* ⟨*sign off* on a memo⟩

sign on* *vi* **:** to announce the start of broadcasting for the day — **sign-on** \'=,=\ *n* -s

si·jo \'sē(,)jō\ *n* -s [Korean] **:** an unrhymed Korean verse form appearing in Korean in 3 lines of 14 to 16 syllables and usu. in English translation in 6 shorter lines

Si·las·tic \sə̇'lastik, sī'-\ *trademark* — used for a soft pliable plastic

silky terrier *also* **silky** *n* **:** a low-set toy terrier that weighs 8 to 10 pounds, has a flat silky glossy coat colored blue with tan on the head, chest, and legs, and is derived from crosses of the Australian terrier with the Yorkshire terrier

sil·vex \'sil,veks\ *n* -ES [prob. fr. L *silva* wood + E *ex*terminator] **:** a selective herbicide $C_9H_7Cl_3O_3$ esp. effective in controlling woody plants but toxic to animals

sil·vi·chemical \¦silvə̇ +\ *n* [L *silva* wood + E *-i-* + *chemical*] **:** any of numerous chemicals derived from wood

si·ma·zine \'sīmə,zēn\ *n* -s [*sim-* (prob. alter. of [2]*sym-*) + tri*azine*] **:** a selective herbicide $C_7H_{12}N_5Cl$ used to control weeds among crop plants

simple* *adj, of a statistical hypothesis* **:** specifying exact values for one or more statistical parameters — compare COMPOSITE *herein*

simple closed curve *n* **:** JORDAN CURVE

simply connected *adj* **:** being or characterized by a surface divided into two separate parts by every closed curve it contains

simply ordered *adj* **:** having any two elements connected by a relationship that is reflexive, antisymmetric, and transitive

simulate* *vt* **:** to make a simulation of (as a physical system) — **sim·u·la·tive** \'simyə,lād·ə̇v\ *adj*

simulation* *n* **1 :** the imitative representation of the functioning of one system or process by means of the functioning of another ⟨a computer ~ of an industrial process⟩ **2 :** examination of a problem often not subject to direct experimentation by means of a simulator (as a programmed computer)

sing–along \ˈ⸗⸗,⸗\ *n* -s [[1]*sing* + *along*] **:** an informal session of group singing esp. of popular songs

single* *n* **:** an unmarried person and esp. one young and socially active — usu. used in pl. ⟨a way of life for young ~*s* —Norman Mailer⟩ ⟨a ~*s* weekend⟩

single–blind \ˈ⸗⸗,⸗\ *adj* **:** of, relating to, or being an experimental procedure in which the experimenters but not the subjects know the makeup of the test and control groups during the actual course of an experiment — compare DOUBLE–BLIND *herein*

single bond* *n* **:** a chemical bond consisting of one covalent bond between two atoms in a molecule esp. when the atoms can have more than one covalent bond

single–cell protein \ˈ⸗⸗ˈ⸗-\ *n* [[1]*single* + *cell*] **:** protein produced by microorganisms cultured on organic material and used esp. as a source of food

single·hood \ˈsiŋgəl,hu̇d\ *n* -s [[1]*single* + *-hood*] **:** the state of being single and esp. unmarried

singles bar *n* **:** a bar that caters esp. to young unmarried men and women

singlet* *n* **:** an elementary particle not part of a multiplet

singleton* *n* **:** a mathematical set that contains one element

singular* *adj* **1** *of a matrix* **:** having a determinant equal to zero **2** *of a linear transformation* **:** having the property that the matrix of coefficients of the new variables has a determinant equal to zero

singularity* *n* **1 :** a point at which the derivative of a given function of a real or complex variable does not exist but every neighborhood of which contains points for which the derivative exists **2 :** a point or region of infinite mass density at which space and time are infinitely distorted by gravitational forces and which is held to be the final state of matter falling into a black hole

singular point *n* **:** SINGULARITY 1 *herein*

sin·se·mil·la \,sinsəˈmēl(y)ə\ *n* -s [MexSp, lit., without seed] **:** high-grade marijuana from female plants that are specially tended and kept seedless by preventing pollination in order to induce a high resin content; *also* **:** a female hemp plant grown to produce sinsemilla

sin tax *n* **:** a tax on substances or activities traditionally considered sinful (as tobacco, liquor, or gambling)

sir·ta·ki \sirˈtäkē\ *n* -s [NGk; perh. akin to Turk *sìrto* a kind of dance] **:** a Greek circle dance similar to a hora

sissy bar *n* **:** a narrow inverted U-shaped bar rising from behind the seat of a motorcycle or bicycle that is designed to support a driver or passenger

sisterhood* *n* **:** a relationship of women united by a common cause or motivation ⟨~ of feminists⟩ ⟨gay ~⟩; *also* **:** women united in a sisterhood

sit·com \ˈsit,käm\ *n* -s [*sit*uation *com*edy] **:** SITUATION COMEDY *herein*

situation comedy *n* **:** a radio or television comedy series that involves a continuing cast of characters in a succession of unconnected episodes

situation ethics *n pl but sing or pl in constr* [trans. of G *situationsethik*] **:** a system of ethics which is based on what is consistent with brotherly love and by which acts are judged within their contexts instead of by categorical principles

sjö·gren's syndrome \ˈshœ̄grənz-\ *also* **sjögren syndrome** *or* **sjögren's disease** *n, usu cap 1st S* [after H.S.C. *Sjögren b*1899 Swed. ophthalmologist] **:** a chronic inflammatory disease that is characterized by dry keratoconjunctivitis, xerostomia, and lymphocytic infiltration of the lacrimal and salivary glands and that is often associated with rheumatoid arthritis

ska \ˈskä\ *n* -s [origin unknown] **:** popular music of Jamaican origin that combines elements of traditional Caribbean rhythms and jazz

skag *var of* SCAG *herein*

skateboard \ˈ⸗,⸗\ *n* [[2]*skate* + *board*] **:** a narrow board about two feet long mounted on roller-skate wheels — **skate·board·er** \-ə(r)\ *n* -s — **skate·board·ing** \-iŋ\ *n* -s

skew field *n* **:** a mathematical field in which multiplication is not commutative

skew lines *n pl* **:** straight lines that do not intersect and are not in the same plane

skibob \ˈ⸗,⸗\ *n* [[1]*ski* + [8]*bob*] **:** a vehicle that has two short skis one behind the other, a steering handle attached to the forward ski, and a low upholstered seat over the rear ski and that is used for gliding downhill over snow by a rider wearing miniature skis for balance — **ski·bob·ber** \-ə(r)\ *n* — **ski·bob·bing** \-iŋ\ *n* -s

skid pad *n* **:** a large usu. circular area of asphalt that is oiled to make it slick and that is used for testing automobiles and motorcycles with controlled skids and spins

skif·fle \ˈskifəl\ *n* -s [perh. imit.] **:** jazz or folk music played by a group all or some of whose members play nonstandard instruments or noisemakers (as jugs, washboards, or jew's harps)

skim* *vt* **:** to remove or conceal (as gambling income) to avoid payment of taxes

ski mask *n* **:** a knit fabric mask worn esp. by skiers for protection from the cold

skimmer* *n* **:** a fitted sleeveless usu. flaring sheathlike dress

skin* *n* **:** a mutual touching or slapping of the palms that takes the place of a handshake — used chiefly in the phrases *give skin* or *give me skin*

skin \ˈskin\ *adj* [[1]*skin*] **:** involving subjects who are nude ⟨expected to conduct ~ searches for weapons —Diane K. Shah⟩; *specif* **:** devoted to showing nudes ⟨~ magazines⟩

skin flick *n* **:** a motion picture characterized by nudity and explicit sexual situations

skin·ner·ian \skəˈnirēən, -ˈner-\ *adj, usu cap* [Burrhus Frederick *Skinner b*1904 Am. psychologist + E *-ian*] **:** of, relating to, or suggestive of the behavioristic theories of B. F. Skinner — **skinnerian** *n* -s *usu cap*

[1]**skin·ny–dip** \ˈskinē,dip\ *vi* [[1]*skin* + [1]*-y* + [1]*dip*] **:** to swim nude — **skin·ny–dip·per** \-ə(r)\ *n* — **skin·ny–dip·ping** \-iŋ\ *n*

[2]**skinny–dip** \"\ *n* **:** a swim in the nude

skin–pop \ˈ⸗,⸗\ *vb* [[1]*skin* + *pop* (herein)] *vi* **:** to inject a drug subcutaneously rather than into a vein ~ *vt* **:** to inject (a drug) by skin-popping — **skin–popper** \ˈ⸗,⸗⸗\ *n*

skint \ˈskint\ *adj* [perh. alter. of *scant*] *Brit* **:** BROKE 2

skirt steak *n* **:** a narrow boneless strip of tender beef from the plate that is usu. broiled

ski touring *n* **:** cross-country skiing for pleasure — **ski tourer** *n*

skiwear \ˈ⸗,⸗\ *n* [[2]*ski* + *wear*] **:** clothing suitable for wear while skiing

skosh \ˈskōsh\ *n* -ES [Jap *sukoshi* smidgen] **:** a small amount **:** [3]BIT 3c, SMIDGEN — used adverbially with *a* ⟨just a ~ bit shook —Josiah Bunting⟩

skunk works *n pl but sing or pl in constr* [locale in *Li'l Abner,* comic strip by Al Capp †1979 Am. cartoonist] **:** a department or facility (as for research and development of a particular product) that is isolated from the rest of a company or corporation

sky·div·ing \ˈskī,dīviŋ\ *n* -s [[1]*sky* + *diving,* gerund of *dive*] **:** the sport of jumping from an airplane at a moderate altitude (as 6000 feet) and executing various tumbles and dives before pulling the rip cord of a parachute — **sky diver** *n*

sky·jack \ˈskī,jak\ *vt* [*sky* + *jack* (as in *hijack*)] **:** to commandeer (an airplane in flight) by the threat of violence — **sky·jack·er** \-ə(r)\ *n* -s — **sky·jack·ing** \-iŋ\ *n* -s

sky marshal *n* **:** an armed federal plainclothesman assigned to prevent skyjackings

skywalk \ˈ=,=\ *n* [[1]*sky* + *walk*] **:** a usu. enclosed aerial walkway connecting two buildings

slam* *n* **:** SLAMMER *herein*

slam dunk *n* **:** DUNK SHOT — **slam–dunk** \(ˈ)=ˈ=\ *vb*

slam·mer \ˈslamə(r), -aa(ə)m-\ *n* -s [[3]*slam* + [2]*-er*] **:** JAIL, PRISON

slap shot *n* **:** a shot in ice hockey that is made with a swinging stroke so that the puck often flies through the air

sleaze \ˈslēz\ *n* -s [back-formation fr. *sleazy*] **:** a sleazy quality or appearance; *also* **:** sleazy material ⟨I don't read ~ —Peter Lawford⟩

sleep around *vi* **:** to engage in sex promiscuously

sleeping pill *also* **sleeping tablet** *n* **:** a drug and esp. a barbiturate that is taken as a tablet or capsule to induce sleep

slide guitar *n* **:** BOTTLENECK *herein*

slim·mer \ˈslimə(r\ *n* -s [[2]*slim* + *-er*] *chiefly Brit* **:** DIETER

slim·nas·tics \,slimˈnastiks\ *n pl but sing in constr* [blend of [1]*slim* and *gymnastics*] **:** exercises designed to reduce one's weight

slingshot* *n* **1 :** a maneuver in auto racing in which a drafting car accelerates past the car in front by taking advantage of reserve power **2 :** a dragster in which the driver sits behind the rear wheels

slipstream* *n* **1 :** an area of reduced air pressure and forward suction immediately behind a rapidly moving racing car **2** *chiefly Brit* **:** BACKWASH 2 ⟨my childhood, which was passed in the ~ of an erratic father —John le Carré⟩

slipstream *vi* **:** to drive in the slipstream of a racing car

slipway* *n* **:** a space between docks

slit card *n* **:** a display card with a slit whereby it is attached to a book

slope* *n* **:** the slope of the line tangent to a plane curve at a point ⟨find the ~ of the curve at the point *x*⟩

slope–intercept form \ˈ=ˈ==,=-\ *n* **:** the equation of a straight line in the form $y = mx + b$ where m is the slope of the line and b is the y-intercept of its graph — compare POINT-SLOPE FORM *herein*

sloppy joe* *n* **:** ground beef cooked in a seasoned sauce (as chili) and usu. served on a bun

sloshed \ˈsläsht\ *adj* [fr. past part. of [2]*slosh*] *slang* **:** DRUNK

slot* *n* **:** a gap between an end and a tackle in an offensive line in football

slotback \ˈ=,=\ *n* **:** an offensive halfback in football who lines up just behind the slot between an offensive end and tackle

slot car *n* **:** an electric toy racing automobile that has an arm underneath fitting into a groove for guidance and metal strips alongside the groove for supplying electricity and that is remotely controlled by the operator's hand=held rheostat

slot racing *n* **:** the racing of slot cars — **slot racer** *n*

slow–pitch *also* **slo–pitch** \ˈslō,pich\ *n* **:** softball which is played with 10 players on each side and in which each pitch must travel in an arc from 3 to 10 feet high in order to be legal and in which base stealing is not permitted

slow virus *n* **:** a virus with a long incubation period between infection and development of the degenerative disease (as multiple sclerosis, rheumatoid arthritis, or kuru) associated with it

slugging average *n* **:** the ratio of the total number of bases reached on base hits to official times at bat for a baseball player expressed as a 3-place decimal — called also *slugging percentage*

slumlord \ˈ=,=\ *n* -s [[1]*slum* + land*lord*] **:** a landlord who receives inflated rents from substandard neglected properties

slump·fla·tion \,sləmpˈflāshən\ *n* -s [*slump* + in*flation*] **:** a state or period of combined economic decline and rising inflation

slurb \ˈslərb\ *n* -s [*sl-* (as in *sloppy, sleazy, slovenly, slipshod*) + sub*urb*] **:** a suburb characterized by wearisomely uniform and usu. poorly constructed houses

slur·vian \ˈslərvēən, -lāv-, -ləiv-\ *n, usu cap* [irreg. fr. *slur* + *-ian*] **:** speech characterized by slurring

slush* *n* **1 :** a partially frozen soft drink **2 :** unsolicited material submitted to a publisher

smack \ˈsmak\ *n* -s [perh. fr. Yiddish *shmek* sniff, whiff, pinch (of snuff)] *slang* **:** HEROIN

smaller european elm bark beetle *n, usu cap 1st E* **:** ELM BARK BEETLE b

smart* *n* **smarts** *pl, slang* **:** INTELLIGENCE, KNOW-HOW ⟨went to show that intellectual heavies could be beautiful in spite of all those ~*s* —Cyra McFadden⟩

smart* *adj* **1 :** operating automatically or by automation ⟨a ~ machine tool⟩ ⟨~ windows to regulate sunlight⟩ **2 :** INTELLIGENT 1 *herein*

smart·ass \ˈ=,=\ *n* -ES [[2]*smart* + [2]*-ass* (herein)] **:** SMART ALECK, WISE GUY — **smartass** *adj*

smart bomb *n* **:** a bomb that can be guided (as by a laser beam) to its target

smashed \ˈsmasht\ *adj* [fr. past part. of [1]*smash*] *slang* **:** DRUNK

s matrix *n, usu cap S* [scattering *matrix*] **:** a unitary matrix in quantum mechanics the absolute values of the squares of whose elements are equal to probabilities of transition between different states — called also *scattering matrix*

smog* *n* **:** a photochemical haze caused by the action of solar ultraviolet radiation on atmosphere polluted with hydrocarbons and oxides of nitrogen from automobile exhaust

smog·less \ˈ=ləs\ *adj* [*smog* + *-less*] **1 :** marked by the absence of smog ⟨a ~ city⟩ **2 :** emitting no fumes that would contribute to the production of smog ⟨~ cars of the future⟩

smoke detector *n* **:** an alarm that activates automatically when it detects smoke

smoke–in \ˈ=,=\ *n* -s [[2]*smoke* + *-in* (herein)] **:** a large gathering of people publicly smoking marijuana usu. in support of legalizing it

smokestack \ˈ=,=\ *adj* **:** of, relating to, being, or characterized by manufacturing and esp. heavy industry ⟨~ industries⟩

smok·ey \'smōkē, -ki\ *n* -s *usu cap* [after *Smokey* the Bear, advertising symbol of U.S. Forest Service who wears a hat shaped like a state trooper's] *slang* **:** a policeman on highway patrol

smoking gun *n* **:** something that serves as conclusive evidence or proof esp. of a crime

smooth* *adj, of a curve* **:** being the representation of a function with a continuous first derivative

snake oil* *n* **:** POPPYCOCK, BUNKUM

SNG *abbr* substitute natural gas; synthetic natural gas

snow* *n, slang* **:** HEROIN

snowbelt \'≈,≈\ *n, often cap* [[1]*snow* + *belt*] **:** a region that receives an appreciable amount of annual snowfall ⟨a state in the ~⟩

snowbird* *n* **:** one who travels to warm climes for the winter

snowblower* *n* **:** SNOW THROWER *herein*

snow cone *n* **:** SNOWBALL 1b

snowmaker \'≈,≈≈\ *n* **:** a device for making snow artificially

snowmaking \'≈,≈≈\ *adj* **:** used for the production of snow usu. for ski slopes ⟨~ machines⟩

snow·mo·bil·ing \'snō(,)mō,bēliŋ\ *n* -s [*snowmobile* + *-ing*] **:** the sport of driving or racing a snowmobile — **snow·mo·bil·er** \-lə(r)\ *also* **snow·mo·bil·ist** \-ləst\ *n* -s

snow pea *n* **:** SUGAR PEA

snow thrower *n* **:** a machine for removing snow (as from a driveway or sidewalk) in which a rotating usu. spiral blade picks up and propels the snow aside

soap* *n* **1 :** SOAP OPERA **2 :** the melodrama and sentimentality characteristic of a soap opera; *also* **:** something (as a novel) having such qualities

soa·ve \'swävā, sə'w-, -ve\ *n* -s *usu cap* [fr. *Soave,* village near Verona, Italy] **:** a dry white wine from the area about Soave, Italy

socialist realism *n* [trans. of Russ *sotsialisticheskiĭ realizm*] **:** a theory of Soviet art, music, and literature that calls for the didactic use of artistic work to develop social consciousness in an evolving socialist state — **socialist realist** *n*

sociobiology* *n* **:** the comparative study of social organization in animals and man esp. with regard to its genetic basis and evolutionary history — **sociobiological*** *adj* — **so·cio·biologist** \¦sōs(h)ē(,)ō+\ *n*

so·cio·linguistic \¦sōs(h)ē(,)ō +\ *adj* [*socio-* + *linguistic*] **1 :** of or relating to the social aspects of language **2 :** of or relating to sociolinguistics

so·cio·linguistics \"+\ *n pl but usu sing in constr* [*socio-* + *linguistics*] **:** the study of linguistic behavior as determined by sociocultural factors (as social class or educational level)

so·ci·ol·o·gese \,sōsē,älə'jēz *also* ,sōshē-\ *n* -s [*sociology* + *-ese*] **:** a style of writing held to be characteristic of sociologists

so·cio·religious \¦sōs(h)ēō +\ *adj* [*socio-* + *religious*] **:** of, relating to, or involving a combination of social and religious factors

sodium dodecyl sulfate *n* **:** SODIUM LAURYL SULFATE

sodium pump *n* **:** a molecular mechanism by which sodium ions are actively transported across a cell membrane; *esp* **:** the one by which the appropriate internal and external concentrations of sodium and potassium ions are maintained in a nerve fiber and which involves the active transport of sodium ions outward with movement of potassium ions to the interior

sodium stearate *n* **:** a white powdery salt $C_{17}H_{35}COONa$ that is soluble in water, is the chief constituent of some laundry soaps, and is used esp. in cosmetics and toothpaste

soft* *adj* **1 :** occurring at such a speed and under such circumstances as to avoid destructive impact ⟨~ landing of a spacecraft on the moon⟩ **2 :** not protected against enemy attack ⟨a ~ aboveground launching site⟩ **3 :** BIODEGRADABLE *herein* ⟨a ~ detergent⟩ ⟨~ pesticides⟩ **4** *of a drug* **:** considered less detrimental than a hard narcotic ⟨marijuana is usually regarded as a ~ drug⟩ **5 a :** being low due to sluggish market conditions ⟨~ prices⟩ **b :** SLUGGISH, SLOW ⟨a ~ market⟩ **6 :** not firmly committed **:** IRRESOLUTE, UNDECIDED ⟨~ voters⟩ **7 :** SOFT-CORE *herein* ⟨~ pornography⟩ **8 a :** being or based on interpretive or speculative data ⟨~ evidence⟩ ⟨~ data⟩ **b :** utilizing or based on soft data ⟨~ science⟩ **9 :** being or using renewable sources of energy (as solar radiation, wind, tides, or biomass conversion) ⟨~ technologies⟩

softbound \'≈¦≈\ *adj* [[1]*soft* + [4]*bound*] **:** not bound in hard covers

soft-coated wheaten terrier *n* **:** any of a breed of compact medium-sized terriers developed in Ireland and having a soft abundant light fawn coat

soft-core \'≈¦≈\ *adj* [[1]*soft* + *-core* (as in *hard-core* — herein)] **1** *of pornography* **:** containing descriptions or scenes of sex acts that are less explicit than hard-core material **2 :** relatively mild **:** MODERATE ⟨*soft-core* support⟩

soft-land \'≈¦≈\ *vb* [back-formation fr. *soft landing*] *vi* **:** to make a soft landing on a celestial body (as the moon) ~ *vt* **:** to cause to soft-land — **soft-land·er** \-ə(r)\ *n* -s

soft landing *n* **:** the averting of a major economic decline through a gradual slowing of the economy

soft-liner \(')≈¦≈≈\ *n* -s [[1]*soft* + *-liner* (as in *hard-liner* — herein)] **:** one who advocates or pursues a flexible policy or course of action

soft paste* *n* **1 :** a fine-grained opaque Chinese ceramic ware related to true porcelain but having part of the kaolin replaced by pegmatite and usu. being fired twice **2 :** a lightweight soft opaque clay body (as of early Staffordshire)

soft rock *n* **:** rock music that is less driving and gentler sounding than hard rock

soft-top \'≈,≈\ *n* [[1]*soft* + *top*] **:** an automobile or motorboat having a top that may be folded back

software \'≈,≈\ *n* [[1]*soft* + [4]*ware*] **1 :** the entire set of programs, procedures, and related documentation associated with a system and esp. a computer system; *specif* **:** computer programs **2 :** something used or associated with and usu. contrasted with hardware; *esp* **:** materials for use with audiovisual equipment

soilborne \¦≈,≈\ *adj* [[3]*soil* + [1]*borne*] **:** transmitted by or in soil

so·ka gak·kai \,sōkə¦gä¦kī\ *n, usu cap S&G* [Jap *Sōka Gakkai,* fr. *sōka* value-creation + *gakkai* learned society] **:** a Japanese sect of Buddhism that emphasizes active proselytism and the use of prayer for the solution of all human problems

solar cell *n* **:** a photovoltaic cell (as one including a junction between two types of silicon semiconductors) that is able to convert light into electrical energy and is used as a power source

solar collector *n* **:** any of various devices that absorb solar radiation for use in the heating of water or buildings or the production of electricity

solar panel *n* **:** a battery of solar cells (as in a spacecraft)

solar pond *n* **:** a pool of salt water heated by the sun and used either as a direct source of heat or to provide power for an electric generator

solar sail *n* **:** a propulsive device that consists of a flat material (as aluminized plastic) designed to receive thrust from solar radiation pressure and that can be attached to a spacecraft

solar wind *n* **:** plasma continuously ejected from the sun's surface into and through interplanetary space

soldier* *n* **:** BUTTON MAN *herein*

solid–state \ˈ==,=\ *adj* **1 :** relating to the properties, structure, or reactivity of solid material; *esp* **:** relating to the arrangement or behavior of ions, molecules, nucleons, electrons, and holes in the crystals of a substance (as a semiconductor) or to the effect of crystal imperfections on the properties of a solid substance **2 a :** utilizing the electric, magnetic, or photic properties of solid materials **:** not using electron tubes ⟨a *solid-state* stereo system⟩

sol·i·ton \ˈsälə̇,tän\ *n* -s [*soli*tary + ²*-on*] **:** a solitary wave (as in a gaseous plasma) that retains its shape and speed after colliding with another such wave

solution set *n* **:** the set of values that satisfy an equation; *also* **:** TRUTH SET *herein*

somali* *n, usu cap* **:** any of a breed of domestic cats that prob. originated as a spontaneous mutation of the Abyssinian and closely resembles it but has a long silky coat and plumelike tail

so·mato·medin \ˌsōməd·əˌmēdᵊn\ *n* -s [*somat-* + *-medin* (perh. as in *intermedin*)] **:** any of several endogenous peptides produced esp. in the liver and dependent on and mediating growth hormone activity (as in sulfate uptake by epiphyseal cartilage)

so·mato·sensory \ˌsoməd·ə +\ *adj* [*somat-* + *sensory*] **:** of, relating to, or being sensory activity not having its origin in the special sense organs (as eyes or ears) and conveying information about the state of the body and its immediate environment

so·mato·statin \ˌsōməd·əˌstatᵊn\ *n* -s[*somat-* + *-stat* + *-in*] **:** a polypeptide neurohormone that is found esp. in the hypothalamus, is composed of a chain of 14 amino= acid residues, and inhibits the secretion of several other hormones (as growth hormone, insulin, and gastrin)

so·mato·therapy \ˌsōməd·ə+\ *n* [*somat-* + *therapy*] **:** therapy for psychological problems that uses physiological intervention (as by drugs or surgery) to modify behavior

somatotropic hormone *n* **:** GROWTH HORMONE 1

something* *pron* — **something else :** something or someone special or extraordinary ⟨the solos . . . were *something else* —Thomas Pynchon⟩ ⟨this guy is *something else* —Claude Brown⟩

son et lumière \sōⁿälüemyer\ *n* [F, lit., sound and light] **:** an outdoor spectacle at an historic site consisting of recorded narration with light and sound effects

son·i·cate \ˈsänə̇,kāt\ *vt* -ED/-ING/-S [*sonic* + ⁴*-ate*] **:** to disrupt (as bacteria) by treatment with high-frequency sound waves — **son·i·ca·tion** \ˌsänə̇ˈkāshən\ *n* -s

so·no·chemistry \ˌsänō, ˌsōnō +\ *n* [*son-* + *chemistry*] **:** a branch of chemistry that deals with the chemical effects of ultrasound — **so·no·chemical** \"+\ *adj*

so·no·gram \ˈsänə,gram, ˈsōn-\ *n* [*son-* + *-gram*] **:** an image produced by ultrasound

so·nog·ra·phy \sōˈnägrəfē\ *n* -ES [*son-* + *-graphy*] **:** ULTRASOUND 1 *herein* — **so·no·graph·ic** \ˌsōnəˈgrafik\ *adj*

so·pai·pil·la \ˌsō,pīˈpē(l)yə\ *also* **so·pa·pil·la** \ˌsōpəˈpilə, -ˈpē(l)yə\ *n* -s [Sp *sopaipilla,* dim. of *sopaipa* fritter soaked in honey, fr. *sopa* sop, food soaked in milk, of Gmc origin; akin to OE *sūpan* to swallow; *sopapilla* by modif.] **:** a square of deep fried dough often sweetened and eaten as dessert

sorghum webworm *n* **:** a noctuid moth (*Celama sorghiella*) whose hairy greenish larva is sometimes a destructive pest of the seed heads of sorghum

sort* *n* **:** an instance of sorting ⟨an alpha ~⟩

soul* *n* **1 :** a strong positive feeling (as of intense sensitivity and emotional fervor) conveyed esp. by black American performers **2 :** NEGRITUDE *herein* **3 :** SOUL MUSIC *herein* **4 :** SOUL FOOD *herein* **5 :** SOUL BROTHER *herein*

soul *adj* [*soul,* n. (herein)] **1 :** of, relating to, or characteristic of black Americans or their culture ⟨vocals are delivered in a raspy, ~ style —Ellen Sander⟩ **2 :** designed for or controlled by blacks ⟨~ radio stations⟩

soul brother *n* **:** a black male

soul food *n* **:** food (as chitterlings, hogs' jowls, ham hocks, collard greens, catfish, and cornbread) traditionally eaten esp. by southern black Americans

soul music *n* **:** music that originated with black American gospel singing, is closely related to rhythm and blues, and is characterized by intensity of feeling and earthiness

soul sister *n* **:** a black female

sounding* *n* **:** SIGNIFYING *herein*

sound pollution *n* **:** NOISE POLLUTION *herein*

soundscape \ˈsau̇n(d),skāp\ *n* -s [³*sound* + *-scape*] **:** a mélange of musical and often nonmusical sounds

soup* *n* **:** the fast-moving white water that moves shoreward after a wave breaks

source language *n* **:** a language which is to be translated into another language — compare TARGET LANGUAGE *herein*

southern pea *n* **:** COWPEA

southwestern corn borer *n* **:** a pyralid moth (*Diatraea grandiosella*) whose larva causes serious damage esp. to corn crops by boring in the stalks

sou·vla·kia \süvˈläkēə\ *n* -s [NGk, fr. *souvla* spit, skewer, fr. Gk *soublizein* to pierce] **:** SHISH KEBAB

soybean cyst nematode *n* **:** a nematode (*Heterodera glycines*) that is a pest of legumes and esp. soybeans causing stunting and yellowing of the plants and reduction in yield

soymilk \ˈ=,=\ *n* [*soy* + ¹*milk*] **:** a milk substitute based on soybeans esp. as a protein source and usu. supplemented (as with calcium and vitamins)

spa* *n* **:** HEALTH SPA *herein*

space* *n* **:** a set of mathematical entities (as points or vectors) with a set of axioms of geometric character — compare METRIC SPACE *herein,* TOPOLOGICAL SPACE *herein,* VECTOR SPACE *herein*

space–age \ˈ=ˈ=\ *adj* **:** of, relating to, or befitting the age of space exploration **:** MODERN ⟨*space-age* gadgetry⟩

spaceborne \ˈ=,=\ *adj* [¹*space* + ¹*borne*] **1 :** carried by a spacecraft ⟨~ radar⟩ **2 :** involving the use of spaceborne equipment ⟨~ television⟩

spaced–out \ˈ=ˈ=\ *adj* [¹*space* + ¹*-ed* + *out*] **1 :** dazed or stupefied by or as if by a narcotic substance **2 :** of a strange or weird character **:** SPACY 2 *herein* ⟨lives with a rather *spaced-out* dog in a stylish penthouse —John Heilpern⟩

spacefaring \'=,==\ *adj* [*space* + *-faring* (as in *seafaring*)] **:** of, relating to, or involved in travel in outer space ⟨~ nations⟩ — **spacefaring** *n* -s

space frame *n* **:** a usu. open framework of struts and braces (as in buildings and racing cars) which defines a structure and in which the weight of the structure is evenly distributed in all directions

spacer* *n* **:** a region of chromosomal DNA between genes that is not transcribed into messenger RNA and is of uncertain function

space shuttle *n* **:** a reusable spacecraft designed to transport people and cargo between earth and space

space sickness *n* **:** unpleasant physiological effects occurring under the conditions of sustained spaceflight

space walk *n* **:** a period of activity outside a spacecraft by an astronaut in space — **space walk** *vi* — **spacewalker** \'=,==\ *n* — **spacewalking** \'=,==\ *n*

spacewoman \'=,==\ *n, pl* **spacewomen** [[3]*space* + *woman*] **:** a woman astronaut

spacy* *or* **spac·ey** \'spāsē, -si\ *adj* **spacier; spaciest** **1 :** SPACED-OUT 1 *herein* **2 :** ODD, WEIRD, OFFBEAT

spa·ghet·ti·ni \spə,ge'tēnē\ *n* -s [It, dim. of *spaghetti*] **:** a pasta thinner than spaghetti but thicker than vermicelli

spaghetti western *n, often cap W* **:** a western motion picture produced by Italians

span* *vt* **:** to be capable of expressing any element of under given operations ⟨a set of vectors that ~*s* a vector space⟩

span·glish \'spaŋ(g)lish\ *n, usu cap* [blend of *Spanish* and *English*] **:** Spanish marked by numerous borrowings from English

spark chamber *n* **:** a device usu. used to detect the path of a high-energy particle that consists of a series of charged metal plates or wires separated by a gas (as neon) in which observable electric discharges follow the path of the particle

spatial summation *n* **:** sensory summation that involves stimulation of several spatially separated neurons at the same time

spatter glass *n* **:** END-OF-DAY GLASS *herein*

speakerphone \'==,=\ *n* [*speaker* + *phone*] **:** a combination microphone and loudspeaker device for two-way communication by telephone lines

spear·ing \'spi(ə)riŋ\ *n* -s [fr. gerund of [3]*spear*] **:** an illegal check in hockey in which one player jabs another in the body with the end of a hockey stick

spec \'spek\ *vt, past part* **specced** *or* **spec'd;** *pres part* **speccing** [by shortening] **:** to write specifications for

special drawing rights *n pl* **:** SDRS *herein*

special education *n* **:** classes for students (as the handicapped) with special educational needs

special theory of relativity : RELATIVITY 3b

spe·cies·ism \'spē(,)s(h)ē,zizəm\ *n* -s [[1]*species* + *-ism* (as in *racism*)] **:** prejudice or discrimination based on species; *esp* **:** discrimination against animals

spec·ti·no·my·cin \,spektənō'mīsᵊn\ *n* -s [NL, fr. *spectabilis* (species name) + *-in* + *-o-* + *-mycin*] **:** a white crystalline broad-spectrum antibiotic $C_{14}H_{24}N_2O_7$ produced by a bacterium of the genus *Streptomyces* (*S. spectabilis*) that is used clinically esp. in the form of its hydrochloride to treat gonorrhea — called also *actinospectacin*

spectrum* *n* **1 :** MASS SPECTRUM **2 :** the representation (as a plot) of a spectrum

speed* *n* **:** METHAMPHETAMINE; *also* **:** a related drug

speed bump *n* **:** a low raised ridge laid across a roadway (as in a parking lot) to limit vehicle speed

speedo \'spē(,)dō\ *n* -s [by shortening] **:** SPEEDOMETER

speed–reading \'=,==\ *n* **:** a method of reading rapidly by skimming — **speed–read** \'=,=\ *vt* — **speed–reader** \'=,==\ *n*

speed shop *n* **:** a shop that sells custom automotive equipment esp. to hot rodders

s phase *n, usu cap S* **:** the period in the cell cycle during which DNA replication takes place — compare G1 PHASE *herein*, G2 PHASE *herein*, M PHASE *herein*

sphe·ro·plast \'sfirə,plast, 'sfer-\ *n* -s [*sphaer-* + *-plast*] **:** a modified gram-negative bacterium that is characterized by major alteration and partial loss of the cell wall and by increased osmotic sensitivity and that can result from various nutritional or environmental factors or be induced artificially by use of a lysozyme

spider hole *n* **:** a camouflaged foxhole

spider plant* *n* **:** a plant of the genus *Chlorophytum* (*C. comosum* var. *variegatum*) that has long green leaves usu. with white or ivory stripes, that produces stems of small white flowers at the end of which small tufts of plantlets follow the flowers, and that is widely grown as a houseplant esp. in hanging baskets

spi·e·di·no \,spēə'dē(,)nō\ *n, pl* **spiedini** \-(,)nē\ [It, lit., skewer, fr. *spiedo* spit, spear, fr. OF *espiet* lance, fr. (assumed) Frankish *speut* lance; akin to G *spies* spit, Sp *espeto* skewer — more at SPIT] **:** a dish of meat rolled around a filling or minced and formed into balls then usu. batter-dipped and cooked on a skewer; *also* **:** slices of bread and mozzarella prepared in a similar way and served with an anchovy sauce

spike* *n* **:** ACTION POTENTIAL *herein*

spin off *vt* **:** to establish or produce as a spin-off ~ *vi* **:** to establish or become a spin-off

spin–off* *n* **1 :** the distribution by a business to its stockholders of particular assets and esp. of stock of another company; *also* **:** a new company created by such a distribution **2 :** a collateral or derived product or effect **:** BY-PRODUCT ⟨new household products that are *spin-offs* from missile research⟩; *also* **:** a number of such by-products ⟨the *spin-off* from the space program⟩ **3 :** something that is imitative or derivative of an earlier work; *esp* **:** a television show starring a character who was popular in a secondary role in an earlier show

spinout \'=,=\ *n* -s [[2]*spin* + [1]*out*] **:** a rotational skid by an automobile that usu. causes it to leave the roadway

spin resonance *n* **:** ELECTRON SPIN RESONANCE *herein*

spin·to \'spēn·(,)tō, -pin-·\ *adj* [It, lit., pushed, fr. past part. of *spingere* to push] *of a singing voice* **:** having both lyric and dramatic qualities — **spinto** *n* -s

spin wave *n* **:** a wave of quantized energy that propagates through a substance as a result of magnetic field shifts within an atom in response to an outside stimulus (as a variable magnetic field or radio waves) — called also *magnon*

spiny–headed worm \',==,==-\ *n* **:** a parasitic worm belonging to the phylum Acanthocephala

spi·ro·no·lactone \spī,ränə, spə,rōnō +\ *n* [*spir-* + *-no-* (prob. arbitrary infix) + *lactone*] **:** an aldosterone antagonist that promotes diuresis and sodium excretion and is sometimes used to relieve ascites

splashdown \'=,=\ *n* -s [fr. the phrase *splash down*] **:** the landing of a manned spacecraft in the ocean — **splash down** *vi*

splice* *vt* **:** to combine (genetic information) from two or more organisms — see GENE-SPLICING *herein*

spliff \'splif\ *n* -s [origin unknown] **:** a marijuana cigarette

spline* *also* **spline function** *n* **:** a function that is defined on an interval, is used to approximate a given function, and is composed of pieces of simple functions defined on subintervals and joined at their endpoints with a suitable degree of smoothness

split* *vt* **:** LEAVE ⟨~ the scene⟩ ~ *vi* **:** LEAVE ⟨the women ~ for New York on Tuesday —Linda Francke⟩

split–brain \ˌ≐ˈ≐\ *adj* **:** of, relating to, concerned with, or having undergone separation of the two cerebral hemispheres by surgical division of the optic chiasma and corpus callosum ⟨behavior in *split-brain* animals⟩ ⟨*split-brain* research⟩

split end *n* **:** an offensive end in football who lines up usu. several yards to the side of the formation

spo·do·sol \'spädəˌsȯl, 'spōd-\ *n* -s [Gk *spodos* wood ash + L *solum* ground, soil — more at SOIL] **:** any of a group of podzols esp. of cool humid regions that have a horizon below the surface composed of an illuvial accumulation of humus with iron or aluminum or both

spoiler* *n* **1 :** an air deflector on the front or on the rear deck of an automobile and esp. a racer for reducing the tendency to lift off the road at high speeds **2 :** one (as a presidential candidate or a baseball team in a pennant race) that has little or no chance of winning but can prevent another's winning

spokes·person \'spōks+ˌ\ *n* [*spokes-* (as in *spokesman*) + *person*] **:** one who speaks as the representative of another

spongeware \'≐ˌ≐\ *n* [[1]*sponge* + [4]*ware*] **:** a typically 19th century earthenware with background color spattered or dabbed (as with a sponge) and usu. a freehand central design

spook* *n* **:** an undercover agent **:** SPY

spoon·er \'spünə(r)\ *n* -s [[1]*spoon* + [2]*-er*] **:** a container that is designed to hold extra teaspoons and forms part of a 19th century table service

spo·ro·pol·len·in \ˌspōrə'pälənən, ˌspȯr-\ *n* -s [ISV *spor-* + *pollen* + *-in*] **:** a relatively chemically inert polymer that makes up the outer layer of pollen grains and spores of higher plants

spotted alfalfa aphid *n* **:** a highly destructive Old World aphid (*Therioaphis maculata*) established in the U.S. from coast to coast in warmer areas that injects a toxic saliva in feeding esp. on alfalfa and causes yellowing and stunting of affected plants

sprang \'spraŋ, -aiŋ\ *n* -s [prob. fr. Norw, tatting, fr. ON, lace-weaving, fr. MD *sprank* ornament; akin to OE *spranca* twig, shoot, and prob. to OE *springan* to spring — more at SPRING] **:** a weaving technique in which threads or cords are intertwined and twisted over one another to form an openwork mesh

spread end *n* **:** SPLIT END *herein*

spreadsheet \'≐ˌ≐\ *n* [fr. *spreadsheet* outsize page used by accountants] **:** an accounting program for a computer; *also* **:** the ledger layout modeled by such a program

sprech·stim·me \'shprekˌshtimə, -ekˌ-\ *n* -s *often cap* [G, lit., speaking voice] **:** a vocal passage or performance in which a declamation is delivered with rhythmic inflections

spring roll *n* **:** EGG ROLL; *also* **:** any of various similar appetizers of oriental cuisine

sprint car *n* **:** a rugged racing automobile that is midway in size between midget racers and ordinary racers, has about the same horsepower as the larger racers, and is usu. raced on a dirt track

spritz \'sprits\ *n* -ES **1** [*spritz* v.] **:** SPRAY, SQUIRT, FIZZ **2** [Yiddish] **:** an improvised usu. humorous harangue

spun·bond·ed \'spənˌbändəd\ *adj* [fr. the material's being bonded by a substance spun from a spinnerette] **:** of, relating to, or being a nonwoven polymeric material that resembles cloth or fabric

square one *n* **:** the initial stage or starting point of a process ⟨had to start all over again, from *square one* —H.C. McDonald⟩

square out *n* **:** a pass pattern in football in which a receiver runs downfield and then breaks sharply for the sidelines

squat* *n* **1 :** a lift in weight lifting in which the lifter performs a knee bend while holding a barbell on the shoulders; *also* **:** a competitive event involving this lift **2** *chiefly Brit* **:** an empty house or building that is occupied and shared by squatters **3** *slang* **:** DIDDLY-SQUAT *herein*, NOTHING

squib kick *n* **:** a kickoff in football in which the ball bounces along the ground

sr* *abbr* steradian

sri lan·kan \(ˈ)srē'läŋkən, (ˈ)shrē-\ *n, cap S&L* [*Sri Lanka* + E [1]*-an*] **:** a native or inhabitant of Sri Lanka — **sri lankan** *adj, usu cap S&L*

sRNA \ˌesˌärˌenˈā\ *n* -s [soluble *RNA*] **:** TRANSFER RNA *herein*

SRO \ˌesˌär'ō\ *n* -s [single-room occupancy] **:** a house, apartment building, or residential hotel in which tenants live in single rooms

SSL *abbr* Licentiate of Sacred Scriptures

SST \ˌeˌse'stē\ *n* -s **:** SUPERSONIC TRANSPORT *herein*

stack* *n* **1 :** a memory or a section of memory in a computer for temporary storage **2 :** a computer memory consisting of arrays of memory elements stacked one on top of another

stacked heel *n* [*stacked,* past part. of [2]*stack*] **:** a heel made of layers of leather and used on shoes

stadium coat *n* **:** a coat of medium length designed for casual winter wear

staff* *n, pl* **staff :** a member of a staff

stag·fla·tion \ˌstag'flāshən\ *n* -s [blend of *stagnation* and *inflation*] **:** persistent inflation combined with stagnant consumer demand and relatively high unemployment — **stag·fla·tio·nary** \-shəˌnerē\ *adj*

staging* *n* **:** the disengaging and discarding of a burned-out rocket unit from a space vehicle during flight

stand–alone \ˈ≐≐ˌ≐\ *adj* [[1]*stand* + *alone*] **:** SELF-CONTAINED; *esp* **:** operating or capable of operating independently of a computer system ⟨a ~ word processor⟩

standing crop* *n* **:** the total amount or number of living things (as an uncut farm crop, the fish in a pond, or organisms in an ecosystem) in a particular situation at any given time

stannous fluoride *n* **:** a white compound SnF_2 of tin and fluorine used in toothpaste to combat tooth decay

sta·pe·dec·to·my \ˌstāpə'dektəmē, -pē'd-\ *n* -ES [ISV *staped-* (fr. NL *staped-, stapes* stapes) + *-ectomy*] **:** surgical removal and prosthetic replacement of the stapes to relieve deafness — **sta·pe·dec·to·mized** \-təˌmīzd\ *adj*

stark·ers \'stärkərz, -täkəz\ *adj* [[1]*stark* + *-ers* (Oxford University slang suffix)] *chiefly Brit* **:** completely unclothed **:** NUDE

starquake \'=,=\ *n* [[1]*star* + [2]*quake*] **:** a seismic event on a star

starter* *n* — **for starters :** to begin with

statement* *n* **1 :** an opinion or message conveyed indirectly usu. by nonverbal means ⟨more than any other garment, the suit makes a ~ — *advt*⟩ **2 :** an instruction in a computer program

state of the art : the level of development (as of a device, procedure, process, technique, art, or science) reached at a particular time usu. as a result of modern methods

state–of–the–art \'===''=\ *adj* **:** made, done with, or using the most up-to-date methods and technology available ⟨a *state-of-the-art* computer⟩

static* *n* **:** heated opposition or criticism ⟨he takes no ~ from anyone —David Wellman⟩

statistic* *n* **:** a random variable that takes on the possible values of a statistic

status offender *n* **:** a young offender (as a runaway or a truant) who is under the jurisdiction of a court for repeated offenses that are not crimes

stave church *n* **:** a church of medieval Nordic origin that is made of wooden staves and has gables, a cupola, and often a series of pitched roofs

staystitching \'=,==\ *n* -s [[5]*stay*] **:** a line of stitching sewn around an edge (as an armhole) of a garment being made in order to prevent the cloth from stretching — **stay-stitch** \'=,=\ *vt*

STD \'es'tē'dē\ *n* -S **:** SEXUALLY TRANSMITTED DISEASE *herein*

steady state theory *n* **:** a theory in astronomy: the universe has always existed and has always been expanding with hydrogen being created continuously and spontaneously — compare BIG BANG THEORY *herein*

steak au poivre \-(,)ō'pwävr(ᵊ), -v(rə)\ *n* [F *au poivre* with pepper] **:** a steak that has had coarsely ground black pepper pressed into it before cooking, is served with a seasoned sauce, and is often flambéed with cognac

steak diane \-(')dī'an\ *n, usu cap D* [prob. fr. the name *Diane*] **:** a steak that is served with a seasoned butter sauce and is often flambéed with cognac

steak tar·tare \-(,)tär'tär, -(,)tä'tä(r\ *n* [F *tartare* Tartar] **:** highly seasoned ground beef eaten raw

Stel·a·zine \'stelə,zēn\ *trademark* — used for trifluoperazine

stel·lar·ator \'stelə,rād·ə(r)\ *n* -s [*stellar* + *-ator* (as in *generator*); fr. its use of temperatures approaching those occurring in some stars] **:** a toroidal device for producing controlled nuclear fusion that involves the confining and heating of a gaseous plasma by means of an externally applied magnetic field

stellar wind *n* **:** plasma ejected at varying rates from a star's surface into interstellar space

stepfamily \'=,=(=)=\ *n* [*step-* + *family*] **:** a family in which there is a stepparent

ste·re·ol·o·gy \,sterē'äləjē, ,stir-\ *n* -ES [ISV *stere-* + *-logy*] **:** a branch of science concerned with inferring the three-dimensional properties of objects or matter ordinarily observed two-dimensionally — **ste·reo·log·i·cal** \-rēə'läjəkəl\ *also* **ste·reo·log·ic** \-jik\ *adj* — **ste·reo·log·i·cal·ly** \-k(ə)lē\ *adv*

stereophone \'===''=\ *n* [[2]*stereo* + *phone*] **:** a stereophonic headphone

stereotactic* *adj* **:** STEREOTAXIC *herein*

stereotape \'===''=\ *n* [[2]*stereo* + *tape*] **:** a stereophonic magnetic tape

ste·reo·tax·ic \'sterēə'taksik, 'stir-\ *adj* [*stereotaxis* (herein) + *-ic* — more at TAXIS] **:** of, relating to, involving, or being a technique or apparatus used in neurological research or surgery for directing the tip of a delicate instrument (as a needle or an electrode) in three planes in attempting to reach a specific locus in the brain — **ste·reo·tax·i·cal·ly** \-k(ə)lē\ *adv*

stereotaxis* *n* **:** a stereotaxic technique or procedure

ste·roido·genesis \stə,rȯidə-, ,stir,ȯid- *also* ,ster- +\ *n* [NL, fr. *steroid* + *-o-* + *genesis*] **:** synthesis of steroids

ste·roido·gen·ic \stə,rȯidə'jenik, ,stir,ȯid- *also* ,ster-\ *adj* [*steroid* + *-o-* + *-genic*] of, relating to, or involved in steroidogenesis

ste·ven·graph \'stēvən,graf\ *or* **ste·vens·graph** \-nz,g-\ *n* -s *usu cap* [Thomas *Stevens,* 19th cent. Am. weaver + E *-graph*] **:** a picture woven in silk

ste·vens–john·son syndrome \'stēvənz'jänsən-\ *n, usu cap S&J* [after Albert Mason *Stevens* †1945 and Frank Chamblis *Johnson* †1934 Am. pediatricians] **:** a severe and sometimes fatal form of erythema multiforme that is characterized esp. by purulent conjunctivitis, Vincent's angina, and ulceration of the genitals and anus and that often results in blindness

stew \'stü\ *n* -s [short for *steward* and *stewardess*] **:** an airline flight attendant

stick* *vb* — **stick it to :** to treat harshly or unfairly

stick shift *n* **:** a manually operated automobile gearshift

sticky wicket *n* **:** a difficult or delicate problem or situation

stiletto heel *n* **:** a high thin heel on women's shoes that is narrower than a spike heel

still bank \'=,=\ *n* [[1]*still*] **:** a bank (as in the shape of an animal) with a slot for coins — compare MECHANICAL BANK *herein*

sting* *n* **:** an elaborate confidence game; *specif* **:** such a game worked by undercover police in order to trap criminals

[1]**stir–fry** \'='=\ *vt* [[1]*stir* + *fry*] **:** to fry quickly over high heat in a lightly oiled pan (as a wok) while stirring continuously

[2]**stir–fry** \"\ *n* **:** a dish of something stir-fried

stish·ov·ite \'stishə,vīt\ *n* -s [S.M. *Stishov,* 20th cent. Russ. mineralogist + E *-ite*] **:** a dense tetragonal mineral SiO_2 consisting of silicon dioxide that is a polymorph of quartz and that is formed under great pressure

stochastic* *adj* **1 :** involving a random variable ⟨a ~ process⟩ **2 :** involving chance or probability **:** PROBABILISTIC ⟨a ~ model of radiation-induced mutation⟩

stoked \'stōkt\ *adj* [fr. past part. of [1]*stoke*] *slang* **:** being in an enthusiastic or exhilarated state

STOL *abbr* short takeoff and landing

stone* *adj* **:** ABSOLUTE, COMPLETE ⟨a zeal that might be called pure ~ craziness —Edwin Shrake⟩

stone \'stōn\ *adv* **:** ABSOLUTELY, COMPLETELY — used as an intensive ⟨it is a ~ positive fact, a scientific certainty —R.A. Aurthur⟩

stonewall* *vi* **:** to be uncooperative, obstructive, or evasive ⟨the Kremlin will be tempted to ~ . . . until after the election —*Business Week*⟩ ~ *vt* **:** to refuse to comply or cooperate with ⟨intention to ~ further requests for . . . evidence —*Newsweek*⟩

stop* *vb* — **stop a stock** *of a stock-market specialist* **:** to agree to a later sale or purchase of a specified number of shares at the price current when the agreement is made

stop out* *vt* **:** to sell securities of (a shareowner) on a stop order ~ *vi* **:** to withdraw temporarily from enrollment at a college or university

stop–out \ˈ=,=\ *n* -s [*stop out* (herein)] **:** a person who stops out of a college or university

storage ring *n* **:** a device for storing a beam of high-energy particles collected from an accelerator until needed for collision with a second beam

stovepipe \ˈ=,=\ *adj* [*stovepipe*, n.] *of trousers* **:** having creaseless legs with essentially the same circumference throughout their length

STP \ˌeˌstēˈpē\ *n* -s [fr. *STP*, trademark for a motor fuel additive] **:** a psychedelic drug chemically related to mescaline and amphetamine — called also *DOM*

straight* *adj* **1 :** HETEROSEXUAL **2 :** not using or under the influence of drugs or alcohol

straight* *n* **1 :** one who adheres to conventional attitudes and mores **2 :** a nonuser of illicit drugs **3 :** HETEROSEXUAL

straight–ahead \ˌ==ˈ=\ *adj* **:** relating to or being music performed in an unembellished manner typical of the idiom or of the performer ⟨committed to playing *straight-ahead*, searching jazz with no gimmicks —David Spitzer⟩; *broadly* **:** STRAIGHTFORWARD, UNADORNED ⟨applauded Hollywood people's *straight-ahead* love for their work —Sheila Weller⟩

straight–arrow \ˌ=ˈ==\ *adj* **:** rigidly proper and conventional — **straight arrow** *n*

straight–leg \ˈ=ˈ=\ *adj* [²*straight* + *leg*] *of trousers* **:** having creased legs with essentially the same diameter throughout their length

straight up** *adj* **:** served without ice **:** not on the rocks ⟨a martini *straight up*⟩

strain·me·ter \ˈstrānˌmēd·ə(r), -ētə-\ *n* [¹*strain* + *-meter*] **:** a mechanical, electrical, or optical instrument for measuring deformation of a body or a change in length over a given length under stress

strand·ed \ˈstrandəd, -aa(ə)n-\ *adj* [⁴*strand* + ¹*-ed*] **:** having a strand or strands esp. of a specified kind or number — usu. used in combination ⟨the double-*stranded* molecule of DNA⟩ — **strandedness** *n*

strange* *adj* **:** having the quantum characteristic of strangeness ⟨~ quark⟩

strangeness* *n* **:** a quantum characteristic of subatomic particles that accounts for the relatively long lifetime of certain particles, is conserved in electromagnetic and strong interactions, and has a value of zero for most known particles

strat·e·gize \ˈstrad·əˌjīz, -atə-\ *vb* -ED/-ING/-S [*strategy* + *-ize*] *vi* **:** to devise a plan or strategy ~ *vt* **:** to devise a plan or strategy for

strategy* *n* **:** an adaptation or complex of adaptations (as of behavior, metabolism, or structure) that serves or appears to serve an important function in achieving evolutionary success ⟨the reproductive *strategies* of beech and yellow birch —L.K. Forcier⟩

strat·i·fi·ca·tion·al grammar \ˌstrad·əfəˈkāshnəl-, -shənᵊl-\ *n* [*stratification* + *-al*] **:** a grammar based on the theory that language consists of a series of hierarchically related strata linked together by representational rules

stratified charge engine *n* **:** an internal-combustion engine in which the fuel charge is divided into two layers with a rich mixture in a small volume close to the spark plug that by its combustion promotes the ignition of a lean mixture in the remainder of the cylinder so that the engine runs on an overall leaner mixture

stra·vin·ski·an *or* **stra·vin·sky·an** \strəˈvin(t)skēən\ *adj, usu cap* [Igor Fëdorovich *Stravinsky* †1971 Am. (Russ.-born) composer + E *-an*] **:** of, relating to, or suggestive of Igor Stravinsky or his music

strawberry jar *n* [prob. fr. their original use as strawberry planters] **:** a ceramic planter with pocketed openings in the sides into which small plants can be inserted for growing

streak* *n* **:** an act or instance of streaking

streak* *vi* **:** to run naked through a public place

streak·er \ˈstrēkə(r)\ *n* -s [fr. *streak* (herein) + *-er*] **:** a person who engages in streaking

streak·ing \ˈstrēkiŋ\ *n* -s [fr. gerund of ²*streak*] **1 :** the lightening (as by chemicals) of a few long strands of hair to produce a streaked effect — compare FROSTING *herein* **2 :** the act or practice of running naked through a public place

stream* *n, Brit* **:** ¹TRACK 3c

streaming* *n, Brit* **:** TRACKING *herein*

street* *n* **:** the streets of a city seen as an environment of poverty, dereliction, or crime (as prostitution and drug trafficking) ⟨heroin worth about $25,000 on the ~ —Loudon Wainwright⟩

streetscape \ˈ=,=\ *n* -s [¹*street* + ⁴*scape*] **1 :** the appearance or view of a street ⟨the first major high-rise incursion in that cherished ~ —William Marlin⟩ **2 :** a work of art depicting a view of a street

street–smart \ˈ=ˈ=\ *adj* [²*street* + *smart*] **:** STREETWISE *herein*

street theater *n* **:** drama or mime often dealing with controversial social and political issues usu. performed in an informal setting outdoors — called also *guerrilla theater*

streetwise \ˈ=ˈ=\ *adj* [²*street* + *wise*] **:** having or showing familiarity with the life and attitudes of street people; *esp* **:** wise and resourceful in surviving and getting what one wants on the street

strep·to·ni·grin \ˌstreptəˈnīgrən\ *n* -s [NL *strepto-* (fr. *Streptomyces flocculus*, actinomycete from which it is produced) + L *nigr-, niger* black + E *-in*; prob. fr. its dark color] **:** a toxic antibiotic $C_{25}H_{22}N_4O_8$ from an actinomycete of the genus *Streptomyces* (*S. flocculus*) that interferes with DNA metabolism and is used as an antineoplastic agent

strep·to·zot·o·cin \ˌstreptəˈzätəsən\ *n* -s [*strept-* + *zo-* + *tocin* (alter. of *toxin*)] **:** a broad-spectrum antibiotic $C_8H_{15}N_3O_7$ with antineoplastic and diabetogenic properties that has been isolated from a bacterium of the genus *Streptomyces* (*S. achromogenes*)

stretch receptor *n* **:** MUSCLE SPINDLE

stretch reflex *n* **:** a spinal reflex involving reflex contraction of a muscle in response to stretching

strewn field *n* [*strewn* fr. past part. of ¹*strew*] **:** an area in which tektites are found

striation* *n* **:** one of the alternate dark and light cross bands of a myofibril of striated muscle

stride piano *also* **stride*** *n* [so called fr. the repeated strides taken by the left hand] **:** a style of jazz piano playing in which the right hand plays the melody while the left hand alternates between a single note and a chord played an octave or more higher

strike* *n* **:** a perfectly thrown ball ⟨fired a ~ to first base⟩

striking price *n* **:** an agreed-upon price at which an option contract (as a put or call) can be exercised

string* *n* **:** a sequence of like items: as **a :** a linear sequence of words, morphemes, or symbols **b :** a sequence of characters esp. when treated as text

strip* *n* **:** a commercially developed area esp. along a highway

strip city *n* **:** an urban area forming a long narrow strip

stripped–down \'=¦=\ *adj* **:** lacking extra or unnecessary features **:** not fancy ⟨a *stripped-down* model of a car⟩

stroke* *vt* **:** to flatter or treat solicitously esp. in order to reassure or persuade ⟨a gift for *stroking* the . . . bankers to whom he resold those loans —Roy Rowan⟩

stro·mat·o·lite \strō'mad·ᵊl,īt\ *n* -s [L *stromat-, stroma* bed covering + E *-o-* + *-lite*] **:** a laminated sedimentary fossil formed from layers of blue-green algae — **stro·mat·o·lit·ic** \-,mad·ᵊl-'id·ik\ *adj*

strong interaction *also* **strong force** *n* **:** a fundamental interaction of elementary particles (as hadrons) that is more powerful than any other known force and is responsible for the binding together of neutrons and protons in the atomic nucleus and for processes of particle creation in high-energy collisions

stro·phoid \'strō,fȯid\ *n* -s [F *strophoïde,* fr. Gk *strophos* twisted band (fr. *strephein* to twist) + *-oïde* -oid] **:** a plane curve that is generated by a point whose distance from the y-axis along a variable straight line which always passes through a fixed point is equal to the y-intercept and that has the equation $\rho = \alpha$ (sec $\theta \pm tan\ \theta$) in polar coordinates

strop·py \'sträpē, -pi\ *adj* [by alter. and shortening of *obstreperous*] *Brit* **:** TOUCHY, CONTRARY, BELLIGERENT ⟨Scotch is the drink but Scots are the people, and very ~ they get about it, too —Leslie Sellers⟩

structural gene *n* **:** a gene determining the amino acid sequence of a protein (as an enzyme) through a specific messenger RNA

structured* *adj* **:** of, relating to, or being a method of computer programming in which each step of a problem's solution is contained in a separate subprogram having only one entry point and one exit point and in which unconditional branches from one part of a program to another are not permitted

strung out *adj* **1 :** addicted to a drug **2 :** physically debilitated from or as if from long-term drug addiction **3 :** intoxicated or stupefied from drug use **4** *slang* **:** being in love

student's t distribution *n, often cap S* [*Student,* pen name of W. S. Gossett †1937 Brit. statistician] **:** T DISTRIBUTION *herein*

student union *n* **:** a building on a college campus that is devoted to student activities and that usu. contains lounges, auditoriums, eating facilities, offices, and game rooms

stuff* *n* **1 :** DUNK SHOT **2 :** any of several habit-forming or narcotic drugs; *specif* **:** HEROIN

stuff* *vt* **:** to throw or drive (a ball or puck) into a goal from very close range

stuff shot *n* **:** DUNK SHOT

Sty·ro·foam \'stīrə,fōm\ *trademark* — used for an expanded rigid polystyrene plastic

subacute scle·ros·ing pan·encephalitis \-sklə- ¦rōsiŋ¦pan +\ *n* [*sclerosing* (pres. part. of *sclerose*) + *panencephalitis,* fr. *pan-* + *encephalitis*] **:** a central nervous system disease of children and young adults caused by infection of the brain by measles virus or a closely related virus and marked by intellectual deterioration, convulsions, and paralysis

sub·cellular \¦səb +\ *adj* [*sub-* + *cellular*] **:** of less than cellular scope or level of organization ⟨~ particles⟩ ⟨~ studies⟩

sub·classification \"+\ *n* [*sub-* + *classification*] **1 :** a primary division of a classification **2 :** arrangement into or assignment to subclassifications

sub·compact \"+\ *n* [*sub-* + [3]*compact*] **:** an automobile smaller than a compact

sub·discipline \"+\ *n* [*sub-* + *discipline*] **:** a subdivision of a branch of learning

subduction* *n* **:** the action or process of the edge of one crustal plate descending below the edge of another — **sub·duct** \səb,dəkt\ *vb*

sub·employed \¦səb +\ *adj* [*sub-* + *employed,* past part. of [1]*employ*] **:** subjected to subemployment

sub·employment \"+\ *n* [*sub-* + *employment*] **:** inadequate employment including unemployment, part-time employment, and full-time employment that does not provide a living wage

sub·field \'səb +,\ *n* [*sub-* + [1]*field*] **1 :** a subset of a mathematical field that is itself a field **2 :** a subdivision of a field (as of study)

sub·government \¦səb +\ *n* [*sub-* + *government*] **:** an informal or unofficial association of persons or institutions that exercises considerable influence on a formal government or organization

sub·graph \'səb +,\ *n* [*sub-* + *graph*] **:** a graph all of whose points and lines are contained in a larger graph

subgroup* *n* **:** a subset of a mathematical group that is itself a group

sub·gum \'səb'gəm\ *n* [Chin (Cant) *shâp kám,* lit., mixture] **:** a dish of Chinese origin prepared with a mixture of vegetables (as peppers, water chestnuts, and mushrooms)

sub·license \¦səb +\ *vt* [*sublicense,* n.] **:** to grant to another a sublicense for

sub·mandibular gland \"+ . . .-\ *also* **submandibular** *n* -s [*sub-* + *mandibular*] **:** SUBMAXILLARY GLAND

submarine* *vi* **:** to dive or slide under something ⟨the danger of *submarining* under a seat belt in a crash⟩

sub·metacentric \¦səb +\ *adj* [*sub-* + *metacentric*] *of a chromosome* **:** having arms of unequal length because the centromere is closer to one end than the other — **submetacentric** *n*

sub·millimeter \"+\ *adj* [*sub-* + *millimeter*] **:** being less than a millimeter in diameter or wavelength ⟨a ~ particle⟩

sub·mitochondrial \"+\ *adj* [*sub-* + *mitochondrial*] **:** of, relating to, composed of, or being parts and esp. fragments of mitochondria ⟨~ membranes⟩ ⟨~ particles⟩

sub·nuclear \"+\ *adj* [*sub-* + *nuclear*] **:** of, relating to, or being a particle smaller than the atomic nucleus

sub·or·di·na·tor \sə'bȯrdᵊn,ād·ər\ *n* -s [[3]*subordinate* + [1]*-or*] **:** one that subordinates; *esp* **:** a subordinating conjunction

sub·program \'səb +,\ *n* [*sub-* + *program* (herein)] **:** a semi-independent portion of a program (as for a computer)

sub·ring \"+\ *n* [*sub-* + [1]*ring*] **:** a subset of a mathematical ring which is itself a ring

sub–saharan \"+\ *adj, usu cap 2d S* [*sub-* + *Saharan*] **:** of, being, or relating to the part of Africa south of the Sahara desert

sub·satellite \¦səb +\ *n* [*sub-* + *satellite*] **1 :** a political entity within the sphere of influence of another entity that is itself a satellite of a stronger power **2 :** an object carried into orbit in and subsequently released from an artificial satellite

subscription TV *n* **:** pay-TV that broadcasts programs directly over the air to customers provided with a special receiver — called also *subscription television;* compare PAY-CABLE *herein*

sub·sequence \'səb +\ *n* [*sub-* + [1]*sequence*] **:** a mathematical sequence that is part of another sequence

sub·shell \'səb +,\ *n* [*sub-* + *shell*] **:** any of the one or more orbitals making up an electron shell of an atom

substance P *n* **:** a mammalian protein present esp. in the gastrointestinal tract and pituitary gland that causes reduction in blood pressure and contraction of smooth muscle and that is thought to function as a neurotransmitter

sub·stan·tia gel·a·ti·no·sa \(,)səb¦stanch(ē)ə,jelət^ən-'ōsə, -'ōzə\ *n* [NL, lit., gelatinous substance] **:** a mass of gelatinous tissue that lies on the dorsal surface of the dorsal column and extends the entire length of the spinal cord into the medulla oblongata and that functions in the transmission of painful sensory information

sub·text \'səb +,\ *n* [*sub-* + *text*] **:** the implicit or metaphorical meaning (as of a literary text) — **sub·textual** \(')səb +\ *adj*

sub·til·i·sin \(,)səb'tiləsən *also* ,səbtə'līsən\ *n* -s [NL *subtilis,* specific epithet of *Bacillus subtilis,* species of which *Bacillus amyloliquefaciens* was formerly considered a variant + E *-in*] **:** an extracellular protease produced by a soil bacterium of the genus *Bacillus* (*B. amyloliquefaciens*)

sub·to·pia \(,)səb'tōpēə\ *n* -s [*sub*urbs + *-topia* (as in *utopia*)] *chiefly Brit* **:** the suburbs of a city — **sub·to·pi·an** \-ēən\ *adj, chiefly Brit*

subtopic *n* [*sub-* + *topic*] **:** a secondary topic **:** one of the subdivisions into which a topic may be divided

sub·viral \¦səb +\ *adj* [*sub-* + *viral*] **:** relating to, being, or caused by a piece or a structural part (as a protein) of a virus

sub·vocalization \"+\ *n* [*sub-* + *vocalization*] **:** the act or process of inaudibly articulating speech with the speech organs — **sub·vocalize** \"+\ *vb*

succinate dehydrogenase *n* **:** SUCCINIC DEHYDROGENASE

succorance* *n* **:** a dependence on or an active seeking for nurturant care — **suc·cor·ant** \'səkərənt\ *adj*

suck* *vt* **:** to perform fellatio upon — often used with *off;* usu. considered vulgar ~ *vi, slang* **:** to be extremely or disgustingly unpleasant or objectionable

sucker* *n* — used as a generalized term of reference ⟨see if you can get that ~ working again⟩

sudden infant death syndrome *n* **:** death due to unknown causes of an infant in apparently good health that occurs usu. before one year of age — called also *crib death*

suicide pact *n* **:** an agreement between two or more individuals wherein they commit suicide together or one kills the other or others and then commits suicide

suicide squad *n* [so called fr. the fact that kickoffs are more dangerous than other plays] **:** a squad used on kickoffs in football

sui·cid·ol·o·gy \,süə,sī'däləjē\ *n* -ES [*suicide* + *-o-* + *-logy*] **:** the study of suicide and suicide prevention — **sui·cid·ol·o·gist** \-jəst\ *n* -s

sul·fa·meth·oxazole \¦səlfə,meth +\ *n* [*sulfa-* + *methyl-* + *oxazole*] **:** a sulfonamide $C_{10}H_{11}N_3O_3S$ used as an antibacterial (as in the treatment of urinary tract infections)

sul·fin·py·ra·zone \,səlfən'pīrə,zōn\ *n* -s [*sulfin*yl + *pyrazole* + *-one*] **:** a uricosuric drug $C_{23}H_{20}N_2O_3S$ used in long-term treatment of chronic gout

sul·fo·bro·mo·phthalein \¦səlfə,brō(,)mō+\ *n* [ISV *sulf-* + *brom-* + *phthalein*] **:** a diagnostic material used in the form of its disodium salt $C_{20}H_8Br_4Na_2O_{10}S_2$ in a liver function test

sul·fo·nyl·urea \,səlfə,nil +\ *n* [NL, fr. ISV *sulfonyl* + NL *urea*] **:** any of several hypoglycemic compounds related to the sulfonamides and used in the oral treatment of diabetes

sulphide* *n* **:** a ceramic form and esp. a portrait bas-relief enclosed in clear glass where it glitters like silver

sum* *n* **:** UNION 1 *herein*

su·mi–e \'sümē'ā\ *n* -s [Jap, fr. *sumi* India ink + *e* drawing] **:** the Japanese art of monochromatic ink painting

sum up* *vt, Brit* **:** ASSESS 4 ⟨that skilled, professional inspection . . . with which we *sum* each other *up* —Doris Lessing⟩

sunbelt \'≈,≈\ *n, often cap* [[1]*sun* + *belt*] **:** the southern and southwestern states of the U.S. — compare FROSTBELT *herein*

sun block *n* **:** a chemical agent (as zinc oxide or PABA) or a preparation of this that is applied to the skin to prevent sunburn by blocking out all or most of the sun's rays — compare SUNSCREEN *in the Dict*

Sunfish \'≈,≈\ *trademark* — used for a light sailboat with one sail and a footwell that is designed to carry no more than two people

sunrise \'≈,≈\ *adj* [*sunrise,* n.] **:** newly created **:** being in a period of growth or development ⟨~ industries⟩

sunroof \'≈,≈\ *n* [so called fr. its letting in the sunlight] **:** an automobile roof having a panel that can be opened

sunseeker \'≈,≈≈\ *n* [[1]*sun* + *seeker*] **:** a person who travels to an area of warmth and sun esp. in winter

sunset \'≈,≈\ *adj* [*sunset,* n.] **1 :** stipulating the periodic review of government agencies and programs in order to continue their existence ⟨~ laws⟩ **2 :** being in a period of decline ⟨~ industries⟩

sunshine* *adj* **:** forbidding or restricting closed meetings of legislative or executive bodies and sometimes providing for public access to records ⟨~ laws⟩

su·per·alloy \¦süper +\ *n* [*super-* + *alloy*] **:** any of various high-strength often complex alloys resistant to high temperature

su·per·city \¦süpə(r) +\ *n* [*super-* + *city*] **:** MEGALOPOLIS

su·per·cluster \¦süpə(r) +\ *n* [*super-* + *cluster*] **:** a group of gravitationally associated clusters of galaxies

su·per·coil \'süpə(r) +\ *n* [*super-* + *coil*] **:** SUPERHELIX *herein* — **supercoil** \¦süpə(r) +\ *vi* — **su·per·coiled** \"+\ *adj*

su·per·computer \"+\ *n* [*super-* + *computer*] **:** a large very fast mainframe used esp. for scientific computations

su·per·continent \"+\ *n* [*super-* + *continent*] **:** a hypothetical former large continent from which other continents broke off and drifted away

su·per·current \"+\ *n* [*super-* + *current*] **:** a current of electricity flowing in a superconductor

su·per·dense \"+\ *adj* [*super-* + *dense*] **:** of extremely great density; *specif* **:** relating to or being a highly compact state of matter in which electrons and protons are pressed together to form neutrons ⟨~ neutron star⟩

su·per·fec·ta \'süpə(r),fektə\ *n* -s [blend of *super-* and *perfecta* (herein)] **:** a variation of the perfecta in which a bettor must select the first four finishers of a race in the correct order of finish in order to win — compare TRIFECTA *herein*

su·per·graphics \ˌsüpə(r) +\ *n pl but sing or pl in constr* [*super-* + *graphics*] **:** billboard-sized graphic shapes usu. of bright color and simple design

su·per·group \ˌsüpə(r) +\ *n* [*super-* + [1]*group*] **:** a rock group made up of former members of other rock groups; *also* **:** an extremely successful rock group

su·per·heavy \"+\ *adj* [*super-* + *heavy*] **:** relating to or being a chemical element with a greater atomic mass than that of any known element; *also* **:** being an atomic nucleus with a higher atomic number than any known — **superheavy** \"\ *n*

su·per·helix \"+\ *n* [*super-* + *helix*] **:** a helix (as of DNA) which has its axis arranged in a helical coil — **su·per·helical** \"+\ *adj* — **su·per·helicity** \"+\ *n*

su·per·hero \"+\ *n* [*super-* + *hero*] **:** a fictional hero (as in a comic book) having extraordinary or supernatural powers; *also* **:** an exceptionally skillful or successful person

su·per·jet \"+\ *n* [*super*sonic + *jet*] **:** a supersonic jet airplane

su·per·massive \"+\ *adj* [*super-* + *massive*] **:** having extraordinarily great mass; *esp* **:** having a hypothetical mass over 50,000 times that of the sun ⟨a ~ black hole⟩

su·per·molecule \"+\ *n* [*super-* + *molecule*] **:** MACROMOLECULE — **su·per·molecular** \"+\ *adj*

su·per·plastic \"+\ *adj* [*super-* + *plastic*] **1 :** capable of plastic deformation under low stress at an elevated temperature — used of metals and alloys **2 :** of or relating to superplastic materials ⟨~ forming⟩ — **su·per·plasticity** \"+\ *n*

su·per·potent \"+\ *adj* [*super-* + *potent*] **:** of greater than normal or acceptable potency ⟨a drug tablet that was ~⟩ — **su·per·potency** \"+\ *n*

supersonic transport *n* **:** a supersonic transport airplane

su·per·star \ˈsüpə(r) +ˌ\ *n* [*super-* + [1]*star*] **:** a star (as in sports or the movies) who is considered extremely talented, has great public appeal, and can usu. command a high salary; *broadly* **:** one that is very prominent or is a prime attraction ⟨a diplomatic ~⟩ ⟨a ~ among growth stocks⟩ — **su·per·stardom** \ˌsüpə(r) +\ *n*

su·per·station \"+\ *n* [*super-* + *station*] **:** a radio or television station whose signal is broadcast nationwide by satellite

supply–side \ˈ=ˌ=\ *adj* [[2]*supply* + [1]*side*] **:** of, relating to, or being an economic theory that recommends the reduction of tax rates esp. in the highest brackets to encourage more earnings, savings, and investment to expand economic activity and therefore the total taxable national income — **supply–sider** \ˈ=ˌ==\ *n*

support* *n* **:** SUPPORT LEVEL *herein*

support hose *n* **:** stockings (as elastic stockings) worn to supply mild compression to assist the veins in the legs — usu. pl. in constr.

support level *or* **support area** *n* **:** a price level on a declining market at which a security resists further decline due to increased attractiveness to traders and investors

suppress* *vt* **:** to inhibit the genetic expression of ⟨~ a mutation⟩

suppressant *n* -s [*suppressant,* adj.] **:** an agent (as a drug) that tends to suppress or reduce in intensity rather than eliminate something ⟨a cough ~⟩

suppressor t cell *or* **suppressor cell** *n, usu cap T* **:** a T cell that suppresses the response of B cells or of other T cells to an antigen resulting in tolerance for the antigen by the organism containing the T cell — compare HELPER T CELL *herein,* KILLER CELL *herein*

su·pra·cellular \ˌsüprə+\ *adj* [*supra-* + *cellular*] **:** of greater than cellular scope or level of organization

su·pre·mo \səˈprē(ˌ)mō, süˈp-\ *n* -s *sometimes cap* [Sp & It, fr. *supremo,* adj., supreme, fr. L *supremus*] *Brit* **:** one who is highest in rank or authority

surf·able \ˈsərfəbəl\ *adj* [[2]*surf* + *-able*] **:** suitable for surfing

surface–effect ship \ˈ===ˌ=-\ *n* **:** an air-cushion vehicle that operates over water

surface feeder *n* **:** DABBLER 2

surface structure *n* **:** a formal representation of the phonetic form of a sentence; *also* **:** the structure which such a representation describes

surface–to–air missile \ˌ===ˈ=-\ *n* **:** a usu. guided missile launched from the ground against a target in the air

surf and turf *n* **:** seafood (as lobster tails or shrimp) and a beefsteak (as filet mignon) served as a single course

sur·jec·tion \(ˌ)sərˈjekshən\ *n* -s [F, fr. **sur** over, on, onto + *-jection* (as in *projection*) — more at SUR-] **:** a mathematical function that is an onto mapping — compare BIJECTION *herein,* INJECTION *herein*

sur·jec·tive \-ˈjektiv\ *adj* [F, fem. of *surjectif,* fr. *sur* onto + *-jectif* (as in *projectif* projective)] **:** ONTO *herein*

sur·ro·ga·tion \ˌsərəˈgāshən\ *n* -s [[1]*surrogate* + *-ation*] **:** the use of surrogates (as abstracts) in place of longer items (as documents) in an information-retrieval system

sur·veil \(ˌ)sə(r)ˈvā(ə)l\ *vt* **surveilled; surveilled; surveilling; surveils** [back-formation fr. *surveillance*] **:** to subject to surveillance

sur·viv·al·ist \sə(r)ˈvīvələ̇st\ *n* -s [*survival* + *-ist*] **:** one who views survival of a catastrophic event as a primary objective — **survivalist** *adj*

su·shi \ˈsüˌshē\ *n* -s [Jap] **:** cold rice dressed with vinegar, shaped into small cakes, and topped or wrapped with garnishes (as raw fish)

suss out \(ˈ)səsˈau̇t\ *vt* **sussed out; sussed out; sussing out; susses out** [perh. short for *suspect*] *Brit* **:** to inspect or study so as to gain more knowledge **:** figure out ⟨when people phone in you've only got five seconds to *suss out* whether they're going to be obscene —Simon Williams⟩

sweat equity *n* **:** an owner's labor on improvements that increase the value of a property

sweep* *n* **:** a television ratings period during which four consecutive one-week surveys are taken to determine advertising rates for local stations — usu. used in pl.

sweeper* *or* **sweeper back** *n* **:** a lone back in soccer who plays between the line of the defenders and the goal

swing* *vi* **1 :** to be lively and up-to-date **2 :** to engage in sex freely

swing* *also* **swing pass** *n* **:** a play in football in which a backfield receiver runs to the outside to take a short pass

swing–by \ˈ=ˌbī\ *n, pl* **swing–bys :** an interplanetary mission in which a space vehicle utilizes the gravitational field of a planet near which it passes for changing course

swinger* *n* **1 :** a lively and up-to-date person who indulges in what is considered fashionable **2 :** one who engages freely in sex

swinging* *n* **:** the practice of engaging in sex freely; *specif* **:** the exchanging of sex partners

swinging* *adj* **:** being lively and up-to-date ⟨~ moderns⟩; *also* **:** abounding in swingers and swinging entertainment

swing·man \'=,man\ *n, pl* **swing·men** \-,men\ [3*swing* + *man*] **:** a player capable of playing effectively in two different positions and esp. of playing both guard and forward on a basketball team

swing–wing \'=,=\ *adj* **:** having an airplane wing whose outer portion folds back along the fuselage to give the plane an arrowlike planform at high speeds

swipe* *n* **:** a sharp often critical remark ⟨taking a few ~*s* at the phony model heroes —J.K. Fairbank⟩

switched–on \(')swicht¦ȯn, -¦än\ *adj* [fr. past part. of the verb phrase *switch on*] **:** attuned to what is new and exciting

switch–hitter* *n, slang* **:** BISEXUAL — **switch–hitting** \,='==\ *n, slang*

sy·li \'sēlē\ *n* [native name in Guinea] **:** the basic monetary unit of Guinea — see MONEY table *in the Dict*

symmetric group *n* **:** a permutation group that is composed of all of the permutations of *n* things

symmetric matrix *n* **:** a matrix that is its own transpose

symmetry* *n* **:** a rigid motion of a geometric figure that determines a one-to-one mapping onto itself

sym·pa·tho·lyt·ic \,simpə(,)thō'lid·ik\ *n* -s **:** a sympatholytic agent

sym·pa·tho·mimetic \"+\ *n* -s **:** a sympathomimetic agent

syn·anthropic \(,)sin, ,sən +\ *adj* [*syn-* + *anthropic*] **:** ecologically associated with man ⟨~ flies⟩ — **syn·an·thro·py** \sə'nan(t)thrəpē\ *n* -ES

synaptic cleft *also* **synaptic gap** *n* **:** the space between neurons at a nerve synapse across which a nerve impulse is transmitted by a neurotransmitter

syn·ap·to·ne·mal complex *or* **syn·ap·ti·ne·mal complex** \sə,naptə¦nēməl-\ *n* [*synaptic* + *-o-* or *-i-* + *-nema* + 1*-al*] **:** a complex tripartite protein structure that spans the region between synapsed chromosomes in meiotic prophase

syn·ap·to·some \sə'naptə,sōm\ *n* -s [*synaptic* + *-o-* + 3*-some*] **:** a nerve ending that is isolated from homogenized nerve tissue — **sy·nap·to·so·mal** \sə,naptə'sōməl\ *adj*

synchrotron radiation *n* [so called from its having been first observed in a synchrotron] **:** electromagnetic radiation emitted by high-energy charged particles (as electrons) when they are accelerated by a magnetic field (as in a nebula)

syndicate* *vt* **:** to sell (as a series of television programs) directly to local stations

syn·ec·tics \sə'nektiks\ *n pl but usu sing in constr* [perh. fr. Gk *synektik*tein to bring forth together (fr. *syn-* + *ektiktein* to bring forth, fr. *ex-* out + *tiktein* to beget) + E *-s* (as in *dialectics*) — more at EX-, THANE] **:** a theory or system of problem-stating and problem-solving based on creative thinking that involves free use of metaphor and analogy in informal interchange within a carefully selected small group of individuals of diverse personality and areas of specialization — **syn·ec·tic** \-tik\ *adj* — **syn·ec·ti·cal·ly** \-tək(ə)lē\ *adv*

synergism* *n* **:** interaction of discrete agencies (as industrial firms) or agents (as drugs) such that the total effect is greater than the sum of the individual effects

syn·fuel \'sin,=\ *n* [*syn*thetic *fuel*] **:** a liquid or gaseous fuel derived from a fossil fuel that is a solid (as coal) or part of a solid (as tar sand or oil shale) or from fermentation (as of grain)

syn·gas \'sin,=\ *n* [*syn*thesis *gas*] **:** SYNTHESIS GAS

syn·ge·ne·ic \¦sinjə¦nēik\ *adj* [Gk *syngeneia* kinship (fr. *syn-* + *genos* kind, kin) + E *-ic* —more at KIN] **:** genetically identical esp. with respect to antigens or immunological reactions ⟨~ tumor cells⟩ — compare ALLOGENEIC *herein*, XENOGENEIC *herein*

syntactic foam *n* [*syntactic* fr. Gk *syntaktikos* putting together — more at SYNTACTIC] **:** a plastic in which preformed cells (as tiny hollow glass spheres) have been incorporated, which can withstand great pressures (as at ocean depths), and which floats

syn·thase \'sin,thās, -āz\ *n* -s [*synth*esis + *-ase*] **:** any of various enzymes that catalyze the synthesis of a substance without involving the breaking of a high-energy phosphate bond (as in ATP)

synthesizer* *n* **:** a usu. computerized electronic apparatus for the production and control of sound (as for producing music)

synthetic division *n* **:** a simplified method of dividing one polynomial by another of the first degree by writing down only the coefficients of the several powers of the variable and changing the sign of the constant term in the divisor so as to replace the usual subtractions by additions

systems analysis *n* **:** the act, process, or profession of studying an activity (as a procedure, a business, or a physiological function) typically by mathematical means in order to define its goals or purposes and to discover operations and procedures for accomplishing them most efficiently — **systems analyst** *n*

T

t* *n, usu cap* **:** T-SHIRT

t* *abbr, cap* **1** tera- *herein* **2** tesla *herein*

TA *abbr or n* -s **:** a teaching assistant

TA* *abbr* transactional analysis *herein*

tab·bou·leh \tə'bülə\ *n* -s *sometimes cap* [Ar *tabbūla;* akin to Ar *taubala* to spice, season] **:** a salad of Lebanese origin that includes cracked wheat, onions, parsley, and tomatoes

ta·bla \'täblə, 'təb-\ *n* -s [Hindi *tabla,* fr. Ar *tabla*] **:** a pair of small different-sized hand drums used esp. in Hindu music

tablet* *n* **:** GRAPHICS TABLET *herein*

ta·can \'ta,kan\ *n* -s [*tac*tical *a*ir *n*avigation] **:** a system of navigation employing ultra-high frequency signals to determine the distance and bearing of an aircraft from a transmitting station

tach \'tak\ *n* -s [by shortening] **:** TACHOMETER

tach·ism \'ta,shizəm\ *n* -s *often cap* [F *tachisme,* fr. *tache* stain, spot, blob + *-isme,* -ism — more at TACHE] **:** ACTION PAINTING *herein* — **tach·ist** \'tashəst\ *adj or n, often cap*

tachy·arrhythmia \¦takē+\ *n* [*tachy-* + *arrhythmia*] **:** arrhythmia characterized by a rapid irregular heartbeat

tachy·on \'takē,än\ *n* -s [*tachy-* + [2]*-on*] **:** a hypothetical particle held to travel faster than light

tad* *n* **:** a small or insignificant amount or degree **:** BIT ⟨might give him some water and a ~ to eat —C.T. Walker⟩ — **a tad :** SOMEWHAT, RATHER ⟨*a tad* overweight⟩

tae kwon do \'tī'kwän'dō\ *n, often cap T&K&D* [Korean] **:** a Korean martial art resembling karate

ta·gli·a·tel·le \,tälyä'tel(,)ā\ *n* -s [It, fr. *tagliato* cut, past part. of *tagliare* to cut, trim, fr. LL *taliare* to split — more at TAILOR] **:** pasta in the shape of noodles

tag·me·mic \(,)tag'mēmik\ *adj* [*tagmeme* + *-ic*] **:** of, relating to, or being a grammar that describes language in terms of the relationship between grammatical function and the class of items which can perform that function — **tag·me·mi·cist** \-'mē- məsəst\ *n* -s — **tag·me·mics** \-'mēmiks\ *n pl.*

tag question *n* [[1]*tag*] **:** a question (as *isn't it* in "it's fine, isn't it?" or *is it* in "Oh it is, is it?") added to a statement or command (as to gain the assent of or challenge the person addressed)

tag sale *n* **:** GARAGE SALE *herein*

ta·hi·ni \tə'hē(,)nē, tä-\ *n* -s [Turk *tāhin* sesame flour or oil] **:** a smooth paste made from sesame seeds

tai chi *or* **t'ai chi** \'tī'jē, -'chē\ *or* **tai chi chuan** *or* **t'ai chi ch'uan** \-'chü'än\ *n, often cap T & Cs* [Chin (Pek) *t'ai*⁴ *chi*² *ch'uan*² Chinese shadowboxing, fr. *t'ai*⁴ greatest, highest + *chi*² reach + *ch'uan*² boxing] **:** an ancient Chinese discipline practiced as a system of exercises for attaining bodily or mental control and well-being

tailgate* *vi* **:** to go on a tailgate picnic (as before a football game)

tail·gate \'=,=\ *adj* [[1]*tailgate*] **:** relating to or being a picnic set up on the tailgate esp. of a station wagon

ta·ka \'täkə\ *n, pl* **taka** *or* **takas** [Bengali *ṭākā* rupee, taka, fr. Skt *ṭaṅka,* a stamped coin] **1 :** the basic monetary unit of Bangladesh — see MONEY table *in the Dict* **2 :** a coin or note representing one taka

take* *vb* — **take a bath :** to suffer a heavy financial loss — **take a position** *of a security dealer* **:** to hold in his own account stock bought in the course of trading — **take the mickey** *chiefly Brit* **:** JOKE, KID — **take the mickey out of** *chiefly Brit* **:** to make fun of **:** TEASE

take* *n* — **on the take :** taking money for illegal favors

take–charge \'=,=\ *adj* [fr. the phrase *take charge*] **:** having the qualities of a forceful leader ⟨a *take-charge* guy who never let anyone else make a decision —A.H. Raskin⟩

take–home \'=,=\ *adj* [[1]*take* + *home*] **:** that may be worked on without supervision outside the classroom ⟨a *take-home* exam⟩

take off* *vi* **1 :** to start rapid activity, development, or growth ⟨the business *took off* and has been flying high ever since —R. H. Jones⟩ **2 :** to spring into wide use or popularity

takeout* *n* **:** an intensive study or report ⟨one of the best ~*s* on urban welfare —Brock Brower⟩

take–out \¦=,=\ *adj* [*take out,* v.] **:** of, relating to, selling, or being food that is not to be consumed on the premises ⟨*take-out* counter⟩ ⟨a *take-out* sandwich⟩

[1]**ta·la** \'tälə\ *n* -s [Skt *tāla* hand-clapping, musical beat, alter. of *tāḍa* beating, fr. *tāḍāyati* he beats] **:** one of the ancient traditional metrical patterns of Hindu music

[2]**tala** *n, pl* **tala** [Samoan, fr. E *dollar*] **1 :** the basic monetary unit of Western Samoa — see MONEY table *in the Dict* **2 :** a coin or note representing one tala

talking head *n* **:** the televised image of the head of a person who is talking

talk show *n* **:** a radio or television program in which usu. well-known persons engage in discussions or are interviewed

tam·ba·la \(,)täm'bälə\ *n, pl* **tambala** [native name in Malawi, lit., cockerel] **1 :** a monetary unit of Malawi equal to $^{1}/_{100}$ kwacha — see MONEY table *in the Dict* **2 :** a coin representing one tambala

tan·door \tän'dů(ə)r\ *n, pl* **tan·doo·ri** \-'dů(ə)rē\ [Punjabi *tandoor* clay oven; akin to Turk *tandir* oven — more at TENDOUR] **:** a cylindrical clay or earthenware oven in which food is cooked over charcoal

tan·doo·ri \tän'dů(ə)rē\ *adj* [*tandoor* (herein)] **:** cooked in a tandoor ⟨~ chicken⟩

tank suit *n* **:** a one-piece bathing suit with shoulder straps

tank top *n* [so called fr. its resemblance to a tank suit] **:** a sleeveless collarless shirt with shoulder straps and no front opening

tape deck *n* **:** a device used to play back and often to record on magnetic tape that usu. has to be connected to an audio system

tape player *n* **:** a self-contained device for the playback of recorded magnetic tapes

tar baby \'=,==\ *n* [fr. *Tar-Baby,* doll made of tar in which Brer Rabbit becomes entangled in a story by Joel Chandler Harris †1908 Am. writer] **:** something from which it is nearly impossible to extricate oneself ⟨the issue became a political *tar baby*⟩

tardive dyskinesia *n* **:** a central nervous system disorder characterized by twitching of the face and tongue and involuntary motor movements of the trunk and limbs and occurring esp. as a side effect of prolonged use of antipsychotic drugs

tar·dy \'tärdē, 'tȧd-, -di\ *n* -ES [*tardy,* adj.] **:** an instance of being tardy (as for class)

tar·get·able \'tärgə̇d·əbəl\ *adj* [²*target* + *-able*] **:** capable of being aimed at a target ⟨missiles with ~ warheads⟩

target language *n* **1 :** a foreign language that is the subject of study **2 :** a language into which a translation is made

tar pit *n* **:** an area in which natural bitumens collect and are exposed at the earth's surface and which tends to trap animals and preserve their hard parts

tart up *vt* [²*tart*] **:** to dress up **:** fancy up ⟨*tarted up* pubs and restaurants for the spenders —Arnold Ehrlich⟩

Tas·lan \'tas,lan\ *trademark* — used for thread and textured yarn

tau particle *n* **:** a short-lived elementary particle of the lepton family that exists in positive and negative charge states and has a mass about 3500 times heavier than an electron

taurean* *n, usu cap* **:** TAURUS *herein*

taurus* *n, usu cap* **:** one born under the astrological sign Taurus

ta·ver·na \tä've(ə)rnə\ *n* -s [modif. (prob. influenced by E *tavern*) of NGk *taberna* tavern] **:** a café in Greece

tax base *n* **:** the wealth (as real estate or income) within a jurisdiction that is liable to taxation

tax haven *n* **:** a country or territory in which taxes are low or nonexistent and thus is attractive to foreign investors

taxi squad *n* [so called fr. the practice of a former owner of a professional team who employed such surplus players as drivers for a taxi fleet which he also owned] **:** a group of professional football players under contract who practice with a team but are ineligible to participate in official games

taxon *abbr* taxonomic; taxonomy

tax selling *n* **:** concerted selling of securities late in the year to establish gains and losses for income-tax purposes

tax shelter *n* **:** a strategy (as formation of a philanthropic foundation), an investment (as in a venture capital enterprise or tax-free municipal bonds), or a tax code provision (as for a depreciation allowance) that reduces one's tax liability — **tax–sheltered** \'=,==\ *adj*

tay·lor's series \'tālə(r)(z)-\ *or* **taylor series** *n, usu cap T* [after Brook *Taylor* †1731 Eng. mathematician] **:** a power series that gives the expansion of a function $f(x)$ in the neighborhood of a point a provided all derivatives exist and the series converges and that has the form

$$f(x) = f(a) + \frac{f^{[1]}(a)}{1!}(x-a) + \frac{f^{[2]}(a)}{2!}(x-a)^2 + \ldots + \frac{f^{[n]}(a)}{n!}(x-a)^n + \ldots$$

where $f^{[n]}(a)$ is the derivative of nth order of $f(x)$ evaluated at a

tay–sachs disease \¦tā'saks-\ *also* **tay–sachs** *n, usu cap T&S* [after Waren *Tay* †1927 Eng. physician and Bernard P. *Sachs* †1944 Am. neurologist] **:** a fatal hereditary disorder of lipid metabolism characterized by the accumulation of sphingolipid esp. in nervous tissue due to an enzyme deficiency

t–bill \'=,=\ *n, usu cap T* [*t*reasury] **:** a U.S. treasury note

TCDD \¦tē¦sē¦dē'dē\ *n* -s [*t*etra- + *c*hlor- + *d*ibenzo- (containing two benzene rings) + *d*ioxin] **:** a carcinogenic dioxin $C_{12}H_4O_2Cl_4$ found esp. as a contaminant in 2,4,5-T

t cell *n, usu cap T* [*t*hymus-derived *cell*] **:** a lymphocyte differentiated in the thymus, characterized by specific surface antigens, and specialized esp. for cell-mediated immunity (as in the defense against viruses and the rejection of foreign tissues) or for cooperation with B cells in immunoglobulin synthesis — compare B CELL *herein*

t distribution *n* **:** a probability density function that is used esp. in testing hypotheses concerning means of normal distributions whose standard deviations are unknown and that is the distribution of a random variable

$$t = \frac{u\sqrt{n}}{v}$$

where u and v are themselves independent random variables and u has a normal distribution with mean 0 and a standard deviation of 1 and v^2 has a chi-square distribution with n degrees of freedom — called also *student's t distribution*

tea break *n, chiefly Brit* **:** a short rest period during the working day for the drinking of tea

tea ceremony *n* **:** CHANOYU

teach–in \'=,=\ *n* -s [*teach* + *-in* (herein)] **:** an extended meeting usu. held on a college campus for lectures, debates, and discussions on important issues (as U.S. foreign policy)

team foul *n* **:** one of a designated number of personal fouls the players on a basketball team may commit during a given period of play before the opposing team begins receiving bonus free throws

team handball *n* **:** a game developed from soccer which is played between two teams of seven players each and in which the ball is thrown, caught, and dribbled with the hands

tear* *vb* — **tear a strip off** *Brit* **:** to bawl out **:** SCOLD

tear·gas \'=,=\ *vt* **:** to use tear gas on

tearoom* *n* **:** a men's room used as a site for homosexual activity

tease* *n* **:** ¹TEASER 4b

tech·ne·tron·ic \¦teknə̇·¦tränik\ *adj* [*techn*ological + elec*tronic*] **:** shaped or influenced by the changes wrought by advances in technology and communications ⟨our modern ~ society⟩

Tech·ni·color \'teknə̇ +,\ *trademark* — used for color motion pictures

tech·nol·o·gize \tek'nälə,jīz\ *vt* -ED/-ING/-S [*technology* + *-ize*] **:** to affect or alter by technology

tech·no·structure \¦teknō +\ *n* [*techno-* + *structure*] **:** a large-scale corporation or system of corporate enterprises; *also* **:** the network of professionally skilled managers (as scientists, engineers, and administrators) that increasingly tends to control the economy both within and beyond individual corporate groups

teeny \'tēnē\ *n* -ES [*teen* + *-y*] **:** TEENAGER

teeny·bop \'==,bäp\ *adj* [back-formation fr. *teenybopper* (herein)] **:** of, relating to, or being a teenybopper

teenybopper \'==,==\ *n* -s [*teeny* (herein) + *bopper*] **:** a teenager and esp. a teenaged girl; *esp* **:** one who is enthusiastically devoted to pop music and to current fads

TEFL \'tefəl\ *abbr* teaching English as a foreign language

tei·cho·ic acid \tā'kōik-, tī'-\ *n* [*teichoic,* fr. Gk *teichos* wall + E *-ic*] **:** any of a class of strongly acidic polymers found in the cell walls, capsules, and membranes of all gram-positive bacteria and containing residues of the phosphates of glycerol and adonitol

tele·com·mut·ing \ˌteləkəˈmyüd·iŋ\ *n* -s [[1]*tel-* + *commuting,* gerund of *commute*] **:** the practice of working at home using a computer and sending completed work to one's employer by telecommunications

tele·con·fer·enc·ing \ˌteləˈkänf(ə)rən(t)siŋ\ *n* -s [[1]*tel-* + *conference* + *-ing*] **:** the holding of a conference among people remote from one another by means of telecommunication devices (as telephones or computer terminals) — **tele·conference** \"+\ *n*

Tele·copier \ˈteləˌkäpēə(r)\ *trademark* — used for transmitting and receiving equipment for producing facsimile copies of documents

tele·diagnosis \ˌtelə +\ *n* [[1]*tel-* + *diagnosis*] **:** the diagnosis of physical or mental ailments based on data received from a patient by means of telemetry and closed-circuit television

tele·facsimile \"+\ *n* [[1]*tel-* + *facsimile*] **:** a system of transmitting and reproducing fixed graphic material (as printing) by means of signals transmitted over telephone lines

tele·film \ˈtelə +ˌ\ *n* [[1]*tel-* + *film*] **:** a motion picture produced for television

tele·marketing \ˌtelə +\ *n* [[1]*tel-* + *marketing*] **:** the marketing of goods or services by telephone

te·lem·e·try \təˈleməˌtrē\ *n* -ES [[1]*tel-* + *-metry*] **1 :** the science or process of telemetering data **2 :** data transmitted by telemetry **3 :** BIOTELEMETRY *herein*

tele·on·o·my \ˌteləˈänəmē\ *n* -ES [*tele-* + *-nomy*] **:** the quality of apparent purposefulness in living organisms that derives from their evolutionary adaptation

tele·processing \ˌtelə +\ *n* [[1]*tel-* + *processing,* gerund of [2]*process*] **:** computer processing via remote terminals

tele·text \ˈtelə +ˌ\ *n* [*tele-* + *text*] **:** an electronic system in which printed matter is broadcast over an unused portion of a television signal and displayed on a viewer's television set that is equipped with a decoder — compare VIDEOTEX *herein*

tel·ex \ˈteˌleks\ *n* -ES [*tele*printer + *ex*change] **1 :** a communication service involving teletypewriters connected by wire through automatic exchanges **2 :** a message sent by telex — **telex** *vt* -ED/-ING/-ES

telophase* *n* **:** a stage in meiosis that is usu. the final stage in the first and second meiotic divisions but may be missing in the first and that is characterized by formation of the nuclear membrane and by changes in coiling and arrangement of the chromosomes

temp* *n* **:** a temporary worker

tem·peh \ˈtemˌpā\ *n* -s [Indonesian *tempé*] **:** an Asian food prepared by fermenting soybeans with a rhizopus

template* *n* **:** a molecule (as of DNA) that serves as a pattern for the generation of another macromolecule (as messenger RNA)

temporal summation *n* **:** sensory summation that involves the addition of single stimuli over a short period of time

ten·der·om·e·ter \ˌtendəˈrämәd·ә(r), -ətə-\ *n* [[1]*tender* + *-o-* + *-meter*] **:** a device for determining the maturity and tenderness of samples of fruits and vegetables

-tene \ˌtēn\ *adj comb form* [*-tene* (in the Dict.)] **:** having (such or so many) chromosomal filaments ⟨poly*tene*⟩ ⟨pachy*tene*⟩

tens digit *n* **:** TEN 8

ten·seg·ri·ty \ten(t)ˈsegrəd·ē\ *n* -ES [*tens*ion + int*egrity*] **:** the property of a skeletal structure having continuous tension members (as wires) and discontinuous compression members (as metal tubes) so that each member performs efficiently in producing a rigid form

ten·sio·met·ric \ˌten(t)sēəˈme·trik\ *adj* [*tension* + *-metric*] **:** of, relating to, or involving the measurement of tension or tensile strength — **ten·si·om·e·try** \ˌten(t)sēˈäma·trē\ *n* -ES

ten–speed \ˈ=ˌ=\ *n* **:** a bicycle with a 10-speed derailleur

tens place *n* **:** the place two to the left of the decimal point in a number expressed in the Arabic system of writing numbers

tent trailer *n* **:** a 2-wheeled automobile-drawn trailer having a canvas shelter that can be opened up above the body to provide camping facilities

ten·ured \ˈtenyə(r)d *also* -ˌyu̇(ə)rd, -ˌyu̇əd\ *adj* [*tenure* + *-ed*] **:** having tenure ⟨~ faculty members⟩

tenure–track \ˈ=(ˌ)=ˌ=\ *adj* [*tenure* + *track*] **:** relating to or being a teaching position that may lead to one's being granted tenure

teo·na·na·catl \ˌtāōˌnänəˈkätᵊl\ *n* -s [Nahuatl, fr. *teotl* god + *nanacatl* mushroom] **:** any of several New World mushrooms (*Psilocybe* and related genera of the family Agaricaceae) that are sources of hallucinogens

te·pa \ˈtēpə\ *n* -s [*t*ri- + *e*thylene + *p*hosphor- + *a*mide] **:** a soluble crystalline compound $C_6H_{12}N_3OP$ that is used esp. as a chemosterilant of insects, a palliative in some kinds of cancer, and in finishing and flameproofing textiles

teph·ra \ˈtefrə\ *n* [Gk *tephra* ashes; akin to L *favilla* ashes —more at DAY] **:** solid material ejected during the eruption of a volcano and transported through the air

tequila sunrise *n* **:** a cocktail consisting chiefly of tequila, orange juice, and grenadine

tera- \ˌterə\ *comb form* [ISV, fr. Gk *teras* monster — more at TERAT-] **:** trillion ⟨*tera*ton⟩ ⟨*tera*hertz⟩

te·rato·carcinoma \ˌterəd·ō+\ *n* [*terato*ma + *carcinoma*] **:** a malignant teratoma; *esp* **:** one involving germinal cells of the testis

te·rato·gen \təˈrad·əjən, ˈterəd·əjən, -ˌjen\ *n* -s [*terat-* + *-gen*] **:** a teratogenic agent (as a drug or virus)

ter·i·ya·ki \ˌterēˈ(y)äkē\ *n* -s [Jap, fr. *teri* glaze + *yaki* grill] **:** a dish of Japanese origin consisting of meat, chicken, or shellfish that is grilled or broiled after being marinated in a spicy soy sauce

terminal* *adj* **:** extremely or excessively severe ⟨~ boredom⟩

terminal* *n* **:** a device (as a video display unit) by which data can be entered into or output from an electronic communications system

ter·ra \ˈterə\ *n, pl* **ter·rae** \-r(ˌ)ē, -rˌī\ [NL, fr. L, land — more at TERRACE] **:** any of the relatively light-grayish highland areas on the surface of the moon

ter·ran \ˈterən\ *n* -s *usu cap* [*Terra,* the planet Earth (fr. L *terra* earth) + E [1]*-an* — more at TERRACE] **:** EARTHMAN

tertiary* *adj* **1 :** being or relating to the recovery of oil and gas from old wells by means of the underground application of heat and chemicals **2 :** being or relating to the purification of wastewater by removal of fine particles, nitrates, and phosphates

TESL \ˈtesəl\ *abbr* teaching English as a second language

tes·la \ˈteslə\ *n* -s [ISV, after Nikola *Tesla* †1943 Am. electrician and inventor] **:** a unit of magnetic flux density in the mks system equivalent to one weber per square meter

TESOL *abbr* teachers of English to speakers of other languages; teaching of English to speakers of other languages

test ban *n* **:** a self-imposed ban on the atmospheric testing of nuclear weapons that is mutually agreed to by countries possessing such weapons

test–drive \ˈ=,=\ *vt* **:** to drive (a motor vehicle) in order to evaluate performance

tet·ra·ben·a·zine \ˌte·trəˌbenə,zēn\ *n* [*tetra-* + *benzo*[*a*]-quinolizine, fr. *benz-* + *a* (an indicator of position) + *quinoline* + *azine*] **:** a serotonin antagonist $C_{19}H_{27}NO_3$ that is used esp. in the treatment of psychosis and anxiety

tet·ra·functional \ˌte·trə +\ *adj* [*tetra-* + *functional*] **:** of, relating to, or being a compound with four sites in a molecule that are highly reactive (as in polymerization)

tet·ra·hy·dro·cannabinol \ˌte·trə,hīdrə +\ *n* -s [*tetrahydr-* + *cannabinol*] **:** THC *herein*

tet·ra·hy·me·na \ˌte·trəˈhīmənə\ *n* [NL, fr. *tetra-* + Gk *hymēn* membrane] **1** *cap* **:** a genus of free-living ciliate protozoans much used for genetic and biochemical research **2** -s **:** a ciliate protozoan of the genus *Tetrahymena*

tet·ra·pyr·role *also* **tet·ra·pyr·rol** \ˌte·trəˌpi,rōl, -rȯl, -əpəˌr-\ *n* [*tetra-* + *pyrrole*] **:** a chemical group consisting of four pyrrole rings joined either in a straight chain (as in phycobilins) or in a ring (as in chlorophyll)

tet·raz·zi·ni \ˌte·trəˌzēnē\ *adj, usu cap* [after Luisa *Tetrazzini* †1940 Ital. opera singer] **:** prepared with pasta and a white sauce seasoned with sherry and served au gratin ⟨chicken *Tetrazzini*⟩

texas citrus mite *n, usu cap T* **:** a red spider (*Eutetrarychus banksi*) that causes leaf injury to citrus trees

tex–mex \ˌteksˌmeks\ *adj, usu cap T&M* [*Tex*an + *Mex*ican] **:** of, relating to, or being the Mexican-American culture or cuisine existing or originating esp. in southern Texas ⟨*Tex-Mex* cooking⟩ ⟨*Tex-Mex* music⟩

text* *n* **:** matter chiefly in the form of words that is treated as data for processing by computerized equipment

textbook \ˈ=ˌ=\ *adj* [*textbook,* n.] **:** of, suggesting, or suitable to a textbook; *esp* **:** CLASSIC ⟨a ~ example of bureaucratic waste⟩

textured vegetable protein *n* **:** protein obtained from some vegetables and esp. soybeans and used as a substitute for or added to meat

tex·tur·ize \ˈtekschə,rīz\ *vt* -ED/-ING/-S [[1]*texture* + *-ize*] **:** [2]TEXTURE 2b ⟨the flat thermoplastic yarn . . . is *texturized* as it approaches the knitting needles —*Technical Survey*⟩

TG* *abbr* **1** transformational-generative **2** transformational grammar *herein*

t–group \ˈ=,=\ *n, usu cap T* [*t*raining *group*] **:** a group of people under the leadership of a trainer who seek to develop self-awareness and sensitivity to others by verbalizing feelings uninhibitedly at group sessions — compare ENCOUNTER GROUP *herein*

thal·as·se·mic \ˌthaləˈsēmik\ *adj* [*thalassem*ia + [1]*-ic*] **:** of, relating to, or affected with thalassemia — **thalassemic** *n*

tha·lid·o·mide \thəˈlidə,mīd, -ˌməd\ *n* -s [ph*thal*im*ide* + *-o-* + *imide*] **:** a sedative and hypnotic drug $C_{13}H_{10}N_2O_4$ that has been the cause of malformation in infants born to mothers using it during pregnancy

thankfully* *adv* **:** thank goodness — used as a sentence modifier ⟨the usual barking dogs, ~ more muted here than in town —Caroline Bates⟩

thatch* *n* **:** a mat of undecomposed plant material (as grass clippings) accumulated next to the soil in a grassy area (as a lawn)

THC \ˌtē(ˌ)āchˈsē\ *n* -s [*t*etra*h*ydro*c*annabinol (herein)] **:** a physiologically active chemical $C_{21}H_{30}O_2$ from hemp plant resin that is the chief intoxicant in marijuana — called also *tetrahydrocannabinol*

the·a·ter \ˈthēə|d·ə(r), ˈthiə|, |tə\ *adj* [*theater,* n.] **:** TACTICAL ⟨~ nuclear weapons⟩

theater of the absurd : theater that seeks to represent the absurdity of man's existence in a meaningless universe by bizarre or fantastic means

the·be \ˈtā(ˌ)bā\ *n, pl* **thebe** [native name in Botswana] **1 :** a monetary unit of Botswana equal to $^1/_{100}$ pula — see MONEY table *in the Dict* **2 :** a coin representing one thebe

theme \ˈthēm\ *adj* [[1]*theme*] *of a restaurant or hotel* **:** having an elaborate, specialized, or fantasy decor and setting

theme park *n* **:** an amusement park in which the structures and settings are based on a central theme

theorem* *n* **1 :** STENCIL **2 :** a painting produced esp. on velvet by the use of stencils for each color

therapeutic index *n* **:** a measure of the relative desirability of a drug for the attaining of a particular medical end that is usu. expressed as the ratio of the largest dose producing no toxic symptoms to the smallest dose routinely producing cures

thermal* *adj* **:** designed (as with insulating air spaces) to prevent dissipation of body heat ⟨~ underwear⟩

thermal pollution *n* **:** the discharge of heated liquid (as wastewater from a factory) into natural waters at a temperature harmful to existing ecosystems

ther·mo·form \ˈthərmə,fȯrm\ *vt* [*therm-* + [2]*form*] **:** to give a final shape to (as a plastic) with the aid of heat and usu. pressure — **thermoform** *n* — **ther·mo·form·able** \ˌ==ˌ=əbəl\ *adj*

thermogram* *n* **1 :** a photographic record made by thermography **2 :** a temperature-weight change graph obtained in thermogravimetry

thermograph* *n* **1 :** the apparatus used in thermography **2 :** THERMOGRAM *herein*

ther·mo·gravimetry \ˌthər(ˌ)mō +\ *n* [ISV *therm-* + *gravimetry;* prob. orig. formed in F] **:** the determination (as with a thermobalance) of weight changes in a substance at a high temperature or during a gradual increase in temperature — **ther·mo·gravimetric** \"+\ *adj*

ther·mo·physical \ˌthərmō, -mə+\ *adj* [*therm-* + *physical*] **:** of, relating to, or being the physical properties of materials as affected by elevated temperatures

ther·mo·regulate \"+\ *vb* [*therm-* + *regulate*] *vt* **:** to subject to thermoregulation ~ *vi* **:** to undergo thermoregulation

ther·mo·remanent \"+\ *adj* [*therm-* + *remanent*] **:** being or relating to magnetic remanence (as in a rock cooled from a molten state or in a baked clay object containing magnetic minerals) that indicates the strength and direction of the earth's magnetic field at a former time — **ther·mo·remanence** \"+\ *n*

ther·mo·sphere \ˈthərmə +ˌ\ *n* [ISV *therm-* + *sphere*] **:** the part of the earth's atmosphere that begins at about 50 miles above the earth's surface, extends to outer space, and is characterized by steadily increasing temperature with height — **ther·mo·spheric** \ˌ==+\ *adj*

theta rhythm *or* **theta wave** *or* **theta*** *n* **:** a relatively high amplitude brain wave pattern between approximately 4 and 9 hertz that is characteristic esp. of the hippocampus but occurs in many regions of the brain including the cortex

thia·ben·da·zole \ˌthīəˈbendəˌzōl\ *n* -s [*thia*zole + *ben*zim- *idazole*] **:** a drug $C_{10}H_7N_3S$ used in the control of parasitic roundworms and fungus infections and as an agricultural fungicide

thi·a·zide \ˈthīəˌzīd, -ˌzəd\ *n* -s [*thia-* + di*az*ine + diox*ide*] **:** any of several drugs used as oral diuretics esp. in the control of high blood pressure

thing* *n* **:** a personal choice of activity **:** SPECIALTY — often used with *do* ⟨letting students do their own ~ —*Newsweek*⟩

think tank *also* **think factory** *n* **:** an institute, corporation, or group organized for interdisciplinary research (as in military strategy or social problems) — **think tank·er** \-ˌtaŋkə(r)\ *n* -s

thin–layer chromatography \ˌ=ˈ=(=)-\ *n* **:** chromatography in which the solution containing the substances to be separated migrates through a thin layer of the absorbent medium (as silica gel, alumina, or cellulose) arranged on a rigid support — compare COLUMN CHROMATOGRAPHY *herein,* PAPER CHROMATOGRAPHY *in the Dict* — **thin–layer chromatogram** \ˌ=ˈ=(=)-\ *n* — **thin–layer chromatographic** *adj*

thi·o·rid·a·zine \ˌthīəˈridəˌzēn, -ˌzən\ *n* -s [*thio-* + piperi*d*ine + phenothi*azine*] **:** a phenothiazine tranquilizer used as the hydrochloride $C_{21}H_{26}N_2S_2{\cdot}HCl$ for relief of anxiety states and in the treatment of schizophrenia

third market *n* [so called in distinction from the organized exchanges and the market in unlisted securities] **:** the over-the-counter market in listed securities — compare FOURTH MARKET *herein*

third–stream \ˈ=ˌ=\ *adj* **:** of, relating to, or being music that incorporates elements of classical music and jazz

third world *n, often cap T&W* [trans. of F *tiers monde*] **1 :** a group of nations esp. in Africa and Asia that are not aligned with either the Communist or the non-Communist blocs **2 :** an aggregate of minority groups within a larger predominant culture **3 :** the aggregate of the underdeveloped nations of the world — **third worlder** \-ˈwər(ə)ldə(r), -ˈwəl-\ *n, often cap T&W*

ThM *abbr* master of theology

thong* *n* **:** a sandal held on the foot by a thong between the toes

thoracic gland *n* **:** PROTHORACIC GLAND *herein*

Tho·ra·zine \ˈthōrəˌzēn, ˈthȯr-\ *trademark* — used for chlorpromazine

thousands digit *n* **:** THOUSAND 4

thousands place *n* **:** the place four to the left of the decimal point in a number expressed in the Arabic system of writing numbers

thread* *n* **threads** *pl* **:** CLOTHES

360 \ˈthrēˈsikstē\ *n, pl* **360s :** a 360 degree turn esp. done very rapidly

thrift* *also* **thrift institution** *n* **:** a mutual savings bank or savings and loan association

thrift shop *n* **:** a shop that sells secondhand articles and esp. clothes and is often run for charitable purposes

throm·box·ane \thrämˈbäkˌsān\ *n* -s [fr. *thrombo*cyte + *ox-* + *-ane*] **:** any of several potent regulators of cellular function formed from endoperoxides and first isolated from blood platelets

throughput* *n* **:** OUTPUT, PRODUCTION ⟨the ~ of a computer⟩

throwaway* *n* **:** a thing made or done without care or interest

throwaway \ˈ==ˌ=\ *adj* [*throw away*] **1 a :** that may be thrown away **:** DISPOSABLE ⟨~ containers⟩ **b :** accustomed to or depending on the discarding rather than the reusing or recycling of materials after initial use ⟨our ~ society⟩ ⟨~ economy⟩ **2 :** written or spoken (as in a play) in a low-key or unemphasized manner ⟨~ lines⟩ **3 :** NONCHALANT, CASUAL ⟨all put together with such style, such ~ chic —Peter Buckley⟩

throw pillow *n* **:** a small pillow used esp. as a decorative accessory

thrust* *n* **1 :** salient or essential element or meaning **2 :** principal concern or objective

thrust chamber *n* **:** ROCKET 4

thrus·tor *also* **thrust·er*** \ˈthrəstə(r)\ *n* -s [[1]*thrust* + [1]*-or*] **:** REACTION ENGINE

thrust stage *n* [*thrust,* past part. of [1]*thrust*] **:** a stage surrounded on three sides by the audience; *also* **:** a forestage that is extended into the auditorium to increase the stage area

thumb piano *n* **:** any of several musical instruments of African origin (as the kalimba, mbira, or zanza) that consist essentially of a resonator and a set of tuned metal or wooden strips that are plucked with the thumbs or fingers

thumbs–up \ˈ=ˈ=\ *n* -s **:** an instance or gesture of approval or encouragement

thy·la·koid \ˈthīləˌkȯid\ *n* -s [ISV *thylak-* (fr. Gk *thylakos* sack) + *-oid;* prob. orig. formed in G] **:** any of the membranous lamellae of plant chloroplasts that are composed of protein and lipid and are the sites of the photochemical reactions of photosynthesis

thy·mec·to·mize \thīˈmektəˌmīz\ *vt* -ED/-ING/-S [*thymectomy* + *-ize*] **:** to subject to thymectomy

thy·mi·co·lymphatic \ˌthīmə(ˌ)kō +\ *adj* [[2]*thymic* + *-o-* + *lymphatic*] **:** of, relating to, or affecting both the thymus and the lymphatic system

thy·mo·sin \ˈthīməsən\ *n* -s [fr. Gk *thymos* thymus + E *-in*] **:** a polypeptide thymic hormone that influences the maturation of T cells destined for an active role in cell-mediated immunity

thy·ris·tor \thīˈristə(r)\ *n* -s [*thyr*atron + tran*sistor*] **:** any of several semiconductor devices that act as switches, rectifiers, or voltage regulators

thy·ro·calcitonin \ˌthīrō +\ *n* [*thyr-* + *calcitonin* (herein)] **:** CALCITONIN *herein*

thyroid–stimulating hormone \ˌ=ˌ=ˈ==ˌ==-\ *n* **:** THYROTROPHIN

thyrotropin–releasing hormone *also* **thyrotropin–releasing factor** *n* **:** a tripeptide hormone synthesized in the hypothalamus that stimulates secretion of thyrotropin by the anterior lobe of the pituitary gland

tic* *n* **:** a frequent usu. unconscious quirk of behavior or speech

ticket pocket *n* **:** a small pocket within or just above the outside pocket of a man's suit jacket

tick off* *vt* **:** to make angry or indignant

[1]**ticky–tacky** \ˈtikēˌtakē\ *also* **ticky–tack** \-ˌtak\ *n, pl* **ticky–tackies** *also* **ticky–tacks** [redupl. of *tacky*] **:** sleazy or shoddy material used esp. in the construction of look-alike tract houses; *also* **:** something built of ticky-tacky

[2]**ticky–tacky** \"\ *also* **ticky–tack** \"\ *adj* **1 :** being of an uninspired or monotonous sameness or commonness **2 :** TACKY **3 :** built of ticky-tacky

tidal volume *n* **:** the volume of the tidal air

tight* *adj* **1 :** marked by friendliness and compatibility **:** CLOSE ⟨the Men's Alpine Ski Team is a ~ bunch, surprisingly free of backbiting —Herbert Burkholz⟩ **2**

: being or performing music in a polished style with precise arrangements ⟨some favor ~ playing, with crisply articulated notes, others open playing, generally faster and more flowing —Eleanor Blau⟩

tight–assed \ˈ≈,≈\ *adj, slang* **:** rigidly proper, conventional, or inhibited

tight end *n* **:** an offensive end in football who lines up within two yards of the tackle

time dilation *also* **time dilatation** *n* **:** a slowing of time in accordance with the theory of relativity that occurs in a system in motion relative to an outside observer and that becomes apparent esp. as the speed of the system approaches that of light

time frame *n* **:** a period of time esp. with respect to some action or project ⟨mandatory *time frames* within which committees must act —Guy Halverson⟩

time line *n* **1** *usu* **timeline :** a schedule of events or procedures **:** TIMETABLE ⟨the *timeline* of a space mission⟩ **2 :** TIME CHART 2

time reversal *n* **:** a formal operation in mathematical physics that reverses the order in which a sequence of events occurs

time reversal invariance *n* **:** a principle in physics: if a given sequence of events is physically possible the same sequence in the opposite order is also possible

time–sharing \ˈ≈,≈≈\ *n* **1 :** simultaneous use of a central computer by many users at remote locations **2** *or* **time–share** \ˈ≈,≈\ **:** joint ownership or rental of a vacation lodging (as a condominium) by several persons with each occupying the premises in turn for a period — **time–share** \ˈ≈,≈\ *vt* — **time–sharer** \ˈ≈,≈≈\ *n*

times sign *n* **:** the symbol × used to indicate multiplication — called also *multiplication sign*

time–tested \ˈ≈,≈≈\ *adj* **:** having effectiveness that has been proved over a long period of time ⟨a *time-tested* formula⟩

time trial *n* **:** a competitive event (as in auto racing) in which individuals are successively timed over a set course or distance

time–trip *vi* [[1]*time* + *trip*] **:** to experience nostalgia

time warp *n* **:** an anomaly, discontinuity, or suspension held to occur in the progress of time

ting ware \ˈting,≈\ *also* **ting yao** \-ˈyau̇\ *n, often cap T* [*Ting* fr. *Ting Chou,* town southwest of Peking, China, where it was originally made; *Ting yao* fr. *Ting* + Chin (Pek) *yao*[2] pottery] **:** a Chinese porcelain ware known since Sung times that is typically expertly potted, often decorated with engraved underglaze designs, and characteristically glazed with a milk-white to creamy white or less often an iron-red glaze

Tin·ker·toy \ˈtiŋkə(r),tȯi\ *trademark* — used for a construction toy of fitting parts

tip of the iceberg [fr. the fact that most of an iceberg is submerged] **:** the earliest, most obvious, or most superficial manifestation of some phenomenon

tissue* *vt* **:** to remove (as cleansing cream) with a tissue

tissue typing *n* **:** the determination of the degree of compatibility of tissues or organs from different individuals based on the similarity of histocompatibility antigens esp. on lymphocytes and used esp. as a measure of potential rejection in an organ transplant procedure

tis·su·lar \ˈtish(y)ələ(r)\ *adj* [[1]*tissue* + *-lar* (as in *cellular*)] **:** of, relating to, or affecting organismic tissue ⟨~ grafts⟩

titer* *n* **:** the dilution of a serum containing a specific antibody at which the solution just retains a specific activity (as neutralizing or precipitating an antigen) but loses it at any greater dilution

tit·fer \ˈtitfə(r)\ *n* -s [by shortening & alter. fr. *tit for tat,* rhyming slang for *hat*] *Brit* **:** HAT

t lymphocyte *n, usu cap T* [*thymus-derived lymphocyte*] **:** T CELL *herein*

TM* *abbr* transcendental meditation *herein*

toaster oven *n* **:** a portable electrical appliance that can function as an oven or a toaster

toea \ˈtȯiə\ *n, pl* **toea** *also* **toeas** [prob. Pidgin English, modif. of E *dollar*] **1 :** a monetary unit of Papua New Guinea equal to $^{1}/_{100}$ kina — see MONEY table *in the Dict* **2 :** a coin representing one toea

toe–to–toe \ˌ≈≈ˈ≈\ *adj (or adv)* **:** characterized by direct and aggressive fighting or conflict ⟨a *toe-to-toe* confrontation⟩

together *adj* [*together,* adv.] **1 :** appropriately prepared, organized, or balanced ⟨a super-delicious, beautifully ~ album —Clayton Riley⟩ **2 :** composed in mind or manner ⟨a warm, sensitive, reasonably ~ girl —*East Village Other*⟩

to·ka·mak \ˈtōkə,mak, ˈtäk-\ *n* -s [Russ] **:** a toroidal device for producing controlled nuclear fusion that involves the confining and heating of a gaseous plasma by means of an internal electric current and its attendant magnetic field

toke \ˈtōk\ *n* -s [origin unknown] **1** *slang* **:** a puff on a marijuana cigarette **2** *slang* **:** a tip given esp. by a gambler to the dealer at a casino

token* *n* **:** a token member of a group; *esp* **:** a token employee

token* *adj* **:** serving or intended to show absence of discrimination ⟨a ~ female employee⟩

to·ken·ism \ˈtōkə,nizəm\ *n* -s [*token* + *-ism*] **:** the policy or practice of making only a token effort (as to desegregate or provide equal employment opportunities) — **to·ken·is·tic** \-istik\ *adj*

to·laz·o·line \tōˈlazə,lēn\ *n* -s [*tol-* + *azole* + *-ine*] **:** a weak alpha-adrenergic blocking agent $C_{10}H_{12}N_2$ used as the hydrochloride to produce peripheral vasodilatation

tom* *n, usu cap* **:** UNCLE TOM

tom *vi* **tommed; tommed; tomming; toms** *often cap* **:** UNCLE TOM *herein*

ton* *n* **1** *Brit* **:** a speed of 100 miles per hour — often used in the phase *do the ton* or *do a ton* ⟨the first cars were doing the ~ barely ten years after Victoria's Diamond Jubilee —*London Times*⟩ **2** *Brit* **:** a score of 100 runs in cricket **:** CENTURY

tone block *n* **:** a rhythm band instrument consisting of a hand-held usu. slotted block of wood struck by a rod or drumstick

tonicity* *n* **:** the osmotic pressure of a solution

tonkinese* *n, pl* **tonkinese** *usu cap* **:** any of a breed of short-haired cats developed in the U.S. by crossing the Siamese with the Burmese that have a brown or bluish gray body coat with darker points and blue-green eyes

tonne \ˈtən\ *n* -s [F, fr. *tonne* tun, fr. OF — more at TUNNEL] **:** METRIC TON

tool \ˈtül\ *n* -s [[2]*tool*] **:** a design (as on the binding of a book) made by tooling

toot* *n* **:** COCAINE; *also* **:** a snort of cocaine

toothpick* *n* **:** a small often elaborate container for a supply of toothpicks at table

top* *adj* **:** having a quantum characteristic whose existence was postulated on the basis of the discovery of the bottom quark ⟨~ quark⟩

top–down* *adj* **:** proceeding by breaking large general aspects (as of a problem) into smaller more manageable constituents **:** working from the general to the specific ⟨~ programming⟩

¹top 40 *n pl, often cap T* **:** the 40 best-selling phonograph records for a given period

²top 40 *adj* **:** constituting, playing, or listing the top 40 ⟨*top 40* tunes⟩ ⟨*top 40* stations⟩

to·po·cen·tric \ˌtäpəˈsen·trik, ˌtōp-\ *adj* [*top-* + *-centric*] **:** relating to, measured from, or as if observed from a particular point on the earth's surface **:** having or relating to such a point as origin ⟨~ coordinates⟩ — compare GEOCENTRIC *in the Dict*

topological* *adj* **:** being or involving properties unaltered under a homeomorphism

topological group *n* **:** a mathematical group which is also a topological space, whose multiplicative operation is continuous such that given any neighborhood of a product there exist neighborhoods of the elements composing the product with the property that any pair of elements representing each of these neighborhoods form a product belonging to the given neighborhood, and whose operation of taking inverses is continuous such that for any neighborhood of the inverse of an element there exists a neighborhood of the element itself in which every element has its inverse in the other neighborhood

topologically equivalent *adj* **:** related by a homeomorphism

topological space *n* **:** a set with a collection of subsets satisfying the conditions that both the empty set and the set itself belong to the collection, the union of any number of the subsets is also an element of the collection, and the intersection of any finite number of the subsets is an element of the collection

topological transformation *n* **:** HOMEOMORPHISM 2

topology* *n* **:** the set of all open sets of a topological space

top·onomastic \(ˌ)täp, -təp+\ *adj* [*top-* + *onomastic*] **:** of or relating to place names ⟨~ study⟩

to·pos \ˈtōˌpōs, ˈtäˌp-\ *n, pl* **to·poi** \-ˌpȯi\ [Gk, place, commonplace, topic — more at TOPIC] **:** a stock rhetorical theme or topic

TOR *abbr* third order regular

torpedo* *n* **:** GRINDER 6

torque *vt* -ED/-ING/-S [²*torque*] **:** to impart torque to **:** cause to twist (as about an axis) — **torqu·er** \ˈtȯrkər\ *n* -s

total* *vt* **:** to make a total wreck of (as a car) **:** DEMOLISH

total environment *n* **:** ENVIRONMENT *herein*

tote* *n* **:** TOTE BAG

tot lot *n* **:** a small playground for young children

tot·ten trust \ˈtätᵊn-\ *n, usu cap 1st T* [fr. the name *Totten*] **:** a trust created by a depositor who opens a savings account in another person's name but retains the right to revoke the trust and to withdraw and use the money

touch* *vb* — **touch base :** to come in contact or communication ⟨coming in from the cold to *touch base* with civilization —Carla Hunt⟩

tough* *adj, slang* **:** EXCELLENT, SPLENDID, GREAT — used as a generalized term of approval

touring car* *n* **:** a usu. 2-door sedan as distinguished from a sports car

tourist trap *n* **:** a place that exploits tourists

tow–away zone \ˈ==ˌ=-\ *n* [fr. the phrase *tow away*] **:** a no-parking zone from which parked vehicles may be towed away

towel·ette \ˌtau̇(ə)ˈlet\ *n* -s [¹*towel* + *-ette*] **:** a usu. premoistened small piece of material used for personal cleansing

tower block *n, Brit* **:** a tall building (as a high-rise apartment building)

town house* *n* **:** a single-family house of two or sometimes three stories connected to another house by a common sidewall

toxic shock syndrome *n* **:** an acute and sometimes fatal disease that is characterized by fever, sore throat, nausea, diarrhea, diffuse erythema, and shock, that is associated esp. with the presence of a bacterium of the genus *Streptomyces* (*S. aureus*), and that occurs esp. in menstruating females using tampons

tra·cheo·esophageal \ˌtrākē(ˌ)ō, trəˈkēō+\ *adj* [*trache-* + *esophageal*] **:** relating to or connecting the trachea and esophagus

track* *n* **1 :** one of a series of parallel or concentric paths along which material (as music or information) is recorded (as on a phonograph record or magnetic tape) **2 :** ¹BAND 8

track* *vt* **1 :** to assign (students) to a curricular track **2 :** to keep track of (as a trend) **:** FOLLOW ~ *vi* **:** to move or progress in accordance with or be consistent with an expected or reasonable pattern

track·ing \ˈtrakiŋ\ *n* -s **:** the policy or practice of assigning students to a curricular track

track record *n* **:** a record of accomplishments ⟨a company with an excellent *track record* in public service⟩

tracksuit \ˈ=ˌ=\ *n* [¹*track* + *suit*] **:** a suit of clothing consisting usu. of a jacket and pants and often worn by athletes (as runners) when working out

tract house *n* **:** one of many similarly designed houses built on a tract of land

trade* *n* **1** *slang* **:** male homosexuals who are prostitutes and often of aggressively masculine manner; *also* **:** a homosexual of this sort **2 :** a passive partner in a male homosexual relationship

trade–off \ˈ=ˌ=\ *n* -s [*trade off*] **1 :** a balancing of desirable considerations or goals all of which are not attainable at the same time ⟨the education versus experience *trade-off* which governs personnel practices —H.S. White⟩ **2 :** a giving up of one thing in return for another **:** EXCHANGE

trail bike *n* **:** a small motorcycle designed for uses other than on highways and for easy transport (as on an automobile bumper)

trail·er·able \ˈtrālərəbəl\ *adj* **:** able to be conveyed by a trailer

trailhead \ˈ=ˌ=\ *n* **:** the point at which a trail begins

train·ee·ship \trāˈnēˌship\ *n* [*trainee* + *-ship*] **:** the position or status of a trainee; *specif* **:** one involving a program of advanced training and study esp. in a medical science and usu. bearing a stipend and allowances (as for travel)

tramp art *n* **:** a style of wood carving flourishing in the U.S. from about 1875 to 1930 that is characterized by ornate layered whittling often of cigar boxes or fruit crates; *also* **:** an object of wood carved in this style

tram·po·lin·ing \ˌtrampəˈlēniŋ, -raam-, -raim-\ *n* -s **:** the sport of jumping and tumbling on a trampoline

transactional analysis *n* **:** a system of psychotherapy involving analysis of individual episodes of social interaction for insight that will aid communication (as by the substitution of constructive mature verbal exchanges for destructive immature ones)

trans·am·i·nate \tran(t)ˈsamə,nāt, traan-, -nˈza-\ *vb* -ED/-ING/-s [back-formation fr. *transamination*] *vi* **:** to induce or catalyze a transamination ~ *vt* **:** to induce or catalyze the transamination of

trans·axle \ˈtran(t),saksəl, ˈtraan-, -n,za-\ *n* [*trans*mission + *axle*] **:** a unit consisting of a combination of transmission and front axle used in front-wheel-drive automobiles

trans·car·ba·myl·ase \(,)tran(t)¦skärbə¦mil,ās, (,)traan, -nz¦k-, -,āz\ *n* -s [*trans-* + *carbamyl* + *-ase*] **:** any of several enzymes that catalyze the addition of a carbamoyl radical to a molecule (as ornithine to form citrulline in urea synthesis)

transcendental meditation *n* **:** a technique of meditation in which a mantra is chanted in order to foster calm, creativity, and spiritual well-being

trans·cortin \¦tran(t)s, -raan-, -nz+\ *n* [*trans-* + *cortin*] **:** an alpha globulin produced in the liver that binds with and transports hydrocortisone in the blood

transcribe* *vt* **:** to cause to undergo genetic transcription

transcript* *n* **:** a sequence of RNA produced by transcription from a DNA template

tran·scrip·tase \tranˈskrip,tās, traan-, -āz\ *n* -s [*transcrip*tion (herein) + *-ase*] **:** REVERSE TRANSCRIPTASE *herein*

transcription* *n* **:** the process of constructing a messenger RNA molecule using a DNA molecule as a template with resulting transfer of genetic information to the messenger RNA — compare TRANSLATION *herein*

tran·scrip·tion·ist \tranˈskripsh(ə)nəst, traan-\ *n* -s [*transcription* + *-ist*] **:** one that transcribes (as dictation)

trans·duce \tran(t)sˈd(y)üs, traan-, -nzˈ-\ *vt* -ED/-ING/-s [L *transducere* to lead across, transfer, fr. *trans-* + *ducere* to lead — more at TOW] **1 :** to convert (as energy or a message) into another form **2 :** to bring about the transfer of (as a gene) from one microorganism to another by means of a viral agent

trans·duc·tant \-ˈdəktənt\ *n* -s [*transduct*ion + *-ant*] **:** a bacterium that has undergone transduction

trans·earth \¦=,=\ *adj* [*trans-* + *earth*] **:** of or relating to the entry into or movement along a trajectory between a celestial body (as the moon) and the earth by a spacecraft ⟨~ injection⟩ ⟨~ burn⟩

trans·fec·tion \tran(t)sˈfekshən, traan-, -nzˈf-\ *n* -s [*trans-* + in*fection*] **:** infection of a cell with isolated viral nucleic acid followed by production of the complete virus in the cell — **trans·fect** \-ˈfekt\ *vt*

transfer factor *n* **:** a polypeptide that is produced and secreted by a lymphocyte functioning in cell-mediated immunity and that upon incorporation into a lymphocyte which has not been sensitized confers upon it the same immunological specificity as the sensitized cell

transfer RNA *n* **:** a relatively small RNA that transfers a particular amino acid to a growing polypeptide chain at the ribosomal site of protein synthesis during translation — compare MESSENGER RNA *herein*

transform* *n* **1 :** a mathematical element obtained from another by transformation **2 :** a linguistic structure (as a sentence) produced by means of a transformation

transform* *vt* **:** to cause to undergo genetic transformation

trans·for·mant \tranzˈfȯrmənt, -raan-, -n(t)sˈf-\ *n* -s [*transform*, vb. (herein) + *-ant*] **:** an individual (as a bacterium) that has undergone genetic transformation

transformation* *n* **1 :** genetic modification of a bacterium by incorporation of free DNA from another ruptured bacterial cell — compare TRANSDUCTION *in the Dict* **2 :** one of an ordered set of rules that specify how to convert the deep structures of a language into surface structures; *also* **:** the process or relation specified by such a rule

trans·for·ma·tion·al \¦tranzfə(r)¦māshənᵊl, ¦traan-, n(t)sf-, -shnəl\ *adj* [*transformation* + ¹*-al*] **:** of, relating to, characterized by, or concerned with transformation and esp. linguistic transformation

transformational grammar *n* **:** a grammar that generates the deep structures of a language and relates these to the surface structures by means of transformations

trans·for·ma·tion·al·ist \,tranzfə(r)māshənᵊləst, ,traan-, -n(t)sf-, -shnəl-\ *n* -s [*transformational* (herein) + ¹*-ist*] **:** an exponent of transformational grammar

trans·fu·sion·al \tranzˈfyüzhənᵊl, traan-, -n(t)sˈf-, -zhnəl\ *adj* [*transfusion* + ¹*-al*] **:** of, relating to, or caused by transfusion

transistor* *or* **transistor radio** *n* **:** a transistorized radio

transition* *n* **:** a genetic mutation in RNA or DNA that results from the substitution of one purine base for the other or of one pyrimidine base for the other

trans·ke·tol·ase \,tran(t)sˈkētə,lās, -raan-, -nzk-, -āz\ *n* -s [*trans-* + *ketol* + *-ase*] **:** an enzyme that catalyzes the transfer of the ketonic residue $CH_3COH-O-$ from the phosphate of xylulose to that of ribose to form the phosphate of sedoheptulose

translate* *vt* **:** to subject (as genetic information) to translation in protein synthesis

translation* *n* **:** the process of forming a protein molecule at a ribosomal site of protein synthesis from information contained in messenger RNA — compare TRANSCRIPTION *herein* — **translational*** *adj*

trans·lunar \(ˈ)tran(t)s, -raan-, -nz+\ *adj* [*trans-* + *lunar*] **:** of or relating to the entry into or movement along a trajectory between a celestial body (as the earth) and the moon by a spacecraft ⟨~ injection⟩ ⟨~ burn⟩

trans·membrane \"+\ *adj* [*trans-* + *membrane*] **:** taking place, existing, or arranged from one side to the other of a membrane

transmission electron microscope *n* **:** a conventional electron microscope which produces an image of a cross-sectional slice of a specimen all points of which are illuminated by the electron beam at the same time — compare SCANNING ELECTRON MICROSCOPE *herein* — **transmission electron microscopy** *n*

transmitter* *n* **:** NEUROTRANSMITTER *herein*

trans·mountain \¦tran(t)s, -raan-, -nz+\ *adj* [*trans-* + *mountain*] **:** crossing or extending over or through a mountain

transmutation* *n* **:** the effect of controlled reduction firing on certain chiefly oriental copper-containing and/or iron-containing ceramic glazes that is typically a variegation of colors (as purple, blue, and red) and a thick often bubbly consistency

transom* *n* — **over the transom :** without solicitation or prior arrangement ⟨the manuscript arrived *over the transom*⟩

trans·peptidase \¦tran(t)s, -raan-, -nz+\ *n* [*trans-* + *peptidase*] **:** an enzyme that catalyzes the transfer of an amino acid residue or a peptide residue from one amino compound to another

transport* *n* **:** a mechanism for moving tape and esp. magnetic tape past a sensing or recording head
transposable element *n* **:** TRANSPOSON *herein*
transpose* *n* **:** a matrix that results in interchanging the rows and columns of a given matrix
trans·pos·on \ˌtran(t)sˈpōˌzän, -raan-, -nz-\ *n* -s [*transpose* + ²*-on*] **:** a segment of mobile DNA that is capable of changing its location in the genome or in some bacteria is capable of undergoing transfer between an extrachromosomal plasmid and a chromosome and that is sometimes used to introduce genes into an organism from an exogenous source (as an individual of another species)
trans·racial \(ˈ)tran(t)s, -raan-, -nz+\ *adj* [*trans-* + *racial*] **:** involving two or more races ⟨~ adoption⟩
trans·sexual \"+\ *n* -s [*trans-* + *sexual*] **:** a person with a psychological urge to belong to the opposite sex that may be carried as far as surgical modification of the sex organs to mimic the other sex — **transsexual** *adj* — **trans·sexualism** \"+\ *n* — **trans·sexuality** \ˈtran(t)(s), -raan-, nz+\ *n*
trans·thoracic \ˈtran(t)s, -raan-, -nz+\ *adj* [*trans-* + *thoracic*] **1 :** performed or made by way of the thoracic cavity **2 :** crossing or having connections that cross the thoracic cavity ⟨a ~ pacemaker⟩ — **trans·tho·rac·i·cal·ly** \-ˈrasək(ə)lē\ *adv*
trans·venous \"+\ *adj* [*trans-* + *venous*] **:** relating to or involving the use of an intravenous catheter containing an electrode carrying electrical impulses from an extracorporeal source to the heart ⟨~ pacing of the heart⟩
tran·yl·cy·pro·mine \ˌtranᵊlˈsīprəˌmēn, -ˌmən\ *n* -s [*trans-* + phen*yl* + *cycl-* + *pro*pyl*amine*] **:** an antidepressant drug $C_9H_{11}N$ that is an inhibitor of monoamine oxidase and is administered as the sulfate
trash* *vt* **1 :** VANDALIZE, WRECK ⟨~ a college building⟩ **2 :** SMASH, DESTROY ⟨~ store windows⟩ **3 :** SPOIL, RUIN ⟨~*ing* the environment⟩ **4 :** to subject to criticism or invective ~ *vi* **:** to trash something esp. as a form of protest — **trasher** \ˈtrashə(r), -raas-, -raīs-\ *n* -s
trashsport \ˈ=ˌ=\ *n* [¹*trash* + *sport*] **:** an exhibition of sports events which is held solely for the purpose of being televised and in which the participants are celebrities
travel trailer *n* **:** a trailer drawn esp. by a passenger automobile and equipped for use (as while traveling) as a dwelling
treat·abil·i·ty \ˌtrēd·əˈbiləd·ē\ *n* [*treatable* + *-ity*] **:** the condition of being treatable
tree ear *n* **:** any of several fungi used esp. in Chinese cooking
trendsetter \ˈ=ˌ==\ *n* **:** one that sets a trend
trendy \ˈtrendē, -di\ *adj* -ER/-EST [²*trend* + ¹*-y*] **1 :** very fashionable **:** UP-TO-DATE, CHIC ⟨he's a ~ dresser —*Sunday Mirror*⟩ **2 :** FADDISH ⟨a newspaper of ~ triviality —J.H. Plumb⟩ — **trend·i·ly** \-dəlē, -dᵊlē\ *adv* — **trend·i·ness** \-dēnəs, -dən-\ *n* -ES — **trendy** *n* -ES
triacetate* *n* **:** a textile fiber or fabric consisting of cellulose that is completely or almost completely acetylated
trial* *n* **:** one of a number of repetitions of an experiment
tri·am·cin·o·lone \ˌtrīamˈsinᵊlˌōn\ *n* -s [*tri-* + *am*yl + *cin*eme, a terpene (fr. *cine*ole + *-ene)* + predniso*lone*] **:** a corticoid drug $C_{21}H_{27}FO_6$ used esp. in treating psoriasis and allergic skin and respiratory disorders
triangle inequality *n* [so called fr. its application to the distances between three points in a coordinate system] **:** an inequality stating that the absolute value of a sum is less than or equal to the sum of the absolute value of the terms
tri·ath·lete \trīˈathˌlēt\ *n* -s [blend of *triathlon* and *athlete*] **:** an athlete who competes in a triathlon
tri·ath·lon \trīˈathlən, -ˌlän\ *n* -s [*tri-* + *-athlon* (as in *decathlon*)] **:** an athletic contest that is a long-distance race consisting of three phases (as swimming, bicycling, and running)
tri·bol·o·gy \trīˈbäləjē, trəˈ-, -ji\ *n* -ES [*tribo-* + *-logy*] *Brit* **:** a study that deals with the design, friction, wear, and lubrication of interacting surfaces in relative motion to each other (as in bearings or gears) — **tri·bo·log·i·cal** \ˌtrībəˈläjəkəl, ˌtrib-\ *adj, Brit* — **tri·bol·o·gist** \trīˈbäləjəst, triˈ-\ *n* -s *Brit*
tri·chlor·fon *also* **tri·chlor·phon** \(ˈ)trīˈklō(ə)rˌfän, -ˈklȯ(ə)r-\ *n* -s [*tri-* + *chlor-* + *-fon* (irreg. fr. *phosphonate*)] **:** a crystalline compound $C_4H_8Cl_3O_4P$ used esp. as an insecticide
trickle-down \ˈ==ˈ=\ *adj* **:** relating to or working on the principle of trickle-down theory ⟨*trickle-down* programs⟩
trickle-down theory \ˈ==ˈ=-\ *n* **:** an economic theory that financial benefits given to big business will in turn pass down to smaller businesses and consumers
tricyclic antidepressant *also* **tricyclic** *n* -s **:** any of a group of antidepressant drugs that potentiate the action of catecholamines and do not inhibit the action of monoamine oxidase
tri·fec·ta \(ˈ)trīˈfektə\ *n* -s [*tri-* + per*fecta*] **:** a variation of the perfecta in which a bettor must select the first 3 finishers of a race in the correct order of finish in order to win — called also *triple;* compare SUPERFECTA *herein*
tri·fluo·per·a·zine \ˈtrīˌflüōˈperəˌzēn, -ˌzən\ *n* -s [*tri-* + *fluo-* + pi*perazine*] **:** a phenothiazine tranquilizer $C_{21}H_{24}F_3N_3S$ used esp. in the treatment of psychotic conditions (as schizophrenia)
tri·flu·ra·lin \trīˈflu̇rələn\ *n* -s [*tri-* + *fluor-* + *ani*l*ine*] **:** an herbicide $C_{13}H_{16}F_3N_3O_4$ used in the control of weeds (as pigweed)
tri·functional \(ˈ)trī +\ *adj* [*tri-* + *functional*] **:** of, relating to, or being a compound with three sites in the molecule that are highly reactive (as in polymerization)
tri·jet \ˈtrī +ˌ\ *n* [*tri-* + *jet*] **:** an aircraft powered with three jet engines — **trijet** \ˈ=ˌ=\ *adj*
tri-level \ˈ=ˈ==\ *adj* [*tri-* + *level*] **:** having three levels or floors ⟨a *tri-level* house⟩ — **tri-level** \"\ *n*
tri·ma·ran \ˈtrīməˈran\ *n* -s [*tri-* + *-maran* (as in *catamaran*)] **:** a fast pleasure sailboat with three hulls side by side
tri·meth·o·prim \trīˈmethəˌprim\ *n* -s [*tri-* + *meth-* + *-prim* (by shortening & alter. fr. *pyrimidine*)] **:** a synthetic antibacterial and antimalarial drug $C_{14}H_{18}N_4O_3$
trip* *n* **1 :** an intense visionary experience undergone by a person who has taken a psychedelic drug (as LSD); *broadly* **:** an exciting experience ⟨orgasm . . . is the ultimate ~ —D.R. Reuben⟩ **2 :** pursuit of an absorbing or obsessive interest **:** KICK ⟨he's on a nostalgia ~⟩ **3 :** SCENE *herein,* LIFE-STYLE ⟨the whole superstar ~ —Joe Eszterhas⟩
trip *vi* **tripped; tripped; tripping, trips** [*trip,* n. (herein)] **:** to get high on a drug **:** turn on — often used with *out* — **trip·per** \ˈtripə(r)\ *n* -s
triple* *n* **:** TRIFECTA *herein*
triple jump *n* **:** HOP, STEP, AND JUMP
triplet* *n* **1 :** a group of three elementary particles (as positive, negative, and neutral pions) with different charge states but otherwise similar properties **2** *or* **trip-**

let state : any state of an elementary particle having one quantum unit of spin **3 :** CODON *herein*

trip wire* *n* **:** something (as a small military force) intended to function as a trip wire (as to set a larger military force in motion)

tri·umph·al·ism \(ˈ)trīˈəm(p)fəˌlizəm *also* ˈtrīˌəm-\ *n* -s [*triumphal* + *-ism*] **:** the doctrine, attitude, or belief that one religious creed is superior to all others — **tri·umph·al·ist** \(ˈ)=ˈ=== *also* ˈ====\ *n or adj*

trivia* *n pl but sing in constr* **:** a quizzing game involving obscure facts

trivial* *adj* **:** relating to or being the mathematically simplest case; *specif* **:** characterized by having all variables equal to zero

triv·i·al·ist \ˈtrivēələ̇st\ *n* -s [*trivial* + *-ist*] **:** one who takes a special interest in trivia or trivial matters

tRNA \ˌtēˌärˌenˈā\ *n* -s [*t*ransfer *RNA* (herein)] **:** TRANSFER RNA *herein*

trog·lo·bite \ˈträgləˌbīt\ *n* -s [by alter. (influenced by *troglodyte*)] **:** TROGLOBIONT — **trog·lo·bit·ic** \ˌ==ˈbid·ik\ *adj*

troika* *n* **1 :** an administrative or ruling body of three ⟨replaced by a ~ of three coequal secretaries-general — *Newsweek*⟩ **2 :** a group of three ⟨astrology, yoga, and poetry are the ~ of humanities that most interest him — A.J. Liebling⟩

trombe wall \ˈtrȯmb-, -rämb-, -rōⁿb-\ *n, usu cap T* [after Felix *Trombe,* 20th cent. Fr. designer] **:** a masonry wall that is usu. glazed on the exterior and is designed to absorb solar heat and release it into the interior of a building

trophic level *n* **:** one of the hierarchical strata of a food web characterized by organisms which are the same number of steps removed from the primary producers

tro·po·collagen \ˌträpə, -rōpə +\ *n* [[1]*trop-* + *collagen*] **:** a soluble substance whose elongated asymmetrical molecules are the fundamental building units of collagen fibers

tro·po·nin \ˈtrōpənə̇n, ˈträp-, -ˌnin\ *n* -s [*trop-* + *-n-* (arbitrary infix) + *-in*] **:** a protein component of skeletal muscle myofibrils that is held to initiate muscle contraction by regulating calcium sensitivity of actomyosin

trouser* *adj* **:** of or relating to a male dramatic role played by a woman ⟨a ~ character in opera⟩

trouser suit *n, chiefly Brit* **:** PANTSUIT *herein*

truck* *vi* **:** to roll along esp. in an easy untroubled way ⟨keep on ~*ing*⟩

trust fund* *n* **:** a governmental fund consisting of moneys accepted for a specified purpose (as civil service retirement) that is administered as a trust separately from other funds and is expended only in furthering the specified purpose

truth set *n* **:** a mathematical or logical set containing all the elements that make a given statement of relationships true when substituted in it

tryp·sin·iza·tion \ˌtripsə̇nəˈzāshən, trə̇pˌsin-, -ˌīˈz-\ *n* -s [*trypsinize* + *-ation*] **:** the action or process of trypsinizing

t–test \ˈ=ˌ=\ *n* **:** a statistical test involving confidence limits for the random variable *t* of a t distribution and used esp. in testing hypotheses about means of normal distributions when the standard deviations are unknown

tube* *n* **:** CATHODE-RAY TUBE; *esp* **:** a television picture tube **b :** TELEVISION **2 :** CURL *herein* **3 :** an article of clothing usu. of knitted material in the shape of a tube ⟨~ top⟩ ⟨~ socks⟩ — **down the tube** *or* **down the tubes :** into a state of collapse, deterioration, or ruin ⟨I know what it means to see a crop go *down the tubes* — B.S. Bergland⟩

tuberous sclerosis *n* **:** EPILOIA

tu·bu·lin \ˈt(y)übyələ̇n\ *n* -s [*tubule* + *-in*] **:** a globular protein that polymerizes to form microtubules

tu·fo·li \t(y)üˈfōlē\ *n, pl* **tufoli** [It (Sicilian), pl. of *tufolo* duct, fr. LL *tubulus,* dim. of L *tubus* tube] **:** a pasta shell large enough for stuffing (as with meat or cheese)

tu·mori·genesis \ˌt(y)ümərə +\ *n* [*tumor* + *-i-* + *genesis*] **:** the formation of tumors

tu·mor·i·gen·ic \ˌt(y)ümərəˈjenik\ *adj* [*tumor* + *-i-* + *-genic*] **:** producing or tending to produce tumors; *also* **:** CARCINOGENIC ⟨~ cells⟩ — **tu·mor·i·ge·nic·i·ty** \ˌ===jə̇ˈnisəd·ē\ *n* -ES

tune* *vt* **:** to adjust the output of (a device) to a chosen frequency or range of frequencies; *also* **:** to alter the frequency of (radiation)

tune out *vt* **:** to become unresponsive to **:** IGNORE ⟨the children *tuned out* their mother's commands⟩ ~ *vi* **:** to dissociate oneself from what is happening

tunnel* *n* **:** CURL *herein*

tunnel diode *n* **:** a semiconductor device that has two stable states when operated in conjunction with suitable circuit elements and a source of voltage, is capable of extremely rapid transformations between the two by means of the tunnel effect of electrons, and is used for amplifying, switching, and computer information storage and as an oscillator

tunnel vision* *n* **:** extreme narrowness of viewpoint — **tunnel–visioned** \ˈ==ˌ==\ *adj*

-tu·ple \ˌtəpəl, ˌtüp-\ *n comb form* [quin*tuple,* sex*tuple*] **:** set of (so many) elements — often used of sets with ordered elements ⟨the ordered 2-*tuple* (*a, b*)⟩

tur·bi·dite \ˈtərbə̇ˌdīt\ *n* -s [*turbid* + *-ite*] **:** a sedimentary deposit consisting of material that has moved down the steep slope at the edge of a continental shelf; *also* **:** a rock formed from this deposit

tur·bo·electric \ˌtərbō +\ *adj* [*turbo-* + *electric*] **:** using or being a turbine generator that produces electricity usu. for motive power ⟨ships with ~ drive⟩

tur·bo·fan \ˈtərbō +ˌ\ *n* [*turbo-* + *fan*] **1 :** a fan that is directly connected to and driven by a turbine and is used to supply air for cooling, ventilation, or combustion **2 :** a jet engine having a turbofan

tur·bo·pump \"+ˌ\ *n* [*turbo-* + *pump*] **:** a pump that is driven by a turbine

tur·bo·shaft \"+ˌ\ *n* [*turbo-* + *shaft*] **:** a gas turbine engine that is similar in operation to a turboprop engine but instead of being used to power a propeller is used through a transmission system for powering other devices (as helicopter rotors and pumps)

tu·ring machine \ˈt(y)u̇riŋ-\ *n, usu cap T* [after A. M. *Turing* †1954 Eng. mathematician] **:** a hypothetical computing machine that has an unlimited amount of information storage

tu·ris·ta \tu̇rˈēstə\ *n* -s [Sp, lit., tourist] **:** intestinal sickness and diarrhea commonly affecting a tourist in a foreign country; *esp* **:** MONTEZUMA'S REVENGE *herein*

turkey* *n* **:** a stupid, foolish, or inept person

turnaround* *n* **:** the action of receiving, processing, and returning something ⟨the user's requirement for rapid ~ time —A.B. Veaner⟩

turner's syndrome \ˈtərnər(z)-; ˈtə̄nə(z)-, ˈtəin-\ *n, usu cap T* [after Henry Herbert *Turner* †1970 Am. physician] **:** a genetically determined condition associated with the presence of one X and no Y chromosome that is characterized by an outwardly female phenotype with incomplete and infertile gonads

turnkey \ˈ=,=\ *adj* **:** supplied or installed complete and ready to operate ⟨a ~ nuclear plant⟩ ⟨a ~ computer system⟩; *also* **:** of or relating to a turnkey installation ⟨a ~ contract⟩ ⟨~ vendors⟩

turn off* *vi* **:** to lose interest **:** WITHDRAW ⟨the kids *turn off* or drift into another world —Edwin Sorensen⟩ ~ *vt* **:** to cause to turn off ⟨dropouts who are *turned off* by . . . political phoniness —Hendrik Hertzberg⟩

turnoff* *n* **:** one that causes loss of interest or enthusiasm ⟨the music was a ~⟩

turn on* *vt* **1 :** to cause to undergo an intense visionary experience esp. by taking a drug; *broadly* **:** to cause to get high **2 :** to excite pleasurably **:** STIMULATE ⟨the ballet . . . was *turning* the audience *on* like magic —Clive Barnes⟩; *also* **:** to excite sexually **3 :** to cause to gain knowledge or appreciation of something specified ~ *vi* **1 :** to undergo an intense visionary experience esp. as a result of taking a drug; *broadly* **:** to get high **2 :** to become pleasurably excited ⟨*turns on* instead with classical music or jazz —Julie M. Heldman⟩ — **turn–on** \ˈ=,=\ *n* -s

turnover* *n* **:** the act or an instance of a team's losing possession of a ball through error or a minor violation of the rules (as in basketball or football)

tush \ˈtu̇sh\ *n* -ES [Yiddish *toches*] *slang* **:** BUTTOCKS

tushy *also* **tush·ie** \ˈtu̇shē\ *n, pl* **tushies** [*tush* (herein) + *-ie*] *slang* **:** BUTTOCKS

tu͵torial* *n* **:** a paper, book, film, or computer program that provides practical information on a specific subject

TV* *abbr or n* -s transvestite

tv dinner *n, usu cap T&V* [so called fr. its saving the television viewer from having to interrupt his viewing to prepare a meal] **:** a quick-frozen packaged dinner that requires only heating before it is served

twee \ˈtwē\ *adj* [baby talk for *sweet*] *chiefly Brit* **:** affectedly or excessively dainty, delicate, cute, or quaint ⟨such a theme might sound ~ or corny —*Times Lit. Supp.*⟩

twin double *n* **:** a system of betting (as on horse races) in which the bettor must select the winners of two consecutive pairs of races in order to win

two–tailed \ˌ=ˈ=\ *also* **two–tail** \ˌ=ˈ=\ *adj* **:** being a statistical test for which the critical region consists of all values of the test statistic greater than a given value plus the values less than another given value—compare ONE=TAILED *herein*

ty·lo·sin \ˈtīləsən\ *n* -s [origin unknown] **:** an antibacterial antibiotic $C_{45}H_{77}NO_{17}$ from an actinomycete of the genus *Streptomyces* (*S. fradiae*) used in veterinary medicine and as a feed additive

type A *adj* **:** relating to, characteristic of, having, or being a personality that is marked by impatience, aggressiveness, and competitiveness and that is held to be associated with increased risk of cardiovascular disease ⟨*type A* behavior⟩

type C \ˈ=ˈ=\ *adj* **:** relating to or being any of the oncornaviruses in which the structure containing the nucleic acid is spherical and centrally located ⟨a *type C* RNA virus⟩

typecast* *vt* **:** STEREOTYPE ⟨administrators . . . fearful of being ~ in the role of autocrats —F.M. Hechinger⟩

type I error \ˌtīpˈwən-\ *n* **:** rejection of the null hypothesis in statistical testing when it is true

type II error \ˌtīpˈtü-\ *n* **:** acceptance of the null hypothesis in statistical testing when it is false

tyrosine hy·drox·y·lase \-hīˈdräksə͵lās, -āz\ *n* -s [*hydroxyl* + *-ase*] **:** an enzyme that catalyzes the first step in the biosynthesis of catecholamines (as dopamine and noradrenaline)

U

u \ˈyü\ *adj, usu cap* [upper class] **:** characteristic of the upper classes — usu. used in contrast to *non-U*

u* *abbr, cap* [*Union of Orthodox Hebrew Congregations*] kosher certification — often enclosed in a circle

ubi·qui·none \yüˈbikwə̇ˌnōn; ¦yübə̇kwə̇ˈn-, -ˈkwiˌn-\ *n* [blend of L *ubique* everywhere and E *quinone;* fr. its occurrence in nature — more at UBIQUITY] **:** a quinone that contains a long isoprenoid side chain and that functions in the part of cellular respiration comprising oxidative phosphorylation as an electron-carrying coenzyme in the transport of electrons from organic substrates to oxygen esp. along the chain of reactions leading from the Krebs cycle — called also *coenzyme Q*

UDP \¦yü¦dēˈpē\ *n* -s [uridine *di*phosphate] **:** a diphosphate of uridine $C_9H_{14}N_2O_{12}P_2$ that functions esp. as a glycosyl carrier in the synthesis of glycogen and starch and is used to form polyuridylic acid

ufol·o·gy \yüˈfäləjē\ *n* -ES *often cap UFO* [*UFO* + *-logy*] **:** the study of unidentified flying objects — **ufo·log·i·cal** \ˌyüfəˈläjə̇kəl\ *adj, often cap UFO* — **ufol·o·gist** \yüˈfäləjə̇st\ *n* -s *often cap UFO*

ULCC \¦yü¦el¦sēˈsē\ *abbr or n* -s [*u*ltra-*l*arge *c*rude *c*arrier] **:** a crude-oil tanker with an extremely large capacity

ul·tra·fiche \ˈəltrə+ˌ\ *n* [*ultra-* + *fiche* (herein)] **:** a microfiche of printed matter reduced 90 or more times

ul·tra·high \¦əltrə +\ *adj* [*ultra-* + *high*] **:** very high **:** exceedingly high ⟨at ~ temperatures⟩

ultrahigh vacuum *n* **:** a vacuum having an atmospheric pressure of 10^{-7} pascal or less

ul·tra·microfiche \¦əltrə +\ *n* [*ultra-* + *microfiche*] **:** ULTRAFICHE *herein*

ul·tra·microtome \"+\ *n* [*ultra-* + *microtome*] **:** a microtome for cutting extremely thin sections for electron microscopy — **ul·tra·microtomy** \"+\ *n*

ul·tra·miniature \"+\ *adj* [*ultra-* + *miniature*] **:** SUBMINIATURE — **ul·tra·miniaturization** \"+\ *n*

ul·tra·pure \"+\ *adj* [*ultra-* + *pure*] **:** extremely pure

ul·tra·so·nog·ra·phy \ˌəltrəsəˈnägrəfē, -sōˈn-\ *n* -ES [²*ultrasonic* + *-o-* + *-graphy*] **:** ULTRASOUND 1 *herein* — **ul·tra·so·no·graph·ic** \-ˌsōnəˈgrafik, -ˌsän-\ *adj*

ultrasound* *n* **1 :** the diagnostic or therapeutic use of ultrasound and esp. a technique involving the formation of a two-dimensional image used for the examination and measurement of internal body structures and the detection of bodily abnormalities — called also *echography, sonography* **2 :** a diagnostic examination using ultrasound

ul·tra·thin \"+\ *adj* [*ultra-* + *thin*] **:** exceedingly thin

umbilical *n* -s **:** UMBILICAL CORD 2

unak·ite \ˈyünəˌkīt\ *n* -s [*Unaka* (Great Smoky) mountains, Tenn. & N.C., + ¹*-ite*] **:** an altered igneous rock that is usu. opaque with green, black, pink, and white flecks and is usu. used as a gemstone

unary* *adj* **:** having or consisting of a single element, item, or component **:** MONADIC

un·bun·dling \ˌənˈbənd(ᵊ)liŋ\ *n* -s [fr. gerund of *unbundle,* fr. ²*un-* + *bundle*] **:** separate pricing of products and services — **un·bun·dle** *vb*

uncle tom *vi* **uncle tommed; uncle tommed; uncle tom- ming; uncle toms** *usu cap U&T* **:** to behave like an Uncle Tom

uncle tom·ism \ˌ==ˈtäˌmizəm\ *n, usu cap U&T* [*Uncle Tom* + *-ism*] **:** behavior or attitudes characteristic of an Uncle Tom — **uncle tom·ish** \-ämish\ *adj, usu cap U&T*

un·conjugated \¦ən +\ *adj* [¹*un-* + *conjugated*] **:** not chemically conjugated

un·cool \"+\ *adj* [¹*un-* + *cool*] **1 :** lacking in assurance, sophistication, or self-control **2 :** failing to accord with the mores of a particular group

un·der·achiev·er \ˌəndərəˈchēvə(r)\ *n* -s [¹*under* + *achieve* + *-er*] **:** a person and esp. a student who fails to achieve his potential or does not do as well as expected — **underachieve** \¦===¦=\ *vi* — **underachievement** \¦===¦==\ *n*

underclass \ˈ==ˌ=\ *n* [prob. trans. of Sw *underklass*] **:** the lowest social stratum usu. made up of disadvantaged minority groups

undercoating* *n* **:** a usu. asphalt-based waterproof coating applied to the underside of a vehicle

underfund \¦==¦=\ *vt* [¹*under* + *fund*] **:** to provide insufficient funds for ⟨Congress has ~*ed* the program⟩

underground* *adj* **1 a :** existing outside the establishment or mainstream ⟨an ~ literary reputation⟩ **b :** existing outside the purview of tax collectors or statisticians ⟨the ~ economy⟩ **2 a :** produced or published outside the establishment esp. by the avant-garde ⟨~ movies⟩ ⟨~ newspapers⟩ **b :** of or relating to the avant-garde underground ⟨an ~ theater⟩

underground* *n* **:** a usu. avant-garde group or movement that functions outside the establishment

underground \¦==¦=\ *vt* [¹*underground*] **:** to place underground ⟨~*ing* power lines⟩

underkill \ˈ==ˌ=\ *n* -s [³*under* + *-kill* (as in *overkill* — herein)] **:** lack of the force required to defeat an enemy

underperform \ˌ===ˈ=\ *vt* [¹*under* + *perform*] **:** to do worse than **:** not do as well as ⟨a mutual fund that ~*ed* the market⟩

underpopulation \¦==ˌ==ˈ==\ *n* [³*under* + *population*] **:** the state of being underpopulated

understeer \ˈ==¦=\ *n* [³*under* + ⁴*steer*] **:** the tendency of an automobile to turn less sharply than the driver intends; *also* **:** the action or an instance of understeer — **understeer** \¦==¦=\ *vi*

un·der·whelm \ˌəndə(r)ˈhwelm *also* -ˈw-\ *vt* -ED/-ING/-S [¹*under* + *-whelm* (as in *overwhelm*)] **:** to fail to impress or stimulate

undock* *vt* **:** UNCOUPLE ⟨~ the lunar module from the command module⟩

un·falsifiable \¦ən +\ *adj* **:** not capable of being proved false

un·flap·pa·ble \ˌənˈflapəbəl\ *adj* [¹*un-* + ²*flap* + *-able*] **:** marked by assurance and self-control **:** IMPERTURBABLE ⟨the most ~ of politicians —Anthony Lewis⟩ — **un·flap·pa·bil·i·ty** \-ˌflapə- ˈbiləd·ē\ *n* -ES — **un·flap·pa·bly** \-ˈflapəblē\ *adv*

un·flapped \ˌənˈflapt\ *adj* [¹*un-* + *flapped,* past part. of ²*flap*] **:** UNRUFFLED 1

unforgiving* *adj* **:** having or making no allowance for error or weakness ⟨lost two friends in avalanches here. The mountains . . . are . . . ~ —Irwin Shaw⟩

un·glued \ˌən'glüd\ *adj* [fr. past part. of *unglue*] **:** being in a confused or agitated state or condition **:** UPSET, DISORDERED ⟨chief executives came ~ at the thought of a strike —H.E. Meyer⟩

un·hip \ˌən +\ *adj* [[1]*un-* + *hip*] **:** not hip **:** UNCOOL *herein*

uniform* *adj* **:** relating to or being convergence of a series whose terms are functions in such manner that the absolute value of the difference between the sum of the first *n* terms of the series and the sum of all terms can be made arbitrarily small for all values of the domain of the functions by choosing the *n*th term sufficiently far along in the series — **uniformly*** *adv*

union* *n* **1 :** the set of all elements belonging to one or more of a given collection of two or more sets — called also *join, sum* **2 :** the mathematical or logical operation of converting separate sets to a union

[1]**uni·sex** \'yünəˌseks\ *n* [*uni-* + *sex*] **:** the quality or state of not being distinguishable (as by hair or clothing) as to sex

[2]**unisex** \"\ *adj* **1 :** not distinguishable as male or female ⟨a ~ face⟩ **2 :** suitable or designed for both males and females ⟨~ clothes⟩; *also* **:** being the same for both males and females ⟨~ insurance rates⟩

uni·sexual* *adj* **:** UNISEX *herein*

uni·tar·i·ly \ˌyünə'terəlē\ *adv* [*unitary* + [2]*-ly*] **:** in a unitary manner

uni·tar·i·ty \ˌyünə'tarəd·ē, -ter-\ *n* -ES [*unitary* + *-ty*] **:** the requirement in quantum mechanics that the S matrix be a unitary transformation between initial and final states of motion

unitary matrix *n* **:** a matrix that has an inverse and a transpose whose corresponding elements are pairs of conjugate complex numbers

unitary transformation *n* **:** a linear transformation of a vector space that leaves scalar products unchanged

unit circle *n* **:** a circle whose radius is one unit of length long

uni·term \'yünə +ˌ\ *n* [*uni-* + *term*] **:** a single term used as a descriptor in document indexing

unit membrane *n* **:** a 3-layered membrane that consists of an inner lipid layer surrounded by a protein layer on each side

unit pricing *n* [*pricing* fr. gerund of [2]*price*] **:** the pricing of products (as packaged foods) whereby the unit price is indicated along with the total price

uni·trust \'yünə+ˌ\ *n* [*uni-* + *trust*] **:** a trust from which the beneficiary receives annually a fixed percentage of the fair market value of its assets

units digit *n* **:** the numeral (as 6 in 456) occupying the units place in a number expressed in the Arabic system of writing numbers

units place *n* **:** the place immediately to the left of the decimal point in a number expressed in the Arabic system of writing numbers

unit train *n* **:** a railway train that transports a single commodity directly from producer to consumer

unit trust *n* **1** *Brit* **:** MUTUAL FUND **2 :** an investment company whose portfolio consists of long-term bonds that are held to maturity

universal product code *n, usu cap U&P&C* **:** a bar code that identifies a product's type and price

universal set *n* **:** a set that contains all elements relevant to a particular discussion or problem **:** UNIVERSE OF DISCOURSE 2

unleaded* *adj* **:** not treated or mixed with lead or lead compounds ⟨~ gasoline⟩

un·linked \ˌən +\ *adj* [[1]*un-* + *linked*, past part. of *link*] **:** not belonging to the same genetic linkage group ⟨~ genes⟩

un·nil·hex·i·um \ˌyünᵊl'heksēəm\ *n* -s [NL *unnil-* (fr. L *unus* one + *nil* nothing, zero) + Gk *hex* six + NL *-ium* — more at ONE, NIL, SIX] **:** the chemical element of atomic number 106 — symbol *Unh*

un·nil·pen·ti·um \ˌyünᵊl'pentēəm\ *n* -s [NL *unnil-* + Gk *pente* five + NL *-ium* — more at FIVE] **:** the chemical element of atomic number 105 — symbol *Unp*

un·nil·qua·di·um \ˌyünᵊl'kwädēəm\ *n* -s [NL *unnil-* + *quadri-* + *-ium*] **:** the chemical element of atomic number 104 — symbol *Unq*

un·person \'ən +ˌ\ *n* [[1]*un-* + *person*] **:** an individual who usu. for political or ideological reasons is removed completely from recognition, consideration, or memory ⟨became an ~ when he was removed from the Lenin Mausoleum —Henry Tanner⟩

up* *adj* **:** being a constituent of nucleons and having the quantum characteristics of an electric charge of $+\frac{2}{3}$ and a baryon number of $\frac{1}{3}$ ⟨~ quark⟩ — compare DOWN *herein*

up* *n* **1 :** a feeling of contentment, excitement, or euphoria **2 :** UPPER *herein*

up·date \'əpˌdāt\ *n* -s [*update*, v.] **1 :** the act or an instance of updating **2 :** current information for updating something ⟨navigational ~ for a spacecraft computer⟩ **3 :** an up-to-date version, account, or report

upfield \'=ˌ=\ *adv or adj* [[4]*up* + *field*] **:** in or into the part of the field toward which the offensive team is headed

up front *adv* **1 :** in or at the front or beginning **2 :** in advance

up–front \ˌ=ˌ=\ *adj* **:** being or coming in or at the front: as **a :** being in a conspicuous or leading position or role ⟨these are very *up-front* and obvious prejudices —Clive Barnes⟩ ⟨I believe I help the city by being *up-front* and visible —Edward Koch⟩ **:** OPEN, FORTHRIGHT, FRANK ⟨wishes Hollywood producers would be a bit more *up=front* on the subject —*People Weekly*⟩ **b :** playing in a front line (as in football, hockey, or soccer) **c :** paid or incurred in advance or at the beginning ⟨*up-front* interest charges⟩ ⟨offered $2 million in *up-front* cash —Tommy Thompson⟩

upgrade* *vt* **:** to extend the usefulness of (as a device) **:** IMPROVE

uplink \'=ˌ=\ *adj* [[2]*up* + *link*] **:** of or relating to transmissions from earth to a spacecraft or satellite — compare DOWNLINK *herein*

up·man·ship \'əpmənˌship\ *n* [by shortening] **:** ONE=UPMANSHIP

upmarket \ˌ=ˌ==\ *adj* [[2]*up* + *market*] **:** UPSCALE *herein* — **upmarket** \"\ *adv*

upper* *n* **1 :** a stimulant drug; *esp* **:** AMPHETAMINE — compare DOWNER *herein* **2 :** something that induces a state of good feeling or exhilaration

upscale \ˌ=ˌ=\ *adj* [[2]*up* + *scale*] **:** of, being, relating to, or appealing to affluent consumers — **upscale** \"\ *adv or vt*

upside \ˌ=ˌ=\ *prep* [prob. fr. [1]*up* + *beside*] *chiefly dial* **:** on or against the side of ⟨he turned . . . and I slapped him right ~ the head —Marques Johnson⟩

upsilon* *or* **upsilon particle** *n* **:** an unstable electrically neutral subatomic particle of the meson family that has a mass about 10 times that of a proton and is held to consist of a bottom quark-antiquark pair

upstream* *adj* **:** of or relating to a portion of the production stream closer to basic extractive or manufacturing processes ⟨an ~ chemical manufacturer⟩ ⟨~ profits⟩ — **upstream*** *adv*

uptick \ˈ≈,≈\ *n* [[2]*up* + [2]*tick*] **1 :** a stock market transaction at a price above the last previous transaction in the same security — compare DOWNTICK *herein* **2 :** INCREASE, RISE ⟨a recovery-induced ~ in demand — *Business Week*⟩

uptight \ˌ≈ˈ≈\ *adj* [[2]*up* + [3]*tight*] **1 :** being in financial difficulties **:** BROKE ⟨surtax was another blow to an industry already ~ —*Chem. & Engineering News*⟩ **2 a :** showing signs of tension or uneasiness **:** APPREHENSIVE ⟨I was a little ~ about it at first —Phyllis Craig⟩ **b :** ANGRY, INDIGNANT ⟨I've been doing that voice in Negro theaters for years. Nobody ever got ~ —Flip Wilson⟩ **3 :** rigidly conventional ⟨~ and antiseptic white community —J.M. Culkin⟩ — **uptight** *n* -s — **uptight·ness** *n* -ES

uptime \ˈ≈ˌ≈\ *n* [[2]*up* + *time*] **:** the time during which a piece of equipment (as a computer) is functioning or is able to function

upvalue \ˌ≈ˈ≈(ˌ)≈\ *vt* [[1]*up* + *value*] **:** to assign a higher value to; *specif* **:** to officially revalue (a currency) upward — **upvaluation** \ˌ≈ˌ≈≈ˈ≈≈\ *n*

upward mobility *n* **:** the capacity or facility for rising to a higher social or economic class of society — **upwardly mobile** *adj*

up·well·ing \ˌəpˈweliŋ\ *n* -s [fr. gerund of *upwell*] **:** the process or an instance of rising or appearing to rise to the surface and flowing outward; *esp* **:** the process of upward movement of marine cold deep usu. nutrient-rich water to the surface near a continental shelf due to offshore drift of surface water (as from the action of winds or the Coriolis force)

ura·nia \yu̇ˈrānēə, -nyə\ *n* -s [NL, fr. *uranium* + *-a*] **:** URANIUM OXIDE a

uranium dioxide *n* **:** URANIUM OXIDE a

uranium trioxide *n* **:** a brilliant orange compound UO_3 that is formed in the course of refining uranium and that has been used as a coloring agent for ceramic wares

uranium 238 *n* **:** an isotope of uranium of mass number 238 that absorbs fast neutrons to form a uranium isotope of mass number 239 which then decays through neptunium to form plutonium of mass number 239

ur·ban·ol·o·gist \ˌərbəˈnäləjəst\ *n* -s [*urbanology* (herein — fr. *urban* + *-o-* + *-logy*) + *-ist*] **:** one who specializes in the problems of cities — **ur·ban·ol·o·gy** \-jē\ *n* -ES

urban renewal *n* **:** a construction program to replace or restore substandard buildings in an urban area

urban sprawl *n* **:** the spreading of urban developments (as houses and shopping centers) on undeveloped land near a city

ureo·tel·ic \yəˌrēəˌtelik, ˌyu̇r-\ *adj* [*ure-* + [2]*tel-* + *-ic;* fr. the fact that urea is the end product] **:** excreting nitrogen mostly in the form of urea ⟨mammals are ~⟩ — **ureo·te·lism** \-lˌizəm, ˌyu̇rēˈätᵊlˌ-\ *n* -s

uri·co·tel·ic \ˌyu̇rəkōˌtelik\ *adj* [*uric-* + [2]*tel-* + *-ic;* fr. the fact that uric acid is the end product] **:** excreting nitrogen mostly in the form of uric acid ⟨birds are ~ animals⟩ — **uri·co·te·lism** \-lˌizəm, ˌyu̇riˈkätᵊlˌ-\ *n* -s

uro·kinase \ˌyu̇rə +\ *n* [[1]*ur-* + *kinase*] **:** an enzyme that is similar to streptokinase, is found in human urine, and is used to dissolve blood clots (as in the heart)

ur·ti·car·io·gen·ic \ˌərd·əˌka(a)rēəˌjenik, -ˌker-\ *adj* [*urticaria* + *-o-* + *-genic*] **:** being an agent or substance that induces or predisposes to urticarial lesions (as wheals on the skin)

u–value \ˈ≈ˌ≈(ˌ)≈\ *n, usu cap U* [fr. unit] **:** a measure of the heat transmission through a building part (as a wall or window) or a given thickness of insulating material expressed as the number of British thermal units transmitted through one square foot per hour per degree Fahrenheit temperature difference between the two sides so that the lower the number the better the insulation

V

vac·ci·nee \ˌvaksəˈnē\ *n* -s [[1]*vaccinate* + *-ee*] : a vaccinated individual

valence band *n* : the range of permissible energy values that are the highest energies an electron of an atom can have and still be associated with the atom and be used to form bonds — compare CONDUCTION BAND *herein*

val·in·o·my·cin \ˌvalə̇(ˌ)nōˈmīsᵊn\ *n* -s [*valine* + *-o-* + *-mycin*] : an antibiotic $C_{54}H_{90}N_6O_{18}$ produced by a bacterium of the genus *Streptomyces* (*S. fulvissimus*)

Val·ium \ˈvalēəm, -lyəm\ *trademark* — used for a preparation of diazepam

value–added tax \ˈ=(ˌ)=ˈ==-\ *n* : an incremental excise that is levied on the value added at each stage of the processing of a raw material or the production and distribution of a commodity

van* *n* **1 :** a multipurpose enclosed boxlike motor vehicle having rear or side doors and side panels often with windows **2 :** a detachable passenger cabin transportable by aircraft or truck

van·co·my·cin \ˌvaŋkəˈmīsᵊn\ *n* -s [*vanco-* (arbitrary prefix) + *-mycin*] : an antimicrobial agent from an actinomycete of the genus *Streptomyces* (*S. orientalis*) that is used esp. as the hydrochloride salt against staphylococci resistant to other antibiotics

va·nil·la \vəˈnilə, -nelə\ *adj* [*vanilla*, n.; fr. the fact that vanilla ice cream is considered the standard flavor] : lacking distinction : ORDINARY, PLAIN ⟨nothing fancy about this design. It's just plain ~ —*Newsweek*⟩ ⟨a plain old ~ terminal —Steven Levy⟩

vanity plate *n* : an automobile registration plate bearing letters, numbers, or a combination of these chosen by the owner

vanner* *n* : one who drives a usu. customized van

vanpool \ˈ=ˌ=\ *n* [[3]*van* + *pool*] : an arrangement by which a group of people commute to work in a passenger van — **van·pool·ing** \-ˌpüliŋ\ *n* -s

va·rac·tor \vəˈraktər, (ˈ)va(a)|(ə)ˈr-, (ˈ)ve|\ *n* -s [*var*ying + re*actor*] : a semiconductor device whose capacitance varies with the applied voltage

variable annuity *n* : an annuity contract which is backed primarily by a fund of common stocks and the payments on which fluctuate with the state of the economy

variable rate mortgage *n* : a periodically renegotiable mortgage that has an interest rate indexed to the cost of funds to the lender

var·i·o·la·tion \ˌvarēōˈlāshən\ *n* -s [*variola* + *-ation*] : the deliberate inoculation of an uninfected person with the smallpox virus (as by contact with pustular matter) that was widely practiced before the era of vaccination as prophylaxis against the severe form of smallpox

vas·cu·li·tis \ˌvaskyəˈlīd·ə̇s\ *n, pl* **vas·cu·li·ti·des** \-ˈlīd·əˌdēz\ [NL, fr. *vascul-* + *-itis*] : ANGIITIS

va·so·active \ˈvā(ˌ)zō, ˈvā(ˌ)sō, ˈva(ˌ)sō, ˈva(ˌ)zō +\ *adj* [*vas-* + *active*] : affecting the blood vessels esp. in respect to the degree of their relaxation or contraction — **va·so·activity** \"+\ *n*

VAT *abbr* value-added tax *herein*

vatican roulette *n, usu cap V, slang* : RHYTHM METHOD

VC* *abbr* Vietcong

VCR \ˌvē(ˌ)sēˈär, -ˈä(r\ *n* -s [videocassette recorder] : a videotape recorder that uses videocassettes

vector* *n* : an element of a vector space

vector space *n* : a set representing a generalization of a system of vectors and consisting of elements which comprise a commutative group under addition, each of which is left unchanged under multiplication by the multiplicative identity of a field, and for which multiplication under the multiplicative operation of the field is commutative, closed, distributive such that both $c(A+B) = cA + cB$ and $(c+d)A = cA + dA$, and associative such that $(cd)A = c(dA)$ where A, B are elements of the set and c, d are elements of the field

vee·na \ˈvēnə\ *n* -s : VINA

ve·gan \ˈvejən, ˈvēgən\ *n* -s [by contraction fr. *vegetarian*] : a strict vegetarian : one that consumes no animal food or dairy products

ve·gan·ism \ˈvejəˌnizəm, ˈvēgə-\ *n* -s [*vegan* (herein) + *-ism*] : strict vegetarianism

vege·bur·ger \ˈvejēˌbərgər; -ˌbəgə(r, -ˌbəig-\ *n* [*veg*etable or *veg*etarian + *-burger*] : a patty of vegetable protein used as a meat substitute; *also* : a sandwich containing such a patty

veg·gie *also* **veg·ie** \ˈvejē\ *n* -s [by shortening and alter.] **1 :** VEGETABLE **2** *slang* : VEGETARIAN

Vel·cro \ˈvel(ˌ)krō\ *trademark* — used for a nylon fabric that can be fastened to itself

ventilate* *vt* : to subject the lungs of (an individual) to ventilation

ventriculo- *comb form* [NL, fr. L, *ventriculus* stomach, ventricle of the heart — more at VENTRICLE] **1 :** ventricle ⟨*ventriculo*tomy⟩ **2 :** ventricular and ⟨*ventriculo*atrial⟩

ve·rap·a·mil \veˈrapəˌmil, və̇-\ *n* -s [*vera*tryl + pro*p*yl + *amin*o] : a coronary vasodilator $C_{27}H_{38}N_2O_4$ used esp. in the form of its hydrochloride

ver·di·cchio \(ˌ)vərˈdē(k)kyō, ver-, -kē(ˌ)ō\ *n* -s *often cap* [It, fr. the name of the grape] : a light dry white wine from Italy

ve·ris·mo \vāˈrēz(ˌ)mō, veˈr-, -ˈriz-\ *n* -s [It — more at VERISM] : VERISM

vernier* *also* **vernier engine** *n* : any of two or more small supplementary rocket engines or gas nozzles on a missile or rocket vehicle for making fine adjustments in the speed or course or controlling the attitude

vé·ro·nique *also* **ve·ro·nique** \vārȯnēk\ *adj, usu cap* [F, fr. *véronique* Veronica] : prepared or garnished with usu. white seedless grapes ⟨chicken ~⟩ ⟨sole ~⟩

very large scale integration *n* : the process of placing a very large number (as thousands) of circuits on a small semiconductor chip — abbr. *VLSI*

vesico- *comb form* [NL, fr. L *vesico* bladder — more at VESICA] : of or relating to the urinary bladder and ⟨*vesico*ureteral⟩

vest–pocket park *n* : a very small urban park

veto–proof \ˈ==ˌ=\ *adj* [[1]*veto* + *proof*] : having enough potential votes to be passed over a veto or to override vetoes consistently

vex·il·lol·o·gy \ˌveksəˈläləjē\ *n* -ES [L *vexillum* flag + E *-o-* + *-logy* — more at VEXILLUM] **:** the study of flags — **vex·il·lo·log·i·cal** \ˌveksəlōˈläjəkəl, (ˌ)vekˌsiləˈlä-\ *adj* — **vex·il·lol·o·gist** \ˌveksəˈläləjəst\ *n* -S
viable* *adj* **:** having a reasonable chance of succeeding ⟨a ~ candidate⟩
vibe \ˈvīb\ *n* -S [by shortening] **:** VIBRATION 4 — usu. used in pl. ⟨the good guy is someone who radiates good ~*s* . . . to others and is not psychotic about doing his own thing —Franklin Chu⟩
vi·bra·harp \ˈvībrəˌhärp, -ˌhȧp\ *n* [fr. *Vibra-Harp,* a trademark] **:** VIBRAPHONE — **vi·bra·harp·ist** \-pəst\ *n*
vi·bron·ic \(ˈ)vīˈbränik\ *adj* [*vibr*ation + electr*onic*] **:** of or relating to transitions between molecular energy states when modified by vibrational energy
vic·tim·less \ˈviktəmləs\ *adj* **:** having no victim ⟨~ crimes⟩
vic·tim·ol·o·gy \ˌviktəˈmäləjē\ *n* -ES [*victim* + *-o-* + *-logy*] **:** the study of the ways in which the behavior of a victim of a crime may have led to or contributed to his victimization — **vic·tim·ol·o·gist** \-jəst\ *n* -S
vic·to·ri·ana \(ˌ)vikˌtōrēˈänə, -tȯr-, -ˈanə, -ˈaa(ə)nə\ *n, usu cap* [Queen *Victoria* + E *-ana*] **:** materials concerning or characteristic of the Victorian age
video* *n* **:** VIDEOTAPE 1 *herein:* as **a :** a recording of a motion picture or television program for playing through a television set **b :** a videotaped performance of a popular song often featuring a dramatic interpretation of the lyrics through visual images
videocassette \ˈ==ˌ==ˈ=\ *n* [*video* + *cassette*] **1 :** a case containing videotape for use with a VCR **2 :** a recording (as of a movie) on a videocassette
videocassette recorder *n* **:** VCR *herein*
videodisc *also* **videodisk** \ˈ==(ˌ)=ˈ=\ *n* [*video* + *disc* or *disk*] **1 :** a disc similar in appearance and use to a phonograph record on which programs have been recorded for playback on a television set; *also* **:** OPTICAL DISC *herein* **2 :** a recording on a videodisc
video game *n* **:** an electronic game esp. emphasizing fast action that is played by means of images on a video screen
vid·eo·land \ˈvidē(ˌ)ōˌland\ *n* [[2]*video* + *land*] **:** the medium of television or the television industry
vid·eo·phone \-ˌfōn\ *n* [*video* + *phone*] **:** a telephone equipped for transmission of video as well as audio signals so that users can see each other
video recorder *n* **:** VIDEO TAPE RECORDER *herein*
[1]**vid·eo·tape** \-ēəˌtāp, -ēōˌt-\ *n* **1 :** a recording of visual images and sound made on magnetic tape **2 :** the magnetic tape used in a video tape recording
[2]**videotape** \"\ *vt* -ED/-ING/-S **:** to make a video tape recording of
videotape recorder *n* **:** a device for recording and playing videotapes
vid·eo·tex \ˈvidēəˌteks, -ēōˌt-\ *also* **vid·eo·text** \-ˌtekst\ *n* [*video-* + *text* or *text*] **:** an electronic data retrieval system in which usu. textual information is transmitted via telephone or cable-television lines and displayed on a television set or video display terminal; *esp* **:** such a system that is interactive — compare TELETEXT *herein*
video ve·ri·té *or* **video ve·ri·te** \-ˌverəˈtā\ *n* [*video* + *verité* or *verite* (as in *cinema verité* — herein)] **:** the art or technique of filming or videotaping a television program (as a documentary) so as to convey candid realism
vi·et·nam·iza·tion \vēˌetnəməˈzāshən, ˌvyet-, -ˌmīˈz- *also* ˌvēət- *or* ˌvēt-\ *n* -S *usu cap* [*Vietnam* country in Indochina + *-ization*] **:** the act or process of transferring war responsibilities from U.S. to Vietnamese hands — **vi·et·nam·ize** \vēˈetnəˌmīz, ˈvyet- *also* ˈvēət-, ˈvēt-\ *vb* -ED/-ING/-S *usu cap*
viewdata \ˈ=ˌ==\ *n* [[2]*view* + *data*] **:** VIDEOTEX *herein*
viewer·ship *R*ˈvyüərˌship, ˈvyu̇(ə)r-; –*R*ˈvyüəˌ-, ˈvyu̇əˌ-\ *n* [*viewer* + *-ship*] **:** a television audience
-ville \ˌvil *esp South* ˌvəl\ *n suffix* -S [*-ville,* suffix occurring in names of towns, fr. F, fr. OF, fr. *ville* farm, village — more at VILLAGE] **:** place or category of a specified nature ⟨squares*ville*⟩
VIN *abbr* vehicle identification number
vin·blas·tine \vinˈblaˌstēn, -ˌstən\ *n* -S [contr. of *vincaleukoblastine* (herein)] **:** an alkaloid $C_{46}H_{58}N_4O_9$ from Madagascar periwinkle used esp. in the form of its sulfate to treat human neoplastic diseases
vin·ca·leu·ko·blas·tine \ˌviŋkəˈlükəˈblaˌstēn, -ˌstən; -ˌlükə-(ˌ)blaˈstēn\ *n* -S [NL *Vinca* + E *leukoblast* + *-ine*] **:** VINBLASTINE *herein*
vin·cris·tine \vinˈkriˌstēn, viŋˈk-, -ˌstən\ *n* -S [NL *Vinca* + L *crista* crest + E *-ine*] **:** an alkaloid $C_{46}H_{56}N_4O_{10}$ from Madagascar periwinkle used esp. in the form of its sulfate to treat some human neoplastic diseases (as leukemias)
vin·da·loo \ˈvindəˌlü\ *n* -S [prob. fr. Pg *vin d'alho* wine and garlic sauce, fr. *vinho* wine + *alho* garlic] **:** a curried meat dish made with garlic and wine or vinegar
vine* *n, slang* **:** an article of clothing; *esp* **:** a man's suit — usu. used in pl.
vi·ol·o·gen \ˈvīələjən\ *n* -S [*viol-* (as in *violet*) + *-o-* + *-gen*] **:** a chloride of any of several bases used as an oxidation-reduction indicator because color is exhibited in the reduced form
virgo* *n, usu cap* **:** one born under the astrological sign Virgo
vir·go·an \ˈvərˌgōən, ˈvəˌ-\ *n* -S *usu cap* [*Virgo* + E *-an*] **:** VIRGO herein
vi·ri·on \ˈvīrēˌän, ˈvir-\ *n* -S [ISV *viri-* (fr. NL *virus*) + [2]*-on*] **:** a complete virus particle that consists of an RNA or DNA core with a protein coat sometimes with external envelopes and that is the extracellular infective form of a virus
viroid* *n* **:** any of several causative agents of plant disease that consist solely of a single-stranded RNA of low molecular weight arranged in a closed loop or a linear chain
virtual* *adj* **1 :** of, relating to, or being a hypothetical particle whose existence is inferred from indirect evidence ⟨~ photon⟩ **2 :** of, relating to, or using virtual memory
virtual memory *n* **:** external memory (as magnetic disks) for a computer that can be used as if it were an extension of the computer's internal memory — called also *virtual storage*
visual literacy *n* **:** the ability to recognize and understand ideas conveyed through visible actions or images (as pictures)
vital signs *n pl* **:** signs of life; *specif* **:** the pulse rate, respiratory rate, body temperature, and sometimes blood pressure of a person
vi·ta·min·iza·tion \ˌvīd·əmənəˈzāshən, *Brit also* ˌvit-\ *n* -S [*vita- minize* + *-ation*] **:** the action or process of vitaminizing
vit·rec·to·my \vəˈtrektəmē\ *n* -ES [NL, fr. *vitr*eous humor + *-ectomy*] **:** surgical removal of all or part of the vitreous humor
VLCC \ˌvēˌel(ˌ)sēˈsē\ *abbr or n* -S [*v*ery *l*arge *c*rude *c*arrier] **:** a crude-oil tanker with a very large capacity

VLSI \ˌvēˌelˌesˈī\ *abbr or n* very large scale integration *herein*

vocabulary* *n* **:** a list or collection of terms or codes available for use (as in an indexing system)

voice mail *n* **:** an electronic communication system in which spoken messages are recorded or digitized and stored for later playback for the intended recipient

voice–over \ˈ=ˌ==\ *n* -s **:** the voice of an unseen narrator heard in a motion picture or television program; *also* **:** the voice of a visible character indicating his thoughts but without motion of his lips

voiceprint \ˈ=ˌ=\ *n* [[1]*voice* + *print*] **:** an individually distinctive pattern of certain voice characteristics that is spectrographically produced

voi·là *also* **voi·la** \ˌvwäˈlä\ *interj* [F, lit., see there] — used to call attention or to express satisfaction or approval

VOLAR *abbr* volunteer army

volcanogenic \ˌvälkənəˈjenik, ˌvȯl-\ *adj* [*volcano* + *-genic*] **:** of volcanic origin ⟨~ sediments⟩

vol·tam·met·ry \vōlˈtämə·trē, -ri\ *n* -ES [*volt-ammeter* + *-y*] **:** the detection of minute quantities of chemicals (as metals) by measuring the currents generated in electrolytic solutions when known voltages are applied — **vol·tam·met·ric** \ˌvōltəˈme·trik, -ēk\ *adj*

-vol·tine \ˈvōlˌtēn, ˈvȯl-\ *adj comb form* [F, fr. It *volta* time, occasion, lit., turn — more at VOLT] **:** having (so many) generations or broods in a season or year ⟨multi*voltine*⟩

vol·un·teer·ism \ˌvälən·ˈti(ə)ˌrizəm\ *n* [[1]*volunteer* + *-ism*] **:** the act or practice of doing volunteer work in community service

VOM *abbr* volt-ohmmeter

vom·it·ous \ˈvämәd·əs, -ətəs\ *adj* [[1]*vomit* + *-ous*] **:** SICKENING, DISGUSTING

von wil·le·brand's disease \fȯnˈviləˌbrän(t)s-\ *n, usu cap W* [after E. A. *von Willebrand* †1949 Finnish physician] **:** a genetic disorder that is inherited as an autosomal recessive trait and is characterized by deficiency of a plasma clotting factor and by mucosal and petechial bleeding due to abnormal blood vessels

voucher* *n* **:** COUPON 2g

VP* *abbr* verb phrase

VSO *abbr* very superior old — usu. used of brandy 12 to 17 years old

VSOP *abbr* very superior old pale — usu. used of brandy 18 to 25 years old

V/STOL \ˈvēˌstōl, -ȯl\ *abbr* vertical or short takeoff and landing

VTOL \ˈvēˌtōl, -ȯl\ *abbr* vertical takeoff and landing

VVSOP *abbr* very very superior old pale — usu. used of brandy 25 to 40 years old

W

w* *or* **w particle** *n, usu cap W* **:** an elementary particle about 80 times heavier than a proton that along with the Z particle is a transmitter of the weak force and that can have a positive or negative charge

[1]wacko \ˈwak(ˌ)ō\ *adj* [by alter.] *slang* **:** WACKY

[2]wacko \"\ *n* -s *slang* **:** a person who is or who acts wacky

wafer* *n* **:** a thin slice of semiconductor (as silicon) used as a base for an electronic component or circuit

wafer* *vt* **1 :** to prepare (as hay or alfalfa) in the form of small compressed cakes suggestive of crackers **2 :** to divide (as a silicon rod) into wafers

waffle* *vi* **:** to talk indecisively or evasively **:** EQUIVOCATE ⟨has *waffled* miserably in his economic and foreign affairs stances —*Christian Science Monitor*⟩

waffle *n* -s **:** empty or pretentious words ⟨a lot of rather vague ~ about how nice he was —Dan Davin⟩

wafflestomper \ˈ==ˌstämpə(r)\ *n* -s [[1]*waffle* + *stomp* + *-er;* fr. the pattern left by the sole] **:** a hiking boot with a lug sole

wahine* *n* **:** a girl surfer

walking catfish *n* **:** an Asian catfish of the genus *Clarias (C. batrachus)* that is able to move about on land and has been inadvertently introduced into Florida waters

walk-up* *adj* **:** designed to allow pedestrians to be served without entering a building ⟨the *walk-up* window of a bank⟩

wall* *n* — **up against the wall :** in or into a tight or difficult situation ⟨high costs . . . have finally driven a ghastly number of colleges and universities *up against the wall* —G. W. Bonham⟩ — **up the wall** *slang* **:** into a state of intense agitation, annoyance, or frustration ⟨the steady crunch-crunch drove [him] *up the wall* —Cyra McFadden⟩

wall system *n* **:** a set of shelves often with cabinets or bureaus that can be variously arranged along a wall

[1]wall-to-wall \¦==¦=\ *adj* **1 :** covering the entire floor ⟨*wall-to-wall* carpeting⟩ **2 a :** covering or filling the entire space or time ⟨a disco crammed with *wall-to-wall* bodies —*Women's Wear Daily*⟩ ⟨relying too heavily on *wall-to-wall* action —Karla Kuskin⟩ **b :** occurring or found everywhere **:** UBIQUITOUS ⟨the *wall-to-wall* comforts that the current affluence made available —W.H. Jones⟩

[2]wall-to-wall \"\ *n* **:** a wall-to-wall carpet

wan·kel engine \¦väŋkəl-, ¦waŋ-\ *n, usu cap W* [after Felix *Wankel* *b*1902 Ger. engineer, its inventor] **:** an internal-combustion rotary engine that has a rounded triangular rotor functioning as a piston and rotating in a space in the engine and that has only two major moving parts

war-game \ˈ=ˌ=\ *vt* **:** to plan or conduct in the manner of a war game ⟨*war-gamed* an invasion —*Newsweek*⟩ ~ *vi* **:** to conduct a war game — **war-gamer** \-ˌgāmə(r)\ *n* -s

warning track *or* **warning path** *n* **:** a usu. dirt or cinder strip around the outside edge of a baseball outfield to warn a fielder running to make a catch that he is nearing a wall or fence

wash·a·te·ria *also* **wash·e·te·ria** \ˌwäshəˈtērēə, ˌwȯsh-, -ˈtir-\ *n* -s [[2]*wash* + *-ateria* or *-eteria* (as in *cafeteria*)] *chiefly South* **:** a self-service laundry usu. with coin-operated machines

wasp \ˈwäsp, ˈwȯsp\ *n* -s *usu cap W or WASP* [white *A*nglo-*S*axon *P*rotestant] **:** an American of northern European and esp. British stock and of Protestant background; *esp* **:** a member of the dominant and most privileged class of people in the U.S. — **wasp·dom** \-spdəm\ *n* -s *usu cap W or WASP* — **wasp·ish** \-spəsh\ *adj, usu cap W or WASP* — **wasp·ish·ness** \-spəshnəs\ *n* -ES *usu cap W or WASP* — **waspy** \-spē, -spi\ *adj, usu cap W or WASP*

waste* *vt* **:** to kill or severely injure

wasted* *adj, slang* **:** intoxicated from drugs or alcohol

wastewater \ˈ=ˌ==\ *n* **:** water that has been used (as in a manufacturing process) **:** SEWAGE

water bed *n* **:** a bed whose mattress is a plastic bag filled with water

water cycle *n* **:** HYDROLOGIC CYCLE

waterflood \ˈ==¦=\ *vi* [[1]*water* + *flood*] **:** to pump water into the ground around an oil well nearing depletion in order to force out additional oil

wa·ter·fowl·er \ˈwȯd·ə(r)ˌfau̇lə(r), ˈwä¦, ¦tə(-\ *n* -s [*waterfowl* + [2]*-er*] **:** a hunter of waterfowl

wa·ter·fowl·ing \-liŋ\ *n* -s [*waterfowl* + [3]*-ing*] **:** the occupation or pastime of hunting waterfowl

wa·ter·gate \ˈwȯd·ə(r)ˌgāt, ˈwä¦, ¦tə(-, *usu* -ād·+V\ *n, usu cap* [fr. *The Watergate,* apartment and office complex in Washington, D.C.; fr. the scandal following the break-in at the Democratic National Committee headquarters there in 1972] **:** a scandal usu. involving abuses of office and the compounding of wrongdoing through a cover-up

wa·ter·zooi \ˈwȯd·ərˌzüē, ˈwäd·-, -zōē\ *n* -s [Flem, prob. modif. of D *waterzootje*] **:** a stew of chicken or seafood and vegetables in a seasoned stock thickened with cream and egg yolks

wat·son-crick \¦wätsənˈkrik, *also* ¦wȯt-\ *adj, usu cap W&C* **:** of or relating to the Watson-Crick model ⟨*Watson-Crick* helix⟩

watson-crick model *n, usu cap W&C* [after J.D. *Watson* *b*1928 Am. biologist and F.H.C. *Crick* *b*1916 Eng. biologist] **:** a model of DNA structure in which the molecule is a cross-linked double-stranded helix, each strand is composed of alternating links of phosphate and deoxyribose, and the strands are cross-linked by pairs of purine and pyrimidine bases projecting inward from the deoxyribose sugars and joined by hydrogen bonds with adenine paired with thymine and with cytosine paired with guanine — compare DOUBLE HELIX *herein*

wave function* *n* **:** a quantum-mechanical function whose square represents the relative probability of finding a given elementary particle within a specified volume of space

waxing* *n* **:** the process of removing body hair with a depilatory wax

way-out \ˈ=¦=\ *adj* [*way out* (adverbial phrase), fr. [4]*way* + [1]*out*] **:** FAR-OUT *herein* — **way-out·ness** \(ˈ)=ˈ=nəs\ *n* -ES

weak interaction *or* **weak force** *n* **:** a fundamental interaction experienced by elementary particles that is responsible for some particle decay processes, for nuclear beta decay, and for emission and absorption of neutrinos

weath·er·ize \'weth̲ə,rīz\ *vt* -ED/-ING/-S [[1]*weather* + *-ize*] **:** to make (as a house) better protected against winter weather esp. by adding insulation and by caulking joints — **weath·er·iza·tion** \,weth̲ərə'zāshən, -ə,rī'z-\ *n* -S

we·del \'vādᵊl *also* 'we-\ *vi* -ED/-ING/-S [back-formation fr. *wedeln*] **:** to ski downhill by means of wedeln

we·deln \'vādᵊl(ə)n *also* 'we-\ *n, pl* **wedelns** *or* **we·deln** [G, fr. *wedeln* to fan, wag the tail, fr. *wedel* fan, tail, fr. OHG *wadal;* akin to ON *vēli* bird's tail] **:** a style of skiing in which the skier moves the rear of the skis from side to side making a series of short quick turns while following the fall line

weirdo \'wi(ə)r(,)dō, 'wiə(,)dō\ *n* -S [[3]*weird* + [1]*-o*] **:** WEIRDIE

well–formed \'=;=\ *adj* **:** produced by the correct application of a set of transformations **:** GRAMMATICAL 2a ⟨grammar . . . specifies the infinite set of *well-formed* sentences —Jerry Fodor & Jerrold J. Katz⟩ — **well–formed·ness** \,wel'fȯ(r)m(ə)dnəs\ *n* -ES

well–ordered \'=;==\ *adj* **:** partially ordered with every subset containing a first element and exactly one of the relationships "greater than", "less than", or "equal to" holding for any given pair of elements

well–ordering \'=;'=(=)=\ *n* -S **:** an instance of being well= ordered

western omelet *n* **:** an omelet made usu. with diced ham, green pepper, and onion

wet* *adj, Brit* **:** lacking strength of character **:** NAMBY= PAMBY ⟨we thought him ~ and violence petrified him —William Golding⟩; *also* **:** somewhat liberal ⟨a character called Jeremy Cardhouse, MP, a ~ . . . Conservative —*Times Lit. Supp.*⟩ — **wet behind the ears :** IMMATURE, INEXPERIENCED

wet* *n, Brit* **:** one who is wet ⟨her . . . nose for bastards or hopeless ~*s* —Eric Korn⟩

wet bar *n* **:** a bar for mixing drinks (as in a home) that contains a sink with running water

wet look *n* **:** a glossy surface on fabrics that is produced by coating with urethane

WF \,dəbə(l)yü'ef, -b(ə)yə'(w)ef\ *n* -S [withdrawn *f*ailing] **:** a grade assigned by a teacher to a student who withdraws from a course with a failing grade

whacked–out \,(h)wak,daůt\ *adj* [fr. past part. of [1]*whack*] **1 :** EXHAUSTED, WORN-OUT 2 **2 :** WACKY **3 :** STONED

whack off *vb* [[1]*whack*] **:** MASTURBATE — usu. considered vulgar

wheeler and dealer *n* **:** WHEELER-DEALER *herein*

wheel·er–dealer \,hwēlə(r),dēlə(r), ,wē-\ *n* [irreg. fr. *wheel and deal* + *-er*] **:** a shrewd operator esp. in business or politics

wheel·ie \'hwēlē, 'wē-\ *n* -S [*wheel* + *-ie*] **:** a maneuver in which a wheeled vehicle (as a motorcycle, bicycle, or dragster) is balanced momentarily on its rear wheel or wheels

wheels* *n* **wheels** *pl, slang* **:** a wheeled vehicle; *esp* **:** AUTOMOBILE

where* *n* — **where it's at 1 a :** a place of central interest or activity **b :** something (as a topic or field of interest) of primary concern or interest **2 :** the true nature of things

whipsawed *adj* [fr. past part. of [2]*whipsaw*] **:** subjected to a double market loss through trying inopportunely to recoup a loss by a subsequent short sale of the same security

whisker* *n* **:** a thin hairlike crystal (as of sapphire or copper) of exceptional mechanical strength used esp. to reinforce composite structural material

whistle–blower \'==,==\ *n* **:** one who reveals something covert or informs on another ⟨*whistle-blowers* who expose . . . hanky-panky in their agencies —Leonard Reed⟩ — **whistle–blowing** \'==,==\ *n*

white amur *n* [*amur* fr. *Amur* river] **:** GRASS CARP *herein*

white backlash *n* **:** the hostile reaction of white Americans to the advances of the civil rights movement

white–bread \,='=\ *adj* **:** being, typical of, or having qualities (as blandness) that appeal to the white middle class ⟨things *white-bread* America doesn't want to hear about —Mike Pritchard⟩

white flight *n* **:** the departure of white families usu. from neighborhoods undergoing racial integration or from cities implementing school desegregation

white hole *n* **:** a hypothetical extremely dense celestial object that radiates enormous amounts of energy and matter — compare BLACK HOLE *herein*

white knight *n* **1 :** one that comes to the rescue; *esp* **:** a corporation invited to buy out a second corporation in order to prevent an unfriendly takeover by a third **2 :** one that champions a cause

white–knuckle \'=;==\ *adj* **:** showing or causing tense nervousness ⟨a *white-knuckle* ride on a roller coaster⟩

white room \'=,=\ *n* **:** CLEAN ROOM *herein*

whit·ey \'hwīd·ē, 'wī-\ *n, often cap* [*white* + *-ie*] **:** the white man **:** white society ⟨Negro leaders who are seen as stooges for *Whitey* —*Times Lit. Supp.*⟩ — usu. used disparagingly

whiz kid *also* **whizz kid** *n* [[4]*whiz*] **:** a person who is unusually intelligent, clever, or successful esp. at an early age

wholesale price index *n* **:** an index measuring the change in the aggregate wholesale price of a large number of commodities in the primary market expressed as a percentage of this price in some base period

whorf·ian hypothesis \'(h)wȯrfēən\ *n, usu cap W* [Benjamin Lee *Whorf* †1941 Am. anthropologist + E *-ian*] **:** a theory in linguistics: an individual's language determines his conception of the world

wic·ca \'wikə\ *n* -S *usu cap* [OE *wicca* wizard; akin to OE *wicce* witch — more at [2]WITCH] **:** the cult or religion of witchcraft — **wic·can** \-kən\ *adj or n, usu cap*

wideband \'=;=\ *adj* [[1]*wide* + *band*] **:** BROADBAND *herein*

wide receiver *n* **:** a football receiver who normally lines up several yards to the side of the offensive formation

wiggy* *adj* **:** WACKY

wig·let \'wiglət\ *n* -S [[2]*wig* + *-let*] **:** a small wig used esp. to enhance a hairstyle

wild card *n* **1 :** one picked to fill a leftover tournament or play-off berth after regularly qualifying competitors have all been determined **2 :** an unknown or unpredictable factor

wild·ean \'wī(ə)ldēən\ *adj, usu cap* [Oscar Fingal O'Flahertie Wills *Wilde* †1900 Eng. (Irish-born) writer + E [2]*-an*] **:** of, relating to, or suggestive of Oscar Wilde or his writings

wil·son's disease \'wilsənz=,=\ *n, usu cap W* [after Samuel A. K. *Wilson* †1937 Eng. neurologist] **:** a hereditary disease that is determined by an autosomal recessive gene and is marked esp. by cirrhotic changes in the liver and severe mental disorder due to a ceruloplasmin deficiency that prevents metabolism of copper

wimp \'wimp\ *n* -s [perh. fr. Brit. slang *wimp* girl, woman, of unknown origin] **:** a weak or ineffectual person — **wimpy** \-pē, -pi\ *adj* -ER/-EST

win·ches·ter \'win,chestə(r)\ *adj, usu cap* [fr. the code name used by the original developer] **:** relating to or being computer disk technology that permits high-density storage by sealing the rigid metal disks against dust

windblast \'=,=\ *n* [[1]*wind* + *blast*] **1 :** a gust of wind **2 :** the destructive effect of air friction on a pilot ejected from a high-speed airplane

windchill** \'=,=\ *or* **windchill factor** *or* **windchill index** *n* [[1]*wind* + *chill*] **:** a still-air temperature with the same cooling effect on exposed human flesh as a given combination of temperature and wind speed

wind down *vt* **:** to cause a gradual lessening of usu. with the intention of bringing to an end **:** DE-ESCALATE *herein* ⟨*wind down* a war⟩ ~ *vi* **1 :** to draw gradually toward an end **2 :** RELAX, UNWIND — **wind–down** \'=,=\ *n* -s

window* *n* **1 :** a range of wavelengths in the electromagnetic spectrum to which a planet's atmosphere is transparent **2 a :** an interval of time within which a rocket or spacecraft must be launched to accomplish a particular mission **b :** a usu. short interval of time during which conditions are favorable or an opportunity exists ⟨a ~ of vulnerability to Soviet attack⟩ ⟨allowed the race committee a three-day ~ —Robert Sullivan⟩ **3 :** an area at the limits of the earth's sensible atmosphere through which a spacecraft must pass for successful reentry **4 :** any of the areas into which a computer display may be divided and on which distinctly different types of information (as text and accounting data) are displayed

windowpane* *n* **:** TATTERSALL

wind shear *n* **:** a radical shift in wind speed and direction that occurs between slightly different altitudes

Wind·surfer \'=,==\ *trademark* — used for a sailboard

wine bar *n* **:** an establishment selling wine and usu. food for consumption on the premises

wing* *vb* — **wing it :** to act or perform without preparation or guidelines **:** IMPROVISE

winklepicker \'==,==\ *n* [[1]*winkle* + *picker;* fr. the notion that the point is sharp enough to be used for picking winkles out of their shells] **:** a shoe with a sharp-pointed toe

winless \'=ləs\ *adj* [[2]*win* + *-less*] **:** being without a win

win·ter·im \'wintə,rim\ *n* -s [blend of [1]*winter* and *interim*] **:** an intersession at some colleges and universities chiefly in January

wipe out *vi* **1 :** to fall from a surfboard **2 :** to fall while skiing

wipeout \'=,=\ *n* -s [fr. *wipe out,* v. (herein)] **1 :** the act or an instance of wiping out; *esp* **:** complete or utter destruction **2 :** a fall from a surfboard caused usu. by losing control, colliding with another surfer, or being knocked off by a wave

wired* *adj* **:** feverishly excited or nervous

wishbone* *n* **:** a variation of the T formation in which the halfbacks line up farther from the line of scrimmage than the fullback does

witch of agne·si \-än'yāzē\ *or* **witch*** *n, usu cap A* [Maria Gaetana *Agnesi* †1799, It. mathematician; *witch* (transl. of It *avversiera* female devil, by confusion with It *versiera,* lit., turning, Agnesi's name for the curve)] **:** a plane cubic curve that is symmetric about the y-axis and approaches the x-axis as an asymptote, that is constructed by drawing lines from the origin intersecting an upright circle tangent to the x-axis at the origin and taking the locus of points of intersection of pairs of lines parallel to the x-axis and y-axis each pair of which consists of a line parallel to the x-axis through the point where a line through the origin intersects the circle and a line parallel to the y-axis through the point where the same line through the origin intersects the line parallel to the x-axis through the point of intersection of the circle and the y-axis, and that has the equation $x^2y = 4a^2(2a - y)$

withhold* *vt* **:** to deduct (withholding tax) from income

wok \'wäk\ *n* -s [Chin (Cant) *wôk*] **:** a bowl-shaped cooking utensil used esp. in the preparation of Chinese food

wolff–par·kin·son–white syndrome \¦wu̇lf¦pärkənsən'(h)wīt-\ *n, usu cap both Ws & P* [after Louis *Wolff* *b*1898 Am. cardiologist, John *Parkinson* *b*1885 Eng. cardiologist, and Paul D. *White* †1973 Am. cardiologist] **:** an abnormal heart condition characterized by premature activation of the ventricle by atrial impulses and an electrocardiographic tracing with a shortened interval between the P wave and the widened QRS complex

wolf–ra·yet star \¦wu̇lfrī'ā-\ *n, usu cap W & R* [after Charles *Wolf* †1918 & Georges *Rayet* †1906 Fr. astronomers] **:** any of a class of white stars whose spectra are characterized by very broad bright lines esp. of hydrogen, helium, carbon, and nitrogen that indicate very hot unstable stars

womanpower \'==¦=(=)\ *n* [[2]*woman* + *power*] **:** women available and prepared for service ⟨huge and growing waste of gifted, educated ~ in contemporary American society —*Current Biog.*⟩

won \'wȯn, 'wän\ *n, pl* **won** [Korean *wǻn*] **1 :** the basic monetary unit of Korea — see MONEY table *in the Dict* **2 :** a coin or note representing one won

wooden rose *n* **:** a tuberous half-hardy trailing vine of the genus *Ipomoea* (*I. tuberosa*) grown in warm regions esp. for its hard showy yellow rose-shaped calyx and seed capsule

woody* *or* **wood·ie** \'wu̇dē, -i\ *n, pl* **woodies :** a wood-paneled station wagon

word* *n* **:** a combination of electrical or magnetic impulses conveying a quantum of information in communications and computer work

word processing *n* **:** the production of typewritten documents (as business letters) with automated and usu. computerized typing and text-editing equipment

word processor *n* **:** a keyboard-operated terminal that usu. has a video display and a magnetic storage device and is used in word processing; *also* **:** software (as for a computer system) to perform word processing

words·man·ship \'wərdzmən,ship, 'wə̄d-, 'wəid-\ *n* [[1]*word* + work*manship*] **:** the art or craft of writing

work·a·hol·ic \¦wərkə'hȯlik, ¦wə̄k-, ¦wəik- *sometimes* -'häl-\ *n* -s [[1]*work* + connective *-a-* + *-holic* (as in *alcoholic*)] **:** a compulsive worker

work·a·hol·ism \'==,=,izəm\ *n* -s [*workaholic* (herein) + *-ism*] **:** an obsessive need to work

work ethic *n* **:** a belief in work as a moral good

work·fare \'=,fa(a)(ə)r, -,fe, ə\ *n* -s [[1]*work* + wel*fare*] **:** a welfare program in which recipients must do usu. public service work

workload** \'=,=\ *n* **:** the amount of work performed or capable of being performed usu. within a specified period

work release *n* **:** a corrections program that releases prisoners daily to work at full-time jobs

workstation \ˈ=ˌ==\ *n* **:** an area with equipment for the performance of a specialized task usu. by a single individual; *also* **:** an intelligent terminal or personal computer usu. connected to a computer network

work-to-rule \ˌ==ˈ=\ *n, chiefly Brit* **:** the practice of working according to the strictest interpretation of the rules so as to slow down production and force employers to comply with demands — **work-to-rule** \"\ *vi, chiefly Brit*

world-class \ˌ=ˈ=\ *adj* **:** of the highest caliber in the world ⟨a *world-class* runner⟩ ⟨*world-class* soccer⟩; *broadly* **:** FIRST-RATE, OUTSTANDING ⟨a *world-class* symphony⟩

world line *n* **:** the aggregate of all positions in space-time of any individual particle that retains its identity

worry beads *n pl* [so called fr. the belief that the fingering releases nervous tension] **:** a string of beads to be fingered so as to keep one's hands occupied

wo·ven \ˈwōvən\ *n* -s [*woven,* past part. of *weave*] **:** a woven fabric

WP \ˌdəbə(l)yüˈpē, -b(ə)yəˈ-\ *n* -s [*w*ithdrawn *p*assing] **:** a grade assigned by a teacher to a student who withdraws from a course with a passing grade

WP* *abbr* **1** wettable powder **2** word processing *herein* **3** word processor *herein*

wrap* *vt* **:** to bring to completion **:** WRAP UP; *esp* **:** to finish filming or videotaping ⟨~ a movie⟩ ~ *vi* **:** to be brought to completion ⟨principal photography is due to ~ soon —*Variety*⟩

wrap* *n* **:** the completion of filming or videotaping

wraparound \ˈ==ˌ=\ *adj* [fr. *wrap around,* v.] **:** of or relating to a flexible printing surface wrapped around a plate cylinder

wrecked \ˈrekt\ *adj* [fr. past part. of [2]*wreck*] *slang* **:** STONED

wrecker's ball *n* **:** SKULL CRACKER

wrist wrestling *n* **:** a form of arm wrestling in which opponents interlock thumbs instead of gripping hands

write* *vt* **:** SELL 2a(1) ⟨~ a stock option⟩

writ·er·ly \ˈrīd·ə(r)lē\ *adj* **:** of, relating to, or typical of a writer

writer's block *n* **:** a psychological inhibition preventing a person from proceeding with a piece of writing

wu-ts'ai \ˈwütˈsī\ *n* -s [Chin (Pek) *wu*[3]*ts'ai*[3] five colors] **:** a 5-colored overglaze enamel decoration used on Chinese porcelain since the Ming period

X

x \ˈeks\ *adj, usu cap, of a motion picture* **:** of such a nature that admission is denied to persons under a specified age (as 17) — compare G *herein,* PG *herein,* PG-13 *herein,* R *herein*

xan·a·du \ˈzanəˌd(y)ü, -aa(ə)n-\ *n, usu cap* [fr. *Xanadu,* locality in *Kubla Khan* (1798) poem by Samuel T. Coleridge †1834 Eng. poet] **:** a place of idyllic beauty

xe·nic \ˈzēnik, ˈzen-\ *adj* [*xen-* + *-ic*] **:** of, relating to, or employing a culture medium containing one or more unidentified organisms — **xe·ni·cal·ly** \-ik(ə)lē\ *adv*

xe·no·biotic \"+\ *n* [*xen-* + *biotic*] **:** a chemical compound (as a drug, pesticide, or carcinogen) that is foreign to a living organism — **xenobiotic** \"\ *adj*

xe·no·ge·ne·ic \ˌ==jəˌnēik\ *also* **xe·no·gen·ic** \ˌ==ˌjenik\ *adj* [*xen-* + *-geneic* (alter. of *-genic*) or *-genic*] **:** derived from, originating in, or being a member of another species ⟨a ~ antibody⟩ ⟨~ hosts⟩ — compare ALLOGENEIC *herein,* SYNGENEIC *herein*

xe·no·graft \ˈzenō, ˈzē- +ˌ\ *n* [*xen-* + *graft*] **:** a tissue graft carried out between members of different species

xenon hexafluoride *n* **:** a highly reactive colorless crystalline compound XeF_6

xenon tetrafluoride *n* **:** a colorless crystalline compound XeF_4 that sublimes readily in air and is formed by heating xenon with fluorine under pressure

xe·no·tro·pic \ˌzēnəˌträpik, -ˌtrōp-\ *adj* [*xen-* + *-tropic*] **:** replicating or reproducing only in cells other than those of the host species ⟨~ viruses⟩

xeroderma pig·men·to·sum \-ˌpigmənˌtōsəm, -ˌmenˌ-\ *n* [NL *pigmentosum,* fr. L *pigmentum* pigment + L *-osum,* neut. of *-osus* -ose] **:** a genetic condition inherited as a recessive autosomal trait that is caused by a defect in mechanisms that repair DNA mutations (as those caused by ultraviolet light) and is characterized by the development of pigment abnormalities and multiple skin cancers in body areas exposed to the sun

Xe·rox \ˈzi(ə)rˌäks, ˈzēˌräks\ *trademark* — used for a xerographic copier

xi* *or* **xi particle** *n* **:** an unstable subatomic particle about 2600 times heavier than an electron that has a strangeness number of 2 and can be negatively charged or neutral

x-rated \ˈ=ˌ==\ *adj, usu cap X* **1 a :** X *herein* **b :** of, relating to, or showing X-rated motion pictures ⟨an *X-rated* theater⟩ **2 a :** relating to or characterized by explicit sexual material or activity ⟨an *X-rated* book⟩ **b :** OBSCENE ⟨an *X-rated* gesture⟩

x-ray astronomy *n, usu cap X* **:** astronomy dealing with investigations of celestial bodies by means of the X rays they emit

x-ray diffraction *n, usu cap X* **:** a scattering of X rays by the atoms of a crystal that produces an interference effect so that the diffraction pattern gives information on the structure of the crystal or the identity of a crystalline substance

x-ray star *n, usu cap X* **:** a luminous starlike celestial object emitting a major portion of its radiation in the form of X rays

xu \ˈsü\ *n, pl* **xu** [Vietnamese, fr. F *sou* sou] **1 :** a coin formerly used in South Vietnam equivalent to the cent **2 :** a unit equal to $^1/_{100}$ dong — see MONEY table *in the Dict*

Xy·lo·caine \ˈzīlōˌkān\ *trademark* — used for a preparation of lidocaine

Y

YA *abbr* young adult

YAG \'yag\ *n* -s [yttrium aluminum garnet] **:** a synthetic yttrium aluminum garnet of marked hardness and high refractive index that is used esp. as a gemstone and in laser technology

ya·ki·to·ri \ˌyäki'tōrē\ *n* -s [Jap, lit., grilled chicken, fr. *yaki* roasting + *tori* bird, chicken] **:** bite-sized marinated chicken pieces grilled on small bamboo skewers

ya·ma·to–e \yä'mätəˌwā\ *also* **ya·ma·to** \-'mä(ˌ)tō\ *n* -s *usu cap* [Jap *yamato-e,* fr. *Yamato* Japan + *e* picture, painting] **:** a movement in Japanese art arising in medieval times and marked by the treatment of Japanese themes with Japanese taste and sentiment

yard sale *n* **:** GARAGE SALE *herein*

ya·yoi \(')yä¦yȯi\ *adj, often cap* [fr. *Yayoi,* site in Tokyo, Japan, where remains of the period were discovered] **:** of, relating to, or being typical of a Japanese cultural period extending from about 200 B.C. to A.D. 200, being generally neolithic but including the beginning of work in metal, and characterized esp. by unglazed wheel-thrown pottery (**Yayoi ware**) usu. without ornamentation but often of florid shape

yech *or* **yecch** \'yək, 'yək\ *interj* [imit.] — used to express rejection or disgust

yellowcake \'==ˌ=\ *n* **:** a bright yellow compound that consists of uranium oxide U_3O_8 and is an intermediate product in uranium refining

yellow pages *n pl, usu cap Y&P* **:** a telephone directory or section of a telephone directory that lists business and professional firms and people alphabetically by category and includes classified advertising

yellow rain *n* **:** a yellow substance that has been reported to occur in Southeast Asia as a mist or as spots on rocks and vegetation and that has been held to have been used as a chemical warfare agent during the Vietnam war but that appears upon chemical and palynological examination to be similar if not identical to the feces of bees

yen·ta \'yen·tə\ *n* -s [Yiddish *yente* vulgar and sentimental woman, fr. the name *Yente*] **:** one that meddles; *also* **:** BLABBERMOUTH, GOSSIP

yer·sin·ia \yər'sinēə, yer-\ *n, cap* [after A.E.J. *Yersin* †1943 Fr. bacteriologist] **:** a genus of gram-negative bacteria of the family Enterobacteriaceae that includes several important pathogens (as the plague bacterium *Y. pestis*) of animals and man formerly included in the genus *Pasteurella*

yé–yé \¦yā(ˌ)yā\ *adj* [F, fr. E *yeah-yeah,* exclamation often interpolated in rock 'n' roll performances] **:** of, relating to, or featuring rock 'n' roll as it developed in France

yield to maturity : the total rate of return to an owner holding a bond to maturity expressed as a percentage of cost

YIG \'yig\ *n* -s [yttrium iron garnet] a synthetic yttrium iron garnet having ferrimagnetic properties that is used esp. as a filter for selecting or tuning microwaves

yi–hsing ware \'yē'shiŋ-\ *also* **yi–hsing** \'='=\ *or* **yi–hsing yao** \'yē'shiŋ'yaü\ *n, usu cap 1st Y* [*Yi-hsing* fr. *Yi-hsing (Ihing),* town in southern Kiangsu province, China; *Yi-hsing yao* fr. *Yi-hsing* + Chin (Pek) *yao*[2] pottery] **:** BOCCARO

yin·glish \'yiŋ(g)lish\ *n* -ES *cap* [blend of *Yiddish* and *English*] **:** English marked by numerous borrowings from Yiddish

yip·pie \'yipē\ *n* -s *often cap* [alter. (influenced by *yippee*) of *hippie*] **:** a person belonging to or identified with a politically active group of hippies

yob·bo \'yäb(ˌ)ō\ *n, pl* **yobbos** *or* **yobboes** [*yob* + *-o*] **1** *Brit* **:** LOUT, YOKEL **2** *or* **yob*** *Brit* **:** HOODLUM

yock \'yək, 'yäk\ *or* **yuck** \'yək\ *or* **yuk** \"\ *vi* **yocked** *or* **yucked** *or* **yukked; yocked** *or* **yucked** *or* **yukked; yocking** *or* **yucking** *or* **yukking; yocks** *or* **yucks** *or* **yuks** [imit.] **:** to laugh esp. in a boisterous or unrestrained manner

youthquake \'=ˌ=\ *n* [*youth* + *quake*] **:** the impact of the values, tastes, and mores of youth on the established norms of society

yo–yo* *n* **:** a stupid or foolish person

yo–yo \'yōˌyō\ *vi* **yo–yoed; yo–yoed; yo–yoing; yo-yos** [*yo-yo,* n.] **:** to move from one position to another repeatedly: as **a :** VACILLATE **b :** FLUCTUATE

[1]**yuck** *var of* [4]YAK

[2]**yuck** \'yək, 'yək\ *also* **yuk*** *interj* [imit.] — used to express rejection or disgust

yucky \'yəkē, 'yəkē\ *adj* [*yuck* (herein) + *-y*] *slang* **:** OFFENSIVE, DISTASTEFUL ⟨not even a decent pool, unless you counted the ~ old bathtub in the phys ed building —W.F. Reed⟩

yup·pie \'yəpē\ *n* -s *often cap* [prob. fr *y*oung *u*rban *p*rofessional + *-ie,* influenced by *yippie* (herein)] **:** a young college-educated adult who is employed in a well-paying profession and who lives and works in or near a large city

Z

z* *or* **z particle** *n, usu cap* Z **:** a neutral elementary particle about 90 times heavier than a proton that along with the W particle is a transmitter of the weak force — called also Z^0 or Z^0 *particle*

zaf·tig *also* **zof·tig** \ˈzäftig, ˈzȯf-\ *adj* [Yiddish *zaftik* juicy, succulent, fr. G *saftig,* fr. *saft* juice, sap, fr. OHG *saf* — more at SAP] *of a woman* **:** having a full rounded figure **:** pleasingly plump

zai·bat·su \(ˈ)zīˈbät(ˌ)sü\ *n pl* [Jap, fr. *zai* money, wealth + *batsu* clique, clan] **:** the powerful financial and industrial conglomerates of Japan

zaire \zäˈi(ə)r *also* ˈzī(ə)r\ *n* -s [F *zaïre,* fr. *Zaïre* (formerly Congo), country in west central Africa, fr. *Zaïre,* former name of Congo river] **1 :** the basic monetary unit of Zaire — see MONEY table *in the Dict* **2 :** a note representing one zaire

zair·ian *or* **zair·ean** \zäˈirēən *also* ˈzir-\ *n* -s *cap* [*Zaire,* central Africa + E *-an*] **:** a native or inhabitant of Zaire — **zairian** *or* **zairean** *adj, usu cap*

[1]**zap** \ˈzap\ *interj* [imit.] **1** — used to express a sound made by or as if by a gun **2** — used to indicate a sudden or instantaneous occurrence

[2]**zap** \ˈ"\ *vb* **zapped; zapped; zapping; zaps** *vt* **1 :** to hit or affect with sudden force: as **a :** to destroy or kill by or as if by shooting **b :** to strike with or as if with electricity or radiation **c :** to criticize sharply **:** ZING *herein* **d :** to defeat in a stunning decisive way **2 :** to propel suddenly or speedily **3 :** to make pungent ⟨a sauce *zapped* with pepper⟩ ~ *vi* **:** to go speedily **:** ZOOM, ZIP

[3]**zap** *n* -s **:** a pungent or zestful quality **:** ZIP; *also* **:** a sudden forceful blow or attack ⟨a ~ or two from a satellite-mounted death ray —Harvey Ardman⟩

ze·atin \ˈzēətən, -tᵊn\ *n* -s [NL *Zea* + E *-tin* (as in *kinetin* — herein)] **:** a cytokinin first isolated from maize endosperm

zebra crossing *n, Brit* **:** a crosswalk marked by a series of broad white stripes

zeit·ge·ber \ˈtsītˌgābər, ˈzīt-\ *n* [G, fr. *zeit* time (fr. OGH *zīt*) + *geber,* lit., giver, donor, fr. *geben* to give, fr. OHG *geban;* akin to OE *giefan* to give — more at TIDE, GIVE] **:** an environmental agent or event (as the occurrence of light or dark) that provides the stimulus setting or resetting a biological clock of an organism

zelkova* *n* -s **:** a plant of the genus *Zelkova; esp* **:** a tall widely spreading Japanese tree (*Z. serrata*) resembling the American elm and replacing the latter as an ornamental and shade tree because of its resistance to Dutch elm disease

zen·do \ˈzen(ˌ)dō\ *n* -s *usu cap* [Jap *zendō,* fr. *zen* Zen sect + *-dō* shrine] **:** a place used for Zen meditation

ze·ner diode \ˈzēnə(r)-, ˈzen-\ *n, often cap* Z [after Clarence Melvin *Zener b*1905 Am. physicist] **:** a silicon semiconductor device used esp. as a voltage regulator

zep·po·le \(t)se(p)ˈpō(ˌ)lā, ze-, ˈ==(ˌ) =\ *also* **zep·po·li** \-(ˌ)lē\ *n, pl* **zeppole** *also* **zeppoli** [It] **:** a doughnut made from deep-fried cream puff dough

zero–based \ˈ==ˌ=\ *or* **zero–base** \ˈ==ˌ=\ *adj* [[2]*zero* + *based* or *base*] **:** having each item justified on the basis of cost or need ⟨*zero-based* budgeting⟩

zero vector *n* **:** a vector which is of zero length and all of whose components are zero

zilch \ˈzilch, ˈziuch\ *n* [origin unknown] **:** ZERO, NIL

zill \ˈzil\ *n* -s [prob. fr. Turk *zil* cymbals] **:** a small metallic cymbal used in pairs with one worn on the thumb and the other on the middle finger

zing* *vb* ~ *vt* **1 :** to hit suddenly **:** ZAP *herein* ⟨~ you with a . . . service fee every time you step out on the court —Barry Tarshis⟩ **2 :** to criticize in a pointed or witty manner ⟨politicians who are ~*ed* in his columns —Ron Nessen⟩ ~ *vi* **1 :** ZIP, SPEED ⟨movie ~*s* right along — *Playboy*⟩ **2 :** to be alive **:** bubble over ⟨~*ing* with raw energy and ambition —David Bellamy⟩

zing·er \ˈziŋə(r)\ *n* -s [[2]*zing* + [2]*-er*] **1 :** a pointed witty remark or retort **2 :** something causing or meant to cause interest, surprise, or shock

zingy \ˈziŋē\ *adj* -ER/-EST [[1]*zing* + [1]*-y*] **1 :** enjoyably exciting ⟨a ~ musical⟩ **2 :** strikingly attractive or appealing ⟨wore a ~ new outfit⟩

zinj·an·thro·pine \zinˈjan(t)thrəˌpīn\ *n* -s [*zinjanthropine* adj., fr. *zinjanthropus* + [1]*-ine*] **:** any of several closely related primitive extinct African hominids including zinjanthropus — **zinjanthropine** *adj*

[1]**zip** \ˈzip\ *n* -s [by shortening] **:** ZIP CODE *herein*

[2]**zip** \ˈ"\ *n* -s [prob. alter. of *zero*] **:** ZERO, NOTHING ⟨a score of 21–*zip*⟩ ⟨so far we have ~ to show for our efforts —Susan Zirinsky⟩

zip code \ˈzipˌ-\ *n, often cap Z&I&P* [*ZIP* fr. zone *i*mprovement *p*lan] **:** a 5-digit code that identifies each U.S. postal delivery area

zip–code \ˈ=ˌ=\ *vt* **:** to furnish with a zip code

zip–out \ˈ=ˌ=\ *adj* **:** attached by means of a zipper ⟨a *zip-out* liner⟩

zir·ca·loy \ˌzərkəˈlȯi\ *n* -s [*zirc*onium + *alloy*] **:** any of several zirconium alloys notable for corrosion resistance and stability over a wide range of radiation and temperature exposures

zit \ˈzit\ *n* -s [origin unknown] *slang* **:** PIMPLE

zi·ti \ˈzēd·ē, -ē(ˌ)tē\ *n, pl* **ziti** [It, lit., boys, pl. of *zito,* modif. of *citto,* boy, youth] **:** medium-sized tubular pasta

z line *n, usu cap* Z **:** any of the dark bands across a striated muscle fiber that mark the junction of actin filaments in adjacent sarcomeres

zol·ling·er–el·li·son syndrome \ˌzäliŋəˈreləsən-\ *n, usu cap Z&E* [R.M. *Zollinger b*1903, Am. surgeon and E.H. *Ellison* †1970, Am. surgeon] **:** a syndrome consisting of fulminating intractable peptic ulcers, gastric hypersecretion and hyperacidity, and hyperplasia of the pancreatic islet cells

zone refining *also* **zone melting** *n* **:** a technique for the purification of a crystalline material and esp. a metal in which a molten region travels through the material to be refined, picks up impurities at its advancing edge, and then allows the purified part to recrystallize at its opposite edge — **zone–refined** *adj*

zon·ian \ˈzōnēən\ *n* -s *cap* [fr. Panama Canal *Zone* + *-ian*] **:** a U.S. citizen who lives in the Panama Canal Zone

zonk \ˈzäŋk, ˈzȯŋk\ *vb* -ED/-ING/-S [back-formation fr. *zonked* (herein)] *vt* **:** STUN, STUPEFY; *also* **:** STRIKE, ZAP —

often used with *out* ~ *vi* **:** to pass out from or as if from alcohol or a drug — often used with *out*

zonked \ˈzäŋ(k)t, ˈzȯŋ-\ *also* **zonked–out** \ˌzäŋ(k)ˌtau̇t, ˌzȯŋ-\ *adj* [origin unknown] **:** stupefied by or as if by alcohol or a drug

zo·ri \ˈzōrē, -ȯr-\ *n, pl* **zori** *also* **zoris** [Jap *zōri,* lit., straw sandals, fr. *sō-* grass, vegetation + *-ri* footwear] **:** a flat thonged sandal usu. made of straw, cloth, leather, or rubber

zorn's lemma \ˈzȯ(ə)rnz-, ˈtsȯ-\ *n, usu cap* Z [after Max August *Zorn* *b*1906 Ger. mathematician] **:** a lemma in set theory: if S is partially ordered and if each subset for which every pair of elements is related by one of the relationships "less than," "equal to," or "greater than" has an upper bound in S, then S contains at least one element for which there is no greater element in S

ZPG *abbr* zero population growth

zup·pa in·gle·se \ˌtsüpə·iŋˈglā(ˌ)zā, ˌzü-, -inˈg-, |(ˌ)sā, |sē, |zē\ *n, often cap I* [It, lit., English soup] **:** a dessert consisting of sponge cake and custard or pudding that is flavored with rum, covered with cream, and garnished with fruit

zy·de·co \ˈzīdəˌkō\ *also* **zod·i·co** \ˈzädəkō\ *n* -s *often cap* [perh. modif. of F *les haricots* beans, fr. the Creole dance tune *Les Haricots Sont Pas Salé*] **:** popular music of southern Louisiana that combines dance tunes of French origin with elements of Caribbean music and the blues and that is usu. played by small groups featuring guitar, washboard, and accordion

zy·mo·gram \ˈzīməˌgram\ *n* [*zym-* + *-gram*] **:** an electrophoretic strip (as of starch gel) or a representation of it exhibiting the pattern of separated proteins or protein components after electrophoresis